Safety Symbols

These symbols appear in laboratory activities. They warn of possible dangers in the laboratory and remind you to work carefully.

 Safety Goggles Wear safety goggles to protect your eyes in any activity involving chemicals, flames or heating, or glassware.

 Lab Apron Wear a laboratory apron to protect your skin and clothing from damage.

 Breakage Handle breakable materials, such as glassware, with care. Do not touch broken glassware.

 Heat-Resistant Gloves Use an oven mitt or other hand protection when handling hot materials such as hot plates or hot glassware.

 Plastic Gloves Wear disposable plastic gloves when working with harmful chemicals and organisms. Keep your hands away from your face, and dispose of the gloves according to your teacher's instructions.

 Heating Use a clamp or tongs to pick up hot glassware. Do not touch hot objects with your bare hands.

 Flames Before you work with flames, tie back loose hair and clothing. Follow instructions from your teacher about lighting and extinguishing flames.

 No Flames When using flammable materials, make sure there are no flames, sparks, or other exposed heat sources present.

 Corrosive Chemical Avoid getting acid or other corrosive chemicals on your skin or clothing or in your eyes. Do not inhale the vapors. Wash your hands after the activity.

 Poison Do not let any poisonous chemical come into contact with your skin, and do not inhale its vapors. Wash your hands when you are finished with the activity.

 Fumes Work in a ventilated area when harmful vapors may be involved. Avoid inhaling vapors directly. Only test an odor when directed to do so by your teacher, and use a wafting motion to direct the vapor toward your nose.

 Sharp Object Scissors, scalpels, knives, needles, pins, and tacks can cut your skin. Always direct a sharp edge or point away from yourself and others.

 Animal Safety Treat live or preserved animals or animal parts with care to avoid harming the animals or yourself. Wash your hands when you are finished with the activity.

 Plant Safety Handle plants only as directed by your teacher. If you are allergic to certain plants, tell your teacher; do not do an activity involving those plants. Avoid touching harmful plants such as poison ivy. Wash your hands when you are finished with the activity.

 Electric Shock To avoid electric shock, never use electrical equipment around water, or when the equipment is wet or your hands are wet. Be sure cords are untangled and cannot trip anyone. Unplug equipment not in use.

 Physical Safety When an experiment involves physical activity, avoid injuring yourself or others. Alert your teacher if there is any reason you should not participate.

 Disposal Dispose of chemicals and other laboratory materials safely. Follow the instructions from your teacher.

 Hand Washing Wash your hands thoroughly when finished with the activity. Use antibacterial soap and warm water. Rinse well.

 General Safety Awareness When this symbol appears, follow the instructions provided. When you are asked to develop your own procedure in a lab, have your teacher approve your plan before you go further.

California

Focus on Earth Science

PEARSON
Education

CALIFORNIA
SCIENCE
EXPLORER

Focus on California
Earth Science

Program Print Resources

Student Edition
Teacher's Edition
Teaching Resources
Color Transparencies
Reading and Note Taking Guide Level A
Reading and Note Taking Guide Level B
Inquiry Skills Activity Books I–III
Vocabulary Flashcards
Laboratory Manual
Laboratory Manual, Teacher's Edition
Probeware Lab Manual
Standards Review Transparencies
Progress Monitoring Assessments
Chapter Tests Level A and B
Teaching Guidebook for Universal Access

Program Technology Resources

Lab zone™ Easy Planner
PresentationExpress CD-ROM
Student Express with Interactive Textbook CD-ROM
TeacherExpress™ CD-ROM
ExamView® Computer Test Bank
Student Edition in MP3
Probeware Lab Manual CD-ROM

Program Video Resources

Lab Activity DVD
Discovery Channel DVD Library

Spanish Program Resources

Spanish Student Edition
Spanish Reading and Note Taking Guide
Spanish Teacher's Guide with Answer Keys
Spanish Student Edition in MP3

Acknowledgments appear on pages 565–566, which constitute an extension of this copyright page.

Pearson Prentice Hall ISBN 0-13-201274-X

5 6 7 8 9 10   11 10 09 08 07

Pearson Scott Foresman ISBN 0-328-24653-0

3 4 5 6 7 8 9 10   11 10 09 08 07

PEARSON
Education

Program Authors

Michael J. Padilla, Ph.D.
Professor of Science Education
University of Georgia
Athens, Georgia

Michael Padilla is a leader in middle school science education. He has served as President of the National Science Teachers Association and as a writer of the National Science Education Standards. As lead author of Science Explorer, Mike has inspired the team in developing a program that meets the needs of middle grade students, promotes science inquiry, and is aligned with the National Science Education Standards.

Ioannis Miaoulis, Ph.D.
President
Museum of Science
Boston, Massachusetts

Originally trained as a mechanical engineer, Ioannis Miaoulis is in the forefront of the national movement to increase technological literacy. As dean of the Tufts University School of Engineering, Dr. Miaoulis spearheaded the introduction of engineering into the Massachusetts curriculum. Currently he is working with school systems across the country to engage students in engineering activities and to foster discussions on the impact of science and technology on society.

Martha Cyr, Ph.D.
Director of K–12 Outreach
Worcester Polytechnic Institute
Worcester, Massachusetts

Martha Cyr is a noted expert in engineering outreach. She has over nine years of experience with programs and activities that emphasize the use of engineering principles, through hands-on projects, to excite and motivate students and teachers of mathematics and science in grades K–12. Her goal is to stimulate a continued interest in science and mathematics through engineering.

Book Authors

Jan Jenner, Ph.D.
Science Writer
Talladega, Alabama

Linda Cronin Jones, Ph.D.
Associate Professor of Science
   and Environmental Education
University of Florida
Gainesville, Florida

Marylin Lisowski, Ph.D.
Professor of Science
   and Environmental Education
Eastern Illinois University
Charleston, Illinois

Barbara Brooks Simons
Science Writer
Boston, Massachusetts

Thomas R. Wellnitz
Science Instructor
The Paideia School
Atlanta, Georgia

Michael Wysession, Ph.D.
Associate Professor of Earth and
   Planetary Sciences
Washington University
St. Louis, Missouri

Reading Consultants

Kate Kinsella

Kate Kinsella, Ed.D., is a faculty member in the Department of Secondary Education at San Francisco State University. A specialist in second-language acquisition and adolescent literacy development across the secondary curricula, Dr. Kinsella earned her master's degree in TESOL from San Francisco State University and her Ed.D. in Second Language Acquisition from the University of San Francisco.

Kevin Feldman

Kevin Feldman, Ed.D., is the Director of Reading and Early Intervention with the Sonoma County Office of Education (SCOE) and an independent educational consultant. At the SCOE, he develops, organizes, and monitors programs related to K-12 literacy. Dr. Feldman has a master's degree from the University of California, Riverside, in Special Education, Learning Disabilities, and Instructional Design. He earned his Ed.D. in Curriculum and Instruction from the University of San Francisco.

Mathematics Consultant

William Tate, Ph.D.
Professor of Education and
   Applied Statistics and
   Computation
Washington University
St. Louis, Missouri

Contributing Writers

W. Russell Blake, Ph.D.
Planetarium Director
Plymouth Community
   Intermediate School
Plymouth, Massachusetts

Rose-Marie Botting
Science Teacher
Broward County School District
Fort Lauderdale, Florida

Jeffrey C. Callister
Former Earth Science Instructor
Newburgh Free Academy
Newburgh, New York

Colleen Campos
Science Teacher
Laredo Middle School
Aurora, Colorado

Holly Estes
Science Teacher
Hale Middle School
Stow, Massachusetts

Edward Evans
Former Science Teacher
Hilton Central School
Hilton, New York

Lauren Magruder
Science Instructor
St. Michael's Country Day School
Newport, Rhode Island

Beth Miaoulis
Technology Writer
Sherborn, Massachusetts

Emery Pineo
Science Teacher
Barrington Middle School
Barrington, Rhode Island

Karen Riley Sievers
Science Teacher
Callanan Middle School
Des Moines, Iowa

Sharon M. Stroud
Science Teacher
Widefield High School
Colorado Springs, Colorado

Reviewers

California Master Teacher Board

Joel Austin
Roosevelt Middle School
San Francisco, California

Donna Baker
Riverview Middle School
Bay Point, California

Luz Castillo
Prairie Vista Middle School
Hawthorne, California

Laura Finco
Stone Valley Middle School
Alamo, California

Tawiah Finley
Central Middle School
Riverside, California

Glen Hanneman
San Lorenzo Middle School
King City, California

Al Janulaw
Sonoma State University (retired)
Rohnert Park, California

Sharon Janulaw
Sonoma County Office of Education
Santa Rosa, California

Cindy Krueger
Washington Middle School
La Habra, California

Diane Maynard
Vineyard Junior High
Alta Loma, California

Catherine Nicholas
Rio Norte Junior High School
Santa Clarita, California

Susan Pritchard, Ph.D
Washington Middle School
La Habra, California

Ingrid Salim
Harper Junior High School
Davis, California

Tia Shields
Nicolas Junior High School
Fullerton, California

Mimi Wentz
TeWinkle Middle School
Costa Mesa, California

Jocelyn Young
El Dorado High School
Placentia, California

California Content Reviewers

Richard Berry, Ph.D.
Department of Geological Sciences
San Diego State University
San Diego, California

Londa Borer-Skov, Ph.D.
Department of Chemistry
California State University Sacramento
Sacramento, California

Eugene Chiang, Ph.D.
Department of Astronomy
University of California Berkeley
Berkeley, California

Susan Collins, Ph.D.
Department of Chemistry and Biochemistry
California State University Northridge
Northridge, California

Debra Fischer, Ph.D.
Department of Physics and Astronomy
San Francisco State University
San Francisco, California

James Hetrick, Ph.D.
Department of Physics
University of the Pacific
Stockton, California

Rita Hoots
Department of Science
Woodland College
Woodland, California

Janet Kruse
Discovery Museum
Sacramento, California

Michael Mastrandrea, Ph.D.
Center for Environmental
    Science and Policy
Stanford University
Stanford, California

George Matsumoto, Ph.D.
Senior Education and Research Specialist
Monterey Bay Aquarium Research Institute
Moss Landing, California

Robert Mellors, Ph.D.
Department of Geological Sciences
San Diego State University
San Diego, California

Donald Merhaut, Ph.D.
Department of Botany and Plant Science
University of California Riverside
Riverside, California

Eric Norman, Ph.D.
Lawrence Berkeley National Lab
University of California Berkeley
Berkeley, California

John Platt
Department of Earth Sciences
University of Southern California
Los Angeles, California

James Prince, Ph.D.
Department of Biology
California State University Fresno
Fresno, California

Gerald Sanders, Sr.
Department of Biology
San Diego State University
San Diego, California

Susan Schwartz, Ph.D.
Department of Earth Sciences
University of California Santa Cruz
Santa Cruz, California

Lynn Yarris, M.A.
Lawrence Berkeley National Lab
University of California Berkeley
Berkeley, California

Content Reviewers

Paul Beale, Ph.D.
Department of Physics
University of Colorado
Boulder, Colorado

Jeff Bodart, Ph.D.
Chipola Junior College
Marianna, Florida

Michael Castellani, Ph.D.
Department of Chemistry
Marshall University
Huntington, West Virginia

Eugene Chiang, Ph.D.
Department of Astronomy
University of California – Berkeley
Berkeley, California

Charles C. Curtis, Ph.D.
Department of Physics
University of Arizona
Tucson, Arizona

Daniel Kirk-Davidoff, Ph.D.
Department of Meteorology
University of Maryland
College Park, Maryland

Diane T. Doser, Ph.D.
Department of Geological Sciences
University of Texas at El Paso
El Paso, Texas

R. E. Duhrkopf, Ph.D.
Department of Biology
Baylor University
Waco, Texas

Michael Hacker
Co-director, Center for
    Technological Literacy
Hofstra University
Hempstead, New York

Michael W. Hamburger, Ph.D.
Department of Geological Sciences
Indiana University
Bloomington, Indiana

Alice K. Hankla, Ph.D.
The Galloway School
Atlanta, Georgia

Donald C. Jackson, Ph.D.
Department of Molecular Pharmacology,
    Physiology, & Biotechnology
Brown University
Providence, Rhode Island

Jeremiah N. Jarrett, Ph.D.
Department of Biological Sciences
Central Connecticut State University
New Britain, Connecticut

David Lederman, Ph.D.
Department of Physics
West Virginia University
Morgantown, West Virginia

Becky Mansfield, Ph.D.
Department of Geography
Ohio State University
Columbus, Ohio

Elizabeth M. Martin, M.S.
Department of Chemistry and Biochemistry
College of Charleston
Charleston, South Carolina

Joe McCullough, Ph.D.
Department of Natural and
    Applied Sciences
Cabrillo College
Aptos, California

Robert J. Mellors, Ph.D.
Department of Geological Sciences
San Diego State University
San Diego, California

Joseph M. Moran, Ph.D.
American Meteorological Society
Washington, D.C.

David J. Morrissey, Ph.D.
Department of Chemistry
Michigan State University
East Lansing, Michigan

Philip A. Reed, Ph.D.
Department of Occupational & Technical
    Studies
Old Dominion University
Norfolk, Virginia

Scott M. Rochette, Ph.D.
Department of the Earth Sciences
State University of New York, College at
    Brockport
Brockport, New York

Laurence D. Rosenhein, Ph.D.
Department of Chemistry
Indiana State University
Terre Haute, Indiana

Ronald Sass, Ph.D.
Department of Biology and Chemistry
Rice University
Houston, Texas

George Schatz, Ph.D.
Department of Chemistry
Northwestern University
Evanston, Illinois

Sara Seager, Ph.D.
Carnegie Institution of Washington
Washington, D.C.

Robert M. Thornton, Ph.D.
Section of Plant Biology
University of California
Davis, California

John R. Villarreal, Ph.D.
College of Science and Engineering
The University of Texas – Pan American
Edinburg, Texas

Kenneth Welty, Ph.D.
School of Education
University of Wisconsin–Stout
Menomonie, Wisconsin

Edward J. Zalisko, Ph.D.
Department of Biology
Blackburn College
Carlinville, Illinois

Safety Reviewers

W. H. Breazeale, Ph.D.
Department of Chemistry
College of Charleston
Charleston, South Carolina

Ruth Hathaway, Ph.D.
Hathaway Consulting
Cape Girardeau, Missouri

Douglas Mandt
Science Education Consultant
Edgewood, Washington

Teacher Reviewers

David R. Blakely
Arlington High School
Arlington, Massachusetts

Jane E. Callery
Two Rivers Magnet Middle School
East Hartford, Connecticut

Melissa Lynn Cook
Oakland Mills High School
Columbia, Maryland

James Fattic
Southside Middle School
Anderson, Indiana

Dan Gabel
Hoover Middle School
Rockville, Maryland

Wayne Goates
Eisenhower Middle School
Goddard, Kansas

Katherine Bobay Graser
Mint Hill Middle School
Charlotte, North Carolina

Darcy Hampton
Deal Junior High School
Washington, D.C.

Karen Kelly
Pierce Middle School
Waterford, Michigan

David Kelso
Manchester High School Central
Manchester, New Hampshire

Benigno Lopez, Jr.
Sleepy Hill Middle School
Lakeland, Florida

Angie L. Matamoros, Ph.D.
ALM Consulting, Inc.
Weston, Florida

Tim McCollum
Charleston Middle School
Charleston, Illinois

Bruce A. Mellin
Brooks School
North Andover, Massachusetts

Ella Jay Parfitt
Southeast Middle School
Baltimore, Maryland

Evelyn A. Pizzarello
Louis M. Klein Middle School
Harrison, New York

Kathleen M. Poe
Fletcher Middle School
Jacksonville, Florida

Shirley Rose
Lewis and Clark Middle School
Tulsa, Oklahoma

Linda Sandersen
Greenfield Middle School
Greenfield, Wisconsin

Mary E. Solan
Southwest Middle School
Charlotte, North Carolina

Mary Stewart
University of Tulsa
Tulsa, Oklahoma

Paul Swenson
Billings West High School
Billings, Montana

Thomas Vaughn
Arlington High School
Arlington, Massachusetts

Susan C. Zibell
Central Elementary
Simsbury, Connecticut

Activity Field Testers

Nicki Bibbo
Witchcraft Heights School
Salem, Massachusetts

Rose-Marie Botting
Broward County Schools
Fort Lauderdale, Florida

Colleen Campos
Laredo Middle School
Aurora, Colorado

Elizabeth Chait
W. L. Chenery Middle School
Belmont, Massachusetts

Holly Estes
Hale Middle School
Stow, Massachusetts

Laura Hapgood
Plymouth Community
    Intermediate School
Plymouth, Massachusetts

Mary F. Lavin
Plymouth Community
    Intermediate School
Plymouth, Massachusetts

James MacNeil, Ph.D.
Cambridge, Massachusetts

Lauren Magruder
St. Michael's Country
    Day School
Newport, Rhode Island

Jeanne Maurand
Austin Preparatory School
Reading, Massachusetts

Joanne Jackson-Pelletier
Winman Junior High School
Warwick, Rhode Island

Warren Phillips
Plymouth Public Schools
Plymouth, Massachusetts

Carol Pirtle
Hale Middle School
Stow, Massachusetts

Kathleen M. Poe
Fletcher Middle School
Jacksonville, Florida

Cynthia B. Pope
Norfolk Public Schools
Norfolk, Virginia

Anne Scammell
Geneva Middle School
Geneva, New York

Karen Riley Sievers
Callanan Middle School
Des Moines, Iowa

David M. Smith
Eyer Middle School
Allentown, Pennsylvania

Gene Vitale
Parkland School
McHenry, Illinois

Unit 1

Focus on the
BIG Idea

What is one main
source of energy
for Earth's natural
processes and
living things?

Focus on the
BIG Idea

What are the
effects of
weathering
of rock?

Focus on the
BIG Idea

What are the forces of erosion and deposition that shape our landscape?

Unit 2

Plate Tectonics and Earth's Structure

Focus on the BIG Idea

What are Earth's plates, and how do their movements change our planet's surface?

Focus on the BIG Idea

How do plate motions affect Earth's crust?

Focus on the
BIG Idea

What causes
volcanoes and
how do they
change Earth's
surface?

Unit 3

Weather and Climate

Focus on the BIG Idea

How do air pressure and temperature vary in the atmosphere?

Focus on the BIG Idea

Which weather factors produce changes in weather?

Focus on the
BIG Idea

What are the major factors that influence a region's climate?

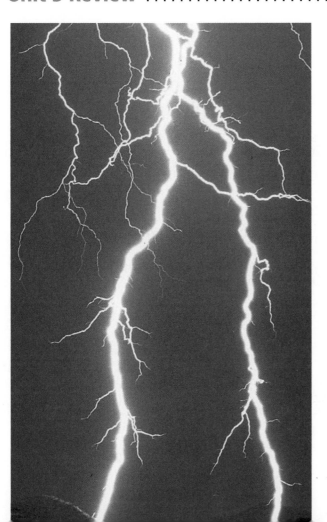

Unit 4

Ecology and Resources

Focus on the BIG Idea

What relationships exist between living things and the environment?

Focus on the BIG Idea

What defines the ecological roles and adaptations of the organisms found in different biomes?

Focus on the
BIG Idea

What are the advantages and disadvantages of various energy resources?

Reference Section

Activities

![Lab zone] **Try This Activity**   Reinforcement of key concepts

![Lab zone] **Skills Activity**   Practice of specific science inquiry skills

active art. Illustrations come alive online

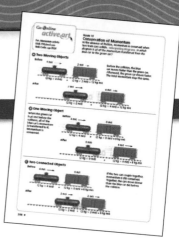

Enhance understanding through dynamic video.

Preview Get motivated with this introduction to the chapter content.

Field Trip Explore a real-world story related to the chapter content.

Assessment Review content and take an assessment.

Get connected to exciting Web resources in every lesson.

SciLINKS Find Web links on topics relating to every section.

Active Art Interact with selected visuals from every chapter online.

Planet Diary® Explore news and natural phenomena through weekly reports.

Science News® Keep up to date with the latest science discoveries.

Experience the complete text-book online and on CD-ROM.

Activities Practice skills and learn content.

Videos Explore content and learn important lab skills.

Audio Support Hear key terms spoken and defined.

Self-Assessment Use instant feedback to help you track your progress.

This textbook is organized to support your understanding of the California Science Content Standards. Understanding this organization can help you master the standards.

Focus on the BIG Idea

S 6.1.d

How do plate motions affect Earth's crust?

Every chapter begins with a Focus on the Big Idea question that is linked to a California Science Standard. Focus on the Big Idea poses a question for you to think about as you study the chapter. You will discover the answer to the question as you read.

CALIFORNIA Standards Focus

S 6.1.g Students know that the effects of an earthquake on any region vary, depending on the size of the earthquake, the distance of the region from the epicenter, the local geology, and the type of construction in the region.

- How do seismographs work?

- How do geologists monitor faults?

- How are seismographic data used?

Each section begins with a Standards Focus. You will learn about these California Science Standards as you read the section.

The Standards Focus is broken down into two to four Key Concept questions. You will find the answers to these questions as you read the section.

Standards Key

Grade Level   Standard Set and Standard

S 6.1.g

Content Area
S for Science
E-LA for English-Language Arts
Math for Mathematics

The next several pages will introduce you to the California Science Content Standards for Grade 6. There are seven sets of standards that cover the material you will be learning this year. Each standard set contains several specific standards that tell you what you need to know. For Grade 6, these standards focus mainly on earth science. Some of the standards also help you learn about relationships between earth science and other branches of science.

STANDARD SET 1

Plate Tectonics and Earth's Structure

1. **Plate tectonics accounts for important features of Earth's surface and major geologic events. As a basis for understanding this concept:**

   1. a. *Students know* evidence of plate tectonics is derived from the fit of the continents; the location of earthquakes, volcanoes, and midocean ridges; and the distribution of fossils, rock types, and ancient climatic zones.
   1. b. *Students know* Earth is composed of several layers: a cold, brittle lithosphere; a hot, convecting mantle; and a dense, metallic core.
   1. c. *Students know* lithospheric plates the size of continents and oceans move at rates of centimeters per year in response to movements in the mantle.

What It Means to You

You will learn about the structure of Earth and how scientists have identified that structure. You will learn that Earth is divided into layers. The top layer is the crust, which is divided into giant sections called plates. These plates move very slowly around Earth's surface. Volcanoes and earthquakes are common where one plate slides past or under another plate.

Where You Will Learn It

Chapter 4

STANDARD SET 1, continued

1. d. *Students know* that earthquakes are sudden motions along breaks in the crust called faults and that volcanoes and fissures are locations where magma reaches the surface.

1. e. *Students know* major geologic events, such as earthquakes, volcanic eruptions, and mountain building, result from plate motions.

1. f. *Students know* how to explain major features of California geology (including mountains, faults, volcanoes) in terms of plate tectonics.

1. g. *Students know* how to determine the epicenter of an earthquake and know that the effects of an earthquake on any region vary, depending on the size of the earthquake, the distance of the region from the epicenter, the local geology, and the type of construction in the region.

What It Means to You

You will learn how the motion of Earth's plates causes earthquakes and volcanoes and builds mountains. Moving plates shaped many features of California's landscape, such as its mountain ranges and faults. You will also learn how scientists measure and locate earthquakes, and what determines how much damage an earthquake does.

Where You Will Learn It

Chapters 4, 5, and 6

2. Topography is reshaped by the weathering of rock and soil and by the transportation and deposition of sediment. As a basis for understanding this concept:

2. a. *Students know* water running downhill is the dominant process in shaping the landscape, including California's landscape.

2. b. *Students know* rivers and streams are dynamic systems that erode, transport sediment, change course, and flood their banks in natural and recurring patterns.

2. c. *Students know* beaches are dynamic systems in which the sand is supplied by rivers and moved along the coast by the action of waves.

2. d. *Students know* earthquakes, volcanic eruptions, landslides, and floods change human and wildlife habitats.

What It Means To You

You will learn about the forces that shape Earth's surface. Moving water is the most important of these forces. You will learn how rivers and oceans shape the land by eroding, or wearing away, material and carrying that material to other places. You will also learn how rapid natural events such as earthquakes, volcanoes, landslides, and floods shape the land. These events can affect all living things, including humans, and can have effects that last long after the event itself.

Where You Will Learn It

Chapters 2, 3, 5, 6, and 10

STANDARD SET 3

Heat (Thermal Energy) (Physical Science)

3. **Heat moves in a predictable flow from warmer objects to cooler objects until all the objects are at the same temperature. As a basis for understanding this concept:**

   3. a. *Students know* energy can be carried from one place to another by heat flow or by waves, including water, light and sound waves, or by moving objects.

   3. b. *Students know* that when fuel is consumed, most of the energy released becomes heat energy.

What It Means to You

You will learn what energy is and how it is transmitted from place to place. Energy can exist in many forms, but in all forms, it is the ability to do work or cause a change. You will learn how waves, heat, and moving objects carry energy. You will also learn how energy can change from one form to another. One example is the burning of a fuel such as coal in a power plant. The fuel's stored energy is changed into other forms. Some of the energy becomes electricity, but most of it becomes heat.

Where You Will Learn It

Chapters 1 and 12

3. c. *Students know know* heat flows in solids by conduction (which involves no flow of matter) and in fluids by conduction and by convection (which involves flow of matter).

3. d. *Students know* heat energy is also transferred between objects by radiation (radiation can travel through space).

What It Means to You

You will learn the three ways in which heat can flow between objects. You will learn that two of these ways, conduction and convection, need matter in order to transfer heat. Conversely, radiation can transfer energy through empty space. You will learn how each of these processes transfers heat, and discover examples of each process.

Where You Will Learn It

Chapters 1, 4, and 7

4. Many phenomena on Earth's surface are affected by the transfer of energy through radiation and convection currents. As a basis for understanding this concept:

4. a. *Students know* the sun is the major source of energy for phenomena on Earth's surface; it powers winds, ocean currents, and the water cycle.

4. b. *Students know* solar energy reaches Earth through radiation, mostly in the form of visible light.

What It Means to You

You will learn that the sun provides most of the energy that powers events on Earth. This energy travels to Earth through radiation. You will also learn that wind, ocean currents, and weather all get their energy directly or indirectly from the Sun. You will understand how the sun's energy drives air and water movements on Earth.

Where You Will Learn It

Chapters 1, 7, 8, and 9

STANDARD SET 4, continued

4. c. *Students know* heat from Earth's interior reaches the surface primarily through convection.

4. d. *Students know* convection currents distribute heat in the atmosphere and oceans.

4. e. *Students know* differences in pressure, heat, air movement, and humidity result in changes of weather.

What It Means to You

You will learn how heat is transferred inside Earth and in Earth's atmosphere and oceans. You will see that convection currents caused by changing amounts of heat bring energy from deep inside Earth to the surface. Similar currents carry heat through the atmosphere and oceans. You will learn how these currents, along with changes in pressure and the amount of water in the air, cause changes in the weather.

Where You Will Learn It

Chapters 4, 7, 8, and 9

STANDARD SET 5

Ecology (Life Sciences)

5. **Organisms in ecosystems exchange energy and nutrients among themselves and with the environment. As a basis for understanding this concept:**

   5. a. *Students know* energy entering ecosystems as sunlight is transferred by producers into chemical energy through photosynthesis and then from organism to organism through food webs.

   5. b. *Students know* matter is transferred over time from one organism to others in the food web and between organisms and the physical environment.

What It Means to You

You have seen how energy is transferred through the nonliving parts of Earth. In this standard set, you will learn how energy is transferred among living things and between living things and their environments. Living things depend on energy from the sun. You will learn how some organisms, such as plants, use this energy to store chemical energy in the form of food. Some organisms gain their energy by eating other organisms. You will learn to trace how energy and matter move between and among living things.

Where You Will Learn It

Chapters 10 and 11

STANDARD SET 5, continued

5. c. *Students know* populations of organisms can be categorized by the functions they serve in an ecosystem.

5. d. *Students know* different kinds of organisms may play similar ecological roles in similar biomes.

5. e. *Students know* the number and types of organisms an ecosystem can support depends on the resources available and on abiotic factors, such as quantities of light and water, a range of temperatures, and soil composition.

What It Means to You

You will learn about the different roles organisms play in the ecosystems in which they live. You will also learn to compare different ecosystems. You will see that different organisms can play the same role in different ecosystems. The types of organisms that can live in an environment depend on both the nonliving parts of the environment (such as its soil and light) and on living parts of the environment (such as plants and animals).

Where You Will Learn It

Chapters 10 and 11

6. **Sources of energy and materials differ in amounts, distribution, usefulness, and the time required for their formation. As a basis for understanding this concept:**

6. a. *Students know* the utility of energy sources is determined by factors that are involved in converting these sources to useful forms and the consequences of the conversion process.

6. b. *Students know* different natural energy and material resources, including air, soil, rocks, minerals, petroleum, fresh water, wildlife, and forests, and know how to classify them as renewable or nonrenewable.

6. c. *Students know* the natural origin of the materials used to make common objects.

What It Means to You

Humans depend on their environments for many useful materials, called natural resources. People use some of these resources to produce energy. Others can be made into objects that people need and want. You will learn that some resources can be replaced relatively quickly, while others cannot be replaced once they are used up. You will be able to list and describe some examples of each type. You will also learn how to tell the difference between these two types of resources.

Where You Will Learn It

Chapters 2, 7, 11, and 12

CALIFORNIA

STANDARD SET 7

Investigation and Experimentation

7. **Scientific progress is made by asking meaningful questions and conducting careful investigations. As a basis for understanding this concept and addressing the content in the other three strands, students should develop their own questions and perform investigations. Students will:**

7. a. Develop a hypothesis.

7. b. Select and use appropriate tools and technology (including calculators, computers, balances, spring scales, microscopes, and binoculars) to perform tests, collect data, and display data.

7. c. Construct appropriate graphs from data and develop qualitative statements about the relationships between variables.

7. d. Communicate the steps and results from an investigation in written reports and oral presentations.

7. e. Recognize whether evidence is consistent with a proposed explanation.

7. f. Read a topographic map and a geologic map for evidence provided on the maps and construct and interpret a simple scale map.

7. g. Interpret events by sequence and time from natural phenomena (e.g., the relative ages of rocks and intrusions).

7. h. Identify changes in natural phenomena over time without manipulating the phenomena (e.g., a tree limb, a grove of trees, a stream, a hillslope).

What It Means to You

You will learn how scientists gather, display, and interpret information. You will perform your own experiments and investigations and learn to draw conclusions from the data you collect. For instance, you will build a weather station and use it to collect data about the weather in your area. You will also learn to read graphs and maps, and to identify how an object or an area changes over time.

Where You Will Learn It

This material is covered in the labs and activities you will do and in Chapter 1.

Your Keys to Success

Read for Meaning

This textbook has been developed to fully support your understanding of the science concepts in the California Science Standards. Each chapter contains built-in reading support.

Before You Read

Use the Standards Focus to preview the California Science Standards that are covered, the key concepts, and key terms in the section.

Standards Focus
The California Science Standards that you will learn are listed at the beginning of each section.

Key Concepts
Each science standard is broken down into smaller ideas called Key Concepts.

Key Terms Use the list of key terms to preview the vocabulary for each section.

Section 1

What Is Science?

CALIFORNIA Standards Focus

§ 6.7 Scientific progress is made by asking meaningful questions and conducting careful investigations. As a basis for understanding this concept and addressing the content in the other three strands, students should develop their own questions and perform investigations. Students will:

a. Develop a hypothesis.

c. Construct appropriate graphs from data and develop qualitative statements about the relationships between variables.

- What skills do scientists use?
- What is scientific inquiry?
- How do scientific theories differ from scientific laws?

Key Terms
- science
- observing
- inferring
- predicting
- scientific inquiry
- hypothesis
- controlled experiment
- variable
- manipulated variable
- responding variable
- data
- scientific theory

Lab zone Standards Warm-Up

How Can Scientists Find Out What's Inside Earth?

1. Your teacher will give you a spherical object, such as a sports ball. You can think of the sphere as a model of Earth.
2. Carefully observe your sphere. What characteristics of the sphere can you observe and measure directly?
3. What characteristics of the sphere cannot be directly observed and measured?

Think It Over
Posing Questions In your notebook, list several questions that you have about Earth. Which of these questions could you answer based on direct observation? Which questions would need to be answered based on indirect evidence?

A helicopter lands near the top of an erupting volcano. With care and speed, a team of scientists get out to do their work. "I've been out there sometimes when lava is shooting out of the ground 100 meters high," says Margaret Mangan, a scientist who studies volcanoes. "The main thing you're struck with is the sound. It's like the roaring of many jet engines. Then there's the smell of sulfur, which is choking. The wind can blow particles from the lava fountain over you, little bits of congealed lava. It feels like a hot sandstorm."

Dr. Mangan has observed many volcanic eruptions of Mount Kilauea in Hawaii. She studies the red-hot lava. She wants to know why lava sometimes erupts in huge fountains, but at other times erupts in gently flowing streams.

As You Read

Key Concepts in boldface sentences allow you to focus on the important ideas of the chapter.

Look for the green and yellow keys to find the key concepts in each section.

Skills Scientists Use

Science is the study of the natural world. Science includes all of the knowledge gained by exploring nature. To think and work like a scientist, you need to use the same skills that they do. **Scientists use the skills of observing, inferring, and predicting to learn more about the natural world.**

Observing Scientists observe things. **Observing** means using one or more senses to gather information. Your senses include sight, hearing, touch, taste, and smell. Each day of your life, you observe things that help you decide what to eat, what to wear, and whether to stay inside or go out.

Scientists usually make observations in a careful, orderly way. They make both qualitative and quantitative observations. Qualitative observations are descriptions that don't involve numbers or measurements. Noticing that a ball is round, that milk smells sour, or that a car is moving is a qualitative observation. Quantitative observations are measurements. You make a quantitative observation when you measure your height or weight. In science, observations may also be called evidence, or data.

Inferring When you explain your observations, you are **inferring,** or making an inference. Inferences are based on reasoning from what you already know. You make inferences all the time without thinking about it. For example, your teacher gives lots of surprise quizzes. So if your teacher walks into the room carrying a stack of paper, you may infer that the pages contain a quiz. But inferences are not always correct. The papers could be announcements to be taken home.

Predicting Every day, people make statements about the future. **Predicting** means making a forecast of what will happen in the future based on past experience or ... ientists predict the ... and current infor... t is based on data, ...ss.

... based on?

Go Online
PHSchool.com

For: More on scientific thinking
Visit: PHSchool.com
Web Code: cgd-6011

FIGURE 1 Inferring
When you explain or interpret your observations, you are making an inference. **Inferring** How do you think these young women obtained the stuffed bear? Explain your reasoning.

Creep

Go Online
active art

For: Mass Movement activity
Visit: PHSchool.com
Web Code: cfp-2031

Creep Creep is the very slow downhill movement of rock and soil. It can even occur on gentle slopes. Creep often results from the freezing and thawing of water in cracked layers of rock beneath the soil. Like the movement of an hour hand on a clock, creep is so slow you can barely notice it. But you can see the effects of creep in objects such as telephone poles, gravestones, and fenceposts. Creep may tilt these objects at spooky angles. Landscapes affected by creep may have the eerie, out-of-kilter look of a funhouse in an amusement park.

Reading Checkpoint What is the main difference between a slump and a landslide?

Section 1 Assessment

S 6.2; E-LA: Reading 6.1.0

Vocabulary Skill Latin Word Origins Review the Latin word *de-*and *positus.* Use what you've learned to explain the meaning of *deposition.*

Reviewing Key Concepts
1. **a.** Listing What are five agents of erosion?
   b. Defining In your own words, write a definition of *erosion.*
   c. Predicting Over time, how will erosion and deposition affect a mountain range? Explain.
2. **a.** Listing What are the four types of mass movement?
   b. Relating Cause and Effect What force causes all types of mass movement?
   c. Inferring A fence runs across a steep hillside. The fence is tilted downhill and forms a curve rather than a straight line. What can you infer happened to the fence? Explain.

Lab zone At-Home Activity

Evidence of Erosion After a rainstorm, take a walk with an adult family member around your neighborhood. Look for evidence of erosion. Try to find areas where there is loose soil, sand, gravel, or rock. **CAUTION:** *Stay away from any large pile of loose sand or soil—it may slide without warning.* Which areas have the most erosion? The least erosion? How does the slope of the ground affect the amount of erosion? Sketch or take photographs of the areas showing evidence of erosion.

After You Read

The Section Assessment tests your understanding of the Key Concepts. Each bank of Reviewing Key Concept questions here focuses on one of the Key Concepts.

If you can't answer these items, go back and review the section.

Your Keys to Success

How to Read Science

 The target reading skills introduced on this page will help you read and understand information in this textbook. Each chapter introduces a reading skill. Developing these reading skills is key to becoming a successful reader in science and other subject areas.

Preview Text Structure By understanding how textbooks are organized, you can gain information from them more effectively. This textbook is organized with red headings and blue subheadings. Before you read, preview the headings. Ask yourself questions to guide you as you read. **(Chapter 1)**

Preview Visuals The visuals in your science textbook provide important information. Visuals are photographs, graphs, tables, diagrams, and illustrations. Before you read, take the time to preview the visuals in a section. Look closely at the title, labels, and captions. Then ask yourself questions about the visuals. **(Chapter 2)**

Sequence Many parts of a science textbook are organized by sequence. Sequence is the order in which a series of events occurs. Some sections may discuss events in a process that has a beginning and an end. Other sections may describe a continuous process that does not have an end. **(Chapters 3 and 10)**

Compare and Contrast Science texts often make comparisons. When you compare and contrast, you examine the similarities and differences between things. You can compare and contrast by using a table or a Venn diagram. **(Chapters 8 and 12)**

Identify Main Ideas As you read, you can understand a section or paragraph more clearly by finding the main idea. The main idea is the most important idea. The details in a section or paragraph support the main idea. Headings and subheadings can often help you identify the main ideas. **(Chapters 5 and 11)**

Identify Supporting Evidence Science textbooks often describe the scientific evidence that supports a theory or hypothesis. Scientific evidence includes data and facts, information whose accuracy can be confirmed by experiments or observation. A hypothesis is a possible explanation for observations made by scientists or an answer to a scientific question. **(Chapter 4)**

Create Outlines You can create outlines to help you clarify the text. An outline shows the relationship between main ideas and supporting details. Use the text structure—headings, subheadings, key concepts, and key terms—to help you figure out information to include in your outline. **(Chapter 6 and 9)**

Take Notes Science chapters are packed with information. Taking good notes is one way to help you remember key ideas and to see the big picture. When you take notes, include key ideas, a few details, and summaries. **(Chapter 7)**

Target Reading Skills

Each chapter provides a target reading skill with clear instruction to help you read and understand the text. You will apply the skill as you read. Then you will record what you've learned in the section and chapter assessments.

Before You Read
Each chapter introduces a target reading skill and provides examples and practice exercises.

As You Read
As you read, you can use the target reading skill to help you increase your understanding.

After You Read
You can apply the target reading skill in the Section Assessments and in the Chapter Assessments.

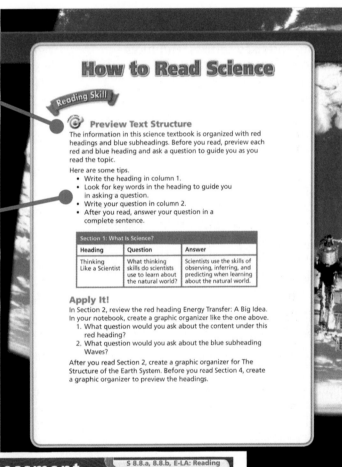

How to Read Science

Reading Skill

Preview Text Structure

The information in this science textbook is organized with red headings and blue subheadings. Before you read, preview each red and blue heading and ask a question to guide you as you read the topic.

Here are some tips.
- Write the heading in column 1.
- Look for key words in the heading to guide you in asking a question.
- Write your question in column 2.
- After you read, answer your question in a complete sentence.

Section 1: What Is Science?

Heading	Question	Answer
Thinking Like a Scientist	What thinking skills do scientists use to learn about the natural world?	Scientists use the skills of observing, inferring, and predicting when learning about the natural world.

Apply It!

In Section 2, review the red heading Energy Transfer: A Big Idea. In your notebook, create a graphic organizer like the one above.
1. What question would you ask about the content under this red heading?
2. What question would you ask about the blue subheading Waves?

After you read Section 2, create a graphic organizer for The Structure of the Earth System. Before you read Section 4, create a graphic organizer to preview the headings.

Section 3 Assessment
S 8.8.a, 8.8.b, E-LA: Reading 8.2.0, Math: 7NS1.2

Target Reading Skill Preview Text Structure
Complete the graphic organizer for this section. What question did you ask about Weight and Mass? What was your answer?

Reviewing Key Concepts
1. a. Identifying What is the standard measurement system used by scientists around the world?
   b. Predicting Suppose that two scientists use different measurement systems in their work. What problems might arise if they shared their data?
2. a. Listing What are the SI units of length, mass, volume, density, time, and temperature?

b. Estimating Estimate the length of a baseball bat and mass of a baseball in SI units. How can you check how close your estimates are?
c. Describing Outline a step-by-step method for determining the density of a baseball.

Math Practice

Two solid cubes have the same mass. They each have a mass of 50 g.

3. Calculating Density Cube A has a volume of 2 cm × 2 cm × 2 cm. What is its density?
4. Calculating Density Cube B has a volume of 4 cm × 4 cm × 4 cm. What is its density?

Your Keys to Success

Build Science Vocabulary

 Studying science involves learning a new vocabulary. Here are some vocabulary skills to help you learn the meaning of words you do not recognize.

Word Analysis You can use your knowledge of word parts—prefixes, suffixes, and roots— to determine the meaning of unfamiliar words.

Prefixes A prefix is a word part that is added at the beginning of a root or base word to change its meaning. Knowing the meaning of prefixes will help you figure out new words. You will practice this skill in Chapter 12.

Suffixes A suffix is a letter or group of letters added to the end of a word to form a new word with a slightly different meaning. Adding a suffix to a word often changes its part of speech. You will practice this skill in Chapter 2.

Word Origins Many science words come to English from other languages, such as Greek and Latin. By learning the meaning of a few common Greek and Latin roots, you can determine the meaning of new science words. You will practice this skill in Chapters 3, 4, and 7.

Use Clues to Determine Meaning

When you come across a word you don't recognize in science texts, you can use context clues to figure out what the word means. First look for clues in the word itself. Then look at the surrounding words, sentences, and paragraphs for clues. You will practice this skill in Chapter 6.

Identify Multiple Meanings

To understand science concepts, you must use terms precisely. Some familiar words may have different meanings in science. Watch for these multiple-meaning words as you read. You will practice this skill in Chapter 8.

Identify Related Word Forms

You can increase your vocabulary by learning related forms of words or word families. If you know the meaning of a verb form, you may be able to figure out the related noun and adjective forms. You will practice this skill in Chapter 10.

atmos + sphaira = atmosphere
vapor   sphere   a layer of
gas   vapor or
                   gases that
                   surrounds
                   Earth

Vocabulary Skills

One of the important steps in reading this science textbook is to be sure that you understand the key terms. Your book shows several strategies to help learn important vocabulary.

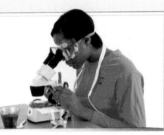

Build Science Vocabulary

The images shown here represent some of the key terms in this chapter. You can use this vocabulary skill to help you understand the meaning of some key terms in this chapter.

Vocabulary Skill

High-Use Academic Words

High-use words are words that are used frequently in academic reading, writing, and discussions. These words are different from key terms because they appear in many subject areas.

Word	Definition	Example Sentence
area (AIR ee uh) p. 21	n. A particular part of a place or surface	In what area of the city is your school located?
factor (FAK tur) p. 9	n. A fact to be considered	In a race, one factor to think about is the distance you will run.
occur (uh KUR) p. 37	v. To take place; to happen	The scientist predicted that an earthquake might occur at the site.

Apply It!

Choose the word from the table that best completes the sentence.
1. Keep your work _____ clean and safe during a laboratory experiment.
2. Accidents sometimes _____ in a science laboratory.
3. Price is a(n) _____ to be considered in buying baseball tickets.

observing

Before You Read

Each chapter introduces a Vocabulary Skill with examples and practice exercises. Key terms come alive through visuals. The beginning of each section lists the key terms.

Creep

Go Online
active art

For: Mass Movement activity
Visit: PHSchool.com
Web Code: cfp-2031

Science is the study of the natural world. Science includes all of the knowledge gained by exploring nature. To think and work like a scientist, you need to use the same skills that they do. **Scientists use the skills of observing, inferring, and predicting to learn more about the natural world.**

Observing Scientists observe things. **Observing** means using one or more senses to gather information. Your senses include sight, hearing, touch, taste, and smell. Each day of your life, you observe things that help you decide what to eat, what to wear, and whether to stay inside or go out.

As You Read

Each key term is highlighted in yellow, appears in boldface type, and is followed by a definition.

Section 1 Assessment
S 6.2; E-LA: Reading 6.1.0

Vocabulary Skill Latin Word Origins Review the Latin word *de-* and *positus*. Use what you've learned to explain the meaning of *deposition*.

Reviewing Key Concepts

1. a. Listing What are five agents of erosion?
   b. Defining In your own words, write a definition of *erosion*.
   c. Predicting Over time, how will erosion and deposition affect a mountain range? Explain.
2. a. Listing What are the four types of mass movement?
   b. Relating Cause and Effect What force causes all types of mass movement?
   c. Inferring A fence runs across a steep hillside. The fence is tilted downhill and forms a curve rather than a straight line. What can you infer happened to the fence? Explain.

Lab zone At-Home **Activity**

Evidence of Erosion After a rainstorm, take a walk with an adult family member around your neighborhood. Look for evidence of erosion. Try to find areas where there is loose soil, sand, gravel, or rock. **CAUTION:** Stay away from any large pile of loose sand or soil—it may slide without warning. Which areas have the most erosion? The least erosion? How does the slope of the ground affect the amount of erosion? Sketch or take photographs of the areas showing evidence of erosion.

After You Read

You can practice the Vocabulary Skill in the Section Assessments. You can apply your understanding of the key terms in the Chapter Assessments.

Build Science Vocabulary

High-Use Academic Words

High-use academic words are words that are used frequently in classroom reading, writing, and discussions. They are different from key terms because they appear in many subject areas.

Learn the Words

Each unit contains a chapter that introduces high-use academic words. The introduction describes the words, provides examples, and includes practice exercises.

Practice Using the Words

You can practice using the high-use academic words in the Section Assessments.

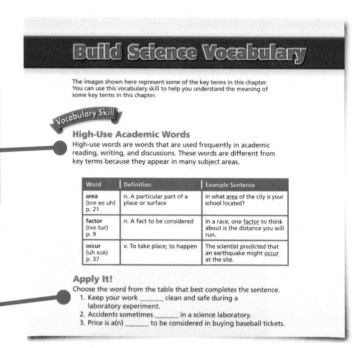

Build Science Vocabulary

The images shown here represent some of the key terms in this chapter. You can use this vocabulary skill to help you understand the meaning of some key terms in this chapter.

 Vocabulary Skill

High-Use Academic Words

High-use words are words that are used frequently in academic reading, writing, and discussions. These words are different from key terms because they appear in many subject areas.

Word	Definition	Example Sentence
area (EHR ee uh) p. 21	*n.* A particular part of a place or surface	In what area of the city is your school located?
factor (FAK tur) p. 9	*n.* A fact to be considered	In a race, one factor to think about is the distance you will run.
occur (uh KUR) p. 37	*v.* To take place; to happen	The scientist predicted that an earthquake might occur at the site.

Apply It!

Choose the word from the table that best completes the sentence.
1. Keep your work _____ clean and safe during a laboratory experiment.
2. Accidents sometimes _____ in a science laboratory.
3. Price is a(n) _____ to be considered in buying baseball tickets.

Focus on Earth Science High-Use Academic Words

Learning the meaning of these words will help you improve your reading comprehension in all subject areas.

alter	contribute	feature	physical	reverse
area	convert	function	positive	series
category	define	generate	predictable	source
channel	detect	indicate	principle	structure
concept	distinct	individual	process	sustain
conduct	diversity	interpret	proportion	technique
constant	enable	layer	range	theory
construct	environment	major	region	transfer
consumer	estimate	method	reject	trigger
contact	expand	obtain	release	uniform
contract	exposure	occur	remove	vary
contrast	factor	percent	resource	

Investigations

You can explore the concepts in this textbook through inquiry. Like a real scientist, you can develop your own scientific questions and perform labs and activities to find answers. Follow the steps below when doing a lab.

1 Read the whole lab.

5 Record your data.

2 Write a purpose. What is the purpose of this activity?

3 Write a hypothesis. What is a possible explanation? Hypotheses lead to predictions that can be tested.

You can present your result orally.

6 Analyze your results. Answering the questions will help you draw conclusions.

4 Follow each step in the procedure. Pay attention to safety icons.

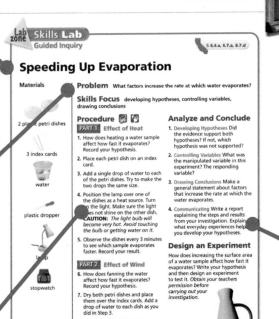

Lab Report
Purpose: To determine how to speed up the evaporation of liquids.
Hypothesis:

7 Communicate your results in a written report or oral presentation.
Your report should include:
◆ a hypothesis
◆ a purpose
◆ the steps of the procedure
◆ a record of your results
◆ a conclusion

For more information on Science Inquiry, Scientific Investigations and Safety refer to the Skills Handbook and Appendix A.

Chapter 1

Introduction to Earth Science

From space, the view of planet Earth consists of vast oceans and swirling clouds. ▶

Focus on the
BIG Idea

S 6.4.a

What is one main source of energy for Earth's natural processes and living things?

Check What You Know

A flashlight beam and a ball can model how sunlight strikes Earth. Sunlight strikes Earth's equator directly. But sunlight is more spread out where it strikes Earth's polar regions. Explain how this uneven distribution of the sun's energy affects Earth's atmosphere and oceans.

Build Science Vocabulary

The images shown here represent some of the key terms in this chapter. You can use this vocabulary skill to help you understand the meaning of some key terms in this chapter.

Vocabulary Skill

High-Use Academic Words

High-use words are words that are used frequently in academic reading, writing, and discussions. These words are different from key terms because they appear in many subject areas.

Word	Definition	Example Sentence
area (EHR ee uh) p. 21	*n.* A particular part of a place or surface	In what <u>area</u> of the city is your school located?
factor (FAK tur) p. 9	*n.* A fact to be considered	In a race, one <u>factor</u> to think about is the distance you will run.
occur (uh KUR) p. 37	*v.* To take place; to happen	The scientist predicted that an earthquake might <u>occur</u> at the site.

Apply It!

Choose the word from the table that best completes the sentence.
1. Keep your work _____ clean and safe during a laboratory experiment.
2. Accidents sometimes _____ in a science laboratory.
3. Price is a(n) _____ to be considered in buying baseball tickets.

observing

thermal energy

plateau

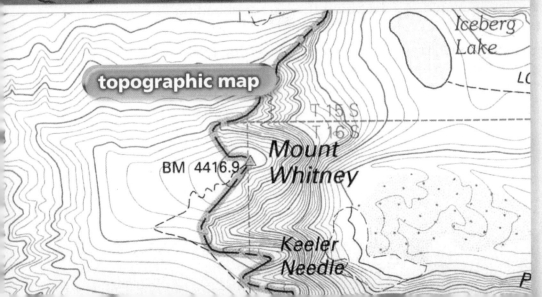

topographic map

Chapter 1
Vocabulary

Build Science Vocabulary
Online
Visit: PHSchool.com
Web Code: cwj-1010

How to Read Science

 Preview Text Structure

The information in this science textbook is organized with red headings and blue subheadings. Before you read, preview each red and blue heading and ask a question to guide you as you read the topic.

Here are some tips.

- Write the heading in column 1.
- Look for key words in the heading to guide you in asking a question.
- Write your question in column 2.
- After you read, answer your question in a complete sentence.

Section 1: What Is Science?		
Heading	**Question**	**Answer**
Thinking Like a Scientist	What thinking skills do scientists use to learn about the natural world?	Scientists use the skills of observing, inferring, and predicting when learning about the natural world.

Apply It!

In Section 2, review the red heading Energy Transfer: A Big Idea. In your notebook, create a graphic organizer like the one above.

1. What question would you ask about the content under this red heading?
2. What question would you ask about the blue subheading Waves?

After you read Section 2, create a graphic organizer for The Structure of the Earth System. Before you read Section 4, create a graphic organizer to preview the headings.

Getting on the Map

For this investigation, you will select a small piece of land and draw a map of its physical features.

Your Goal

To create a scale map of a small area of your neighborhood

To complete this investigation, you must

- work with your teacher or an adult family member
- choose and measure a small square piece of land
- use a compass to locate north
- draw a map to scale
- use symbols and a key to represent natural and human-made features of the land
- follow the safety guidelines in Appendix A

Plan It!

Start by looking for a suitable site. Your site should be about 300 to 1,000 square meters in area. It could be part of a park, playground, or backyard. Look for an area that includes interesting natural features such as trees, a stream, and changes in elevation. There may be some human-made structures on your site, such as a park bench or sidewalk. Once you have chosen a site, measure its boundaries and sketch its physical features. Then brainstorm ideas for symbols to include on your map. When you have completed your map, including a key and map scale, present it to your class.

What Is Science?

CALIFORNIA
Standards Focus

S 6.7 Scientific progress is made by asking meaningful questions and conducting careful investigations. As a basis for understanding this concept and addressing the content in the other three strands, students should develop their own questions and perform investigations. Students will:

a. Develop a hypothesis.

c. Construct appropriate graphs from data and develop qualitative statements about the relationships between variables.

- What skills do scientists use?
- What is scientific inquiry?
- How do scientific theories differ from scientific laws?

Key Terms

- science
- observing
- inferring
- predicting
- scientific inquiry
- hypothesis
- controlled experiment
- variable
- manipulated variable
- responding variable
- data
- scientific theory

Lab zone Standards **Warm-Up**

How Can Scientists Find Out What's Inside Earth?

1. Your teacher will give you a spherical object, such as a sports ball. You can think of the sphere as a model of Earth.
2. Carefully observe your sphere. What characteristics of the sphere can you observe and measure directly?
3. What characteristics of the sphere cannot be directly observed and measured?

Think It Over

Posing Questions In your notebook, list several questions that you have about Earth. Which of these questions could you answer based on direct observation? Which questions would need to be answered based on indirect evidence?

A helicopter lands near the top of an erupting volcano. With care and speed, a team of scientists get out to do their work. "I've been out there sometimes when lava is shooting out of the ground 100 meters high," says Margaret Mangan, a scientist who studies volcanoes. "The main thing you're struck with is the sound. It's like the roaring of many jet engines. Then there's the smell of sulfur, which is choking. The wind can blow particles from the lava fountain over you, little bits of congealed lava. It feels like a hot sandstorm."

Dr. Mangan has observed many volcanic eruptions of Mount Kilauea in Hawaii. She studies the red-hot lava. She wants to know why lava sometimes erupts in huge fountains, but at other times erupts in gently flowing streams.

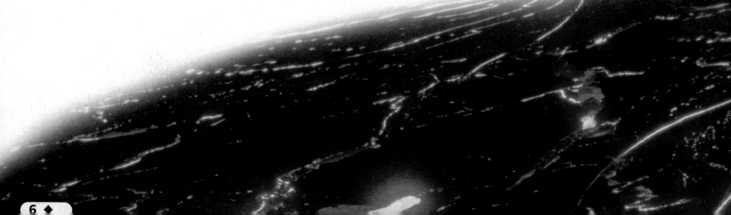

Thinking Like a Scientist

Watching a volcanic eruption, you might ask yourself questions such as: "What is lava?" and "Where does lava form?" In asking these questions, you are thinking like a scientist—a person who uses science to explore problems and answer questions about the natural world. **Science** is a way of learning about the natural world. Science is also the knowledge gained through that process. As scientists seek to understand the natural world, they use skills such as observing, inferring, and predicting.

Observing Using one or more of your senses to gather information is **observing**. Your senses include sight, hearing, touch, taste, and smell. For example, Dr. Mangan not only saw lava erupting, but she heard the noise it makes, smelled volcanic gases, and felt the lava's heat.

Inferring When you explain or interpret the things you observe, you are **inferring**, or making an inference. Making an inference doesn't mean guessing wildly. An inference is based on reasoning from what you already know. For example, Margaret Mangan inferred that differences in the gas content of the lava result in different types of eruptions. But inferences are not always correct. There could be other factors that affect the strength of a volcanic eruption.

Predicting If Dr. Mangan's inferences are correct, her results may help scientists predict whether a volcanic eruption will be strong or gentle. **Predicting** means making a forecast of what will happen in the future based on past experience or evidence.

Reading Checkpoint) **What is a prediction?**

FIGURE 1
Observing Volcanic Eruptions
Margaret Mangan studies samples of lava from Mount Kilauea, Hawaii.
Forming Operational Definitions
Based on the photograph, how would you define lava?

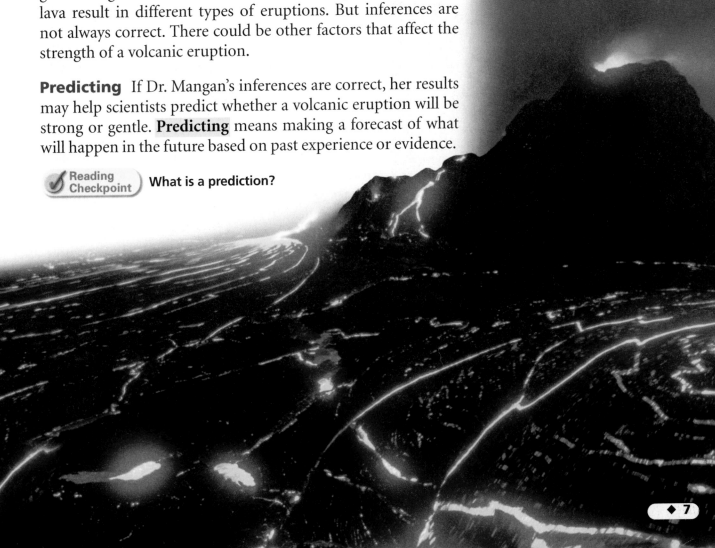

Scientific Inquiry

Asking questions about what you observe is the start of **scientific inquiry** . Scientific inquiry **refers to the many ways in which scientists study the natural world and propose explanations based on the evidence they gather.**

Posing Questions Scientific inquiry often begins with a problem or question about an observation. The questions may come from observations and inferences that you make, or just from curiosity. For example, scientists studying giant sequoia (sih KWOY uh) trees made an observation. They noticed that very few sequoia seedlings grew inside Sequoia National Park.

The scientists knew that these sequoias, shown in Figure 2, have been mostly protected from fire for more than 100 years. They also knew that sequoia seeds require fire in order to sprout. In the past, natural fires regularly burned in the sequoia groves. These fires did not kill the largest trees, but opened spaces between them. The fires also exposed bare soil. When seeds fell from cones in the remaining trees, the seeds could grow where they had sunlight and nutrients.

The scientists asked: What intensity, or strength, of fire would produce the greatest increase in sequoia seedlings? The answer to this question would help improve the use of controlled burns to get more seeds to sprout. A controlled burn is a fire that is set within a limited area to manage a forest.

Developing a Hypothesis The scientists' question about sequoia seedlings and fire can be stated as a hypothesis: The intensity of fires in sequoia groves affects the number of sequoia seedlings. A **hypothesis** (plural: *hypotheses*) is a possible explanation for a set of observations or answer to a scientific question. Hypotheses lead to predictions that can be tested. This means that scientists must be able to carry out investigations and gather evidence that will either support or disprove the hypothesis.

Designing an Experiment The scientists studying giant sequoias designed an experiment to test their hypothesis about fire and sequoia seedlings. They selected several sites where the National Park Service had used controlled burns. They compared these sites with similar sites that had not burned in more than 50 years. They rated each burned area according to the intensity of the burn. They also counted sequoia seedlings within a certain distance of mature sequoia trees in all the sites.

This experiment tested the scientists' hypothesis. A **controlled experiment** is a test of a hypothesis under conditions established by the scientist. In a controlled experiment, a scientist determines how one particular variable affects the outcome of the experiment. A **variable** is one of the factors that can change in an experiment. For example, in the experiment involving the sequoias, burn intensity was the variable that determined the outcome of the experiment.

In an experiment, the variable that a scientist changes is called the **manipulated variable** (**independent variable**). The variable that changes because of the manipulated variable is the **responding variable** (**dependent variable**). In the sequoia experiment, the manipulated variable is burn intensity. The responding variable is the growth of sequoia seedlings. In a controlled experiment, scientists control, or keep constant, all other variables. By controlling variables, scientists can eliminate the effects of the other variables as factors in their results.

 **Reading Checkpoint** What is a variable?

Lab zone **Skills Activity**

Controlling Variables
Suppose you are a scientist designing an experiment involving sequoia seedlings. You want to determine whether the seedlings grow better in ordinary forest soil or in soil covered with ash from a recent fire. What is your manipulated variable? What is your responding variable? What other variables would you need to control?

FIGURE 3
Controlled Burns
Scientists try to imitate the natural pattern of fires in sequoia groves by a program of carefully controlled burns.
Applying Concepts *What was the manipulated variable in the sequoia experiment? Explain.*

FIGURE 4
Sequoia Seedlings and Cones
After a fire, sequoia seeds can sprout and grow on the forest floor.

Collecting and Interpreting Data If you wanted to investigate the weather in your area, you would need to collect data. **Data** are the facts, figures, and other evidence gathered through observations. A data table provides an organized way to collect and record observations.

After all the data have been collected, they need to be interpreted. One useful tool that can help you interpret data is a graph. Graphs like the one in the Analyzing Data feature on this page can reveal patterns or trends in data.

In the sequoia experiment, the scientists' data were their observations of the effects of fires and of the numbers of sequoia seedlings. They interpreted these data by relating the number of seedlings to the different levels of fire intensity. The graph in the Analyzing Data feature below summarizes the scientists' observations.

Drawing Conclusions After you have gathered and interpreted your data, you can draw a conclusion about your hypothesis. A conclusion is a decision about how to interpret what you have learned from an experiment. You may decide that the data support the hypothesis. Or you may decide that the data show that the hypothesis was incorrect. Sometimes, no conclusion can be reached and more data are needed.

The scientists decided that their data showed that more seedlings sprouted around the sequoia trees after the more intense fires. Therefore, they concluded that their hypothesis was correct.

 Reading Checkpoint What is a conclusion?

Mathematical Reasoning 6.2.4

Math Analyzing Data

Sequoias and Fire

The graph shows the growth of sequoia seedlings in relation to the intensity of controlled burns. Use the graph to answer the questions.

1. **Reading Graphs** What do the bars on the graph represent?

2. **Reading Graphs** What does the height of each bar represent?

3. **Interpreting Data** Which level of burn intensity led to the most seedling production? The least seedling production?

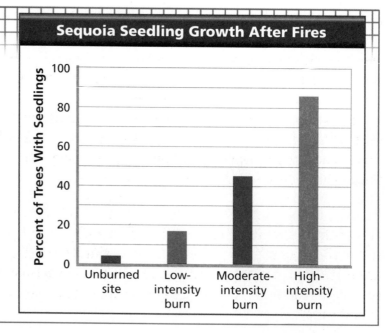

Sequoia Seedling Growth After Fires

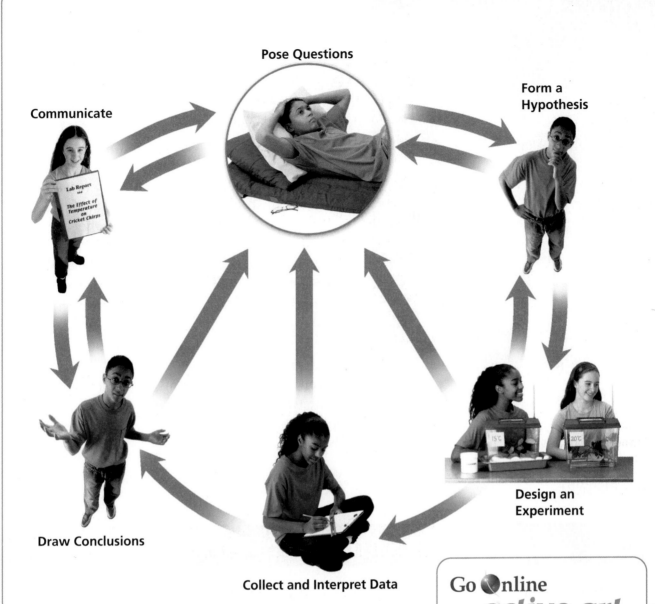

Pose Questions

Communicate

Lab Report
***
The Effect of
Temperature
on
Cricket Chirps

Form a Hypothesis

Draw Conclusions

Collect and Interpret Data

Design an Experiment

Go Online
active art

For: The Nature of Inquiry activity
Visit: PHSchool.com
Web Code: cgp-6012

Communicating An important part of scientific inquiry is communicating the results. Communicating is the sharing of ideas and experimental findings with others through writing and speaking. Scientists share their ideas in many ways. For example, they give talks at scientific meetings, exchange information on the Internet, or publish articles in scientific journals.

The scientists involved in the study of sequoias and fire presented their findings at a meeting of scientists and in a book. That made their results available to other scientists and to those who manage California's giant sequoias.

Posing New Questions Even after you have drawn a conclusion from one experiment, scientific inquiry usually doesn't end. Other scientists may repeat the experiment to determine if its results were correct. Often, the results of an experiment suggest new questions. These new questions can lead to new hypotheses.

FIGURE 5
The Nature of Inquiry
Observations at any stage of a scientific inquiry may lead you to change your hypothesis or experiment. **Applying Concepts** *Why is observation important during scientific inquiry?*

FIGURE 6
Law of Gravity
The force of gravity pulls the water in this waterfall toward Earth's center.

Scientific Theories and Laws

As scientists study the natural world, they develop concepts that explain their observations. These concepts are called scientific theories. A **scientific theory** is a well-tested scientific concept that explains a wide range of observations. An accepted theory has withstood repeated tests. But if tests fail to support a theory, scientists change the theory or abandon it.

When scientists repeatedly observe the same result in specific circumstances, they may arrive at a scientific law. **Unlike a theory, a scientific law describes an observed pattern in nature, but does not provide an explanation for it.** A scientific law is a statement that describes what scientists expect to happen every time under a particular set of conditions. For example, the law of gravity states that the force of gravity acts between all objects in the universe. As a result of gravity, any two objects in the universe attract each other. Scientists have repeatedly tested this law and found it to be true.

 Reading Checkpoint) **What is a scientific law?**

Section 1 Assessment

S 6.7.a, 6.7.c E-LA: Reading 6.1.0, Writing 6.2.0

Vocabulary Skill High-Use Academic Words In a complete sentence, explain what happens in a controlled experiment. Use the word *factor* in your explanation.

Reviewing Key Concepts

1. a. Reviewing What is science?
   b. Explaining Explain three main skills that scientists use.
   c. Applying Concepts Can you make an inference without having made any observations? Explain your answer.
2. a. Defining Define the term *scientific inquiry*.
   b. Explaining You may have heard the saying "Red sky at morning, sailors take warning." This means that stormy weather may follow if the sky looks red at sunrise. Could you test this using scientific inquiry? Explain.
   c. Problem Solving To determine whether the saying in part (b) is true, what kinds of data would you need to collect?

3. a. Defining What is a scientific theory? What is a scientific law?
   b. Comparing and Contrasting How do scientific theories differ from scientific laws?

Writing in Science

Volcano Inquiry Look at the photograph in Figure 1. With a partner, think of a question about volcanoes that you would like to answer. Write your question in your notebook. List anything you already know about the topic of your question that might help you answer it. Then state your question as a hypothesis.

Section 2
Studying Earth

CALIFORNIA
Standards Focus

S 6.3.a Students know energy can be carried from one place to another by heat flow or by waves, including water, light and sound waves, or by moving objects.

S 6.4.a Students know the sun is the major source of energy for phenomena on Earth's surface; it powers winds, ocean currents, and the water cycle.

🔑 What are the parts of the Earth system?

🔑 How is energy transferred in the Earth system?

🔑 What are the branches of Earth science?

Key Terms
- energy
- atmosphere
- hydrosphere
- lithosphere
- biosphere
- matter
- wave
- heat
- thermal energy
- Earth science

Lab zone Standards **Warm-Up**

What Is the Source of Earth's Energy?

1. Pour 100 mL of tap water into a clear plastic jar and tighten the lid.
2. Place the jar in the sun for 10 minutes.
3. Move the jar to a shaded location and wait several minutes
4. Observe the sides of the jar. What do you see?

Think It Over
Inferring What can you infer about the energy source for the changes you observed in the bottle? Explain how the bottle could serve as model of Earth's ocean and atmosphere.

Joshua Tree National Park, in California's Mojave Desert, is a popular spot for people who enjoy the outdoors. If you visit the park, you can take a nature trail to observe desert animals and wildflowers. You can also ride a mountain bike past cactuses and Joshua trees, or explore huge granite boulders. But whatever you do, be sure to apply sunblock, wear a hat, and drink plenty of water!

When you get thirsty, you can pause in the cool shade of a boulder for a drink of water. But when you step out of the shade into the bright sun, your skin feels warm right away. You may wonder why you feel warmer in the sun than in the shade. To understand this, you need to know how sunlight is related to the concept of energy.

▼ **Joshua Tree National Park**

The Structure of the Earth System

Sunlight heats up any surface it strikes, including your skin, because it is a form of energy. **Energy** is the ability to do work, or cause change. Energy from the sun is transferred to Earth as radiation, a form of energy that can move through space. When you stepped out of the shade, the sun's radiation hit you directly. That's why you felt warmer.

Every second, the sun's radiation transfers a huge amount of energy to Earth. Sunlight provides energy for many processes on Earth. For example, in the water cycle, water moves from the oceans, to the atmosphere, to the land, and back to the oceans. The sun provides the energy for the water cycle.

Earth as a System Although the sun is millions of kilometers away, it affects everything on Earth's surface. The sun is part of a system that includes Earth's air, water, land, and living things. A system is a group of parts that work together as a whole. As in the water cycle, a change in one part of the Earth system affects other parts of the system.

🔑 **The Earth system has four main parts, or "spheres": the atmosphere, hydrosphere, lithosphere, and biosphere. As one source of energy for processes on Earth, the sun can also be considered part of the Earth system.** Figure 7 shows some of the ways in which parts of the Earth system affect each other.

FIGURE 7
Earth as a System
The atmosphere, hydrosphere, lithosphere, and biosphere together make up the Earth system. Changes in any part of the system can affect the other parts. **Interpreting Diagrams** *How does the hydrosphere affect the atmosphere?*

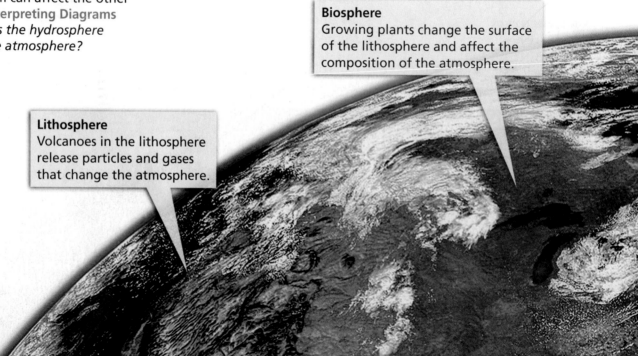

Biosphere
Growing plants change the surface of the lithosphere and affect the composition of the atmosphere.

Lithosphere
Volcanoes in the lithosphere release particles and gases that change the atmosphere.

Atmosphere The outermost sphere is the **atmosphere** (AT muh sfeer), the mixture of gases that surrounds the planet. By far the most abundant gases are nitrogen and oxygen, but the atmosphere also contains water vapor, carbon dioxide, and other gases.

Hydrosphere Earth's oceans, lakes, rivers, and ice form the **hydrosphere** (HY druh sfeer). Most of the hydrosphere consists of the salt water in the oceans, but fresh water is also part of the hydrosphere. Oceans cover more than two thirds of Earth.

Lithosphere Earth's solid, rocky outer layer is called the **lithosphere** (LITH uh sfeer). The lithosphere is made up of the continents as well as smaller landmasses called islands. The lithosphere extends under the entire ocean floor. The surface of the lithosphere varies from smooth plains to wrinkled hills and valleys to jagged mountain peaks.

The energy for some processes that shape the lithosphere comes from the heat of Earth's interior. For example, deep inside Earth, some rock melts, forming the lava that erupts from volcanoes.

Biosphere All living things—whether in the air, in the oceans or on and beneath the land surface—make up the **biosphere** (BY uh sfeer). The biosphere extends into each of the other three spheres.

 **Reading Checkpoint** What is the biosphere?

Hydrosphere
Earth's vast oceans affect the temperature of the atmosphere; flowing rivers shape the surface of the lithosphere.

Atmosphere
Storms in the atmosphere bring rains that change the surface of the lithosphere.

Moving Objects ▲
A moving object such as this baseball transfers energy from the pitcher's arm to the catcher—or the hitter's bat.

Waves ▲
When the fans cheer, sound waves transfer energy as they move through the air.

FIGURE 8
Energy Transfer
The different forms of energy transfer occur around us constantly—even at a baseball game.
Applying Concepts *What type of energy transfer is involved when ice cream melts?*

Energy Transfer: A Big Idea

Matter and energy constantly move from one part of the Earth system to another. **Matter** is what makes up everything in the universe. Matter is made up of tiny particles called atoms. Two or more atoms that are joined and act as a unit make up a molecule. For example, a water molecule consists of two hydrogen atoms and one oxygen atom.

The movement of matter cannot occur without energy transfer. Energy transfer is the movement of energy from one location to another. **Energy can be transferred from place to place by moving objects, by waves, or by heat flow.**

Moving Objects Any moving object or particle transfers energy. When a pitcher throws a baseball, the baseball carries energy with it from the pitcher to the catcher. Many types of motion in Earth's systems transfer energy in this way. For example, wind and flowing water transfer energy through the movement of particles.

Waves Energy can also be transferred by waves. A **wave** is an up-and-down or back-and-forth motion that carries energy from place to place but leaves the matter behind. For example, sound waves from one vibrating object, such as a guitar string, can travel to your ear. In order to reach your ear, sound waves require a medium, such as air, to travel through. A medium is the material through which a wave travels.

Heat Flow ▲
Heat flow transfers energy from the warm air into the cold ice cream, causing the ice cream to melt.

▲ Electromagnetic Waves
Electromagnetic waves transfer energy as they carry the TV announcer's voice and image to people outside the ballpark.

Waves can travel through many different materials. In the ocean, water is the medium for the waves. Although the wave travels through the water, the water particles vibrate in place. The waves produced by an earthquake also require a medium. These waves transfer energy as they shake the lithosphere.

Electromagnetic Waves Electromagnetic waves are waves that transfer electrical and magnetic energy. You are probably most familiar with this type of energy in the form of visible light. The sunlight that warms your skin travels to Earth as electromagnetic waves. These waves do not require a medium to travel through.

Heat Flow Heat flow takes place whenever two objects of different temperatures are brought into contact. What is heat? **Heat** is the thermal energy transferred from one object to another as a result of the difference in temperature. **Thermal energy** is the total energy of all of the atoms that make up an object. Atoms possess thermal energy because they are in constant in motion. These vibrations contain energy.

If two objects have different temperatures, heat will flow from the warmer object to the colder one. The heat will continue to flow until the objects are at the same temperature. For example, when you hold an ice cube in your hand, heat from your hand warms the ice cube, causing it to melt.

Reading Checkpoint What is heat?

FIGURE 9
Careers in Earth Science

If you worked as an Earth scientist, you might chip samples of rock from a mountain, explore the ocean floor, or use satellite data to track a storm.

Oceanographers ▲
These oceanographers are wearing scuba gear to observe the interactions of living things on the ocean floor.

Geologists ▲
The work of geologists often takes them outdoors—in this case, to a rocky mountainside.

The Branches of Earth Science

Over thousands of years, scientists have built a body of knowledge about Earth and the forces that change our planet. **Earth science** is the term for this knowledge about Earth's land, air, water, and living things. **Earth science has several different branches. In this book, you will learn about geology, meteorology, and environmental science.**

Geology Geology is the study of the solid Earth. Geologists study the forces that have shaped Earth throughout its long history. Geologists study the constructive forces that build up mountains and landmasses. Geologists also study the destructive forces that wear away features on Earth's surface.

Meteorology Meteorology is the study of Earth's atmosphere. Meteorologists are scientists who forecast the weather based on data about conditions in the atmosphere.

Environmental Science Some Earth scientists, called environmental scientists, study Earth's environment and resources. Environmental scientists learn how human activities affect Earth's land, air, water, and living things.

◄ **Meteorologists**
Meteorologists use data from weather satellites to monitor storms such as hurricanes. Computers process and display weather data.

Environmental Scientists ►
These environmental scientists are testing water samples to find evidence of environmental change or pollution.

Section 2 Assessment

S 6.3.a, 6.4.a; E-LA: Reading 6.2.0, Writing 6.2.2

Target Reading Skill **Preview Text Structure** In your graphic organizer, what question did you ask about the heading The Structure of the Earth System?

Reviewing Key Concepts

1. a. **Listing** What are the four "spheres" that make up the Earth system?
   b. **Relating Cause and Effect** Give an example of how one of the spheres of the Earth system can affect at least one of the other spheres.
2. a. **Listing** What are three different ways energy can be transferred from one location to another?
   b. **Explaining** In which direction does heat flow between two objects of different temperatures?
   c. **Predicting** Describe the flow of heat that occurs if you drop a block of ice into a pot of boiling water.
3. a. **Reviewing** What are three branches of Earth science?
   b. **Summarizing** What do geologists do?
   c. **Classifying** What type of Earth scientist would probably study the effects of human activities on coral reefs? Explain.

Writing in Science

A Day in the Life Research one of the Earth science careers in Figure 9. Based on your research, write a paragraph describing a typical workday for that type of Earth scientist. In your description, include the science inquiry skills the scientist would use on the job.

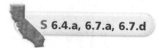
S 6.4.a, 6.7.a, 6.7.d

Speeding Up Evaporation

Materials

2 plastic petri dishes

3 index cards

water

plastic dropper

lamp

stopwatch

Problem What factors increase the rate at which water evaporates?

Skills Focus developing hypotheses, controlling variables, drawing conclusions

Procedure

PART 1 Effect of Heat

1. How does heating a water sample affect how fast it evaporates? Record your hypothesis.

2. Place each petri dish on an index card.

3. Add a single drop of water to each of the petri dishes. Try to make the two drops the same size.

4. Position the lamp over one of the dishes as a heat source. Turn on the light. Make sure the light does not shine on the other dish. **CAUTION:** *The light bulb will become very hot. Avoid touching the bulb or getting water on it.*

5. Observe the dishes every 3 minutes to see which sample evaporates faster. Record your result.

PART 2 Effect of Wind

6. How does fanning the water affect how fast it evaporates? Record your hypothesis.

7. Dry both petri dishes and place them over the index cards. Add a drop of water to each dish as you did in Step 3.

8. Use an index card to fan one of the dishes for 5 minutes. Be careful not to fan the other dish.

9. Observe the dishes to see which sample evaporates faster. Record your result.

Analyze and Conclude

1. **Developing Hypotheses** Did the evidence support both hypotheses? If not, which hypothesis was not supported?

2. **Controlling Variables** What was the manipulated variable in this experiment? The responding variable?

3. **Drawing Conclusions** Make a general statement about factors that increase the rate at which the water evaporates.

4. **Communicating** Write a report explaining the steps and results from your investigation. Explain what everyday experiences helped you develop your hypotheses.

Design an Experiment

How does increasing the surface area of a water sample affect how fast it evaporates? Write your hypothesis and then design an experiment to test it. *Obtain your teachers permission before carrying out your investigation.*

Section 3
Exploring Earth's Surface

CALIFORNIA
Standards Focus

S 6.2 Topography is reshaped by the weathering of rock and soil and by the transportation and deposition of sediment.

S 6.7.f Read a topographic map and a geologic map for evidence provided on the maps and construct and interpret a simple scale map.

🔑 What does the topography of an area include?

🔑 What are the main types of landforms?

🔑 How do maps represent Earth's surface and help find locations?

Key Terms
- topography • elevation
- relief • plain • mountain
- plateau • map • scale
- degree • latitude
- longitude

Lab zone Standards **Warm-Up**

What Is the Land Like Around Your School?

1. On a piece of paper, draw a small square to represent your school. Choose a word to describe the land near the school, such as flat, hilly, or rolling, and write it next to the square.
2. Use a magnetic compass to determine the direction of north. Assume that north is at the top of your paper.
3. Choose a word to describe the land 1 km north of your school. Write that word to the north of the square.
4. Repeat Step 3 for areas 1 km to the east, south, and west.

Think It Over
Forming Operational Definitions What phrase could you use to describe the land in your area?

Suppose that you traveled from California's coast across the state to the Sierra Nevada mountains. On your trip, you would observe many changes in topography. **Topography** (tuh PAHG ruh fee) is the shape of the land. An area's topography may be flat, sloping, hilly, or mountainous.

🔑 **The topography of an area includes the area's elevation, relief, and landforms.** (A landform is a feature of topography, such as a hill or valley.) The height above sea level of a point on Earth's surface is its **elevation.** Look at the diagram below to see the changes in elevation on a trip across California. The difference in elevation between the highest and lowest parts of an area is its **relief.** The diagram includes both flat land, which has low relief, and mountains, which have high relief.

Elevations Across California ▼

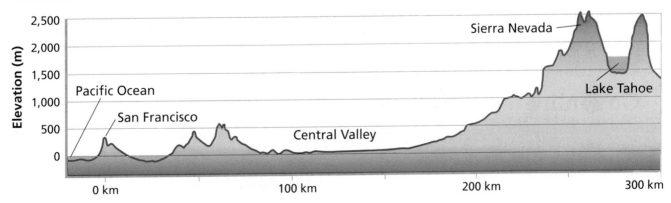

FIGURE 10
Landforms

Plains, mountains, and plateaus are just a few of the many landforms that make up the topography of Earth's surface.
Forming Operational Definitions
Based on this illustration, how would you define "mountains"?

Plains
Plains may occur along a continent's edges or in the interior.

Types of Landforms

Different landforms have different combinations of elevation and relief. Landforms vary greatly in size and shape—from level plains extending as far as the eye can see, to low, rounded hills that you could climb on foot, to jagged mountains that would take you many days to walk around.  **There are three main types of landforms: plains, mountains, and plateaus.**

Plains A **plain** is a landform made up of nearly flat or gently rolling land with low relief. A plain that lies along a seacoast is called a coastal plain. In North America, a coastal plain extends around the continent's eastern and southeastern shores. Coastal plains have both low elevation and low relief.

A plain that lies away from the coast is called an interior plain. Although interior plains have low relief, their elevation can vary. The broad interior plains of North America are called the Great Plains. The Great Plains extend north from Texas into Canada.

✓ **Reading Checkpoint** **What is an interior plain?**

Go Online
SciLINKS _{NSTA}

For: Links on landforms
Visit: www.SciLinks.org
Web Code: scn-0711

Mountains
A mountain's base usually covers an area of at least several square kilometers, but its peak may rise to a point. Mountains often have steeply sloping sides.

Plateaus
The top of a plateau forms a level surface.

Mountains A **mountain** is a landform with high elevation and high relief. Mountains usually occur as part of a mountain range. A mountain range is a group of mountains that are closely related in shape, structure, and age. For example, the Cascade Range is a mountain range that runs from Washington State through Oregon to northern California.

The different mountain ranges in a region make up a mountain system. In California, the Santa Lucia Mountains south of Monterey Bay are one mountain range in the mountain system known as the Coast Ranges.

Mountain ranges and mountain systems in a long, connected chain form a larger unit called a mountain belt. The Rocky Mountains are part of a great mountain belt that stretches down the western sides of North America and South America.

Plateaus A landform that has high elevation and a more or less level surface is called a **plateau.** A plateau is rarely perfectly smooth on top. Streams and rivers may cut into the plateau's surface. The Columbia Plateau in Washington State is an example. The many layers of rock that make up the Columbia Plateau are stacked about 1,500 meters thick.

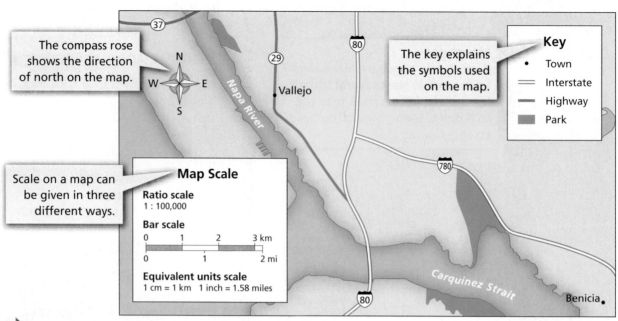

The compass rose shows the direction of north on the map.

Scale on a map can be given in three different ways.

The key explains the symbols used on the map.

Key
- • Town
- ═ Interstate
- ─ Highway
- ▓ Park

Map Scale

Ratio scale
1 : 100,000

Bar scale
0   1   2   3 km
0   1   2 mi

Equivalent units scale
1 cm = 1 km   1 inch = 1.58 miles

FIGURE 11
What's in a Map?
A map is drawn to scale, uses symbols explained in a map key, and usually has a compass rose to show direction. This map shows the area around Vallejo, California.
Interpreting Maps *What is the scale of this map?*

What Is a Map?

A **map** is a flat model of all or part of Earth's surface as seen from above. 🔵 **Maps are drawn to scale and use symbols to represent topography and other features on Earth's surface.** A map's **scale** relates distance on a map to a distance on Earth's surface. Scale is often given as a ratio. For example, one unit on a map could equal 25,000 units on the ground. So one centimeter on the map would represent 0.25 kilometer. This scale, "one to twenty-five thousand," would be written "1 : 25,000." Figure 11 shows three ways of giving a map's scale.

Mapmakers use shapes and pictures called symbols to stand for features on Earth's surface. A symbol can represent a physical feature, such as a river, lake, mountain, or plain. A symbol also can stand for a human-made feature, such as a highway, city, or airport. A map's key, or legend, is a list of all the symbols used on the map with an explanation of their meaning.

Maps also include a compass rose or north arrow. The compass rose helps relate directions on the map to directions on Earth's surface. North usually is located at the top of the map.

 **Reading Checkpoint** **What is a map's scale?**

Math Skills

Scale and Ratios

A ratio compares two numbers by division. For example, the scale of a map given as a ratio is 1 : 250,000. At this scale, the distance between two points on the map measures 23.5 cm. How would you find the actual distance?

1. Write the scale as a fraction.

$$\frac{1}{250,000}$$

2. Write a proportion. Let d represent the distance between the two points.

$$\frac{1}{250,000} = \frac{23.5 \text{ cm}}{d}$$

3. Write the cross products.

$$1 \times d = 250,000 \times 23.5 \text{ cm}$$
$$d = 5,875,000 \text{ cm}$$

(*Hint:* To convert cm to km, divide d by 100,000.)

Practice Problem A map's scale is 1 : 25,000. If two points are 4.7 cm apart on the map, how far apart are they on the ground?

Earth's Grid

When you play checkers, the grid of squares helps you to keep track of where each piece should be. To find a point on Earth's surface, you need a grid like the one on a checkerboard. Most maps and globes show a grid. Because Earth is a sphere, the grid curves to cover the entire planet.

Measuring in Degrees To locate positions on Earth's surface, scientists use units called degrees. You probably know that degrees are used to measure the distance around a circle. As you can see in Figure 12, a **degree** (°) is $\frac{1}{360}$ of the distance around a circle. Degrees can also be used to measure distances on the surface of a sphere. On Earth's surface, each degree is a measure of an angle formed by lines drawn from the center of Earth to points on the surface.

The Equator Halfway between the North and South poles, the equator forms an imaginary line that circles Earth. The equator divides Earth into the Northern and Southern hemispheres. A hemisphere (HEM ih sfeer) is one half of the sphere that makes up Earth's surface. If you started at the equator and traveled to one of the poles, you would travel 90 degrees. That is one quarter of the distance in a full circle.

The Prime Meridian Another imaginary line, called the prime meridian, makes a half circle from the North Pole to the South Pole. The prime meridian passes through Greenwich, England. Places east of the prime meridian are in the Eastern Hemisphere. Places west of it are in the Western Hemisphere. If you started at the prime meridian and traveled west along the equator, you would travel through 360 degrees before returning to your starting point.

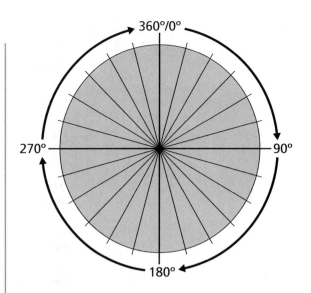

FIGURE 12
Degrees Around Earth
Distances around Earth are measured in degrees.

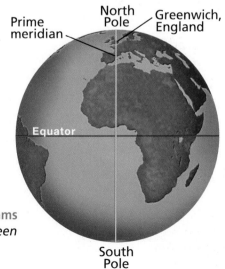

FIGURE 13
Equator and Prime Meridian
Two lines, the equator and prime meridian, are the baselines for measuring distances on Earth's surface. Interpreting Diagrams *How many degrees are there between the equator and the North Pole?*

Lab zone Try This Activity

Where in the World?

Using a globe, determine what city is found at each of the following points:

2° S, 79° W

38° N, 9° W

34° N, 135° E

34° S, 58° W

55° N, 3° W

1° N, 103° E

What word is spelled by the first letters of these cities?

Locating Points on Earth's Surface By using the equator and prime meridian, mapmakers have constructed a grid made up of lines of latitude and longitude.  **The lines of latitude and longitude on a map form a grid that can be used to find locations anywhere on Earth.**

The equator is the starting line for measuring **latitude,** or distance in degrees north or south of the equator. The latitude of the equator is 0°. Between the equator and each pole are 90 evenly spaced, parallel lines called lines of latitude. Each degree of latitude is equal to about 111 kilometers.

The distance in degrees east or west of the prime meridian is called **longitude.** There are 360 lines of longitude that run from north to south, meeting at the poles. Each line represents one degree of longitude. At the equator, a degree of longitude equals about 111 kilometers. But at the poles, where the lines of longitude come together, the distance decreases to zero.

The prime meridian, which is the starting line for measuring longitude, is at 0°. The longitude lines in each hemisphere are numbered up to 180 degrees.

Using Latitude and Longitude The location of any point on Earth's surface can be expressed in terms of the latitude and longitude lines that cross at that point. For example, you can see on the map in Figure 15 that New Orleans is located where the line for 30° North latitude crosses the line for 90° West longitude. Notice that each longitude line crosses the latitude lines, including the equator, at a right angle.

✓ Reading Checkpoint **How are longitude lines numbered?**

FIGURE 14
Locating a Point
Points on Earth's surface can be located using latitude and longitude.

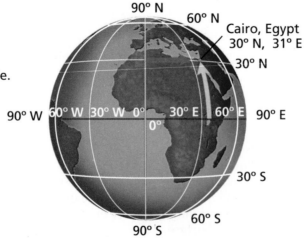

◀ Cairo, Egypt, is located where the latitude line 30° N crosses the longitude line 31° E.

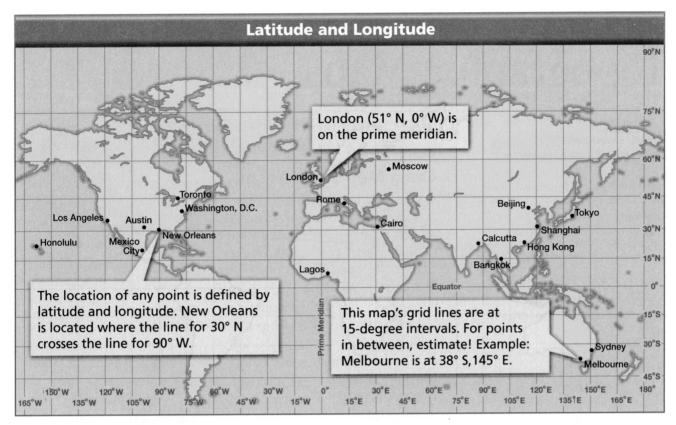

Latitude and Longitude

London (51° N, 0° W) is on the prime meridian.

The location of any point is defined by latitude and longitude. New Orleans is located where the line for 30° N crosses the line for 90° W.

This map's grid lines are at 15-degree intervals. For points in between, estimate! Example: Melbourne is at 38° S, 145° E.

FIGURE 15
Every point on Earth's surface has a particular latitude and longitude.
Interpreting Maps *What are the latitude and longitude of Los Angeles? Of Sydney?*

Section 3 Assessment

S 6.2, 6.7.f; E-LA: Reading 6.1.0

Vocabulary Skill High-Use Academic Words
Use the word *area* correctly in a sentence explaining topography.

🔑 **Reviewing Key Concepts**

1. a. **Defining** What is topography?
   b. **Comparing and Contrasting** What is relief? How does it differ from elevation?
   c. **Calculating** What is the relief in an area where the highest point is 1,200 m above sea level and the lowest point is 200 m above sea level?
2. a. **Listing** What are the three main types of landforms?
   b. **Describing** What are the characteristics of a mountain?
   c. **Sequencing** Place these features in order from smallest to largest: mountain system, mountain range, mountain belt, mountain.

3. a. **Identifying** On a world map, what two lines are the starting lines for measurements on Earth's surface?
   b. **Explaining** How are these lines used to locate points on Earth's surface?

Math Practice

4. **Scales and Ratios** A globe has a scale of 1 : 40,000,000. Using a piece of string, you determine that the shortest distance between two cities on the globe is 7 cm. What is the actual distance between the two cities?

Topographic Maps

CALIFORNIA
Standards Focus

S 6.7.f Read a topographic map and a geologic map for evidence provided on the maps and construct and interpret a simple scale map.

How do mapmakers represent elevation, relief, and slope?

How do you read a topographic map?

Key Terms
- topographic map
- contour line
- contour interval
- index contour

Lab zone Standards **Warm-Up**

Can a Map Show Relief?

1. Carefully cut the corners off 8 pieces of cardboard so that they look rounded. Each piece should be at least 1 centimeter smaller than the one before.
2. Trim the long sides of the two largest pieces so that the long sides appear wavy. Don't cut more than 0.5 centimeter into the cardboard.
3. Trace the largest cardboard piece on a sheet of paper.
4. Trace the next largest piece inside the drawing of the first. Don't let any lines cross.
5. Trace the other cardboard pieces, from largest to smallest, one inside the other, on the same paper.
6. Stack the cardboard pieces beside the paper in the same order they were traced. Compare the stack of cardboard pieces with your drawing. How are they alike? How are they different?

Think It Over
Making Models If the cardboard pieces are a model of a landform, what do the lines on the paper represent?

FIGURE 16
Orienteering
Orienteering helps people develop the skill of using a map and compass.

An orienteering meet is not an ordinary race. Teams compete to see how quickly they can find a series of locations called control points. The control points are scattered over a large park or state forest. Orienteers choose a set number of control points and then visit the points in any order. In this sport, your ability to read a map and use a compass is often more important than how fast you can run. In a major meet, there may be several hundred orienteers on dozens of teams.

At the start of a meet, you would need to consult your map. But the maps used in orienteering are different from road maps or maps in an atlas—they're topographic maps. A **topographic map** (tahp uh GRAF ik) is a map showing the surface features of an area. Topographic maps use symbols to show the land as if you were looking down on it from above.

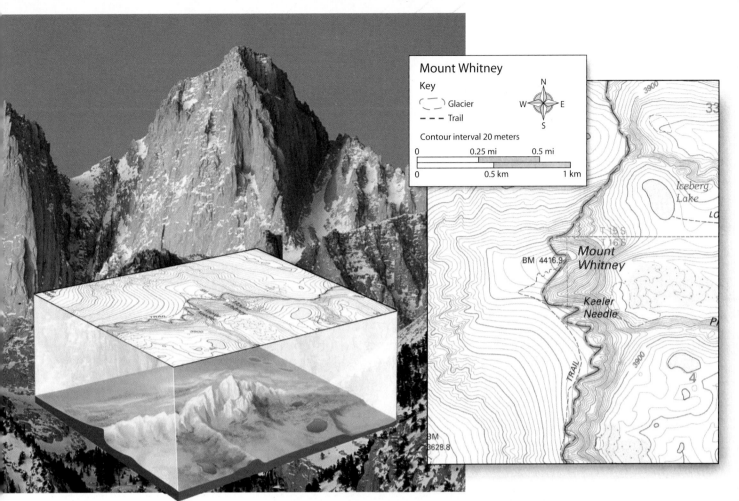

FIGURE 17

Contour Lines

The contour lines on a topographic map represent elevation and relief. **Forming Operational Definitions** *What information does the topographic map provide that the photograph does not?*

Mapping Earth's Topography

Topographic maps provide information on the elevation, relief, and slope of the ground surface. 👄 **Mapmakers use contour lines to represent elevation, relief, and slope on topographic maps.** On a topographic map, a **contour line** connects points of equal elevation. In the United States, most topographic maps give contour intervals in feet rather than meters.

The change in elevation from contour line to contour line is called the **contour interval.** The contour interval for a given map is always the same. For example, the map in Figure 18 has a contour interval of 20 meters. If you start at one contour line and count up 10 contour lines, you have reached an elevation 200 meters above where you started. Usually, every fifth contour line, known as an index contour, is darker and heavier than the others. **Index contours** are labeled with the elevation in round units, such as 1,600 or 2,000 meters above sea level.

Topographic maps have many uses. For example, geologists use them to identify landforms. You could use a topographic map to plan the route of a hike or bicycle trip.

Go Online
active art

For: Topographic Map activity
Visit: PHSchool.com
Web Code: cfp-2014

Reading Checkpoint **What do all the points connected by a contour line have in common?**

Reading a Topographic Map

Looking at a topographic map with many squiggly contour lines, you may feel as if you are gazing into a bowl of spaghetti. But with practice, you can learn to read a topographic map like the one in Figure 18. **To read a topographic map, you must familiarize yourself with the map's scale and symbols and interpret the map's contour lines.**

Scale Topographic maps are usually large-scale maps. Large-scale maps show a close-up view of part of Earth's surface. In the United States, many topographic maps are at a scale of 1 : 24,000, or 1 centimeter equals 0.24 kilometers. At this scale, a map can show the details of elevation and features such as rivers and coastlines. Large buildings, airports, and major highways appear as outlines at the correct scale. Symbols are used to show houses and other small features.

FIGURE 18
Topographic Map

The different types of symbols on topographic maps provide data on elevation, relief, slopes, and human-made features. This United States Geological Survey map shows part of Morro Bay, California.

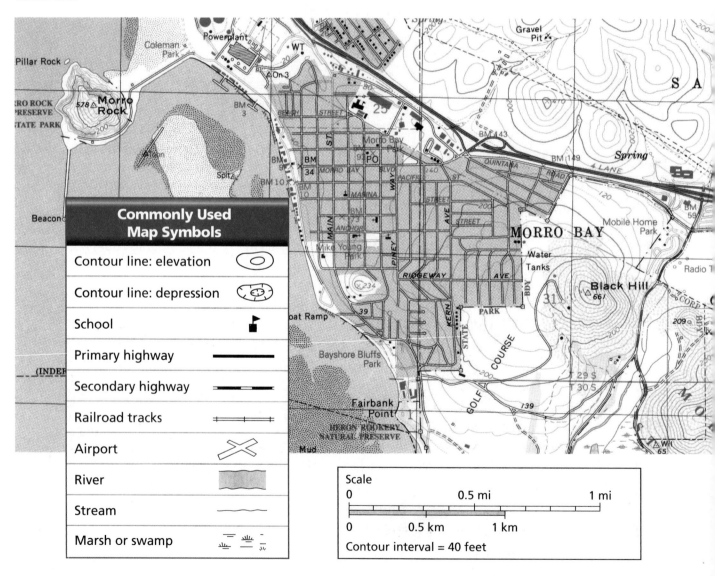

Commonly Used Map Symbols

Contour line: elevation	
Contour line: depression	
School	
Primary highway	
Secondary highway	
Railroad tracks	
Airport	
River	
Stream	
Marsh or swamp	

Scale

0   0.5 mi   1 mi

0   0.5 km   1 km

Contour interval = 40 feet

Symbols Mapmakers use a great variety of symbols on topographic maps. If you were drawing a map, what symbols would you use to represent a forest, a campground, an orchard, a swamp, or a school? Look at Figure 18 to see some commonly used map symbols.

Interpreting Contour Lines To find the elevation of a feature, begin at the labeled index contour, which is a heavier line than regular contour lines. Then, count the number of contour lines up or down to the feature.

Reading contour lines is the first step toward "seeing" an area's topography. Look at the map in Figure 18. The closely spaced contour lines are used for steep slopes. The widely spaced contour lines are used for gentle slopes or flatter areas. A contour line that forms a closed loop with no other contour lines inside it is used to show a hilltop. A closed loop with dashes inside shows a depression, or hollow in the ground.

The shape of contour lines also help to show ridges and valleys. V-shaped contour lines pointing downhill show a ridge line. V-shaped contour lines pointing uphill show a valley. A stream in the valley flows toward the open end of the V.

 **Reading Checkpoint** How are hilltops and depressions shown using contour lines?

Video Field Trip
Discovery Channel School
Mapping Earth's Surface

Section 4 Assessment

S 6.7.f; E-LA: Reading 6.2.0, Writing 6.2.2

Target Reading Skill Preview Text Structure In your graphic organizer, what question did you ask about the heading Interpreting Contour Lines?

Reviewing Key Concepts

1. **a.** Defining What is a topographic map?
   b. Explaining How do topographic maps represent elevation and relief?
   c. Calculating If the contour interval on a topographic map is 50 meters, how much difference in elevation do 12 contour lines represent?
2. **a.** Reviewing What do you need to know about a topographic map in order to read it?
   b. Comparing and Contrasting Compare the way steep slopes are represented on a topographic map with the way gentle slopes are represented.
   c. Inferring Reading a map, you see V-shaped contour lines that point uphill. What land feature would you find in this area?

Writing in Science

Giving Directions Write a descriptive paragraph of a simple route from one point on the map in Figure 18 to another point. Your paragraph should provide the starting point, but not the end point. Include details such as distance, compass direction, and topography along the route. Share your paragraph with classmates to see if they can follow your directions.

A Map in a Pan

Materials

modeling clay

deep-sided pan

water and food coloring

clear, hard sheet of plastic

marking pencil

sheet of unlined white paper

Problem How can you make and read a topographic map?

Skills Focus making models, interpreting maps

Procedure

1. Place a lump of clay on the bottom of a pan. Shape the clay into a model of a hill.

2. Pour colored water into the pan to a depth of 1 centimeter to represent sea level.

3. Place a sheet of hard, clear plastic over the container.

4. Trace the outline of the pan on the plastic sheet with a marking pencil. Then, looking straight down into the pan, trace the outline the water makes around the edges of the clay model. Remove the plastic sheet from the pan.

5. Add another centimeter of water to the pan, bringing the depth of the water to 2 centimeters. Replace the plastic sheet exactly as before and then trace the water level again.

6. Repeat Step 5 several times. Stop when the next addition of water would completely cover your model.

7. Remove the plastic sheet. Trace the outlines that you drew on the plastic sheet onto a sheet of paper to make a topographic map.

Analyze and Conclude

1. **Interpreting Maps** Read your topographic map. How can you tell which parts of your model hill have a steep slope? A gentle slope?

2. **Interpreting Maps** How can you tell from the map which point on the hill is the highest?

3. **Interpreting Maps** Are there any ridges or valleys on your map? How do you know?

4. **Applying Concepts** Is there any depression on your map where water would collect after it rained? What symbol should you use to identify this depression?

5. **Communicating** Read your topographic map and compare it with the clay landform. Write a paragraph comparing your topographic map and landform model. In your paragraph, explain how the map and model are alike and how they are different.

More to Explore

Obtain a topographic map that includes an interesting landform such as a mountain, canyon, river valley, or coastline. After reading the contour lines on the map, make a sketch of what you think the landform looks like. Then build a scale model of the landform using clay or layers of cardboard or foamboard. How does your model landform compare with your sketch?

Section 5

Safety in the Science Laboratory

CALIFORNIA
Standards Focus

S 6.7 Scientific progress is made by asking meaningful questions and conducting careful investigations. As a basis for understanding this concept and addressing the content in the other three strands, students should develop their own questions and perform investigations. Students will:

b. Select and use appropriate tools and technology (including calculators, computers, balances, spring scales, microscopes, and binoculars) to perform tests, collect data, and display data.

- Why is preparation important when carrying out scientific investigations in the lab and in the field?

- What should you do if an accident occurs?

Lab zone Standards **Warm-Up**

Where Is the Safety Equipment in Your School?

1. Look around your classroom or school for any safety-related equipment.
2. Draw a floor plan of the room or building and clearly label where each item is located.

Think It Over
Predicting Why is it important to know where safety equipment is located?

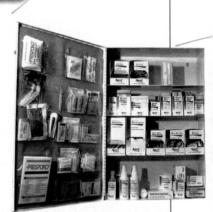

You probably have a favorite summer outdoor activity. Some people enjoy watching baseball or picnicking at the beach. Others look forward to team sports or bicycling. But what if you wanted to try a new activity, such as canoeing? Before trying a new recreation, there are several things that you need to do to prepare. For example, before learning how to paddle a canoe, you would need to pass a swimming test. Then you would need to take a class to learn basic safety rules, such as always wearing a life vest.

Proper preparation for ▶
a canoe trip is important.

For: Links on laboratory safety
Visit: www.SciLinks.org
Web Code: scn-1624

FIGURE 19
Safety in the Lab
Conducting careful investigations in the laboratory is important in science. It is also important to use and select appropriate tools and techniques to ensure safety.
Observing List the equipment each student has selected to ensure safety while performing the labs.

Safety in the Lab

Just as when you go canoeing, you have to be prepared before you begin any scientific investigation. **Good preparation helps you stay safe when doing activities in the laboratory.**

Thermometers, balances, and glassware are some of the tools you will use in science labs. Do you know how to use these items? What should you do if something goes wrong? Thinking about these questions ahead of time is an important part of being prepared.

Preparing for the Lab Preparing for a lab should begin the day before you will perform the lab. It is important to read through the procedure carefully and make sure you understand all the directions. Also, review the general safety guidelines in Appendix A, including those related to the specific tools and other equipment you will use. If anything is unclear, ask your teacher about it before you begin the lab.

Reading
Checkpoint   **Why is it important to know how to use laboratory equipment?**

Wear an apron to protect yourself and your clothes from chemicals.

Wear heat-resistant gloves when handling hot objects. Wear plastic gloves to protect your skin when handling chemicals.

Make sure electric cords are untangled and out of the way.

Review and Assessment

Go Online
PHSchool.com
For: Self-Assessment
Visit: PHSchool.com
Web Code: cwa-1010

⟳ Target Reading Skill

Preview Text Structure Create a graphic organizer to preview the headings in Section 3.

Section 3: Exploring Earth's Surface		
Heading	**Question**	**Answer**
Topography	What is topography?	
Types of Landforms		
What Is a Map?		
Earth's Grid		

Reviewing Key Terms

Choose the letter of the best answer.

1. If you interpret something based on your experience, you are making a(n)
   a. hypothesis.
   b. prediction.
   c. inference.
   d. scientific law.

2. A possible explanation for a set of observations or answer to a scientific question is a
   a. variable.
   b. scientific theory.
   c. prediction.
   d. hypothesis.

3. The transfer of energy from the sun to Earth is an example of the movement of energy by
   a. moving objects.
   b. evaporation.
   c. waves.
   d. heat flow.

4. A landform that has high elevation but a mostly flat surface is a
   a. plain.
   b. mountain.
   c. mountain range.
   d. plateau.

5. A measurement based on distance north or south of the equator is called
   a. scale.
   b. latitude.
   c. longitude.
   d. contour interval.

6. On a topographic map, relief is shown using
   a. lines of latitude.
   b. lines of longitude.
   c. prime meridian.
   d. contour lines.

Complete the following sentences so that your answers clearly explain the key terms.

7. A scientist often conducts a **controlled experiment,** which is _____.

8. Topography is partly made up of the land's **relief,** which is _____.

9. One of Earth's four spheres is the **hydrosphere,** which is _____.

10. If an airplane flew around Earth in a straight line from east to west, it would change its **longitude,** which is _____.

11. When reading a topographic map, you might look for an **index contour,** which is _____.

Writing in Science

Advertisement Suppose that you are a manufacturer of topographic maps. Write an advertisement that describes as many uses for your maps as you can think of.

Video Assessment
Discovery Channel School
Mapping Earth's Surface

Review and Assessment

Checking Concepts

12. In science, can a hypothesis be accepted as true after one test? Explain.

13. What is a controlled experiment?

14. What is the role of the responding variable in a controlled experiment?

15. What are three ways in which scientists communicate their ideas?

16. What do meteorologists do?

17. What is one source of energy for processes in Earth's lithosphere, hydrosphere, atmosphere, and biosphere?

18. Compare the elevation of a coastal plain with that of an interior plain.

19. What are five things you should do when you complete a lab experiment?

Thinking Critically

20. **Applying Concepts** Once an experiment is complete, what must a scientist do to determine whether the data support the hypothesis?

21. **Predicting** A volcano erupts in the Pacific Ocean and forms a new island. How could this change in the lithosphere lead to a change in the biosphere?

22. **Inferring** Auckland, New Zealand, is located at 37° S, 175° E. What two hemispheres is it in? Explain.

23. **Applying Concepts** Which would be more likely to show a shallow, 1.5-meter hollow in the ground: a 1-meter contour interval or a 5-meter contour interval?

24. **Interpreting Graphics** If you saw the safety icons below at the beginning of an experiment's procedure, what safety steps would you need to take?

Math Practice

25. **Scale and Ratios** Earth's diameter is about 13,000 km. If a globe has a diameter of 0.5 m, write the globe's scale as a ratio. What distance on Earth would 1 cm on the globe represent?

Applying Skills

Use the graph to answer Questions 26–28.

A scientist measured the distance a lava flow traveled in 5 minutes and recorded the data in the graph below.

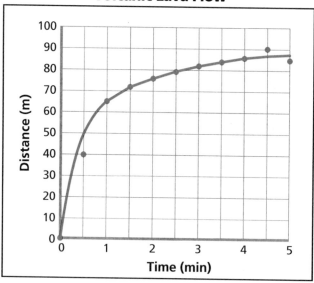

26. **Reading Graphs** What is plotted on each axis?

27. **Interpreting Data** Did the lava flow travel the same distance every minute?

28. **Predicting** Predict how far the lava will flow between 5 and 6 minutes.

Lab zone Standards Investigation

Performance Assessment Present your map to the class. What scale did you use? What symbols did you use to represent the natural and physical features of your site? How did you measure and locate them on your map? Does your map give others a clear idea of the topography of the land?

Choose the letter of the best answer.

1. What would a scientist usually do after conducting a controlled experiment?
   A interpret the data from the experiment
   B communicate the results of the experiment
   C draw a conclusion and, if needed, revise the hypothesis
   D all of the above   **S 6.7.a**

2. In which of the following is energy transferred from particle to particle through a medium?
   A ocean waves
   B sunlight
   C wind
   D electromagnetic waves   **S 6.3.a**

3. Which of the following is NOT a process for which the sun provides energy?
   A a volcanic eruption
   B the water cycle
   C winds
   D ocean currents   **S 6.4.a**

4. In an experiment, the variable that the scientist changes is called the
   A responding variable.
   B inquiry variable.
   C manipulated variable.
   D controlled variable.   **S 6.7.c**

5. Which phrase provides the best definition of *relief*?
   A the elevation of the lowest point in an area
   B the sum of the highest and lowest points in an area
   C the elevation of the highest point in an area
   D the difference in elevation between the highest and lowest points in an area   **S 6.2**

6. If an accident occurs in a science laboratory, the first thing you should do is
   A determine the cause of the accident.
   B notify your teacher.
   C locate the first-aid kit.
   D put a bandage on the affected area.   **S 6.7.a**

Use the map below and your knowledge of science to answer Questions 7 and 8.

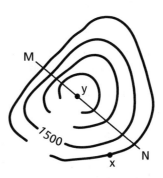

Contour interval = 15 meters

7. A topographic profile shows the shape or relief of the land along a given line. Along line M-N on the map, which of the following would the profile most closely resemble?

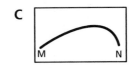
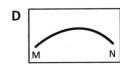
                                                S 6.7.f

8. What is the elevation of the point marked *x* on the map?
   A 1,400 meters   B 1,500 meters
   C 1,485 meters   D 1,515 meters
                                                S 6.7.f

9. On a map, what is the height above sea level of a point on Earth's surface called?
   A topography   B relief
   C elevation   D latitude   **S 6.2**

Apply the BIG Idea

10. Choose one of the lithosphere, hydrosphere, atmosphere, or biosphere. Describe how you think the sun's energy affects that part of the Earth system. Then explain how a change in that part of the system might affect one of the other parts.   **S 6.4.a**

Chapter 2

Weathering and Soil

CALIFORNIA
Standards Preview

S 6.2 Topography is reshaped by the weathering of rock and soil and by the transportation and deposition of sediment. As a basis for understanding this concept:

a. Students know water running downhill is the dominant process in shaping the landscape, including California's landscape.

Framework Water contributes to two processes that help shape the landscape—the breaking down of rock into smaller pieces by mechanical and chemical weathering and the removal of rock and soil by erosion.

S 6.5.e Students know the number and types of organisms an ecosystem can support depends on the resources available and on abiotic factors, such as quantities of light and water, a range of temperatures, and soil composition.

Framework To support vigorous plant growth, soils must contain sufficient minerals (e.g., nitrogen, phosphorus, potassium) and humus (decomposed organic materials) without excess acidity or alkalinity.

S 6.6 Sources of energy and materials differ in amounts, distribution, usefulness, and time required for their formation. As a basis for understanding this concept:

b. Students know different natural energy and material resources, including air, soil, rocks, minerals, petroleum, fresh water, wildlife, and forests, and know how to classify them as renewable or nonrenewable.

c. Students know the natural origin of materials used to make common objects.

Wildflowers bloom in the Anza-Borrego Desert State Park, California. ▶

Focus on the
BIG Idea

S 6.2.a

How does the weathering of rock help to reshape Earth's topography and form soil?

Check What You Know

Suppose that you carve a model of a mountain in a bar of soap. Then, you leave the model outside in the rain overnight. Based on what you think would happen to the model, predict how rock on Earth's surface might change over time.

Build Science Vocabulary

The images shown here represent some of the key terms in this chapter. You can use this vocabulary skill to help you understand the meaning of some key terms in this chapter.

Vocabulary Skill

Suffixes

A suffix is a letter or group of letters added to the end of a word to change its meaning and usually its part of speech. The suffixes *-ation* or *-ing* added to a verb can form a noun that means "process of" or "action of." For example, the suffix *-ation* added to the verb *observe* forms the noun *observation*.

Example: Students in the lab will record their observations.

In this chapter, you will learn key terms that have the suffixes *-ation*, *-sion*, and *-ing*.

Suffix	Meaning	Part of Speech	Key Terms
-ation	Process of, action of	Noun	Conservation, oxidation, rotation
-sion	Process of, action of	Noun	Abrasion, erosion
-ing	Showing continuous action	Noun or adjective	Melting, plowing, smelting, weathering, wedging

Apply It!

Complete the sentences with the correct words.
1. People who _____ electricity are contributing to energy _____. (*conserve/conservation*)
2. Rain, snow, and other types of _____ contribute to the _____ of Earth's surface. (*weather/weathering*)

crystal

mechanical weathering

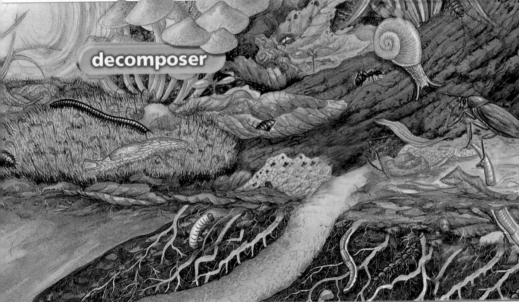

decomposer

contour plowing

Chapter 2 Vocabulary

interactive Textbook

Build Science Vocabulary
Online
Visit: PHSchool.com
Web Code: cwj-1020

How to Read Science

 Preview Visuals

Before you read your science textbook, it's important to take the time to preview the visuals. Visuals are photographs, graphs, tables, diagrams, and illustrations. Visuals contain important information that helps you understand the content. Follow these steps to preview visuals.

- Read the title.
- Read labels and captions.
- Ask yourself questions about the visuals to give yourself a purpose for reading.

Preview the illustration titled The Rock Cycle, Figure 6. Use a graphic organizer like this one to ask questions about the rock cycle.

The Rock Cycle
Q: What is the subject of this illustration?
A:
Q: Why are there a lot of different arrows?
A:
Q: What processes do the arrows show?
A:
Q: What do the four diagrams show about the rock cycle?
A:

Apply It!

Copy the graphic organizer into your notebook. Look carefully at the illustration and write the answer to the question "What processes do the arrows show?"

After you read Section 1, complete your graphic organizer and revise it as necessary. Before you read Section 3, create graphic organizers to preview the visuals.

Standards **Investigation**

Soil for Seeds

The process of weathering affects all rocks exposed on Earth's surface. Weathering breaks rock into smaller and smaller particles. When the rock particles mix with other ingredients, such as leaves, the mixture is called soil. In this investigation, you will test how soil and other growing materials affect the growth of plants.

Your Goal

To determine how soil composition affects the growth of bean seeds

To complete this investigation, you must

- compare the particle size, shape, and composition of different growing materials
- compare how bean seeds grow in several different growing materials
- determine what type of soil or growing material is best for young bean plants
- follow the safety guidelines in Appendix A

Plan It!

In a group, brainstorm what types of soil and other growing materials you will use in your experiment. What are the different variables that affect the growth of plants? How will you measure the growth of your bean plants? Plan your experiment and obtain your teacher's approval. As you carry out your experiment, observe and record the growth of your plants. Then present your results to your class.

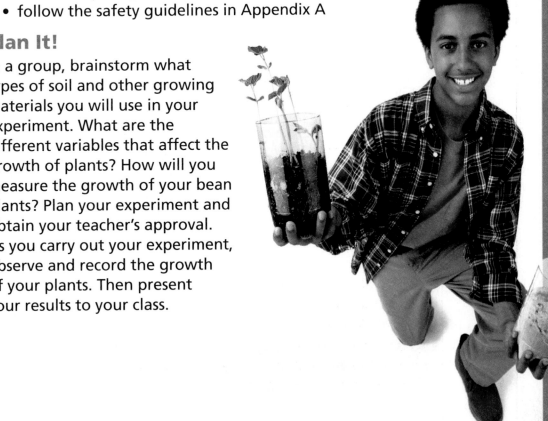

Minerals and Rocks

CALIFORNIA
Standards Focus

S 6.6.b Students know different natural energy and material resources, including air, soil, rocks, minerals, petroleum, fresh water, wildlife, and forests, and know how to classify them as renewable or nonrenewable.

c. Students know the natural origin of materials used to make common objects.

🔑 What is a mineral?

🔑 What are the three major groups of rock, and how do they form through the rock cycle?

🔑 How are minerals and rocks used and processed?

Key Terms
- mineral
- crystal
- rock cycle
- igneous rock
- sedimentary rock
- sediment
- metamorphic rock
- nonrenewable resource
- ore
- smelting

Lab zone Standards **Warm-Up**

What's a Rock?

1. Your teacher will give you three different rocks.
2. Observe each rock under a hand lens. In your notebook, describe the color or colors that you see in the rocks. Also describe any shapes or patterns in the rocks.
3. Make a sketch of each of your rocks.
4. Are your rocks made up of one material or several materials? How can you tell?
5. How are the rocks similar? How are they different?

Forming Operational Definitions Based on your observations, how would you define the word *rock*?

You may think of a golf course as a place covered by smooth, green grass. But that's not true of the Devil's Golf Course in Death Valley National Park. Instead of grass, a jagged crust of salt covers this "golf course." The salt forms lacy sheets, spikes, and other strange shapes.

Where did the salt that forms the Devil's Golf Course come from? About 3,000 years ago, a large lake filled the area. The lake's water contained dissolved salt. Over time, the climate became drier and the lake slowly dried up. As the water evaporated, the salt was left behind. This salt, the same as ordinary table salt, is also called halite. To a geologist, halite is a mineral.

FIGURE 1
Devil's Golf Course
The fantastic shapes on this dry lake bed in Death Valley National Park, California, are formed mostly of salt crystals.

What Is a Mineral?

Minerals can be as rare as a precious diamond. Or they can be as common as the halite that makes up the Devil's Golf Course. Geologists have identified more than 3,000 different minerals. But all of these minerals share certain characteristics.

 **A mineral is a naturally occurring, inorganic solid that forms on or beneath Earth's surface. Almost all minerals have a crystal shape. Each mineral also has a definite chemical composition.** For a substance to be a **mineral,** it must have all five of these characteristics.

Inorganic Solid Halite occurs naturally in areas once occupied by lakes or seas. Halite is inorganic. This means that the mineral did not form from materials that were once part of a living thing. If you pour some halite into your hand, you can see that it is made up of small, solid particles.

Crystal Shape Halite also has a crystal shape. In Figure 2, you can see that halite crystals are shaped like cubes. A **crystal** is a solid made up of particles that line up in a pattern that repeats over and over again.

Definite Chemical Composition Halite has a definite chemical composition. This means that it is made up of certain elements in definite proportions. Halite is made up of one atom of sodium for every atom of chlorine. Many other minerals are made up of several elements. A few minerals are made up of only one element. Copper, silver, gold, and sulfur sometimes occur naturally in this form.

Each mineral has different properties depending on its chemical composition. For example, minerals differ in color, hardness, and crystal shape.

Reading Checkpoint What is a crystal?

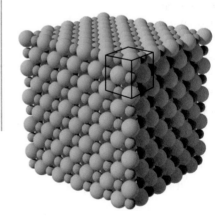

FIGURE 2
Mineral Crystals
Crystals of the mineral halite—which you know as table salt—are shaped like cubes.

FIGURE 3
Granite and Basalt
Granite is made up of large crystals of several minerals, including quartz, mica, and feldspar. The crystals in basalt are too small to be seen without a hand lens.

Granite   Basalt

Rocks and the Rock Cycle

Minerals are one of the main building blocks of rock. Rock is the solid material made up of one or more minerals or other substances. Rock makes up Earth's hard crust. How do the different kinds of rocks form? Forces deep inside Earth and at the surface produce a slow cycle that builds, destroys, and changes rocks. The **rock cycle** is a series of processes on and beneath Earth's surface that slowly change rocks from one kind to another. 🔑 **Geologists classify rocks into three major groups: igneous rock, sedimentary rock, and metamorphic rock. The rocks in each group form through different steps in the rock cycle.**

Forming Igneous Rock The rock cycle begins when molten material forms inside Earth. Then, this material slowly cools and hardens at or beneath the surface. The result is **igneous rock** (IG nee us). The granite in Figure 3 formed when molten material cooled slowly beneath the surface. Because it cools slowly, granite is made up of large crystals.

Other igneous rocks form when molten material erupts onto Earth's surface. Basalt forms when molten material cools and hardens on the surface. Because it cools quickly, basalt is made up of very small crystals.

Forming Sedimentary Rock The rock cycle continues as **sedimentary rock** (sed uh MEN tur ee) forms. Water and weather cause rocks on Earth's surface to break down, forming sediment. **Sediment** is small, solid pieces of material that come from rocks or living things.

Water and wind carry sediment and deposit it in layers. Layers of sediment build up and are squeezed together by their own weight. At the same time, minerals in the rock slowly dissolve in water. These minerals harden and glue the sediment together. Over millions of years, the sediment slowly changes to sedimentary rock.

Lab zone
Try This Activity

Rock Absorber

Here's how to find out if water can soak into rock.

1. Using a hand lens, compare samples of sandstone and shale.
2. Use a balance to measure the mass of each rock.
3. Place the rocks in a pan of water and watch closely. Which sample has bubbles escaping? Predict which sample will gain mass.
4. Leave the rocks submerged in the pan overnight.
5. The next day, remove the rocks from the pan and find the mass of each rock.

Drawing Conclusions How did the masses of the two rocks change after soaking? What can you conclude about each rock?

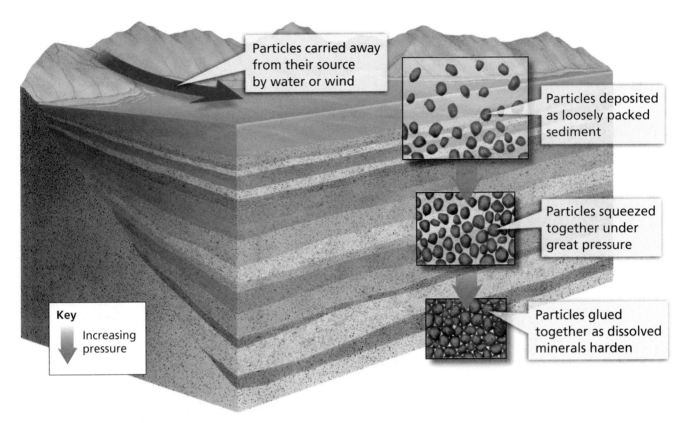

FIGURE 4
How Sedimentary Rocks Form
Sedimentary rocks form over millions of years
as particles of sediment are deposited and
then squeezed and glued together.
Relating Cause and Effect *What conditions
are necessary for sedimentary rocks to form?*

Some sedimentary rocks, such as sandstone, are made up of
particles of other rocks. The remains of plants and animals can
also form sedimentary rock. For example, limestone forms in
the oceans from the shells and skeletons of coral and other animals. Another type of sedimentary rock forms when minerals
dissolved in water form crystals. That's how rock salt, made of
the mineral halite, is formed.

Forming Metamorphic Rock As the rock cycle continues,
any rock can change into **metamorphic rock** (met uh MAWR fik).
Forces inside Earth can push rocks down toward the heat of
Earth's interior. The deeper a rock is buried, the greater the
pressure on that rock. Under great heat and pressure, the minerals in a rock can be changed into other minerals. The rock
has become metamorphic rock. For example, heat and pressure
can change granite into gneiss, as shown in Figure 5.

 **What is sediment?**

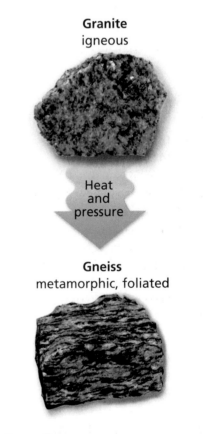

Granite
igneous

Heat
and
pressure

Gneiss
metamorphic, foliated

FIGURE 5
Forming Metamorphic Rock
Heat and pressure change granite
to a metamorphic rock, gneiss.

FIGURE 6

The Rock Cycle

Rocks change continuously through the rock cycle.
Interpreting Diagrams
What process leads to the formation of sediment?

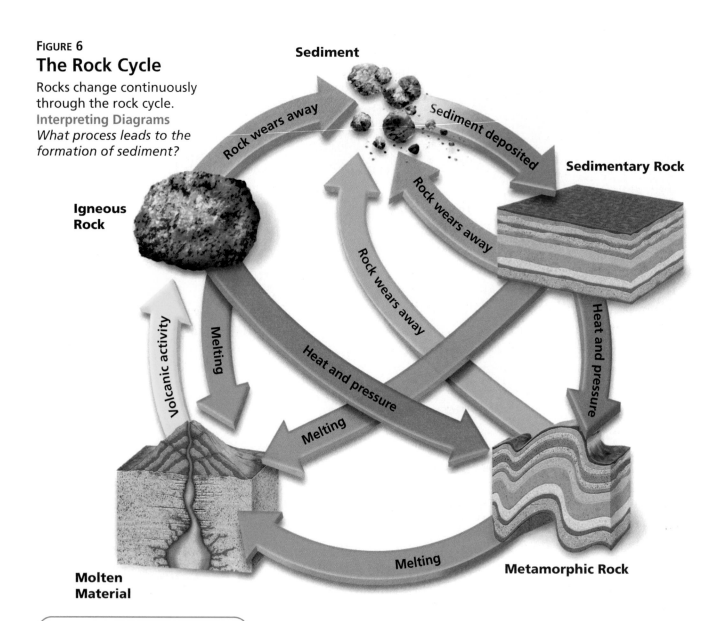

Sediment

Rock wears away

Sediment deposited

Sedimentary Rock

Igneous Rock

Rock wears away

Rock wears away

Volcanic activity

Melting

Heat and pressure

Heat and pressure

Melting

Melting

Molten Material

Metamorphic Rock

Go Online
active art

For: Rock Cycle activity
Visit: PHSchool.com
Web Code: cfp-1056

Pathways of the Rock Cycle As you can see in Figure 6, there are many pathways through the rock cycle. Here is one possible pathway: The igneous rock granite formed beneath the surface millions of years ago. Then, the forces of mountain building slowly pushed the granite upward, forming a mountain. Slowly, water and weather wore away the granite, forming sand. Streams carried the sand to the ocean.

Over millions of years, layers of sandy sediment piled up on the ocean floor. Slowly the sediments were pressed together and cemented to form sandstone, a sedimentary rock. Over time, the sandstone became deeply buried. Heat and pressure changed the rock's texture from gritty to smooth. Over millions of years, the sandstone changed into the metamorphic rock quartzite.

Metamorphic rock does not end the rock cycle. For example, the heat of Earth's interior could melt the rock. This molten material could then form new igneous rock.

Using Minerals and Rocks

People use minerals and rocks in thousands of ways. But because minerals and rocks can take millions of years to form, they are considered nonrenewable resources. A **nonrenewable resource** is one that is not replaced in a useful time frame.

Uses of Minerals You might be surprised at how many common products contain minerals.  **Minerals are the source of gemstones, metals, and other materials used to make many products.**

Gemstones such as rubies and sapphires have amazed people throughout the ages. Usually, a gemstone is a hard, colorful mineral. Gemstones are used mainly for jewelry. They are also used for mechanical parts and for grinding and polishing.

Minerals are also the source of metals such as iron, copper, and silver. Metal tools, aluminum foil, and the steel used to make cars all began as minerals. Many other minerals are used in foods, medicines, fertilizers, and building materials. Quartz, a mineral found in sand, is used in making glass. Gypsum, a soft, white mineral, is used to make wallboard and cement.

> **Reading Checkpoint** What are gemstones?

Uses of Rocks Throughout history, people have found many uses for rocks. For thousands of years, people made arrowheads out of flint, a sedimentary rock. **Today, people use rocks for building materials and in industrial processes.** Hard, durable granite is used in curbstones, floors, and kitchen counters. Limestone can be cut easily into blocks or slabs for use in buildings. Limestone is also used in making cement and steel. Slate splits easily into flat pieces. These pieces can be used for flooring and roofing.

FIGURE 7
Gemstones
Minerals have many uses. Precious gems like the rubies and emeralds in this necklace are used in jewelry.

FIGURE 8
Durable Granite
The faces of four presidents were carved in granite on Mount Rushmore, South Dakota.

Products From Minerals

To understand how minerals must be processed before they are used, compare bauxite and an aluminum can.

1. Examine a piece of the mineral bauxite carefully. Describe its properties, such as color, texture, and hardness.

2. Examine an aluminum can. (The metal aluminum comes from bauxite.) Compare the properties of the aluminum can with the properties of bauxite.

Posing Questions

To understand how bauxite is made into a useful material, what questions would you need to ask?

Producing Metals From Ores

A rock that contains a metal or other useful mineral that can be mined and sold at a profit is called an **ore.** Most metals do not occur in a pure form. A metal usually occurs as a mineral that is a combination of that metal and other elements. Copper often comes from ores containing iron and sulfur as well as copper.

How is an ore made into a finished product? **To produce metal from an ore, the ore must be mined, or removed from the ground. Then the ore must be processed to extract the metal.**

Mining Once geologists locate an ore deposit, miners decide how to remove the ore from the ground. There are three types of mines: strip mines, open-pit mines, and shaft mines. In strip mining, earthmovers scrape away soil to expose ore. In open-pit mining, miners use giant earthmoving equipment to dig a huge pit. Then they remove the ore deposits. For ore deposits that occur in veins, miners dig shaft mines. Shaft mines often have a network of tunnels that extend deep into the ground.

Each type of mining has environmental effects. For example, strip mines expose the soil, which can then be blown or washed away. Plants may not be able to grow in a strip-mined area for many years. To restore the land, mine operators replace soil removed during mining. Then they plant grass and trees.

Smelting Ores must be smelted before the metals they contain can be used. In the process of **smelting,** an ore is mixed with other substances and then melted to separate the useful metal from other elements the ore contains. For example, iron ores must be smelted to separate the iron from the oxygen and other substances in the ores.

Smelting releases gases and particles of metals into the air and water. Some of these substances can be harmful to living things. Smelters often have devices called "scrubbers" located on exhaust vents to reduce the release of harmful substances.

Reading Checkpoint What is smelting?

FIGURE 9
Processing Ore
Once an ore has been processed in a smelter, the molten metal can be poured into a mold and formed into bars called ingots.

FIGURE 10
Smelting Iron Ore

Iron ore must be smelted to separate the iron from the oxygen and other substances in the ore. *Interpreting Diagrams During which step is iron separated from the other substances in iron ore?*

1. Iron ore and limestone are mixed with coke (baked coal).

2. The mixture is placed in the blast furnace and heated.

3. As the coke burns, chemical changes produce carbon dioxide gas and molten iron.

4. Molten iron sinks to the bottom. Impurities combine with the limestone to form slag.

5. The slag and molten iron are poured off through taps.

Section 1 Assessment

S 6.6.b, S 6.6.c
E-LA: Reading 6.2.0

Target Reading Skill Preview Visuals Review your questions and answers about the rock cycle. What are two processes that occur during the rock cycle?

Reviewing Key Concepts

1. a. Listing List the five characteristics of a mineral.
   b. Explaining What does it mean to say that a mineral is inorganic?
   c. Classifying Coal is a solid, naturally occuring substance. Coal forms from the remains of plants and animals. Is coal a mineral? Explain.

2. a. Defining Write a definition of the rock cycle.
   b. Explaining What must happen for any rock in the rock cycle to form sedimentary rock?
   c. Sequencing Begin with an igneous rock and explain how it could change through two more steps in the rock cycle.

3. a. Listing List three main uses of minerals and two main uses of rocks.
   b. Identifying What is an ore?
   c. Summarizing Explain the steps that must take place before an ore can be made into a product.

Lab zone At-Home Activity

The Rocks Around Us Many common household products contain minerals found in igneous rock. For example, glass contains quartz, which is found in granite. Research one of the following materials and the products in which it is used: garnet, granite, perlite, pumice, or vermiculite. Explain to family members how the rock or mineral formed and how it is used.

Rocks and Weathering

CALIFORNIA
Standards Focus

S 6.2 Topography is reshaped by the weathering of rock and soil and by the transportation and deposition of sediment. As a basis for understanding this concept:

a. Students know water running downhill is the dominant process in shaping the landscape, including California's landscape.

🔑 How do weathering and erosion affect Earth's surface?

🔑 What are the causes of mechanical weathering and chemical weathering?

🔑 What determines how fast weathering occurs?

Key Terms

- weathering
- erosion
- uniformitarianism
- mechanical weathering
- abrasion
- ice wedging
- chemical weathering
- oxidation
- permeable

Lab zone Standards **Warm-Up**

How Fast Can It Fizz?

1. Place a fizzing antacid tablet in a small beaker. Then grind up a second tablet and place it in another beaker. The whole tablet is a model of solid rock. The ground-up tablet is a model of rock fragments.

2. Add 100 mL of warm water to the beaker containing the whole tablet. Then stir with a stirring rod until the tablet dissolves completely. Use a stopwatch to time how long it takes.

3. Add 100 mL of warm water to the beaker containing the ground-up tablet. Then stir until all of the ground-up tablet dissolves. Time how long it takes.

Think It Over

Drawing Conclusions Which dissolved faster, the whole antacid tablet or the ground-up tablet? What variable affected how long it took each of them to dissolve?

Imagine a hike that lasts for months and covers hundreds of kilometers. Each year, many hikers go on such treks. They hike trails that run the length of America's great mountain ranges. For example, the John Muir Trail follows the Sierra Nevada mountains. The Sierras extend about 640 kilometers along the eastern side of California. In the east, the Appalachian Trail follows the Appalachian Mountains. The Appalachians stretch more than 3,000 kilometers from Alabama to Canada.

The two trails cross very different landscapes. The Sierras are rocky and steep, with many peaks rising 3,000 meters above sea level. The Appalachians are more rounded and gently sloping, and are covered with soil and plants. The highest peaks in the Appalachians are less than half the elevation of the highest peaks in the Sierras. Which mountain range do you think is older? The Appalachians formed more than 250 million years ago. The Sierras formed only within the last 10 to 20 million years. The forces that wear down rock on Earth's surface have had much longer to grind down the Appalachians.

Weathering and Erosion

The process of mountain building thrusts rock up to the surface of Earth. There, the rock is exposed to weathering. **Weathering** is the process that breaks down rock and other substances at Earth's surface. Heat, cold, water, and ice all contribute to weathering. So do the oxygen and carbon dioxide in the atmosphere. Repeated freezing and thawing, for example, can crack rock apart into smaller pieces. Rainwater can dissolve minerals that bind rock together. You don't need to go to the mountains to see examples of weathering. The forces that wear down mountains also cause bicycles to rust, paint to peel, sidewalks to crack, and potholes to form.

The forces of weathering break rocks into smaller and smaller pieces of sediment. Then the forces of erosion carry the pieces away. **Erosion** (ee ROH zhun) is the transportation of sediment by wind, water, ice, or gravity. ⬤ **Topography is reshaped by weathering and erosion. These processes work together continuously to wear down and carry away the rocks at Earth's surface.** The weathering and erosion that geologists observe today also shaped Earth's surface millions of years ago. How do geologists know this? Geologists make inferences based on the principle of **uniformitarianism** (yoon uh fawrm uh TAYR ee un iz um). This principle states that the same processes that operate today operated in the past.

There are two kinds of weathering: mechanical weathering and chemical weathering. Both types of weathering act slowly, but over time they break down even the biggest, hardest rocks.

Reading Checkpoint What is the difference between weathering and erosion?

FIGURE 11
Effects of Weathering
The jagged peaks of the Sierra Nevadas (bottom) formed within the last 10 million years. The more gently sloping Appalachians (top) have been exposed to weathering for 250 million years.
Inferring *How can you tell that the Sierra Nevadas formed much more recently than the Appalachians?*

FIGURE 12

Forces of Mechanical Weathering

Mechanical weathering affects all the rock on Earth's surface.

Forming Operational Definitions *Study the examples of mechanical weathering. Then write a definition of each term in your own words.*

Freezing and Thawing
When water freezes in a crack in a rock, it expands and makes the crack bigger. The process of ice wedging also widens cracks in sidewalks and causes potholes in streets.

Release of Pressure
As the surface of a mass of rock erodes, pressure on the rock is reduced. This release of pressure causes the outside of the rock to crack and flake off like the layers of an onion. This form of weathering is seen in the granite domes of Yosemite National Park in California.

Animal Actions
Animals that burrow in the ground— including moles, gophers, prairie dogs, and some insects—loosen and break apart rocks in the soil.

Mechanical Weathering

If you hit a rock with a hammer, the rock may break into pieces. Like a hammer, some forces of weathering break rock into pieces. The type of weathering in which rock is physically broken into smaller pieces is called **mechanical weathering**. These smaller pieces of rock have the same composition as the rock they came from. If you have seen rocks that are cracked or split in layers, then you have seen rocks that are undergoing mechanical weathering. Mechanical weathering works slowly. But over very long periods of time, it does more than wear down rocks. Mechanical weathering eventually wears away whole mountains.

Abrasion
Sand and other rock particles that are carried by wind, water, or ice can wear away exposed rock surfaces like sandpaper on wood. Wind-driven sand helped shape the rocks shown here.

Plant Growth
Roots of trees and other plants enter cracks in rocks. As roots grow, they force the cracks farther apart. Over time, the roots of even small plants can pry apart cracked rocks.

🔑 **The causes of mechanical weathering include freezing and thawing, release of pressure, plant growth, actions of animals, and abrasion.** The term **abrasion** (uh BRAY zhun) refers to the grinding away of rock by rock particles carried by water, ice, wind, or gravity.

In cool climates, the most important force of mechanical weathering is the freezing and thawing of water. Water seeps into cracks in rocks and then freezes when the temperature drops. Water expands when it freezes. Ice therefore acts like a wedge that forces things apart. Wedges of ice in rocks widen and deepen cracks. This process is called **ice wedging**. When the ice melts, the water seeps deeper into the cracks. With repeated freezing and thawing, the cracks slowly expand until pieces of rock break off.

Go Online
PHSchool.com

For: More on weathering
Visit: PHSchool.com
Web Code: cfd-2021

Reading Checkpoint How does ice wedging weather rock?

Chemical Weathering

In addition to mechanical weathering, another type of weathering attacks rock. **Chemical weathering** is the process that breaks down rock through chemical changes. ⊂▬ **The causes of chemical weathering include the action of water, oxygen, carbon dioxide, living organisms, and acid rain.**

Each rock is made up of one or more minerals. Chemical weathering can produce new minerals as it breaks down rock. For example, granite is made up of several minerals, including feldspar, quartz, and mica. As a result of chemical weathering, granite eventually changes the feldspar minerals to clay minerals.

Chemical weathering creates holes or soft spots in rock, so the rock breaks apart more easily. Chemical and mechanical weathering often work together. As mechanical weathering breaks rock into pieces, more surface area becomes exposed to chemical weathering. The Standards Warm-Up activity at the beginning of this section shows how increasing the surface area increases the rate of a chemical reaction.

FIGURE 13
Weathering and Surface Area
As weathering breaks apart rock, the surface area exposed to weathering increases. The total volume of the rock stays the same even though the rock is broken into smaller and smaller pieces.
Predicting *What will happen to the surface area if each cube is again divided into eight cubes?*

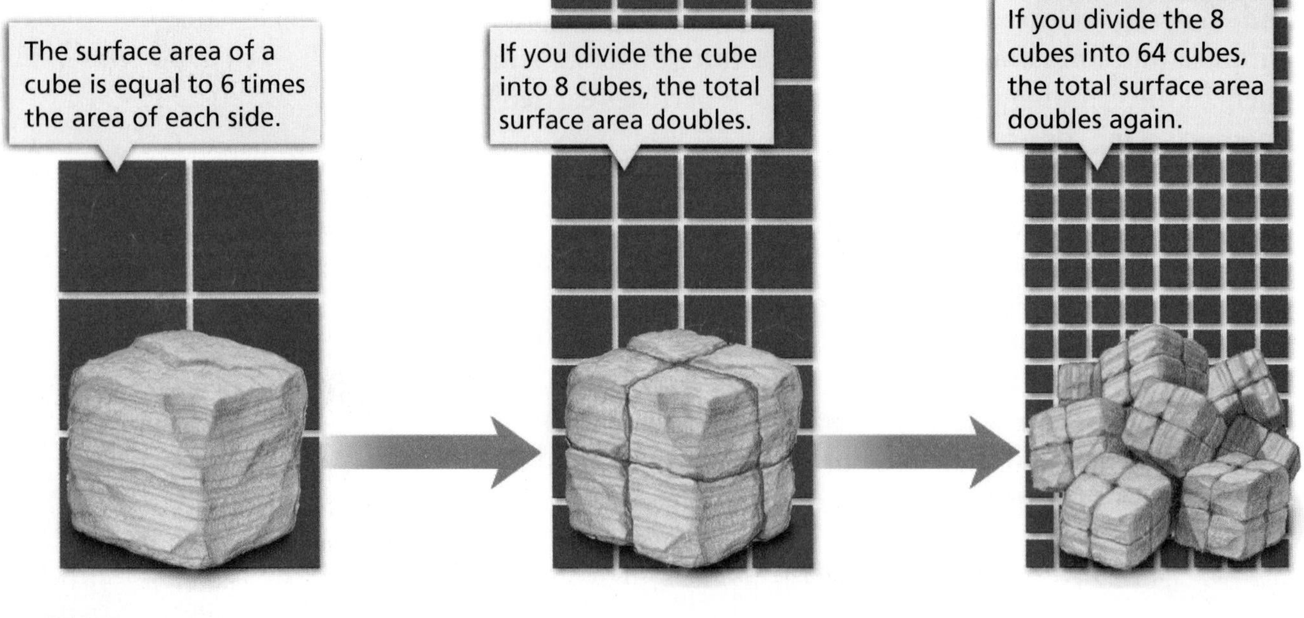

The surface area of a cube is equal to 6 times the area of each side.

If you divide the cube into 8 cubes, the total surface area doubles.

If you divide the 8 cubes into 64 cubes, the total surface area doubles again.

FIGURE 14
Effects of Chemical Weathering
Acid rain chemically weathered these stone gargoyles on the cathedral of Notre Dame in Paris, France.

Water Water is the most important cause of chemical weathering. Water weathers rock by dissolving it. When a rock or other substance dissolves in water, it mixes uniformly throughout the water to make a solution. Over time, many rocks will dissolve in water.

Oxygen The oxygen gas in air is an important cause of chemical weathering. If you have ever left a bicycle or metal tool outside in the rain, then you have seen how oxygen can weather iron. Iron combines with oxygen in the presence of water in a process called **oxidation.** The product of oxidation is rust. Rock that contains iron also oxidizes, or rusts. Rust makes rock soft and crumbly and gives it a red or brown color.

Carbon Dioxide Another gas found in air, carbon dioxide, also causes chemical weathering. Carbon dioxide dissolves in rainwater and in water that sinks through air pockets in the soil. The result is a weak acid called carbonic acid. Carbonic acid easily weathers rocks such as marble and limestone.

Living Organisms Imagine a seed landing on a rock face. As it sprouts, its roots push into cracks in the rock. As the plant's roots grow, they produce weak acids that slowly dissolve rock around the roots. Lichens—plantlike organisms that grow on rocks—also produce weak acids that chemically weather rock.

Acid Rain Over the past 150 years, people have been burning large amounts of coal, oil, and gas for energy. Burning these fuels can pollute the air with sulfur, carbon, and nitrogen compounds. Such compounds react chemically with the water vapor in clouds, forming acids. These acids mix with raindrops and fall as acid rain. Acid rain causes very rapid chemical weathering.

Reading Checkpoint How can plants cause chemical weathering?

Math / Analyzing Data

Which Weathered Faster?

The graph shows the rate of weathering for two identical pieces of limestone that weathered in different locations.

1. **Reading Graphs** What does the *x*-axis of the graph represent?

2. **Reading Graphs** What does the *y*-axis of the graph represent?

3. **Reading Graphs** How much thickness did Stone A lose in 1,000 years? How much thickness did Stone B lose in the same period?

4. **Drawing Conclusions** Which stone weathered at a faster rate?

5. **Inferring** Since the two identical pieces of limestone weathered at different rates, what can you infer caused the difference in their rates of weathering?

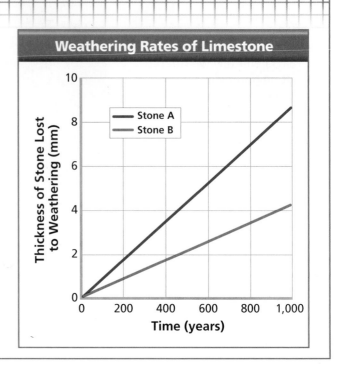

Weathering Rates of Limestone

Stone A
Stone B

y-axis: Thickness of Stone Lost to Weathering (mm)
x-axis: Time (years)

Rate of Weathering

Visitors to New England's historic cemeteries may notice a surprising fact. Slate tombstones carved in the 1700s are less weathered and easier to read than marble gravestones from the 1800s. Why is this so? Some kinds of rocks weather more rapidly than others. ◐ **The most important factors that determine the rate at which weathering occurs are the type of rock and the climate.**

Type of Rock The minerals that make up the rock determine how fast it weathers. Rock made of minerals that do not dissolve easily in water weathers slowly. Rock made of minerals that dissolve easily in water weathers faster.

Some rock weathers more easily because it is permeable. **Permeable** (PUR mee uh bul) means that a material is full of tiny, connected air spaces that allow water to seep through it. Permeable rock weathers chemically at a fast rate. Why? As water seeps through the spaces in the rock, it dissolves and removes material broken down by weathering.

Climate Climate refers to the average weather conditions in an area. Both chemical and mechanical weathering occur faster in wet climates. Rainfall provides the water needed for chemical changes as well as for freezing and thawing.

Granite

Marble

Chemical reactions occur faster at higher temperatures. That is why chemical weathering occurs more quickly where the climate is both hot and wet. Granite, for example, is a very hard rock that forms when molten material cools inside Earth. Granite weathers so slowly in cool climates that it is often used as a building stone. But in hot and wet climates, granite weathers more rapidly and eventually crumbles apart.

FIGURE 15
Which Rock Weathers Faster?
These two tombstones are about the same age and are in the same cemetery, yet one has weathered much less than the other.
Inferring Which type of stone weathers faster, granite or marble? Explain.

 **Reading Checkpoint** **How does rainfall affect the rate of weathering?**

Section 2 Assessment

S 6.2, S 6.2.a
E-LA: Reading 6.1.0

Vocabulary Skill Suffixes Complete the sentence with the correct words (*wedges/ice wedging*). _____ of ice in rocks widen and deepen cracks in the process of _____ .

🔑 **Reviewing Key Concepts**

1. a. **Defining** What is weathering?
   b. **Defining** What is erosion?
   c. **Predicting** Over millions of years, how do weathering and erosion change a mountain made of solid rock?
2. a. **Defining** What is chemical weathering?
   b. **Comparing and Contrasting** Compare and contrast mechanical weathering and chemical weathering.
   c. **Classifying** Classify each as chemical or mechanical weathering: freezing or thawing, oxidation, water dissolving chemicals in rock, abrasion, acid rain.
3. a. **Identifying** What are two factors that affect the rate of weathering?
   b. **Relating Cause and Effect** A granite monument is placed outside for 200 years in a region with a cool, dry climate. What would its rate of weathering be? Explain.

Lab zone **At-Home Activity**

Ice in a Straw Demonstrate one type of weathering for your family. Plug one end of a drinking straw with a small piece of clay. Fill the straw with water. Now plug the top of the straw with clay. Make sure that the clay plugs do not leak. Lay the straw flat in the freezer overnight. Remove the straw the next day. What happened to the clay plugs? What process produced this result? Be sure to dispose of the straw so that no one will use it for drinking.

Rock Shake

Materials

4 watertight plastic containers with screw-on caps, 500 mL

marking pen or pencil and masking tape

80 small pieces of water-soaked limestone

plastic graduated cylinder, 250 mL

300 mL of water

300 mL of vinegar, an acid

balance

2 pieces of thin cloth

paper towels

Problem
How will shaking and acid conditions affect the rate at which limestone weathers?

Skills Focus
developing hypotheses, interpreting data, calculating, drawing conclusions

Procedure

PART 1 Day 1

1. Using masking tape, label the four 500-mL containers A, B, C, and D.

2. Separate the 80 pieces of limestone into four sets of 20.

3. Copy the data table in your notebook. Then place the first 20 pieces of limestone on the balance and record their mass in the data table. Place the rocks in container A.

4. Repeat Step 3 for the other sets of rocks and place them in containers B, C, and D.

5. Pour 150 mL of water into container A and container B. Put caps on both containers.

6. Pour 150 mL of vinegar into container C and container D. Put caps on both containers.

7. Develop a hypothesis explaining the effect of weathering on the mass of the limestone pieces. Predict which will weather more: the limestone in water or the limestone in vinegar. (*Hint:* Vinegar is an acid.) Also develop a hypothesis explaining the effect of shaking on the limestone in containers B and D. Record your hypotheses in your notebook.

8. Allow the pieces to soak overnight.

Data Table				
Container	Total Mass at Start	Total Mass Next Day	Change in Mass	Percent Change in Mass
A (water, no shaking)				
B (water, shaking)				
C (vinegar, no shaking)				
D (vinegar, shaking)				

PART 2 Day 2

9. Screw the caps tightly on containers B and D. Shake both containers for 10 to 15 minutes. Make sure that each container is shaken for exactly the same amount of time and at the same intensity. After shaking, set the containers aside. Do not shake containers A and C.

10. Open the top of container A. Place one piece of thin cloth over the opening of the container. Carefully pour all of the water out through the cloth into a waste container. Be careful not to let any of the pieces flow out with the water. Dry these pieces carefully and record their mass in your data table.

11. Next, determine how much limestone was lost through weathering in container A. (*Hint:* Subtract the mass of the limestone pieces remaining on Day 2 from the mass of the pieces on Day 1.)

12. Repeat Steps 10 and 11 for containers B, C, and D.

Analyze and Conclude

1. Calculating Calculate the percent change in mass of the 20 pieces for each container.

$$\% \text{ change} = \frac{\text{Change in mass} \times 100}{\text{Total mass at start}}$$

Record the results in the data table.

2. Interpreting Data Do your data show a change in mass of the 20 pieces in each of the four containers?

3. Interpreting Data Is there a greater change in total mass for the pieces in one container than for the pieces in another? Explain.

4. Drawing Conclusions Did your results support your hypotheses explaining how shaking and acid would affect the weathering of limestone? Explain.

5. Developing Hypotheses If your data showed a greater change in the mass of the pieces in one of the containers, how might this change be explained?

6. Drawing Conclusions Based on your data, which variable do you think was more responsible for breaking down the limestone: the vinegar or the shaking? Explain.

7. Communicating Write a paragraph that explains why you allowed two of the containers to stand without shaking, and why you were careful to shake the other two containers for the same amount of time.

Design an Experiment

Would your results for this experiment change if you changed the variables? For example, you could soak or shake the pieces for a longer time, or test rocks other than limestone. You could also test whether adding more limestone pieces (30 rather than 20 in each set) would make a difference in the outcome. Develop a new hypothesis to explain the effects of changing one of those variables on the rate of weathering. Then design an experiment to test your hypothesis. *Have your teacher approve your plan before you begin.*

How Soil Forms

CALIFORNIA
Standards Focus

S 6.6.b Students know different natural energy and material resources, including air, soil, rocks, minerals, petroleum, fresh water, wildlife, and forests, and know how to classify them as renewable or nonrenewable.

- What is soil made of, and how does it form?
- How do scientists classify soils?
- What is the role of plants and animals in soil formation?

Key Terms

- soil
- bedrock
- humus
- fertility
- loam
- soil horizon
- topsoil
- subsoil
- acidic
- basic
- litter
- decomposer

Lab zone **Standards Warm-Up**

What Is Soil?

1. Use a toothpick to separate a sample of soil into individual particles. With a hand lens, try to identify the different types of particles in the sample. Wash your hands when you are finished.
2. Write a "recipe" for the sample of soil, naming each of the "ingredients" that you think the soil contains. Include what percentage of each ingredient would be needed to make up the soil.
3. Compare your recipe with those of your classmates.

Think It Over

Forming Operational Definitions Based on your observations, how would you define the word *soil*?

A bare rock surface does not look like a spot where a plant could grow. But look more closely. In that hard surface is a small crack. Over many years, mechanical and chemical weathering will slowly enlarge the crack. Rain and wind will bring bits of weathered rock, dust, and dry leaves. The wind also may carry tiny seeds. With enough moisture, a seed will sprout and take root. Then, a few months later, the plant blossoms.

What Is Soil?

The crack in the rock seems to have little in common with a flower garden containing thick, rich soil. But soil is what the weathered rock and other materials in the crack have started to become. **Soil** is the loose, weathered material on Earth's surface in which plants can grow.

One of the main ingredients of soil comes from bedrock. **Bedrock** is the solid layer of rock beneath the soil. Once exposed at the surface, bedrock gradually weathers into smaller and smaller particles that are the basic material of soil.

Soil Composition Soil is more than particles of weathered bedrock. 🔵 **Soil is a mixture of rock particles, minerals, decayed organic material, water, and air.** Together, sand, silt, and clay make up the portion of soil that comes from weathered rock.

The decayed organic material in soil is called humus. **Humus** (HYOO mus) is a dark-colored substance that forms as plant and animal remains decay. Humus helps create spaces in soil for the air and water that plants must have. Humus also contains substances called nutrients, including nitrogen, sulfur, phosphorus, and potassium. Plants need nutrients in order to grow. As plants grow, they absorb nutrients from the soil.

Fertile soil is rich in the nutrients that plants need to grow. The **fertility** of soil is a measure of how well the soil supports plant growth. Soil that is rich in humus has high fertility. Sandy soil containing little humus has low fertility.

Soil Texture Sand feels coarse and grainy, but clay feels smooth and silky. These differences are differences in texture. Soil texture depends on the size of individual soil particles.

The particles of rock in soil are classified by size. As you can see in Figure 17, the largest soil particles are gravel. The smallest soil particles are clay. Clay particles are smaller than the period at the end of this sentence.

Soil texture is important for plant growth. Soil that is mostly clay has a dense, heavy texture. Some clay soils hold a lot of water, so plants grown in them may "drown" for lack of air. In contrast, sandy soil has a coarse texture. Water quickly drains through it, so plants may die for lack of water.

Soil that is made up of about equal parts of clay, sand, and silt is called **loam.** It has a crumbly texture that holds both air and water. Loam is best for growing most types of plants.

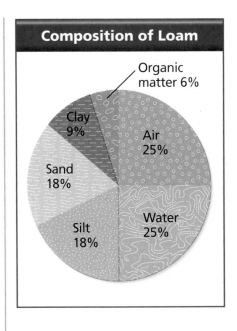

Composition of Loam

- Organic matter 6%
- Clay 9%
- Air 25%
- Sand 18%
- Silt 18%
- Water 25%

FIGURE 16
Loam, a type of soil, is made up of air, water, and organic matter as well as materials from weathered rock. **Interpreting Graphs** *What two materials make up the major portion of this soil?*

FIGURE 17
Soil particles range in size from gravel to clay particles too small to be seen by the unaided eye. The sand, silt, and clay shown here have been enlarged.

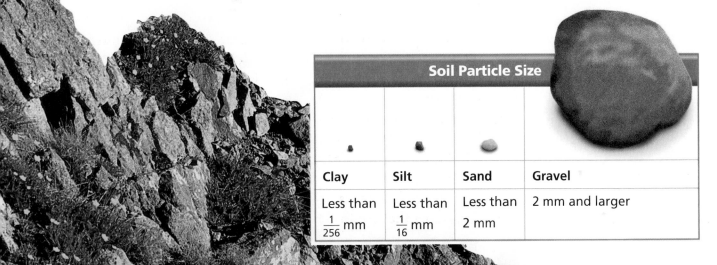

Soil Particle Size

Clay	Silt	Sand	Gravel
Less than $\frac{1}{256}$ mm	Less than $\frac{1}{16}$ mm	Less than 2 mm	2 mm and larger

The Process of Soil Formation

Soil forms as rock is broken down by weathering and mixes with other materials on the surface. Soil is constantly being formed wherever bedrock is exposed. Soil formation continues over a long period of time.

Gradually, soil develops layers called horizons. A **soil horizon** is a layer of soil that differs in color and texture from the layers above or below it.

If you dug a hole in the ground about half a meter deep, you would see the different soil horizons. Figure 18 shows how soil scientists classify the soil into three horizons. The A horizon is made up of **topsoil,** a crumbly, dark brown soil that is a mixture of humus, clay, and other minerals. The B horizon, often called **subsoil,** usually consists of clay and other particles washed down from the A horizon, but little humus. The C horizon contains only partly weathered rock.

The rate at which soil forms depends on the climate and type of rock. Remember that weathering occurs most rapidly in areas with a warm, rainy climate. As a result, soil develops more quickly in these areas. In contrast, weathering and soil formation take place slowly in areas where the climate is cold and dry.

Some types of rock weather and form soil faster than others. For example, limestone, a type of rock formed from the shells and skeletons of once-living things, weathers faster than granite. Thus, soil forms more quickly from limestone than from granite.

Go Online
active art

For: Soil Layers activity
Visit: PHSchool.com
Web Code: cfp-2022

FIGURE 18
Soil Layers
Soil horizons form in three steps.
Inferring *Which soil horizon is responsible for soil's fertility? Explain.*

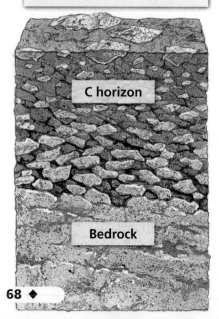

❶ The C horizon forms as bedrock weathers and rock breaks up into soil particles.

C horizon

Bedrock

❷ The A horizon develops as plants add organic material to the soil and plant roots weather pieces of rock.

A horizon

C horizon

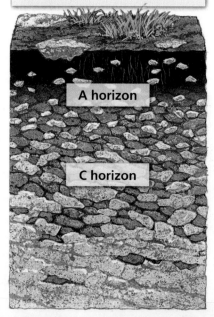

❸ The B horizon develops as rainwater washes clay and minerals from the A horizon to the B horizon.

A horizon

B horizon

C horizon

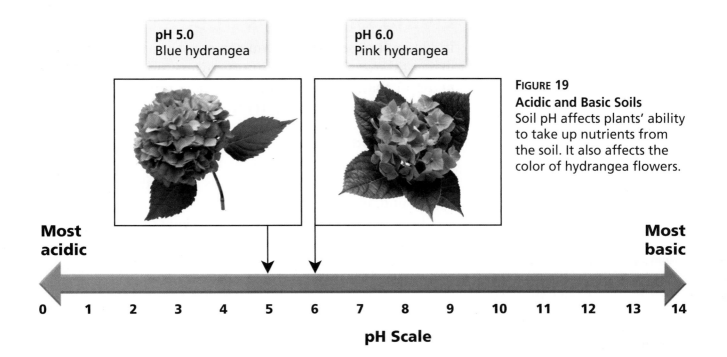

pH 5.0
Blue hydrangea

pH 6.0
Pink hydrangea

FIGURE 19
Acidic and Basic Soils
Soil pH affects plants' ability to take up nutrients from the soil. It also affects the color of hydrangea flowers.

Most acidic

Most basic

0   1   2   3   4   5   6   7   8   9   10   11   12   13   14

pH Scale

Soil Types

There are thousands of different soil types. ⊂ **Scientists classify the different types of soil into major groups based on climate, plants, soil composition, and whether the soil is acidic or basic.** Fertile soil can form in regions with hot, wet climates, but rain may wash humus and minerals out of the A horizon. In mountains and polar regions with cold, dry climates, the soil is often very thin. The thickest, most fertile soil forms in climate regions with moderate temperatures and rainfall.

The most common plants found in a region are also used to help classify the soil. For example, grassland soils are very different from forest soils. In addition, scientists classify soil by its composition—whether it is rocky, sandy, or rich in clay.

Soils can also be classified as either acidic or basic. A substance is **acidic** if it reacts strongly with some metals and changes blue litmus paper red. A substance is **basic** if it feels slippery and changes red litmus paper blue. Scientists use the pH scale, shown in Figure 19, to measure how acidic or basic a substance is. A substance with a pH of 0 is strongly acidic. A substance with a pH of 14 is strongly basic. A substance with a pH of 7 is neutral. This means that it is in between acidic and basic. For plants to grow well, soil must not be too acidic or too basic. Most garden plants grow best if the soil's pH is between 6 and 7.5, or slightly acidic to slightly basic. But some soils can have a pH as low as 4, which is quite acidic.

Lab zone **Try This Activity**

Red or Blue?

You can use litmus paper to determine whether soil is acidic or basic. **CAUTION:** Never taste a substance to test whether it is acidic or basic. Strongly acidic or basic substances are poisonous and can cause burns.

1. Place a small spoonful of soil in a plastic cup, add enough water to fill the cup halfway, and stir carefully for 10 seconds.
2. Dip a strip of blue litmus paper in the mixture of soil and water.
3. Observe the color change in the litmus paper.
4. Repeat Steps 2 and 3 using red litmus paper.

Inferring What can you infer about the pH of the soil?

 **Reading Checkpoint** What does the pH scale measure?

Living Organisms in Soil

If you look closely at soil, you can see that it is teeming with living things. ⬮ **Some soil organisms make humus, the material that makes soil fertile. Other soil organisms mix the soil and make spaces in it for air and water.**

Forming Humus Plants contribute most of the organic remains that form humus. As plants shed leaves, they form a loose layer called **litter.** When plants die, their remains fall to the ground and become part of the litter. Plant roots also die and begin to decay underground. Although plant remains are full of stored nutrients, they are not yet humus.

FIGURE 20
Life in Soil

Every cubic meter of soil contains billions of organisms. All organisms that live in soil enrich humus with their remains or wastes. This illustration shows some of the organisms typically found in northern forest soil.
Relating Cause and Effect Which organisms in the art help air and water to enter the soil?

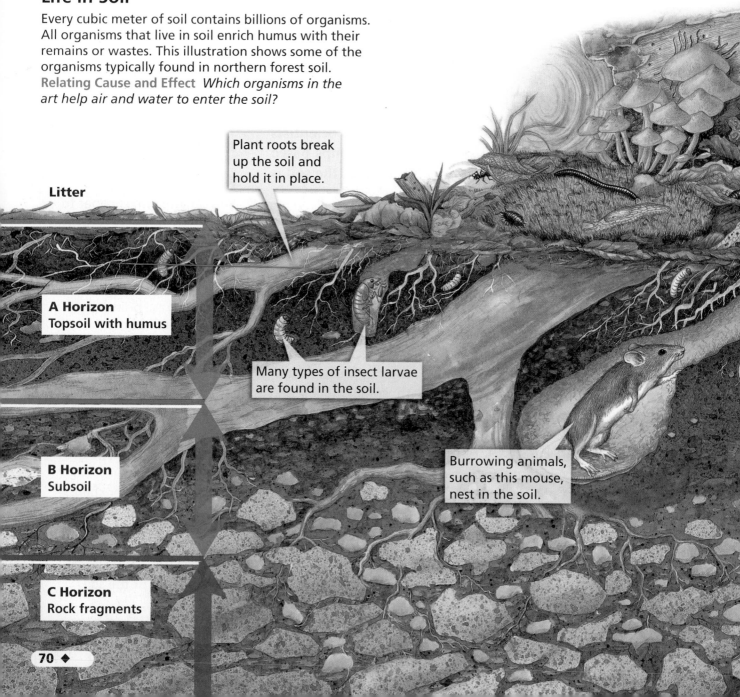

Litter

Plant roots break up the soil and hold it in place.

A Horizon
Topsoil with humus

Many types of insect larvae are found in the soil.

B Horizon
Subsoil

Burrowing animals, such as this mouse, nest in the soil.

C Horizon
Rock fragments

Humus forms in a process called decomposition. During decomposition, organisms that live in soil turn dead organic material into humus. These organisms are called decomposers. **Decomposers** are the organisms that break the remains of dead organisms into smaller pieces and digest them with chemicals.

Soil decomposers include fungi, bacteria, worms, and other organisms. Fungi are organisms such as molds and mushrooms. Fungi grow on, and digest, plant remains. Bacteria are microscopic decomposers that cause decay. Bacteria attack dead organisms and their wastes in soil. Very small animals, such as mites and worms, also decompose dead organic material and mix it with the soil.

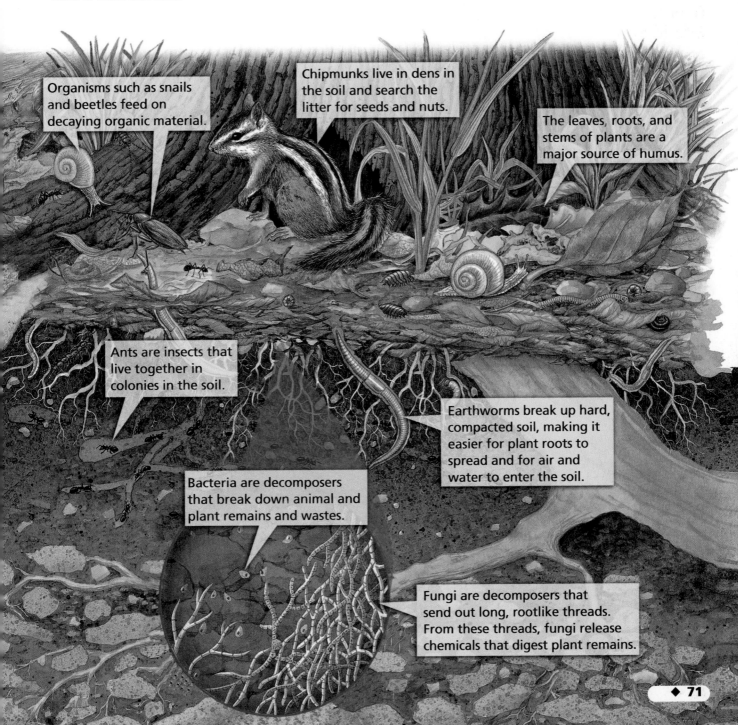

Organisms such as snails and beetles feed on decaying organic material.

Chipmunks live in dens in the soil and search the litter for seeds and nuts.

The leaves, roots, and stems of plants are a major source of humus.

Ants are insects that live together in colonies in the soil.

Earthworms break up hard, compacted soil, making it easier for plant roots to spread and for air and water to enter the soil.

Bacteria are decomposers that break down animal and plant remains and wastes.

Fungi are decomposers that send out long, rootlike threads. From these threads, fungi release chemicals that digest plant remains.

FIGURE 21
Soil Mixers
Earthworms break up the soil, allowing in air and water. An earthworm eats its own weight in soil every day. **Predicting** *How fertile is soil that contains many earthworms likely to be? Explain.*

Mixing the Soil Earthworms do most of the work of mixing humus with other materials in soil. As earthworms eat their way through the soil, they carry humus down to the subsoil and subsoil up to the surface. Earthworms also pass out the soil they eat as waste. The waste soil is enriched with substances that plants need to grow, such as nitrogen.

Many burrowing mammals such as mice, moles, prairie dogs, and gophers break up hard, compacted soil and mix humus through it. These animals also add nitrogen to the soil when they produce waste. They add organic material when they die and decay.

Earthworms and burrowing animals also help to aerate, or mix air into, the soil. Plant roots need the oxygen that this process adds to the soil.

 **Reading Checkpoint** **Which animals are most important in mixing humus into the soil?**

Section **3** **Assessment**

S 6.6.b, E-LA: Reading 6.2.0, Writing 6.2.0

↻ **Target Reading Skill** Preview Visuals Review your questions and answers for Figure 20, Life in Soil. What two organisms in the illustration are decomposers?

Reviewing Key Concepts

1. **a.** Describing What five materials make up soil?
   b. Explaining How do soil horizons form?
   c. Sequencing Place these terms in the correct order starting from the surface: C horizon, subsoil, bedrock, topsoil.
2. **a.** Reviewing What are four main factors used to classify soils?
   b. Classifying The pH values of four soil samples are Sample 1, 7.7; Sample 2, 6.0; Sample 3, 7.0; and Sample 4, 4.9. Classify the samples as acidic, basic, or neutral. (*Hint:* Refer to the pH scale in Figure 19.)

3. **a.** Identifying What are two main ways in which soil organisms contribute to soil formation?
   b. Describing Give examples of three types of decomposers and describe their effects on soil.
   c. Predicting What would happen to the fertility of a soil if all decomposers were removed? Explain.

Writing in Science

Product Label Write a product label for a bag of topsoil. Your label should give the soil a name that will make consumers want to buy it, state how and where the soil formed, give its composition, and suggest how it can be used.

Consumer Lab
Guided Inquiry

S 6.5.e, 6.7.b

Comparing Soils

Materials

20–30 grams of local soil

graph paper ruled with 1- or 2-mm spacing

plastic petri dish or jar lid

plastic spoon and plastic dropper

water

stereomicroscope

20–30 grams of bagged topsoil

Problem

What are the characteristics of two samples of soil?

Skills Focus observing, inferring, developing hypotheses

Procedure

1. Obtain a sample of local soil. As you observe the sample, record your observations in your lab notebook.

2. Spread half of the sample on the graph paper. Spread the soil thinly so that you can see the lines on the paper through the soil. Using the graph paper as a background, estimate the sizes of the particles that make up the soil.

3. Place the rest of the sample in the palm of your hand, rub it between your fingers, and squeeze it. Is it soft or gritty? Does it clump together or crumble when you squeeze it?

4. Place about half the sample in a plastic petri dish. Using the dropper, add water one drop at a time. Watch how the sample changes. Does any material in the sample float? As the sample gets wet, do you notice any odor? (*Hint:* If the wet soil has an odor or contains material that floats, it is likely to contain organic material.)

5. Look at some of the soil under the stereomicroscope. (*Hint:* Use a toothpick to separate the particles in the soil.) Sketch what you see. Label the particles, such as gravel, organic matter, or strangely shaped grains.

6. Repeat Steps 1–5 with the topsoil. Be sure to record your observations.

7. Clean up and dispose of your samples as directed by your teacher. **CAUTION:** *Wash your hands when you finish handling the soil.*

Analyze and Conclude

1. Observing Did you observe any similarities between the local soil sample and the topsoil? Any differences?

2. Inferring What can you infer about the composition of both types of soil from the different sizes of their particles? From your observations of texture? From how the samples changed when water was added?

3. Inferring Do you think that both types of soil were formed in the same way? Explain.

4. Developing Hypotheses Based on your observations and study of the chapter, develop a hypothesis to explain which soil would be better for growing a specific vegetable.

5. Communicating Write a report for consumers that summarizes the steps in your analysis of the two soil samples and your results. Be sure to describe what factors you analyzed and give a suggestion for which soil consumers should use for growing flowers and vegetables.

Design an Experiment

Design an experiment to test the hypothesis that you developed for Question 4. Be sure to indicate how you would control variables. *After you receive your teacher's approval, carry out your experiment.*

Section 4

Soil Conservation

CALIFORNIA
Standards Focus

S 6.6 Sources of energy and materials differ in amounts, distribution, usefulness, and the time required for their formation. As a basis for understanding this concept:

b. Students know different natural energy and material resources, including air, soil, rocks, minerals, petroleum, fresh water, wildlife, and forests, and know how to classify them as renewable or nonrenewable.

- Why is fertile soil considered a nonrenewable resource?
- How can soil lose its value?
- What are some ways that soil can be conserved?

Key Terms

- sod
- natural resource
- Dust Bowl
- soil conservation
- contour plowing
- conservation plowing
- crop rotation

Prairie grasses and wildflowers ▼

Lab zone Standards Warm-Up

How Can You Keep Soil From Washing Away?

1. Pour about 500 mL of soil into a pie plate, forming a pile.
2. Devise a way to keep the soil from washing away when water is poured over it. To protect the pile of soil, you may use craft sticks, paper clips, pebbles, modeling clay, strips of paper, or other materials approved by your teacher.
3. After arranging your materials to protect the soil, hold a container filled with 200 mL of water about 20 cm above the center of the soil. Slowly pour the water in a stream onto the pile of soil.
4. Compare your pan of soil with those of your classmates.

Think It Over

Observing Based on your observations, what do you think is the best way to prevent soil on a slope from washing away?

Suppose you were a settler traveling west in the mid 1800s. Much of your journey would have been through vast, open grasslands called prairies. After the forests and mountains of the East, the prairies were an amazing sight. Grass taller than a person rippled and flowed in the wind like a sea of green.

The prairie soil was very fertile. It was rich with humus because of the tall grass. The **sod**—the thick mass of tough roots at the surface of the soil—kept the soil in place and held on to moisture.

The prairies covered a vast area in the American Midwest. Today, farms growing crops such as corn, soybeans, and wheat have replaced the prairies. But prairie soils are still among the most fertile in the world.

Soil as a Resource

A **natural resource** is anything in the environment that humans use. Soil is one of Earth's most valuable natural resources because everything that lives on land, including humans, depends directly or indirectly on soil. Plants depend directly on the soil to live and grow. Humans and animals depend on plants—or on other animals that depend on plants—for food.

Fertile soil is valuable because there is a limited supply. Less than one eighth of the land on Earth has soils that are well suited for farming. Soil is also in limited supply because it takes a long time to form. It can take hundreds of years for just a few centimeters of soil to form. The thick, fertile soil of the prairies took many thousands of years to develop. **Because fertile soil is in limited supply and takes a long time to form, it is considered a nonrenewable resource.**

Video Field Trip
Discovery Channel School
Weathering and Soil Formation

Soil Damage and Loss

Human activities and changes in the environment can affect the soil. **The value of soil is reduced when soil loses its fertility and when topsoil is lost due to erosion.**

Loss of Fertility Soil can be damaged when it loses its fertility. Soil that has lost its fertility is said to be exhausted. This type of soil loss occurred in large parts of the South in the late 1800s. Soils in which only cotton had been grown were exhausted. Many farmers left their farms. Early in the 1900s in Alabama, a scientist named George Washington Carver developed new crops and farming methods that helped to restore soil fertility in the South. Peanuts were one crop that helped make the soil fertile again. Peanut plants are legumes. Legumes have small lumps on their roots that contain nitrogen-fixing bacteria. These bacteria make nitrogen, an important nutrient, available in a form that plants can use.

FIGURE 22
Restoring Soil Fertility
George Washington Carver (1864–1943) taught new methods of soil conservation. He also encouraged farmers to plant peanuts, which helped restore soil fertility.
Applying Concepts *What nutrient do peanut plants add to the soil?*

The Dust Bowl

Key
- Dust Bowl
- Other areas affected by dust storms

Montana, North Dakota, Wyoming, South Dakota, Iowa, Nebraska, Rocky Mountains, Colorado, Kansas, Missouri, Oklahoma, New Mexico, Mississippi River, Texas

FIGURE 23
The Dust Bowl
The Dust Bowl ruined farmland in western Oklahoma and parts of the surrounding states. Wind blew dry particles of soil into great clouds of dust that traveled thousands of kilometers.

Go Online

sciLINKS NSTA

For: Links on soil conservation
Visit: www.SciLinks.org
Web Code: scn-0723

Loss of Topsoil Where soil is exposed, water and wind can quickly carry soil away in the process of erosion. Plant cover can protect soil from erosion. Plants break the force of falling rain, and plant roots hold the soil together. Wind also causes soil loss. Wind erosion is most likely in areas where farming methods are not suited to dry conditions. For example, wind erosion led to the Dust Bowl on the Great Plains.

Soil Loss in the Dust Bowl Toward the end of the 1800s, farmers settled the Great Plains. The soil of the Great Plains is fertile. But rainfall decreases steadily from east to west across the Great Plains. The region also has droughts—years when rainfall is scarce. Plowing removed the grass from the Great Plains and exposed the soil. In times of drought, the topsoil quickly dried out, turned to dust, and blew away.

By 1930, almost all of the Great Plains had been turned into farms or ranches. Then, a long drought turned the soil on parts of the Great Plains to dust. The wind blew the soil east in great, black clouds that reached Chicago and New York City. The erosion was most serious in the southern Plains states. This area, shown in Figure 23, was called the **Dust Bowl.** The Dust Bowl helped people appreciate the value of soil. With government support, farmers in the Great Plains and throughout the country began to take better care of their land. They adopted methods of farming that helped save the soil. Some methods were new. Others had been practiced for hundreds of years.

 **Reading Checkpoint** **What caused the Dust Bowl?**

Soil Conservation

Since the Dust Bowl, farmers have adopted modern methods of soil conservation. **Soil conservation** is the management of soil to prevent its destruction.  **Soil can be conserved through contour plowing, conservation plowing, and crop rotation.**

In **contour plowing,** farmers plow their fields along the curves of a slope. This helps slow the runoff of excess rainfall and prevents it from washing the soil away.

In **conservation plowing,** farmers disturb the soil and its plant cover as little as possible. Dead weeds and stalks of the previous year's crop are left in the ground to help return soil nutrients, retain moisture, and hold soil in place. This method is also called low-till or no-till plowing.

In **crop rotation,** a farmer plants different crops in a field each year. Different types of plants absorb different amounts of nutrients from the soil. Some crops, such as corn and cotton, absorb large amounts of nutrients. The year after planting these crops, the farmer plants crops that use fewer soil nutrients, such as oats, barley, or rye. The year after that the farmer sows legumes such as alfalfa or beans to restore the nutrient supply.

Reading Checkpoint How does conservation plowing help conserve soil?

FIGURE 24
Soil Conservation Methods
This farm's fields show evidence of contour plowing and crop rotation. **Predicting** *How might contour plowing affect the amount of topsoil?*

Section 4 Assessment

S 6.6.b; E-LA: Reading 6.1.0

Vocabulary Skill Suffixes Complete the following sentence with the correct word (*conserve/conservation*). Farmers can _____ soil by crop rotation.

Reviewing Key Concepts

1. a. **Reviewing** What is a natural resource?
   b. **Explaining** Why is fertile soil considered a nonrenewable resource?
2. a. **Listing** What are two ways in which the value of soil can be reduced?
   b. **Explaining** Explain how topsoil can be lost.
   c. **Relating Cause and Effect** What caused the Dust Bowl?
3. a. **Defining** What is soil conservation?
   b. **Listing** What are three methods by which farmers can conserve soil?
   c. **Problem Solving** A farmer growing corn wants to maintain soil fertility and reduce erosion. What conservation methods could the farmer try? Explain.

Writing in Science

Public Service Announcement
A severe drought in a farming region threatens to produce another Dust Bowl. Write a paragraph about soil conservation to be read as a public service announcement on radio stations. The announcement should identify the danger of soil loss due to erosion. It should also describe the steps farmers can take to conserve the soil.

Study Guide

🔑 The **BIG Idea** The weathering of rock helps to reshape Earth's topography and form soil.

① Minerals and Rocks

🔑 **Key Concepts** ✎ S 6.6.b

- A mineral is a naturally occurring, inorganic solid that forms on or beneath Earth's surface. Almost all minerals have a crystal shape. Each mineral also has a definite chemical composition.

- Geologists classify rocks into three groups: igneous rock, sedimentary rock, and metamorphic rock. The rocks in each group form through different steps in the rock cycle.

- Minerals are the source of gemstones, metals, and other materials used to make products.

- People use rocks for building materials and in industrial processes.

- To produce metal from an ore, the ore must be mined and then smelted to extract the metal.

Key Terms
- mineral • crystal • rock cycle
- igneous rock • sedimentary rock • sediment
- metamorphic rock • nonrenewable resource
- ore • smelting

② Rocks and Weathering

🔑 **Key Concepts** ✎ S 6.2, 6.2.a

- Weathering and erosion work together continuously to wear down and carry away the rocks at Earth's surface.

- The causes of mechanical weathering include freezing and thawing, release of pressure, plant growth, actions of animals, and abrasion.

- The causes of chemical weathering include the action of water, oxygen, carbon dioxide, living organisms, and acid rain.

- The most important factors that determine the rate at which weathering occurs are the type of rock and the climate.

Key Terms
- weathering • erosion • uniformitarianism
- mechanical weathering • abrasion
- ice wedging • chemical weathering
- oxidation • permeable

③ How Soil Forms

🔑 **Key Concepts** ✎ S 6.6.b

- Soil is a mixture of rock particles, minerals, decayed organic material, water, and air.

- Soil forms as rock is broken down by weathering and mixes with other materials on the surface. Soil is constantly being formed wherever bedrock is exposed.

- Scientists classify the different types of soil into major groups based on climate, plants, soil composition, and whether the soil is acidic or basic.

- Some soil organisms make humus, the material that makes soil fertile. Other soil organisms mix the soil and make spaces in it for air and water.

Key Terms
- soil • bedrock • humus • fertility • loam
- soil horizon • topsoil • subsoil • acidic
- basic • litter • decomposer

④ Soil Conservation

🔑 **Key Concepts** ✎ S 6.6.b

- Because fertile soil is in limited supply and takes a long time to form, it is considered a nonrenewable resource.

- The value of soil is reduced when soil loses its fertility and when topsoil is lost due to erosion.

- Soil can be conserved through contour plowing, conservation plowing, and crop rotation.

Key Terms
- sod • natural resource • Dust Bowl
- soil conservation • contour plowing
- conservation plowing • crop rotation

Review and Assessment

For: Self-Assessment
Visit: PHSchool.com
Web Code: cwa-1020

Target Reading Skill

Previewing Visuals Complete your graphic organizer for Life in Soil with more questions and answers to show that you understand the role of organisms in forming soil.

Life in Soil

Q. What is the subject of this illustration?
A.
Q. What kinds of organisms live underground?
A.
Q.
A.

Reviewing Key Terms

Choose the letter of the best answer.

1. In the rock cycle, a rock that is changed by heat and pressure becomes a(n)
   a. sedimentary rock.
   b. metamorphic rock.
   c. chemical rock.
   d. igneous rock.

2. The process that splits rock through freezing and thawing is called
   a. erosion.
   b. chemical weathering.
   c. ice wedging.
   d. abrasion.

3. Soil that is made up of roughly equal parts of clay, sand, and silt is called
   a. sod.
   b. loam.
   c. tropical soil.
   d. subsoil.

4. The B horizon consists of
   a. subsoil.
   b. topsoil.
   c. litter.
   d. bedrock.

5. The humus in soil is produced by
   a. mechanical weathering.
   b. bedrock.
   c. chemical weathering.
   d. decomposers.

Complete the following sentences so that your answers clearly explain the key terms.

6. Minerals and rocks are considered **nonrenewable resources,** which means _____ .

7. One way rock breaks down is through **mechanical weathering,** which is _____ .

8. Rock that is **permeable** weathers easily because _____ .

9. Fertile soil is rich in **humus,** which is _____ .

10. In **conservation plowing,** farmers conserve soil fertility by _____ .

Writing in Science

Journal Entry You are a farmer on the tall grass prairie in the midwestern United States. Write a journal entry describing prairie soil. Include the soil's composition, how it formed, and how animals helped it develop.

Video Assessment
Discovery Channel School
Weathering and Soil Formation

Review and Assessment

Checking Concepts

11. What is a crystal?

12. How are granite and basalt similar? How are they different? Explain.

13. What are the environmental effects of mining and smelting?

14. What is the principle of uniformitarianism?

15. Explain how plants can act as agents of both mechanical and chemical weathering.

16. What is the role of gases such as oxygen and carbon dioxide in chemical weathering?

17. Briefly describe how soil is formed.

18. Which contains more humus, topsoil or subsoil? Which has higher fertility? Explain.

19. What role did grass play in conserving the soil of the prairies?

20. How do conservation plowing and crop rotation contribute to soil conservation?

Thinking Critically

21. **Predicting** If mechanical weathering breaks a rock into pieces, how would this affect the rate at which the rock weathers chemically?

22. **Comparing and Contrasting** Compare the layers in the diagram below in terms of their composition and humus content.

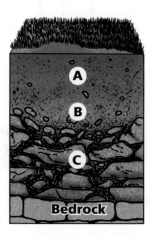

23. **Making Judgments** The mineral calcite forms large, glassy crystals that can be scratched by a copper penny. Would calcite be useful as a gemstone? Explain.

Applying Skills

Use the following information to answer Questions 24–26.

You have two samples of soil. One is mostly sand and one is mostly clay.

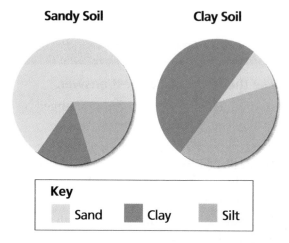

24. **Predicting** Which soil sample would lose water more quickly? Why?

25. **Designing Experiments** Design an experiment to test how quickly water passes through each soil sample.

26. **Posing Questions** A farmer wants to grow soybeans in one of these two soils. What questions would the farmer need to answer before choosing where to plant the soybeans?

Lab zone Standards Investigation

Performance Assessment You are ready to present your data and conclusions about what type of material is best for growing bean plants. How did your group's results compare with those of the other groups in your class? What did you learn from this investigation about soil characteristics that help plants to grow? How could you improve your experiment?

Choose the letter of the best answer.

Use the diagram below and your knowledge of science to answer Questions 1 and 2.

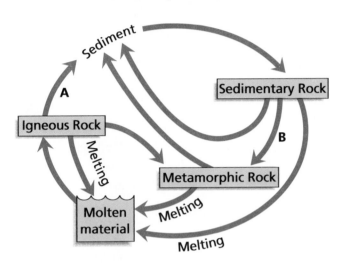

1. In the rock cycle, molten material forms through the melting of
A igneous rock.
B sedimentary rock.
C metamorphic rock.
D all of the above   S 6.2

2. In the rock cycle diagram, what does the letter B represent?
A melting
B cooling and hardening
C heat and pressure
D formation of sediment   S 6.2

3. Which of the following is a type of mechanical weathering?
A abrasion
B freezing and thawing
C plant growth
D all of the above   S 6.2

4. A plant grows best in soil with a pH of 6. The pH of this soil can be described as
A slightly basic.
B neutral.
C slightly acidic.
D strongly acidic.   S 6.5.e

Soil Erosion by State			
	Tons per Acre per Year		
State	Water Erosion	Wind Erosion	Total Erosion
Montana	1.08	3.8	4.9
Wyoming	1.57	2.4	3.97
Texas	3.47	14.9	18.4
New Mexico	2.00	11.5	13.5
Colorado	2.5	8.9	11.4
Tennessee	14.12	0.0	14.12
Hawaii	13.71	0.0	13.71

Use the data table above and your knowledge of science to answer Questions 5 and 6.

5. Of the states listed in the table, which two have the greatest amount of erosion by water?
A Texas and Tennessee
B Texas and Hawaii
C New Mexico and Colorado
D Tennessee and Hawaii   S 6.2.a

6. Which state in the table has the greatest soil erosion?
A Texas
B Hawaii
C Tennessee
D New Mexico   S 6.2.a

Apply the
BIG Idea

7. Two rocks, each in a different location, have been weathering for the same amount of time. Mature soil has formed from one rock, but only immature soil has formed from the other. What factors might have caused this difference in rate of soil formation? In your answer, include examples of both mechanical and chemical weathering.   S 6.2.a

Erosion and Deposition

S 6.2 Topography is reshaped by the weathering of rock and soil and by the transportation and deposition of sediment. As a basis for understanding this concept:

a. Students know water running downhill is the dominant process in shaping the landscape, including California's landscape.

Framework Surface water flow, glaciers, wind, and ocean waves have all been and continue to be active throughout California and the rest of the world in shaping landscapes.

b. Students know rivers and streams are dynamic systems that erode, transport sediment, change course, and flood their banks in natural and recurring patterns.

c. Students know beaches are dynamic systems in which the sand is supplied by rivers and moved along the coast by the action of waves.

d. Students know earthquakes, volcanic eruptions, landslides, and floods change human and wildlife habitats.

Ocean waves slowly break down California's rocky coast, forming the boulders and sand that make up this beach. ▶

Focus on the
BIG Idea

S 6.2.a

What are the forces of erosion and deposition that shape our landscape?

Check What You Know

Suppose that you fill a jar halfway with layers of gravel, sand, and soil. Then you fill the jar with water, cover it tightly, and shake for 5 seconds. What effect would shaking the jar have on the soil, sand, and gravel? What would happen to them after the shaking stops? Explain your answer.

The images shown here represent some of the key terms in this chapter. You can use this vocabulary skill to help you understand the meaning of some key terms in this chapter.

Vocabulary Skill

Latin Word Origins

Many science words come to English from Latin. In this chapter you will learn the term *mass movement*. *Movement* comes from the Latin words *movere* meaning "to move" and *-mentum* meaning "the act of." *Movement* means "the act of moving."

Example The movement of wind and water shape Earth's surface.

movere	+	-mentum	=	movement
to move		act of		the act of moving

Learn these Latin words to help you remember the key terms.

Latin Origin	Meaning	Examples
de-	From, down, away	Deflation, deposition
flare	Blow	Deflation
-mentum	The act of, the result of	Movement
positus	Put	Deposition
sedere	Sit, settle	Sediment

Apply It!

Review the Latin words and meanings. Look at the word *sedere* and the second meaning of *mentum*. Predict the meaning of *sediment*. Revise your definition as you read the chapter.

sediment

meander

sand dunes

glacier

Chapter 3
Vocabulary

interactive Textbook

Build Science Vocabulary
Online
Visit: PHSchool.com
Web Code: cwj-1030

How to Read Science

 Sequence

Many parts of a science textbook are organized by sequence. Sequence is the order in which a series of events occurs. Sometimes the text uses signal words, such as *begin*, *next*, *then*, and *later* to show sequence. Look for the sequence of events in the paragraph below.

Stream Formation

The formation of a stream <u>begins</u> when raindrops strike the ground. <u>Next</u>, the water collects as runoff on the ground and <u>then begins</u> to run downhill. <u>Later</u>, this flowing water causes tiny grooves, called rills, to form in the ground surface.

A flowchart can help you understand sequence. To make a flowchart, write a description of each step in a box. Place the boxes in order.

Stream Formation
Raindrops strike ground.
↓
Runoff forms.
↓
Water begins to run downhill.

Apply It!

In your notebook, write the fourth step in stream formation. As you read about water erosion in Section 2, complete a seven-step flowchart showing the process of stream formation.

Standards **Investigation**

Changes in the Land

What force shaped the rocky cliffs of the California coast? For millions of years, powerful ocean waves have been cutting and grinding the coast. The waves carry away broken particles of rock. The waves also pile up boulders, pebbles, and sand to form beaches. In this investigation, you will model how erosion and deposition shape the landscape.

Your Goal

To make three-dimensional models that show how the forces of erosion and deposition can change a landscape

To complete this investigation you must

- make a three-dimensional landscape
- predict how the model would be affected by erosion
- construct a second model showing how your landscape might look after erosion has continued for millions of years
- follow the safety guidelines in Appendix A

Plan It!

To begin, draw a landscape that shows the land before erosion. Then make a list of materials that you will use to build your model. Once your teacher has approved your drawing and your list of materials, build your first model. Next, make a second model to show the effects of erosion. Finally, explain your models to your class.

Changing Earth's Surface

CALIFORNIA
Standards Focus

S 6.2 Topography is reshaped by the weathering of rock and soil and by the transportation and deposition of sediment.

- What processes wear down and build up Earth's surface?
- What causes the different types of mass movement?

Key Terms

- erosion
- sediment
- deposition
- gravity
- mass movement

Lab zone Standards **Warm-Up**

How Does Gravity Affect Materials on a Slope?

1. Place a small board flat on your desk. Place a marble on the board and slowly tip one end of the board up slightly. Observe what happens.
2. Place a block of wood on the board. Slowly lift one end of the board and observe the result.
3. Next, cover the board and the wood block with sandpaper and repeat Step 2.

Think It Over

Developing Hypotheses How do the results of each step differ? Develop a hypothesis to explain your observations.

The ground you stand on is solid. But under certain conditions, solid earth can quickly change to thick, soupy mud. For example, high rains soaked into the soil and triggered the devastating mudflow in Figure 1. A river of mud raced down the mountainside, burying homes and cars. Several lives were lost. In moments, the mudflow moved a huge volume of soil mixed with water and rock downhill.

Wearing Down and Building Up

A mudflow is a spectacular example of erosion. **Erosion** is the process by which natural forces move weathered rock and soil from one place to another. You may have seen water carrying soil and gravel down a driveway after it rains. That's an example of erosion. A mudflow is a very rapid type of erosion. Other types of erosion move soil and rock more slowly. Gravity, running water, glaciers, waves, and wind are all causes, or agents, of erosion. In geology, an agent is a force or material that causes a change in Earth's surface.

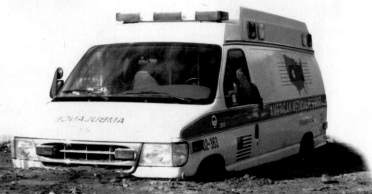

FIGURE 1
Mudflow
A mudflow caused by heavy rains in San Bernardino, California, brought this ambulance to a stop.

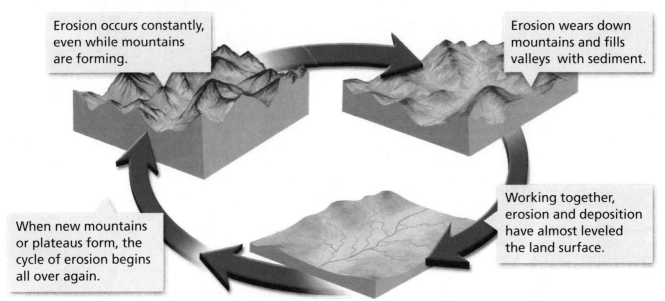

Erosion occurs constantly, even while mountains are forming.

Erosion wears down mountains and fills valleys with sediment.

When new mountains or plateaus form, the cycle of erosion begins all over again.

Working together, erosion and deposition have almost leveled the land surface.

FIGURE 2
Cycle of Erosion and Deposition
Over millions of years, erosion gradually wears away mountains while deposition fills in valleys with sediment.
Predicting *What would happen to the surface of the land if uplift did not occur?*

The material moved by erosion is **sediment.** Sediment may consist of pieces of rock or soil or the remains of plants and animals. Both weathering and erosion produce sediment. **Deposition** occurs where the agents of erosion deposit, or lay down, sediment. Deposition changes the shape of the land. You may have watched a playing child who picked up several toys, carried them across a room, and then put them down. This child was acting something like an agent of erosion and deposition.

☞ **Weathering, erosion, and deposition act together in a cycle that wears down and builds up Earth's surface. This cycle, called the geologic cycle, has continued for billions of years.** As a mountain wears down in one place, new landforms build up in other places. Erosion and deposition are at work everywhere on Earth.

 **Reading Checkpoint** What is sediment?

Mass Movement

Imagine that you are sitting on a bicycle at the top of a hill. With only a slight push, you can coast down the hill. If the slope of the hill is very steep, you will reach a high speed before reaching the bottom. The force that pulls you downward is gravity. Gravity pulls everything toward the center of Earth.

Gravity is the force that moves rock and other materials downhill. Gravity causes **mass movement,** any one of several processes that move sediment downhill. ☞ **The different types of mass movement include landslides, mudflows, slump, and creep.** Mass movement can be rapid or slow.

Lab zone Skills Activity

Making Models
You can make a model of mass movement. Design a plan to model one of the types of mass movement using sand, pebbles, and water. With your teacher's approval, make and test your model.

How well did your model represent the type of mass movement you chose? How could you improve your model?

Landslide

Slump

FIGURE 3

FIGURE 3
Mass Movement
In addition to mudflows, types of mass movement include landslides, slump, and creep. The La Conchita landslide buried 23 homes and killed 10 people.
Making Judgments Which form of mass movement produces the most drastic change in the surface?

Landslides A landslide is a kind of mass movement that occurs when rock and soil slide rapidly down a steep slope. Some landslides contain huge masses of rock. But many landslides contain only a small amount of rock and soil. Some landslides occur where road builders have cut highways through hills or mountains. Figure 3 shows a landslide that struck La Conchita, California, in 2005.

Mudflows A mudflow is the rapid downhill movement of a mixture of water, rock, and soil. The amount of water in a mudflow can be as high as 60 percent. Mudflows often occur after heavy rains in a normally dry area. In clay soils with a high water content, mudflows may occur even on very gentle slopes. Under certain conditions, clay soils suddenly turn to liquid and begin to flow. An earthquake can trigger both mudflows and landslides. Mudflows can be very dangerous.

Slump If you slump your shoulders, the entire upper part of your body drops down. A slump is a type of mass movement in which a mass of rock and soil rapidly slips down a slope. Unlike a landslide, the material in a slump moves down in one large mass. It looks as if someone pulled the bottom out from under part of the slope. A slump often occurs when water soaks the bottom of soil that is rich in clay.

Creep

Go Online
active art

For: Mass Movement activity
Visit: PHSchool.com
Web Code: cfp-2031

Creep   Creep is the very slow downhill movement of rock and soil. It can even occur on gentle slopes. Creep often results from the freezing and thawing of water in cracked layers of rock beneath the soil. Like the movement of an hour hand on a clock, creep is so slow you can barely notice it. But you can see the effects of creep in objects such as telephone poles, gravestones, and fenceposts. Creep may tilt these objects at spooky angles. Landscapes affected by creep may have the eerie, out-of-kilter look of a funhouse in an amusement park.

Reading Checkpoint   **What is the main difference between a slump and a landslide?**

Section 1 Assessment

S 6.2; E-LA: Reading 6.1.0

Vocabulary Skill Latin Word Origins Review the Latin word *de*-and *positus*. Use what you've learned to explain the meaning of *deposition*.

Reviewing Key Concepts

1. a. **Listing** What are five agents of erosion?
   b. **Defining** In your own words, write a definition of *erosion.*
   c. **Predicting** Over time, how will erosion and deposition affect a mountain range? Explain.
2. a. **Listing** What are the four types of mass movement?
   b. **Relating Cause and Effect** What force causes all types of mass movement?
   c. **Inferring** A fence runs across a steep hillside. The fence is tilted downhill and forms a curve rather than a straight line. What can you infer happened to the fence? Explain.

Lab zone **At-Home Activity**

Evidence of Erosion After a rainstorm, take a walk with an adult family member around your neighborhood. Look for evidence of erosion. Try to find areas where there is loose soil, sand, gravel, or rock. **CAUTION:** *Stay away from any large pile of loose sand or soil—it may slide without warning.* Which areas have the most erosion? The least erosion? How does the slope of the ground affect the amount of erosion? Sketch or take photographs of the areas showing evidence of erosion.

Sand Hills

Materials

tray (about 15 cm x 45 cm x 60 cm)

cardboard tube

dry sand, 500 mL

spoon and ruler

several sheets of white paper

masking tape

pencil or crayon

wooden barbecue skewer

Problem What is the relationship between the height and width of a sand hill?

Skills Focus developing hypotheses, interpreting data, predicting

Procedure

1. Begin by observing how gravity causes mass movement. To start, place the cardboard tube vertically in the center of the tray.

2. Using the spoon, fill the cardboard tube with the dry sand. Take care not to spill the sand around the outside of the tube.

3. Carefully lift the sand-filled tube straight up so that all the sand flows out. As you lift the tube, observe the sand's movement.

4. Develop a hypothesis explaining how you think the width of the sand pile is related to its height for different amounts of sand.

5. Empty the sand in the tray back into a container. Then set up your system for measuring the sand hill.

6. Copy the data table into your lab notebook.

Data Table					
Test	1	2	3	4	5
Width					
Height					

7. Following Steps 1 through 3, make a new sand hill.

8. Measure and record the sand hill's height and width for Test 1. (See the instructions in the yellow box to help you accurately measure the height and width.)

9. Now test what happens when you add more sand to the sand hill. Place your cardboard tube vertically at the center of the sand hill. Be careful not to push the tube down into the sand hill! Using the spoon, fill the tube with sand as before.

10. Carefully raise the tube and observe the sand's movement.

11. Measure and record the sand hill's height and width for Test 2.

12. Repeat Steps 9 through 11 at least three more times. After each test, record your results. Be sure to number each test.

Analyze and Conclude

1. **Graphing** Make a graph showing how the sand hill's height and width changed with each test. (*Hint:* Use the *x*-axis of the graph for height. Use the *y*-axis of the graph for width.)

2. **Interpreting Data** What does your graph show about the relationship between the variables, sand hill height and width?

3. **Drawing Conclusions** Does your graph support your hypothesis about the sand hill's height and width? Why or why not?

4. **Developing Hypotheses** How would you revise your original hypothesis after examining your data? Give reasons for your answer.

5. **Predicting** Predict what would happen if you continued the experiment for five more tests. Extend your graph with a dashed line to show your prediction. How could you test your prediction?

6. **Communicating** Write a paragraph in which you discuss the steps you took to measure your sand hill. Did any problems you had in making your measurements affect your results? How did you adjust your measurement technique to solve these problems?

How to Measure a Sand Hill

1. Cover the bottom of the tray with unlined white paper and tape it firmly in place.

2. Mark off points 0.5 cm apart along one side of the paper in the tray.

3. Carefully draw the sand hill's outline on the paper. The line should go completely around the base of the hill.

4. Now measure the width of the hill against the marks you made along the edge of the paper.

5. Measure the sand hill's height by inserting a barbecue skewer through its center. Make a mark on the skewer at the top of the hill.

6. Remove the skewer and use the ruler to measure how much of the skewer was buried in the hill. Try not to disturb the sand.

Design an Experiment

Do you think the use of different materials, such as wet sand or gravel, would produce different results from those using dry sand? Make a new hypothesis about the relationship between slope and width in hills made of materials other than dry sand. Design an experiment in which you test how these different materials form hills. Obtain your teacher's approval before you try the experiment.

For : Data sharing
Visit: PHSchool.com
Web Code: cfd-2031

Section 2

Water Erosion

S 6.2.a Students know water running downhill is the dominant process in shaping the landscape, including California's landscape.

S 6.2.b Students know rivers and streams are dynamic systems that erode, transport sediment, change course, and flood their banks in natural and recurring patterns.

- What process is mainly responsible for shaping the surface of the land?
- What features are formed by water erosion and deposition?
- What factors affect a river's ability to erode and carry sediment?

Key Terms

- runoff
- rill
- gully
- stream
- energy
- flood plain
- meander
- oxbow lake
- alluvial fan
- delta
- load

▼ **FIGURE 4**
Sediment in Motion
Streams carry sediment in several ways.

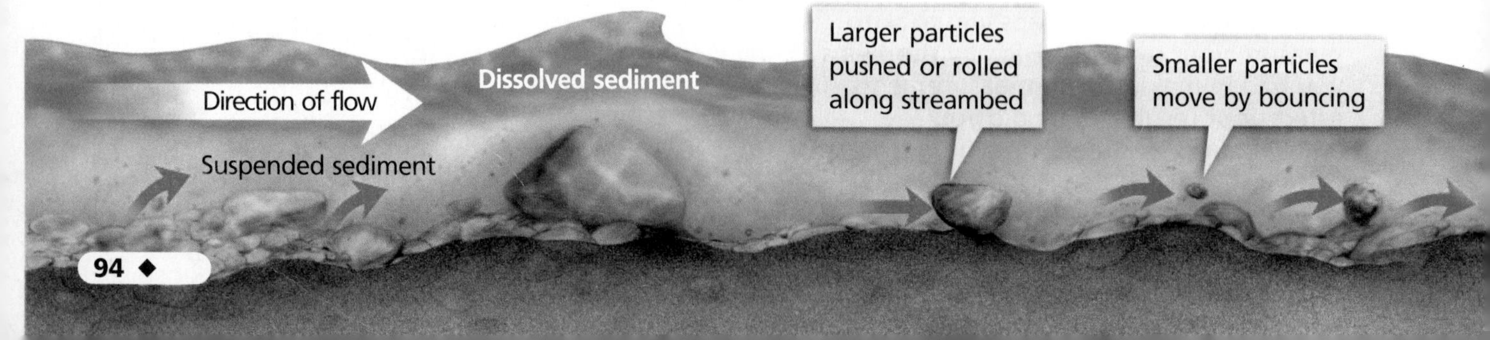

Lab zone Standards **Warm-Up**

How Does Moving Water Wear Away Rocks?

1. Obtain two bars of soap that are the same size and brand.
2. Open a faucet just enough to let the water drip out very slowly. How many drops of water does the faucet release per minute?
3. Place one bar of soap in a dry place. Place the other bar of soap under the faucet. Predict the effect of the dripping water droplets on the soap.
4. Let the faucet drip for 10 minutes.
5. Turn off the faucet and observe both bars of soap. What difference do you observe between them?

Think It Over

Predicting What would the bar of soap under the dripping faucet look like if you left it there for another 10 minutes? For an hour? How could you speed up the process? Slow it down?

Walking in the woods in summer, you can hear the racing water of a stream before you see the stream itself. The water roars as it foams over rock ledges and boulders. When you reach the stream, you see water rushing by. Sand and pebbles tumble along the bottom of the stream. As it swirls downstream, the water also carries twigs, leaves, and bits of soil. In sheltered pools, insects such as water striders skim the water's calm surface. Beneath the surface, a rainbow trout swims in the clear water.

In winter, the stream freezes. Chunks of ice scrape and grind away at the stream's bed and banks. In spring, the stream floods. Then the flow of water may be strong enough to move large rocks. But throughout the year, the stream continues to erode its small part of Earth's surface.

Direction of flow   Dissolved sediment

Larger particles pushed or rolled along streambed

Smaller particles move by bouncing

Suspended sediment

A stream causes erosion because of the sediment it carries. Look at Figure 4. Notice how large sediment moves by rolling and sliding along the bottom. Grains of sand or small stones move by bouncing. Fast-moving water can lift and carry sand or smaller sediment. Water dissolves some sediment completely.

Runoff and Erosion

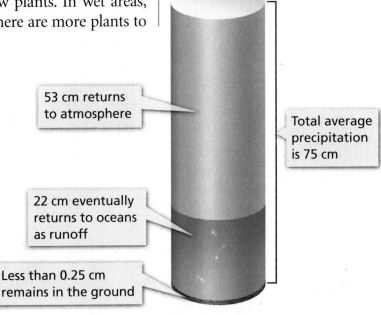

Water running downhill is the major agent of the erosion that has shaped Earth's land surface. Erosion by water begins with the splash of rain. Some rainfall sinks into the ground. Some evaporates or is taken up by plants. The force of a falling raindrop can loosen and pick up soil particles. As water moves over the land, it carries these particles with it. This moving water is called runoff. **Runoff** is water that moves over Earth's surface. When runoff flows in a thin layer over the land, it may cause a type of erosion called sheet erosion.

Amount of Runoff The amount of runoff in an area depends on five main factors. The first factor is the amount of rain an area receives. A second factor is vegetation. Grasses, shrubs, and trees reduce runoff by absorbing water and holding soil in place. A third factor is the type of soil. Some types of soils absorb more water than others. A fourth factor is the shape of the land. Land that is steeply sloped has more runoff than flatter land. Finally, a fifth factor is how people use the land. For instance, a paved parking lot absorbs no water, so all the rain that falls on it becomes runoff.

The amount of plant cover in an area affects runoff and erosion. Even though deserts have little rainfall, they often have high runoff and erosion because they have few plants. In wet areas, runoff and erosion may be low because there are more plants to protect the soil.

FIGURE 5
Where the Runoff Goes
Precipitation over the United States averages about 75 cm per year. About 22.5 cm becomes runoff. Most returns to the atmosphere by evaporation or through the leaves of plants.
Reading Graphs *How much runoff remains in the ground?*

53 cm returns to atmosphere

Total average precipitation is 75 cm

22 cm eventually returns to oceans as runoff

Less than 0.25 cm remains in the ground

Raindrops Falling

Find out how the force of falling raindrops affects soil.

1. Fill a petri dish with fine-textured soil to a depth of about 1 cm. Make sure the soil has a smooth flat surface, but do not pack it firmly in the dish.
2. Place the dish in the center of a newspaper.
3. Fill a dropper with water. Squeeze a large water drop from a height of 1 m onto the surface of the soil. Repeat 4 times.
4. Use a meter stick to measure the distance the soil splashed from the dish. Record your observations.
5. Repeat Steps 1 through 4, this time from a height of 2 m.

Drawing Conclusions Which test produced the greater amount of erosion? Why?

Rills and Gullies Because of gravity, runoff and the material it contains move downhill. During sheet erosion, runoff forms tiny grooves in the soil called **rills.** As many rills flow into one another, they grow larger, forming gullies. A **gully** is a large groove, or channel, in the soil that carries runoff after a rainstorm. As water flows through gullies, it moves soil and rocks with it, thus enlarging the gullies through erosion. Gullies contain water only after it rains.

Streams and Rivers Gullies join together to form a larger channel called a stream. A **stream** is a channel along which water is continually flowing down a slope. Unlike gullies, streams rarely dry up. Small streams are also called creeks or brooks. As streams flow together, they form larger and larger bodies of flowing water. A large stream is often called a river.

Reading Checkpoint What is a gully?

Erosion by Rivers

As a river flows from the mountains to the sea, the river forms a variety of features. **Through erosion, a river creates valleys, waterfalls, flood plains, meanders, and oxbow lakes.** How does a river cause erosion? A river's water has energy. **Energy** is the ability to do work or cause change. When energy does work, the energy is transferred from one object to another.

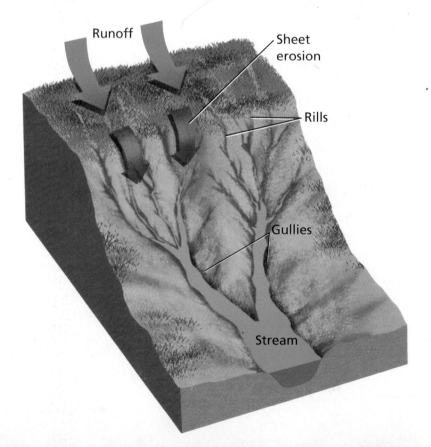

FIGURE 6
Runoff, Rills, and Gullies
Water flowing across the land runs together to form rills, gullies, and streams. **Predicting** *What will happen to the land between the gullies as they grow wider?*

All along a river, the water's energy does work. A river is always moving sediment from the mountains to the sea. At the same time, sediments grind and chip away at the rock of the riverbed, deepening and widening the river's channel.

Rivers often form on steep mountain slopes. Near its source, a river is often fast flowing and generally follows a straight, narrow course. The steep slopes along the river erode rapidly. The result is a deep, V-shaped valley.

Waterfalls Waterfalls may occur where a river meets an area of rock that is very hard and erodes slowly. The river flows over this rock and then flows over softer rock downstream. As you can see in Figure 7, the softer rock wears away faster than the harder rock. Eventually a waterfall develops where the softer rock was removed. Areas of rough water called rapids also occur where a river tumbles over hard rock.

Flood Plain Lower down on its course, a river usually flows over more gently sloping land. The river spreads out and erodes the land, forming a wide river valley. The flat, wide area of land along a river is a **flood plain.** A river often covers its flood plain when it overflows its banks during floods. On a wide flood plain, the valley walls may be kilometers away from the river itself. A flooding river may cut into its banks, changing the river's course through the flood plain.

Go Online
PLANET DIARY

For: More on floods
Visit: PHSchool.com
Web Code: cfd-2032

FIGURE 7
How a Waterfall Forms
A waterfall forms where a flat layer of tough rock lies over a layer of softer rock that erodes easily. When the softer rock erodes, pieces of the harder rock above break off, creating the waterfall's sharp drop.

Harder rock layers eventually break off.

Softer rock layers erode first.

Rapids are areas of turbulence below the falls where water rushes over rocks.

FIGURE 8
Meanders and Oxbow Lakes
Erosion often forms meanders and oxbow lakes where a river winds across its flood plain.

1 A small obstacle creates a slight bend in the river.

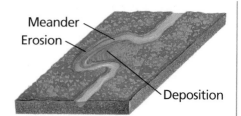

Meander
Erosion
Deposition

2 As water erodes the outer edge of a meander, the bend becomes bigger. Deposition occurs along the inner edge.

3 Gradually, the meander becomes more curved. The river breaks through and takes a new course.

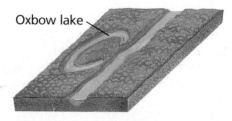

Oxbow lake

4 An oxbow lake remains.

Meanders A river often develops meanders where it flows through easily eroded rock or sediment. A **meander** is a loop-like bend in the course of a river. As the river winds from side to side, it tends to erode the outer bank and deposit sediment on the inner bank of a bend. Over time, the meander becomes more and more curved.

Because of the sediment a river carries, it can erode a very wide flood plain. Along this part of a river's course, its channel is deep and wide. Meanders are common. The southern stretch of the Mississippi River is one example of a river that meanders on a wide, gently sloping flood plain.

Oxbow Lakes Sometimes a meandering river forms a feature called an oxbow lake. As Figure 8 shows, an **oxbow lake** is a meander that has been cut off from the river. An oxbow lake may form when a river floods. During the flood, high water finds a straighter route downstream. As the flood waters fall, sediments dam up the ends of a meander. The meander has become an oxbow lake.

 **Reading Checkpoint** How does an oxbow lake form?

Deposits by Rivers

As water moves, it carries sediments with it. Any time moving water slows down, it drops, or deposits, some of the sediment. As the water slows down, fine particles fall to the river's bed. Larger stones quit rolling and sliding. ● **Deposition creates landforms such as alluvial fans and deltas. It can also add soil to a river's flood plain.** In Figure 11 on pages 100–101, you can see these and other features shaped by rivers and streams.

Alluvial Fans Where a stream flows out of a steep, narrow mountain valley, the stream suddenly becomes wider and shallower. The water slows down. Here sediments are deposited in an alluvial fan. An **alluvial fan** is a wide, sloping deposit of sediment formed where a stream leaves a mountain range. As its name suggests, this deposit is shaped like a fan. You can see an alluvial fan in Figure 9.

Deltas A river ends its journey when it flows into a still body of water, such as an ocean or a lake. Because the river water is no longer flowing downhill, the water slows down. At this point, the sediment in the water drops to the bottom. Sediment deposited where a river flows into an ocean or lake builds up a landform called a **delta**. Deltas can be a variety of shapes. The delta of the Nile River in Egypt is shaped like a triangle. The delta of the Mississippi River, shown in Figure 10, is an example of a type of delta called a "bird's foot" delta.

Soil on Flood Plains Deposition can also occur during floods. Then heavy rains or melting snow cause a river to rise above its banks and spread out over its flood plain. When the flood water finally retreats, it deposits sediment as new soil. Deposition of new soil over a flood plain is what makes a river valley fertile. Dense forests can grow in the rich soil of a flood plain. The soil is also perfect for growing crops.

 **Reading Checkpoint** How can a flood be beneficial?

FIGURE 9
Alluvial Fan
This alluvial fan in Death Valley, California, was formed from deposits by streams from the mountains.

FIGURE 10
Mississippi Delta This satellite image shows the part of the Mississippi River delta where the river empties into the Gulf of Mexico. In 2005, parts of the delta and the city of New Orleans were flooded as a result of Hurricane Katrina. **Observing** *What happens to the Mississippi River as it flows through its delta? Can you find the river's main channel?*

Waterfalls and Rapids
Waterfalls and rapids are common where the river passes over harder rock. Many California rivers have waterfalls and rapids. Rapids are common on fast-flowing rivers like the Trinity and American rivers.

V-Shaped Valley
Near its source, the river flows through a deep, V-shaped valley. As the river flows, it cuts the valley deeper. Many California rivers in the Sierra Nevada have steep, V-shaped valleys, except where glaciers have carved the valley walls. Examples include the Merced and Tuolomne rivers.

Flood Plain
A flood plain forms where the river's power of erosion widens its valley rather than deepening it. The San Joaquin and Sacramento rivers both have vast flood plains.

Meanders
Where the river flows across easily eroded sediment, its channel bends from side to side in a series of meanders. The Sacramento River has both meanders and oxbow lakes where it winds through California's Central Valley.

Beaches
Sand carried downstream by the river spreads along the coast to form beaches.

FIGURE 11
The Course of a River
The slope and size of a river, as well as the sediment it carries, determine how a river shapes the land. **Classifying** *Which features result from erosion? From deposition?*

Tributary
The river receives water and sediment from a tributary—a smaller river or stream that flows into it.

Oxbow Lake
An oxbow lake is a meander cut off from the river by deposition of sediment.

Valley Widening
As the river approaches sea level, it meanders more and develops a wider valley and broader flood plain.

Bluffs
Erosion forms cliffs called bluffs along the edge of a flood plain.

Delta
Where the river flows into the ocean, it deposits sediment, forming a delta. In California, the Sacramento River and the San Joaquin River join to form a large delta with many channels.

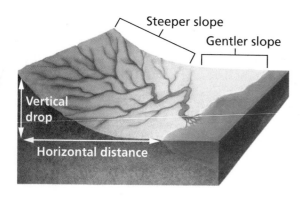

FIGURE 12
The Slope of a River
A river's slope is usually greatest near the river's source. As a river approaches its mouth, its slope lessens.

Erosion and Sediment Load

The power of a river to cause erosion and carry sediment depends on several factors. **A river is a dynamic system. A river's slope, volume of flow, and the shape of its streambed all affect how fast the river flows and how much sediment it can erode.**

The amount of sediment that a river carries is its **load.** A fast-flowing river carries more and larger particles of sediment. When a river slows down, it drops its sediment load. The larger particles of sediment are deposited first.

Slope Generally, if a river's slope increases, the water's speed also increases. A river's slope is the amount the river drops toward sea level over a given distance. If a river's speed increases, its sediment load and power to erode may increase.

Volume of Flow A river's flow is the volume of water that moves past a point on the river in a given time. Volume of flow is also called *discharge*. As more water flows through a river, its speed increases. During a flood, the increased volume of water helps the river to cut more deeply into its banks and bed. The river's power to erode increases greatly. A flooding river can carry huge amounts of sand, soil, and other sediments. It may move giant boulders as if they were pebbles.

Math: Algebra and
Functions 6.2.2

Sediment on the Move

The velocity, or speed, of a stream affects the size of the sediment particles the stream can carry. Study the graph, then answer the questions below.

1. **Reading Graphs** What variable is shown on the *x*-axis of the graph?

2. **Reading Graphs** What variable is shown on the *y*-axis of the graph?

3. **Interpreting Data** What is the speed at which a stream moves small pebbles? Large boulders?

4. **Predicting** A stream's speed increases to about 600 cm per second during a flood. What are the largest particles the stream can move?

5. **Developing Hypotheses** Write a hypothesis that states the relationship between a stream's speed and the size of sediment it can move.

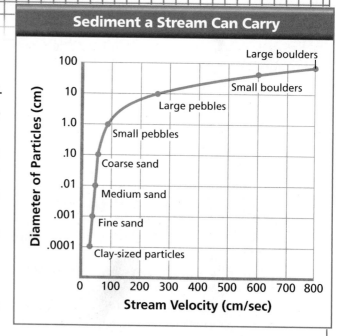

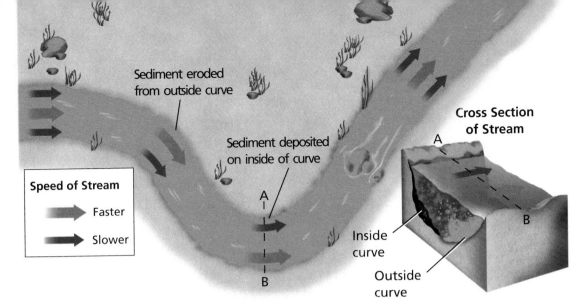

Sediment eroded from outside curve

Sediment deposited on inside of curve

Speed of Stream

→ Faster

→ Slower

A

B

Cross Section of Stream

A

B

Inside curve

Outside curve

Streambed Shape Whether a river flows in a straight line or a curved line affects the way it erodes and deposits sediment. Where a river flows in a straight line, the water flows faster near the center of the river than along its sides. Deposition occurs along the sides of the river, where the water moves more slowly.

If a river curves, the water moves fastest along the outside of the curve. There, the river tends to cut into its bank, causing erosion. Sediment is deposited on the inside curve, where the water speed is slowest. You can see this process in Figure 13.

FIGURE 13
Stream Erosion and Deposition
A river erodes sediment from its banks on the outside curve and deposits sediment on the inside curve.
Relating Cause and Effect *Why does a river deposit sediment on the inside of a curve?*

 **Reading Checkpoint** Where a stream curves, in what part of the stream does the water flow fastest?

Section 2 Assessment

S 6.2.a, 6.2.b E-LA: Reading 6.2.0, Writing 6.2.2.

Target Reading Skill Sequence Look at the illustration showing Meanders and Oxbow Lakes. Write down in order the steps that occur to form an oxbow lake.

Reviewing Key Concepts

1. a. **Reviewing** What is the major agent of erosion on Earth's surface?
   b. **Sequencing** List these in order of size: tributary, stream, rill, gully, runoff, river.
   c. **Predicting** Where would gullies be more likely to form: a field with plowed soil and no plants, or a field covered with thick grass?
2. a. **Listing** What are five features that erosion forms along a river?
   b. **Listing** What are three features that result from deposition along a river?
   c. **Relating Cause and Effect** Why does a delta often form where a river meets the ocean?

3. a. **Identifying** What three factors affect how fast a river flows?
   b. **Interpreting Diagrams** Study Figure 13 above. Over time, what will happen to the river's bank at point B? Why?

Writing in Science

Comparison Paragraph A river carries different types of sediment particles from its source to its mouth: tiny clay particles, grains of sand, pebbles, and boulders. Write a paragraph that compares clay particles and pebbles in terms of how they move, how fast they travel, and where they would be deposited.

Streams in Action

Materials

plastic container

diatomaceous earth

plastic measuring cup and spray bottle

2 wood blocks about 2.5 cm thick

wire, 13–15 cm long, 20 gauge

plastic stirrers, 10–12 cm long, with two small holes each, and ruler

hand lens, scissors, and clock or watch

blue food coloring and liquid detergent

Problem How do rivers and streams erode the land?

Skills Focus making models, observing

Procedure

PART 1 Creating Streams Over Time

1. Your teacher will give you a plastic tub containing diatomaceous earth that has been soaked with water. Place the tub on a level surface. **CAUTION:** *Dry diatomaceous earth produces dust that may be irritating if inhaled.* To keep the diatomaceous earth from drying out, spray it lightly with water.

2. One end of the tub will contain more diatomaceous earth. Use a block of wood to raise this end of the tub 2.5 cm.

3. Place the cup at the upper end of the slope with the notches pointing to the left and right.

4. Press the cup firmly down into the earth to secure its position.

5. Start the dripper (see Step 6 in the yellow box on the opposite page). Allow the water to drip to the right onto the diatomaceous earth.

6. Allow the dripper to drip for 5 minutes. (*Hint:* When you need to add more water, be careful not to disturb the dripper.)

7. Observe the flow of water and the changes it makes. Use the hand lens to look closely at the stream bed.

8. After 5 minutes, remove the dripper.

9. In your lab notebook, draw a picture of the resulting stream and label it "5 minutes."

10. Now switch the dripper to the left side of the cup. Restart the dripper and allow it to drip for 10 minutes. Then remove the dripper.

11. Draw a picture and label it "10 minutes."

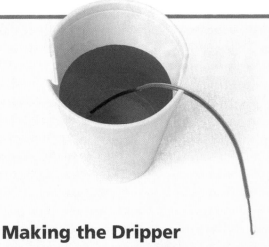

PART 2 Changing the Angle of Slope

1. Remove the cup from the stream table.

2. Save the stream bed on the right side of the tub. Using the bowl of the spoon, smooth out the diatomaceous earth on the left side.

3. To increase the angle of slope of your stream table, raise the end of the tub another 2.5 cm.

4. In your lab notebook, predict the effects of increasing the angle of slope.

5. Replace the cup and restart the dripper, placing it in the notch on the left side of the cup. Allow the dripper to drip for 5 minutes. Notice any changes in the new stream bed.

6. After 5 minutes, remove the dripper.

7. Draw the new stream bed in your lab notebook. Label it "Increased Angle."

8. Follow your teacher's instructions for clean-up after this activity. Wash your hands when you have finished.

Analyze and Conclude

1. **Observing** Compare the 5-minute stream with the 10-minute stream. How did the length of time that the water flowed affect erosion along the stream bed?

2. **Drawing Conclusions** Were your predictions about the effects of increasing the angle of slope correct? Explain your answer.

3. **Observing** What happened to the eroded material that was carried downstream?

4. **Making Models** What features of streams were you able to observe using your model? How could you modify the model to observe additional features?

5. **Controlling Variables** What other variables besides time and angle of slope might affect the way rivers and streams erode the land?

6. **Communicating** Describe an example of water erosion that you have seen, such as water flowing down a hillside or street after a heavy rain. Include in your answer details such as the slope of the land, the color of the water, and the effects of the erosion.

Making the Dripper

1. Insert the wire into one of the two holes in a plastic stirrer. The ends of the wire should protrude from the stirrer.

2. Gently bend the stirrer into a U shape. Be careful not to make any sharp bends. This is the dripper.

3. With scissors, carefully cut two small notches on opposite sides of the top of the foam cup.

4. Fill the cup to just below the notches with water colored with two drops of blue food coloring. Add more food coloring later as you add more water to the cup.

5. Add one drop of detergent to keep air bubbles out of the dripper and increase flow.

6. To start the dripper, fill it with water. Then quickly tip it and place it in one of the notches in the cup, as shown above.

7. Adjust the flow rate of the dripper to about 2 drips per 1 second. (*Hint:* Bend the dripper into more of a U shape to increase flow. Lessen the curve to reduce flow.)

Design an Experiment

Design an experiment in which you use your model to measure how the amount of sediment carried by a river changes as the volume of flow of the river increases. *Obtain your teacher's approval before you try the experiment.*

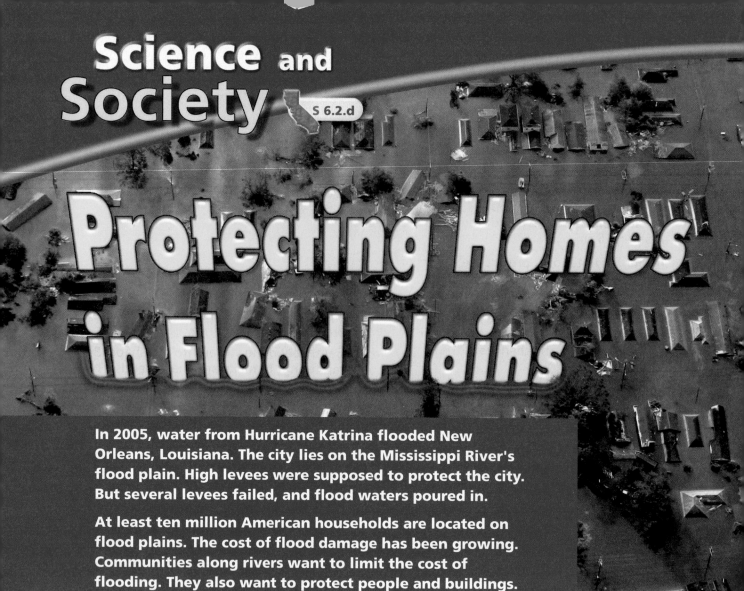

Science and Society

S 6.2.d

Protecting Homes in Flood Plains

In 2005, water from Hurricane Katrina flooded New Orleans, Louisiana. The city lies on the Mississippi River's flood plain. High levees were supposed to protect the city. But several levees failed, and flood waters poured in.

At least ten million American households are located on flood plains. The cost of flood damage has been growing. Communities along rivers want to limit the cost of flooding. They also want to protect people and buildings.

The Issues

Should the Government Insure People Against Flood Damage?

The United States government offers insurance to households in flood plains. The insurance pays part of the cost of repairs after a flood. However, government flood insurance is available only to towns and cities that take steps to reduce flood damage. Cities must allow new building only on high ground. In addition, the insurance will not pay to rebuild homes that are badly damaged by flood water. Instead, these people must use the money to find a home somewhere else.

Critics say that government insurance just encourages development in areas that flood. Another problem with the insurance is cost. It is very expensive, so most people who live in flood plains don't buy the government insurance. Supporters say government insurance rewards towns and cities that make rules to control building on flood plains. Over time, this approach would mean fewer homes and other buildings on flood plains—and less damage from flooding.

In 2005, floodwaters from Hurricane Katrina rose to the rooftops of many New Orleans houses. Thousands of people were stranded and had to be evacuated by boat.

How Much of the Flood Plain Should Be Protected?

Government flood insurance is available only in areas where scientists expect flooding at least once in 100 years. But such figures are just estimates. Three floods occurred in only 12 years in a government flood insurance area near Sacramento, California.

Should the Government Say Where People Can Live?

The frequency and severity of flooding is an important factor in land-use decisions. Sometimes, no construction on a flood plain is advisable. Some programs of flood control forbid all new building. Other programs may also encourage people to move to safer areas. The 1997 flood on the Red River in Grand Forks, North Dakota, is one example. After the flood, the city of Grand Forks offered to buy all the damaged buildings near the river. The city wants to build high walls of earth to protect the rest of the town.

The Grand Forks plan might prevent future damage, but is it fair? Supporters say that since the government has to pay for flood damage, it has the right to make people leave flood plains. Critics of such plans say that people should be free to live where they want, even in risky areas.

Who should decide that no new houses can be built in a certain area—the local, state, or federal government? Some believe scientists should make the decision.

Floodwaters engulfed much of New Orleans after the historic city's levees were breached by Hurricane Katrina.

You Decide

1. **Identify the Problem** In your own words, describe the controversy surrounding flood plains and housing.
2. **Analyze the Options** List several steps that could be taken to reduce the damage done to buildings in flood plains. For each step, include who would benefit from the step and who would pay the costs.
3. **Find a Solution** Your town has to decide what to do about a neighborhood damaged by the worst flood in 50 years. Write a speech that argues for your solution.

Go Online
PHSchool.com

For: More on protecting homes in flood plains
Visit: PHSchool.com
Web Code: cfh-2030

Section 3

Waves and Wind

CALIFORNIA
Standards Focus

S 6.2.a Framework Surface water flow, glaciers, wind, and ocean waves have all been and continue to be active throughout California and the rest of the world in shaping landscapes.

S 6.2.c Students know beaches are dynamic systems in which the sand is supplied by rivers and moved along the coast by the action of waves.

- What gives waves their energy?
- How do waves shape a coast?
- What are the causes and effects of wind erosion?

Key Terms
- headland
- beach
- longshore drift
- spit
- sand dune
- deflation
- loess

▼ A wave nears the shore.

Lab zone Standards **Warm-Up**

What Is Sand Made Of?

1. Collect a spoonful of sand from each of two different beaches.
2. Examine the first sample of beach sand with a hand lens.
3. Record the properties of the sand grains, for example, color and shape.
4. Hold a magnet close to the sand. Are any of the sand grains magnetic?
5. Examine the second sample and repeat Step 3. How do the two samples compare?

Think It Over
Posing Questions What questions do you need to answer to understand beach sand? Use what you know about erosion and deposition to help you think of questions.

Ocean waves contain energy—sometimes a great deal of energy. Created by ocean winds, they carry energy vast distances across the Pacific Ocean. Acting like drills or buzz saws, the waves erode the solid rock of the coast into cliffs and caves. Waves also carry sediment that forms features such as beaches.

How Waves Form

The energy in waves comes from wind that blows across the water's surface. As the wind makes contact with the water, some of its energy transfers to the water. Large ocean waves are the result of powerful storms far out at sea. But ordinary breezes can produce waves in lakes or small ponds.

The energy that water picks up from the wind causes water particles to move up and down as the wave goes by. But the water particles themselves don't move forward.

A wave changes as it approaches land. In deep water, a wave only affects the water near the surface. But as it approaches shallow water, the wave begins to drag on the bottom. The dragging between the wave and the bottom causes the wave to slow down. Now the water actually does move forward with the wave. This forward-moving water provides the force that shapes the land along the shoreline.

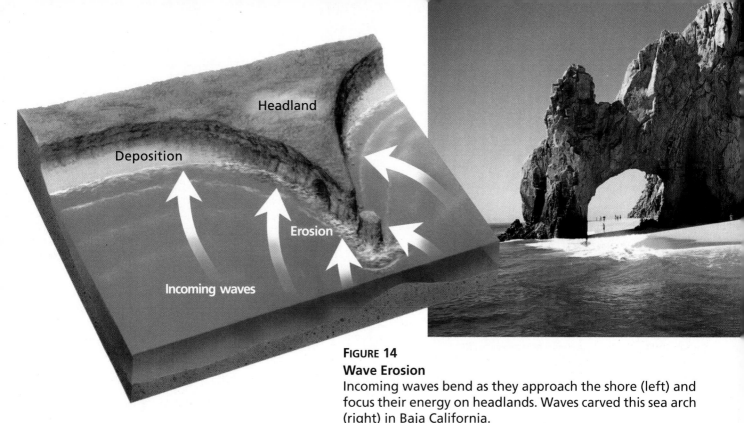

FIGURE 14
Wave Erosion
Incoming waves bend as they approach the shore (left) and focus their energy on headlands. Waves carved this sea arch (right) in Baja California.
Predicting *What will eventually happen to the headlands?*

Erosion by Waves

Waves are the major force of erosion along coasts, including the California coast. ⟶ **Waves shape the coast through erosion by breaking down rock and transporting sand and other sediment.**

How Waves Erode One way waves erode the land is by impact. Large waves can hit rocks along the shore with great force. This energy in waves can break apart rocks. Over time, waves can make small cracks larger. Eventually, the waves cause pieces of rock to break off.

Waves also erode by abrasion. Recall that abrasion is the wearing away of rock by a grinding action. As a wave approaches shallow water, it picks up sediment, including sand and gravel. This sediment is carried forward by the wave. When the wave hits land, the sediment wears away rock like sandpaper wearing away wood.

Waves coming to shore gradually change direction. The change in direction occurs as different parts of a wave begin to drag on the bottom. Notice how the waves in Figure 14 change direction as they approach the shore. The energy of these waves is concentrated on headlands. A **headland** is a part of the shore that sticks out into the ocean. Headlands stand out from the coast because they are made of harder rock that resists erosion by the waves. But, over time, waves erode the headlands and even out the shoreline.

Go Online
SciLINKS NSTA

For: Links on waves
Visit: www.SciLinks.org
Web Code: scn-0735

Erosional Features

Sea cave
Formed as wave action hollows out the cliff

Wave-cut cliff

Sea arch
Formed when sea caves on either side of a headland join

Headland

Sea stack
Left standing when a sea arch collapses

FIGURE 15
The Changing Coast
Erosion (left) and deposition (right) create a variety of features along a coast. You can often see these features along rocky parts of the California coast.
Predicting *What will eventually happen to the sea arch?*

Landforms Created by Wave Erosion When waves hit a steep, rocky coast, they strike the area again and again. Think of an ax striking the trunk of a tree. The cut gets bigger and deeper with each strike of the blade. Finally the tree falls. In a similar way, ocean waves erode the base of the land along a steep coast. Where the rock is softer, the waves erode the land faster. Over time the waves may erode a hollow area in the rock called a sea cave.

Eventually, waves may erode the base of a cliff so much that the rock above collapses. The result is a wave-cut cliff. You can see an example of such a cliff in Figure 15.

Another feature created by wave erosion is a sea arch. A sea arch forms when waves erode a layer of softer rock that underlies a layer of harder rock. If an arch collapses, the result might be a sea stack, a pillar of rock rising above the water.

 Reading Checkpoint **Over a long period of time, what effect do waves have on a steep, rocky coast?**

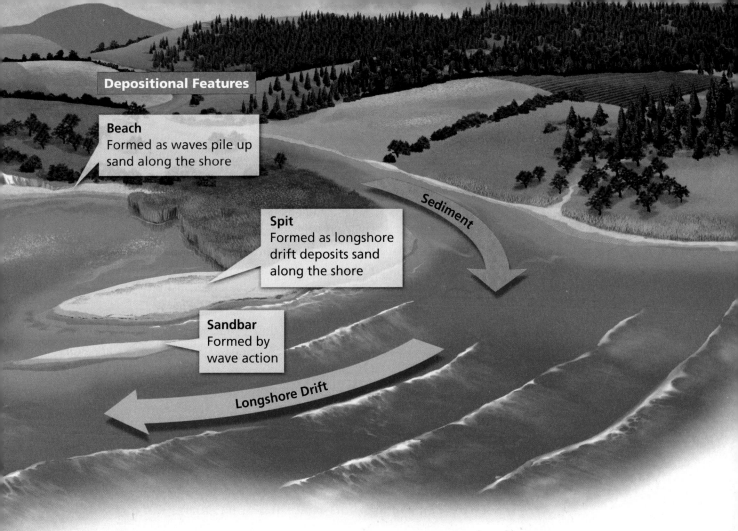

Depositional Features

Beach
Formed as waves pile up sand along the shore

Spit
Formed as longshore drift deposits sand along the shore

Sandbar
Formed by wave action

Sediment

Longshore Drift

Deposits by Waves

⊂⊃ **Waves shape a coast when they deposit sediment, forming coastal features such as beaches, spits, sandbars, and barrier beaches.** Deposition occurs when waves slow down, causing the water to drop its sediment. This process is similar to the deposition that occurs on a river delta when the river slows down and drops its sediment load.

Beaches As waves reach the shore, they drop the sediment they carry, forming a beach. A **beach** is an area of wave-washed sediment along a coast. The sediment deposited on beaches is usually sand. Most sand comes from rivers that carry eroded particles of rock into the ocean.

Beaches are dynamic systems. Beaches are constantly changing as rivers supply sand and the action of waves moves sand along the coast.

The sediment on a beach usually moves down the beach after it has been deposited. Waves usually hit the beach at an angle instead of straight on. These angled waves create a current that runs parallel to the coastline. As waves repeatedly hit the beach, some of the beach sediment moves down the beach with the current, in a process called **longshore drift.**

Lab zone Skills **Activity**

Calculating A sandy coast erodes at a rate of 1.25 m per year. But a severe storm can erode an additional 3.75 m from the shore. If 12 severe storms occur during a 50-year period, how much will the coast erode? If you wish, you may use an electronic calculator to find the answer.

FIGURE 16
Spits
This aerial photograph shows how longshore drift can carry sand and deposit it to form a spit.
Inferring *What feature along the coast do you think caused the spit to form? Explain.*

Spits One result of longshore drift is the formation of a spit. A **spit** is a beach that projects like a finger out into the water. Spits form as a result of deposition by longshore drift. Spits occur where a headland or other obstacle interrupts longshore drift, or where the coast turns abruptly.

Sandbars and Barrier Beaches Incoming waves carrying sand may build up sandbars, long ridges of sand parallel to the shore. A barrier beach is similar to a sandbar. A barrier beach forms when storm waves pile up large amounts of sand above sea level forming a long, narrow island parallel to the coast. Barrier beaches are found in many places along the seacoasts of the United States, such as the Outer Banks of North Carolina.

In California, barrier beaches can be found at the mouths of rivers and bays. Examples range from Silver Strand Beach in San Diego to the barrier beach that shelters Humboldt Bay in northern California.

People have built homes on many of these barrier beaches. But the storm waves that build up the beaches can also wash them away. Barrier beach communities must be prepared for the damage that hurricanes and other storms can bring.

Erosion by Wind

Imagine a landscape made almost entirely of sand. A **sand dune** is a deposit of wind-blown sand. Over thousands of years, wind sweeps sand across a desert, piling up huge, ever-changing dunes.

Wind by itself is the weakest agent of erosion. Water, waves, moving ice, and even mass movement have more effect on the land. Yet wind can be a powerful force in shaping the land in areas where there are few plants to hold the soil in place. For example, few plants grow in deserts, so wind can easily move the grains of dry sand. ☞ **Wind causes erosion by deflation and abrasion.**

FIGURE 17
Sand Dunes
In California, areas of sand dunes are found in parts of the Mojave Desert.

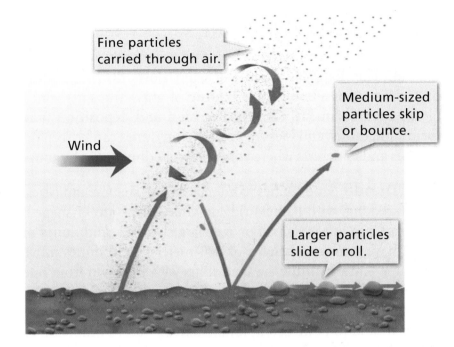

Fine particles carried through air.

Medium-sized particles skip or bounce.

Wind

Larger particles slide or roll.

FIGURE 18
Wind Erosion
Wind erosion moves sediment particles of different sizes in the three ways shown at the left. *Comparing and Contrasting Compare the movement of sediment by wind with the movement of sediment by water in Figure 4 earlier in the chapter. How are the processes similar? How are they different?*

Deflation The main way that wind causes erosion is by deflation. Geologists define **deflation** as the process by which wind removes surface materials. When wind blows over the land, it picks up the smallest particles of sediment. This sediment is made of bits of clay and silt. The stronger the wind, the larger the particles that it can pick up. Slightly heavier particles, such as sand, might skip or bounce for a short distance. But sand soon falls back to the ground. Strong winds can even roll heavier sediment particles over the ground. Figure 18 shows how wind erodes by deflation.

Deflation does not usually have a great effect on land. However, in parts of the Great Plains in the 1930s, deflation caused the loss of about 1 meter of topsoil in just a few years. In deserts, deflation can sometimes create an area of rock fragments called desert pavement, shown in Figure 19. There, wind has blown away the smaller sediment. All that remains are rocky materials that are too heavy to be moved. Areas of desert pavement are common in California's Mojave Desert. Where there is already a slight depression in the ground, deflation can produce a bowl-shaped hollow called a blowout.

Abrasion Abrasion by wind-carried sand can polish rock, but it causes little erosion. At one time, geologists thought that the sediment carried by wind cut the stone shapes seen in deserts. But now evidence shows that most desert landforms are the result of weathering and water erosion.

Reading Checkpoint Where would you be most likely to see evidence of wind erosion?

FIGURE 19
Desert Pavement
Wind erosion formed this desert pavement in the Arizona desert. Wind-driven sand may polish and shape individual stones.

Crescent-shaped dunes form where the wind usually blows in the same direction.

Star-shaped dunes form where the wind direction changes frequently.

Wind direction

FIGURE 20
Movement of Sand Dunes
Wind direction helps determine the shape and size of sand dunes.

Deposition by Wind

All the sediment picked up by wind eventually falls to the ground. This happens when the wind slows down or some obstacle, such as a boulder or a clump of grass, traps the wind-blown sand sediment. **Wind erosion and deposition may form sand dunes and loess deposits.** Sand dunes can be seen on beaches and in deserts where wind-blown sediment has built up.

Sand Dunes Sand dunes come in many shapes and sizes. Some are long, with parallel ridges, while others are U-shaped. They can also be very small or very large—some sand dunes in China have grown to heights of 500 meters. Sand dunes move over time. Little by little, the sand shifts with the wind from one side of the dune to the other. This process is shown in Figure 20. In California, sand dunes occur along the coast where rivers have supplied sand to bays. Examples include the dunes near Monterey Bay, Humboldt Bay, and San Diego Bay. Areas of sand dunes can also be found in Death Valley and the Mojave desert.

Loess Deposits Sediment that is finer than sand, such as particles of clay and silt, is sometimes deposited in layers far from its source. This fine, wind-deposited sediment is **loess** (les). Large loess deposits are found in central China and in the midwestern United States. Loess helps to form fertile soil. Many areas with thick loess deposits are valuable farmlands.

Section 3 Assessment

S 6.2.a, 6.2.c; E-LA: Reading 6.1.0, Writing 6.2.2

Vocabulary Skill Latin Word Origins Use what you've learned to complete the following sentence. A process in which wind wears down surface materials is called _____.

Reviewing Key Concepts

1. a. Explaining What is the source of the energy in ocean waves?
   b. Describing How does an ocean wave change when it reaches shallow water?
   c. Applying Concepts What are two ways in which waves cause erosion?
2. a. Identifying What are two results of wave erosion along a coast?
   b. Listing What are three features formed by wave deposition?
   c. Relating Cause and Effect Beginning with the source of sand, explain how a spit forms.

3. a. Reviewing What are two kinds of wind erosion?
   b. Identifying What are two types of features that result from wind deposition?
   c. Predicting In a desert, soil containing a mixture of sand and small rocks is exposed to wind erosion. Over time, how would the land surface change? Explain.

Writing in Science

Explaining a Process Suppose that you live in a coastal area that has a barrier beach. Write a paragraph in which you explain the processes that formed the barrier beach. Also describe how the forces might change it over time.

Glaciers

CALIFORNIA
Standards Focus

S 6.2.a Framework Surface water flow, glaciers, wind, and ocean waves have all been and continue to be active throughout California and the rest of the world in shaping landscapes.

- What are the two kinds of glaciers?
- How does a valley glacier form and move?
- How do glaciers cause erosion and deposition?

Key Terms

- glacier
- continental glacier
- ice age
- valley glacier
- plucking
- till
- moraine
- kettle

Lab zone Standards Warm-Up

How Do Glaciers Reshape the Land?

1. Put some sand in a small plastic container.
2. Fill the container with water and place the container in a freezer until the water turns to ice.
3. Remove the block of ice from the container. Hold the ice with a paper towel.
4. Rub the ice, sand side down, over a bar of soap. Observe what happens to the surface of the soap.

Think It Over

Inferring Based on your observations, how do you think moving ice could change the surface of the land?

You are on a boat trip near the coast of Alaska. You sail by vast evergreen forests and snow-capped mountains. Then, as your boat rounds a point of land, you see an amazing sight. A great mass of ice flows like a river between rows of mountains. Suddenly you hear a noise like thunder. Where the ice meets the sea, a giant chunk of ice breaks off and plunges into the water. Carefully, the pilot steers your boat around the iceberg and toward the mass of ice. It towers over your boat. You see that it is made up of solid ice that is deep blue and green as well as white. What is this river of ice?

▼ **The Hubbard Glacier in Alaska**

How Glaciers Form and Move

Geologists define a **glacier** as any large mass of ice that moves slowly over land. 👁 **There are two kinds of glaciers—continental glaciers and valley glaciers.**

Continental Glaciers A **continental glacier** is a glacier that covers much of a continent or large island. A continental glacier can cover millions of square kilometers. Today, continental glaciers cover about 10 percent of Earth's land. They cover Antarctica and most of Greenland. The glacier covering Antarctica is over 3 kilometers thick! Continental glaciers can flow in all directions. Continental glaciers spread out much as pancake batter spreads out in a frying pan.

Many times in the past, continental glaciers have covered larger parts of Earth's surface. These times are known as **ice ages.** Beginning about 2.5 million years ago, continental glaciers advanced and retreated, or melted back, several times. They finally retreated about 10,000 years ago.

Valley Glaciers A **valley glacier** is a long, narrow glacier that forms when snow and ice build up high in a mountain valley. The sides of mountains keep these glaciers from spreading out in all directions. Instead, they usually move down valleys that have already been cut by rivers. Valley glaciers are found on many high mountains. Although they are much smaller than continental glaciers, valley glaciers can be tens of kilometers long. In California, small valley glaciers occur on many of the highest peaks in the Sierra Nevada and on Mount Shasta.

High in mountain valleys, temperatures seldom rise above freezing. Snow builds up year after year. The weight of more and more snow compacts the snow at the bottom into ice. 👁 **Glaciers can form only in an area where more snow falls than melts. Once the depth of snow and ice reaches more than 30 to 40 meters, gravity begins to pull the glacier downhill.**

Valley glaciers flow at a rate of a few centimeters to a few meters per day. But sometimes a valley glacier slides down more quickly in what is called a surge. A surging glacier can flow as much as 6 kilometers per year.

 Reading Checkpoint — On what type of landform are valley glaciers found?

The Ice Age in North America

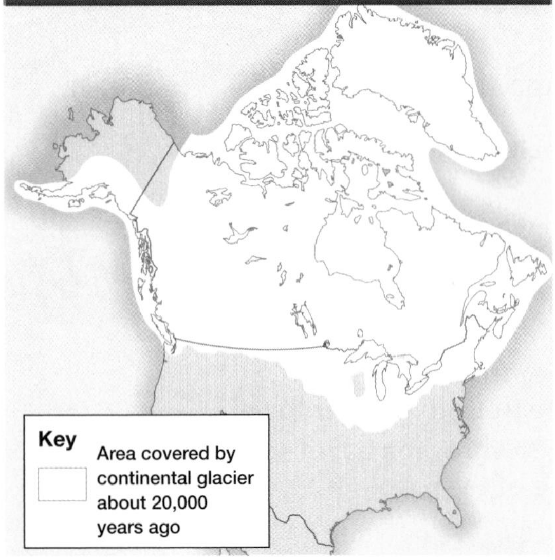

Key Area covered by continental glacier about 20,000 years ago

FIGURE 21
Continental Glaciers
During the last ice age, a continental glacier covered most of northern North America.

How Glaciers Shape the Land

The movement of a glacier changes the land beneath it. Although glaciers work slowly, they are a major force of erosion. ⊙ **The two processes by which glaciers erode the land are plucking and abrasion.**

Glacial Erosion As a glacier flows over the land, it picks up rocks in a process called **plucking.** Beneath a glacier, the weight of the ice can break rocks apart. These rock fragments freeze to the bottom of the glacier. When the glacier moves, it carries the rocks with it. Figure 22 shows plucking by a glacier.

Many rocks remain on the bottom of the glacier, and the glacier drags them across the land. This process, called abrasion, gouges and scratches the bedrock. You can see the results of erosion by glaciers in Figure 22. In a similar way, glacial erosion formed Yosemite Valley in the Sierra Nevada.

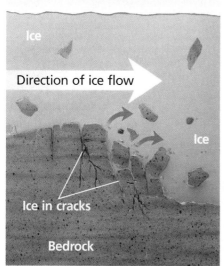

Ice

Direction of ice flow

Ice

Ice in cracks

Bedrock

FIGURE 22
Glacial Erosion

As a glacier moves (left), plucking breaks pieces of bedrock from the ground. Erosion by glaciers can carve a mountain peak into a sharp horn (below) and grind out a **V**-shaped valley to form a **U**-shaped valley.
Predicting *What other changes did the glacier produce in this landscape?*

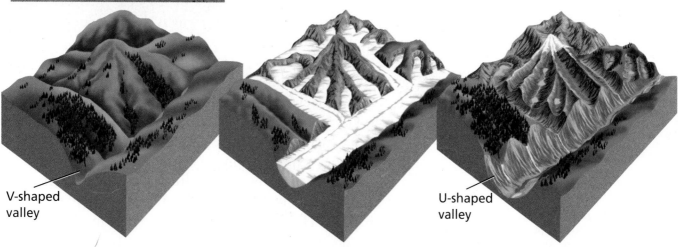

V-shaped valley

U-shaped valley

Before Glaciers Form   **During Glaciation**   **After Glaciers Have Melted**

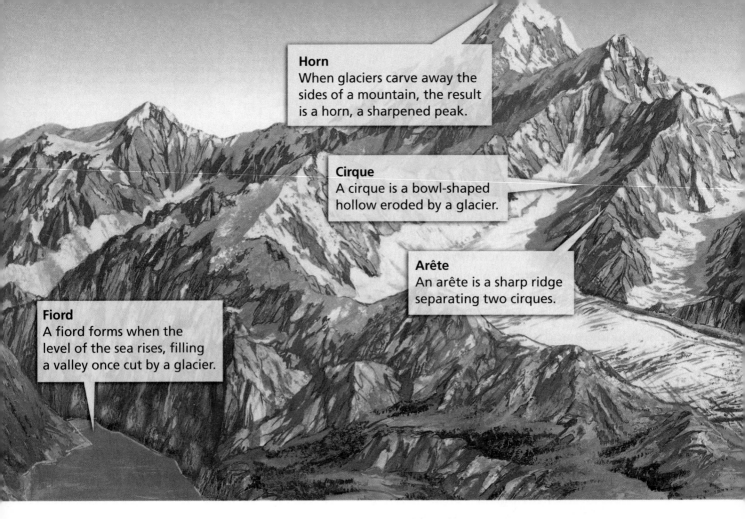

Horn
When glaciers carve away the sides of a mountain, the result is a horn, a sharpened peak.

Cirque
A cirque is a bowl-shaped hollow eroded by a glacier.

Arête
An arête is a sharp ridge separating two cirques.

Fiord
A fiord forms when the level of the sea rises, filling a valley once cut by a glacier.

FIGURE 23
Glacial Landforms

As glaciers advance and retreat, they sculpt the landscape by erosion and deposition.
Classifying *Classify these glacial features according to whether they result from erosion or deposition: drumlin, horn, cirque, moraine, U-shaped valley.*

Go Online
SciLINKS

For: Links on glaciers
Visit: www.SciLinks.org
Web Code: scn-0734

Glacial Deposition A glacier gathers a huge amount of rock and soil as it erodes the land in its path. ⊙ **When a glacier melts, it deposits the sediment it eroded from the land, creating various landforms.** These landforms remain for thousands of years after the glacier has melted. The mixture of sediments that a glacier deposits directly on the surface is called **till.** Till is made up of particles of many different sizes. Clay, silt, sand, gravel, and boulders can all be found in till.

The till deposited at the edges of a glacier forms a ridge called a **moraine.** A terminal moraine is the ridge of till at the farthest point reached by a glacier. A terminal moraine that formed at the end of the last ice age extends across part of Yosemite Valley in California.

Retreating glaciers also create features. A **kettle** is a small depression that forms when a chunk of ice is left in glacial till. When the ice melts, the kettle remains. The continental glacier of the last ice age left behind many kettles. Kettles often fill with water, forming small lakes called kettle lakes. Small lakes also form in the bowl-shaped hollow eroded by a glacier at the base of a high peak. There are many of these lakes in California's Sierra Nevada.

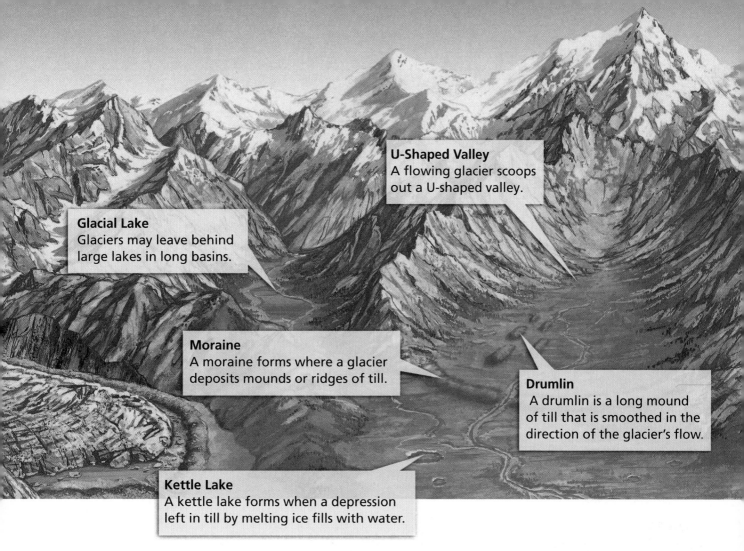

U-Shaped Valley
A flowing glacier scoops out a U-shaped valley.

Glacial Lake
Glaciers may leave behind large lakes in long basins.

Moraine
A moraine forms where a glacier deposits mounds or ridges of till.

Drumlin
A drumlin is a long mound of till that is smoothed in the direction of the glacier's flow.

Kettle Lake
A kettle lake forms when a depression left in till by melting ice fills with water.

Section 4 Assessment

S 6.2.a; E-LA: Reading 6.2.0, Writing 6.2.5

Target Reading Skill Sequence Review Valley Glaciers under the heading How Glaciers Form and Move. Then organize the text in a flowchart called How a Valley Glacier Forms. In the first box write, "Snow builds up." Write the next 3 steps in the process.

Reviewing Key Concepts

1. a. Defining What is a continental glacier?
   b. Defining What is a valley glacier?
   c. Comparing and Contrasting How are the two types of glaciers similar? How are they different?

2. a. Reviewing How does a glacier form?
   b. Explaining How does a glacier move?
   c. Relating Cause and Effect Why does the snow that forms a glacier change to ice?

3. a. Identifying What are two ways in which glaciers erode Earth's surface?
   b. Describing How does glacial deposition occur?

Writing in Science

Travel Brochure A travel agency wants people to go on a tour of a mountain region with many glaciers. Write a paragraph for a travel brochure describing what people will see on the tour. In your answer, include features formed by glacial erosion and deposition.

🔑 The **BIG Idea** Moving water, wind, and ice are forces that shape our landscape.

① Changing Earth's Surface

🔑 **Key Concepts** 🗝 S 6.2

- Weathering, erosion, and deposition act together in a cycle that wears down and builds up Earth's surface.
- Gravity causes mass movement, including landslides, mudflows, slump, and creep.

Key Terms

erosion   gravity
sediment   mass movement
deposition

② Water Erosion

🔑 **Key Concepts** 🗝 S 6.2.a, 6.2.b

- Moving water is the major agent of the erosion that has shaped Earth's land surface.
- Through erosion, a river creates valleys, water–falls, flood plains, meanders, and oxbow lakes.
- Deposition creates alluvial fans and deltas. It can also add soil to a river's flood plain.
- A river's slope, volume of flow, and the shape of its streambed all affect how fast the river flows and how much sediment it can erode.

Key Terms

runoff   meander
rill   oxbow lake
gully   alluvial fan
stream   delta
energy   load
flood plain

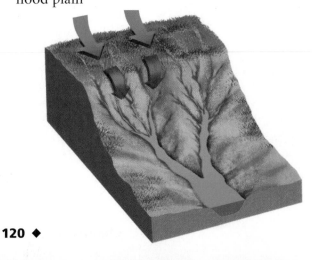

③ Waves and Wind

🔑 **Key Concepts** 🗝 S 6.2.a, 6.2.c

- The energy in waves comes from wind that blows across the water's surface.
- Waves shape the coast through erosion by breaking down rock and transporting sand and other sediment.
- Waves shape a coast when they deposit sediment, forming coastal features such as beaches, sand bars, spits, and barrier beaches.
- Wind causes erosion by deflation and abrasion.
- Wind erosion and deposition may form sand dunes and loess deposits.

Key Terms

headland   sand dune
beach   deflation
longshore drift   loess
spit

④ Glaciers

🔑 **Key Concepts** 🗝 S 6.2.a

- There are two kinds of glaciers—continental glaciers and valley glaciers.
- Glaciers can form only in an area where more snow falls than melts. Once the depth of snow and ice reaches more than 30 to 40 meters, gravity begins to pull the glacier downhill.
- The two processes by which glaciers erode the land are plucking and abrasion.
- When a glacier melts, it deposits the sediment it eroded from the land, creating various landforms.

Key Terms

glacier   plucking
continental glacier   till
ice age   moraine
valley glacier   kettle

Review and Assessment

Target Reading Skill

Sequence Complete a six-step graphic organizer for Stream Formation.

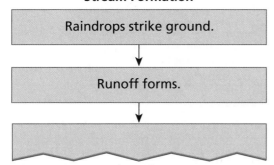

Stream Formation

Raindrops strike ground.

↓

Runoff forms.

↓

Reviewing Key Terms

Choose the letter of the best answer.

1. The eroded materials carried by water or wind are called
   a. till.
   b. desert pavement.
   c. sediment.
   d. moraines.

2. The downhill movement of eroded materials is known as
   a. mass movement.
   b. abrasion.
   c. deposition.
   d. deflation.

3. As runoff flows over the surface, it forms tiny grooves in soil called
   a. gullies.
   b. deltas.
   c. rills.
   d. fans.

4. Where a streambed curves, deposition occurs
   a. in the middle.
   b. along the inside of the curve.
   c. along the outside of the curve.
   d. as the water speeds up.

5. The erosion of sediment by wind is
   a. deposition.
   b. deflation.
   c. plucking.
   d. glaciation.

6. A mass of rock and soil deposited directly by a glacier is called
   a. load.
   b. till.
   c. loess.
   d. erosion.

7. Glaciers pick up rocks by a process called
   a. creep.
   b. plucking.
   c. drift.
   d. meandering.

Complete the following sentences so that your answers clearly explain the key terms.

8. Water carrying sediment eventually slows down, causing **deposition,** which is _____ .

9. Rain that falls to the surface can form **runoff,** which is _____ .

10. Where a river flows across its floodplain, it may form a **meander,** which is _____ .

11. Waves' hitting a beach at an angle creates a current parallel to the coastline, causing **longshore drift,** which is _____ .

12. One feature formed when a glacier deposits sediment is a **moraine,** which is _____ .

Writing in Science

Article Suppose that you have just returned from a visit to a limestone cave, such as Mammoth Cave in Kentucky. Write an article describing your visit to the cave. Include how the cave formed, what you saw during your visit, and how features inside the cave developed.

Video Assessment
Discovery Channel School
Erosion and Deposition

Review and Assessment

Checking Concepts

13. What agents of erosion are assisted by the force of gravity?

14. Beginning with rain hitting the land surface, describe the process by which a stream forms.

15. How does an alluvial fan form?

16. How do a river's slope and volume of flow affect the river's sediment load?

17. Where is the speed of the flowing water in a river the slowest? Explain.

18. How does a loess deposit form?

19. What are ice ages?

20. How does a kettle lake form?

Thinking Critically

21. Comparing and Contrasting Compare and contrast landslides and mudflows.

22. Applying Concepts Describe a beneficial effect that flooding can have on a flood plain.

23. Making Judgments A salesperson offers to sell your family a new house right on a riverbank for very little money. Why might your family hesitate to buy this house?

24. Relating Cause and Effect What caused the features labeled A, B, and C in the diagram below? Explain.

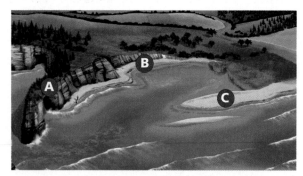

25. Inferring You see a sandy beach along a coastline. Where did the sand come from?

26. Problem Solving Suppose you are a geologist studying a valley glacier. What method could you use to tell if it is advancing or retreating?

Applying Skills

Use the table below to answer Questions 27–29.

The table shows how a river's volume of flow and sediment load change over six months.

Month	Volume of Flow (cubic meters/second)	Sediment Load (metric tons/day)
January	1.5	200
February	1.7	320
March	2.6	725
April	4.0	1,600
May	3.2	1,100
June	2.8	900

27. Graphing Make one graph with the month on the x-axis and the volume of flow on the y-axis. Make a second graph with the sediment load on the y-axis. Compare your two graphs. When were the river's volume of flow and load the greatest? The lowest?

28. Developing Hypotheses Use your graphs to develop a hypothesis about the relationship between volume of flow and sediment load.

29. Relating Cause and Effect What may have occurred in the river's drainage basin in April to cause the changes in volume of flow and sediment load? Explain.

Lab zone — Standards Investigation

Performance Assessment Now you are ready to explain your models of erosion to your class. Explain to your classmates the features that formed as the result of erosion. Predict how the topography of your model could change as the cycle of erosion continues.

Choose the letter of the best answer.

1. What is the slow, downhill mass movement of rock and soil, caused by gravity?
   A a landslide
   B creep
   C runoff
   D a glacier   **S 6.2**

2. Which statement best describes the process that forms a stream?
   A Sheet erosion digs a deep channel.
   B Tiny rills enlarge to form gullies, which join to form a stream.
   C Small gullies enlarge to form rills, which deepen to form a stream.
   D Water flows down a V-shaped valley.   **S 6.2.a**

3. A meander that is cut off from the main course of a river becomes a(n)
   A kettle lake.
   B delta.
   C oxbow lake.
   D alluvial fan.   **S 6.2.a**

4. As a stream flows from a mountainous area to a flatter area, what happens to the size of the sediment the stream normally carries?
   A The sediment size does not change.
   B The sediment size carried by the stream increases.
   C The sediment size carried by the stream decreases.
   D The stream drops all the sediment it was carrying.   **S 6.2.b**

5. Which of the following is an effect of longshore drift?
   A Deep deposits of loess are formed.
   B A meander forms in a river.
   C A delta builds up at a river's mouth.
   D Beach sand moves along a coastline. **S 6.2.c**

Use the diagram below and your knowledge of science to answer Questions 6 and 7.

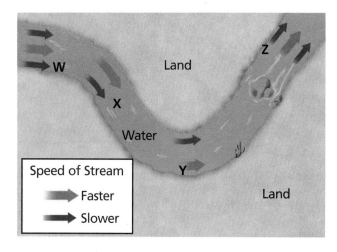

6. What is the erosional feature in the diagram?
   A a meander
   B a delta
   C a flood plain
   D an alluvial fan   **S 6.2.a**

7. In the diagram, where is the speed of the stream the greatest?
   A at Y
   B at X
   C at W
   D at Z   **S 6.2.b**

8. Scientists determine that a certain flood plain will probably have a severe flood two or three times in a hundred years. The best type of land use for the flood plain would be
   A a shopping center.
   B homes and schools.
   C farmland and forest.
   D tall office buildings.   **S 6.2.d**

Apply the
BIG Idea

9. Describe how gravity is involved in the erosion of Earth's surface by mass movement, running water, and glaciers. Be sure to first explain what erosion is.   **S 6.2**

Earth Systems and Processes
Unit 1 Review

Chapter 1
Introduction to Earth Science
The BIG Idea

Sunlight provides energy for many processes on Earth's surface that affect the land, air, water, and living things.

- What skills do scientists use to learn about the world?
- How is energy transferred in the Earth system?
- What does the topography of an area include?

Chapter 2
Weathering and Soil
The BIG Idea

The weathering of rock helps to reshape Earth's topography and form soil.

- What are the three major groups of rock, and how do they form through the rock cycle?
- How do weathering and erosion affect Earth's surface?
- What is soil made of, and how does it form?
- Why is soil a valuable resource?

Chapter 3
Erosion and Deposition
The BIG Idea

Moving water, wind, and ice are forces that shape our landscape.

- What processes wear down and build up Earth's surface?
- What features are formed by water erosion and deposition?
- How do glaciers cause erosion and deposition?

Connecting the
BIG Ideas

Thank you for choosing the Rivers and Redwoods Tour! We hope you enjoy your visit to the Klamath River. The river reaches the ocean in Redwood National Park, where the giant coast redwoods and many other plants thrive in the rich soil. Water from the river and ocean cycles back into the atmosphere, bringing moisture to the trees.

As you can see from the map below, our trip to the river's mouth will pass several interesting geologic features. These features include a large meander, a delta made up of several islands, a spit, and a long ocean beach.

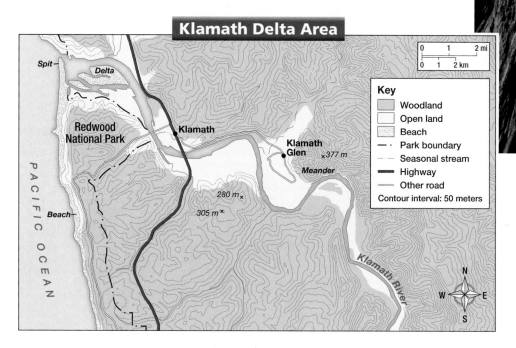

Klamath Delta Area

Key
- Woodland
- Open land
- Beach
- Park boundary
- Seasonal stream
- Highway
- Other road

Contour interval: 50 meters

1. What provides the energy for water to move from the river and ocean to the atmosphere? *(Chapter 1)*

    a. gravity   **b.** sunlight
    c. condensation   **d.** Earth's interior

2. What process contributes to the formation of soil in Redwood National Park? *(Chapter 2)*

    a. creep   **b.** slump
    c. weathering   **d.** widening

3. What formed the delta of the Klamath River, shown in yellow on the map? *(Chapter 3)*

    a. deposition   **b.** mudflow
    c. longshore drift   **d.** abrasion

4. **Summary** Write a paragraph that describes a trip down the Klamath River. Describe the features of erosion and deposition that you would see on your trip and explain how they formed.

Chapter 4

Plate Tectonics

CALIFORNIA
Standards Preview

S 6.1 Plate tectonics accounts for important features of Earth's surface and major geologic events. As a basis for understanding this concept:

a. Students know evidence of plate tectonics is derived from the fit of the continents; the location of earthquakes, volcanoes, and mid-ocean ridges; and the distribution of fossils, rock types, and ancient climatic zones.

b. Students know Earth is composed of several layers: a cold, brittle lithosphere; a hot, convecting mantle; and a dense, metallic core.

c. Students know lithospheric plates the size of continents and oceans move at rates of centimeters per year in response to movements in the mantle.

S 6.4 Many phenomena on Earth's surface are affected by the transfer of energy through radiation and convection currents. As a basis for understanding this concept:

c. Students know heat from Earth's interior reaches the surface primarily through convection.

The diagonal line in the photo marks California's San Andreas fault. Two large pieces of Earth's crust slide past each other along the fault. ▶

Focus on the
BIG Idea

S 6.1.c

What are Earth's plates, and how do their movements change our planet's surface?

Check What You Know

Imagine knocking a hardboiled egg against a table so that the shell cracks in several places. Then suppose that you slice the egg in half to make a cross section of the shell, egg white, and yolk. Explain how your sliced egg with the cracked shell can serve as a model of Earth.

Build Science Vocabulary

The images shown here represent some of the key terms in this chapter. You can use this vocabulary skill to help you understand the meaning of some key terms in this chapter.

Vocabulary Skill

Use Greek Word Origins

Many science words come to English from ancient Greek. In this chapter you will learn the word *lithosphere*. You probably know the meaning of *sphere*, a globe or ball. The Greek word *litho* means "stone." Therefore, the *lithosphere* is the stony outer shell, or sphere, that forms Earth's surface.

litho + **sphere** = **lithosphere**
stone   globe   the stony outer part of Earth

Learn these Greek words to help you remember the key terms.

Greek Root	Meaning	Examples
asthenes	weak	asthenosphere
litho-	stone	lithosphere
seismos	earthquake	seismic
sphaira	sphere	lithosphere
tektón	carpenter, builder	tectonics

Apply It!

Review the Greek roots and meanings in the chart. Then predict the meaning of seismic waves. As you read, revise your definition as needed.

Use these Greek words to help you figure out unfamiliar words in this chapter.

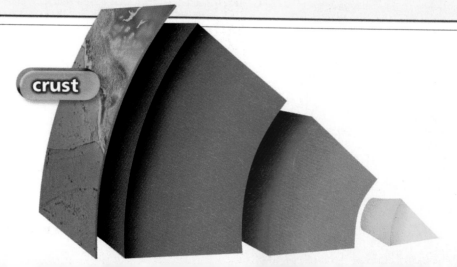

crust

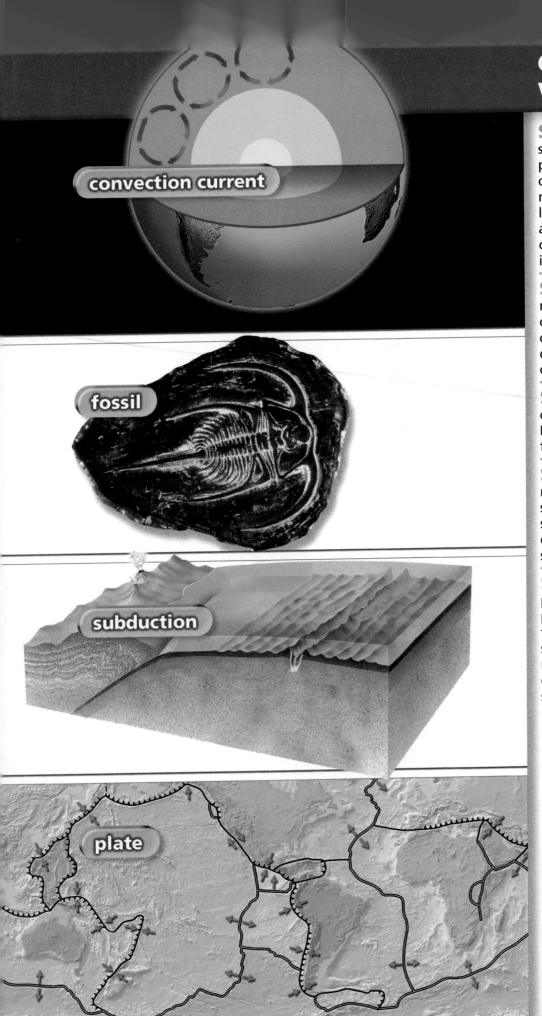

convection current

fossil

subduction

plate

Build Science Vocabulary
Online
Visit: PHSchool.com
Web Code: cwj-2040

How to Read Science

Identify Supporting Evidence

Science textbooks often describe the scientific evidence that supports a theory or hypothesis. Remember that scientific evidence includes data and facts that have been confirmed by observation or experiments.

You can use a graphic organizer like the one below to help you understand how supporting evidence is related to a theory.

Include
- a title
- supporting evidence on the left
- the hypothesis or theory on the right

This chapter discusses Wegener's hypothesis of continental drift.

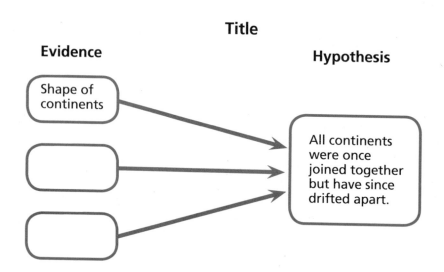

Apply It!
Review the graphic organizer and answer the questions.
1. What is a good title for the graphic organizer?
2. What information should you include in the ovals on the left?

As you read Section 3, complete the graphic organizer on continental drift. In Section 4, create a graphic organizer to explain the theory of sea-floor spreading.

Make a Model of Earth

In this chapter, you will learn how movements deep within Earth help to form mountains and other surface features. As you read this chapter, you will build a model that shows Earth's interior.

Your Goal

To build a model that shows Earth's surface features, as well as a cutaway view of Earth's interior

Your model must

- be built to scale to show the layers of Earth's interior
- include at least three of the plates that form Earth's surface, as well as two landmasses or continents
- show how the plates push together, pull apart, or slide past each other and indicate their direction of movement
- be built following the safety guidelines in Appendix A

Plan It!

Think about the materials you could use to make a three-dimensional model. How will you show what happens beneath the crust? As you learn about sea-floor spreading and plate tectonics, add the appropriate features to your model.

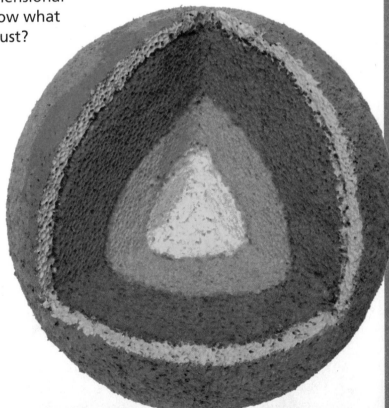

Section 1

Earth's Interior

CALIFORNIA
Standards Focus

S 6.1.b. Students know Earth is composed of several layers: a cold, brittle lithosphere; a hot, convecting mantle; and a dense, metallic core.

How have geologists learned about Earth's inner structure?

What are the characteristics of Earth's crust, mantle, and core?

Key Terms

- seismic waves
- pressure
- crust
- mantle
- lithosphere
- asthenosphere
- outer core
- inner core

FIGURE 1
Lava From Inside Earth
A lava flow like this one on Mount Kilauea, Hawaii, transfers some of the heat of Earth's interior to the surface.

Lab zone Standards **Warm-Up**

How Do Scientists Find Out What's Inside Earth?

1. Your teacher will provide you with three closed film canisters. Each canister contains a different material. Your goal is to determine what is inside each canister—even though you can't directly observe what it contains.
2. Tape a paper label on each canister.
3. To gather evidence about what is in the canisters, you may tap, roll, shake, or weigh them. Record your observations.
4. What differences do you notice between the canisters? Apart from their appearance on the outside, are the canisters similar in any way? How did you obtain this evidence?

Think It Over
Inferring From your observations, what can you infer about the contents of the canisters? How is a canister like Earth?

Volcanic eruptions like those at Mount Kilauea in Hawaii make people wonder, What's inside Earth? Yet this question is very difficult to answer. Much as geologists would like to, they cannot dig a hole to the center of Earth. The extreme conditions in Earth's interior prevent exploration far below the surface.

The deepest mine in the world, a gold mine in South Africa, reaches a depth of 3.8 kilometers. But that mine only scratches the surface. You would have to travel more than 1,600 times that distance—over 6,000 kilometers—to reach Earth's center.

Exploring Inside Earth

Geologists have used two main types of evidence to learn about Earth's interior: direct evidence from rock samples and indirect evidence from seismic waves. Geologists have used this evidence to build a picture of Earth's interior.

Evidence From Rock Samples Rocks from inside Earth give geologists clues about Earth's structure. Geologists have drilled holes as much as 12 kilometers into Earth. The drills bring up samples of rock. From these samples, geologists can learn about conditions deep inside Earth, where these rocks formed. In addition, forces inside Earth sometimes blast rock to the surface from depths of more than 100 kilometers. These rocks provide clues about the interior.

Evidence From Seismic Waves Geologists cannot look inside Earth. Instead, they must rely on indirect methods of observation. Have you ever hung a heavy picture on a wall? If you have, you know that you can knock on the wall to locate the wooden beam underneath the plaster that will support the picture. When you knock on the wall, you listen carefully for a change in the sound.

To study Earth's interior, geologists also use an indirect method. But instead of knocking on walls, they use seismic waves. When earthquakes occur, they produce **seismic waves** (SYZ mik). Geologists record the seismic waves and study how they travel through Earth. Different types of seismic waves behave differently. The speed of the waves and the paths they take reveal the structure of the planet. You will learn about the different types of seismic waves in Chapter 5, Earthquakes.

Using data from seismic waves, geologists have learned that Earth's interior is made up of layers. Each layer surrounds the layers beneath it, much like the layers of an onion. In Figure 2, you can see how seismic waves travel through the layers that make up Earth.

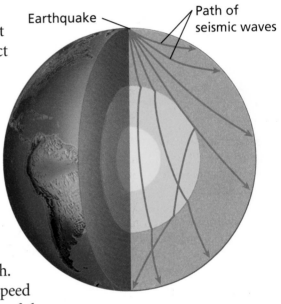

Earthquake

Path of seismic waves

 Reading Checkpoint What causes seismic waves?

Go Online

*SCi*LINKS NSTA

For: Links on the structure of Earth
Visit: www.SciLinks.org
Web Code: scn-1011

A Journey to the Center of Earth

🔵 **The three main layers of Earth are the crust, the mantle, and the core. These layers vary greatly in size, composition, temperature, and pressure.** If you could travel through these layers to the center of Earth, what would your trip be like? To begin, you will need a vehicle that can travel through solid rock. The vehicle will carry scientific instruments to record changes in temperature and pressure as you descend.

Temperature   As you start to tunnel beneath the surface, the surrounding rock is cool. Then at about 20 meters down, your instruments report that the rock is getting warmer. For every 40 meters that you descend from that point, the temperature rises 1 Celsius degree. This rapid rise in temperature continues for several tens of kilometers. After that, the temperature increases more slowly, but steadily. The high temperatures inside Earth are the result of heat left over from the formation of the planet. In addition, radioactive substances inside Earth release energy. This further heats the interior.

Pressure   During your journey to the center of Earth, your instruments record an increase in pressure in the surrounding rock. **Pressure** results from a force pressing on an area. Because of the weight of the rock above, pressure inside Earth increases as you go deeper. The deeper you go, the greater the pressure. Pressure inside Earth increases much as it does in the swimming pool in Figure 3.

FIGURE 3
Pressure and Depth
The deeper this swimmer goes, the greater the pressure from the surrounding water.
Comparing and Contrasting *How is the water in the swimming pool similar to Earth's interior? How is it different?*

Depth

0

0.5 m

1 m

Pressure
Increases

1.5 m

2 m

The Crust

Your journey to the center of Earth begins in the crust. The **crust** is the layer of rock that forms Earth's outer skin. ⚷ **The crust is a layer of solid rock that includes both dry land and the ocean floor.** On the crust you find rocks and mountains. The crust also includes the soil and water on Earth's surface.

This outer layer of rock is much thinner than the layer that lies beneath it. In fact, you can think of Earth's crust as being similar to the paper-thin skin of an onion. The crust is thickest under high mountains and thinnest beneath the ocean. In most places, the crust is between 5 and 40 kilometers thick. But it can be up to 70 kilometers thick beneath mountains.

The crust beneath the ocean is called oceanic crust. Oceanic crust consists mostly of rocks such as basalt. Recall that basalt (buh SAWLT) is a dark igneous rock with a fine texture. Continental crust, the crust that forms the continents, consists mainly of rocks such as granite. Recall that granite is an igneous rock that usually is a light color and has a coarse texture.

Reading Checkpoint What is the main type of rock in oceanic crust?

FIGURE 4
Earth's Crust
Half Dome in Yosemite National Park forms part of Earth's continental crust. Soil and plants cover much of the crust.

The Mantle

Your journey downward continues. About 40 kilometers beneath the surface, you cross a boundary. Below the boundary is the solid material of the **mantle,** a layer of hot rock. **Earth's mantle is made up of rock that is very hot, but solid. Different layers of the mantle have different physical characteristics.** Overall, the mantle is nearly 3,000 kilometers thick.

The Lithosphere The uppermost part of the mantle and the crust together form a rigid layer called the **lithosphere** (LITH uh sfeer). In Greek, *lithos* means "stone." As you can see in Figure 5, the lithosphere averages about 100 kilometers thick.

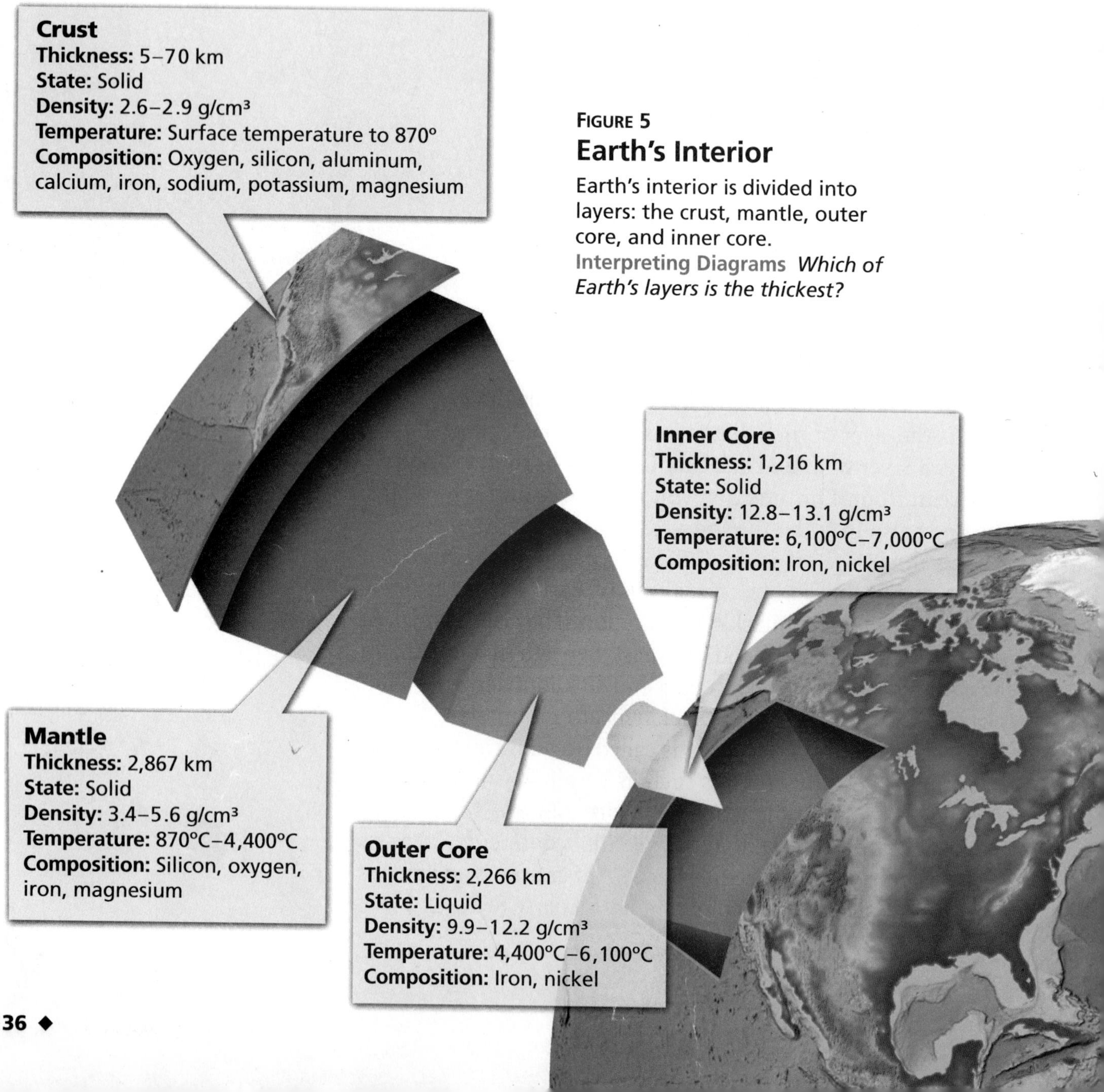

Crust
Thickness: 5–70 km
State: Solid
Density: 2.6–2.9 g/cm³
Temperature: Surface temperature to 870°
Composition: Oxygen, silicon, aluminum, calcium, iron, sodium, potassium, magnesium

FIGURE 5
Earth's Interior

Earth's interior is divided into layers: the crust, mantle, outer core, and inner core.
Interpreting Diagrams *Which of Earth's layers is the thickest?*

Inner Core
Thickness: 1,216 km
State: Solid
Density: 12.8–13.1 g/cm³
Temperature: 6,100°C–7,000°C
Composition: Iron, nickel

Mantle
Thickness: 2,867 km
State: Solid
Density: 3.4–5.6 g/cm³
Temperature: 870°C–4,400°C
Composition: Silicon, oxygen, iron, magnesium

Outer Core
Thickness: 2,266 km
State: Liquid
Density: 9.9–12.2 g/cm³
Temperature: 4,400°C–6,100°C
Composition: Iron, nickel

The Asthenosphere Below the cold, brittle lithosphere, your vehicle encounters material that is hotter and under increasing pressure. As a result, the part of the mantle just beneath the lithosphere is less rigid than the rock above. Like road tar softened by the heat of the sun, this part of the mantle is somewhat soft—it can bend like plastic. This soft layer is called the **asthenosphere** (as THEN uh sfeer). In Greek, *asthenes* means "weak." Although the asthenosphere is softer than the rest of the mantle, it's still solid. If you kicked it, you would stub your toe.

The Lower Mantle Beneath the asthenosphere, the mantle is solid. This solid material extends all the way to Earth's core.

Reading Checkpoint — **What is the asthenosphere?**

Lab zone Skills **Activity**

Creating Data Tables

Imagine that you are in a super-strong vehicle that is tunneling deep into Earth's interior. You stop several times on your trip to collect data. Copy the data table. For each depth, identify the layer and what that layer is made of. Then complete the table.

Data Table		
Depth	Name of Layer	What Layer Is Made Of
20 km		
150 km		
2,000 km		
4,000 km		
6,000 km		

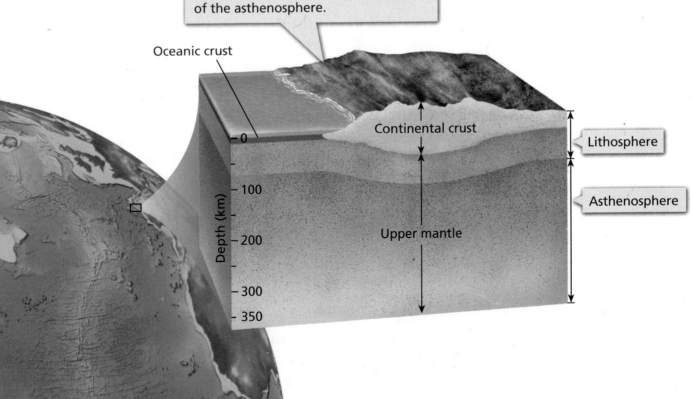

Lithosphere and Asthenosphere
The rigid lithosphere, which includes the crust, rests on the softer material of the asthenosphere.

Oceanic crust

Continental crust

Lithosphere

Asthenosphere

Upper mantle

Depth (km)

0

100

200

300

350

Math Analyzing Data

Temperature Inside Earth

The graph shows how temperatures change between Earth's surface and the bottom of the mantle. On this graph, the temperature at Earth's surface is 0°C. Study the graph carefully and then answer the questions.

1. **Reading Graphs** As you move from left to right on the *x*-axis, how does depth inside Earth change?

2. **Estimating** What is the temperature at the boundary between the lithosphere and the asthenosphere?

3. **Estimating** What is the temperature at the boundary between the lower mantle and the core?

4. **Interpreting Data** How does temperature change with depth in Earth's interior?

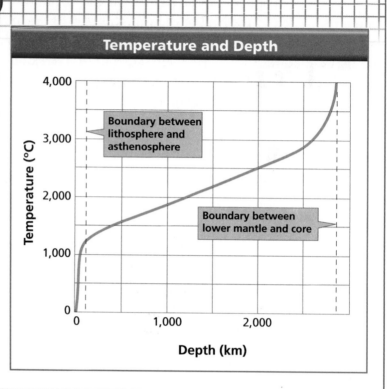

Temperature and Depth

Boundary between lithosphere and asthenosphere

Boundary between lower mantle and core

y-axis: Temperature (°C) — 0, 1,000, 2,000, 3,000, 4,000
x-axis: Depth (km) — 0, 1,000, 2,000

The Core

After traveling through the mantle, you reach Earth's dense, metallic core.  **The core is made mostly of the metals iron and nickel. It consists of two parts—a liquid outer core and a solid inner core.** Together, the inner and outer core are 3,486 kilometers thick.

Outer Core and Inner Core The **outer core** is a layer of molten metal that surrounds the inner core. Despite enormous pressure, the outer core is liquid. The **inner core** is a dense ball of solid metal. In the inner core, extreme pressure squeezes the atoms of iron and nickel so much that they cannot spread out and become liquid.

Most of the current evidence suggests that both parts of the core are made of iron and nickel. But scientists have found data showing that the core also contains substances such as oxygen, sulfur, and silicon. Scientists must seek more data before they decide which of these other substances is most abundant.

Reading Checkpoint What is the main difference between the outer core and the inner core?

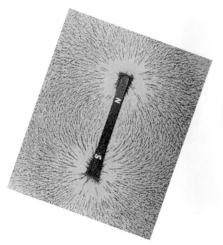

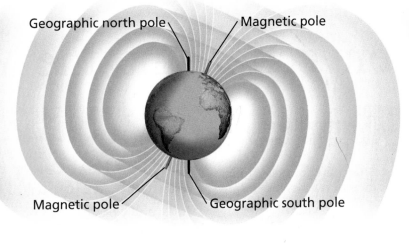

Geographic north pole

Magnetic pole

Magnetic pole

Geographic south pole

Bar Magnet's Magnetic Field
The pattern of iron filings was made by sprinkling them on paper placed under a bar magnet.

Earth's Magnetic Field
Like a magnet, Earth's magnetic field has north and south poles.

The Core and Earth's Magnetic Field Consider an ordinary bar magnet. If you place it on a piece of paper and sprinkle iron filings on the paper, the iron filings line up with the bar's magnetic field. Earth also has a magnetic field. If you could cover the entire planet with iron filings, they would form a similar pattern. In fact, the planet acts like a giant bar magnet. When you use a compass, the compass needle aligns with the lines of force in Earth's magnetic field.

Scientists think that movements in the liquid outer core create Earth's magnetic field. As you can see in Figure 6, the magnetic field affects the whole Earth.

FIGURE 6
Earth's Magnetic Field

Just as a bar magnet is surrounded by its own magnetic field, Earth's magnetic field surrounds the planet.
Relating Cause and Effect *If you shifted the magnet beneath the paper, what would happen to the iron filings?*

Section 1 Assessment

S 6.1.b, E-LA: Reading 6.1.0, Writing 6.2.1

Vocabulary Skill Use Greek Word Origins
Use what you know about the Greek words *asthenes* and *sphaira* to write the definition of *asthenosphere*.

Reviewing Key Concepts
1. a. **Explaining** Why is it difficult to determine Earth's inner structure?
   b. **Inferring** How are seismic waves used to provide evidence about Earth's interior?
2. a. **Listing** List Earth's three main layers.
   b. **Comparing and Contrasting** How are the lithosphere and the asthenosphere similar? How are they different?

c. **Classifying** Classify each of the following layers as liquid, rigid, or solid but able to flow slowly: lithosphere, asthenosphere, lower mantle, outer core, inner core.

Writing in Science

Narrative Write a narrative of your own imaginary journey to the center of Earth. Your narrative should describe the layers of Earth through which you travel and how temperature and pressure change beneath the surface.

Convection and the Mantle

CALIFORNIA
Standards Focus

S 6.4.c. Students know heat from Earth's interior reaches the surface primarily through convection.

- How is heat transferred?
- What causes convection currents?
- What causes convection currents in Earth's mantle?

Key Terms

- radiation
- conduction
- convection
- density
- convection current

Lab zone Standards **Warm-Up**

How Can Heat Cause Motion in a Liquid?

1. Carefully pour some hot water into a small, shallow pan. Fill a clear, plastic cup about half full with cold water. Place the cup in the pan.
2. Allow the water to stand for two minutes until all motion stops.
3. Fill a plastic dropper with some food coloring. Then, holding the dropper under the water's surface and slightly away from the edge of the cup, gently squeeze a small droplet of the food coloring into the water.
4. Observe the water for one minute.
5. Add another droplet at the water's surface in the middle of the cup and observe again.

Think It Over

Inferring How do you explain what happened to the droplets of food coloring? Why do you think the second droplet moved in a way that was different from the way the first droplet moved?

Earth's molten outer core is nearly as hot as the surface of the sun. What makes an object become hotter? Whether the object is Earth's core or a cooking pot, the cause is the same. When an object is heated, the particles that make up the object move faster. The faster-moving particles have more energy.

Have you ever touched a hot pot accidentally? If so, you have learned for yourself (in a painful way) that heat moves. In this case, it moved from the hot pot to your hand. The movement of energy from a warmer object to a cooler object is called heat transfer. To explain how heat moves from Earth's core through the mantle, you need to know how heat is transferred.

Types of Heat Transfer

Heat always moves from a warmer substance to a cooler substance. For example, holding an ice cube will make your hand begin to feel cold in a few seconds. But is the coldness in the ice cube moving to your hand? No! Cold is the absence of heat. It's the heat in your hand that moves to the ice cube. This is one of the ways that heat is transferred. 🔑 **There are three types of heat transfer: radiation, conduction, and convection.**

Radiation The transfer of energy through space is called **radiation.** Heat transfer by radiation takes place with no direct contact between a heat source and an object. Sunlight is radiation that warms Earth's surface. Other familiar forms of radiation include the heat you feel around a flame or open fire.

Conduction Heat transfer within a material or between materials that are touching is called **conduction.** For example, a spoon in a pot of soup heats up by conduction, as shown in Figure 7. Heat moves from the hot soup and the pot to the particles that make up the spoon. The particles near the bottom of the spoon vibrate faster as they are heated, so they bump into other particles and heat them, too. Gradually the entire spoon heats up. When your hand touches the spoon, conduction transfers heat from the spoon directly to your skin. Then you feel the heat. Conduction also causes an ice cube in your hand to melt. Conduction is responsible for some of the heat transfer inside Earth.

✓ **Reading Checkpoint** What is conduction?

FIGURE 7
Conduction
In conduction, the heated particles of a substance transfer heat through contact with other particles in the substance. Conduction heats the spoon and the pot itself. That's why you need a mitt to protect your hand from the hot handle.

Go Online
PHSchool.com

For: More on convection currents in the mantle
Visit: PHSchool.com
Web Code: cfd-1012

Convection Heat can also be transferred by the movement within fluids—liquids and gases. **Convection** is heat transfer by the movement of currents within a fluid. During convection, heated particles of fluid begin to flow. This flow transfers heat from one part of the fluid to another.

Heat transfer by convection is caused by differences of temperature and density within a fluid. **Density** is a measure of how much mass there is in a volume of a substance. For example, rock is more dense than water because a given volume of rock has more mass than the same volume of water.

When a liquid or gas is heated, the particles move faster and spread apart. As a result, the particles of the heated fluid occupy more space. The fluid's density decreases. But when a fluid cools, its particles move more slowly and settle together more closely. As the fluid becomes cooler, its density increases.

Convection Currents

When you heat soup on a stove, changes in density cause convection in the soup, as shown in Figure 8. As the soup at the bottom of the pot gets hot, it expands and therefore becomes less dense. The warm, less dense soup moves upward and floats over the cooler, denser soup. At the surface, the warm soup cools, becoming denser. Then gravity pulls this cooler, denser soup back down to the bottom of the pot, where it is heated again.

A constant flow begins as the cooler, denser soup sinks to the bottom of the pot and the warmer, less dense soup rises. A **convection current** is the flow that transfers heat within a fluid. 🔑 **Heating and cooling of the fluid, changes in the fluid's density, and the force of gravity combine to set convection currents in motion.** Convection currents continue as long as heat is added. Without heat, convection currents eventually stop.

✓ **Reading Checkpoint** **What is the role of gravity in creating convection currents?**

FIGURE 8
Convection Currents
Differences in temperature and density cause convection currents. In the pot, convection currents arise because the soup close to the heat source is hotter and less dense than the soup near the surface.

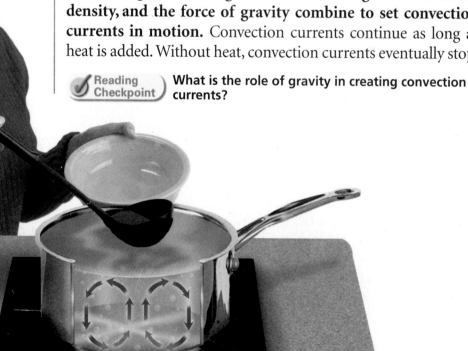

Convection Currents in Earth

In Earth's mantle, large amounts of heat are transferred by convection currents, as shown in Figure 9. 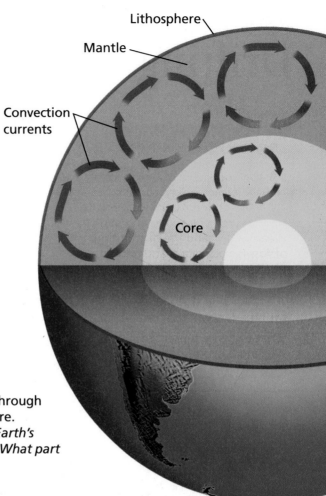 **Heat from the core and the mantle itself causes convection currents in the mantle.**

How can mantle rock flow? Recall that temperature increases steadily as you go deeper in the mantle. Rock in the lower mantle is hotter and therefore less dense than the rock above it. As a result, solid mantle rock rises slowly from the bottom of the mantle toward the top. The hot rock eventually cools and sinks back through the mantle. These cycles of rising and sinking take place over millions of years. Convection currents like these have been moving inside Earth for most of Earth's history.

Lithosphere

Mantle

Convection currents

Core

FIGURE 9
Mantle Convection
Convection currents rise and sink through the mantle and the liquid outer core.
Applying Concepts *What part of Earth's interior is like the soup in the pot? What part is like the burner on the stove?*

Section 2 Assessment

S 6.4.c; E-LA: Reading 6.1.0

Vocabulary Skill Use Greek Word Origins Use what you know about the Greek words *litho* and *sphaira* to write the definition of *lithosphere*.

Reviewing Key Concepts

1. a. Listing What are the three types of heat transfer?
   b. Explaining How is heat transferred through space?
2. a. Defining What is a convection current?
   b. Relating Cause and Effect In general, what happens to the density of a fluid as it becomes hotter?
   c. Summarizing Describe how convection currents form.
3. a. Identifying Name two layers of Earth in which convection currents take place.
   b. Relating Cause and Effect What causes convection currents in the mantle?
   c. Predicting What will happen to the convection currents in the mantle if Earth's interior eventually cools down? Explain.

Lab zone **At-Home Activity**

Tracing Heat Flow Convection currents may keep the air inside your home at a comfortable temperature. Air is made up of gases, so it is a fluid. Regardless of the type of home heating system, heated air circulates through a room by convection. You may have tried to adjust the flow of air in a stuffy room by opening a window. When you did so, you were making use of convection currents. With an adult family member, study how your home is heated. Look for evidence of convection currents.

Section 3
Drifting Continents

CALIFORNIA
Standards Focus

S 6.1.a Students know evidence of plate tectonics is derived from the fit of the continents; the location of earthquakes, volcanoes, and mid-ocean ridges; and the distribution of fossils, rock types, and ancient climatic zones.

- What was Alfred Wegener's hypothesis about the continents?
- What evidence supported Wegener's hypothesis?
- Why was Wegener's hypothesis rejected by most scientists of his day?

Key Terms
- continental drift
- Pangaea
- fossil

Lab zone Standards **Warm-Up**

How Are Earth's Continents Linked Together?

1. Find the oceans and the seven continents on a globe showing Earth's physical features.
2. How much of the globe is occupied by the Pacific Ocean? Does most of Earth's dry land lie in the Northern or Southern Hemisphere?
3. Find the points or areas where most of the continents are connected. Find the points at which several of the continents almost touch, but are not connected.
4. Examine the globe more closely. Find the great belt of mountains running from north to south along the western side of North and South America. Can you find another great belt of mountains on the globe?

Think It Over

Posing Questions What questions can you pose about how oceans, continents, and mountains are distributed on Earth's surface?

Five hundred years ago, the sea voyages of Columbus and other explorers changed the map of the world. The continents of Europe, Asia, and Africa were already known to mapmakers. Soon mapmakers were also showing the outlines of the continents of North and South America. Looking at these world maps, many people wondered why the coasts of several continents matched so neatly. For example, the coasts of Africa and South America look as if they could fit together like jigsaw-puzzle pieces. In the 1700s, geologists thought that the continents had always remained in the same place. But early in the 1900s, one scientist became curious about the matching shapes of the continents.

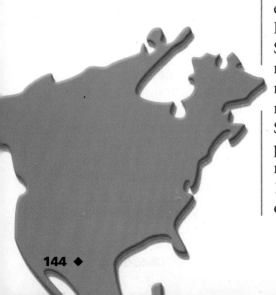

FIGURE 10
Continental Puzzle Today's continents provide clues about Earth's history.
Observing *Which coastlines of continents seem to match up like jigsaw-puzzle pieces? (Hint: Refer to the map in Figure 11.)*

Continental Drift

In 1910, a young German scientist named Alfred Wegener (VAY guh nur) attempted to solve the jigsaw puzzle of the continents. He hypothesized that Earth's continents had moved! **Wegener's hypothesis was that all the continents were once joined together in a single landmass and have since drifted apart.** Wegener's idea that the continents slowly moved over Earth's surface became known as **continental drift.**

According to Wegener, the continents drifted together to form the supercontinent **Pangaea** (pan JEE uh). *Pangaea* means "all lands." According to Wegener, Pangaea existed about 300 million years ago. This was the time when reptiles and winged insects first appeared. Tropical forests, which later formed coal deposits, covered large parts of Earth's surface.

Over tens of millions of years, Pangaea began to break apart. The pieces of Pangaea slowly moved toward their present-day locations. These pieces became the continents as they are today.

How did Wegener attempt to prove his amazing idea? **Wegener gathered evidence from different scientific fields to support his ideas about continental drift. He studied land features, fossils, and evidence of climate change.** In 1915, Wegener published his evidence for continental drift in a book called *The Origin of Continents and Oceans.*

Go Online
SciLINKS NSTA

For: Links on continental drift
Visit: www.SciLinks.org
Web Code: scn-1013

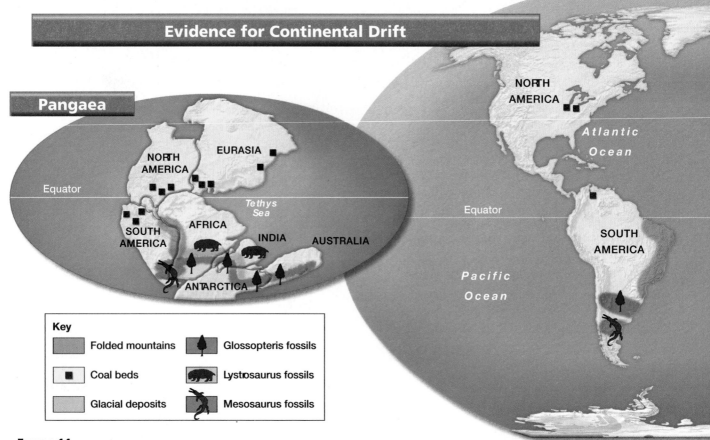

Evidence for Continental Drift

Pangaea

NORTH AMERICA

EURASIA

Equator

SOUTH AMERICA

AFRICA

INDIA

AUSTRALIA

Tethys Sea

ANTARCTICA

NORTH AMERICA

Atlantic Ocean

Equator

SOUTH AMERICA

Pacific Ocean

Key

Folded mountains

Coal beds

Glacial deposits

Glossopteris fossils

Lystrosaurus fossils

Mesosaurus fossils

FIGURE 11
Fossils and rocks found on different continents provide evidence that Earth's landmasses once were joined together in the supercontinent Pangaea.
Inferring What do the matching mountain ranges in Africa and South America show, according to Wegener's hypothesis?

Evidence From Land Features As shown in Figure 11, mountains and other features on the continents provided evidence for continental drift. For example, when Wegener pieced together maps of Africa and South America, he noticed that mountain ranges on both continents line up. He noticed that European coal fields match up with coal fields in North America.

Evidence From Fossils Wegener also used fossils to support his argument for continental drift. A **fossil** is any trace of an ancient organism that has been preserved in rock. For example, *Glossopteris* (glaw SAHP tuh ris), was a fernlike plant that lived 250 million years ago. *Glossopteris* fossils have been found in rocks in Africa, South America, Australia, India, and Antarctica. The occurrence of *Glossopteris* on these widely separated landmasses convinced Wegener that Pangaea had existed.

Other examples include fossils of the freshwater reptiles *Mesosaurus* and *Lystrosaurus*. These fossils have also been found in places now separated by oceans. Neither reptile could have swum great distances across salt water. Wegener inferred that these reptiles lived on a single landmass that has since split apart.

Lystrosaurus

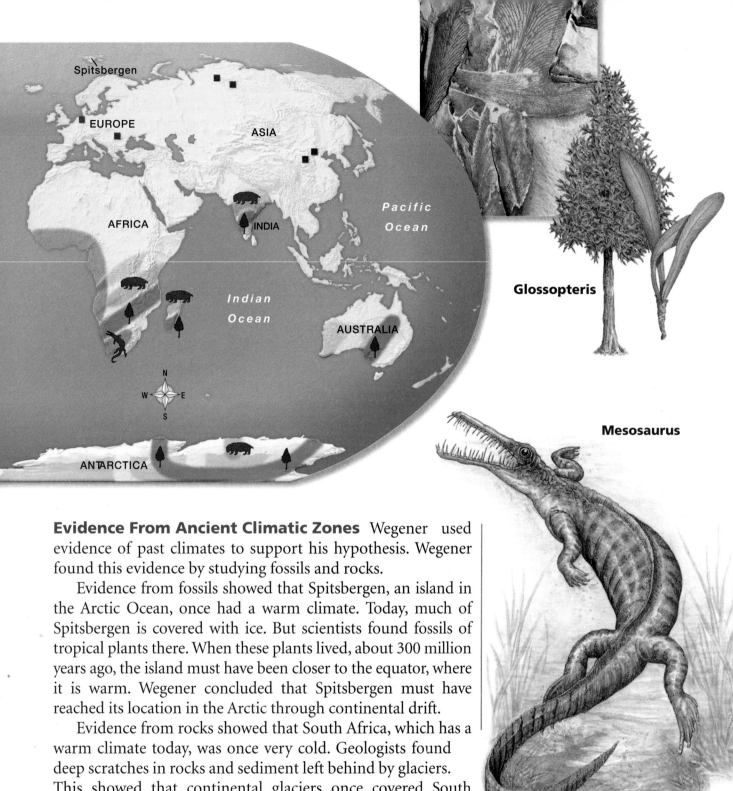

Glossopteris

Mesosaurus

Evidence From Ancient Climatic Zones Wegener used evidence of past climates to support his hypothesis. Wegener found this evidence by studying fossils and rocks.

Evidence from fossils showed that Spitsbergen, an island in the Arctic Ocean, once had a warm climate. Today, much of Spitsbergen is covered with ice. But scientists found fossils of tropical plants there. When these plants lived, about 300 million years ago, the island must have been closer to the equator, where it is warm. Wegener concluded that Spitsbergen must have reached its location in the Arctic through continental drift.

Evidence from rocks showed that South Africa, which has a warm climate today, was once very cold. Geologists found deep scratches in rocks and sediment left behind by glaciers. This showed that continental glaciers once covered South Africa. Continental glaciers are thick layers of ice that cover all or part of a continent. But the climate of South Africa is too mild today for continental glaciers to form. Wegener concluded that continental drift had moved South Africa away from the South Pole.

 **Reading Checkpoint** How would continental drift affect a continent's climate?

FIGURE 12
Alfred Wegener
Although scientists rejected his theory, Wegener continued to collect evidence on continental drift and to update his book until his death in 1930.

Wegener's Hypothesis Rejected

Wegener attempted to explain how continental drift took place. He suggested that the continents plowed across the ocean floors. **Unfortunately, Wegener could not provide a satisfactory explanation for the force that pushes or pulls the continents.** Because Wegener could not identify the cause of continental drift, most geologists rejected his idea. Geologists also rejected Wegener's idea because it contradicted their ideas about how mountains form.

More than 30 years would pass before geologists accepted new evidence that supported Wegener's ideas. In the early 1900s, many geologists thought that mountains formed because Earth was slowly cooling and shrinking. According to this hypothesis, mountains formed when the crust wrinkled like the skin of a dried-up apple.

Wegener said that if these geologists were correct, then mountains should be found all over Earth's surface. But mountains usually occur in narrow bands along the edges of continents. Wegener proposed that when continents collide, their edges crumple and fold. The folding continents push up huge mountains.

Section 3 Assessment

S 6.1.a; E-LA: Reading 6.2.0

Target Reading Skill Identify Supporting Evidence What supporting evidence did you include in your graphic organizer for the hypothesis of continental drift?

Reviewing Key Concepts

1. a. Identifying Who proposed the concept of continental drift?
   b. Summarizing According to the hypothesis of continental drift, how would a world map have changed over the last 250 million years?
2. a. Reviewing What evidence supported the hypothesis of continental drift?
   b. Explaining How did fossils provide evidence for continental drift?
   c. Forming Hypotheses Deposits of coal have been found beneath the ice of Antarctica. But coal only forms in warm swamps. Use Wegener's hypothesis to explain how coal could be found so near to the South Pole.

3. a. Explaining Why did most scientists reject Wegener's hypothesis of continental drift?
   b. Making Judgments Do you think the scientists of Wegener's time should have accepted his hypothesis? Why or why not?

Lab zone At-Home Activity

Moving the Continents Using a world map and tracing paper, trace the outlines of the continents that border the Atlantic Ocean. Label the continents. Then use scissors to carefully cut your map along the edges of the continents. Throw away the Atlantic Ocean. Place the two remaining pieces on a dark surface and ask family members to try to fit the two halves together. Explain to them about continental drift and Pangaea.

Sea-Floor Spreading

CALIFORNIA
Standards Focus

S 6.1.a Students know evidence of plate tectonics is derived from the fit of the continents; the location of earthquakes, volcanoes, and mid-ocean ridges; and the distribution of fossils, rock types, and ancient climatic zones.

🔑 What is the process of sea-floor spreading?

🔑 What is the evidence for sea-floor spreading?

🔑 What happens at deep-ocean trenches?

Key Terms
- mid-ocean ridge
- sonar
- sea-floor spreading
- deep-ocean trench
- subduction

Lab zone Standards **Warm-Up**

What Is the Effect of a Change in Density?

1. Partially fill a sink or dishpan with water.
2. Open up a dry washcloth in your hand. Does the washcloth feel light or heavy?
3. Moisten one edge of the washcloth in the water. Then gently place the washcloth so that it floats on the water's surface. Observe the washcloth carefully (especially at its edges) as it starts to sink.
4. Remove the washcloth from the water and open it up in your hand. Is the mass of the washcloth the same as, less than, or greater than when it was dry?

Think It Over

Observing How did the washcloth's density change? What effect did this change in density have on the washcloth?

Deep in the ocean, the temperature is near freezing. There is no light, and living things are generally scarce. Yet some areas of the deep-ocean floor are teeming with life. One of these areas is the East Pacific Rise. This area forms part of the Pacific Ocean floor off the coasts of Mexico and South America. Here, ocean water sinks through cracks, or vents, in the crust. The water is heated by contact with hot material from the mantle. The hot water then spurts back into the ocean.

Around these hot-water vents live some of the most bizarre creatures ever discovered. Giant, red-tipped tube worms sway in the water. Nearby sit giant clams nearly a meter across. Strange spider-like crabs scuttle by. Surprisingly, the geological features around hot water vents provided some of the best evidence for Wegener's hypothesis of continental drift.

FIGURE 13
The Deep-Ocean Floor
Shrimp, crabs, and other organisms cluster near hot water vents in the ocean floor.

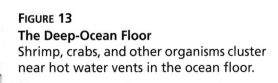

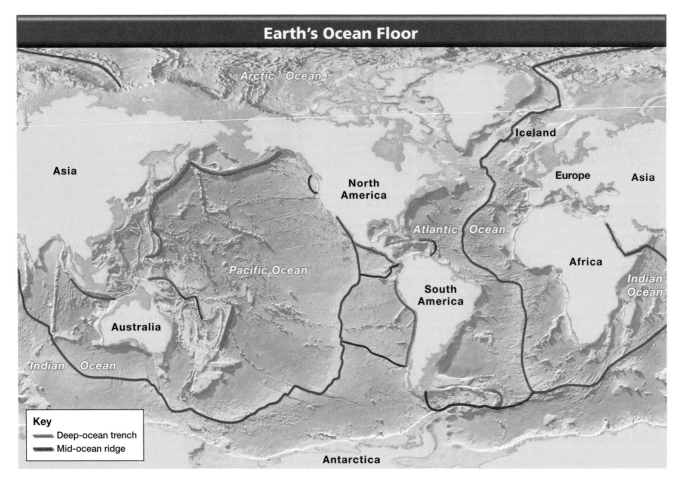

Earth's Ocean Floor

Key
- Deep-ocean trench
- Mid-ocean ridge

FIGURE 14
The mid-ocean ridge system is more than 50,000 kilometers long.
Interpreting Maps *What is unusual about Iceland?*

Mid-Ocean Ridges

The East Pacific Rise is just one of many mid-ocean ridges. A **mid-ocean ridge** is an undersea mountain chain that is part of a long system of mountains that winds beneath Earth's oceans. In the mid-1900s, scientists mapped the mid-ocean ridges using sonar. **Sonar** is a device that bounces sound waves off underwater objects and then records the echoes of these sound waves. The time it takes for the echo to arrive indicates the distance to the object.

Mid-ocean ridges curve like the seam of a baseball along the sea floor. They extend into all of Earth's oceans. Figure 14 shows the location of these ridges. Most of the mountains in the mid-ocean ridge system lie hidden under hundreds of meters of water. But in a few places the ridge pokes above the surface. For example, the island of Iceland is a part of the mid-ocean ridge. Iceland rises above the surface in the North Atlantic Ocean. A steep-sided valley splits the top of some ridges.

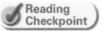 **Reading Checkpoint** **What device is used to map the ocean floor?**

What Is Sea-Floor Spreading?

The mapping of mid-ocean ridges made some scientists curious to know more about them. What are the ridges? How do they form? These scientists carefully examined maps of the mid-ocean ridge system. A few scientists began to think about the ocean floor in relation to the problem of continental drift. They began to think that maybe Wegener was right! Perhaps the continents do move.

In 1960, one geologist proposed a radical idea. He suggested that a process he called **sea-floor spreading** continually adds new material to the ocean floor. **In sea-floor spreading, the sea floor spreads apart along both sides of a mid-ocean ridge as new crust is added. As a result, the ocean floors move like conveyor belts, carrying the continents along with them.** Look at Figure 15 to see the process of sea-floor spreading.

Sea-floor spreading begins at a mid-ocean ridge, which forms along a crack in the oceanic crust. Along the ridge, molten material that forms several kilometers beneath the surface rises and erupts. At the same time, older rock moves outward on both sides of the ridge. As the molten material cools, it forms a strip of solid rock in the center of the ridge. When more molten material flows into the crack, it forms a new strip of rock.

Go Online
PHSchool.com

For: More on sea-floor spreading
Visit: PHSchool.com
Web Code: cfd-1014

FIGURE 15
Sea-Floor Spreading
Molten material erupts through the center of a mid-ocean ridge. This material hardens to form the rock of the ocean floor.
Applying Concepts *What happens to the rock along the ridge when new molten material erupts?*

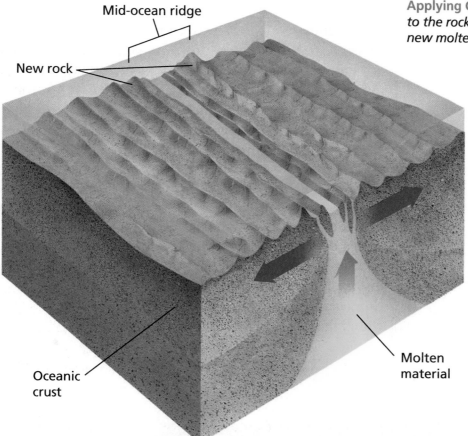

Mid-ocean ridge

New rock

Oceanic crust

Molten material

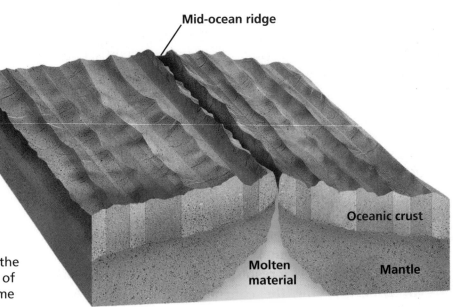
Mid-ocean ridge

Oceanic crust

Molten material

Mantle

Rock formed when Earth's magnetic field was normal

Rock formed when Earth's magnetic field was reversed

FIGURE 16
Magnetic Stripes
Magnetic stripes in the rock of the ocean floor show the direction of Earth's magnetic field at the time the rock hardened.
Interpreting Diagrams *How are these matching stripes evidence of sea-floor spreading?*

Evidence for Sea-Floor Spreading

🔑 **Several types of evidence supported the theory of sea-floor spreading: eruptions of molten material, magnetic stripes in the rock of the ocean floor, and the ages of the rocks themselves.** In the 1960s, this evidence led scientists to look again at Wegener's hypothesis of continental drift.

Evidence From Molten Material The scientists discovered evidence that new material is indeed erupting along mid-ocean ridges. The scientists dived to the ocean floor in *Alvin*, a small submarine. *Alvin* was built to withstand the crushing pressures four kilometers down in the ocean. In a ridge's central valley, *Alvin's* crew found strange rocks shaped like pillows. Other rocks looked like toothpaste squeezed from a tube. Such rocks form only when molten material hardens quickly under water. These rocks showed that molten material has erupted again and again along the mid-ocean ridges.

Evidence From Magnetic Stripes Patterns in the rocks of the ocean floor provided more support for sea-floor spreading. You read earlier that Earth behaves like a giant magnet, with a north pole and a south pole. Surprisingly, Earth's magnetic poles have reversed themselves many times during Earth's history. The last reversal happened 780,000 years ago. What if the magnetic poles suddenly reversed themselves today? You would find that your compass needle pointed south.

Scientists discovered that the rock that makes up the ocean floor lies in a pattern of magnetized "stripes," shown in Figure 16. These stripes hold a record of reversals in Earth's magnetic field. The rock of the ocean floor contains iron. The rock began as molten material that cooled and hardened. As the rock cooled, the iron bits inside lined up in the direction of Earth's magnetic poles. This locked the iron bits in place, giving the rocks a permanent "magnetic memory."

Scientists then used instruments to record the magnetic memory of rocks on both sides of a ridge. They found stripes of rock that formed when Earth's magnetic field pointed north. These stripes alternate with stripes of rock that formed when the magnetic field pointed south. Look at Figure 16. Notice how the pattern is the same on both sides of the ridge.

Evidence From Drilling Samples The final proof of sea-floor spreading came from rock samples obtained by drilling into the ocean floor. The *Glomar Challenger*, a drilling ship built in 1968, gathered the samples. The *Glomar Challenger* sent drilling pipes through water six kilometers deep to drill holes in the ocean floor. This feat has been compared to digging a hole into the sidewalk from the top of the Empire State Building.

Samples from the sea floor were brought up through the pipes. Then the scientists determined the age of the rocks in the samples. They found that the farther away from a ridge the samples were taken, the older the rocks were. The youngest rocks were always in the center of the ridges. This showed that sea-floor spreading really has taken place.

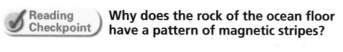

Reading Checkpoint — **Why does the rock of the ocean floor have a pattern of magnetic stripes?**

FIGURE 17
Sea-Floor Drilling
The *Glomar Challenger* was the first research ship designed to drill samples of rock from the deep-ocean floor.

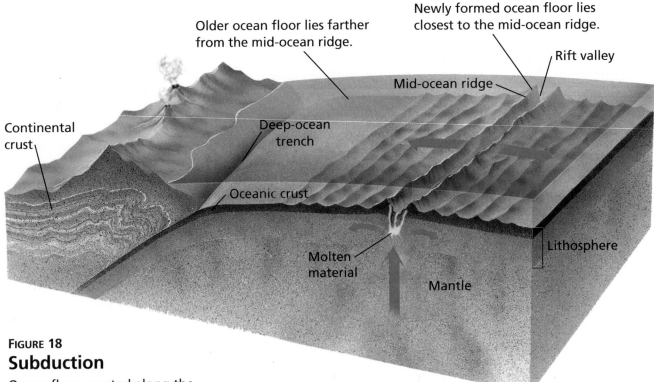

Older ocean floor lies farther from the mid-ocean ridge.

Newly formed ocean floor lies closest to the mid-ocean ridge.

Rift valley

Mid-ocean ridge

Continental crust

Deep-ocean trench

Oceanic crust

Molten material

Mantle

Lithosphere

FIGURE 18
Subduction
Ocean floor created along the mid-ocean ridge is destroyed at a deep-ocean trench. In the process of subduction, ocean floor sinks down beneath the trench into the mantle.
Drawing Conclusions *Where would the densest ocean floor be found?*

Subduction at Trenches

How can the ocean floor keep getting wider and wider? The answer is that the ocean floor generally does not just keep spreading. Instead, the ocean floor sinks beneath deep under-water canyons called **deep-ocean trenches.** At a deep-ocean trench, the ocean floor bends downward. What occurs at trenches? 🔑 **In a process taking tens of millions of years, part of the ocean floor sinks back into the mantle at deep-ocean trenches.**

The Process of Subduction The process by which the ocean floor sinks beneath a deep-ocean trench and back into the mantle is called **subduction** (sub DUK shun). During subduction, ocean floor closer to a mid-ocean ridge moves away from the ridge and toward a trench. Sea-floor spreading and subduction work together. They move the ocean floor as if it were on a giant conveyor belt.

New ocean floor is hot. But as it moves away from the mid-ocean ridge, it cools and becomes more dense. Eventually, as shown in Figure 18, gravity pulls this older, denser ocean floor down beneath the trench. The sinking ocean floor is like the washcloth in the Standards Warm-Up at the beginning of this section. As the dry washcloth floating on the water gets wet, its density increases and it begins to sink.

Subduction and Earth's Oceans Together, subduction and sea-floor spreading change the size and shape of the oceans. These processes renew the ocean floor about every 200 million years. That is the time it takes for new rock to form at a mid-ocean ridge, move across the ocean, and sink into a deep-ocean trench.

The vast Pacific Ocean covers almost one third of the planet. And yet it is shrinking. How can that be? The Pacific Ocean has many deep-ocean trenches around its edges. Subduction occurs through these trenches faster than new crust can be added. The result is that the width of the Pacific Ocean will gradually shrink over millions of years.

As you can see in Figure 19, the Atlantic Ocean is expanding. The main reason for this is that the Atlantic Ocean has only a few short trenches. As a result, most of the spreading ocean floor has nowhere to go. In most places, the oceanic crust of the Atlantic Ocean floor is attached to the continental crust of the continents around the ocean. So as the Atlantic's ocean floor spreads, the continents along its edges also move. Over time, the whole ocean gets wider.

FIGURE 19
Growing an Ocean
Because of sea-floor spreading, the distance between Europe and North America is increasing by a few centimeters per year.

 **Why is the Pacific Ocean shrinking?**

Section 4 Assessment

S 6.1.a, E-LA: Reading 6.2.0, Writing 6.2.2

Target Reading Skill Identify Supporting Evidence Create a graphic organizer for the theory of sea-floor spreading. What evidence did you include?

Reviewing Key Concepts

1. a. **Identifying** Along what feature of the ocean floor does sea-floor spreading begin?
   b. **Describing** How is new rock added to the ocean floor?
   c. **Sequencing** What are the steps in the process of sea-floor spreading?
2. a. **Reviewing** What three types of evidence provided support for the theory of sea-floor spreading?
   b. **Applying Concepts** How do rocks along the central valley of the mid-ocean ridge provide evidence of sea-floor spreading?
   c. **Predicting** Where would you expect to find the oldest rock on the ocean floor?
3. a. **Defining** What is a deep-ocean trench?
   b. **Relating Cause and Effect** What happens to oceanic crust at a deep-ocean trench?

Writing in Science

Description Write a description of what you might see if you could explore a mid-ocean ridge in a vessel like the *Alvin*. In your description, be sure to include the main features of the ocean floor along and near the ridge.

Modeling Sea-Floor Spreading

Materials

colored markers

2 sheets of
unlined paper

scissors

metric ruler

Problem

How does sea-floor spreading add material to the ocean floor?

Skills Focus

making models

Procedure

1. Draw stripes across one sheet of paper, parallel to the short sides of the paper. The stripes should vary in spacing and thickness.

2. Fold the paper in half lengthwise and write the word "Start" at the top of both halves of the paper. Using the scissors, carefully cut the paper in half along the fold line to form two strips.

3. Lightly fold the second sheet of paper into eighths. Then unfold it, leaving creases in the paper. Fold this sheet in half lengthwise.

4. Starting at the fold, draw lines 5.5 cm long on the middle crease and the two creases closest to the ends of the paper.

5. Now carefully cut along the lines you drew. Unfold the paper. There should be three slits in the center of the paper.

6. Put the two striped strips of paper together so their Start labels touch one another. Insert the Start ends of the strips up through the center slit and then pull them toward the side slits.

7. Insert the ends of the strips into the side slits. Pull the ends of the strips and watch what happens at the center slit.

8. Practice pulling the strips until you can make the two strips come up through the center and go down through the sides at the same time.

Analyze and Conclude

1. **Making Models** What feature of the ocean floor does the center slit stand for? What prominent feature of the ocean floor is missing from the model along the center slit?

2. **Making Models** What do the side slits stand for? What does the space under the paper stand for?

3. **Comparing and Contrasting** As shown by your model, how does the ocean floor close to the center slit differ from the ocean floor near a side slit? How does this difference affect the depth of the ocean?

4. **Making Models** What do the stripes on the strips stand for? Why is it important that your model have an identical pattern of stripes on both sides of the center slit?

5. **Applying Concepts** Explain how differences in density and temperature provide some of the force needed to cause sea-floor spreading and subduction.

6. **Communicating** Use your own words to describe the process of sea-floor spreading. What parts of the process were not shown by your model?

More to Explore

How could you modify your model to show an island that formed where a large amount of molten rock erupted from the mid-ocean ridge? How could you show what would happen to the island over a long period of time?

The Theory of Plate Tectonics

CALIFORNIA
Standards Focus

S 6.1.c. Students know lithospheric plates the size of continents and oceans move at rates of centimeters per year in response to movements in the mantle.

🔑 What is the theory of plate tectonics?

🔑 What are the three types of plate boundaries?

Key Terms
- plate
- plate tectonics
- fault
- spreading boundary
- rift valley
- colliding boundary
- sliding boundary

Lab zone Standards **Warm-Up**

How Well Do the Continents Fit Together?

1. Using a world map in an atlas, trace the shapes of the continents North America, South America, Africa, and Europe.
2. ✂ Carefully cut apart the landmasses.
3. Piece together these landmasses as they may have looked before Pangaea split apart, creating the Atlantic Ocean.
4. Attach your partial reconstruction of Pangaea to a piece of paper.
5. Obtain a map that shows the continental shelf. The continental shelf is the apron of continental crust that extends under water around the edges of the continents. Trace around the shelves of the same continents used in Step 1.
6. Repeat steps 2 through 4 to compare the fit of the continents with and without their continental shelves.

Think It Over

Drawing Conclusions Do your observations support the idea that the continents were once joined together? When did they fit together better: when you cut them out along their coastlines or along their continental shelves? Explain.

▼ A cracked eggshell

Have you ever dropped a hard-boiled egg? If so, the eggshell probably cracked in many places. Earth's lithosphere, its solid outer shell, is not one unbroken layer. It is more like that cracked eggshell. It's broken into jagged pieces.

There are cracks in the continents similar to those on the ocean floor. In the 1960s, scientists proposed that these cracks break the lithosphere into separate sections called **plates.** The plates fit together along cracks in the lithosphere. As shown in Figure 20, the plates carry the continents or parts of the ocean floor, or both. One scientist combined what geologists knew about sea-floor spreading, Earth's plates, and continental drift into a single theory. Recall that a scientific theory is a well-tested concept that explains a wide range of observations.

How Plates Move

The theory of **plate tectonics** (tek TAHN iks) states that pieces of Earth's lithosphere are in slow, constant motion, driven by convection currents in the mantle. 👁 **The theory of plate tectonics explains the formation, movement, and subduction of Earth's plates.**

What force is great enough to move Earth's heavy plates? Geologists think that movement of convection currents in the mantle is the major cause of plate motion. Mantle motion is transferred to the lithosphere at its boundary with the asthenosphere. The plates are carried along in much the same way that ice floats on slow-moving water. During subduction, gravity pulls one edge of a plate down into the mantle. The rest of the plate also moves. This slow movement is similar to what happens in a pot of soup when gravity causes the cooler, denser soup near the surface to sink.

As the plates move, they change Earth's surface. These changes include earthquakes, volcanoes, mountain ranges, and deep-ocean trenches.

FIGURE 20
Plate boundaries divide the lithosphere into large plates.
Interpreting Maps *Which plates include both continents and ocean floor?*

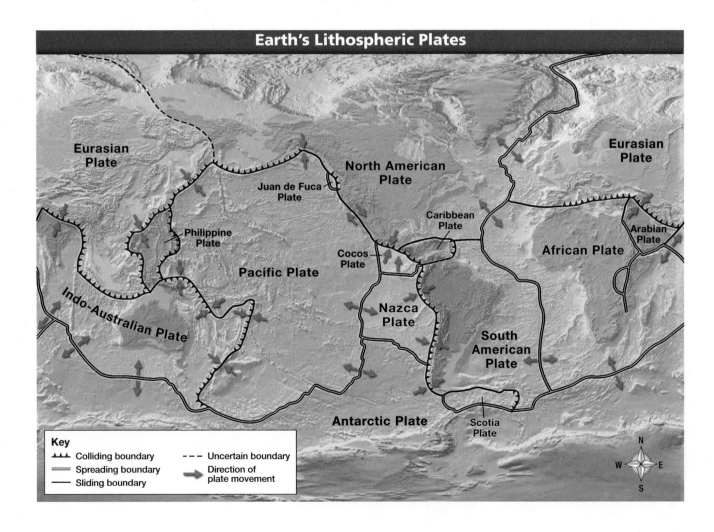

Earth's Lithospheric Plates

Eurasian Plate
North American Plate
Juan de Fuca Plate
Caribbean Plate
Eurasian Plate
Arabian Plate
Philippine Plate
Cocos Plate
African Plate
Pacific Plate
Indo-Australian Plate
Nazca Plate
South American Plate
Antarctic Plate
Scotia Plate

Key
- ▲▲▲ Colliding boundary
- ═══ Spreading boundary
- ─── Sliding boundary
- - - - Uncertain boundary
- → Direction of plate movement

N
W E
S

Plate Boundaries

The edges of Earth's plates meet at plate boundaries. Plate boundaries extend deep into the lithosphere. Faults form along these boundaries. **Faults** are breaks in Earth's crust where rocks have slipped past each other. 👁 **There are three kinds of plate boundaries: spreading boundaries, colliding boundaries, and sliding boundaries. A different type of plate movement occurs along each type of boundary.**

Scientists have used instruments on satellites to measure plate motion. The plates move about 1 to 24 centimeters per year in response to movements in the mantle. The North American and Eurasian plates are moving apart at a rate of 2.5 centimeters per year. That's about as fast as your fingernails grow. But these plates have been moving for millions of years.

Spreading Boundaries The place where two plates move apart is called a **spreading boundary.** Most spreading boundaries occur along the mid-ocean ridges where sea-floor spreading occurs. Spreading boundaries are also called divergent boundaries.

Spreading boundaries also occur on land. When a spreading boundary develops on land, two of Earth's plates slide apart. A deep valley called a **rift valley** forms along the spreading boundary. For example, the Great Rift Valley in East Africa marks a deep crack in the African continent.

FIGURE 21
Plate Tectonics

Plate movements have built many of the features of Earth's land surfaces and ocean floors.
Predicting *What will eventually happen if a rift valley continues to pull apart?*

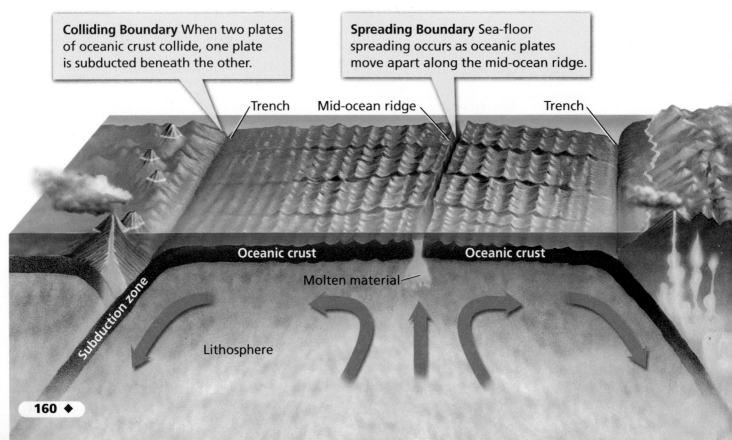

Colliding Boundary When two plates of oceanic crust collide, one plate is subducted beneath the other.

Spreading Boundary Sea-floor spreading occurs as oceanic plates move apart along the mid-ocean ridge.

Trench   Mid-ocean ridge   Trench

Oceanic crust   Oceanic crust

Molten material

Subduction zone

Lithosphere

Colliding Boundaries The place where two plates come together, or collide, is called a **colliding boundary.** Another term for colliding boundary is convergent boundary. When two plates collide, the density of the plates determines which one comes out on top. There are three types of collision between plates.

In the first type of collision, two plates made up of oceanic crust meet at a trench. The plate that is more dense sinks under the other plate. The reason for this is that oceanic crust becomes cooler and denser during sea-floor spreading.

In the second type of collision, an oceanic plate collides with a continental plate. Subduction occurs as the denser oceanic plate sinks beneath the less dense continental plate.

In the third type of collision, two plates carrying continental crust collide, but subduction does not take place. Neither piece of crust is dense enough to sink very far into the mantle. Instead, the collision squeezes the crust into mighty mountain ranges.

Sliding Boundaries A **sliding boundary** is a place where two plates slip past each other, moving in opposite directions. Along sliding boundaries, crust is neither created nor destroyed. Sliding boundaries can also be called transform boundaries.

 **Reading Checkpoint** What features form where two continental plates come together?

 **Math Skills**

Calculating a Rate
To calculate the rate of plate motion, divide the distance the plate moves by the time it takes to move that distance.

$$\text{Rate} = \frac{\text{Distance}}{\text{Time}}$$

For example, a plate takes 2 million years to move 156 km. Calculate its rate of motion.

$$\frac{156 \text{ km}}{2{,}000{,}000 \text{ years}} = 7.8 \text{ cm per year}$$

Practice Problem The Pacific plate is sliding past the North American plate. It has taken 10 million years for the plate to move 600 km. What is the Pacific plate's rate of motion?

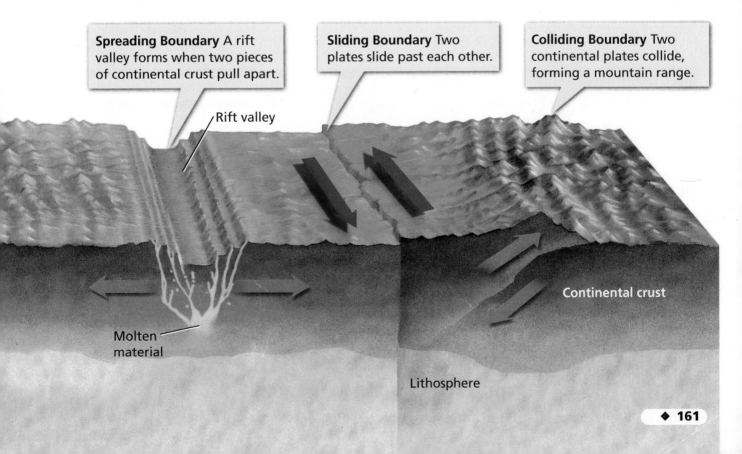

Spreading Boundary A rift valley forms when two pieces of continental crust pull apart.

Sliding Boundary Two plates slide past each other.

Colliding Boundary Two continental plates collide, forming a mountain range.

Rift valley

Molten material

Continental crust

Lithosphere

225 Million Years Ago

Plate Motions Over Time The movement of Earth's plates has greatly changed Earth's surface. Geologists have evidence that, before Pangaea existed, other supercontinents formed and split apart over billions of years. Pangaea itself formed when Earth's landmasses drifted together about 260 million years ago. Then, about 225 million years ago, Pangaea began to break apart. Figure 22 shows how major landmasses have moved since the breakup of Pangaea.

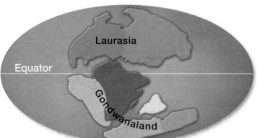

180–200 Million Years Ago

FIGURE 22
Continental Drift
Geologists have used computer modeling to trace the movements of the continents since the breakup of Pangaea. **Posing Questions** *What questions would you need to answer in order to predict where the continents will be in 50 million years?*

135 Million Years Ago

For: Continental Drift activity
Visit: PHSchool.com
Web Code: cfp-1015

Earth Today

Section 5 Assessment

S 6.1.c, E-LA: Reading 6.1.0

Vocabulary Skill Use Greek Word Origins This chapter is about the theory of plate tectonics. Use what you know about the Greek word origin of *tectonics* to explain the meaning of *plate tectonics*.

Reviewing Key Concepts

1. a. **Defining** What are plates?
   b. **Summarizing** What is the theory of plate tectonics?
   c. **Relating Cause and Effect** What do scientists think causes the movement of Earth's plates?
2. a. **Listing** What are the three types of plate boundaries?
   b. **Describing** Describe the type of movement that occurs at each type of plate boundary.
   c. **Predicting** What is likely to occur at a plate boundary where oceanic crust collides with continental crust?

Math Practice

3. **Calculating a Rate** There are two islands on opposite sides of a mid-ocean ridge in the Atlantic Ocean. During the last 8 million years, the distance between the islands has increased by 200 kilometers. Calculate the rate at which the two plates are moving apart.

Modeling Mantle Convection Currents

Materials

large bottle or container with tap water

small glass jar

red food coloring

aluminum foil or plastic wrap

rubber band

small pieces of paper or several paper hole punches

pencil

Problem
How might convection in Earth's mantle affect tectonic plates?

Skills Focus
making models, observing

Procedure

1. Fill the large jar about half full with cold tap water.

2. Partly fill the small jar with hot tap water and stir in 6 drops of food coloring. Carefully add enough hot water to fill the jar to the brim.

3. Cover the top of the jar with aluminum foil or plastic wrap and secure with a rubber band.

4. Carefully lower the jar into the bottle of tap water.

5. Place the pieces of paper on the surface of the water.

6. Without disturbing the water, use the tip of the pencil to make two small holes about 2–4 mm in diameter in the material covering the jar.

7. Predict what will happen to the colored water and to the pieces of paper floating on the surface.

8. Observe the contents of the jar, as well as the paper pieces on the surface of the water.

Analyze and Conclude

1. **Observing** Describe what happened to the colored water and to the pieces of paper after the holes were punched in the material covering the jar.

2. **Drawing Conclusions** How did your prediction compare with what actually happened to the colored water and pieces of paper?

3. **Inferring** What type of heat transfer took place in the bottle? Describe how the transfer occurred.

4. **Making Models** Which part of your model represents a tectonic plate? Which part represents Earth's mantle?

5. **Communicating** How well do you think this lab modeled the movement of Earth's plates? What similarities exist between this model and actual plate movement? What factors weren't you able to model in this lab?

Design an Experiment

Repeat this activity, but develop a plan to measure the temperature of the water inside the large jar. Is there a difference in temperature between the water's surface and the water near the top of the small jar? Do you observe any change in the convection currents as the water temperature changes? With your teacher's approval, carry out your plan.

Study Guide

 **The BIG Idea** Earth's plates are large pieces of the lithosphere that move slowly, producing faults, mountain ranges, volcanoes, and deep-ocean trenches.

1 Earth's Interior

Key Concepts S 6.1.b

- Geologists have used two main types of evidence to learn about Earth's interior: direct evidence from rock samples and indirect evidence from seismic waves.

- The three main layers of Earth are the crust, the mantle, and the core. These layers vary greatly in size, composition, temperature, and pressure.

- The crust is a layer of solid rock that includes both dry land and the ocean floor.

- Earth's mantle is made up of rock that is very hot, but solid. Scientists divide the mantle into layers based on physical characteristics.

- The core is made mostly of the metals iron and nickel. It consists of two parts—a liquid outer core and a solid inner core.

Key Terms
- seismic waves • pressure • crust • mantle
- lithosphere • asthenosphere • outer core
- inner core

2 Convection and the Mantle

Key Concepts S 6.4.c

- There are three types of heat transfer: radiation, conduction, and convection.

- Heating and cooling of the fluid, changes in the fluid's density, and the force of gravity combine to set convection currents in motion.

- Heat from the core and the mantle itself causes convection currents in the mantle.

Key Terms
- radiation • conduction • convection
- density • convection current

3 Drifting Continents

Key Concepts S 6.1.a

- Wegener's hypothesis was that all the continents had once been joined together in a single landmass and have since drifted apart.

- Wegener gathered evidence from different scientific fields to support his ideas about continental drift. He studied land features, fossils, and evidence of climate change.

- Wegener could not provide a satisfactory explanation for the force that pushes or pulls the continents.

Key Terms
- continental drift • Pangaea • fossil

4 Sea-Floor Spreading

Key Concepts S 6.1.a

- In sea-floor spreading, the sea floor spreads apart along both sides of a mid-ocean ridge as new crust is added. As a result, the ocean floors move like conveyor belts, carrying the continents along with them.

- Several types of evidence supported the theory of sea-floor spreading: eruptions of molten material, magnetic stripes in the rock of the ocean floor, and the ages of the rocks.

- In a process taking tens of millions of years, part of the ocean floor sinks back into the mantle at deep-ocean trenches.

Key Terms
- mid-ocean ridge • sonar • sea-floor spreading
- deep-ocean trench • subduction

5 The Theory of Plate Tectonics

Key Concepts S 6.1.c

- The theory of plate tectonics explains the formation, movement, and subduction of Earth's plates.

- There are three kinds of plate boundaries: spreading boundaries, colliding boundaries, and sliding boundaries. A different type of plate movement occurs along each.

Key Terms
- plate • plate tectonics • fault
- spreading boundary • rift valley
- colliding boundary • sliding boundary

Review and Assessment

Target Reading Skill

Identify Supporting Evidence
Complete the graphic organizer on the theory of plate tectonics.

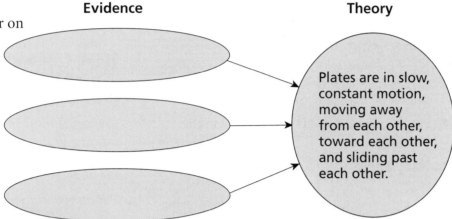

The Theory of Plate Tectonics

Evidence

Theory

Plates are in slow, constant motion, moving away from each other, toward each other, and sliding past each other.

Reviewing Key Terms

Choose the letter of the best answer.

1. The relatively soft layer of the upper mantle is the
   a. asthenosphere.   **b.** lithosphere.
   c. inner core.   **d.** continental crust.

2. The transfer of heat by the direct contact of particles of matter is
   a. pressure.
   b. radiation.
   c. conduction.
   d. convection.

3. Subduction of the ocean floor takes place at
   a. the lower mantle.   **b.** mid-ocean ridges.
   c. rift valleys.   **d.** trenches.

4. The process that powers plate tectonics is
   a. radiation.
   b. convection.
   c. conduction.
   d. subduction.

5. Two plates crash into each other at
   a. a spreading boundary.
   b. a colliding boundary.
   c. the boundary between the mantle and the crust.
   d. a sliding boundary.

Complete the following sentences so that your answers clearly explain the key terms.

6. Granite is one of the main rocks that makes up **continental crust,** which is _____ .

7. Heat is transferred in the mantle by **convection currents,** which are _____ .

8. Continental drift formed the landmass called **Pangaea,** which was _____ .

9. Oceanic crust returns to the mantle at **deep-ocean trenches,** which are _____ .

10. A rift valley forms at a **spreading boundary,** which is _____ .

Writing in Science

Prediction Now that you have learned about the theory of plate tectonics, write a paragraph predicting what the shape and positions of Earth's continents will be 50 million years in the future.

Video Assessment
Discovery Channel School
Plate Tectonics

Review and Assessment

Checking Concepts

11. What kinds of indirect evidence do geologists use to study the structure of Earth?

12. How do temperature and pressure change as you go deeper into Earth?

13. What happens in Earth's interior to produce Earth's magnetic field? Describe the layer where the magnetic field is produced.

14. Why are there convection currents in the mantle?

15. How do magnetic stripes form on the ocean floor? Why are these stripes significant?

16. What type of geologic feature will form where two continental plates collide? Explain.

Thinking Critically

17. **Comparing and Contrasting** How are oceanic and continental crust alike? How do they differ?

18. **Sequencing** Place these terms in correct order so they begin at Earth's surface and move toward the center: inner core, asthenosphere, lower mantle, lithosphere, outer core.

19. **Predicting** In the diagram below, a plate of oceanic crust is colliding with a plate of continental crust. What will happen? Why?

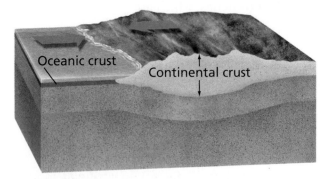

20. **Relating Cause and Effect** What do many geologists think is the driving force of plate tectonics? Explain.

21. **Making Judgments** Scientists refer to plate tectonics as a *theory*. What is a theory? How is plate tectonics a theory? Why isn't continental drift considered a theory? (*Hint*: Refer to the Skills Handbook for more on theories.)

Math Practice

22. **Calculating a Rate** It takes 100,000 years for a plate to move about 14 kilometers. Calculate the rate of plate motion.

Applying Skills

Use the map to answer Questions 23–25.

Geologists think that a new plate boundary is forming in the Indian Ocean. The part of the plate carrying Australia is twisting away from the part of the plate carrying India.

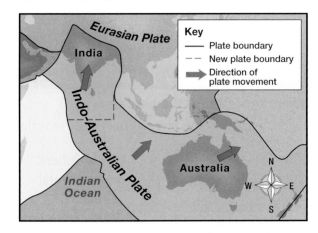

23. **Interpreting Maps** In what direction is the part of the plate carrying Australia moving? In what direction is the part carrying India moving?

24. **Predicting** As India and Australia move in different directions, what type of plate boundary will form between them?

25. **Inferring** What features could occur where the northern part of the Indo-Australian plate is colliding with the Eurasian plate?

Lab zone Standards Investigation

Performance Assessment Present your model to the class. Point out the types of plate boundaries on your model. Discuss the plate motions and landforms that result in these areas.

Choose the letter that best answers the question or completes the statement.

1. An island on the Pacific plate moves a distance of 550 cm in 50 years. What is the plate's rate of speed?
   A 44 cm per year
   B 110 cm per year
   C 2,750 cm per year
   D 11 cm per year

   S 6.1.c

2. The subduction of oceanic crust beneath continental crust occurs because
   A continental crust is denser than oceanic crust.
   B oceanic crust is denser than continental crust.
   C the heavy mountains on continental crust push the oceanic crust down.
   D oceanic crust is warmer than continental crust.

   S 6.1.c

3. Which statement best explains how convection currents can occur in Earth's mantle?
   A The mantle is made up of hot liquid.
   B The mantle is made of hot but solid rock that can flow slowly.
   C The density of rock increases as temperature increases in the mantle.
   D Earth's rotation causes mantle convection.

   S 6.1.b

4. Which of the following is evidence for sea-floor spreading?
   A matching patterns of magnetic stripes in the ocean floor
   B volcanic eruptions along mid-ocean ridges
   C older rock found farther from mid-ocean ridges
   D all of the above

   S 6.1.a

5. Wegener thought the continents moved because fossils of the same organisms are found on widely separated continents. Wegener's use of fossil evidence is an example of a(n)
   A prediction.
   B observation.
   C inference.
   D controlled experiment.

   S 6.1.a

6. In Earth's outer core heat is transferred mainly by
   A seismic waves.
   B radiation.
   C conduction.
   D convection currents.

   S 6.4.c

7. Which of the following best describes the process in the diagram below?
   A Colliding plates form a transform boundary.
   B Colliding plates form volcanoes.
   C Spreading plates form a mid-ocean ridge.
   D Spreading plates form a rift valley.

   S 6.1.c

Apply the BIG Idea

8. Today, the Mediterranean Sea lies between Europe and Africa. But the African plate is moving toward the Eurasian plate at a rate of a few centimeters per year. Predict how this area will change in 100 million years. In your answer, first explain how the Mediterranean Sea will change. Then explain what will happen on land.

   S 6.1.c

Chapter 5

Earthquakes

An earthquake destroyed this freeway in Oakland, California, in 1989. ▶

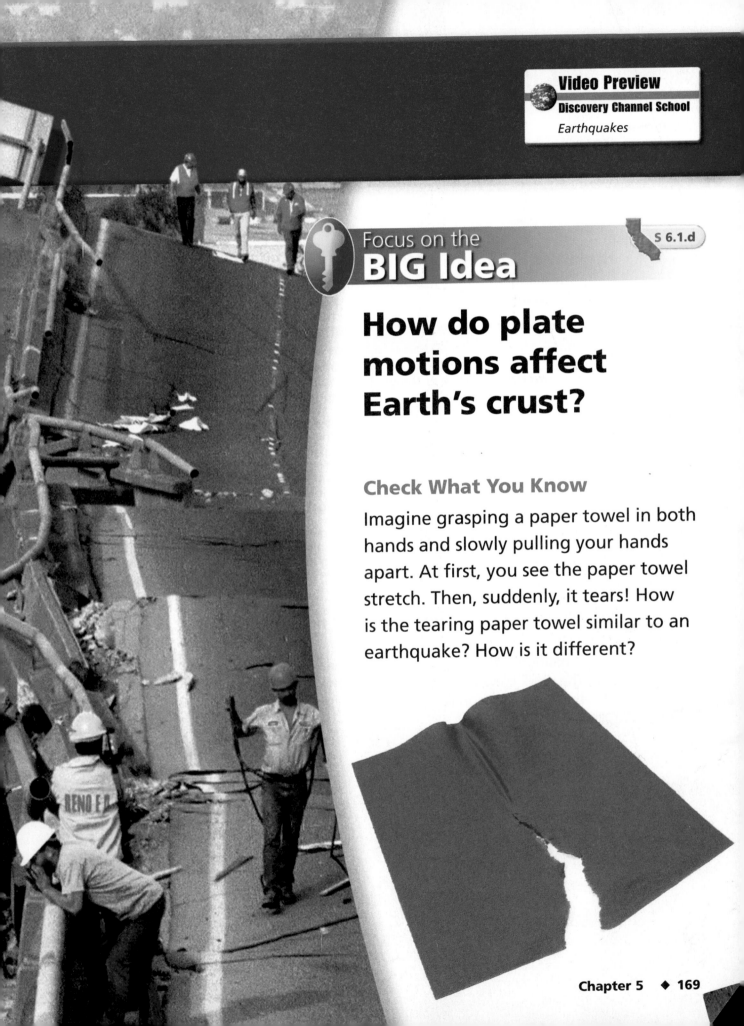

S 6.1.d

Focus on the
BIG Idea

How do plate motions affect Earth's crust?

Check What You Know

Imagine grasping a paper towel in both hands and slowly pulling your hands apart. At first, you see the paper towel stretch. Then, suddenly, it tears! How is the tearing paper towel similar to an earthquake? How is it different?

Build Science Vocabulary

The images shown here represent some of the key terms in this chapter. You can use this vocabulary skill to help you understand the meaning of some key terms in this chapter.

High-Use Academic Words

High-use academic words are words that are used frequently in academic reading, writing, and discussions.

Word	Definition	Example Sentence
category (KAT uh gawr ee) p. 184	*n.* A class or group of things	The books on the shelf are separated into two <u>categories</u>—math and science.
construct (kun STRUCT) p. 205	*v.* To build	The goal was to <u>construct</u> a building that would stand up during an earthquake.
expand (ek SPAND) p. 185	*v.* To spread out	The experiment <u>expanded</u> into a long-term scientific investigation.
method (METH ud) p. 186	*n.* A way or system of doing things	Writing a letter and sending an e-mail are two <u>methods</u> of sharing information.

Apply It!

From the list above, choose the word that best completes the sentence.

1. A balloon will _____ until it breaks.
2. The work crew will _____ the bridge to be safe during an earthquake.

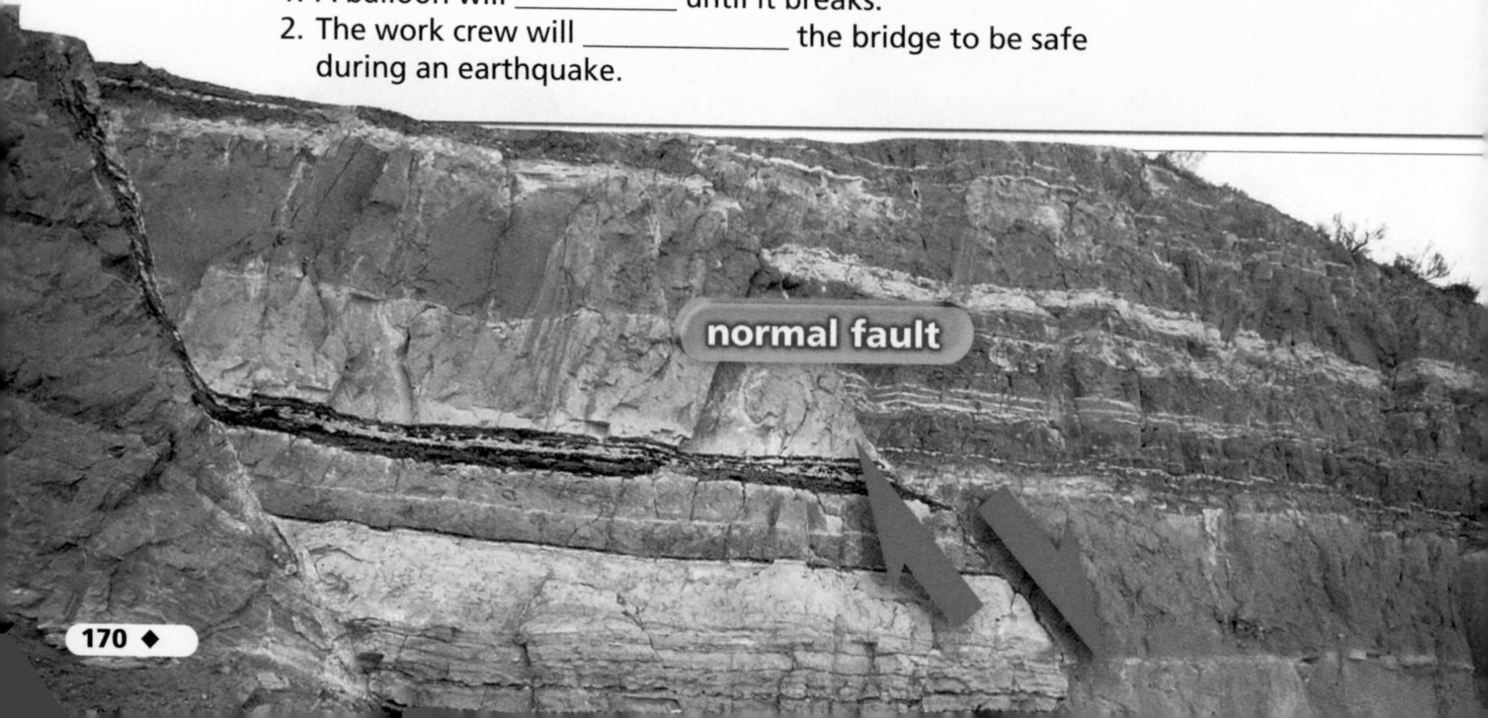

normal fault

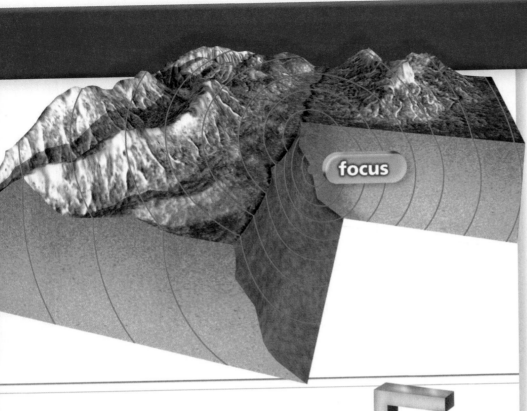

Chapter 5 Vocabulary

focus

seismogram

tsunami

Build Science Vocabulary
Online
Visit: PHSchool.com
Web Code: cwj-2050

How to Read Science

Reading Skill

TARGET SKILL Identify Main Idea

The main idea in a paragraph is the most important, or biggest, idea. Sometimes the main idea is stated directly. At other times you must identify the main idea yourself.

Here are some tips.

- Look at the heading or subheading.
- Read carefully the first and last few sentences in the paragraph.
- Identify the main idea of the paragraph.
- Identify a few important details about the topic.

Read the paragraph below. Then identify the main idea. In your notebook, write the main idea in the first box and a few supporting details and examples in the boxes under it.

Earthquake-Safe House

There are ways to make a house safer before an earthquake occurs. Supporting brick chimneys with metal brackets adds strength. Fastening bookshelves and cabinets to wood in the wall keeps them from falling. Adding plywood boards to walls strengthens them.

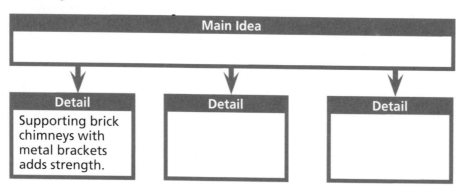

Main Idea

Detail	Detail	Detail
Supporting brick chimneys with metal brackets adds strength.		

Apply It!

Look for main ideas and supporting details in paragraphs in this chapter.

S 6.1.g

Design and Build an Earthquake-Safe House

Earthquakes are proof that our planet is subject to great forces from within. Earthquakes remind us that we live on the moving pieces of Earth's crust. In this chapter you will design a structure that can withstand earthquakes.

Your Goal

To design, build, and test a model structure that is earthquake resistant

Your structure must

- be made of materials that have been approved by your teacher
- be built to specifications agreed on by your class
- be able to withstand several "earthquakes" of increasing intensity
- be built following the safety guidelines in Appendix A

Plan It!

Before you design your model, find out how earthquakes damage structures such as homes, office buildings, and highways. Preview the chapter to find out how engineers design structures to withstand earthquakes. Then choose materials for your structure and sketch your design. When your teacher has approved your design, build and test your structure.

Forces in Earth's Crust

CALIFORNIA
Standards Focus

S 6.1.e Students know major geologic events, such as earthquakes, volcanic eruptions, and mountain building, result from plate motions.

S 6.1.f Students know how to explain major features of California geology (including mountains, faults, and volcanoes) in terms of plate tectonics.

🔑 How does stress in the crust change Earth's surface?

🔑 Where are faults usually found, and why do they form?

🔑 What land features result from the forces of plate movement?

Key Terms

- stress
- tension
- compression
- shearing
- normal fault
- hanging wall
- footwall
- reverse fault
- strike-slip fault
- plateau

Lab zone | Standards **Warm-Up**

How Does Stress Affect Earth's Crust?

1. Put on your goggles.
2. Holding a popsicle stick at both ends, slowly bend it into an arch.
3. Release the pressure on the popsicle stick and observe what happens.
4. Repeat Steps 1 and 2. This time, however, keep bending the ends of the popsicle stick toward each other. What happens to the wood?

Think It Over

Predicting Think of the popsicle stick as a model for part of Earth's crust. What do you think might eventually happen as the forces of plate movement bend the crust?

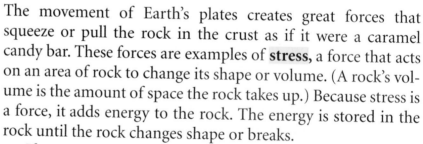

The movement of Earth's plates creates great forces that squeeze or pull the rock in the crust as if it were a caramel candy bar. These forces are examples of **stress,** a force that acts on an area of rock to change its shape or volume. (A rock's volume is the amount of space the rock takes up.) Because stress is a force, it adds energy to the rock. The energy is stored in the rock until the rock changes shape or breaks.

If you try to break a caramel candy bar in two, it may only bend and stretch at first. Like a candy bar, many types of rock can bend or fold. But beyond a certain limit, even these rocks will break.

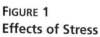

FIGURE 1
Effects of Stress
Powerful forces in Earth's crust caused the ground beneath this athletic field in Taiwan to change its shape.

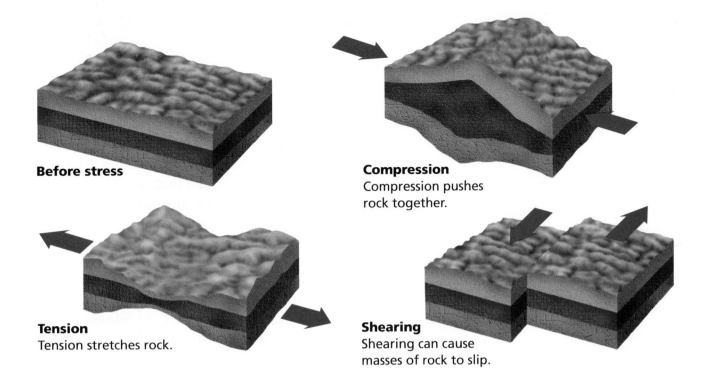

Before stress

Compression
Compression pushes rock together.

Tension
Tension stretches rock.

Shearing
Shearing can cause masses of rock to slip.

Types of Stress

Three different kinds of stress can occur in the crust—tension, compression, and shearing. 🔑 **Tension, compression, and shearing work over millions of years to change the shape and volume of rock.** Stress causes some rocks to become brittle and snap. Other rocks bend slowly, like road tar softened by the sun. Figure 2 shows how stress affects the crust.

Most changes in the crust occur so slowly that they cannot be observed directly. But if you could speed up time so a billion years passed by in minutes, you would see the crust bend, stretch, break, tilt, fold, and slide. The slow shift of Earth's plates causes these changes.

Tension The type of stress called **tension** pulls on the crust, stretching rock so that it becomes thinner in the middle. The effect of tension on rock is somewhat like pulling apart a piece of warm bubble gum. Tension occurs where two plates are moving apart.

Compression A type of stress called **compression** squeezes rock until it folds or breaks. One plate pushing against another can compress rock like a giant trash compactor.

Shearing Stress that pushes a mass of rock in two opposite directions is called **shearing.** Shearing can cause rock to break and slip apart or to change its shape.

 **Reading Checkpoint** How does shearing affect rock in Earth's crust?

FIGURE 2
Stress in Earth's Crust
Stress pushes, pulls, or twists the rocks in Earth's crust.
Relating Cause and Effect
Which type of stress tends to shorten part of the crust?

Kinds of Faults

When enough stress builds up in rock, the rock breaks, creating a fault. Recall that a fault is a break in the rock of the crust where rock surfaces slip past each other. The rocks on both sides of a fault can move up or down or sideways. ⊙ **Most faults occur along plate boundaries, where the forces of plate motion push or pull the crust so much that the crust breaks. There are three main types of faults: normal faults, reverse faults, and strike-slip faults.**

Normal Faults Tension in Earth's crust pulls rock apart, causing **normal faults.** In a normal fault, the fault is at an angle, so one block of rock lies above the other block of rock. The block of rock that lies above is called the **hanging wall.** The rock that lies below is called the **footwall.** Look at Figure 3 to see how the hanging wall lies above the footwall. When movement occurs along a normal fault, the hanging wall slips downward. Normal faults occur where plates diverge, or pull apart. For example, normal faults are found along the Owens Valley in California where Earth's crust is under tension.

FIGURE 3
Kinds of Faults

There are three main kinds of faults: normal faults, reverse faults, and strike-slip faults.
Inferring Which half of a normal fault would you expect to form the floor of a valley? Why?

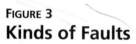

Key

➡ Force deforming the crust

➤ Movement along the fault

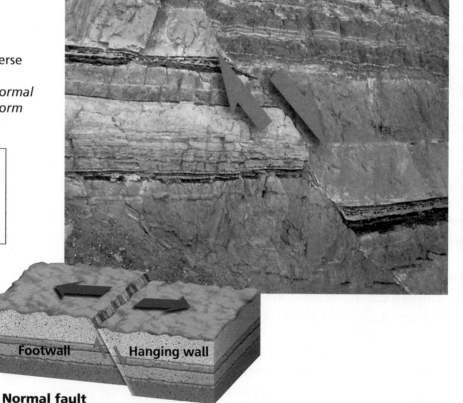

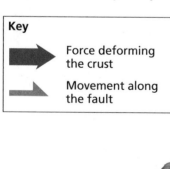

Footwall   Hanging wall

Normal fault
In a normal fault, the hanging wall slips down relative to the footwall.

Reverse Faults In places where the rock of the crust is pushed together, compression causes reverse faults to form. A **reverse fault** has the same structure as a normal fault, but the blocks move in the opposite direction. Look at Figure 3 to see how the rocks along a reverse fault move. As in a normal fault, one side of a reverse fault lies at an angle above the other side. However, in a reverse fault, the rock forming the hanging wall slides up and over the footwall. Movement along reverse faults produced part of the northern Rocky Mountains in the western United States and Canada. Reverse faults also helped produce the Klamath Mountains in northern California.

Strike-Slip Faults In places where plates move past each other, shearing creates strike-slip faults. In a **strike-slip fault,** the rocks on either side of the fault slip past each other sideways, with little up or down motion. A strike-slip fault that forms the boundary between two plates is called a sliding boundary. The San Andreas fault in California is an example of a strike-slip fault that is a sliding boundary.

Go Online
SCi LINKS™ NSTA

For: Links on faults
Visit: www.SciLinks.org
Web Code: scn-1021

✓ Reading Checkpoint   **What is the difference between a hanging wall and a footwall?**

Footwall   Hanging wall

Reverse fault
In a reverse fault, the hanging wall moves up relative to the footwall.

Strike-slip fault
Rocks on either side of a strike-slip fault, such as the San Andreas fault (above), slip past each other.

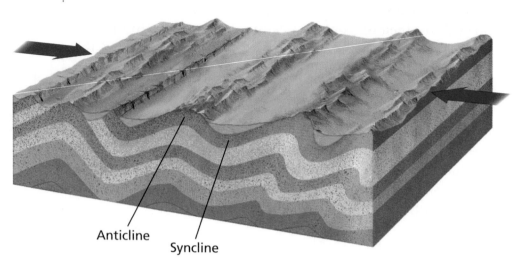

FIGURE 4
Effects of Folding
Compression and folding of the crust produce anticlines, which arch upward, and synclines, which dip downward. Over millions of years, folding can push up high mountain ranges.
Predicting If the folding in the diagram continued, what kind of fault might form?

Anticline

Syncline

Changing Earth's Surface

The forces produced by the movement of Earth's plates can fold, stretch, and uplift the crust.  **Over millions of years, the forces of plate movement can change a flat plain into landforms produced by folding, stretching, and uplifting Earth's crust. These landforms include anticlines and synclines, folded mountains, fault-block mountains, and plateaus.**

Folding Earth's Crust Sometimes plate movement causes the crust to fold. Have you ever skidded on a rug that wrinkled up as your feet pushed it across the floor? Much as the rug wrinkles, rock stressed by compression may bend without breaking. Folds are bends in rock that form when compression shortens and thickens part of Earth's crust. A fold can be only a few centimeters across or hundreds of kilometers wide. You can often see small folds in the rock exposed where a highway has been cut through a hillside.

Geologists use the terms anticline and syncline to describe upward and downward folds in rock. A fold in rock that bends upward into an arch is an anticline, shown in Figure 4. A fold in rock that bends downward to form a valley is a syncline. Anticlines and synclines are found in many places where compression forces have folded the crust.

The collision of two plates can cause compression and folding of the crust over a wide area. Folding produced some of the world's largest mountain ranges, such as the Himalayas in Asia and the Alps in Europe. The mountains in California's northern Coast Range are partly the result of folding.

Lab zone Try This **Activity**

Modeling Stress
You can model the stresses that create faults.

1. Knead a piece of plastic putty until it is soft.
2. Push the ends of the putty toward the middle.
3. Pull the ends apart.
4. Push half of the putty one way and the other half in the opposite direction.

Classifying Which step in this activity models the type of stress that would produce anticlines and synclines?

 **Reading Checkpoint** What is an anticline?

Stretching Earth's Crust When two normal faults cut through a block of rock, a fault-block mountain forms. You can see a diagram of this process in Figure 5. How does this process begin? Where two plates move away from each other, tension forces create many normal faults. When two of these normal faults form parallel to each other, a block of rock is left lying between them. As the hanging wall of each normal fault slips downward, the block in between moves upward, forming a fault-block mountain. The Panamint Range, which forms the western side of Death Valley, is an example of a fault-block mountain range in California.

If you traveled by car from Salt Lake City to Los Angeles, you would cross the Great Basin. This region contains many ranges of fault-block mountains separated by broad valleys, or basins. This "basin and range" region covers much of Nevada and western Utah. The region extends into California's Mojave Desert and the area east of the Sierra Nevada.

FIGURE 5
Fault-Block Mountains
As tension forces pull the crust apart, two parallel normal faults can form a range of fault-block mountains.

Key

Tension forces in the crust

Movement along normal fault

Normal fault

Normal fault

Normal fault

FIGURE 6

The Kaibab Plateau
The flat land on the horizon is the Kaibab Plateau, which forms the North Rim of the Grand Canyon in Arizona. The Kaibab Plateau is part of the Colorado Plateau.

Uplifting Earth's Crust The forces that raise mountains can also uplift, or raise, plateaus. A **plateau** is a large area of flat land elevated high above sea level. Some plateaus form when forces in Earth's crust push up a large, flat block of rock. Like a fancy sandwich, a plateau consists of many different flat layers, and is wider than it is tall.

Forces deforming the crust uplifted the Colorado Plateau in the "Four Corners" region of Arizona, Utah, Colorado, and New Mexico. Much of the Colorado Plateau lies more than 1,500 meters above sea level. Figure 6 shows one part of that plateau in northern Arizona.

Section 1 Assessment

S 6.1.e, 6.1.f; E-LA: Reading 6.2.0

⟳ **Target Reading Skill** Identify Main Ideas
Review the text under Types of Stress. Identify three details that support the main idea that different types of stress can occur in Earth's crust.

🔑 **Reviewing Key Concepts**

1. **a. Reviewing** What are the three main types of stress in rock?
   b. Relating Cause and Effect How does tension change the shape of Earth's crust?
   c. Comparing and Contrasting Compare the way that compression affects the crust to the way that tension affects the crust.
2. **a. Describing** What is a fault?
   b. Explaining Why do faults often occur along plate boundaries?
   c. Relating Cause and Effect What type of fault is formed when plates diverge, or pull apart? What type of fault is formed when plates are pushed together?

3. **a. Listing** Name five kinds of landforms caused by plate movement.
   b. Relating Cause and Effect What are three landforms produced by compression in the crust? What landform is produced by tension?

Lab zone **At-Home Activity**

Modeling Faults To model Earth's crust, roll modeling clay into layers and then press the layers together to form a rectangular block. Use a plastic knife to slice through the block at an angle, forming a fault. Explain which parts of your model represent the land surface, the hanging wall, and the footwall. Then show the three ways in which the sides of the fault can move.

Section 2
Earthquakes and Seismic Waves

CALIFORNIA
Standards Focus

S 6.1.d Students know that earth-quakes are sudden motions along breaks in the crust called faults and that volcanoes and fissures are locations where magma reaches the surface.

S 6.1.g Students know that the effects of an earthquake on any region vary, depending on the size of the earthquake, the distance of the region from the epicenter, the local geology, and the type of construction in the region.

- How does the energy of an earthquake travel through Earth?
- What are the scales used to measure the strength of an earthquake?
- How do scientists locate the epicenter of an earthquake?

Key Terms
- earthquake
- focus
- epicenter
- P wave
- S wave
- surface wave
- Mercalli scale
- magnitude
- Richter scale
- seismograph
- moment magnitude scale

Lab zone Standards **Warm-Up**

How Do Seismic Waves Travel?

1. Stretch a spring toy across the floor while a classmate securely holds the other end. Do not stretch the toy too much.
2. Have a third classmate measure and record the distance along the stretched-out toy.
3. Gather together about four coils of the spring toy and release them. Observe the coils' motion. Repeat this step, having a classmate use a stopwatch to time one wave's movement along the spring toy, and then record the time.
4. Jerk one end of the toy from side to side once. Observe the coils' motion. Repeat this step, again having a classmate time and record one wave's movement. (Keep the distance along the spring toy the same as in Step 3).

Think It Over
Calculating Calculate the speed of the waves in Steps 3 and 4. (*Hint:* Divide the distance along the spring toy by the time the wave took to travel that distance.) Which type of wave traveled faster? How can you explain this difference?

Earth is never still. Every day, worldwide, there are several thousand earthquakes. An **earthquake** is the shaking that results from the sudden movement of rock along a fault. Most earthquakes are too small to notice. But a large earthquake can change Earth's surface and cause great damage.

The forces of plate movement cause earthquakes. Plate movements produce stress in Earth's crust, adding energy to rock and forming faults. Stress increases along a fault until the rock breaks. An earthquake begins. In seconds, the earthquake releases a large amount of stored energy.

Most earthquakes begin in the lithosphere within about 100 kilometers of Earth's surface. The **focus** (FOH kus) is the area beneath Earth's surface where rock that is under stress breaks, triggering an earthquake. The point on the surface directly above the focus is called the **epicenter** (EP uh sen tur).

Types of Seismic Waves

Like a pebble thrown into a pond, an earthquake produces vibrations called waves. These waves carry energy as they travel outward. During an earthquake, seismic waves race out from the focus in all directions. Seismic waves are vibrations that travel through Earth carrying the energy released during an earthquake. **Seismic waves carry energy from an earthquake away from the focus, through Earth's interior, and across the surface.** That's what happened in 2002, when a powerful earthquake ruptured the Denali fault in Alaska, shown in Figure 7.

There are three main categories of seismic waves: P waves, S waves, and surface waves. An earthquake sends out two types of waves from its focus: P waves and S waves. When these waves reach Earth's surface at the epicenter, surface waves develop.

FIGURE 7
Seismic Waves

This diagram shows an earthquake along the Denali fault. An earthquake occurs when rocks fracture deep in the crust. The seismic waves move out in all directions from the focus. **Interpreting Diagrams** *At what point do seismic waves first reach the surface?*

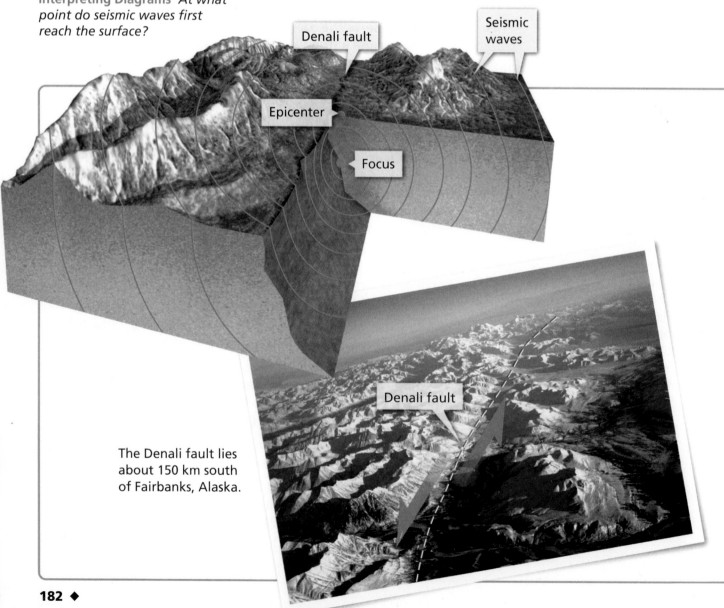

Denali fault

Seismic waves

Epicenter

Focus

Denali fault

The Denali fault lies about 150 km south of Fairbanks, Alaska.

P Waves The first waves to arrive are primary waves, or P waves, shown in Figure 7. **P waves** are seismic waves that compress and expand the ground like an accordion. Like the other types of seismic waves, P waves can damage buildings. P waves can move through solids and liquids.

S Waves After P waves come secondary waves, or S waves. **S waves** are seismic waves that vibrate from side to side as well as up and down. They shake the ground back and forth. When S waves reach the surface, they shake structures violently. Unlike P waves, S waves cannot move through liquids.

Surface Waves When P waves and S waves reach the surface, some of them become surface waves. **Surface waves** move more slowly than P waves and S waves, but they can produce severe ground movements. Some surface waves make the ground roll like ocean waves. Other surface waves shake buildings from side to side.

Reading Checkpoint Which type of seismic wave causes the ground to roll like ocean waves?

Go Online
active.art

For: Seismic Waves activity
Visit: PHSchool.com
Web Code: cfp-1022

P waves ▼
The crust vibrates forward and back along the path of the wave.

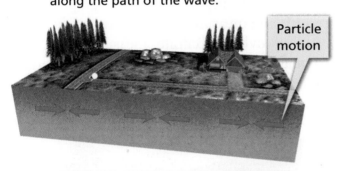

Particle motion

Direction of waves ⟶

S waves ▼
The crust vibrates from side to side and up and down.

Particle motion

Direction of waves ⟶

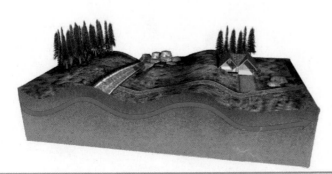

◄ **Surface waves**
The ground surface rolls with a wavelike motion.

Measuring Earthquakes

When an earthquake occurs, people want to know "How big was the quake?" **There are three commonly used methods of measuring earthquakes: the Mercalli scale, the Richter scale, and the moment magnitude scale.**

The Mercalli Scale The **Mercalli scale** was developed to rate earthquakes according to their intensity, or strength at a given place. The 12 steps of the Mercalli scale, shown in Figure 9, describe the levels of damage an earthquake can cause. The same earthquake can have different Mercalli ratings because its intensity varies at different locations.

For example, an earthquake's intensity generally decreases with distance from the epicenter. This happens because Earth materials absorb some of the waves' energy. Also, the earthquake's energy spreads over a wider area as the waves move out from the epicenter.

The Richter Scale An earthquake's **magnitude** is a number that geologists assign to an earthquake based on the earthquake's size. Geologists determine magnitude by measuring the seismic waves and fault movement that occur during an earthquake. The **Richter scale** assigns a magnitude number to an earthquake based on the size of seismic waves. The seismic waves are measured by a **seismograph.** A seismograph is an instrument that records and measures seismic waves.

The Richter scale provides accurate measurements for small, nearby earthquakes. But it does not work well for large or distant earthquakes.

Slight Damage

Moderate Damage

FIGURE 8
Levels of Earthquake Damage
The level of damage caused by an earthquake varies depending on the magnitude of the earthquake and the distance from the epicenter.

Great Destruction

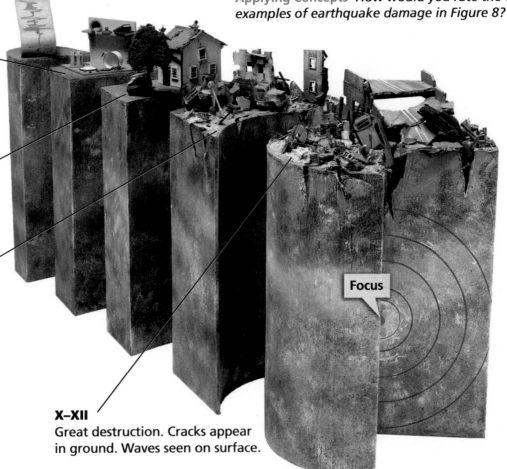

FIGURE 9
The Mercalli Scale
The Mercalli scale uses Roman numerals to rank earthquakes by how much damage they cause.
Applying Concepts *How would you rate the three examples of earthquake damage in Figure 8?*

I–III
People notice vibrations like those from a passing truck. Unstable objects disturbed.

IV–VI
Slight damage. People run outdoors.

VII–IX
Moderate to heavy damage. Buildings jolted off foundations or destroyed.

X–XII
Great destruction. Cracks appear in ground. Waves seen on surface.

Focus

The Moment Magnitude Scale Geologists today often use the **moment magnitude scale,** a rating system that estimates the total energy released by an earthquake. The moment magnitude scale can be used to rate earthquakes of all sizes, near or far. You may hear news reports that mention the Richter scale. But the number they quote is almost always the moment magnitude for that earthquake.

To rate an earthquake on the moment magnitude scale, geologists first study data from seismographs. They also use data on how much movement occurred along the fault and the strength of the rocks that broke when the fault slipped.

 **Reading Checkpoint** What evidence do geologists use to rate an earthquake on the moment magnitude scale?

Lab zone **Skills Activity**

Classifying
Classify the earthquake damage at these locations using the Mercalli scale.

1. Many buildings are destroyed; cracks form in the ground.
2. Several old brick buildings and a bridge collapse.
3. Canned goods fall off shelves; walls crack; people go outside to see what's happening.

Comparing Earthquakes An earthquake's magnitude tells geologists how much stored energy was released by the earthquake. Magnitude values can range from near zero to between 9.0 and 10.0. For each one number increase in magnitude, ground shaking increases by a factor of 10. But for each one number increase in magnitude, the amount of energy released increases by a factor of about 30! A magnitude 8 quake releases 30 times as much energy as a magnitude 7 quake, and about 1,000,000 times as much as a magnitude 4 quake.

The effects of an earthquake increase with magnitude. People scarcely notice earthquakes with magnitudes below 3. Earthquakes with a magnitude below 5 are small and cause little damage. Those with a magnitude between 5 and 6 can cause moderate damage. Earthquakes with a magnitude above 6 can cause great damage. Fortunately, the most powerful earthquakes, with a magnitude of 8 or above, are rare.

FIGURE 10
Collecting Seismic Data
This geologist is checking data collected after an earthquake. These data can be used to pinpoint the epicenter of an earthquake.

Locating the Epicenter

Geologists use seismic waves to locate an earthquake's epicenter. Seismic waves travel at different speeds. P waves arrive at a seismograph first, with S waves following close behind. To tell how far the epicenter is from the seismograph, scientists measure the difference between the arrival times of the P waves and S waves. The farther away an earthquake is, the greater the time between the arrival of the P waves and the S waves.

Math: Mathematical Reasoning 6.2.4

Math ▸ Analyzing Data

Seismic Wave Speeds

Seismographs at five observation stations recorded the arrival times of the P and S waves produced by an earthquake. These data are shown in the graph.

1. **Reading Graphs** What variable is shown on the *x*-axis of the graph? The *y*-axis?

2. **Reading Graphs** How long did it take the S waves to travel 2,000 km?

3. **Estimating** How long did it take the P waves to travel 2,000 km?

4. **Calculating** What is the difference in the arrival times of the P waves and the S waves at 2,000 km? At 4,000 km?

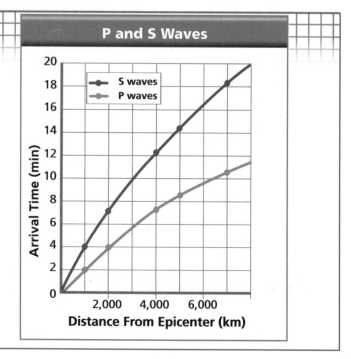

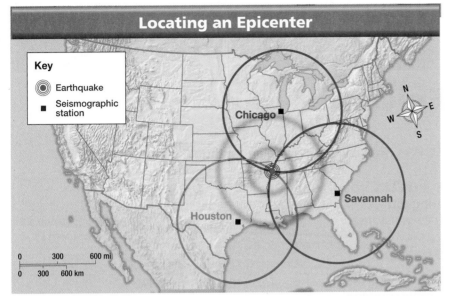

Locating an Epicenter

Key
- ◎ Earthquake
- ■ Seismographic station

Chicago

Savannah

Houston

| 0 | 300 | 600 mi |
| 0 | 300 | 600 km |

FIGURE 11
The map shows how to find the epicenter of an earthquake using data from three seismographic stations. **Measuring** *Use the map scale to determine the distances from Savannah and Houston to the epicenter. Which is closer?*

Geologists then draw at least three circles using data from different seismographs set up at stations all over the world. The center of each circle is a particular seismograph's location. The radius of each circle is the distance from that seismograph to the epicenter. As you can see in Figure 11, the point where the three circles intersect is the location of the epicenter.

 **Reading Checkpoint** What do geologists measure to determine the distance from a seismograph to an epicenter?

Section 2 Assessment

S 6.1.d, 6.1.g; E-LA: Reading 6.1.0, Writing 6.2.1

Vocabulary Skill High-Use Academic Words
Explain the difference between *expand* and *compress* in the following sentence: P waves are seismic waves that compress and expand the ground.

Reviewing Key Concepts

1. a. **Reviewing** How does energy from an earthquake reach Earth's surface?
   b. **Describing** What kind of movement is produced by each of the three types of seismic waves?
   c. **Sequencing** When do P waves arrive at the surface in relation to S waves and surface waves?
2. a. **Defining** What is magnitude?
   b. **Describing** How is magnitude measured using the Richter scale?
   c. **Applying Concepts** What are the advantages of using the moment magnitude scale to measure an earthquake?

3. a. **Explaining** What type of data do geologists use to locate an earthquake's epicenter?
   b. **Interpreting Maps** Study the map in Figure 11 above. Then describe the method that scientists use to determine the epicenter of an earthquake.

Writing in Science

News Report As a television news reporter, you are covering an earthquake rated between IV and V on the Mercalli scale. Write a short news story describing the earthquake's effects. Your lead paragraph should tell *who, what, where, when,* and *how.* (*Hint:* Refer to Figure 9 for examples of earthquake damage.)

Finding the Epicenter

Materials

drawing compass
with pencil

outline map of
the United States

Problem How can you locate an earthquake's epicenter?

Skills Focus
interpreting data,
drawing conclusions

Procedure

1. Make a copy of the data table showing differences in earthquake arrival times.

Data Table		
City	Difference in P and S Wave Arrival Times	Distance to Epicenter
Denver, Colorado	2 min 40 s	
Houston, Texas	1 min 50 s	
Chicago, Illinois	1 min 10 s	

2. The graph shows how the difference in arrival time between P waves and S waves depends on the distance from the epicenter of the earthquake. Find the difference in arrival time for Denver on the *y*-axis of the graph. Follow this line across to the point at which it crosses the curve. To find the distance to the epicenter, read down from this point to the *x*-axis of the graph. Enter this distance in the data table.

3. Repeat Step 2 for Houston and Chicago.

4. Set your compass at a radius equal to the distance from Denver to the earthquake epicenter that you previously recorded in your data table.

5. Draw a circle with the radius determined in Step 4, using Denver as the center. Draw the circle on your copy of the map. (*Hint:* Draw your circles carefully. You may need to draw some parts of the circles off the map.)

6. Repeat Steps 4 and 5 for Houston and Chicago.

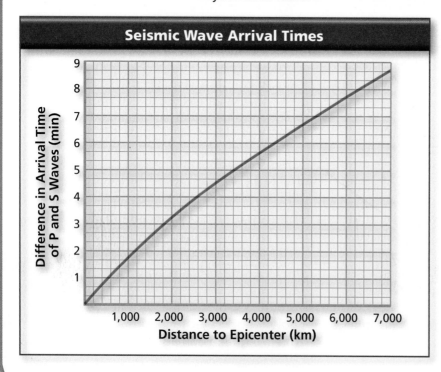

Seismic Wave Arrival Times

Difference in Arrival Time of P and S Waves (min)

Distance to Epicenter (km)

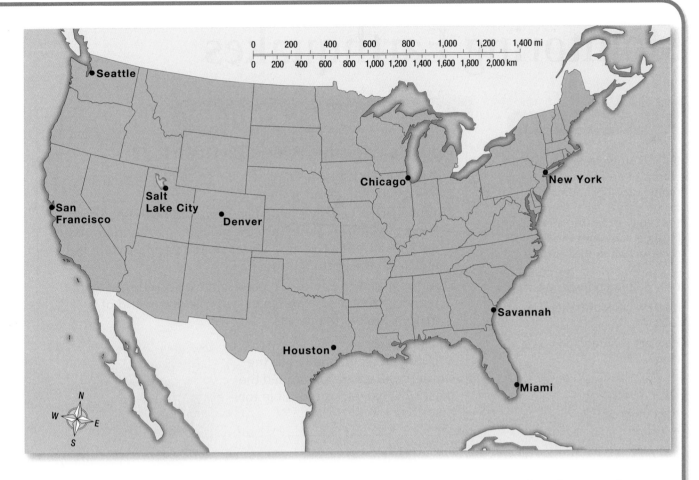

Analyze and Conclude

1. **Drawing Conclusions** Observe the three circles you have drawn. Where is the earthquake's epicenter?

2. **Measuring** Which city on the map is closest to the earthquake epicenter? How far, in kilometers, is this city from the epicenter?

3. **Inferring** In which of the three cities listed in the data table would seismographs detect the earthquake first? Last?

4. **Estimating** About how far from San Francisco is the epicenter that you found? What would be the difference in arrival times of the P waves and S waves for a recording station in San Francisco?

5. **Interpreting Data** What happens to the difference in arrival times between P waves and S waves as the distance from the earthquake increases?

6. **Communicating** Review the procedure you followed in this lab and then answer the following question. When you are trying to locate an epicenter, why is it necessary to know the distance from the epicenter for at least three recording stations?

More to Explore

You have just located an earthquake's epicenter. Find this earthquake's location on the map of Earthquake Risk in the United States (Figure 18). What is the risk of earthquakes in the area of this quake?

Now look at the map of Earth's Lithospheric Plates (Figure 22 in the chapter "Plate Tectonics"). What conclusions can you draw from this map about the cause of earthquakes in this area?

Monitoring Earthquakes

CALIFORNIA
Standards Focus

S 6.1.g Students know that the effects of an earthquake on any region vary, depending on the size of the earthquake, the distance of the region from the epicenter, the local geology, and the type of construction in the region.

🔑 How do seismographs work?

🔑 How do geologists monitor faults?

🔑 How are seismographic data used?

Key Terms
- seismogram
- friction

Lab zone Standards **Warm-Up**

How Can Seismic Waves Be Detected?

1. ✂ Using scissors, cut 4 plastic stirrers in half. Each piece should be about 5 cm long.
2. Your teacher will give you a pan containing gelatin. Gently insert the 8 stirrer pieces into the gelatin, spacing them about 2–3 cm apart in a row. The pieces should stand upright, but not touch the bottom of the pan.
3. At the opposite end of the pan from the stirrers, gently tap the surface of the gelatin once with the eraser end of a pencil. Observe the results.

Think It Over
Inferring What happened to the stirrer pieces when you tapped the gelatin? What was responsible for this effect?

Look at the beautiful vase in the photo. You might be surprised to learn that the vase is actually a scientific instrument. Can you guess what it was designed to do? Zhang Heng, an astronomer, designed and built this earthquake detection device in China nearly 2,000 years ago. It is said to have detected an earthquake centered several hundred kilometers away.

Earthquakes are dangerous, so people want to monitor them. To *monitor* means to "watch closely." Like the ancient Chinese, many societies have used technology to determine when and where earthquakes have occurred. During the late 1800s, scientists developed seismographs that were much more sensitive and accurate than any earlier devices.

FIGURE 12
Earthquake Detector
Nearly 2,000 years ago, a Chinese scientist invented this instrument to detect earthquakes.

The Seismograph

A simple seismograph can consist of a heavy weight attached to a frame by a spring or wire. A pen connected to the weight rests its point on a drum that can rotate. As the drum rotates slowly, the pen draws a straight line on paper wrapped tightly around the drum. **Seismic waves cause the seismograph's drum to vibrate. But the suspended weight with the pen attached moves very little. Therefore, the pen stays in place and records the drum's vibrations.**

Measuring Seismic Waves When you write a sentence, the paper stays in one place while your hand moves the pen. But in a seismograph, it's the pen that remains still while the paper moves. Why is this? All seismographs make use of a basic principle of physics: Whether it is moving or at rest, every object resists any change to its motion. A seismograph's heavy weight resists motion during a quake. But the rest of the seismograph is anchored to the ground and vibrates when seismic waves arrive.

Reading a Seismogram You have probably seen a zigzag pattern of lines used to represent an earthquake. The pattern of lines, called a **seismogram,** is the record of an earthquake's seismic waves produced by a seismograph. Study the seismogram in Figure 13 and notice when the P waves, S waves, and surface waves arrive. The height of the jagged lines drawn on the seismograph's drum is greater for a more severe earthquake or for an earthquake close to the seismograph.

 **What is a seismogram?**

FIGURE 13
Recording Seismic Waves
A seismograph records seismic waves, producing a seismogram. Today, electronic seismographs contain sensors instead of pens. **Interpreting Diagrams** *What is the function of the weight in the seismograph?*

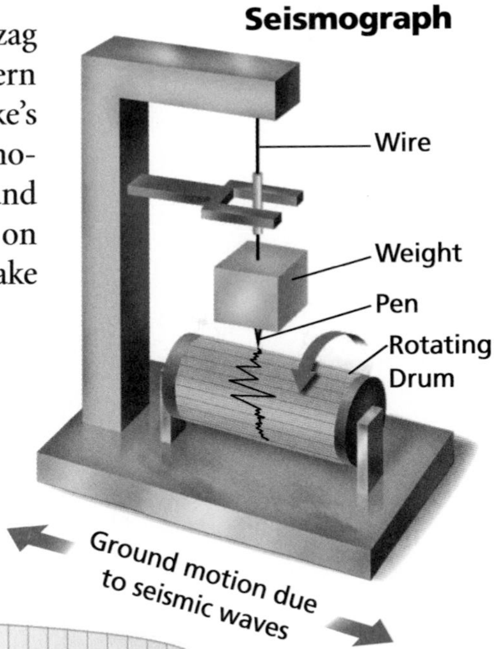

Seismograph

Wire

Weight

Pen

Rotating Drum

Ground motion due to seismic waves

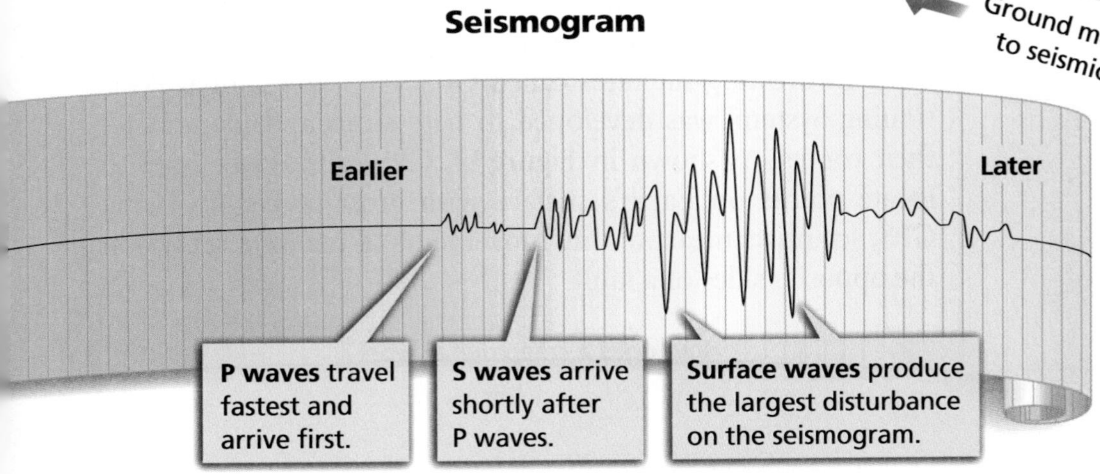

Seismogram

Earlier

Later

P waves travel fastest and arrive first.

S waves arrive shortly after P waves.

Surface waves produce the largest disturbance on the seismogram.

Instruments That Monitor Faults

Along a fault, scientists may detect a slight rise or fall in the elevation and tilt of the land. Geologists think that such changes signal a buildup of stress in rock. Increasing stress could eventually lead to an earthquake. **To monitor faults, geologists have developed instruments to measure changes in elevation, tilting of the land surface, and ground movements along faults.** Some of the instruments that geologists use to monitor these movements include tiltmeters, creep meters, laser-ranging devices, and satellites.

Tiltmeters A tiltmeter measures tilting or raising of the ground. If you have ever used a carpenter's level, you have used a type of tiltmeter. The tiltmeters used by geologists consist of two bulbs that are filled with a liquid and connected by a hollow stem. Notice that if the land rises or falls slightly, the liquid will flow from one bulb to the other. Each bulb contains a measuring scale to measure the depth of the liquid in that bulb. Geologists read the scales to measure the amount of tilt occurring along the fault.

Creep Meters A creep meter uses a wire stretched across a fault to measure horizontal movement of the ground. On one side of the fault, the wire is anchored to a post. On the other side, the wire is attached to a weight that can slide if the fault moves. Geologists determine how much the fault has moved by measuring how much the weight has moved against a scale.

Laser-Ranging Devices A laser-ranging device uses a laser beam to detect horizontal fault movements. The device times a laser beam as it travels to a reflector and back. Thus, the device can detect any change in distance to the reflector.

GPS Satellites Scientists can monitor changes in elevation as well as horizontal movement along faults using a network of Earth-orbiting satellites called GPS. GPS, the Global Positioning System, was developed to help ships and planes find their routes. As shown in Figure 14, GPS can also be used to locate points on Earth's surface with great precision. Using GPS, scientists measure tiny movements of markers set up on the opposite sides of a fault.

 **How does a creep meter work?**

Go Online
SciLINKS
NSTA
For: Links on earthquake measurement
Visit: www.SciLinks.org
Web Code: scn-1023

FIGURE 14
Monitoring Faults

To detect slight motions along faults in
California, geologists use several types of
devices.
Comparing and Contrasting *Which of these
devices measure horizontal movement? Which
ones measure vertical movement?*

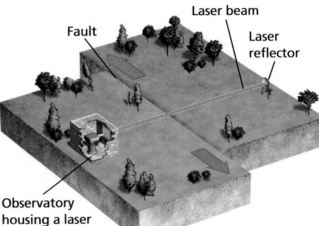

Tiltmeter
A tiltmeter measures
vertical movement.

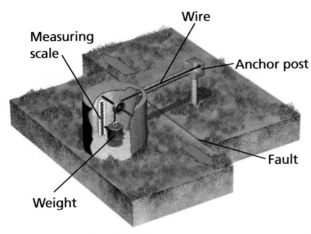

Creep Meter
A creep meter measures
horizontal movement.

Laser-Ranging Device
A laser-ranging device measures
horizontal movement.

GPS Satellites
Ground-based receivers use the GPS
satellite system to measure changes
in elevation and tilt of the land as
well as horizontal movement along a fault.

Using Seismographic Data

Scientists collect and use seismographic data in a variety of ways. **Seismographs and fault-monitoring devices provide data used to map faults and detect changes along faults. Geologists are also trying to use these data to develop a method of predicting earthquakes.**

Mapping Faults Faults are often hidden by a thick layer of rock or soil. How can geologists map a hidden fault?

When seismic waves hit a fault, the waves are reflected off the fault. Seismographs can detect these reflected seismic waves. Geologists then use these data to map the fault's length and depth. Knowing the location of hidden faults helps scientists determine the earthquake risk for the area.

Monitoring Changes Along Faults Geologists study the types of movement that occur along faults. How rocks move along a fault depends on how much friction there is between the sides of the fault. **Friction** is the force that opposes the motion of one surface as it moves across another surface. Friction exists because surfaces are not perfectly smooth.

Along parts of some faults, the rocks on both sides of the fault slide by each other without much sticking. Therefore stress does not build up, and big earthquakes are unlikely. Along many faults, the rocks lock together. In this case, stress increases until it is large enough to overcome the friction force. For example, in most places along the San Andreas fault in California, the plates lock. Stress builds up until an earthquake occurs.

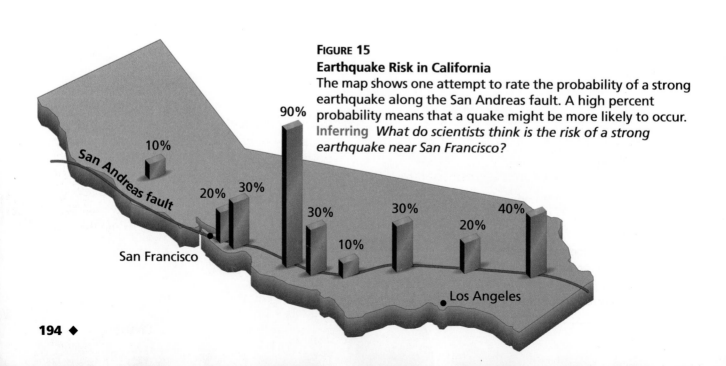

FIGURE 15
Earthquake Risk in California
The map shows one attempt to rate the probability of a strong earthquake along the San Andreas fault. A high percent probability means that a quake might be more likely to occur. *Inferring What do scientists think is the risk of a strong earthquake near San Francisco?*

Figure 15 shows how geologists in California have used data about how the San Andreas fault moves. They have tried to estimate the earthquake risk along the fault. Unfortunately, this attempt at forecasting earthquakes has not worked yet.

Trying to Predict Earthquakes Even with data from many sources, geologists can't predict when and where a quake will strike. Usually, stress along a fault increases until an earthquake occurs. Yet sometimes stored energy builds up along a fault, but an earthquake fails to occur. Or, one or more small earthquakes would relieve only some of the stored energy along the fault. There is always the chance that a large, destructive earthquake will suddenly release most of the stored energy. So exactly what will happen remains uncertain.

The problem of predicting earthquakes is one of many scientific questions that remain unsolved. If you become a scientist, you can work to find answers to these questions. Much remains to be discovered!

FIGURE 16
Seismographic Data
A geologist interprets a seismogram. Understanding changes that precede earthquakes may help in efforts to predict them.

 **Reading Checkpoint** Why is it difficult to predict earthquakes?

Section 3 Assessment

S 6.1.g; E-LA: Reading 6.2.0, Writing 6.2.2

Target Reading Skill Identify Main Ideas Review the text under Monitoring Changes Along Faults. Identify two or three details that support the main idea that friction along faults helps to determine the risk of earthquakes.

Reviewing Key Concepts

1. a. Defining What is a seismograph?
   b. Explaining How does a seismograph record seismic waves?
   c. Predicting A seismograph records a strong earthquake and a weak earthquake. How would the seismograms for the two earthquakes compare?
2. a. Reviewing What four instruments are used to monitor faults?
   b. Describing What changes does each instrument measure?
   c. Inferring A satellite that monitors a fault detects an increasing tilt in the land surface along the fault. What could this change in the land surface indicate?

3. a. Listing What are three ways in which geologists use seismographic data?
   b. Explaining How do geologists use seismographic data to make maps of faults?
   c. Making Generalizations Why do geologists collect data on friction along the sides of faults?

Writing in Science

Patent Application You are an inventor who has created a simple device that can detect an earthquake. To protect your rights to the invention, you apply for a patent. In your patent application, describe your device and how it will indicate the direction and strength of an earthquake. You may include a sketch.

Earthquake Safety

CALIFORNIA
Standards Focus

S 6.1.g Students know that the effects of an earthquake on any region vary, depending on the size of the earthquake, the distance of the region from the epicenter, the local geology, and the type of construction in the region.

S 6.2.d Students know earthquakes, volcanic eruptions, landslides, and floods change human and wildlife habitats.

- How do geologists determine earthquake risk?
- What kinds of damage does an earthquake cause?
- What can be done to increase earthquake safety and reduce earthquake damage?

Key Terms
- liquefaction
- aftershock
- tsunami
- base-isolated building

Lab zone Standards **Warm-Up**

Can Bracing Prevent Building Collapse?

1. Tape four straws together to make a square frame. Hold the frame upright on a flat surface.
2. Hold the bottom straw down with one hand while you push the top straw to the left with the other. Push it as far as it will go without breaking the frame.
3. Tape a fifth straw horizontally across the middle of the frame. Repeat Step 2.

Think It Over

Predicting What effect did the fifth straw have? What effect would a piece of cardboard taped to the frame have? Based on your observations, how would an earthquake affect the frame of a house?

Imagine being sound asleep in your bed in the middle of the night. Suddenly, you are jolted wide awake as your home begins to rattle and shake. As objects fall off shelves and walls crack, you crouch under a desk for protection. Around the city, large buildings collapse and fires break out. The quake lasts less than a minute, but leaves behind great damage. That's what happened in September 1999 when a magnitude 7.6 earthquake hit Taipei, Taiwan. The effects of an earthquake on any region vary, depending on the size of the earthquake, distance from the epicenter, local geology, and the type of construction in the region.

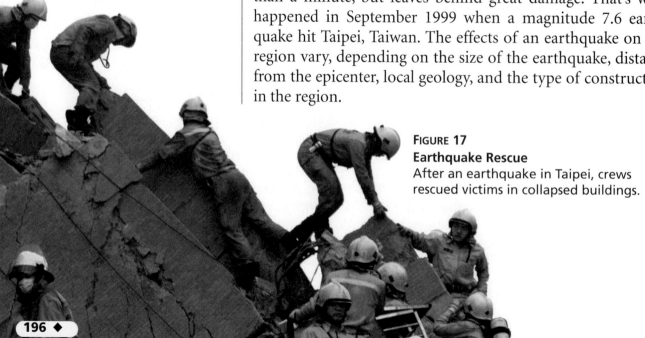

FIGURE 17
Earthquake Rescue
After an earthquake in Taipei, crews rescued victims in collapsed buildings.

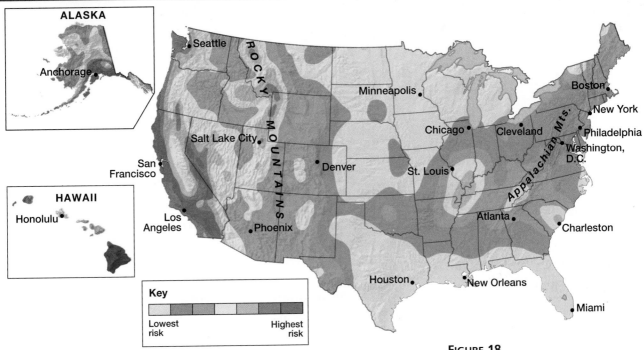

ALASKA
Anchorage

HAWAII
Honolulu

Seattle

R O C K Y   M O U N T A I N S

Salt Lake City

San Francisco

Los Angeles

Phoenix

Denver

Minneapolis

Chicago

St. Louis

Cleveland

Atlanta

Houston

New Orleans

Boston

New York

Philadelphia

Washington, D.C.

Appalachian Mts.

Charleston

Miami

Key

Lowest risk   Highest risk

FIGURE 18
The map shows areas where serious earthquakes are likely to occur, based on the locations of previous earthquakes.
Interpreting Maps *Where are damaging earthquakes least likely to occur? Most likely to occur?*

Earthquake Risk

Geologists know that earthquakes are likely wherever plate movement stores energy in the rock along faults. **Geologists can determine earthquake risk by locating where faults are active, where past earthquakes have occurred, and where the most damage was caused.**

Plate Boundaries and Faults Look at Figure 18. In the United States, the risk is highest along the Pacific coast in California, Washington, and Alaska. Plates meet along the Pacific coast, causing many active faults. In California, the Pacific plate and North American plate meet along the San Andreas fault. In Washington, earthquakes result from the subduction of the Juan de Fuca plate. In Alaska, subduction of the Pacific plate causes many earthquakes.

The eastern United States mostly has a low risk of earthquakes because this region lies far from plate boundaries. But the East has had some of the most powerful quakes in the nation's history. Scientists think that the continental plate forming most of North America is under stress. This stress could disturb faults hidden beneath soil and rock.

Go Online
PLANET DIARY

For: More on earthquake risk
Visit: PHSchool.com
Web Code: cfd-1024

Reading Checkpoint What areas of the United States have the highest earthquake risk?

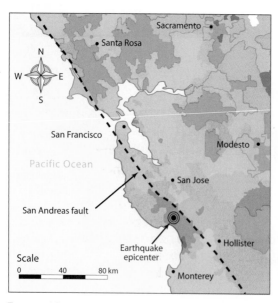

Intensity	Shaking	Damage
I	Not felt	None
II–III	Weak	None
IV	Light	None
V	Moderate	Very light (some windows break)
VI	Strong	Light (some plaster falls)
VII	Very Strong	Moderate (chimneys break)
VIII	Severe	Moderate to heavy (chimneys and walls fall)
IX	Violent	Heavy (building foundations shift; ground cracks)
X+	Extreme	Very heavy (most structures destroyed; rails bend)

FIGURE 19

Loma Prieta Earthquake
The 1989 Loma Prieta earthquake struck along the San Andreas fault. The map shows the intensity of shaking felt in areas affected by the earthquake.

Major Earthquakes	
Earthquake	**Moment Magnitude**
San Francisco, California, 1906	7.8
Messina, Italy, 1908	7.2
Tokyo, Japan, 1923	7.9
Southern Chile, 1960	9.5
Anchorage, Alaska, 1964	9.2
Loma Prieta, California, 1989	6.9
Northridge, California, 1994	6.7
Indian Ocean, near Sumatra, Indonesia, 2004	9.0

FIGURE 20

Major Earthquakes
The table shows strong earthquakes of the past 100 years and their magnitudes.
Calculating *About how much more powerful is a magnitude 9.0 earthquake than a magnitude 7.0 earthquake?*

Mapping Earthquake Intensity Geologists can use modified Mercalli scale data to map the intensity of an earthquake. Intensity maps show how the ground shaking and damage from an earthquake vary from place to place. You can see an example of this type of map in Figure 19.

Why are intensity maps important? These maps show that areas near faults generally suffer the most serious earthquake damage. And the same areas might suffer damage again if struck by another strong quake.

Historic Earthquakes Why do geologists study earthquakes that happened many years ago? Past earthquakes can help geologists estimate the risk of future earthquakes. One way that geologists learn about past earthquakes is from historic reports. These reports may describe where the quake was strongest and what damage it caused. Geologists also study the rock and soil along faults for evidence of past earthquakes. Geologists can use these data to estimate the magnitudes of earthquakes that occurred before the seismograph was invented.

 **Why do geologists make intensity maps?**

How Earthquakes Cause Damage

When a major earthquake strikes, it can cause great damage. But distance from an earthquake's epicenter is not the only factor involved. ⬤ **Causes of earthquake damage include shaking, liquefaction, aftershocks, and tsunamis.**

Shaking The shaking produced by seismic waves can trigger landslides or avalanches. These disasters can bury and destroy both human-made buildings and the natural areas wildlife need in order to live. Shaking itself can also damage or destroy buildings and bridges, topple utility poles, and fracture gas and water mains. S waves and surface waves, with their side-to-side and up-and-down movement, can cause severe damage to buildings near the epicenter.

The types of rock and soil determine where and how much the ground shakes. The most violent shaking may occur kilometers away from the epicenter. Loose soil shakes more violently than solid rock. This means a house built on sandy soil will shake more than a house built on solid rock.

Liquefaction In 1964, when a powerful earthquake roared through Anchorage, Alaska, wide cracks opened in the ground. The cracks were created by liquefaction. **Liquefaction** (lik wih FAK shun) occurs when an earthquake's violent shaking suddenly turns loose, soft soil into liquid mud. Liquefaction is likely where the soil is full of moisture. As the ground gives way, buildings sink and pull apart.

Aftershocks Sometimes, buildings weakened by an earthquake collapse during an aftershock. An **aftershock** is an earthquake that occurs after a larger earthquake in the same area. Aftershocks may strike hours, days, or even months later.

Lab zone Try This **Activity**

Mapping Magnitude

1. Obtain an outline map of the world with latitude and longitude.
2. Use reference sources to find out the locations of the earthquakes in Figure 20 and plot them on the map. Use a different symbol to mark quakes with a magnitude of 9.0 or more.
3. Compare your map with the map of plate boundaries in Figure 22 on p. 159. Notice what type of plate boundary lies near the magnitude 9.0 earthquakes.

Inferring What process takes place at the plate boundaries near the 9.0 magnitude earthquakes? How does this help to explain why these quakes are so powerful?

FIGURE 21
Liquefaction Damage
An earthquake caused the soil beneath this building to liquefy. Liquefaction can change soil to liquid mud.
Posing Questions *What are some questions people might ask before building in a quake-prone area?*

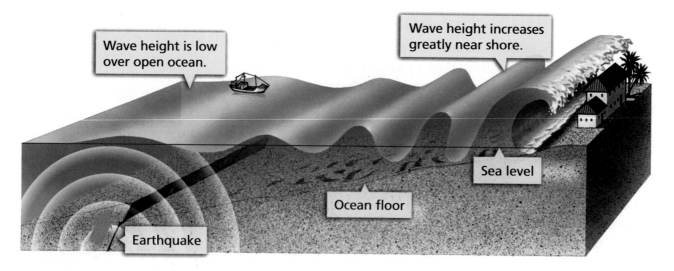

Wave height is low over open ocean.

Wave height increases greatly near shore.

Sea level

Ocean floor

Earthquake

FIGURE 22

How a Tsunami Forms
A tsunami begins as a low wave, but turns into a huge wave as it nears the shore. In 2004, a powerful earthquake in the Indian Ocean triggered several tsunamis. The tsunamis caused great loss of life and destruction to coastal areas around the Indian Ocean.

Tsunamis When an earthquake jolts the ocean floor, plate movement causes the ocean floor to rise slightly and push water out of its way. The water displaced by the earthquake may form a large wave called a **tsunami** (tsoo NAH mee), shown in Figure 22. A tsunami spreads out from an earthquake's epicenter and speeds across the ocean. In the open ocean, the height of the wave is low. As a tsunami approaches shallow water, the wave grows into a mountain of water.

Steps to Earthquake Safety

What should you do if an earthquake strikes? The main danger is from falling objects and flying glass. **The best way to protect yourself is to drop, cover, and hold.**

If you are indoors when a quake strikes, drop down and crouch beneath a sturdy table or desk and hold on to it. If no desk or table is available, crouch against an inner wall, away from the outside of a building, and cover your head and neck with your arms. Avoid windows, mirrors, wall hangings, and furniture that might topple.

If you are outdoors, move to an open area such as a playground. Avoid vehicles, power lines, trees, and buildings. Sit down to avoid being thrown down.

After a quake, water and power supplies may fail, food stores may be closed, and travel may be difficult. People may have to wait days for these services to be restored. To prepare, store an earthquake kit containing canned food, water, and first aid supplies where it is easy to reach.

 **Reading Checkpoint** **How can furniture be dangerous during a quake? How can it protect you?**

Designing Safer Buildings

Most earthquake-related deaths and injuries result from damage to buildings or other structures. 🔑 **To reduce earthquake damage, new buildings must be made stronger and more flexible. Older buildings may be modified so as to withstand stronger quakes.** Figure 23 shows some of the steps that can make houses earthquake-safe.

Generally, the effects of an earthquake depend on the type of construction. Buildings made of brittle materials such as concrete or brick suffer the most damage in an earthquake. Buildings made of more flexible materials, such as wood, tend to suffer less damage. Tall buildings are more subject to damage than single-story buildings.

FIGURE 23
An Earthquake-Safe House
People can take a variety of steps to make their homes safer in an earthquake.
Predicting *During a quake, what might happen to a house that was not bolted to its foundation?*

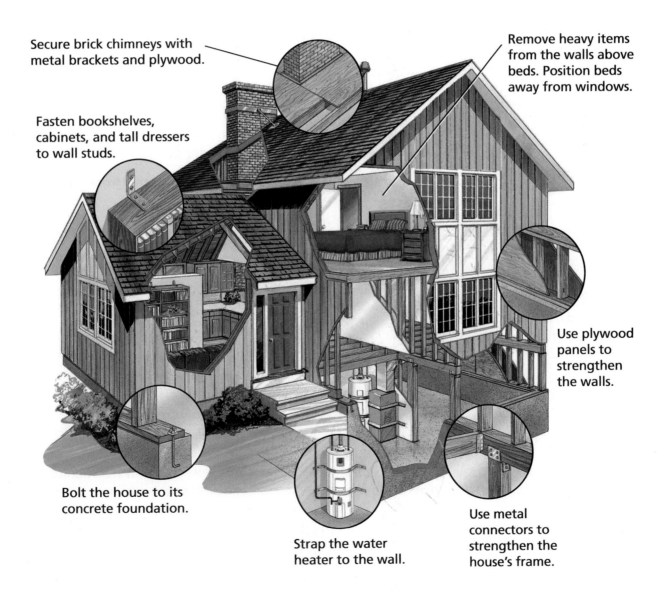

Secure brick chimneys with metal brackets and plywood.

Remove heavy items from the walls above beds. Position beds away from windows.

Fasten bookshelves, cabinets, and tall dressers to wall studs.

Use plywood panels to strengthen the walls.

Bolt the house to its concrete foundation.

Strap the water heater to the wall.

Use metal connectors to strengthen the house's frame.

Stable or Unstable?

1. Make a model of a fault by placing two small, folded towels side by side on a flat surface.
2. Pile a stack of books on the fault by placing light books on the bottom and heavy ones on top.
3. Gently pull the towels in opposite directions until the pile topples.
4. Repeat the process, but this time with the heavier books on the bottom.

Relating Cause and Effect Which one of your structures was more stable? Why?

Protecting Structures The way in which a building is constructed determines whether it can withstand an earthquake. During an earthquake, brick buildings and some wood-frame buildings may collapse if their walls have not been reinforced, or strengthened. To combat damage caused by liquefaction, new homes built on soft ground should be anchored to solid rock below the soil. Bridges and highway overpasses can be built on supports that go through soft soil to firmer ground. To find out more about how buildings can withstand earthquakes, look at *Seismic-Safe Buildings* on the following pages.

A **base-isolated building** is designed to reduce the amount of energy that reaches the building during an earthquake. A base-isolated building rests on shock-absorbing rubber pads or springs. Like the suspension of a car, the pads and springs smooth out a bumpy ride. During a quake, the building moves gently back and forth without any violent shaking.

Making Utilities Safer Earthquakes can cause fire and flooding when gas pipes and water mains break. Flexible joints can be installed in gas and water lines to keep them from breaking. Automatic shut-off valves also can be installed on these lines to cut off gas and water flow.

Reading Checkpoint How can utilities be protected from earthquake damage?

Section 4 Assessment

S 6.1.g, 6.2.d; E-LA: Reading 6.1.0

Vocabulary Skill High-Use Academic Words
What are two things you would do to construct a building so that it could withstand an earthquake? Use the word *construct* in your answer.

Reviewing Key Concepts

1. a. **Identifying** What factors help geologists determine earthquake risk for a region?
   b. **Comparing and Contrasting** Why does the risk of quakes vary across the United States?
2. a. **Listing** What are four ways that earthquakes cause damage?
   b. **Relating Cause and Effect** How does liquefaction cause damage during an earthquake?
   c. **Developing Hypotheses** How might heavy rain before an earthquake affect the danger of liquefaction?

3. a. **Reviewing** How can you protect yourself during an earthquake?
   b. **Describing** What will happen to a base-isolated building when seismic waves strike the building during an earthquake?

Quake Safety Plan Work with an adult family member to develop an earthquake safety plan. The plan should tell family members what to do during an earthquake. It should list items your family would need if a quake cut electrical power and water lines. It should also explain where to shut off the gas if your home has a natural gas line. Share your earthquake safety plan with the rest of your family.

Earthshaking Events

Problem How can you use a map of faults and historic earthquakes to analyze earthquake risk in California?

Skills Focus interpreting maps, inferring

Procedure

1. Using a piece of tracing paper and a pencil, trace the outline of California in Figure 18 on page 237. Trace and label the latitude and longitude lines and the map scale. Mark the location of your community on your map.

2. In a second color, trace the state's active faults. Label the faults.

3. Use the map scale to measure the distance from your community to the nearest fault. Record the distance.

4. In a third color, plot the epicenters of the earthquakes in the table. Also draw a line along the southern San Andreas fault to shade approximately the part of the fault that moved during the Fort Tejon earthquake.

5. Measure the distance from your community to the nearest epicenter of a historic earthquake. Record the distance.

Analyze and Conclude

1. **Interpreting Maps** What major fault is closest to your community?

2. **Interpreting Maps** What historic earthquake was closest to your community? What was the earthquake's magnitude?

3. **Inferring** Based on your distance from an active fault and historic earthquake, how would you rate the earthquake risk in your area?

4. **Communicating** Write a paragraph explaining the earthquake risk in your community. In your answer, include factors such as the role of plate tectonics, active faults, and historic earthquakes.

More to Explore

You can further analyze earthquake risk in your community. Conduct research on nearby active faults and past earthquake activity, ground motion, and faulting. Write a report based on your research findings.

Earthquake	Epicenter	Magnitude
Fort Tejon, 1857	Somewhere along the southern San Andreas fault	7.9
Owens Valley, 1872	118° W, 37° N	7.9
San Francisco, 1906	Approximately 123° W, 38° N	7.8
Calaveras fault, 1911	122° W, 37° N	6.5
Long Beach, 1933	118° W, 33° N	6.4
Imperial Valley, 1940	116° W, 33° N	7.1
Concord, 1954	122° W, 38° N	5.4
San Fernando, 1971	118° W, 34° N	6.7
Gorda Plate, 1980	125° W, 41° N	7.2
Loma Prieta, 1989	122° W, 37° N	6.9
Northridge, 1994	119° W, 34° N	6.7
Parkfield, 2004	120° W, 36° N	6.0

S 6.1.g

Seismic-Safe Buildings

Breaking one thin twig doesn't require much force. Breaking a bundle of twigs does. Like one thin twig, the walls, beams, and other supporting parts of a building can snap as seismic energy travels through the structure. Reinforcing a building's parts makes them more like the bundle of twigs—stronger and less likely to snap when a quake occurs.

What Are Seismic-Safe Buildings?

Seismic-safe buildings have types of construction that reduce earthquake damage. Some of these features strengthen a building. Others allow the building to move, or shield the building from the energy of seismic waves. In earthquake-prone areas, most tall steel-frame buildings may have one or more of the seismic-safe features shown here.

Shear Walls A shear wall transfers some of a quake's energy from roofs and floors to the building's foundation.

Tension Ties These devices firmly "tie" the floors and ceilings of a building to the walls. Tension ties absorb and scatter earthquake energy and thus reduce damage.

Tension tie

Steel frame

Base Isolators These pads separate, or isolate, a building from its foundation and prevent some of an earthquake's energy from entering the building.

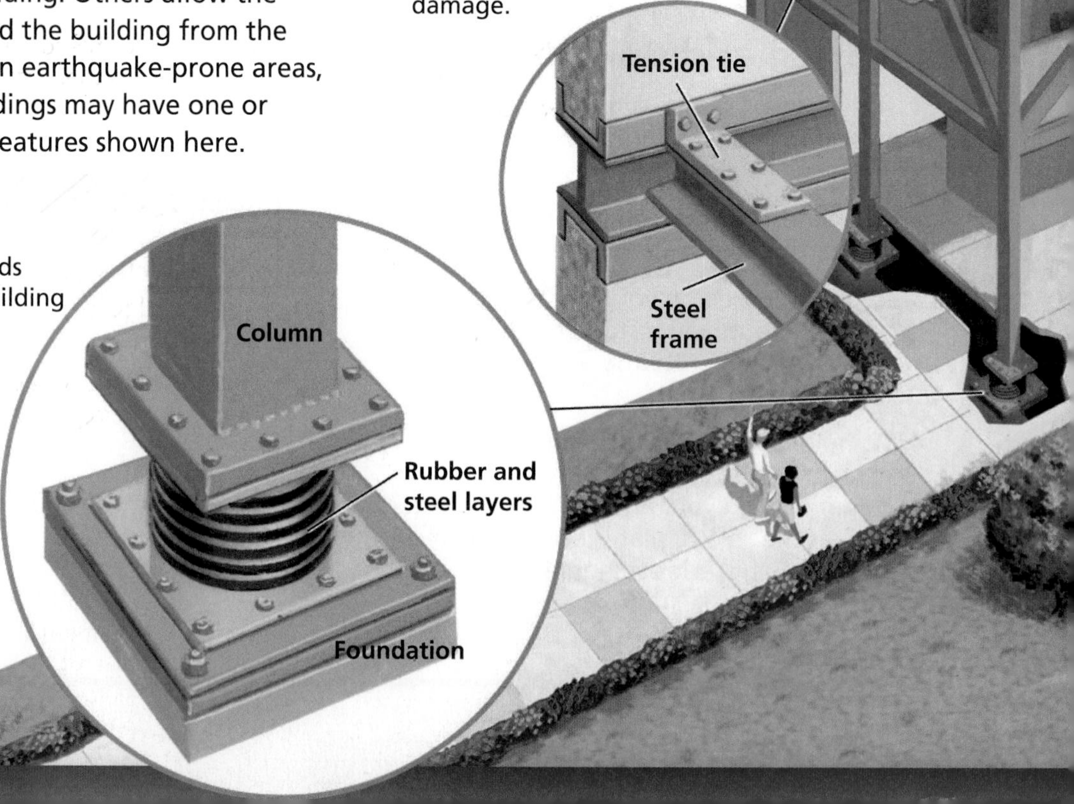

Column

Rubber and steel layers

Foundation

Cross Braces Steel cross braces are placed between stories to stiffen a building's frame and absorb energy during an earthquake.

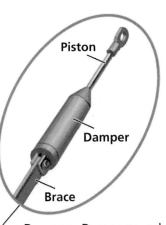

Piston

Damper

Brace

Dampers Dampers work like the shock absorbers in a car to absorb some of the energy of seismic waves.

Flexible Pipes Water and gas pipes have flexible joints. Flexible pipes bend as energy passes through them, greatly reducing damage.

Seismic-Safe, But at What Cost?

Seismic-safe buildings save lives and reduce damage. Despite these benefits, the technologies have drawbacks. Seismic-safe features, such as cross braces, may reduce the amount of usable space in a building. It is also expensive to add seismic-safe features to an existing building. Communities must make trade-offs between the benefits and the costs of seismic-safe buildings.

Even steel-frame buildings need seismic-safe design features.

Weigh the Impact

1. **Identify the Need** Your city has hired you to decide which buildings or other structures most need to be able to withstand an earthquake. List three types of structures that you think need to be seismic-safe.

2. **Research** Research how the structures on your list can be made safe. Choose one structure from your list and make notes on how it can be made safe.

3. **Write** Using your notes, write a report that explains how your structure can be designed or modified to withstand earthquakes.

For: More on seismic-safe buildings
Visit: PHSchool.com
Web Code: cfh-1020

🔑 The **BIG Idea**   Plate motions produce stress in Earth's crust that leads to faults, mountain building, and earthquakes.

① Forces in Earth's Crust

🔑 **Key Concepts**   🗝 S 6.1.e, 6.1.f

- Tension, compression, and shearing work over millions of years to change the shape and volume of rock.

- Faults usually occur along plate boundaries, where the forces of plate motion push or pull the crust so much that the crust breaks. There are three main types of faults: normal faults, reverse faults, and strike-slip faults.

- Over millions of years, the forces of plate movement can change a flat plain into landforms such as anticlines and synclines, folded mountains, fault-block mountains, and plateaus.

Key Terms

stress	hanging wall
tension	footwall
compression	reverse fault
shearing	strike-slip fault
normal fault	plateau

② Earthquakes and Seismic Waves

🔑 **Key Concepts**   🗝 S 6.1.d, 6.1.g

- Seismic waves carry energy from an earthquake away from the focus, through Earth's interior, and across the surface.

- Three commonly used ways of measuring earthquakes are the Mercalli scale, the Richter scale, and the moment magnitude scale.

- Geologists use seismic waves to locate an earthquake's epicenter.

Key Terms

earthquake	Mercalli scale
focus	magnitude
epicenter	Richter scale
P wave	seismograph
S wave	moment magnitude scale
surface wave	

③ Monitoring Earthquakes

🔑 **Key Concepts**   🗝 S 6.1.g

- During an earthquake, seismic waves cause the seismograph's drum to vibrate. But the suspended weight with the pen attached moves very little. Therefore, the pen stays in place and records the drum's vibrations.

- To monitor faults, geologists have developed instruments to measure changes in elevation, tilting of the land surface, and ground movements along faults.

- Seismographs and fault-monitoring devices provide data used to map faults and detect changes along faults.

Key Terms

seismogram	friction

④ Earthquake Safety

🔑 **Key Concepts**   🗝 S 6.1.g, 6.2.d

- Geologists can determine earthquake risk by locating where faults are active, where past earthquakes have occurred, and where past earthquakes have caused the most damage.

- Causes of earthquake damage include shaking, liquefaction, aftershocks, and tsunamis.

- The best way to protect yourself is to drop, cover, and hold.

- To reduce earthquake damage, new buildings must be made stronger and more flexible. Older buildings may be modified to withstand stronger quakes.

Key Terms

liquefaction	tsunami
aftershock	base-isolated building

Review and Assessment

Go Online
PHSchool.com

For: Self-Assessment
Visit: PHSchool.com
Web Code: cwa-2050

Target Reading Skill

Identifying Main Ideas Reread the text under the heading Kinds of Faults in Section 1. Complete the graphic organizer.

Kinds of Faults

Detail	Detail	Detail
Normal faults—hanging wall slips down relative to footwall		

Reviewing Key Terms

Choose the letter of the best answer.

1. The force that causes part of the crust to become shorter and thicker is
   a. tension.
   b. compression.
   c. shearing.
   d. normal force.

2. When the hanging wall of a fault slips down with respect to the footwall, the result is a
   a. reverse fault.
   b. syncline.
   c. normal fault.
   d. strike-slip fault.

3. Which of the following is a rating of earthquake damage at a particular location?
   a. moment magnitude scale
   b. focus scale
   c. Mercalli scale
   d. Richter scale

4. The largest waves on a seismogram are
   a. P waves.
   b. S waves.
   c. surface waves.
   d. tsunamis.

5. In the hours after an earthquake, people should not go inside a building, even if it appears undamaged, because of
   a. aftershocks.   b. liquefaction.
   c. tsunamis.   d. deformation.

Complete the following sentences so that your answers clearly explain the key terms.

6. **Compression** is a force that changes Earth's crust by _____ .

7. Tension in Earth's crust can produce a **normal fault,** which is _____ .

8. Beneath an earthquake's epicenter lies the quake's **focus,** which is _____ .

9. After an earthquake, the first seismic waves to arrive are **P waves,** which are _____ .

10. An earthquake beneath the ocean floor can trigger a **tsunami,** which is _____ .

Writing in Science

Cause-and-Effect Paragraph Now that you have learned about the awesome power of earthquakes, write a paragraph about how earthquakes cause damage. Discuss both the natural and human-made factors that contribute to an earthquake's destructive power.

Video Assessment
Discovery Channel School
Earthquakes

Review and Assessment

Checking Concepts

11. What process causes stress in Earth's crust?

12. Explain how a fault-block mountain forms.

13. What type of stress in the crust results in the formation of folded mountains? Explain.

14. What are plateaus, and how do they form?

15. Describe what happens along a fault beneath Earth's surface when an earthquake occurs.

16. How is the amount of energy released by an earthquake related to its magnitude?

17. What does the height of the jagged lines on a seismogram indicate?

18. How can homes and other structures be protected from liquefaction?

Thinking Critically

19. **Classifying** Look at the diagram of a fault below. Describe how the hanging wall moves in relation to the footwall. What kind of fault is this?

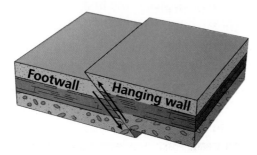

20. **Analyzing Data** A geologist has data about an earthquake from two seismographic stations. Is this enough information to determine the location of the epicenter? Why or why not?

21. **Predicting** A community has just built a street across a strike-slip fault that has frequent earthquakes. How will movement along the fault affect the street?

22. **Making Generalizations** How can filled land and loose, soft soil affect the amount of damage caused by an earthquake? Explain.

Applying Skills

Use the graph to answer Questions 23–26.

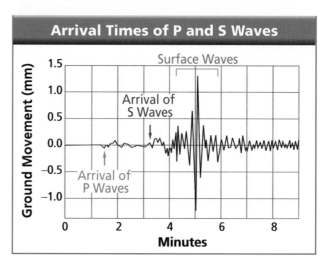

Arrival Times of P and S Waves

23. **Interpreting Diagrams** In what order did the seismic waves arrive at the seismograph station?

24. **Interpreting Diagrams** Which type of seismic wave produced the largest ground movement?

25. **Analyzing Data** What was the difference in arrival times for the P waves and S waves?

26. **Predicting** What would the seismogram look like several hours after this earthquake? How would it change if an aftershock occurred?

 Standards Investigation

Performance Assessment Before testing how your model withstands an earthquake, explain to your classmates how and why you changed your model. When your model is tested, observe how it withstands the earthquake. How would a real earthquake compare with the method used to test your model? If it were a real building, could your structure withstand an earthquake? How could you improve your model?

Choose the letter of the best answer.

1. The diagram below shows how stress affects a mass of rock in a process called
   - **A** compression
   - **B** tension.
   - **C** squeezing.
   - **D** shearing   S 6.1.d

2. The diagram below shows a strike-slip fault like the San Andreas fault in California. Movement along the fault occurs because of
   - **A** tension in the crust.
   - **B** uplift of the crust.
   - **C** plate motions.
   - **D** volcanic activity.   S 6.1.f

3. Stress will build until an earthquake occurs if friction along a fault is
   - **A** decreasing.
   - **B** high.
   - **C** low.
   - **D** changed to heat.   S 6.1.e

4. To estimate the total energy released by an earthquake, a geologist should use the
   - **A** Mercalli scale.
   - **B** Richter scale.
   - **C** epicenter scale.
   - **D** moment magnitude scale.   S 6.1.g

Use the information below and your knowledge of science to answer Questions 5 and 6.

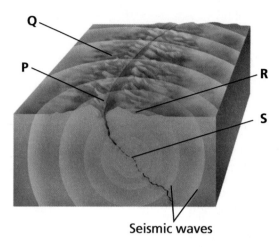

Seismic waves

5. In the diagram, the epicenter is located at point
   - **A** Q.
   - **B** P.
   - **C** R.
   - **D** S.   S 6.1.g

6. When an earthquake occurs, seismic waves travel
   - **A** from P in all directions.
   - **B** from R to S.
   - **C** from S in all directions.
   - **D** from Q to P.   S 6.1.g

7. Which answer best explains how earthquakes can change an area where wild animals live?
   - **A** A landslide covers a forest.
   - **B** A tsunami washes away a sand dune.
   - **C** Soil turns to liquid mud.
   - **D** All of the above   S 6.2.d

Apply the BIG Idea

8. Plate motions can cause tension in Earth's crust. Explain how tension could lead to the formation of a fault, a type of mountain, and an earthquake.   S 6.1.d

Chapter 6

Volcanoes

A spectacular lava fountain erupts from Mount Kilauea, a volcano in Hawaii. ▶

Focus on the
BIG Idea

S 6.1.d

What causes volcanoes, and how do they change Earth's surface?

Check What You Know

You know that if you want to open a bottle of soda, you must do so carefully. Otherwise, the soda might spray out of the bottle as soon as you loosen the cap. What causes the soda to rush out with such force? How is this similar to what happens when a volcano erupts? Explain.

Build Science Vocabulary

The images shown here represent some of the key terms in this chapter. You can use this vocabulary skill to help you understand the meaning of some key terms in this chapter.

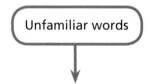

Use Clues to Determine Meaning

Science textbooks often contain unfamiliar words. When you are reading, use clues to figure out what these words mean. First look for clues in the word itself. Then look at the surrounding words, sentences, and paragraphs.

Look at the clues to the meaning of *hot spot* in the following text.

> Unfamiliar words

Some volcanoes result from hot spots in Earth's mantle. A **hot spot** is an area where material from within the mantle rises and then melts. A volcano forms above a hot spot when the hot material erupts through the crust and reaches the surface.

A hot spot in the ocean floor can gradually form a series of volcanic mountains. For example, the Hawaiian Islands formed one by one over millions of years as the Pacific plate drifted over a hot spot.

> *Hot spot* is the subject of the sentence.

> Definition, follows boldface

> Explanation

> Example

Apply It!

Review the clues to the meaning of *hot spot*. Then complete the following.

1. What clue tells you that *hot spot* might be followed by a definition?
2. What example helps you understand hot spots?

As you come across an unfamiliar word in this chapter, look for clues to its meaning.

Chapter 6
Vocabulary

lava

crater

dike

basin

interactive Textbook

Build Science Vocabulary
Online
Visit: PHSchool.com
Web Code: cwj-2060

How to Read Science

Create Outlines

You have learned to use headings and to identify main ideas and details to guide you as you read. An outline uses these skills to show the relationship between main ideas and supporting details.

An outline usually is set up like the one below. Roman numerals show the main topics or headings. Capital letters show the subheadings. Numbers show supporting details and key terms.

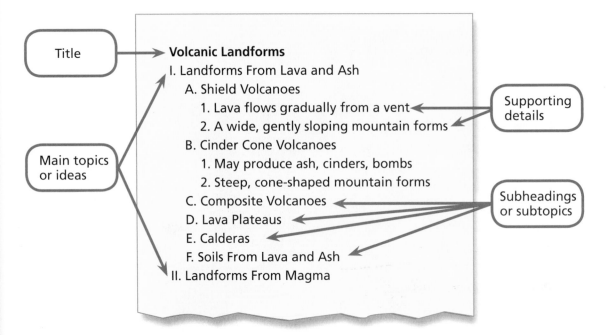

Volcanic Landforms

I. Landforms From Lava and Ash
   A. Shield Volcanoes
      1. Lava flows gradually from a vent
      2. A wide, gently sloping mountain forms
   B. Cinder Cone Volcanoes
      1. May produce ash, cinders, bombs
      2. Steep, cone-shaped mountain forms
   C. Composite Volcanoes
   D. Lava Plateaus
   E. Calderas
   F. Soils From Lava and Ash
II. Landforms From Magma

Title

Main topics or ideas

Supporting details

Subheadings or subtopics

Apply It!

Answer each of the following questions.

1. What are the most important ideas in this outline?
2. What details support the subheading Shield Volcanoes?

Copy the outline above into your notebook. Use the headings, subheadings, and key terms to help you select information to complete the outline for Landforms From Magma in Section 3. Create an outline for Kinds of Volcanic Eruptions in Section 2.

Volcanoes and People

The eruptions of a volcano can be dangerous. Yet volcanoes and people have been closely connected throughout history. People often live near volcanoes because of the benefits they offer, from rich soil to minerals to hot springs. In this investigation, you will research the people living in a volcanic region.

Your Goal

To make a documentary about life in a volcanic region

Your documentary must

- describe the type of volcano you chose and give its history
- focus on one topic, such as how people have benefited from living near the volcano or how people include the volcano in their art and stories
- use a variety of media
- follow the safety guidelines in Appendix A

Plan It!

Brainstorm with a group of other students which geographic area you would like to learn about. Your teacher may suggest some volcanic regions for you to check out. Decide what research resources you will need. For media, you might consider video, computer art, a skit, or a mural. Be creative! When your documentary is finished, present it to your class.

The Volcano

PROD. NO.	TAKE	ROLL
SCENE		
3	2	A

DATE *November 28*   SOUND *yes*
PROD. CO. *José*
DIRECTOR *Sarah*
CAMERAMAN *Mark*

Volcanoes and Plate Tectonics

CALIFORNIA
Standards Focus

S 6.1 Plate tectonics accounts for important features of Earth's surface and major geologic events. As a basis for understanding this concept:

e. Students know major geologic events, such as earthquakes, volcanic eruptions, and mountain building, result from plate motions.

- Where are most of Earth's volcanoes found?
- How do hot spot volcanoes form?

Key Terms
- volcano
- magma
- lava
- Ring of Fire
- island arc
- hot spot

Lab zone Standards **Warm-Up**

Where Are Volcanoes Found on Earth's Surface?

1. Look at the map of Earth's Active Volcanoes in Figure 2. What symbols are used to represent volcanoes? What other symbols are shown on the map?

2. Do the locations of the volcanoes form a pattern? Do the volcanoes seem related to any other features on Earth's surface?

Think About It

Developing Hypotheses Develop a hypothesis to explain where Earth's volcanoes are located.

In 2002, Mount Etna erupted in glowing fountains and rivers of molten rock. Located on the island of Sicily in the Mediterranean Sea, Mount Etna is Europe's largest volcano. Over the last 2,500 years, it has erupted often. The ancient Greeks believed that Mount Etna was one home of Hephaestus, the Greek god of fire. Beneath the volcano was the forge where Hephaestus made beautiful metal objects for the other Greek gods.

The eruption of a volcano is among the most awe-inspiring events on Earth. A **volcano** is a weak spot in the crust where molten material, or magma, comes to the surface. **Magma** is a molten mixture of rock-forming substances, gases, and water from the mantle. When magma reaches the surface, it is called **lava.** After lava has cooled, it forms solid rock. Lava released during volcanic activity builds up Earth's surface.

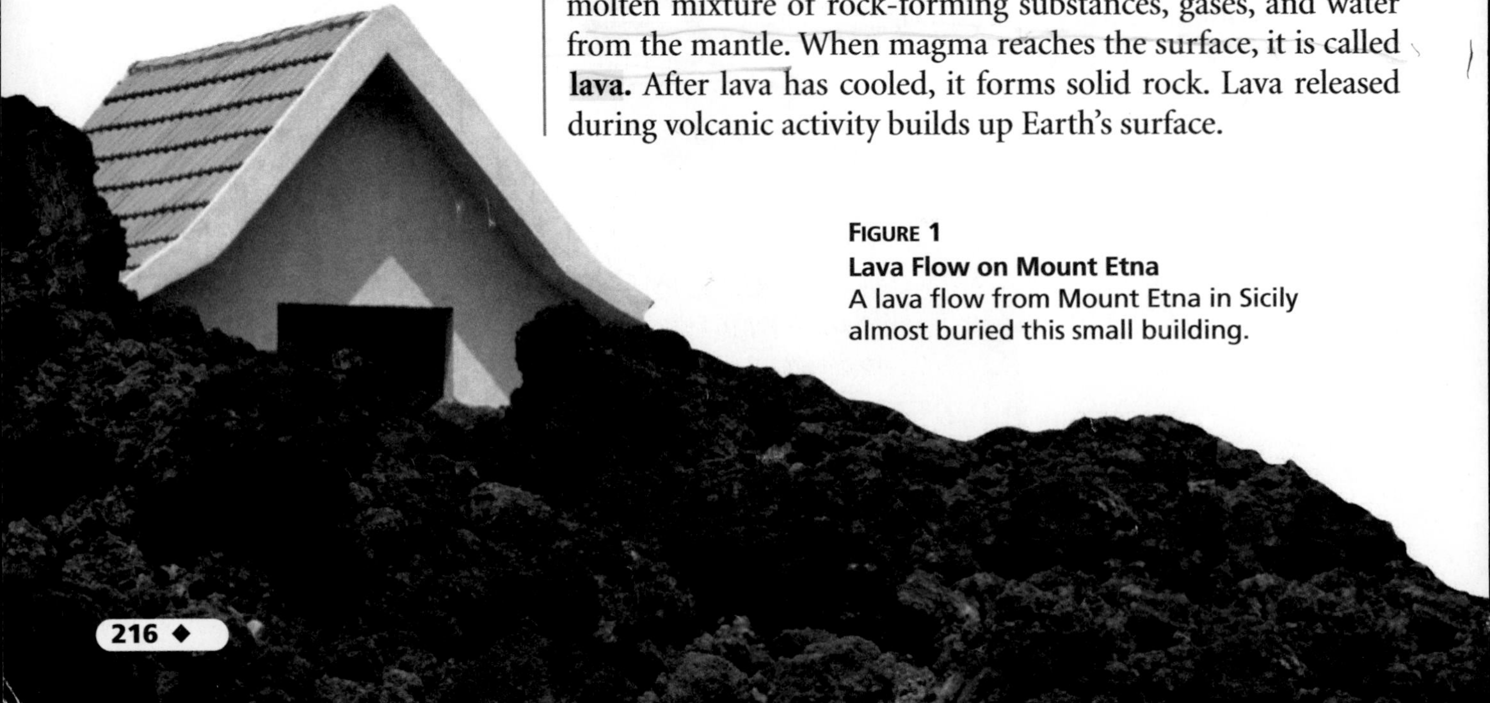

FIGURE 1
Lava Flow on Mount Etna
A lava flow from Mount Etna in Sicily almost buried this small building.

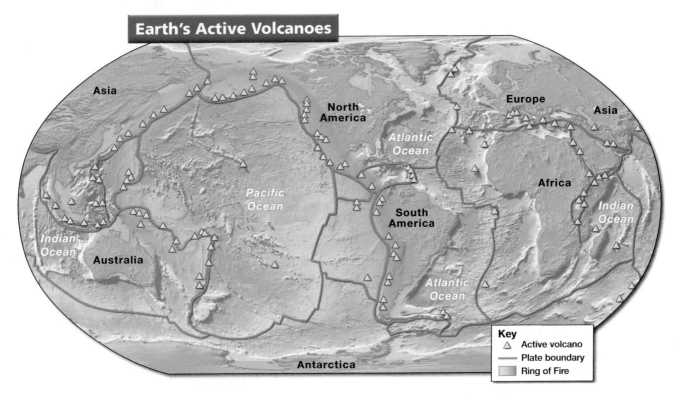

Earth's Active Volcanoes

Asia

North America

Atlantic Ocean

Europe

Asia

Africa

Indian Ocean

Pacific Ocean

South America

Indian Ocean

Australia

Atlantic Ocean

Antarctica

Key
△ Active volcano
— Plate boundary
▢ Ring of Fire

Volcanoes and Plate Boundaries

There are about 600 active volcanoes on land. Many more lie beneath the sea, where it is difficult for scientists to observe and map them. Figure 2 shows the location of some of Earth's major volcanoes. Notice how volcanoes occur in belts that extend across continents and oceans. One major volcanic belt is the **Ring of Fire,** formed by the many volcanoes that rim the Pacific Ocean.

👁 **Volcanic belts form along the boundaries of Earth's plates.** At plate boundaries, huge pieces of the crust spread apart or collide. As a result, the crust often fractures, allowing magma to reach the surface. Most volcanoes form along spreading boundaries such as mid-ocean ridges and along colliding boundaries where subduction takes place. For example, Mount Etna formed near the boundary of the Eurasian and African plates.

Spreading Boundaries Volcanoes form along the mid-ocean ridges, which mark spreading boundaries. Recall that ridges are long, underwater mountain ranges that sometimes have a rift valley down their center. Along the rift valley, lava pours out of cracks in the ocean floor, gradually building new mountains. Volcanoes also form along spreading boundaries on land. For example, there are several large volcanoes along the Great Rift Valley in East Africa.

FIGURE 2
Many of Earth's volcanoes are located along the boundaries of tectonic plates. The belt of volcanoes that circles the Pacific Ocean is called the Ring of Fire.
Observing *What other regions have a large number of volcanoes?*

Go Online
PLANET DIARY

For: More on volcanoes
Visit: PHSchool.com
Web Code: cfd-1031

Colliding Boundaries Many volcanoes form near colliding boundaries where oceanic plates return to the mantle. Volcanoes may form where two oceanic plates collide or where an oceanic plate collides with a continental plate. Figure 3 shows how colliding plates produce volcanoes.

Many volcanoes occur near boundaries where two oceanic plates collide. Through subduction, the older, denser plate sinks beneath a deep-ocean trench into the mantle. Some of the rock above the subducting plate melts and forms magma. Because the magma is less dense than the surrounding rock, it rises toward the surface. Eventually, the magma breaks through the ocean floor, creating volcanoes.

The resulting volcanoes create a string of islands called an **island arc.** The curve of an island arc echoes the curve of its deep-ocean trench. Major island arcs include Japan, New Zealand, Indonesia, the Philippines, the Aleutians, and the Caribbean islands.

Volcanoes also occur where an oceanic plate is subducted beneath a continental plate. Collisions of this type produced the volcanoes of the Andes in South America and the volcanoes of Northern California, Oregon, and Washington.

Reading Checkpoint **How did the volcanoes in the Andes Mountains form?**

FIGURE 3
Volcanoes at Colliding Boundaries
Volcanoes often form where two oceanic plates collide or where an oceanic plate collides with a continental plate. In both situations, an oceanic plate sinks beneath a trench. Rock above the plate melts to form magma, which later erupts as lava.

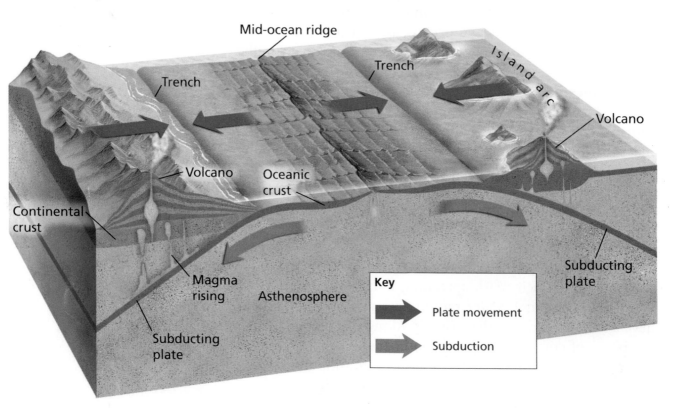

Pacific Ocean

Maui

Kauai   Oahu

H a w a i i a n   I s l a n d s

Hawaii

Hot spot

Motion of Pacific plate

FIGURE 4
Hot Spot Volcanoes
Eventually, the Pacific plate's movement will carry the island of Hawaii away from the hot spot.
Inferring Which island on the map formed first?

Hot Spot Volcanoes

Some volcanoes result from "hot spots" in Earth's mantle. A **hot spot** is an area where material from deep within the mantle rises and then melts, forming magma. 🔑 **A volcano forms above a hot spot when magma erupts through the crust and reaches the surface.** Some hot spot volcanoes lie in the middle of plates far from any plate boundaries. Other hot spots occur on or near plate boundaries.

A hot spot in the ocean floor can gradually form a series of volcanic mountains. For example, the Hawaiian Islands formed, one by one, over millions of years as the Pacific plate drifted over a hot spot. Hot spots can also form under the continents. Yellowstone National Park in Wyoming marks a hot spot under the North American plate.

Section 1 Assessment

S 6.1.e: E-LA: Reading 6.1.4, Writing 6.2.2

Vocabulary Skill Use Clues to Determine Meaning
Reread the paragraph on island arcs, under the heading Colliding Boundaries. What are some examples of island arcs?

🔑 **Reviewing Key Concepts**

1. a. **Defining** What is a volcano?
   b. **Reviewing** Where are most volcanoes located?
   c. **Relating Cause and Effect** What causes volcanoes to form at a spreading plate boundary?
2. a. **Defining** What is a hot spot?
   b. **Summarizing** How does a hot spot volcano form?
   c. **Predicting** What features form at a hot spot?

Writing in Science

Travel Brochure As a travel agent, you are planning a Pacific Ocean cruise that will visit volcanoes in the Ring of Fire and Hawaii. Write a travel brochure describing the types of volcanoes the group will see and explaining why the volcanoes formed where they did.

S 6.1.e

Mapping Earthquakes and Volcanoes

Problem Is there a pattern in the locations of earthquakes and volcanoes?

Skills Focus interpreting data

Procedure

1. Use the information in the table to mark the location of each earthquake on a world map. Use a colored pencil to draw a letter E inside a circle at each earthquake location.

2. Use a pencil of a second color to mark the volcanoes on the world map. Indicate each volcano with the letter V inside a circle.

3. Use a third pencil to lightly shade the areas in which earthquakes are found.

4. Use a fourth colored pencil to lightly shade the areas in which volcanoes are found.

Analyze and Conclude

1. **Interpreting Data** How are earthquakes distributed on the map? Are they scattered evenly or concentrated in zones?

2. **Interpreting Data** How are volcanoes distributed? Are they scattered evenly or concentrated in zones?

3. **Inferring** From your data, what can you infer about the relationship between earthquakes and volcanoes?

4. **Communicating** Suppose the locations of additional earthquakes and volcanoes were added to the map. Would the overall pattern of earthquakes and volcanoes change? Explain in writing why you think the pattern would or would not change.

More to Explore

Pick one earthquake and one volcanic eruption to investigate. (You can use the list of earthquakes in Figure 19 on page 198 and the Science & History timeline on volcanoes on pages 226–227). Plot and label the events on the map you just made. Research how the events relate to plate motions and how powerful they were. Report your findings to your class.

Earthquakes and Volcanoes			
Earthquakes		Volcanoes	
Longitude	Latitude	Longitude	Latitude
122° W	37° N	150° W	60° N
110° E	5° S	70° W	35° S
77° W	4° S	155° W	19° N
88° E	23° N	61° W	15° N
121° E	14° S	105° W	20° N
34° E	7° N	75° W	0°
74° W	44° N	122° W	40° N
70° W	30° S	120° E	15° N
10° E	45° N	60° E	30° N
85° W	13° N	160° E	55° N
125° E	23° N	37° E	3° S
30° E	35° N	145° E	40° N
140° E	35° N	120° E	10° S
102° W	18° N	14° E	41° N
75° E	28° N	105° E	5° S
150° W	61° N	35° E	15° N
68° W	47° S	70° W	30° S
175° E	41° S	175° E	39° S
143° E	3° S	168° W	53° N
160° E	53° N	16° W	64° N

Section 2
Volcanic Eruptions

CALIFORNIA
Standards Focus

S 6.1.d Students know that earthquakes are sudden motions along breaks in the crust called faults and that volcanoes and fissures are locations where magma reaches the surface.

S 6.2.d Students know earthquakes, volcanic eruptions, landslides, and floods change human and wildlife habitats.

- What happens when a volcano erupts?
- What are the two types of volcanic eruptions?
- What are a volcano's stages of activity?

Key Terms
- magma chamber
- pipe
- vent
- lava flow
- crater
- silica
- pyroclastic flow
- dormant
- extinct
- geyser

Lab zone Standards Warm-Up

What Are Volcanic Rocks Like?

Volcanoes produce lava, which hardens into rock. Two of these rocks are pumice and obsidian.

1. Observe samples of pumice and obsidian with a hand lens.
2. How would you describe the texture of the pumice? What could have caused this texture?
3. Observe the surface of the obsidian. How does the surface of the obsidian differ from pumice?

Think It Over

Developing Hypotheses What could have produced the difference in texture between the two rocks? Explain your answer.

Pumice

Obsidian

In Hawaii, there are many myths about Pele (PAY lay), the fire goddess of volcanoes. According to legend, Pele lives in the depths of Hawaii's erupting volcanoes. When Pele is angry, she causes a volcanic eruption. One result of an eruption is "Pele's hair," a fine, threadlike rock formed by lava. Pele's hair forms when lava sprays out of the ground like water from a fountain. As it cools, the lava stretches and hardens into thin strands, as shown in Figure 5.

Where does this lava come from? Lava begins as magma, which usually forms in the asthenosphere. The materials of the asthenosphere are under great pressure. Liquid magma is less dense than the solid material around it. Therefore, magma flows upward into any cracks in the rock above. As magma rises, it sometimes becomes trapped beneath layers of rock. But if an opening in weak rock allows the magma to reach the surface, a volcano forms.

FIGURE 5
Pele's Hair
Pele's hair is a type of rock formed from lava. Each strand is as fine as spun glass.

Try This Activity

Lab zone

Gases in Magma

This activity models the gas bubbles in a volcanic eruption.

1. In a 1- or 2-liter plastic bottle, mix 10 g of baking soda into 65 mL of water.

2. Put about six raisins in the water.

3. While swirling the water and raisins, add 65 mL of vinegar and stir vigorously.

4. Once the liquid stops moving, observe the raisins.

Making Models What happens after you add the vinegar? What do the raisins and bubbles represent? How is this model similar to the way magma behaves in a volcano?

Magma Reaches Earth's Surface

A volcano is more than a large, cone-shaped mountain. Inside a volcano is a system of passageways through which magma moves.

Inside a Volcano All volcanoes have a pocket of magma beneath the surface and one or more cracks through which the magma forces its way. Beneath a volcano, magma collects in a pocket called a **magma chamber.** The magma moves upward through a **pipe,** a long tube in the ground that connects the magma chamber to Earth's surface. You can see these features in Figure 7.

Molten rock and gas leave the volcano through an opening called a **vent.** Often, there is one central vent at the top of a volcano. However, many volcanoes also have other vents that open on the volcano's sides. A **lava flow** is the area covered by lava as it pours out of a vent. A **crater** is a bowl-shaped area that may form at the top of a volcano around the central vent.

A Volcanic Eruption What pushes magma to the surface? The explosion of a volcano is similar to the soda water bubbling out of a warm bottle of soda pop. You cannot see the carbon dioxide gas in a bottle of soda pop because it is dissolved in the liquid. But when you open the bottle, pressure is released. The carbon dioxide expands and forms bubbles, which rush to the surface. Like the carbon dioxide in soda pop, dissolved gases are trapped in magma. These dissolved gases are under tremendous pressure.

FIGURE 6
Lava Burp
During an eruption of Mount Kilauea, the force of a bursting gas bubble pushes up a sheet of red-hot lava.

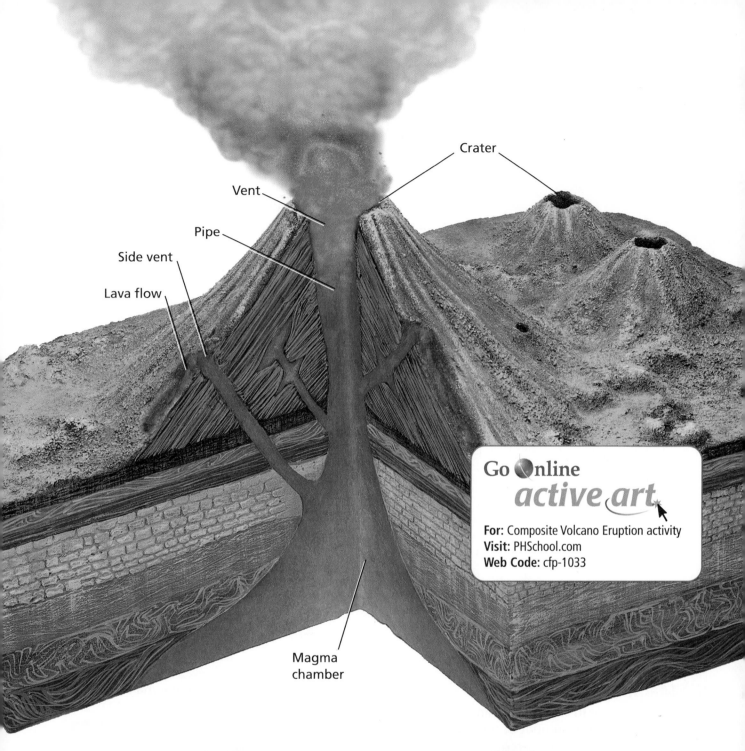

Crater

Vent

Pipe

Side vent

Lava flow

Magma chamber

Go Online
active art

For: Composite Volcano Eruption activity
Visit: PHSchool.com
Web Code: cfp-1033

As magma rises toward the surface, the pressure of the sur-rounding rock on the magma decreases. The dissolved gases begin to expand, forming bubbles. As pressure falls within the magma, the size of the gas bubbles increases greatly. These expanding gases exert an enormous force. ◉ **When a volcano erupts, the force of the expanding gases pushes magma from the magma chamber through the pipe until it flows or explodes out of the vent.** Once magma escapes from the volcano and becomes lava, the remaining gases bubble out.

 **Reading Checkpoint**   What happens to the pressure in magma as the magma rises toward the surface?

FIGURE 7
A Volcano Erupts
A volcano forms where magma breaks through Earth's crust and lava flows over the surface.
Interpreting Diagrams *What part of a volcano connects the vent with the magma chamber?*

Pahoehoe

Aa

FIGURE 8
Pahoehoe and Aa
Both pahoehoe and aa can come
from the same volcano. Pahoehoe
flows easily and hardens into a
rippled surface. Aa hardens into
rough chunks.

Kinds of Volcanic Eruptions

Some volcanic eruptions occur gradually. Others are dramatic explosions. ⬤ **Geologists classify volcanic eruptions as quiet or explosive.** The properties of magma determine how a volcano erupts. Whether an eruption is quiet or explosive depends on the magma's silica content and whether the magma is thin and runny or thick and sticky. **Silica** is a material found in magma that is formed from the elements oxygen and silicon.

Quiet Eruptions A volcano erupts quietly if its magma is low in silica. Low-silica magma is thin and runny and flows easily. The gases in the magma bubble out gently. Low-silica lava oozes quietly from the vent and can flow for many kilometers.

Quiet eruptions can produce two different types of lava that differ in temperature. Pahoehoe (pah HOH ee hoh ee) is fast-moving, hot lava that is thin and runny. The surface of a lava flow formed from pahoehoe looks like a solid mass of wrinkles and ropelike coils. Lava that is cooler and slower-moving is called aa (AH ah). Aa is thicker than pahoehoe. When aa hardens, it forms a rough surface consisting of jagged lava chunks.

The Hawaiian Islands were formed from quiet eruptions. On the Big Island of Hawaii, lava pours out of the crater on Mount Kilauea. But lava also flows out of long cracks, called fissures, on the volcano's sides. Quiet eruptions have built up the Big Island over hundreds of thousands of years.

⬤ Math: Mathematical Reasoning 6.2.4

Math Analyzing Data

Magma Composition

Magma varies in composition and is classified according to the amount of silica it contains. The graphs show the average composition of two types of magma. Use the graphs to answer the questions.

1. **Reading Graphs** Study both graphs. What materials make up both types of magma?

2. **Reading Graphs** Which type of magma has more silica? About how much silica does this type of magma contain?

3. **Estimating** A third type of magma has a silica content that is halfway between that of the other two types. About how much silica does this magma contain?

4. **Predicting** What type of magma would be more thick and sticky? Explain.

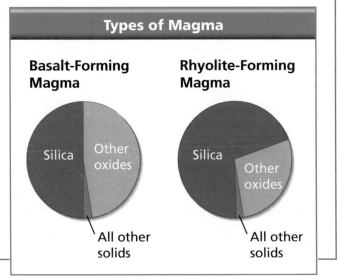

Types of Magma

Basalt-Forming Magma

Silica / Other oxides / All other solids

Rhyolite-Forming Magma

Silica / Other oxides / All other solids

Before Eruption

During Eruption

After Eruption

Explosive Eruptions A volcano erupts explosively if its magma is high in silica. High-silica magma is thick and sticky. It builds up in the volcano's pipe, plugging it like a cork in a bottle. Dissolved gases, including water vapor, cannot escape from the thick magma. The trapped gases build up pressure until they explode. The erupting gases and steam push the magma out of the volcano with incredible force. That's what happened during the eruption of Mount St. Helens, shown in Figure 9.

An explosive eruption breaks lava into fragments that quickly cool and harden into pieces of different sizes. The smallest pieces are volcanic ash—fine, rocky particles as small as a speck of dust. Pebble-sized particles are called cinders. Larger pieces, called bombs, may range from the size of a base-ball to the size of a car. A **pyroclastic flow** (py roh KLAS tik) is a type of explosive eruption that hurls out a mixture of hot gases, ash, cinders, and bombs.

Pumice and obsidian, which you observed if you did the Standards Warm-Up activity, form from high-silica lava. Obsidian forms when lava cools very quickly, giving it a smooth, glossy surface like glass. Pumice forms when gas bub-bles are trapped in fast-cooling lava, leaving spaces in the rock.

FIGURE 9
An Explosive Eruption
Mount St. Helens in Washington State erupted at 8:30 A.M. on May 18, 1980. The explosion blew off the top of the mountain.
Relating Cause and Effect *Why did Mount St. Helens erupt so explosively?*

 **What is a pyroclastic flow?**

Volcano Hazards Although quiet eruptions and explosive eruptions produce different hazards, both types of eruption can cause damage far from the crater's rim.

During a quiet eruption, lava flows from vents, setting fire to, and then burying, everything in its path. A quiet eruption can cover large areas with a thick layer of lava.

During an explosive eruption, a volcano can belch out hot clouds of deadly gases as well as ash, cinders, and bombs. Volcanic ash can bury entire towns. If it becomes wet, the heavy ash can cause roofs to collapse. If a jet plane sucks ash into its engine, the engine may stall. Eruptions can cause landslides and avalanches of mud, melted snow, and rock. The Science and History timeline shows the effects of several explosive eruptions.

Reading Checkpoint How does volcanic ash cause damage?

Science and History

The Power of Volcanoes
Within the last 150 years, major volcanic eruptions have greatly affected the land and people around them.

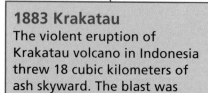

1883 Krakatau
The violent eruption of Krakatau volcano in Indonesia threw 18 cubic kilometers of ash skyward. The blast was heard 5,000 kilometers away.

1902 Mount Pelée
Mount Pelée, a Caribbean volcano, spewed out a burning cloud of hot gas and pyroclastic flows. The cloud killed 29,000 residents of St. Pierre, a city on the volcano's flank. Only two people survived.

1912 Mount Katmai
Today, a river in Alaska cuts through the thick layer of volcanic ash from the eruption of Mount Katmai.

| 1850 | 1875 | 1900 |

Stages of Volcanic Activity

The activity of a volcano may last from less than a decade to more than 10 million years. Geologists try to determine a volcano's past and whether the volcano will erupt again.

Life Cycle of a Volcano 🔄 **Geologists often use the terms** *active,* **dormant,** *or* **extinct** *to describe a volcano's stage of activity.* An active, or live, volcano is one that is erupting or has shown signs that it may erupt in the near future. A dormant, or sleeping, volcano is like a sleeping bear. Scientists expect a **dormant** volcano to awaken in the future and become active. An **extinct,** or dead, volcano is unlikely to erupt again.

In California, Lassen Peak and Mount Shasta are considered active volcanoes. Lassen Peak erupted between 1915 and 1921, and Mount Shasta erupted during the late 1700s. Craters near Long Valley on the eastern side of the Sierras are dormant but could become active again.

Writing in Science

Research and Write People have written eyewitness accounts of famous volcanic eruptions. Research one of the eruptions in the timeline. Then write a letter describing what someone observing the eruption might have seen.

2002 Mount Etna
Bulldozers constructed a wall against a scalding river of lava creeping down the slopes of Mount Etna in Sicily.

1991 Mount Pinatubo
Pinatubo in the Philippines spewed out huge quantities of ash that rose high into the atmosphere and buried nearby areas.

1980 Mount St. Helens
When Mount St. Helens in Washington exploded, it blasted one cubic kilometer of volcanic material skyward.

1950   1975   2000

Hot Springs and Geysers Hot springs and geysers are often found in areas of present or past volcanic activity. A hot spring forms when water deep underground is heated by a nearby body of magma or by hot rock. The hot water rises to the surface and collects in a natural pool. Sometimes, rising hot water and steam become trapped in a narrow crack. Pressure builds until the mixture suddenly sprays above the surface as a geyser. A **geyser** (GY zur) is a fountain of water and steam that erupts from the ground.

Monitoring Volcanoes Geologists use instruments to detect changes in and around a volcano. These changes may give warning a short time before a volcano erupts. But geologists cannot be certain about the type of eruption or how powerful it will be.

Geologists use tiltmeters and other instruments to detect slight surface changes in elevation and tilt caused by magma moving underground. They monitor any gases escaping from the volcano. A temperature increase in underground water may be a sign that magma is nearing the surface. Geologists also monitor the many small earthquakes that occur around a volcano before an eruption. The upward movement of magma triggers these quakes.

FIGURE 10
A Geyser Erupts
Old Faithful, a geyser in Yellowstone National Park, erupts about every 33 to 93 minutes.

Section 2 Assessment

S 6.1.d, 6.2.d; E-LA: Reading 6.2.4, Writing 6.2.2

Target Reading Skill Create Outlines
Complete your outline for the section Volcanic Eruptions. What are three important details that you included under the heading Life Cycle of a Volcano?

Reviewing Key Concepts

1. **a. Listing** What are the parts of a volcano?
   b. Sequencing Describe the order of parts through which magma travels as it moves to the surface.
   c. Relating Cause and Effect As a volcano erupts, what force pushes magma out of a volcano onto the surface?
2. **a. Identifying** What are the two main kinds of volcanic eruptions?
   b. Explaining What properties of magma help to determine the type of eruption?
   c. Inferring What do lava flows made of pahoehoe and aa indicate about the type of volcanic eruption that occurred?

3. **a. Naming** What are the three stages of volcanic activity?
   b. Predicting Which is more likely to be dangerous—a volcano that erupts frequently or a volcano that has been inactive for a hundred years? Why?

Writing in Science

Interview You are a television news reporter who will be interviewing a geologist. The geologist has just returned from studying a nearby volcano that may soon erupt. Write the questions that you would ask. Be sure to ask about the evidence that an eruption is coming, the type of eruption expected, and any hazards that will result. Write an answer you expect for each question.

Section 3
Volcanic Landforms

CALIFORNIA
Standards Focus

S 6.1.f Students know how to explain major features of California geology (including mountains, faults, and volcanoes) in terms of plate tectonics.

S 6.7.g Interpret events by sequence and time from natural phenomena (e.g., the relative age of rocks and intrusions).

What landforms do lava and ash create?

How does magma that hardens beneath the surface create landforms?

Key Terms

- shield volcano
- cinder cone
- composite volcano
- caldera
- volcanic neck
- dike
- sill
- intrusion
- batholith

Lab zone **Standards Warm-Up**

How Can Volcanic Activity Change Earth's Surface?

1. Use tape to secure the neck of a balloon over one end of a straw.
2. Place the balloon in the center of a box with the straw protruding.
3. Partially inflate the balloon.
4. Put damp sand on top of the balloon until it is covered.
5. Slowly inflate the balloon more. Observe what happens to the surface of the sand.

Think It Over
Making Models This activity models one of the ways in which volcanic activity can cause a mountain to form. What do you think the sand represents? What does the balloon represent?

Volcanoes have created some of Earth's most spectacular landforms. The perfect cone of Mount Fuji in Japan, shown in Figure 11, is famous around the world.

For much of Earth's history, volcanic activity on and beneath the surface has built up Earth's land areas. Volcanic activity also formed the rock of the ocean floor. Some volcanic landforms arise when lava flows build up mountains and plateaus on Earth's surface. Other volcanic landforms are the result of the buildup of magma beneath the surface.

FIGURE 11
Mount Fuji
The snow-capped volcanic cone of Mount Fuji in Japan has long been a favorite subject for artists.

Landforms From Lava and Ash

Volcanic eruptions create landforms made of lava, ash, and other materials. These landforms include shield volcanoes, cinder cone volcanoes, composite volcanoes, and lava plateaus. Look at Figure 12 to see these features. Another landform, called a caldera, results from the collapse of a volcanic mountain.

Shield Volcanoes At some places on Earth's surface, thin layers of lava pour out of a vent and harden on top of previous layers. Such lava flows gradually build a wide, gently sloping mountain called a **shield volcano.** Shield volcanoes created the Hawaiian Islands and the Medicine Lake volcano in northern California.

Cinder Cone Volcanoes If a volcano's lava is high in silica, it may produce ash, cinders, and bombs. These materials build up around the vent in a steep, cone-shaped hill or small mountain called a **cinder cone.** For example, Paricutín in Mexico erupted in 1943 in a farmer's cornfield. The volcano built up a cinder cone about 400 meters high.

FIGURE 12
Volcanic Mountains

Volcanic activity is responsible for building up much of Earth's surface. Lava from volcanoes cools and hardens into three types of mountains. It can also form lava plateaus. **Classifying** *What type of volcano is formed from thin, low-silica lava?*

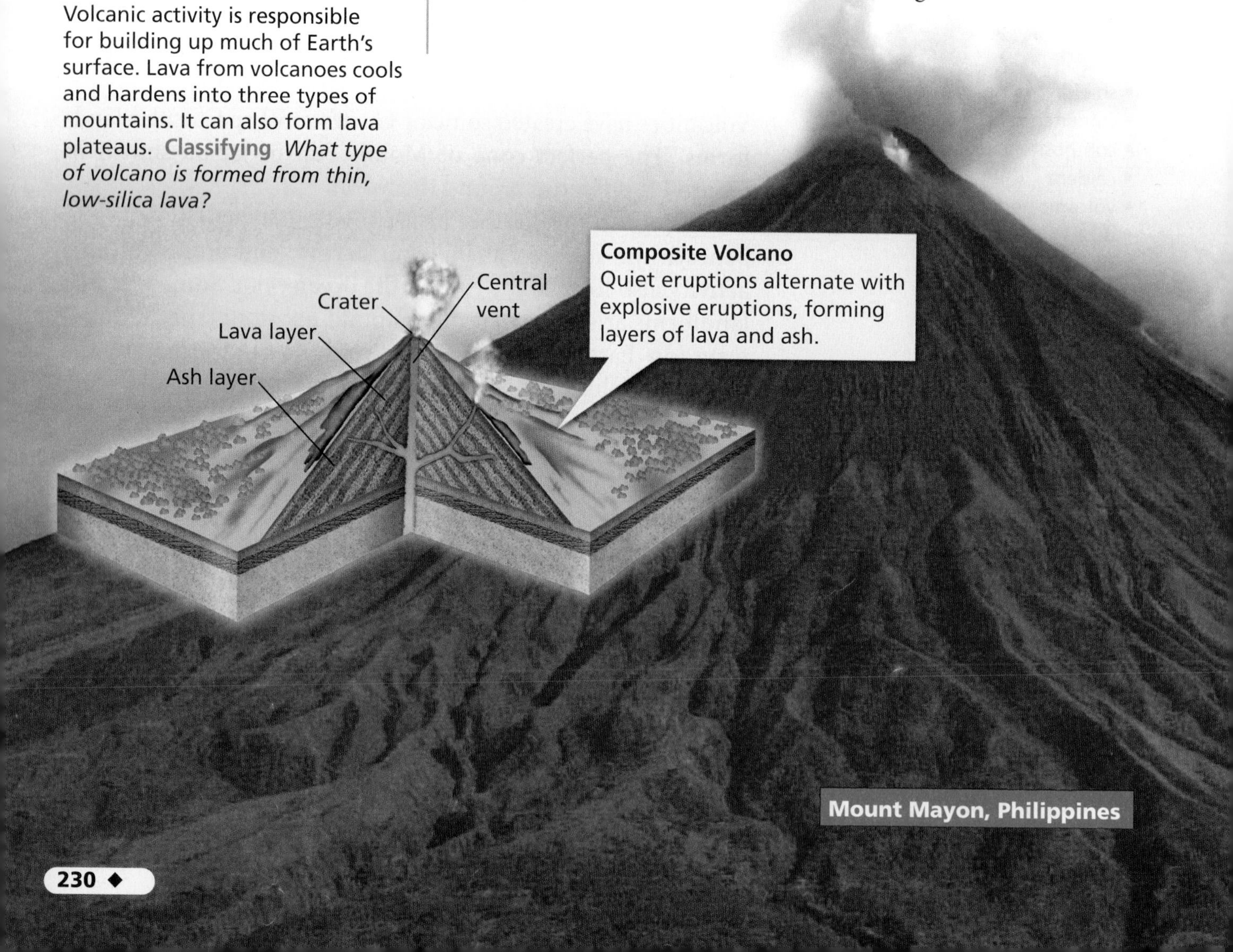

Crater

Lava layer

Ash layer

Central vent

Composite Volcano
Quiet eruptions alternate with explosive eruptions, forming layers of lava and ash.

Mount Mayon, Philippines

Composite Volcanoes Sometimes, lava flows alternate with explosive eruptions of ash, cinder, and bombs. The result is a composite volcano. **Composite volcanoes** are tall, cone-shaped mountains in which layers of lava alternate with layers of ash. Examples include Mount Fuji in Japan and Mount Shasta and Lassen Peak in California.

Lava Plateaus Some eruptions of lava form high, level areas called lava plateaus. First, lava flows out of several long cracks, or fissures, in an area. The thin, runny lava travels far before cooling and solidifying. Again and again, floods of lava flow on top of earlier floods. After millions of years, these layers of lava can form high plateaus. Examples include the Columbia Plateau in Washington, Oregon, and Idaho, and the Modoc Plateau in northeastern California.

Video Field Trip
Discovery Channel School

Volcanoes

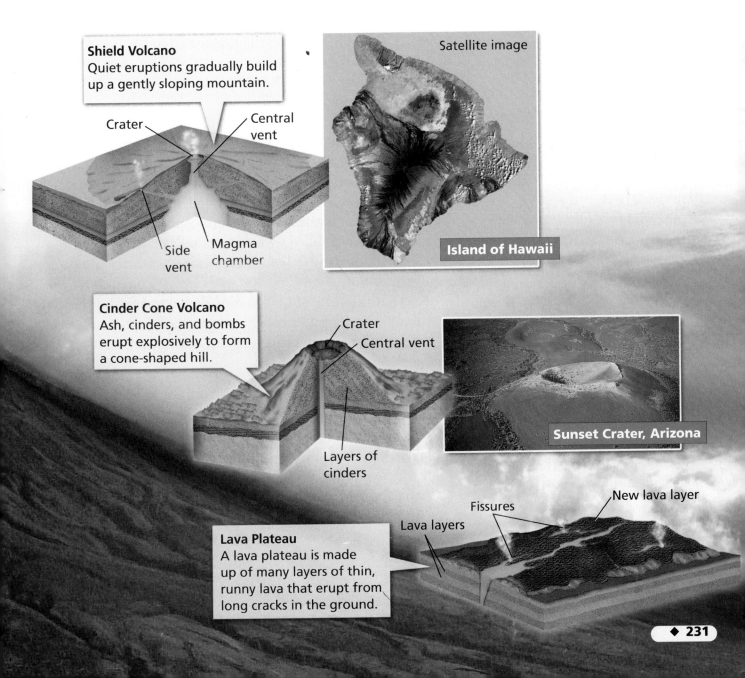

Shield Volcano
Quiet eruptions gradually build up a gently sloping mountain.

Crater

Central vent

Side vent

Magma chamber

Satellite image

Island of Hawaii

Cinder Cone Volcano
Ash, cinders, and bombs erupt explosively to form a cone-shaped hill.

Crater

Central vent

Layers of cinders

Sunset Crater, Arizona

New lava layer

Fissures

Lava layers

Lava Plateau
A lava plateau is made up of many layers of thin, runny lava that erupt from long cracks in the ground.

FIGURE 13
How a Caldera Forms
Today, Crater Lake (right) fills an almost circular caldera. A caldera forms when a volcano's magma chamber empties and the roof of the chamber collapses.

Crater Lake

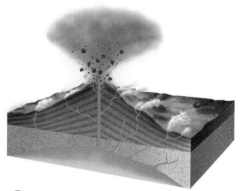

1 The top of a composite volcano explodes. Lava flows partially empty the magma chamber.

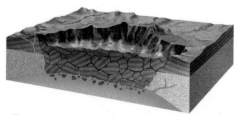

2 The roof of the magma chamber collapses, forming a caldera.

3 Later, a small cinder cone forms in the caldera, which partly fills with water.

Calderas The huge hole left by the collapse of a volcanic mountain is called a **caldera** (kal DAIR uh). The hole is filled with the pieces of the volcano that have fallen inward, as well as some lava and ash.

How does a caldera form? Enormous eruptions may empty the main vent and the magma chamber beneath a volcano. The mountain becomes a hollow shell. With nothing to support it, the top of the mountain collapses inward, forming a caldera.

In Figure 13 you can see steps in the formation of Crater Lake, a caldera in Oregon. Crater Lake formed about 7,700 years ago when a huge explosive eruption partly emptied the magma chamber of a volcano called Mount Mazama. When the volcano exploded, the top of the mountain was blasted into the atmosphere. The caldera that formed then filled with water from rain and snow.

In California, the Long Valley caldera formed after a huge eruption about 760,000 years ago. Geologists have detected the release of carbon dioxide gas and earthquakes centered near the caldera. These events are signs that volcanic eruptions might someday occur in the same area.

Soils From Lava and Ash Why would anyone live near an active volcano? People often settle close to volcanoes to take advantage of the fertile volcanic soil. The lava, ash, and cinders that erupt from a volcano are initially barren. Over time, however, the hard surface of the lava breaks down to form soil. When volcanic ash breaks down, it releases potassium, phosphorus, and other substances that plants need. As soil develops, plants are able to grow. Some volcanic soils are among the richest soils in the world. Rich soil is fertile, or able to support plant growth.

 **Reading Checkpoint** How are volcanic soils important?

Landforms From Magma

Sometimes magma forces its way through cracks in the upper crust, but fails to reach the surface. There the magma cools and hardens into rock. Over time, the forces that wear away Earth's surface—such as flowing water, ice, or wind—may strip away the layers above the hardened magma and finally expose it. **Features formed by magma include volcanic necks, dikes, sills, and batholiths.**

Volcanic Necks A volcanic neck looks like a giant tooth stuck in the ground. A **volcanic neck** forms when magma hardens in a volcano's pipe. The softer rock around the pipe wears away, exposing the hard rock of the volcanic neck. Ship Rock in New Mexico, shown in Figure 14, is a volcanic neck.

Dikes and Sills Magma can force its way across or between rock layers. Magma that forces itself across rock layers hardens into a **dike.** Sometimes, a dike can be seen slanting through bedrock along a highway cut. When magma squeezes between horizontal layers of rock, it forms a **sill.**

Dikes and sills are examples of igneous intrusions. An **intrusion** forms when magma hardens underground to form igneous rock. An intrusion is always younger than the rocks around it.

Go Online
SCi LINKS
NSTA

For: Links on volcanic effects
Visit: www.SciLinks.org
Web Code: scn-1034

FIGURE 14
Volcanic Necks, Dikes, and Sills
Magma that hardens beneath the surface may form volcanic necks, dikes, and sills. A dike extends outward from Ship Rock, a volcanic neck in New Mexico.
Applying Concepts *In the photograph of the sill below, which is older: the sill or the rock layers above and below it?*

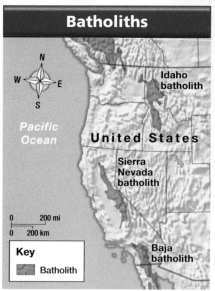

Batholiths

FIGURE 15
Batholiths
Several large batholiths form the core of mountain ranges in western North America, including the Sierra Nevada, shown here.

Batholiths Large rock masses called batholiths form the core of many mountain ranges. A **batholith** (BATH uh lith) is a mass of rock formed when a large body of magma cools inside the crust. The map in Figure 15 shows just how big batholiths really are. The Sierra Nevada batholith extends for roughly 600 kilometers along the eastern side of California. The photograph shows how a batholith looks when the layers of rock above it have worn away.

Section 3 Assessment

S 6.1.f, 6.7.g; E-LA: Reading 6.1.4, Writing 6.2.2

Vocabulary Skill Use Clues to Determine Meaning Reread the paragraphs under the heading Calderas. Find clues for a definition, an explanation, and an example of a caldera.

Reviewing Key Concepts

1. a. Identifying What are the three main types of volcanoes?

  b. Comparing and Contrasting Compare the three types of volcanic mountains in terms of shape, type of eruption, and the materials that make up the volcano.

2. a. Listing What features form as a result of magma hardening beneath Earth's surface?

  b. Explaining What are two ways in which mountains can form as a result of magma hardening beneath Earth's surface?

c. Predicting After millions of years, what landform forms from hardened magma in the pipe of an extinct volcano?

Writing in Science

Explaining a Process Write an explanation of the process that formed Crater Lake. In your answer, include the type of volcanic mountain and eruption involved, as well as the steps in the process. (*Hint:* Look at the diagram in Figure 13 before you write.)

California Geology

S 6.1.f Students know how to explain major features of California geology (including mountains, faults, and volcanoes) in terms of plate tectonics.

How does plate tectonics help to explain features of California's geology?

Key Terms

- basin
- Central Valley

Lab zone Standards **Warm-Up**

How Do Plate Motions Affect California?

1. Look at the map of plate boundaries in Figure 17 on page 236. Study the map and the map key.
2. What are the names of the plates that make up California and the nearby part of the Pacific Ocean? Write the names of the plates in your notebook.
3. Determine what types of plate boundaries are found in or near California. Write the types of boundaries in your notebook.

Think It Over

Relating Cause and Effect Recall that there are volcanoes in northern California. Which feature on the map causes the volcanoes there? Explain.

If you flew in an airplane across the Mojave Desert, you might spot Amboy Crater. This extinct cinder cone would be easy to see—it's nearly half a kilometer across. Why is there a volcano here? Plate movement caused the crust to stretch and crack, allowing magma to reach the surface.

Many volcanic landforms dot the California landscape. But volcanoes are only one type of geologic feature that makes up a landscape.

Plate Tectonics and California

You have probably seen many maps of California. Plate tectonics helps to explain the geologic features on those maps.

The movements of the Pacific and North American plates produced California's major geological features. These features include faults, volcanoes, mountain ranges, and basins. These features took shape over millions of years.

FIGURE 16
Amboy Crater
Amboy Crater formed in the Mojave Desert about 10,000 years ago.

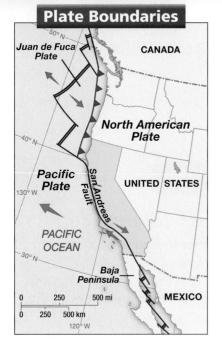

Plate Boundaries

Key
— Sliding plate boundary
━ Spreading plate boundary
▼ Colliding plate boundary
→ Direction of plate motion

FIGURE 17
Plate Tectonics and California
The movements of three plates have shaped the geologic features of California over millions of years.
Predicting *What will happen to the Baja peninsula as sea-floor spreading occurs in the nearby Gulf of California?*

Faults Faults are often found along or near the boundaries of plates. As you can see in Figure 17, the Pacific and North American plates slide past each other along the San Andreas fault. They push and pull on the crust with enormous force. The crust breaks, forming many other faults, shown in Figure 18.

Volcanoes In the Pacific Ocean north of California, the Juan de Fuca plate is being subducted beneath the North American plate. Mount Shasta and Lassen Peak in northern California are volcanoes that resulted from this process.

Mountain Ranges Plate motion provides the force that pushes up California's mountains. The Sierra Nevada began to form several million years ago as plate movements pushed up a batholith. Plate motions folded the crust to push up the northern Coast Ranges. The Transverse Ranges formed as plate motions rotated a block of crust and squeezed it upward.

Basins Plate movements sometimes cause the crust to warp, or bend, downward. The result is a basin. A **basin** is a broad, bowl-shaped valley. For example, the **Central Valley** of California is a huge basin with the Sierras and Coast Ranges on either side. As these mountains rose, the crust forming the Central Valley's floor was bent downward. Slowly, a thick layer of sediment built up on the valley floor.

Millions of years ago, some of California's basins slowly sank below sea level. Later, plate motions pushed the crust above sea level again.

Section 4 Assessment

S 6.1.f, E-LA: Reading 6.1.4

Vocabulary Skill **Use Clues to Determine Meaning**
Reread the paragraphs under the heading Basins. Find clues for a definition, an explanation, and an example of a basin.

Reviewing Key Concepts

1. a. **Listing** What four features of California geology does plate tectonics explain?
   b. **Explaining** How does the San Andreas fault help to explain why there are so many other faults in California?
   c. **Predicting** Los Angeles lies on the Pacific plate. San Jose lies on the North American plate. How will the distance between the two cities change over millions of years?

Lab zone **At-Home Activity**

Modeling California
Use plastic putty to make a model of California, showing the state's major geologic features. Use one color of putty for the part of the state that is on the Pacific plate and another color for the part that is on the North American plate. Explain your model to family members.

California's Geologic Features

FIGURE 18
Many geologic processes worked together to form California's landscape of volcanoes, faults, mountain ranges, and basins.

1 Volcanoes

Mount Shasta formed as a result of the subduction of the Juan de Fuca plate.

2 Faults

The San Andreas fault slices through the San Francisco peninsula.

3 Mountain Ranges

Plate motions pushed up the Transverse Range in California.

Basins 4

Like the Central Valley, the Los Angeles basin formed where the crust was bent downward.

42° N

CASCADE RANGE

Goose Lake

Klamath R.

Medicine Lake
Glass Mtn.
△ 2,323 m

KLAMATH MTS.
△ Mt. Shasta
4,317 m

Trinity R.

1

Lassen Peak
△ 3,187 m

40° N

C O A S T   R A N G E S

Eel R.

Sacramento R.

S I E R R A

Clear Lake △

Yuba R.

Lake Tahoe

American R.

Sacramento ★
Hayward Fault

San Andreas

38° N

San Francisco
San Francisco Peninsula
San Jose

Oakland

Calaveras Fault

Fault

San Joaquin R.

C E N T R A L   V A L L E Y

Tuolumne R.

Merced R.

Mono Lake

Long Valley
Caldera △

N E V A D A

Owens Valley

GREAT BASIN

PACIFIC OCEAN

C O A S T   R A N G E S

36° N

Kings R.

Mt. Whitney
▲ 4,418 m

Death Valley

86 m below sea level
(Lowest point in U.S.) ▼

CALIFORNIA

Kern R.

San

Garlock Fault

Andreas

MOJAVE DESERT

Fault

TRANSVERSE RANGES

Ventura Basin

San Jacinto Fault
3

Los Angeles
Los Angeles Basin
4

Eisinore

Coyote Creek Fault

Fault

Salton Sea

Colorado River

Channel Islands

Imperial Fault

N
W   E
S

120° W

San Diego

118° W

Imperial Valley

Key
- – – – Fault
- ▲ Volcano
- △ Area of potential volcanic activity

Elevation (m)
- More than 3,000
- 2,000–3,000
- 1,000–2,000
- 500–1,000
- 200–500
- 0–200

0   50   100 mi
0   50   100 km

Gelatin Volcanoes

Materials

unflavored gelatin mold in bowl

aluminum pizza pan with holes punched at 2.5-cm intervals

3 small cardboard oatmeal boxes

tray or shallow pan and rubber gloves

red food coloring, plastic cup, and water

plastic syringe, 10 cc, and plastic knife

unlined paper

Problem   How does magma move inside a volcano?

Skills Focus   developing hypotheses, making models, observing

Procedure

1. Before magma erupts as lava, how does it travel up from underground magma chambers? Record your hypothesis.

2. Remove the gelatin from the refrigerator. Loosen the gelatin from its container by briefly placing the container of gelatin in a larger bowl of hot water.

3. Place the pizza pan over the gelatin so the mold is near the center of the pizza pan. While holding the pizza pan against the top of the mold, carefully turn the mold and the pizza pan upside down.

4. Carefully lift the bowl off the gelatin mold to create a gelatin volcano.

5. Place the pizza pan with the gelatin mold on top of the oatmeal boxes as shown below.

6. Mix the red food coloring and water in the plastic cup. Then fill the syringe with "magma" (the red water). Remove air bubbles from the syringe by holding it upright and squirting out a small amount of water.

7. Insert the tip of the syringe through a hole in the pizza pan near the center of the gelatin volcano. Inject the magma into the gelatin very slowly. Observe what happens to the magma.

8. Repeat steps 6 and 7 as many times as possible. Observe the movement of the magma each time. Note any differences in the direction the magma takes when the syringe is inserted into different parts of the gelatin volcano. Record your observations.

Data Table			
Test	Initial Location of Magma	Position and Shape of Magma Bodies	Other Observations
1.			
2.			
3.			
4.			

9. Look down on your gelatin volcano from above. Make a sketch of the positions and shapes of the magma bodies. Label your drawing "Top View."

10. Carefully use a knife to cut your volcano in half. Separate the pieces and examine the cut surfaces for traces of the magma bodies.

11. Sketch the positions and shapes of the magma bodies on one of the cut faces. Label your drawing "Cross Section."

Analyze and Conclude

1. **Observing** Describe how the magma moved through your model. Did the magma move straight up through the center of your model volcano or did it branch off in places? Explain why you think the magma moved in this way.

2. **Developing Hypotheses** What knowledge or experience did you use to develop your hypothesis? How did the actual movement compare with your hypothesis?

3. **Inferring** How would you explain any differences in the direction the magma flowed when the syringe was inserted in different parts of the gelatin volcano?

4. **Making Models** How does what you observed in your model compare to the way magma moves through real volcanoes? How could you change your model to be more like a real volcano?

5. **Communicating** Prepare your model as a display to teach other students about volcanoes. Make a list of the volcanic features in your model. For each feature, write a description of how the feature would form in a real volcano.

More to Explore

Plan to repeat the investigation using a mold made of two layers of gelatin. Before injecting the magma, develop a hypothesis about the effect of layering on the movement of magma. Record your observations to determine if your hypothesis was correct. What volcanic feature is produced by this version of the model? Can you think of other volcanic features that you could model using gelatin layers? *Obtain your teacher's permission before carrying out your investigation.*

An eruption of
Mount Kilauea, Hawaii

Study Guide

🔑 The **BIG Idea** Volcanic eruptions result from plate motions and produce landforms such as volcanic mountains and lava plateaus.

1 Volcanoes and Plate Tectonics

🔹 **Key Concepts** S 6.1.e

- Volcanic belts form along the boundaries of Earth's plates.
- A volcano forms above a hot spot when magma erupts through the crust and reaches the surface.

Key Terms

volcano	Ring of Fire
magma	island arc
lava	hot spot

2 Volcanic Eruptions

🔹 **Key Concepts** S 6.1.d, 6.2.d

- When a volcano erupts, the force of the expanding gases pushes magma from the magma chamber through the pipe until it flows or explodes out of the vent.
- Geologists classify volcanic eruptions as quiet or explosive.
- Geologists often use the terms *active, dormant,* or *extinct* to describe a volcano's stage of activity.

Key Terms

magma chamber	silica
pipe	pyroclastic flow
vent	dormant
lava flow	extinct
crater	geyser

3 Volcanic Landforms

🔹 **Key Concepts** S 6.1.f, 6.7.g

- Volcanic eruptions create landforms made of lava, ash, and other materials. These landforms include shield volcanoes, cinder cone volcanoes, composite volcanoes, and lava plateaus.
- Features formed by magma include volcanic necks, dikes, sills, and batholiths.

Key Terms

shield volcano	dike
cinder cone	sill
composite volcano	intrusion
caldera	batholith
volcanic neck	

4 California Geology

🔹 **Key Concepts** S 6.1.f

- The movements of the Pacific and North American plates produced California's major geological features. These features include faults, volcanoes, mountain ranges, and basins.

Key Terms
basin
Central Valley

Review and Assessment

Target Reading Skill

Create Outlines In your notebook, add details and definitions to your outline for Kinds of Volcanic Eruptions in Section 2.

> **Volcanic Eruptions**
>
> I. Kinds of Volcanic Eruptions
>   A. Quiet Eruptions
>   B. Explosive Eruptions

Reviewing Key Terms

Choose the letter of the best answer.

1. Volcanoes found where two oceanic plates collide form a(n)
   a. cinder cone. **b.** island arc.
   c. hot spot. **d.** Ring of Fire.

2. Magma becomes lava when it reaches a volcano's
   a. geyser. **b.** magma chamber.
   c. pipe. **d.** vent.

3. Lava that forms smooth, ropelike coils when it hardens is called
   a. aa.
   b. silica.
   c. pahoehoe.
   d. pyroclastic flow.

4. A volcanic mountain made up of volcanic ash, cinders, and bombs is called a
   a. shield volcano.
   b. cinder cone.
   c. composite volcano.
   d. caldera.

5. The collapse of a volcano's magma chamber may produce a(n)
   a. crater.
   b. island arc.
   c. caldera.
   d. batholith.

6. A volcano that has not erupted for many years but might erupt again in the future is
   a. extinct.
   b. dormant.
   c. pyroclastic.
   d. active.

7. Magma that hardens in a volcano's pipe forms a
   a. volcanic neck.
   b. sill.
   c. volcanic crater.
   d. hot spot.

Complete the following sentences so that your answers clearly explain the key terms.

8. Far from plate boundaries, a volcano may form over a **hot spot,** which is _____ .

9. An explosive eruption may produce a **pyroclastic flow,** which is _____ .

10. When magma that is high in silica erupts, it can form a **cinder cone,** which is _____ .

11. A thin sheet of magma can harden underground to form a **dike,** which is _____ .

12. Between California's Coast Ranges and the Sierra Nevada lies the **Central Valley,** which is _____ .

13. In a volcanic area, underground water and steam can form a **geyser,** which is _____ .

Writing in Science

Comparison Write a comparison of the three different kinds of volcanoes. Discuss the ways in which all three are similar and the ways in which they are different. Use the correct terms to describe each type of volcano.

Video Assessment
Discovery Channel School
Volcanoes

Review and Assessment

Checking Concepts

14. What is the Ring of Fire?

15. What process causes volcanoes to form along the mid-ocean ridge?

16. What are two ways volcanoes can form near converging plate boundaries?

17. What effect does temperature have on the characteristics of magma?

18. How does a shield volcano form?

19. Describe the three stages in the "life cycle" of a volcano.

20. Why can earthquakes be a warning sign that an eruption is about to happen?

21. What type of geologic feature is the Central Valley of California? How did it form?

Thinking Critically

22. **Predicting** Is a volcanic eruption likely to occur on the East Coast of the United States? Explain your answer.

23. **Comparing and Contrasting** Compare the way in which an island arc forms with the way in which a hot spot volcano forms.

24. **Making Generalizations** How might a volcanic eruption affect the area around a volcano, including its plant and animal life?

25. **Relating Cause and Effect** Look at the diagram of a lava plateau below. Why doesn't the type of eruption that produces a lava plateau produce a volcanic mountain instead?

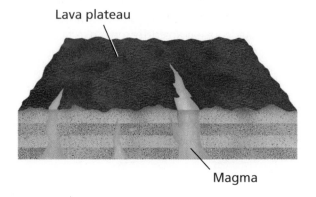

Lava plateau

Magma

Applying Skills

Refer to the diagram to answer Questions 26–29.

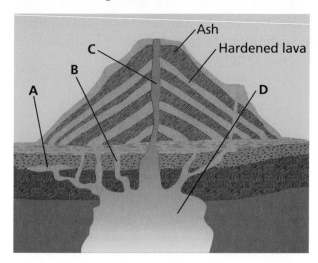

26. **Classifying** What is this volcano made of? How do geologists classify a volcano made of these materials?

27. **Developing Hypotheses** What is the feature labeled A in the diagram? What is the feature labeled B? How do these features form?

28. **Predicting** What is the feature labeled C in the diagram? If this feature becomes plugged with hardened magma, what could happen to the volcano? Explain.

29. **Inferring** What is the feature labeled D in the diagram? What can you infer about this feature if the volcano becomes dormant?

Lab zone Standards Investigation

Performance Assessment Present your documentary about a volcanic region to your class. Evaluate how well your documentary presented the information you collected. As you watched the other documentaries, did you see any similarities between how people in different regions live with volcanoes?

Choose the letter of the best answer.

1. A volcano is most likely to form
   A in the center of a plate.
   B where an oceanic plate collides with a continental plate.
   C where two pieces of crust slide past each other.
   D in a basin.   **S 6.1.e**

2. Mount Shasta is a composite volcano in northern California. Mount Shasta formed as a result of a
   A hot spot.
   B sliding plate boundary.
   C spreading plate boundary.
   D colliding plate boundary.   **S 6.1.f**

3. Which answer is a benefit that explains why people might live in the region around a volcano?
   A A volcano removes trees.
   B Volcanic eruptions are interesting to watch.
   C Volcanic soil is good for growing crops.
   D Volcanoes release various gases.   **S 6.2.d**

4. Study the diagram below. Which answer best describes the age of the sedimentary rock layers below Layer A relative to the intrusion?
   A much younger
   B older
   C the same age
   D slightly younger   **S 6.7.g**

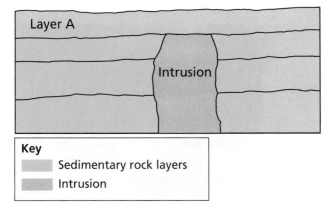

Layer A

Intrusion

Key
Sedimentary rock layers
Intrusion

5. Magma that hardens between layers of rock forms a
   A volcanic neck.
   B dike.
   C batholith.
   D sill.   **S 6.1.d**

6. The diagram below shows the formation of what volcanic feature?
   A caldera
   B island arc volcano
   C hot spot
   D mid-ocean ridge   **S 6.1.e**

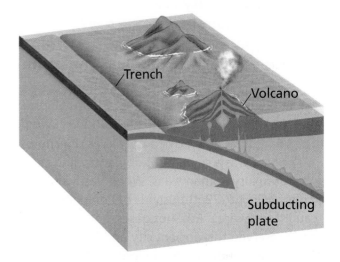

Trench

Volcano

Subducting plate

Apply the **BIG Idea**

7. A geologist was observing the area around a dormant volcano. She decided that this volcano must have had an explosive eruption. Describe the evidence geologists would use to make this decision. In your answer, discuss the properties of the magma and the types of rock that would result from an explosive eruption.   **S 6.1.d**

Pompeii

In the Shadow of Vesuvius

Which ancient city . . .
- **was destroyed in one day?**
- **lay buried for centuries?**
- **is a window on ancient Roman life?**

Nearly 2,000 years ago, the city of Pompeii prospered on the fertile slopes near the volcano Vesuvius. About 100 kilometers north of Pompeii was the city of Rome.

Pompeii was a small but popular trading center and site for luxury Roman villas. When Vesuvius erupted violently in A.D. 79, thousands of Pompeians were caught unawares. Ash, hot gases, and rocks trapped and preserved this ancient city and its inhabitants. Today, excavations at Pompeii reveal the daily life of a bustling city at the height of the Roman Empire.

The Forum
Mount Vesuvius looms behind the ruins of the Forum at Pompeii.

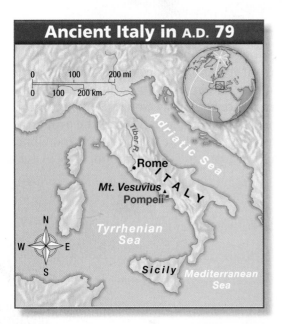

Ancient Italy in A.D. 79

0   100   200 mi
0   100   200 km

Tiber R.

Adriatic Sea

Rome

Mt. Vesuvius
Pompeii

ITALY

Tyrrhenian
Sea

Sicily   Mediterranean
Sea

N
W E
S

Fresco From Pompeii
This fresco portrays an educated couple. Here the wife holds a stylus and wax tablet, and the husband holds a scroll.

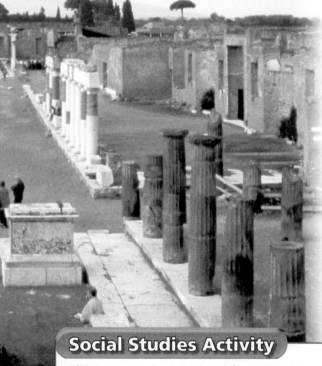

Daily Life in Pompeii

Excavations at Pompeii began in the mid-1700s and continue today. The findings have been astounding. Life stopped abruptly that fateful day. Thousands abandoned their meals or left food simmering on the fire. A baker had just placed the day's round loaves of bread in the oven. A jeweler left his work unfinished on a bench. Houses and public buildings that remained intact reveal daily life through frescoes (wall paintings), sculpture, mosaic floors, and expansive indoor courtyards.

At the center of city life was the Forum, a large, rectangular open space where Pompeians conducted business and politics. Here people sold meat and fish as well as fruits, vegetables, grapes, and olives grown on the fertile slopes of Vesuvius. Some merchants sold cloth made from the wool of sheep raised nearby. Others sold copper pots, oil lamps, furniture, and glassware. People of all classes gathered at the Forum to exchange ideas, notices, and gossip. Some even wrote graffiti on the walls!

Bakery and Bread
This fresco, found in Pompeii, shows a man purchasing bread. A carbonized loaf of bread, below, indicates how bread was cut into wedges.

Social Studies Activity

The Forum was central to life in Pompeii. Research another structure in Pompeii. Write a short report that describes its structure and function. Explain the building's importance to Roman society. Possible topics include

- amphitheater
- city walls
- temples
- basilica
- public baths
- water system

Vesuvius Erupts!

Most volcanoes and earthquakes occur along plate boundaries, where Earth's crust is fractured and weak. Unknown to the people of Pompeii, their city and surrounding areas rested directly over a subduction zone where the Eurasian plate meets the African plate. Although Mount Vesuvius had erupted in the past, the volcano had lain dormant for hundreds of years.

Around noon on August 24, A.D. 79, the volcano suddenly exploded. Volcanic ash and gases shot 27 kilometers into the air. During the rest of the day and into the night, 3 meters of ash blanketed the city. But the destruction wasn't over. Around midnight, a deadly pyroclastic flow poured over the entire area, trapping about 2,000 Pompeians who had not yet escaped. Afterward, an additional 3 meters of volcanic debris rained down on Pompeii. This layer of material sealed the city, preserving it nearly intact for centuries.

The Great Eruption of Mt. Vesuvius
This eighteenth-century painting is by Louis-Jean Desprez.

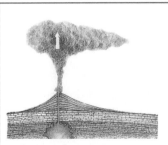

1 Magma explodes from the vent in Mount Vesuvius. A column of pumice and ash rises.

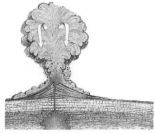

2 Pumice and ash blow southeast and fall on Pompeii.

3 The column of ash collapses and pyroclastic flows cover the region.

Science Activity

Different kinds of lava vary in silica content and temperature and therefore spread at different rates. Use molasses to model lava flow rates.

1. Measure one tablespoon of molasses and slowly pour it onto a plastic plate. Time and record how long it takes for the molasses to stop spreading.

2. Add one tablespoon of sand to one tablespoon of molasses. Stir the mixture thoroughly. Repeat the pouring and timing of Step 1.

How does the sand affect the molasses' rate of flow? What does the sand represent in your model? How would a volcano with this type of lava be likely to erupt?

3. Heat one tablespoon of molasses over a hot plate. Repeat Step 1. How does the rate of flow of the heated molasses compare with that of the molasses in Step 1? What can you conclude about the effect of temperature on the flow rate of lava?

Eyewitness Account

Pliny the Younger (around A.D. 62–113) was a nephew of the scholar and historian Pliny the Elder. When he was about 17 years old, he witnessed the eruption of Mount Vesuvius while visiting a city across the bay from Pompeii. Some 25 years later, Pliny the Younger described the terrifying scene in a letter to the historian Tacitus.

Excerpt from Pliny the Younger's letter to Tacitus, about A.D. 104

"I look back: a dense cloud looms behind us, following us like a flood poured across the land. . . . A darkness came that was not like a moonless or cloudy night, but more like the black of closed and unlighted rooms. You could hear women lamenting, children crying, men shouting. Some were calling for parents, others for children or spouses. . . . There were some so afraid of death that they prayed for death. . . . It grew lighter, though that seemed not a return of day, but a sign that the fire was approaching. The fire itself actually stopped some distance away, but darkness and ashes came again, a great weight of them. We stood up and shook the ash off again and again, otherwise we would have been covered with it and crushed by the weight. . . .

At last the cloud thinned out and dwindled to no more than smoke or fog. Soon there was real daylight. The sun was even shining, though with the lurid glow it has after an eclipse. The sight that met our still terrified eyes was a changed world, buried in ash like snow."

▲ Pliny the Younger

Language Arts Activity

An eyewitness account is a firsthand, factual account of an event or experience. Pliny the Younger filled his letter with vivid sensory details—details that help the reader see, feel, smell, taste, and hear—in order to convey what the Vesuvius eruption was like.

Choose an interesting event that you've witnessed. Write an eyewitness account of it. Provide readers with key facts, such as the time and place of the event, along with interesting and vivid details.

Dog at Pompeii
This is a plaster cast of a dog left chained to a post during the eruption of Vesuvius.

Plate Tectonics and Earth's Structure

Chapter 4
Plate Tectonics

The BIG Idea

Earth's plates are large pieces of the lithosphere that move slowly, producing faults, mountain ranges, volcanoes, and deep-ocean trenches.

- What causes convection currents in Earth's mantle?
- What was Alfred Wegener's hypothesis about the continents?
- What is the process of sea-floor spreading?
- What are the three types of plate boundaries?

Chapter 5
Earthquakes

The BIG Idea

Plate motions produce stress in Earth's crust that leads to faults, mountain building, and earthquakes.

- What land features result from the forces of plate movement?
- How does the energy of an earthquake travel through Earth?
- What kinds of damage does an earthquake cause?

Chapter 6
Volcanoes

The BIG Idea

Volcanic eruptions result from plate motions and produce landforms such as volcanic mountains and lava plateaus.

- Where are most of Earth's volcanoes found?
- What happens when a volcano erupts?
- What landforms do lava and ash create?

Unit 2 Assessment

A junction is a point where things come together. At the Mendocino Triple Junction, three of Earth's plates come together off the coast of northern California.

As you can see in the map, the triple junction marks one end of the San Andreas fault. The Pacific plate slides north along the fault until it reaches the junction. There, the Pacific plate twists to the west. But north of the junction, the Gorda plate pushes east and collides with the North American plate. This collision forms a subduction zone.

Why is the Mendocino Triple Junction important? Plate movements around the junction cause earthquakes and volcanoes.

Strong earthquakes occur as the Gorda plate sinks beneath the North American plate. Many earthquakes also happen along the boundary of the Gorda and Pacific plates and along the San Andreas fault.

Huge active volcanoes—Mount Shasta and Lassen Peak—have formed through subduction of the Gorda plate. Geologists have also detected volcanic activity in the ocean along the western edge of the Gorda plate.

Mendocino Triple Junction

Key
→ Direction of plate motion
━ Spreading boundary
▲▲ Colliding boundary
— Sliding boundary
▲ Volcano

1. What type of plate boundary is found where the Gorda Plate meets the North American Plate? *(Chapter 4)*

   a. colliding   b. spreading
   c. sliding   d. uplifting

2. What type of fault is the San Andreas fault? *(Chapter 5)*

   a. tension   b. normal
   c. reverse   d. strike-slip

3. What caused the volcanic activity along the western edge of the Gorda plate? (*Hint:* Look at the map to see the type of plate boundary there.) *(Chapter 6)*

   a. lava erupting from a deep-ocean trench
   b. magma forming above a subducting plate
   c. lava erupting from a mid-ocean ridge
   d. plates moving over a hot spot

4. **Summary** Write a paragraph summarizing plate movements at the Mendocino Triple Junction and the effects of those plate movements on the geology of northern California.

Chapter 7

The Atmosphere

An aurora illuminates the winter sky over a forest in Manitoba, Canada. ▶

Video Preview
Discovery Channel School
The Atmosphere

Focus on the BIG Idea

S 6.4.d, 6.4.e

How do air pressure and temperature vary in the atmosphere?

Check What You Know

Suppose you dove into a pool. The deeper you went, the more water there would be above you. The weight of the water above causes the pressure to increase as you go deeper.

Like water, air has weight, and pushes on you from all directions. Considering the example above, how do you think the pressure of the air above you would change if you climbed a mountain?

Build Science Vocabulary

The images shown here represent some of the key terms in this chapter. You can use this vocabulary skill to help you understand the meaning of some key terms in this chapter.

Vocabulary Skill

Greek Word Origins

Many science words come to English from ancient Greek. In this chapter, you will learn the word *atmosphere*. You've learned that *sphaira* means "sphere" or "ball" (see Chapter 4). The Greek word *atmos* means "vapor" or "gas." Therefore, the *atmosphere* is the layer of gases that surrounds Earth.

atmos	+	sphaira	=	atmosphere
vapor, gas		sphere		a layer of vapor or gases that surrounds Earth

Greek Origin	Meaning	Examples
atmos	Vapor, gas	Atmosphere
exo-	Out, outer	Exosphere
meter	Measure	Anemometer, barometer, thermometer
photo-	Light	Photochemical
thermos	Heat	Thermosphere

Apply It!

Review the Greek origins and meanings in the table. Then predict the meaning of *exosphere*. Revise your definition as needed.

In your notebook, create a table like the one above. After reading Section 3, add the Greek prefixes *tropo-* and *meso-*. Then complete the table with meanings and examples.

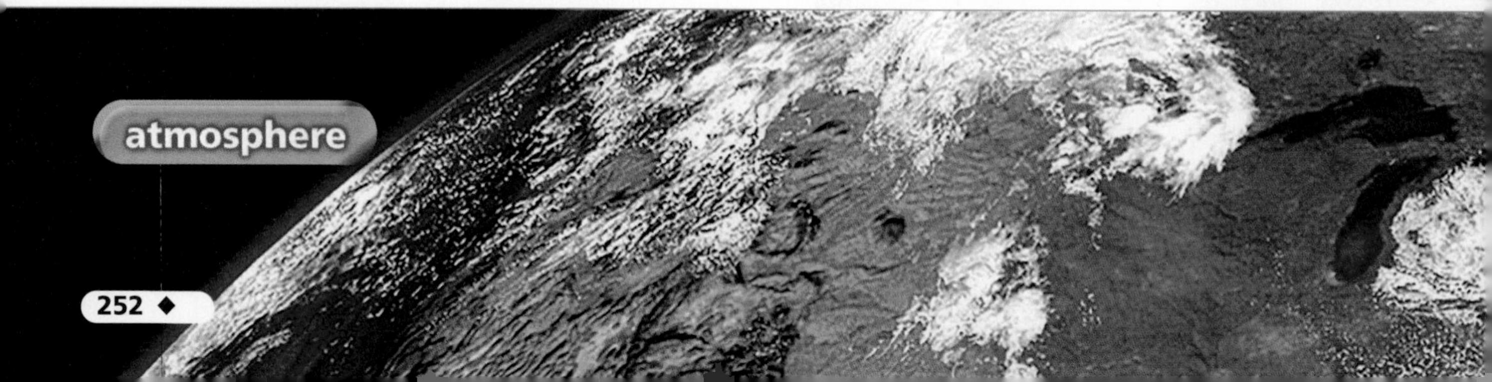

atmosphere

barometer

ionosphere

electromagnetic wave

convection

sea breeze

Chapter 7
Vocabulary

Interactive Textbook

Build Science Vocabulary
Online
Visit: PHSchool.com
Web Code: cwj-3070

How to Read Science

 Take Notes

Science chapters are packed with information. Each section needs to be read at least twice. After finding the main idea and important details in a section, take notes so you have something to study.

In your notebook, create a two-column note-taking organizer.

- Label the left side "Recall Clues and Questions."
- Label the right side "Notes."
- Under "Notes," write key ideas, using phrases and abbreviations. Include a few important details.
- Use your notes to write a summary statement for each red heading.
- Under "Recall Clues and Questions," write review and study questions.

As you take notes, think about the key concepts and key terms in the section. Look at the example for the first part of Section 1.

Recall Clues and Questions	Notes: The Air Around You
What is weather?	Weather: condition of Earth's atmosphere
What is the atmosphere?	Atmosphere: gases around Earth
What is the atmosphere made of?	Atmosphere made of • nitrogen • oxygen • carbon dioxide • water vapor • other gases
	<u>Summary Statement:</u> Earth's atmosphere is made up of nitrogen, oxygen, carbon dioxide, water vapor, and many other gases, plus liquids and solids.

Apply It!

What are two important ideas found in the Notes column?
What questions in the left column help you recall the content?

Take notes as you read each section in this chapter.

Build Your Own Weather Station

In this chapter you will learn about a variety of weather factors — such as air pressure, temperature, and wind speed. As you learn about these factors, you will build your own weather station. Your weather station will include simple instruments that you will use to monitor the weather.

Your Goal

To design and build a weather station to monitor at least three weather factors and to look for patterns that can be used to predict the next day's weather

In completing your investigation, you will

- develop a plan for measuring weather factors
- design and build instruments for your weather station
- use your instruments to collect and record data in a daily log
- display your data in a set of graphs
- use your data and graphs to try to predict the weather
- follow the safety guidelines in Appendix A

Plan It!

Begin your investigation by deciding where your weather station will be located. Plan which instruments you will build and how you will make your measurements.

Prepare a log to record your observations. Collect and record measurements each day. Graph the data and look for any patterns that you can use to predict the next day's weather. Compare your predictions with the actual weather conditions the next day. At the end of the chapter, you will present your observations and explain how well you predicted the weather.

The Air Around You

CALIFORNIA
Standards Focus

S 6.4.e Students know differences in pressure, heat, air movement, and humidity result in changes in weather.

S 6.6.b Students know different natural energy and material resources, including air, soil, rocks, minerals, petroleum, fresh water, wildlife, and forests, and know how to classify them as renewable or nonrenewable.

- What is the composition of Earth's atmosphere?
- How is the atmosphere important to living things?
- What causes smog and acid rain?

Key Terms
- weather
- atmosphere
- ozone
- water vapor
- pollutant
- photochemical smog
- acid rain

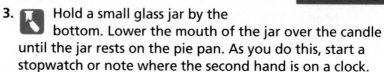

Lab zone **Standards Warm-Up**

How Long Will the Candle Burn?

1. Put on your goggles.
2. Stick a small piece of modeling clay onto an aluminum pie pan. Push a short candle into the clay. Carefully light the candle.
3. Hold a small glass jar by the bottom. Lower the mouth of the jar over the candle until the jar rests on the pie pan. As you do this, start a stopwatch or note where the second hand is on a clock.
4. Watch the candle carefully. How long does the flame burn?
5. Wearing an oven mitt, remove the jar. Relight the candle and then repeat Steps 3 and 4 with a larger jar.

Think It Over

Inferring How would you explain any differences between your results in Steps 4 and 5?

The sky is full of thick, dark clouds. In the distance you see a bright flash. Thirty seconds later, you hear a crack of thunder. You begin to run and reach your home just as the downpour begins. That was close! From your window you look out to watch the storm.

Does the weather where you live change often, or is it fairly constant from day to day? **Weather** is the condition of Earth's atmosphere at a particular time and place. But what is the atmosphere? Earth's **atmosphere** (AT muh sfeer) is the envelope of gases that surrounds the planet. To understand the relative size of the atmosphere, imagine that Earth is the size of an apple. If you breathe on the apple, a thin film of water droplets will form on its surface. Earth's atmosphere is like that water on the apple—a thin layer of gases on Earth's surface.

◀ **From space, Earth's atmosphere appears as a thin layer near the horizon.**

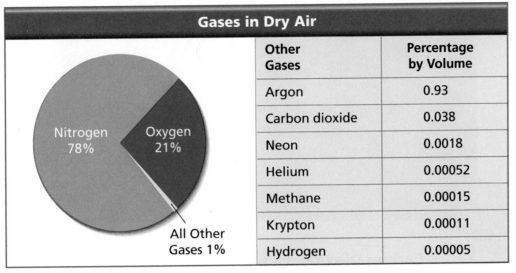

Gases in Dry Air

Other Gases	Percentage by Volume
Argon	0.93
Carbon dioxide	0.038
Neon	0.0018
Helium	0.00052
Methane	0.00015
Krypton	0.00011
Hydrogen	0.00005

Nitrogen 78%

Oxygen 21%

All Other Gases 1%

FIGURE 1
Dry air in the lower atmosphere generally has about the same composition of gases.
Interpreting Data
What two gases make up most of the air?

Composition of the Atmosphere

The atmosphere is made up of a mixture of atoms and molecules of different kinds. An atom is the smallest unit of a chemical element that can exist by itself. Molecules are made up of two or more atoms. ⬮ **Earth's atmosphere is made up of nitrogen, oxygen, carbon dioxide, water vapor, and many other gases, as well as particles of liquids and solids.**

Nitrogen As you can see in Figure 1, nitrogen is the most common gas in the atmosphere. It makes up a little more than three fourths of the air we breathe. Each nitrogen molecule consists of two nitrogen atoms. Nitrogen moves in a cycle from the air to the soil, into living things, and then back into the air.

Oxygen Even though oxygen is the second most abundant gas in the atmosphere, it makes up less than one fourth of the volume. Plants and other organisms use light to convert water and carbon dioxide into oxygen and to produce food. Thus, like nitrogen, the oxygen in the air moves through a natural cycle involving living things.

Oxygen is also involved in many other important processes. Any fuel you can think of, from the gasoline in a car to the candles on a birthday cake, uses oxygen as it burns. Without oxygen, a fire will go out. Burning uses oxygen rapidly. During other processes, oxygen is used slowly. For example, steel reacts slowly with oxygen to form iron oxide, or rust.

Most oxygen molecules have two oxygen atoms. **Ozone** is a form of oxygen that has three oxygen atoms in each molecule instead of the usual two.

FIGURE 2
Burning Uses Oxygen
Oxygen is necessary in order for the wood to burn.

 **Reading Checkpoint** What is ozone?

FIGURE 3
Water Vapor in the Air
There is very little water vapor in the air over the desert where this lizard lives. In the tropical rain forest (right), where the frog lives, as much as four percent of the air may be water vapor.

Carbon Dioxide Each molecule of carbon dioxide has one atom of carbon and two atoms of oxygen. Carbon dioxide is essential to life. Plants take in carbon dioxide from the air to make food. When plant and animal cells break down food to produce energy, they give off carbon dioxide as a waste product.

When fuels such as coal and gasoline are burned, they release carbon dioxide. Burning these fuels increases the amount of carbon dioxide in the atmosphere.

Other Gases Oxygen and nitrogen together make up 99 percent of dry air. Argon and carbon dioxide make up most of the other one percent. The remaining gases are called trace gases because only small amounts of them are present.

Water Vapor So far, we have discussed the composition of dry air. In reality, air is not dry because it contains water vapor. **Water vapor** is water in the form of a gas. Water vapor is invisible. It is not the same thing as steam, which is made up of tiny droplets of liquid water. Each water molecule contains two atoms of hydrogen and one atom of oxygen.

The amount of water vapor in the air varies greatly from place to place and from time to time. Water vapor plays an important role in Earth's weather. Clouds form when water vapor condenses out of the air to form tiny droplets of liquid water or crystals of ice. If these droplets or crystals become heavy enough, they can fall as rain or snow.

Particles Pure air contains only gases. But pure air exists only in laboratories. The air we breathe also contains tiny solid and liquid particles of dust, smoke, salt, and other chemicals. You can see some of these particles in the air around you, but most of them are too small to see.

 **Reading Checkpoint** What is water vapor?

Lab zone Try This **Activity**

Breathe In, Breathe Out

How can you detect carbon dioxide in the air you exhale?

1. Put on your goggles.
2. Fill a glass or beaker halfway with limewater.
3. ☠ Using a straw, slowly blow air through the limewater for about a minute. **CAUTION:** *Do not suck on the straw or drink the limewater.*
4. What happens to the limewater?

Developing Hypotheses
What do you think would happen if you did the same experiment after jogging for 10 minutes? What would your results tell you about exercise and carbon dioxide?

Importance of the Atmosphere

Earth's atmosphere makes conditions on Earth suitable for living things. The atmosphere contains oxygen and other gases that living things need to survive. Living things also need warmth and liquid water. By trapping energy from the sun, the atmosphere keeps most of Earth's surface warm enough for water to exist as a liquid. In addition, Earth's atmosphere protects living things from ultraviolet radiation from the sun. The atmosphere also prevents Earth's surface from being hit by most meteoroids, which are rocks from outer space.

The atmosphere is constantly changing, with gases such as nitrogen, oxygen, and carbon dioxide moving in and out of living things, the land, and the water. From this point of view, air can be considered a renewable resource.

Air Quality

Breathing brings air into your lungs, where the oxygen you need is taken into your body. But not everything in the air is healthful. You may also breathe in tiny particles or even a small amount of harmful gases.

If you live in a large city, you may have noticed a brown haze in the air. Even if you live far from a city, the air around you may contain pollutants. **Pollutants** are harmful substances in the air, water, or soil. Air that contains harmful particles and gases is said to be polluted. Air pollution can affect the health of humans and other living things.

Sources of Pollution Some pollution occurs naturally. For example, many natural processes add particles to the atmosphere. Forest fires, soil erosion, and dust storms release a great deal of smoke and dust into the air. The wind carries particles of molds and pollen. Erupting volcanoes spew out clouds of dust and ash along with poisonous gases.

Go Online

SciLINKS NSTA

For: Links on the atmosphere
Visit: www.SciLinks.org
Web Code: scn-0911

Most air pollution is the result of burning fossil fuels, such as coal, oil, gasoline, and diesel fuel. Almost half of this pollution comes from cars and other motor vehicles. Factories and power plants that burn coal and oil also release pollution. Burning fossil fuels produces a variety of pollutants, including carbon monoxide, nitrogen oxides, and sulfur oxides.

Smog and Acid Rain High levels of air pollution decrease the quality of the air. 🔊 **The burning of fossil fuels can cause smog and acid rain.** One hundred years ago, the city of London, England, was dark and dirty. Factories burned coal, and most houses were heated by coal. The air was full of soot. In 1905, the term *smog* was created by combining the words *smoke* and *fog* to describe this type of air pollution.

Fortunately, London-type smog is no longer common. Instead, many cities today have another type of smog. The brown haze that develops in sunny cities is called **photochemical smog** (foh toh KEM ih kul). The *photo-* in photochemical means "light." Photochemical smog is formed by the action of sunlight on pollutants such as hydrocarbons and nitrogen oxides. These chemicals react to form a brownish mixture of ozone and other pollutants. Smog can irritate the eyes, throat, and lungs. It can also harm plants and other living things.

Another result of air pollution is acid rain. Rain is naturally slightly acidic, but rain that contains more acid than normal is known as **acid rain.** How does acid rain form? The burning of coal that contains a lot of sulfur produces sulfur oxides, substances composed of oxygen and sulfur. Acid rain forms when nitrogen oxides and sulfur oxides combine with water in the air to form nitric acid and sulfuric acid.

Acid rain is sometimes strong enough to damage the surfaces of buildings and statues. It also harms lakes and ponds. Acid rain can make water so acidic that many plants and animals can no longer live in it.

FIGURE 4
Results of Acid Rain
This scientist is studying trees damaged by acid rain. Needle-leafed trees such as pines and spruces are especially sensitive to acid rain. Acid rain may make tree needles turn brown or fall off.

Improving Air Quality

In the United States, the federal and state governments have passed a number of laws and regulations to reduce air pollution. The Environmental Protection Agency (EPA) monitors air pollutants in the United States. Air quality in this country has generally improved over the past 30 years. The amounts of most major air pollutants have decreased. Many newer cars cause less pollution than older models. Recently-built power plants are less polluting than power plants that have been in operation for many years.

However, there are now more cars on the road and more power plants burning fossil fuels than in the past. Unfortunately, the air in many American cities is still polluted. Voluntary measures, such as greater use of public transportation in place of driving, could reduce the total amount of air pollution produced. Many people think that stricter regulations are needed to control air pollution. Others argue that reducing air pollution can be very expensive and that the benefits of stricter regulations may not be worth the costs.

FIGURE 5
Public Tranportation
Public transportation, like the light rail system above, can reduce air pollution.

 **Reading Checkpoint** **Explain one way that air quality could be improved.**

Section 1 Assessment

S 6.4.e, 6.6.b, E-LA: Reading 6.1.0, Writing 6.2.2

Vocabulary Skill Greek Word Origins Use what you know about the Greek prefix *photo-* to explain the meaning of *photochemical smog.*

Reviewing Key Concepts

1. a. Defining What is the atmosphere?
   b. Listing What are the four most common gases in dry air?
   c. Explaining Why are the amounts of gases in the atmosphere usually shown as percentages of dry air?

2. a. Describing What are three ways in which the atmosphere is important to life on Earth?
   b. Predicting How would the amount of carbon dioxide in the atmosphere change if there were no plants?
   c. Developing Hypotheses How would Earth be different without the atmosphere?

3. a. Identifying What human activity is responsible for the formation of smog and acid rain?
   b. Explaining What kinds of harm does photochemical smog cause?
   c. Inferring Do you think that photochemical smog levels are higher during the winter or during the summer? Explain.

Writing in Science

Summary Write a paragraph that summarizes in your own words how oxygen from the atmosphere is important. Include its importance to living things and in other processes.

Air Pressure

CALIFORNIA
Standards Focus

S 6.4.e Students know differences in pressure, heat, air movement, and humidity result in changes in weather.

- What are some of the properties of air?
- What instruments are used to measure air pressure?
- How does increasing altitude affect air pressure and density?

Key Terms

- density
- pressure
- air pressure
- barometer
- mercury barometer
- aneroid barometer
- altitude

Like a heavy backpack pressing on your shoulders, the weight of the atmosphere causes air pressure. ▼

Lab zone Standards **Warm-Up**

Does Air Have Mass?

1. Use a balance to find the mass of a deflated balloon.
2. Blow up the balloon fully and tie the neck closed. Predict whether the mass of the balloon plus the air you have compressed into it will differ from the mass of the deflated balloon.
3. Find the mass of the inflated balloon. Compare this to the mass of the deflated balloon. Was your prediction correct?

Think It Over
Drawing Conclusions What can you conclude about whether air has mass? Explain your conclusion.

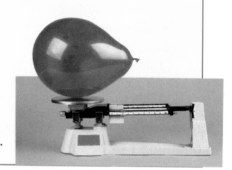

The air is cool and clear—just perfect for an overnight hiking trip. You've stuffed your backpack with your tent, sleeping bag, stove, and food. When you hoist your pack onto your back, its weight presses into your shoulders. That pack sure is heavy! By the end of the day, you'll be glad to take it off and get rid of all that weight.

But here's a surprise: Even when you take off your pack, your shoulders will still have pressure on them. The weight of the atmosphere itself is constantly pressing on your body.

Properties of Air

It may seem to you that air has no mass. But in fact, air consists of atoms and molecules, which have mass. So air must have mass.  **Because air has mass, it also has other properties, including density and pressure.**

Density Recall that the amount of mass in a given volume of air is its **density.** You can calculate the density of a substance by dividing its mass by its volume.

$$\text{Density} = \frac{\text{Mass}}{\text{Volume}}$$

If there are more molecules in a given volume, the density is greater. If there are fewer molecules, the density is less.

Pressure The force pushing on an area or surface is known as **pressure.** The weight of the atmosphere exerts a force on surfaces. **Air pressure** is the result of the weight of a column of air pushing down on an area. The column of air extends upward through the entire atmosphere, as shown in Figure 6.

The atmosphere is heavy. The weight of the column of air above your desk is about the same as the weight of a large schoolbus. So why doesn't air pressure crush your desk? The reason is that the molecules in air push in all directions—down, up, and sideways. The air pushing down on top of your desk is balanced by the air pushing up on the bottom of your desk.

Air pressure can change from day to day. A denser substance has more mass per unit volume than a less dense one. So denser air exerts more pressure than less dense air.

Reading Checkpoint How does the density of air affect air pressure?

FIGURE 6
Air Pressure
There is a column of air above you all the time. The weight of the air in the atmosphere causes air pressure.

FIGURE 7
Mercury Barometer
Air pressure pushes down on the surface of the mercury in the dish, causing the mercury in the tube to rise. The air pressure is greater on the barometer on the right, so the mercury is higher in the tube.
Predicting What happens to the level of mercury in the tube when the air pressure decreases?

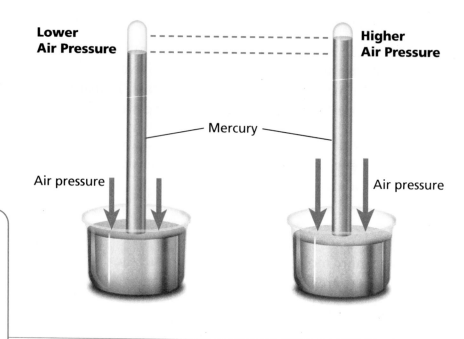

Lower Air Pressure

Higher Air Pressure

Mercury

Air pressure

Air pressure

Go **O**nline
active.art

For: Measuring Air Pressure activity
Visit: PHSchool.com
Web Code: cfp-4012

Measuring Air Pressure

A **barometer** (buh RAHM uh tur) is an instrument that is used to measure air pressure. ● **Two kinds of barometers are mercury barometers and aneroid barometers.**

Mercury Barometers Figure 7 shows the way a mercury barometer works. A **mercury barometer** consists of a glass tube open at the bottom end and partially filled with mercury. The space in the tube above the mercury is almost a vacuum—it contains very little air. The open end of the tube rests in a dish of mercury. The air pressure pushing down on the surface of the mercury in the dish is equal to the pressure exerted by the weight of the column of mercury in the tube. When the air pressure increases, it presses down more on the surface of the mercury. Greater air pressure forces the column of mercury higher. At sea level the mercury column is about 76 centimeters high, on average.

Aneroid Barometers If you have a barometer at home, it is probably an aneroid barometer. The word *aneroid* means "without liquid." An **aneroid barometer** (AN uh royd) has an airtight metal chamber. The metal chamber is sensitive to changes in air pressure. When air pressure increases, the thin walls of the chamber are pushed in. When the pressure drops, the walls bulge out. The chamber is connected to a dial by a series of springs and levers. As the shape of the chamber changes, the needle on the dial moves.

Units of Air Pressure Weather reports use several different units for air pressure. Most weather reports for the general public use inches of mercury. For example, if the column of mercury in a mercury barometer is 30 inches high, the air pressure is "30 inches of mercury" or just "30 inches."

National Weather Service maps indicate air pressure in millibars. One inch of mercury is approximately 33.87 millibars, so 30 inches of mercury is approximately equal to 1,016 millibars.

 What are two common units that are used to measure air pressure?

FIGURE 8
Aneroid Barometer
In an aneroid barometer, changes in air pressure cause the walls of an airtight metal chamber to flex in and out. This causes the needle on the barometer's dial to move.

Altitude and the Properties of Air

At the top of a mountain, the air pressure is less than the air pressure at sea level. **Altitude,** or elevation, is the distance above sea level, the average level of the surface of the oceans. **Air pressure decreases as altitude increases. As air pressure decreases, so does density.**

Altitude Affects Air Pressure Imagine a stack of books. Which book has more weight on it, the second book from the top or the book at the bottom? The second book from the top has only the weight of one book on top of it. The book at the bottom of the stack has the weight of all the books pressing on it.

Air at sea level is like the bottom book. Sea-level air has the weight of the whole atmosphere pressing on it. So air pressure is greater at sea level. Air near the top of the atmosphere is like the second book from the top. There, the air has less weight pressing on it, and thus has lower air pressure.

FIGURE 9
Air Pressure and Altitude
Air pressure is greater at sea level and decreases as the altitude increases.

Sea Level

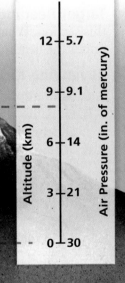

Altitude (km)	Air Pressure (in. of mercury)
12	5.7
9	9.1
6	14
3	21
0	30

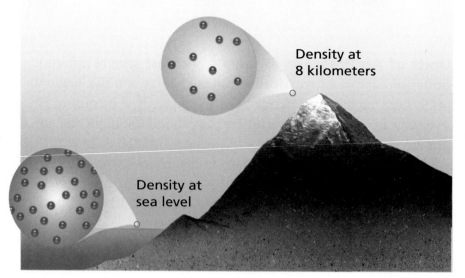

FIGURE 10
Altitude and Density
The density of air decreases as altitude increases. Air at sea level has more gas molecules in each cubic meter than air at the top of a mountain.

Density at 8 kilometers

Density at sea level

Video Field Trip
Discovery Channel School
The Atmosphere

Altitude Also Affects Density As you go up through the atmosphere, the density of the air decreases. This means the gas molecules that make up the atmosphere are farther apart at high altitudes than they are at sea level. If you were near the top of a tall mountain and tried to run, you would quickly get out of breath. Why? The air contains 21 percent oxygen, whether you are at sea level or on top of a mountain. However, since the air is less dense at a high altitude, there are fewer oxygen molecules to breathe in each cubic meter of air than at sea level. So you would become short of breath quickly at high altitudes.

Reading Checkpoint **Why is it hard to breathe at the top of a mountain?**

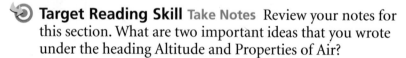
Section 2 Assessment S 6.4.e, E-LA: Reading 6.2.4

Target Reading Skill Take Notes Review your notes for this section. What are two important ideas that you wrote under the heading Altitude and Properties of Air?

Reviewing Key Concepts

1. a. **Defining** What is air pressure?
   b. **Explaining** How does increasing the density of a gas affect its pressure?
2. a. **Listing** What are two instruments that can be used to measure air pressure?
   b. **Measuring** What units are commonly used to measure air pressure?
   c. **Calculating** How many millibars are equal to 27.23 inches of mercury?
3. a. **Defining** What is altitude?
   b. **Relating Cause and Effect** As altitude increases, how does air pressure change? How does density change?
   c. **Predicting** What changes in air pressure would you expect if you carried a barometer down a mine shaft?

Lab zone **At-Home Activity**

Model Air Pressure Here's how you can show your family that air has pressure. Fill a glass with water. Place a piece of cardboard over the top of the glass. Hold the cardboard in place with one hand as you turn the glass upside down. **CAUTION:** *Be sure the cardboard does not bend.* Now remove your hand from the cardboard. What happens? Explain to your family that the cardboard doesn't fall because the air pressure pushing up on it is greater than the weight of the water pushing down.

Layers of the Atmosphere

CALIFORNIA
Standards Focus

S 6.4.e Students know differences in pressure, heat, air movement, and humidity result in changes in weather.

- What are the four main layers of the atmosphere?
- What are the characteristics of each layer?

Key Terms
- troposphere
- stratosphere
- mesosphere
- thermosphere
- temperature
- ionosphere
- exosphere

Lab zone Standards **Warm-Up**

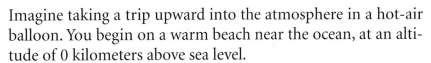

Is Air There?

1. Use a heavy rubber band to tightly secure a plastic bag over the top of a wide-mouthed jar.
2. Gently try to push the bag into the jar. What happens? Is the air pressure higher inside or outside the bag?
3. Remove the rubber band and line the inside of the jar with the plastic bag. Use the rubber band to tightly secure the edges of the bag over the rim of the jar.
4. Gently try to pull the bag out of the jar with your fingertips. What happens? Is the air pressure higher inside or outside the bag?

Think It Over

Predicting Explain your observations in terms of air pressure. How do you think differences in air pressure would affect a balloon as it traveled up through the atmosphere?

Imagine taking a trip upward into the atmosphere in a hot-air balloon. You begin on a warm beach near the ocean, at an altitude of 0 kilometers above sea level.

You hear a roar as the balloon's pilot turns up the burner to heat the air in the balloon. The balloon begins to rise, and Earth's surface gets farther and farther away. As the balloon rises to an altitude of 3 kilometers, you realize that the air is getting colder. As you continue to rise, the air gets colder still. At 6 kilometers you begin to have trouble breathing. The air is becoming less dense. It's time to go back down.

What if you could have continued your balloon ride up through the atmosphere? As you rose higher, the air pressure and temperature would change dramatically.

 Scientists divide Earth's atmosphere into four main layers classified according to changes in temperature. These layers are the troposphere, the stratosphere, the mesosphere, and the thermosphere. Read on to learn more about each of these layers.

▲ Hot-air balloon

The Troposphere

You live in the inner, or lowest, layer of Earth's atmosphere, the **troposphere** (TROH puh sfeer). *Tropo-* means "turning" or "changing." Conditions in the troposphere are more variable than in the other layers.  **The troposphere is the layer of the atmosphere in which Earth's weather occurs.**

Although hot-air balloons cannot travel very high into the troposphere, other types of balloons can. To measure weather conditions, scientists launch weather balloons that carry instruments up into the atmosphere. The balloons are not fully inflated before they are launched. Recall that air pressure decreases as you rise through the atmosphere. Leaving the balloon only partly inflated gives the gas inside the balloon room to expand as the air pressure outside the balloon decreases.

The depth of the troposphere varies from 16 kilometers above the equator to less than 9 kilometers above the North and South poles. Although it is the shallowest layer, the troposphere contains almost all of the mass of the atmosphere.

As altitude increases in the troposphere, the temperature decreases. On average, for every 1-kilometer increase in altitude, the air gets about 6.5 Celsius degrees cooler. At the top of the troposphere, the temperature stops decreasing and stays at about −60°C. Water here forms thin, feathery clouds of ice.

The Stratosphere

The **stratosphere** extends from the top of the troposphere to about 50 kilometers above Earth's surface. *Strato-* means "layer" or "spread out."  **The stratosphere is the second layer of the atmosphere and contains the ozone layer.**

The lower stratosphere is cold, about −60°C. Surprisingly, the upper stratosphere is warmer than the lower stratosphere. Why is this? The middle portion of the stratosphere contains a layer of air where there is much more ozone than in the rest of the atmosphere. (Recall that ozone is the three-atom form of oxygen.) When the ozone absorbs energy from the sun, the energy is converted into heat, warming the air. The ozone layer is also important because it protects Earth's living things from dangerous ultraviolet radiation from the sun.

As a weather balloon rises through the stratosphere, the air pressure outside the balloon continues to decrease. The volume of the balloon increases. Finally, the balloon bursts, and the instrument package falls back to Earth's surface.

Reading Checkpoint Why is the upper stratosphere warmer than the lower stratosphere?

FIGURE 11
Weather Balloon
This weather balloon will carry a package of instruments to measure weather conditions high in the atmosphere.
Applying Concepts Which is the first layer of the atmosphere that the balloon passes through on its way up?

Go Online
PLANET DIARY

For: More on the ozone layer
Visit: PHSchool.com
Web Code: cfd-4013

FIGURE 12

Layers of the Atmosphere

The atmosphere is divided into four layers: the troposphere, the stratosphere, the mesosphere, and the thermosphere. The thermosphere is further divided into the ionosphere and the exosphere.

Interpreting Diagrams *How deep is the mesosphere?*

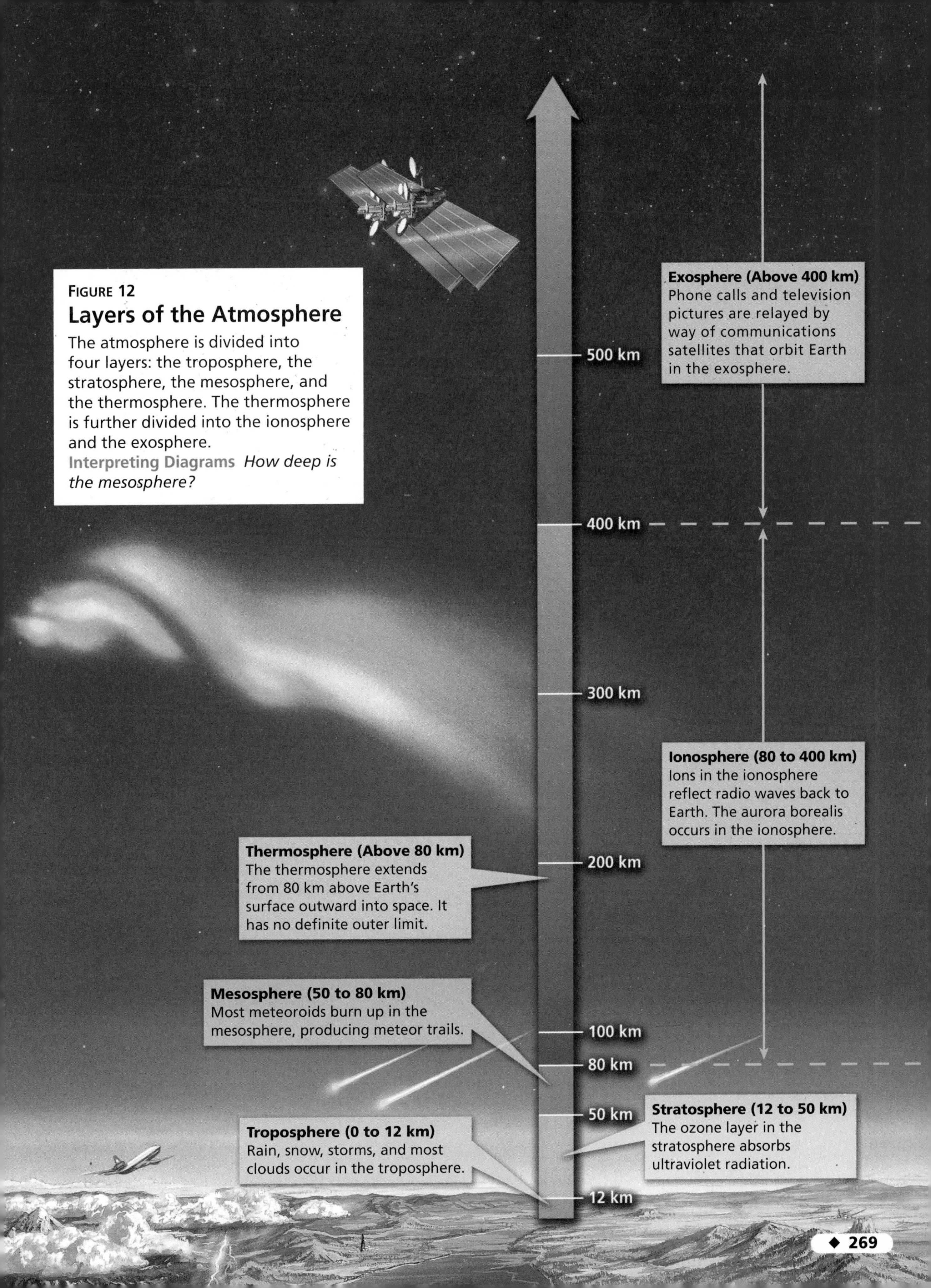

Exosphere (Above 400 km)
Phone calls and television pictures are relayed by way of communications satellites that orbit Earth in the exosphere.

Ionosphere (80 to 400 km)
Ions in the ionosphere reflect radio waves back to Earth. The aurora borealis occurs in the ionosphere.

Thermosphere (Above 80 km)
The thermosphere extends from 80 km above Earth's surface outward into space. It has no definite outer limit.

Mesosphere (50 to 80 km)
Most meteoroids burn up in the mesosphere, producing meteor trails.

Troposphere (0 to 12 km)
Rain, snow, storms, and most clouds occur in the troposphere.

Stratosphere (12 to 50 km)
The ozone layer in the stratosphere absorbs ultraviolet radiation.

500 km
400 km
300 km
200 km
100 km
80 km
50 km
12 km

Math — Analyzing Data

Changing Temperatures

The graph shows how temperatures in the atmosphere change with altitude. Use it to answer the questions below.

1. **Reading Graphs** What two variables are being graphed? In what unit is each measured?

2. **Reading Graphs** What is the temperature at the bottom of the stratosphere?

3. **Interpreting Data** Which layer of the atmosphere has the lowest temperature?

4. **Making Generalizations** Describe how temperature changes as altitude increases in the troposphere.

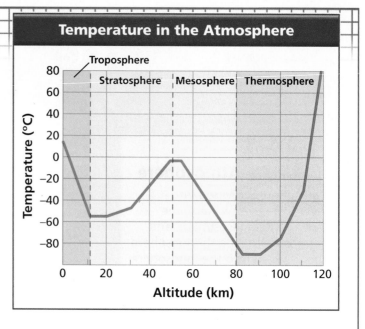

Temperature in the Atmosphere

The Mesosphere

Above the stratosphere, a drop in temperature marks the beginning of the next layer, the **mesosphere.** *Meso-* means "middle," so the mesosphere is the middle layer of the atmosphere. The mesosphere begins 50 kilometers above Earth's surface and ends at an altitude of 80 kilometers. In the outer mesosphere, temperatures approach −90°C.

🔑 **The mesosphere is the layer of the atmosphere that protects Earth's surface from being hit by most meteoroids.** Meteoroids are chunks of stone and metal from space. What you see as a shooting star, or meteor, is the trail of hot, glowing gases the meteoroid leaves behind in the mesosphere.

The Thermosphere

Near the top of the atmosphere, the air is very thin. At 80 kilometers above Earth's surface, the air is only about 0.001 percent as dense as the air at sea level. It's as though you took a cubic meter of air at sea level and expanded it into 100,000 cubic meters at the top of the mesosphere. 🔑 **The outermost layer of Earth's atmosphere is the thermosphere.** The **thermosphere** extends from 80 kilometers above Earth's surface outward into space. It has no definite outer limit, but blends gradually with outer space.

The *thermo-* in thermosphere means "heat." Even though the air in the thermosphere is thin, it is very hot, up to 1,800°C. This is because sunlight strikes the thermosphere first. Nitrogen and oxygen molecules convert this energy into heat.

Despite the high temperature, you would not feel warm in the thermosphere. An ordinary thermometer would show a temperature well below 0°C. Why is that? **Temperature** is the average amount of energy of motion of each molecule of a substance. The gas molecules in the thermosphere move very rapidly, so the temperature is very high. However, the molecules are spaced far apart in the thin air. There are not enough of them to collide with a thermometer and warm it very much.

The thermosphere is divided into two layers. The lower layer, called the **ionosphere** (eye AHN uh sfeer), begins about 80 kilometers above the surface and extends to about 400 kilometers. Energy from the sun causes gas molecules in the ionosphere to become electrically charged particles called ions. Radio waves bounce off ions in the ionosphere back to Earth's surface. Brilliant light displays, such as those shown in Figure 13, also occur in the ionosphere. In the Northern Hemisphere, these displays are called the Northern Lights, or the aurora borealis. Auroras are caused by particles from the sun that enter the ionosphere near the poles. These particles strike atoms in the ionosphere, causing them to glow.

Exo- means "outer," so the **exosphere** is the outer portion of the thermosphere. The exosphere extends from about 400 kilometers outward for thousands of kilometers.

FIGURE 13
Aurora Borealis
The aurora borealis, seen from Fairbanks, Alaska, creates a spectacular display in the night sky.

 **Reading Checkpoint** **What is the ionosphere?**

Section 3 Assessment

S 6.4.e, E-LA: Reading 6.1.0, Writing 6.2.2

Vocabulary Skill Greek Word Origins Add *tropo-* and *meso-* to your word origins chart. Then describe the four main layers of the atmosphere.

Reviewing Key Concepts

1. a. Listing List the four main layers of the atmosphere, beginning with the layer closest to Earth's surface.
   b. Classifying What property is used to distinguish the layers of the atmosphere?
   c. Interpreting Diagrams According to Figure 12, in which layer of the atmosphere do communications satellites orbit?
2. a. Identifying Give at least one important characteristic of each of the four main layers of Earth's atmosphere.

b. Comparing and Contrasting How does temperature change as height increases in the troposphere? Compare this to how temperature changes with height in the stratosphere.
   c. Applying Concepts Why would you not feel warm in the thermosphere, even though temperatures can be up to 1,800°C?

Writing in Science

Cause and Effect Paragraph How do you think Earth's surface might be different if it had no atmosphere? Write a paragraph explaining your ideas.

Energy in Earth's Atmosphere

CALIFORNIA
Standards Focus

S 6.3.d Students know heat energy is also transferred between objects by radiation (radiation can travel through space).

S 6.4.b Students know solar energy reaches Earth through radiation, mostly in the form of visible light.

- In what form does energy from the sun travel to Earth?

- What happens to the sun's energy when it reaches Earth?

Key Terms
- electromagnetic wave
- radiation
- infrared radiation
- ultraviolet radiation
- scattering
- greenhouse effect

Lab zone Standards **Warm-Up**

Does a Plastic Bag Trap Heat?

1. Record the initial temperatures on two thermometers. (You should get the same readings.)

2. Place one of the thermometers in a plastic bag. Put a small piece of paper in the bag so that it shades the bulb of the thermometer. Seal the bag.

3. Cover the bulb of the second thermometer with a small piece of paper. Place both thermometers on a sunny window ledge or near a light bulb. Predict what you think will happen.

4. Wait five minutes. Then record the temperatures on the two thermometers.

Think It Over
Measuring Were the two temperatures the same? How could you explain any difference?

In the deserts of California, summer nights can be chilly. In the morning, the sun is low in the sky and the air is cool. As the sun rises, the temperature increases. By noon it is quite hot. As you will learn in this chapter, heat is a major factor in the weather. The movement of heat in the atmosphere causes temperatures to change, winds to blow, and rain to fall.

Energy From the Sun

Where does this heat come from? Nearly all the energy in Earth's atmosphere comes from the sun. This energy travels to Earth as **electromagnetic waves,** a form of energy that can move through the vacuum of space. Electromagnetic waves are classified according to wavelength, or distance between waves. **Radiation** is the direct transfer of energy by electromagnetic waves, so the electromagnetic waves given off by the sun are called solar radiation.

What kinds of energy do we receive from the sun? Is all of the energy the same? **Most of the energy from the sun travels to Earth in the form of visible light.** However, a full spectrum of electromagnetic energy is present in solar radiation.

As the sun rises, energy in the form of electromagnetic waves reaches Earth's surface.

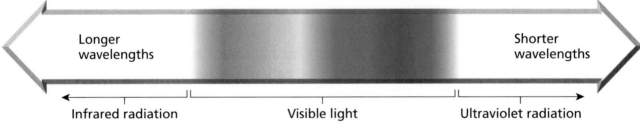

Longer wavelengths

Shorter wavelengths

Infrared radiation   Visible light   Ultraviolet radiation

Visible Light Visible light includes all of the colors that you see in a rainbow: red, orange, yellow, green, blue, indigo, and violet. The different colors are the result of different wavelengths. Red and orange light have the longest wavelengths, while blue and violet light have the shortest wavelengths, as shown in Figure 14.

Non-Visible Radiation One form of electromagnetic energy, **infrared radiation,** has wavelengths that are longer than red light. Infrared radiation is not visible, but can be felt as heat. The sun also gives off **ultraviolet radiation,** which is an invisible form of energy with wavelengths that are shorter than violet light. Ultraviolet radiation can cause sunburns. This radiation can also cause skin cancer and eye damage. Solar radiation includes a full spectrum of wavelengths, from below the infrared to above the ultraviolet.

 **Reading Checkpoint**   Which color of visible light has the longest wavelengths?

FIGURE 14
Solar Radiation
Energy from the sun travels to Earth across a full spectrum of wavelengths.
Interpreting Diagrams *What type of radiation has wavelengths that are shorter than visible light?*

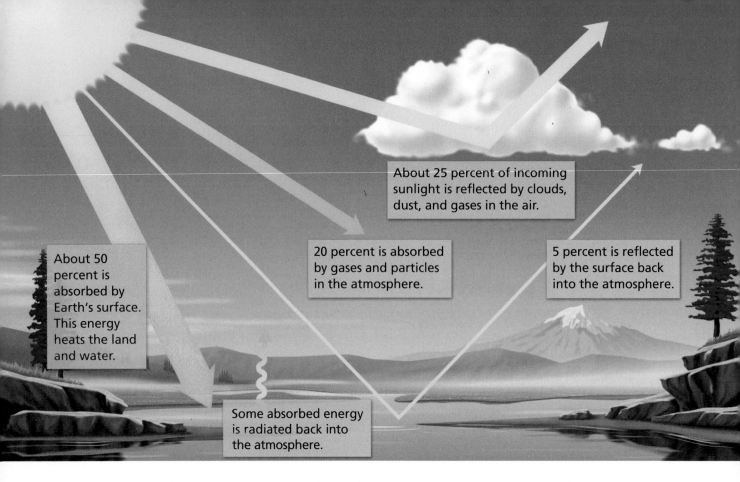

About 25 percent of incoming sunlight is reflected by clouds, dust, and gases in the air.

About 50 percent is absorbed by Earth's surface. This energy heats the land and water.

20 percent is absorbed by gases and particles in the atmosphere.

5 percent is reflected by the surface back into the atmosphere.

Some absorbed energy is radiated back into the atmosphere.

FIGURE 15
Energy in the Atmosphere
The sun's energy interacts with Earth's atmosphere and surface in several ways. About half is either reflected back into space or absorbed by the atmosphere. The rest reaches Earth's surface.

For: Links on energy in Earth's atmosphere
Visit: www.SciLinks.org
Web Code: scn-0921

Energy in the Atmosphere

Before reaching Earth's surface, sunlight must pass through the atmosphere. The path of the sun's rays is shown in Figure 15. **Some sunlight is absorbed or reflected by the atmosphere before it can reach the surface. The rest passes through the atmosphere to the surface.**

Some solar radiation is absorbed by the atmosphere. The ozone layer in the stratosphere absorbs most of the ultraviolet radiation. Water vapor and carbon dioxide absorb some infrared radiation. Clouds, dust, and other gases also absorb energy.

Some sunlight is reflected. Clouds act like mirrors, reflecting sunlight back into space. Dust particles and gases in the atmosphere reflect light in all directions, a process called **scattering.** When you look at the sky, the light you see has been scattered by gas molecules in the atmosphere. Gas molecules scatter short wavelengths of visible light (blue and violet) more than long wavelengths (red and orange). Scattered light therefore looks bluer than ordinary sunlight. This is why the daytime sky looks blue.

When the sun is rising or setting, its light passes through a greater thickness of the atmosphere than when the sun is higher in the sky and looks yellow. More light from the blue end of the spectrum is removed by scattering before it reaches your eyes. The remaining light is mostly red and orange. The sun looks red, and clouds around it become very colorful.

Energy at Earth's Surface

Some of the sun's energy reaches Earth's surface and is reflected back into the atmosphere. About half of the sun's energy, however, is absorbed by the land and water and changed into heat.

🔑 **When Earth's surface is heated, it radiates most of the energy back into the atmosphere as infrared radiation.** As shown in Figure 16, much of this infrared radiation cannot travel all the way through the atmosphere back into space. Instead, it is absorbed by water vapor, carbon dioxide, methane, and other gases in the air. The energy from the absorbed radiation heats the gases in the air. These gases form a "blanket" around Earth that holds heat in the atmosphere. The process by which gases hold heat in the air is called the **greenhouse effect**.

The greenhouse effect is a natural process that keeps Earth's atmosphere at a temperature that is comfortable for most living things. Over time, the amount of energy absorbed by the atmosphere and Earth's surface is nearly in balance with the amount of energy radiated into space. In this way, Earth's average temperatures remain fairly constant. However, as you will learn, emissions from human activities may be altering this process.

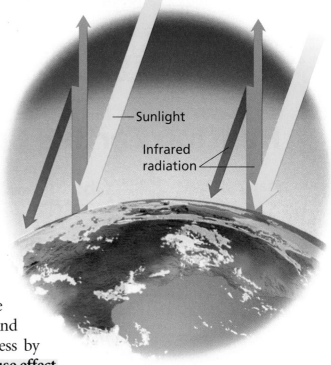

FIGURE 16
Greenhouse Effect
Sunlight travels through the atmosphere to Earth's surface. Earth's surface then gives off infrared radiation. Much of this energy is held by the atmosphere, warming it.

—Sunlight

Infrared radiation

✔ **Reading Checkpoint** What is the greenhouse effect?

Section 4 Assessment

S 6.3.d, 6.4.b,
E-LA: Reading 6.2.4

 **Target Reading Skill** Take Notes Use your notes to help you answer the following questions.

🔑 **Reviewing Key Concepts**

1. a. **Listing** List three forms of radiation from the sun.
   b. **Comparing and Contrasting** Which form of radiation from the sun has the longest wavelength? The shortest wavelength?
2. a. **Summarizing** What happens to most of the sunlight that reaches Earth?
   b. **Interpreting Diagrams** What percentage of incoming sunlight is reflected by clouds, dust, and gases in the atmosphere?
   c. **Applying Concepts** Why are sunsets red?

3. a. **Describing** What happens to the energy from the sun that is absorbed by Earth's surface?
   b. **Predicting** How might conditions on Earth be different without the greenhouse effect?

Lab zone **At-Home Activity**

Heating Your Home With an adult family member, explore the role radiation from the sun plays in heating your home. Does it make some rooms warmer in the morning? Are other rooms warmer in the afternoon? How does opening and closing curtains or blinds affect the temperature of a room? Explain your observations to your family.

Heating Earth's Surface

Materials

2 thermometers or temperature probes and 2 beakers, 400 mL

sand and water, 300 mL

ring stand and two ring clamps

string

metric ruler

lamp with 150-W bulb

stopwatch or clock

graph paper

Problem How do the heating and cooling rates of sand and water compare?

Skills Focus developing hypotheses, graphing, drawing conclusions

Procedure

1. Which do you think will heat up faster—sand or water? Record your hypothesis. Then follow these steps to test your hypothesis.

2. Copy the data table into your notebook. Add enough rows to record data for 15 minutes.

3. Fill one beaker with 300 mL of dry sand.

4. Fill the second beaker with 300 mL of water at room temperature.

5. Arrange the beakers side by side beneath the ring stand.

6. Place one thermometer in each beaker. If you are using a temperature probe, see your teacher for instructions.

7. Suspend the thermometers from the ring stand with string. This will hold the thermometers in place so they do not fall.

8. Adjust the height of the clamp so that the bulb of each thermometer is covered by about 0.5 cm of sand or water in a beaker.

9. Position the lamp so that it is about 20 cm above the sand and water. There should be no more than 8 cm between the beakers. **CAUTION:** *Be careful not to splash water onto the hot light bulb.*

10. Record the temperature of the sand and water in your data table.

11. Turn on the lamp. Read the temperature of the sand and water every minute for 15 minutes. Record the temperatures in the Temperature With Light On column in the data table.

Data Table					
Temperature With Light On (°C)			Temperature With Light Off (°C)		
Time (min)	Sand	Water	Time (min)	Sand	Water
Start			16		
1			17		
2			18		
3			19		
4			20		
5			21		

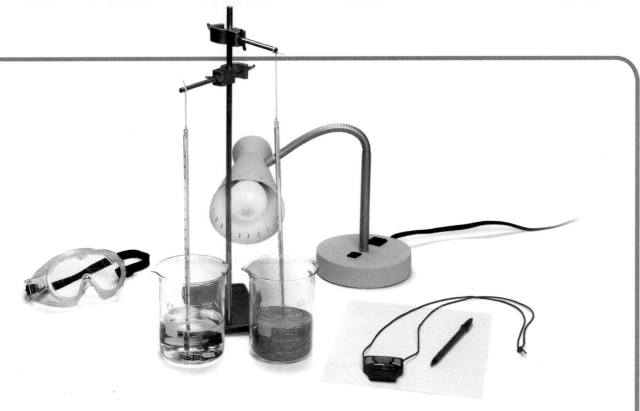

12. Which material do you think will cool off more quickly? Record your hypothesis. Again, give reasons why you think your hypothesis is correct.

13. Turn the light off. Read the temperature of the sand and water every minute for another 15 minutes. Record the temperatures in the Temperature With Light Off column (16–30 minutes).

Analyze and Conclude

1. **Graphing** Draw two line graphs to show the data for the temperature change in sand and water over time. Label the horizontal axis from 0 to 30 minutes and the vertical axis in degrees Celsius. Draw both graphs on the same piece of graph paper. Use a dashed line to show the temperature change in water and a solid line to show the temperature change in sand.

2. **Calculating** Calculate the total change in temperature for each material.

3. **Interpreting Data** Based on your data, which material had the greater increase in temperature?

4. **Drawing Conclusions** What can you conclude about which material absorbed heat faster? How do your results compare with your hypothesis?

5. **Interpreting Data** Review your data again. In 15 minutes, which material cooled faster?

6. **Drawing Conclusions** How do these results compare to your second hypothesis?

7. **Developing Hypotheses** Based on your results, which do you think will heat up more quickly on a sunny day: the water in a lake or the sand surrounding it? After dark, which will cool off more quickly?

8. **Communicating** If your results did not support either of your hypotheses, why do you think the results differed from what you expected? Write a paragraph in which you discuss the results and how they compared to your hypotheses.

Design an Experiment

Do you think all solid materials heat up as fast as sand? For example, consider gravel, crushed stone, or different types of soil. Write a hypothesis about their heating rates.

With the approval and supervision of your teacher, develop a procedure to test your hypothesis. Was your hypothesis correct?

Heat Transfer in the Atmosphere

CALIFORNIA
Standards Focus

S 6.3.c Students know heat flows in solids by conduction (which involves no flow of matter) and in fluids by conduction and by convection (which involves flow of matter).

S 6.4.d Students know that convection currents distribute heat in the atmosphere and oceans.

🔑 How is temperature measured?

🔑 In what three ways is heat transferred?

🔑 How is heat transferred in the troposphere?

Key Terms

- thermal energy
- thermometer
- heat
- conduction
- convection
- convection current

Lab zone Standards **Warm-Up**

What Happens When Air Is Heated?

1. Use heavy scissors to cut the flat part out of an aluminum pie plate. Use the tip of the scissors to poke a small hole in the middle of the flat part of the plate.
2. Cut the part into a spiral shape, as shown in the photo. Tie a 30-centimeter piece of thread to the middle of the spiral.
3. Hold the spiral over a source of heat, such as a candle, hot plate, or incandescent light bulb.

Think It Over

Inferring What happened to the spiral? Why do you think this happened?

You pour a cup of steaming tea from a teapot. Your teacup is warm to the touch. Somehow, heat was transferred from one object (the cup) to another (your hand) that it was touching. This is an example of conduction, one of three ways that heat can be transferred. As you'll learn in this section, heat transfer in the troposphere plays an important role in influencing Earth's weather.

It takes only a small amount of energy to heat up a cup of tea. ▼

FIGURE 17
Movement of Molecules
The iced tea is cold, so its molecules move slowly. The herbal tea is hot, so its molecules move faster than the molecules in the iced tea. **Inferring** *Which liquid has a higher temperature?*

Thermal Energy and Temperature

The tea in the cup and in the teapot are the same temperature but have different amounts of total energy. To understand this, you need to know that all substances are made up of tiny particles that are constantly moving. The faster the particles are moving, the more energy they have. Figure 17 shows how the motion of the particles is related to the amount of energy they hold. Recall that temperature is the *average* amount of energy of motion of each particle of a substance. That is, temperature is a measure of how hot or cold a substance is. In contrast, the *total* energy of motion in the particles of a substance is called **thermal energy.** The hot tea in the teapot has more thermal energy than the hot tea in the cup because it has more particles.

Measuring Temperature Temperature is one of the most important factors affecting the weather. 🔊 **Air temperature is usually measured with a thermometer.** A **thermometer** is a thin glass tube with a bulb on one end that contains a liquid, usually colored alcohol.

Thermometers work because liquids expand when they are heated and contract when they are cooled. When the air temperature increases, the temperature of the liquid in the bulb also increases. This causes the liquid to expand and rise up the tube of the thermometer.

Temperature Scales Temperature is measured in units called degrees. Two temperature scales are commonly used: the Celsius scale and the Fahrenheit scale. Scientists use the Celsius scale. On the Celsius scale, the freezing point of pure water is 0°C (read "zero degrees Celsius"). The boiling point of pure water at sea level is 100°C. Weather reports in the United States use the Fahrenheit scale. On the Fahrenheit scale, the freezing point of water is 32°F and the boiling point is 212°F.

Which temperature scale do scientists use?

Math Skills

Converting Units

Temperatures in weather reports use the Fahrenheit scale, but scientists use the Celsius scale. Temperature readings can be converted from the Fahrenheit scale to the Celsius scale using the following equation:

$$°C = \frac{5}{9}(°F - 32)$$

If the temperature is 68°F, what is the temperature in degrees Celsius?

$$°C = \frac{5}{9}(68 - 32)$$

$$°C = 20°C$$

Practice Problem Use the equation to convert the following temperatures from Fahrenheit to Celsius: 35.0°F, 60.0°F, and 72.0°F.

Lab zone Try This **Activity**

Temperature and Height

How much difference is there between air temperatures near the ground and higher up? Give reasons for your prediction.

1. Take all of your measurements outside at a location that is sunny all day.

2. [icon] Early in the morning, measure the air temperature 1 cm and 1.25 m above the ground. Record the time and temperature for each height. Repeat your measurements late in the afternoon.

3. Repeat Step 2 for two more days.

4. Graph your data for each height with temperature on the vertical axis and time of day on the horizontal axis. Use the same graph paper and same scale for each graph. Label each graph.

Interpreting Data At which height did the temperature vary the most? How can you explain the difference?

How Heat Is Transferred

Recall that **heat** is the transfer of thermal energy from a hotter object to a cooler one. ⬭ **Heat is transferred in three ways within the atmosphere: radiation, conduction, and convection.**

Radiation Have you ever felt the warmth of the sun's rays on your face? You were feeling energy coming directly from the sun as radiation. Recall that radiation is the direct transfer of energy by electromagnetic waves.

Conduction Have you ever walked barefoot on hot sand? Your feet felt hot because heat moved directly from the sand into your feet. The direct transfer of heat from one substance to another substance that it is touching is called **conduction.** When a fast-moving sand molecule bumps into a slower-moving particle, the faster particle transfers some of its energy.

The closer together the particles in a substance are, the more effectively they can conduct heat. Conduction works well in some solids, such as metals, but not as well in liquids and gases. Air and water do not conduct heat very well.

Convection In fluids (liquids and gases), particles can move easily from one place to another. As the particles move, their energy goes along with them. The transfer of heat by the movement of a fluid is called **convection.**

Heating the Troposphere Radiation, conduction, and convection work together to heat the troposphere. During the day, the sun's radiation heats Earth's surface. The land becomes warmer than the air. Air near Earth's surface is warmed by both radiation and conduction. However, heat is not easily transferred from one air particle to another by conduction. Only the first few meters of the troposphere are heated by conduction. Thus, the air close to the ground is usually warmer than the air a few meters up.

⬭ **Within the troposphere, heat is transferred mostly by convection.** When the air near the ground is heated, its particles move more rapidly. As a result, they bump into each other and move farther apart. The heated air becomes less dense. Cooler, denser air sinks toward the surface, forcing the warmer air to rise. As the warm air rises, it cools and becomes more dense. This denser cool air sinks back toward the ground where it may be heated once again. This upward movement of warm air and the downward movement of cool air form **convection currents.** Convection currents move heat throughout the troposphere.

 **Reading Checkpoint** How is the air near Earth's surface heated?

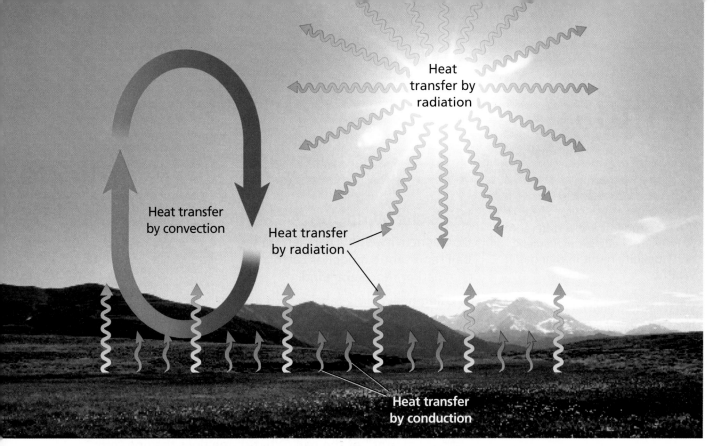

Heat transfer by radiation

Heat transfer by convection

Heat transfer by radiation

Heat transfer by conduction

Radiation

Conduction

Convection

FIGURE 18
Heat Transfer
All three types of heat transfer—radiation, conduction, and convection—help to warm the troposphere.

Section 5 Assessment

S 6.4.d, Math: 6AF1.1, E-LA: Reading 6.1.0

Vocabulary Skill Greek Word Origins Use what you've learned about the Greek word *thermos* to explain the meaning of *thermal energy.*

Reviewing Key Concepts

1. **a. Defining** What is temperature?
   b. Identifying What instrument is used to measure air temperature?
   c. Comparing and Contrasting A pail of water is the same temperature as a lake. Compare the amount of thermal energy of the water in the lake and the water in the pail.

2. **a. Naming** Name three ways that heat can be transferred.
   b. Describing How do the three types of heat transfer work together to heat the troposphere?

   c. Identifying What is the major way that heat is transferred in the troposphere?
   d. Applying Concepts Explain how a hawk or eagle could use convection currents to soar upward without flapping its wings.

Math Practice

3. **Converting Units** Use the equation from the Math Skills Activity to convert the following temperatures from Fahrenheit to Celsius: 52°F, 86°F, 77°F, and 97°F.

Winds

CALIFORNIA
Standards Focus

S 6.4.e Students know differences in pressure, heat, air movement, and humidity result in changes in weather.

- What causes winds?
- How do local winds and global winds differ?
- Where are the major global wind belts located?

Key Terms
- wind
- anemometer
- wind-chill factor
- local wind
- sea breeze
- land breeze
- global wind
- Coriolis effect
- latitude
- jet stream

Lab zone Standards **Warm-Up**

Does the Wind Turn?

Do this activity with a partner. Let the ball represent a model of Earth and the marker represent wind.

1. Using heavy-duty tape, attach a pencil to a large smooth ball so that you can spin the ball from the top without touching it.
2. One partner should hold the pencil. Slowly turn the ball counterclockwise when seen from above.
3. While the ball is turning, the second partner should use a marker to try to draw a straight line from the "North Pole" to the "equator" of the ball. What shape does the line form?

Think It Over

Making Models If cold air were moving south from Canada into the continental United States, how would its movement be affected by Earth's rotation?

Have you ever flown a kite? Start by unwinding a few meters of string with the kite downwind from you. Have a friend hold the kite high overhead. Then, as your friend releases the kite, run directly into the wind. If you're lucky, the kite will start to rise. Once the kite is stable, you can unwind your string to let the wind lift the kite high into the sky. But what exactly is the wind that lifts the kite, and what causes it to blow?

A kite festival in Cape Town, South Africa ▶

What Is Wind?

Because air is a fluid, it can move easily from place to place. Differences in air pressure cause the air to move. A **wind** is the horizontal movement of air from an area of high pressure to an area of lower pressure. 🔑 **Winds are caused by differences in air pressure.**

Most differences in air pressure are caused by the unequal heating of the atmosphere. Convection currents form when an area of Earth's surface is heated by the sun's rays. Air over the heated surface expands and becomes less dense. As the air becomes less dense, its air pressure decreases. If a nearby area is not heated as much, the air above the less-heated area will be cooler and denser. The cool, dense air with a higher pressure flows underneath the warm, less dense air. This forces the warm air to rise.

Measuring Wind Winds are described by their direction and speed. Wind direction is determined with a wind vane. The wind swings the wind vane so that one end points into the wind. The name of a wind tells you where the wind is coming from. For example, a south wind blows from the south toward the north. A north wind blows to the south.

Wind speed can be measured with an **anemometer** (an uh MAHM uh tur). An anemometer has three or four cups mounted at the ends of spokes that spin on an axle. The force of the wind against the cups turns the axle. A meter on the axle shows the wind speed.

Wind-Chill Factor On a warm day, a cool breeze can be refreshing. But in winter, the same breeze can make you feel uncomfortably cold. The wind blowing over your skin removes body heat. The stronger the wind, the colder you feel. The increased cooling a wind can cause is called the **wind-chill factor**.

 **Reading Checkpoint** **Toward what direction does a west wind blow?**

Lab zone Try This Activity

Build a Wind Vane

1. ✂ Use scissors to cut out a pointer and a slightly larger tail fin from construction paper.
2. Make a slit 1 cm deep in each end of a soda straw.
3. Slide the pointer and tail fin into place on the straw, securing them with small pieces of tape.
4. Hold the straw on your finger to find the point at which it balances.
5. Carefully push a pin through the balance point and into the eraser of a pencil. Make sure the wind vane can spin freely.

Observing How can you use your wind vane to tell the direction of the wind?

FIGURE 19
Wind Speed
The anemometer on the right measures wind speed. The cups catch the wind, turning faster when the wind blows faster.

◆ 283

Local Winds

Have you ever noticed a breeze at the beach on a hot summer day? Even if there is no wind inland, there may be a cool breeze blowing in from the water. This breeze is an example of a local wind. **Local winds** are winds that blow over short distances. 🌀 **Local winds are caused by the unequal heating of Earth's surface within a small area.** Local winds form only when large-scale winds are weak.

Sea Breeze Unequal heating often occurs along the shore of a large body of water. It takes more energy to warm up a body of water than it does to warm up an equal area of land. As the sun heats Earth's surface during the day, the land warms up faster than the water. As a result, the air over the land becomes warmer than the air over the water. The warm air expands and rises, creating a low-pressure area. Cool air blows inland from over the water and moves underneath the warm air, causing a sea breeze. A **sea breeze** or a lake breeze is a local wind that blows from an ocean or lake. Figure 20 shows a sea breeze.

Land Breeze At night, the process is reversed. Land cools more quickly than water, so the air over the land becomes cooler than the air over the water. As the warmer air over the water expands and rises, cooler air from the land moves beneath it. The flow of air from land to a body of water is called a **land breeze.**

Sea Breeze
Warm air rises
Cooler air moves beneath warm air

Land Breeze
Warm air rises
Cooler air moves beneath warm air

FIGURE 20
Local Winds
During the day, cool air moves from the sea to the land, creating a sea breeze. At night, cooler air moves from the land to the sea.
Forming Operational Definitions *What type of breeze occurs at night?*

Global Winds

Global winds are winds that blow steadily from specific directions over long distances. ⊙ **Like local winds, global winds are created by the unequal heating of Earth's surface. But unlike local winds, global winds occur over a large area.** Recall how the sun's radiation strikes Earth. In the middle of the day near the equator, the sun is almost directly overhead. The direct rays from the sun heat Earth's surface intensely. Near the poles, the sun's rays strike Earth's surface at a lower angle. The sun's energy is spread out over a larger area, so it heats the surface less. As a result, temperatures near the poles are much lower than they are near the equator.

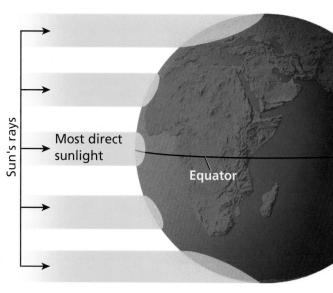

Global Convection Currents How do global winds develop? Temperature differences between the equator and the poles produce giant convection currents in the atmosphere. Warm air rises at the equator, and cold air sinks at the poles. Therefore air pressure tends to be lower near the equator and greater near the poles. This difference in pressure causes winds at Earth's surface to blow from the poles toward the equator. Higher in the atmosphere, however, air flows away from the equator toward the poles. Those air movements produce global winds.

The Coriolis Effect If Earth did not rotate, global winds would blow in a straight line from the poles toward the equator. Because Earth is rotating, however, global winds do not follow a straight path. As the winds blow, Earth rotates from west to east underneath them, making it seem as if the winds have curved. The way Earth's rotation makes winds curve is called the **Coriolis effect** (kawr ee OH lis).

Because of the Coriolis effect, global winds in the Northern Hemisphere gradually turn toward the right. As Figure 22 shows, a wind blowing toward the south gradually turns toward the southwest. In the Southern Hemisphere, winds curve toward the left.

 **Reading Checkpoint** **Which way do winds turn in the Southern Hemisphere?**

FIGURE 21
Angle of Sun's Rays
Near the equator, energy from the sun strikes Earth almost directly. Near the poles, the same amount of energy is spread out over a larger area.

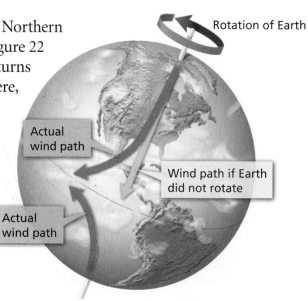

FIGURE 22
Coriolis Effect
As Earth rotates, the Coriolis effect turns winds in the Northern Hemisphere toward the right.

Global Wind Belts

Global convection currents and other factors combine to produce a pattern of calm areas and wind belts around Earth, as shown in Figure 24. The calm areas include the doldrums and the horse latitudes. ⊙ **The major global wind belts are the trade winds, the polar easterlies, and the prevailing westerlies.**

Doldrums Near the equator, the sun heats the surface strongly. Warm air rises steadily, creating an area of low pressure. Cool air moves into the area, but is warmed rapidly and rises before it moves very far. There is very little horizontal motion, so the winds near the equator are very weak. Regions near the equator with little or no wind are called the doldrums.

Horse Latitudes Warm air that rises at the equator divides and flows both north and south. **Latitude** is distance from the equator, measured in degrees. At about 30° north and south latitudes, the air stops moving toward the poles and sinks. In each of these regions, another belt of calm air forms. Hundreds of years ago, sailors becalmed in these waters ran out of food and water for their horses and had to throw the horses overboard. Because of this, the latitudes 30° north and south of the equator came to be called the horse latitudes.

Trade Winds When the cold air over the horse latitudes sinks, it produces a region of high pressure. This high pressure causes surface winds to blow both toward the equator and away from it. The winds that blow toward the equator are turned west by the Coriolis effect. As a result, winds in the Northern Hemisphere between 30° north latitude and the equator generally blow from the northeast. In the Southern Hemisphere between 30° south latitude and the equator, the winds blow from the southeast. For hundreds of years, sailors relied on these winds to move ships carrying valuable cargoes from Europe to the West Indies and South America. As a result, these steady easterly winds are called the trade winds.

Prevailing Westerlies In the mid-latitudes, between 30° and 60° north and south, winds that blow toward the poles are turned toward the east by the Coriolis effect. Because they blow from the west to the east, they are called prevailing westerlies. The prevailing westerlies blow generally from the southwest in north latitudes and from the northwest in south latitudes. The prevailing westerlies play an important part in the weather of the United States.

FIGURE 23
Ocean Sailing
Sailing ships relied on global winds to speed their journeys to various ports around the world. **Applying Concepts** *How much effect do you think the prevailing winds have on shipping today?*

FIGURE 24
Global Winds

A series of wind belts circles Earth. Between the wind belts are calm areas where air is rising or falling. **Interpreting Diagrams** *Which global wind belt would a sailor choose to sail from eastern Canada to Europe?*

Go Online
active art

For: Global Winds activity
Visit: PHSchool.com
Web Code: cfp-4023

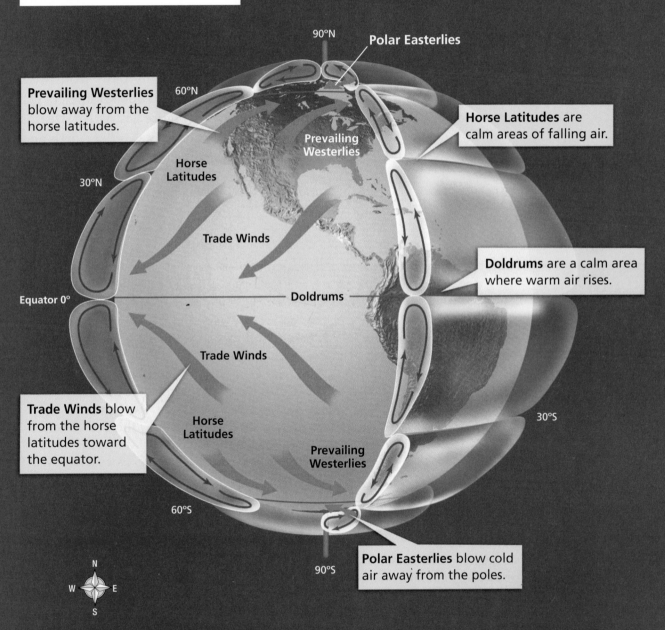

90°N — **Polar Easterlies**

Prevailing Westerlies blow away from the horse latitudes.

60°N

Prevailing Westerlies

Horse Latitudes are calm areas of falling air.

Horse Latitudes

30°N

Trade Winds

Doldrums are a calm area where warm air rises.

Equator 0° — **Doldrums**

Trade Winds

Trade Winds blow from the horse latitudes toward the equator.

Horse Latitudes

Prevailing Westerlies

30°S

60°S

90°S

Polar Easterlies blow cold air away from the poles.

N
W E
S

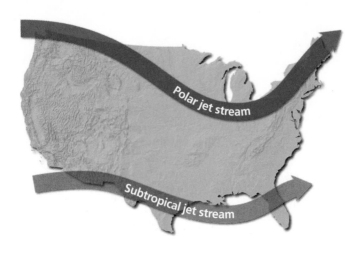

FIGURE 25
Jet Streams
The jet streams are high-speed bands of winds occurring at the top of the troposphere. By traveling east in a jet stream, pilots can save time and fuel.

Polar jet stream

Subtropical jet stream

Polar Easterlies Cold air near the poles sinks and flows back toward lower latitudes. The Coriolis effect shifts these polar winds to the west, producing the polar easterlies. The polar easterlies meet the prevailing westerlies at about 60° north and 60° south latitudes, along a region called the polar front. The mixing of warm and cold air along the polar front has a major effect on weather in the United States.

Jet Streams About 10 kilometers above Earth's surface are bands of high-speed winds called **jet streams.** These winds are hundreds of kilometers wide but only a few kilometers deep. Jet streams generally blow from west to east at speeds of 200 to 400 kilometers per hour, as shown in Figure 25. As jet streams travel around Earth, they wander north and south along a wavy path.

 **Reading Checkpoint**   **What are the jet streams?**

Section 6 Assessment

S 6.4.e, E-LA: Reading 6.2.4, Writing 6.2.2

Target Reading Skill Take Notes Review your notes for this section. What important idea did you include about the Coriolis effect?

Reviewing Key Concepts

1. **a.** Defining What is wind?
   b. Relating Cause and Effect How is wind related to air temperature and air pressure?
   c. Applying Concepts It's fairly warm but windy outside. Use the concept of wind-chill factor to explain why it may be a good idea to wear a jacket.

2. **a.** Defining What are local winds?
   b. Summarizing What causes local winds?
   c. Comparing and Contrasting Compare the conditions that cause a sea breeze with those that cause a land breeze.

3. **a.** Identifying Name the three major global wind belts.
   b. Describing Briefly describe the three major global wind belts and where they are located.
   c. Interpreting Diagrams Use Figure 22 and Figure 24 to describe how the Coriolis effect influences the direction of the trade winds in the Northern Hemisphere. Does it have the same effect in the Southern Hemisphere? Explain.

Writing in Science

Explanation Imagine that you are a hot-air balloonist. You want to fly your balloon across the continental United States. To achieve the fastest time, would it make more sense to fly east-to-west or west-to-east? Explain how the prevailing winds influenced your decision.

Technology Lab
Guided Inquiry

S 6.4.e, 6.7.d

Measuring the Wind

Problem Can you design and build an anemometer to measure the wind?

Design Skills evaluating the design, redesigning

Materials

- pen • round toothpick • masking tape
- 2 wooden coffee stirrers • meter stick
- corrugated cardboard sheet, 15 cm × 20 cm
- wind vane

Procedure

1. Begin by making a simple anemometer that uses wooden coffee stirrers to indicate wind speed. On a piece of cardboard, draw a curved scale like the one shown in the diagram. Mark it in equal intervals from 0 to 10.

2. Carefully use a pencil to make a small hole where a toothpick will go. Insert a toothpick through the hole.

3. Tape two wooden coffee stirrers to the toothpick as shown in the diagram, one on each side of the cardboard.

4. Copy the data table into your notebook.

Data Table		
Location	Wind Direction	Wind Speed

5. Take your anemometer outside the school. Stand about 2–3 m away from the building and away from any corners or large plants.

6. Use the wind vane to find out what direction the wind is coming from. Hold your anemometer so that the card is straight, vertical, and parallel to the wind direction.

7. Observe the wooden stirrer on your anemometer for one minute. Record the highest wind speed that occurs.

8. Repeat your measurements on all the other sides of the building. Record your data.

Analyze and Conclude

1. **Interpreting Data** Was the wind stronger on one side of the school than on the other sides? Explain your observations.

2. **Applying Concepts** Based on your data, which side of the building provides the best location for a door?

3. **Evaluating the Design** Do you think your anemometer accurately measured all of the winds you encountered? How could you improve its accuracy?

4. **Redesigning** What was the hardest part of using your anemometer? How could you change your design to make it more useful at very low or at very high wind speeds? Explain.

5. **Working With Design Constraints** How did having to use the materials provided by your teacher affect your anemometer? How would your design have changed if you could have used any materials you wanted to?

Communicate

Write a brochure describing the benefits of your anemometer. Make sure your brochure explains how the anemometer works and its potential uses.

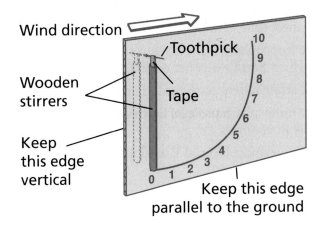

Wind direction

Toothpick

Wooden stirrers

Tape

Keep this edge vertical

Keep this edge parallel to the ground

10 9 8 7 6 5 4 3 2 1 0

Study Guide

The BIG Idea

Air pressure and temperature vary with altitude and location, resulting in distinct atmospheric layers and predictable wind patterns.

1 The Air Around You

Key Concepts S 6.4.e, 6.6.b

- Earth's atmosphere is made up of nitrogen, oxygen, carbon dioxide, water vapor, and many other gases, as well as liquid particles and solids.
- Earth's atmosphere makes conditions on Earth suitable for living things.
- Burning fossil fuels causes smog and acid rain.

Key Terms
- weather • atmosphere • ozone • water vapor
- pollutant • photochemical smog • acid rain

2 Air Pressure

Key Concepts S 6.4.e

- Because air has mass, it also has other properties, including density and pressure.
- Two kinds of barometers are mercury barometers and aneroid barometers.
- Air pressure decreases as altitude increases. As air pressure decreases, so does density.

Key Terms
- density • pressure • air pressure
- barometer • mercury barometer
- aneroid barometer • altitude

3 Layers of the Atmosphere

Key Concepts S 6.4.e

- Scientists divide Earth's atmosphere into four main layers: the troposphere, the stratosphere, the mesosphere, and the thermosphere.
- The troposphere is the layer of the atmosphere in which Earth's weather occurs.
- The stratosphere contains the ozone layer.
- The mesosphere protects Earth's surface from most meteoroids.
- The outermost layer of Earth's atmosphere is the thermosphere.

Key Terms
- troposphere • stratosphere • mesosphere
- thermosphere • ionosphere • exosphere

4 Energy in Earth's Atmosphere

Key Concepts S 6.3.d, 6.4.b

- Most energy from the sun travels to Earth in the form of visible light.
- Some sunlight is absorbed or reflected by the atmosphere before it can reach the surface.
- When the surface is heated, it radiates energy back into the atmosphere as infrared radiation.

Key Terms
- electromagnetic waves • radiation
- infrared radiation • ultraviolet radiation
- scattering • greenhouse effect

5 Heat Transfer in the Atmosphere

Key Concepts S 6.3.c, 6.4.d

- Air temperature is usually measured with a thermometer.
- Heat is transferred in three ways: radiation, conduction, and convection.
- Radiation, conduction, and convection work together to heat the troposphere.

Key Terms
- temperature • thermal energy
- thermometer • heat • conduction
- convection • convection current

6 Winds

Key Concepts S 6.4.e

- Winds are caused by differences in air pressure.
- Local winds are caused by the unequal heating of Earth's surface within a small area.
- Global winds are created by the unequal heating of Earth's surface over a large area.
- Major global wind belts are the trade winds, the polar easterlies, and the prevailing westerlies.

Key Terms
- wind • anemometer • wind-chill factor
- local wind • sea breeze • land breeze
- global wind • Coriolis effect • latitude
- jet stream

Review and Assessment

Target Reading Skill

In your notebook, complete the two-column note-taking organizer that you started earlier for Section 1. Include summary statements.

Recall Clues and Questions	Notes: The Air Around You
What are pollutants?	Pollutants: harmful substances in the air, water, or soil
What are some sources of air pollution?	Sources of Pollution • Natural sources—

Reviewing Key Terms

Choose the letter of the best answer.

1. The most abundant gas in the atmosphere is
   a. ozone.
   b. water vapor.
   c. oxygen.
   d. nitrogen.

2. Air pressure is typically measured with a
   a. thermometer.
   b. satellite.
   c. barometer.
   d. hot-air balloon.

3. The layers of the atmosphere are classified according to changes in
   a. altitude.
   b. temperature.
   c. air pressure.
   d. pollutants.

4. Energy from the sun travels to Earth's surface by
   a. radiation.
   b. convection.
   c. evaporation.
   d. conduction.

5. Rising warm air transports thermal energy by
   a. conduction.
   b. convection.
   c. radiation.
   d. condensation.

Complete the following sentences so that your answers clearly explain the key terms.

6. Air contains varying amounts of **water vapor,** which is _____ .

7. The daytime sky looks blue because of **scattering,** a process in which _____ .

8. Earth is warmed by the **greenhouse effect,** which is _____ .

9. **Convection currents,** which are _____, move heat throughout the troposphere.

10. At night you may experience a **sea breeze,** which occurs when _____ .

Writing in Science

Descriptive Paragraph Suppose you are on a hot-air balloon flight to the upper levels of the troposphere. Describe how the properties of the atmosphere, such as air pressure and amount of oxygen, would change during your trip.

Video Assessment
Discovery Channel School
The Atmosphere

Review and Assessment

Checking Concepts

11. Explain why it is difficult to include water vapor in a graph that shows the percentages of various gases in the atmosphere.

12. Name two ways in which carbon dioxide is added to the atmosphere.

13. Describe the temperature changes that occur as you move upward through the troposphere.

14. Describe examples of radiation, conduction, and convection from your daily life.

15. Explain how movements of air at the equator and poles produce global wind patterns.

Math Practice

16. **Converting Units** What is 60°F in degrees Celsius?

17. **Converting Units** What is 30°C in degrees Fahrenheit?

Thinking Critically

18. **Applying Concepts** Why can an aneroid barometer be used to indicate changes in elevation as well as air pressure?

19. **Reading Graphs** According to the graph below, what is the air pressure at an altitude of 4 km? In general, how does air pressure change with altitude?

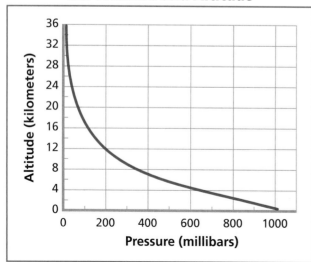

Air Pressure and Altitude

20. **Inferring** Why are clouds at the top of the troposphere made of ice crystals rather than drops of water?

21. **Inferring** Venus has an atmosphere that is mostly carbon dioxide. How do you think the greenhouse effect has altered Venus?

22. **Relating Cause and Effect** What circumstances could cause a nighttime land breeze in a city near the ocean?

Applying Skills

Use the table below to answer the questions that follow.

The table shows the temperature at various altitudes above Omaha, Nebraska, on a January day.

Altitude (kilometers)	0	1.6	3.2	4.8	6.4	7.2
Temperature (°C)	0	−4	−9	−21	−32	−40

23. **Graphing** Make a line graph of the data in the table. Put temperature on the horizontal axis and altitude on the vertical axis. Label your graph.

24. **Reading Graphs** At about what height above the ground was the temperature −15°C?

25. **Reading Graphs** What was the approximate temperature 2.4 kilometers over Omaha?

26. **Calculating** Suppose an airplane was about 6.8 kilometers above Omaha on this day. What was the approximate temperature at 6.8 kilometers? How much colder was the temperature at 6.8 kilometers above the ground than at ground level?

Lab zone · Standards Investigation

Performance Assessment Decide how to present the findings from your weather station to the class. For example, you could put your graphs and predictions on a poster or use a computer to make a slide show. Make sure your graphs are neatly drawn and easy to understand.

CALIFORNIA Standards Practice

Choose the letter of the best answer.

1. What two gases make up approximately 99% of Earth's atmosphere?
   A nitrogen and carbon dioxide
   B oxygen and carbon dioxide
   C nitrogen and hydrogen
   D nitrogen and oxygen   S 6.4.e

2. In the troposphere, as altitude increases
   A air pressure decreases.
   B temperature decreases.
   C air density decreases.
   D all of the above   S 6.4.e

Layers of the Atmosphere

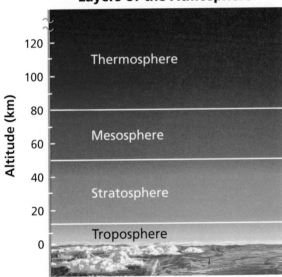

Use the diagram above and your knowledge of science to answer Questions 3 and 4.

3. Use the diagram to estimate the depth of the stratosphere.
   A about 50 kilometers
   B about 40 kilometers
   C about 30 kilometers
   D about 20 kilometers   S 6.4.e

4. According to the diagram, where is a meteoroid when it is 75 kilometers above Earth's surface?
   A the mesosphere
   B the stratosphere
   C the thermosphere
   D the troposphere   S 6.4.e

Use the table below and your knowledge of science to answer Questions 5 and 6. The row with a wind speed of 0 km/h shows the actual air temperature.

Wind-Chill Temperature Index

Wind Speed	Equivalent Air Temperature (°C)			
0 km/h	5°	0°	−5°	−10°
10 km/h	2.7°	−3.3°	−9.3°	−15.3°
15 km/h	1.7°	−4.4°	−10.6°	−16.7°
20 km/h	1.1°	−5.2°	−11.6°	−17.9°

5. On a windy winter's day, the actual air temperature is −5°C and the wind speed is 15 kilometers per hour. What would the wind-chill factor make the temperature feel like to a person outdoors?
   A 1.7°C   B −5°C
   C −10.6°C   D −16.7°C   S 6.4.e

6. Use trends shown in the data table to predict how cold the air temperature would feel if the actual temperature was 0°C and the wind speed was 25 km/h.
   A about 0°C   B about −6°C
   C about −15°C   D about 25°C   S 6.4.e

7. The solar energy that reaches Earth is mostly in the form of
   A visible light.
   B gamma rays.
   C ultraviolet radiation.
   D infrared radiation.   S 6.3.d, 6.4.b

8. What is the main method by which heat is transferred within the troposphere?
   A radiation
   B conduction
   C convection
   D the greenhouse effect   S 6.3.c, 6.4.d

Apply the BIG Idea

9. Explain how the uneven heating of the atmosphere produces global winds.   S 6.4.d

Chapter 8

Weather

Hurricane Nora approaches
Baja California on
September 22, 1997. ▶

S 6.4.e

Focus on the BIG Idea

Which weather factors produce changes in weather?

Check What You Know

Think about the last time you took a hot shower. You may have noticed when you got out that the mirror was covered with a thin film of moisture. Where do you think this moisture came from? How did it get there? Would the same film of moisture appear if you took a cold shower? Why or why not?

The images shown here represent some of the key terms in this chapter. You can use this vocabulary skill to help you understand the meaning of some key terms in this chapter.

Vocabulary Skill

Identify Multiple Meanings

Some words have more than one meaning. Words you use everyday may have different meanings in science. Look at the different meanings of the words below.

Word	Everyday Meaning	Scientific Meaning
cyclone	*n.* A windstorm with a violent whirling movement; a tornado **Example:** When the <u>cyclone</u> touched down, it destroyed the barn.	*n.* A center of low air pressure **Example:** The forecaster said the <u>cyclone</u> would have clouds, light rain, and moderate winds.
front	*n.* The forward part or surface **Example:** Enter by the door in the <u>front</u> of the house, not the one in back.	*n.* The boundary between two air masses of different temperatures and humidities **Example:** Storms often develop along <u>fronts</u>.
relative	*n.* A member of your family **Example:** Her brother is her closest <u>relative</u>.	*adj.* Having a particular quality compared to something else **Example:** The temperature here is mild <u>relative</u> to the temperature in Alaska.

Apply It!

Complete the sentences below with the correct word from the list above. Identify the sentence that uses the scientific meaning.

1. A warm _____ will arrive in this area tomorrow.
2. The _____ of the store has a window display of skateboards.

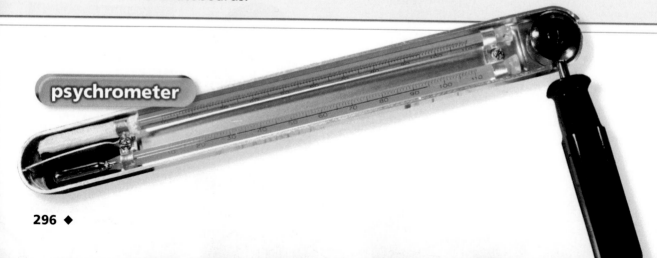

psychrometer

precipitation

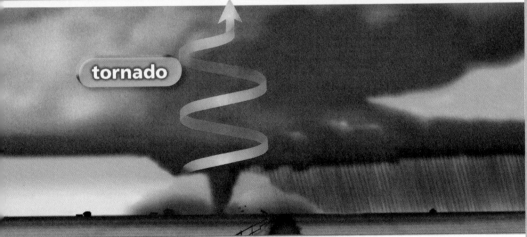

front

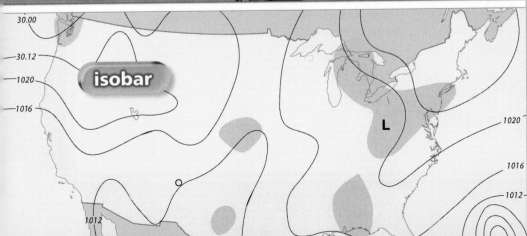

tornado

isobar

30.00
30.12
1020
1016

L

1020

1016

1012

1012

Chapter 8
Vocabulary

interactive Textbook

Build Science Vocabulary
Online
Visit: PHSchool.com
Web Code: cwj-3080

How to Read Science

 Compare and Contrast

Science texts often make comparisons. When you compare and contrast, you examine the similarities and differences between things. You can compare and contrast by using a table.

Follow these steps to set up a compare/contrast table.
- List the characteristics to be compared across the top of the table
- List the things to be compared in the left column.
- Complete the table by filling in information about each characteristic.

In this chapter you will learn the term *front*, which is the area where unlike air masses meet. There are four types of fronts. Look at Figure 14. Then look at the following table.

Front	How Forms	Type of Weather
Cold front	A cold air mass overtakes a warm air mass.	
Warm front		
Stationary front		
Occluded front		

Apply It!

Answer the following questions in complete sentences.
1. What are the items being compared in this table?
2. What are the characteristics that are being compared?
3. How does a cold front form?

After reading Section 2, make a compare/contrast table for types of precipitation. Complete the compare/contrast table above after you read Section 3.

The Weather Tomorrow

When the sky turns dark and threatening, it's not hard to predict the weather. A storm is likely on its way. But wouldn't you rather know about an approaching storm before it arrives? In this investigation, you will get a chance to make your own weather forecasts and compare them to the forecasts of professionals. Good luck!

Your Goal

Predict the weather for your own community and two other locations in the United States.

To complete this investigation you must

- compare weather maps for several days at a time
- look for patterns in the weather
- draw maps to show your weather predictions

Plan It!

Begin by previewing the chapter to learn about weather maps and symbols. Start a project folder to store daily national weather maps and a description of the symbols used on the maps. Choose two locations that are at least 1,000 kilometers away from your town and from each other. As you collect weather maps, look for patterns in day-to-day weather changes. Then predict the next day's weather and compare your predictions to the professional forecasts and to the actual weather.

Section 1
Water in the Atmosphere

CALIFORNIA
Standards Focus

S 6.4.a Students know the sun is the major source of energy for phenomena on Earth's surface; it powers winds, ocean currents, and the water cycle.

S 6.4.e Students know differences in pressure, heat, air movement, and humidity result in changes in weather.

- What is humidity and how is it measured?
- How do clouds form?
- What are the three main types of clouds?

Key Terms

- water cycle
- evaporation
- humidity
- relative humidity
- psychrometer
- condensation
- dew point
- cirrus
- cumulus
- stratus

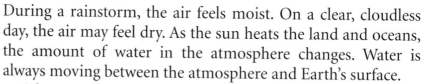

Lab zone **Standards Warm-Up**

How Does Fog Form?

1. Fill a narrow-necked plastic bottle with hot tap water. Pour out most of the water, leaving about 3 cm at the bottom. **CAUTION:** *Avoid spilling hot water. Do not use water that is so hot that you cannot safely hold the bottle.*
2. Place an ice cube on the mouth of the bottle. What happens?
3. Repeat Steps 1 and 2 using cold water instead of hot water. What happens?

Think It Over
Developing Hypotheses How can you explain your observations? Why is there a difference between what happens with the hot water and what happens with the cold water?

During a rainstorm, the air feels moist. On a clear, cloudless day, the air may feel dry. As the sun heats the land and oceans, the amount of water in the atmosphere changes. Water is always moving between the atmosphere and Earth's surface.

The continuous movement of water between the atmosphere and Earth's surface is called the **water cycle.** The sun's energy in the form of radiation powers the water cycle. However, the cycle itself has no real beginning or end.

As you can see in Figure 1, water vapor enters the air by evaporation from the oceans and other bodies of water. **Evaporation** is the process by which water molecules in liquid water absorb energy and escape into the air as water vapor. Water vapor is also added to the air by living things. Water enters the roots of plants, rises to the leaves, and is released as water vapor.

As part of the water cycle, some of the water vapor in the atmosphere condenses to form clouds. Rain and snow fall from the clouds toward the surface. The water then runs off the surface or moves through the ground, back into the lakes, streams, and eventually the oceans.

Humidity

How is the quantity of water vapor in the atmosphere measured? **Humidity** is a measure of the amount of water vapor in the air. Air's ability to hold water vapor depends on its temperature. Warm air can hold more water vapor than cool air.

Relative Humidity Weather reports usually refer to the water vapor in the air as relative humidity. **Relative humidity** is the percentage of water vapor that is actually in the air compared to the maximum amount of water vapor the air can hold at a particular temperature. For example, at 10°C, 1 cubic meter of air can hold at most 8 grams of water vapor. If there actually were 8 grams of water vapor in the air, then the relative humidity of the air would be 100 percent. Air with a relative humidity of 100 percent is said to be saturated. If the air had 4 grams of water vapor, the relative humidity would be half, or 50 percent.

FIGURE 1
Water Cycle

In the water cycle, water moves from oceans, lakes, rivers, and plants into the atmosphere and then falls back to Earth.

Go **O**nline
active art

For: Water Cycle activity
Visit: PHSchool.com
Web Code: cfp-4024

Condensation

Precipitation

Evaporation from plants

Evaporation from oceans, lakes, and streams

Surface runoff

FIGURE 2
Sling Psychrometer
A sling psychrometer is used to measure relative humidity.

Measuring Relative Humidity Relative humidity can be measured with an instrument called a psychrometer. A **psychrometer** (sy KRAHM uh tur) has two thermometers, a wet-bulb thermometer and a dry-bulb thermometer, as shown in Figure 2. The bulb of the wet-bulb thermometer has a cloth covering that is moistened with water. When the psychrometer is "slung," or spun by its handle, air blows over both thermometers. Because the wet-bulb thermometer is cooled by evaporation, its reading drops below that of the dry-bulb thermometer.

If the relative humidity is high, the water on the wet bulb evaporates slowly, and the wet-bulb temperature does not change much. If the relative humidity is low, the water on the wet bulb evaporates rapidly, and the wet-bulb temperature drops. The relative humidity can be found by comparing the temperatures of the wet-bulb and dry-bulb thermometers.

Reading Checkpoint What instrument measures relative humidity?

 Math: Mathematical Reasoning 6.1.1

Math Analyzing Data

Determining Relative Humidity

Relative humidity is affected by temperature. Use the data table to answer the questions below. First, find the dry-bulb temperature in the left column of the table. Then find the difference between the wet- and dry-bulb temperatures across the top of the table. The number in the table where these two readings intersect indicates the relative humidity in percent.

1. **Interpreting Data** At noon, the readings on a sling psychrometer are 18°C for the dry-bulb thermometer and 14°C for the wet-bulb thermometer. What is the relative humidity?

2. **Interpreting Data** At 5 P.M., the psychrometer is used again. The reading on the dry-bulb thermometer is 12°C, and the reading on the wet-bulb thermometer is 11°C. Determine the new relative humidity.

3. **Interpreting Data** How did the temperature change between noon and 5 P.M.?

Relative Humidity					
Dry-Bulb Reading (°C)	Difference Between Wet- and Dry-Bulb Readings (°C)				
	1	2	3	4	5
10	88	76	65	54	43
12	88	78	67	57	48
14	89	79	69	60	50
16	90	80	71	62	54
18	91	81	72	64	56
20	91	82	74	66	58
22	92	83	75	68	60

4. **Interpreting Data** How did relative humidity change during the course of the day?

5. **Drawing Conclusions** How was the relative humidity affected by air temperature? Explain your answer.

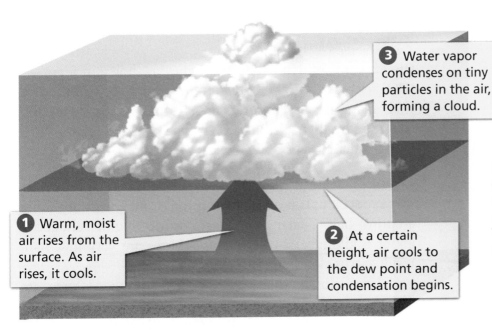

③ Water vapor condenses on tiny particles in the air, forming a cloud.

① Warm, moist air rises from the surface. As air rises, it cools.

② At a certain height, air cools to the dew point and condensation begins.

FIGURE 3
Cloud Formation
Clouds form when warm, moist air rises and cools. Water vapor condenses onto tiny particles in the air.

How Clouds Form

When you look at a cloud, you are seeing millions of tiny water droplets or ice crystals. ⊙ **Clouds form when water vapor in the air condenses to form liquid water or ice crystals.** Molecules of water vapor in the air become liquid water in the process of **condensation.** How does water in the atmosphere condense? Two conditions are required for condensation: cooling of the air and the presence of particles in the air.

The Role of Cooling As you have learned, cold air holds less water vapor than warm air. As air cools, the amount of water vapor it can hold decreases. The water vapor condenses into tiny droplets of water or ice crystals.

The temperature at which condensation begins is called the **dew point.** If the dew point is above freezing, the water vapor forms water droplets. If the dew point is below freezing, the water vapor may change directly into ice crystals.

The Role of Particles But something else besides a change in temperature is needed for cloud formation. For water vapor to condense, tiny particles must be present so the water has a surface on which to condense. In cloud formation, most of these particles are salt crystals, dust from soil, and smoke. Water vapor also condenses onto solid surfaces, such as blades of grass or window panes. Liquid water that condenses from the air onto a cooler surface is called dew. Ice that has been deposited on a surface that is below freezing is called frost.

FIGURE 4
Condensation
Water vapor condensed on this insect to form dew. **Predicting** *What would happen if the surface were below freezing?*

 **Reading Checkpoint** **What two factors are required for condensation to occur?**

Cirrus Clouds

Cumulus Clouds

Stratus Clouds

Types of Clouds

Clouds come in many different shapes, as shown in Figure 5. 🔵 **Scientists classify clouds into three main types based on their shape: cirrus, cumulus, and stratus. Clouds are further classified by their altitude.** Each type of cloud is associated with a different type of weather.

Cirrus Clouds Wispy, feathery clouds are known as **cirrus** (SEER us) clouds. *Cirrus* comes from a word meaning a curl of hair. Cirrus clouds form only at high levels, above about 6 kilometers, where temperatures are very low. As a result, cirrus clouds are made of ice crystals.

Cirrus clouds that have feathery "hooked" ends are sometimes called mare's tails. Cirrocumulus clouds, which look like rows of cotton balls, often indicate that a storm is on its way. The rows of cirrocumulus clouds look like the scales of a fish. For this reason, the term "mackerel sky" is used to describe a sky full of cirrocumulus clouds.

Cumulus Clouds Clouds that look like fluffy, rounded piles of cotton are called **cumulus** (KYOO myuh lus) clouds. The word *cumulus* means "heap" or "mass" in Latin. Cumulus clouds form less than 2 kilometers above the ground, but they may grow in size and height until they extend upward as much as 18 kilometers. Cumulus clouds that are not very tall usually indicate fair weather. These clouds, which are common on sunny days, are called "fair weather cumulus." Towering clouds with flat tops, called cumulonimbus clouds, often produce thunderstorms. The suffix *-nimbus* means "rain."

Stratus Clouds Clouds that form in flat layers are called **stratus** (STRAT us) clouds. Recall that *strato* means "spread out." Stratus clouds usually cover all or most of the sky and are a uniform dull, gray color. As stratus clouds thicken, they may produce drizzle, rain, or snow. They are then called nimbostratus clouds.

 **Reading Checkpoint** What are stratus clouds?

FIGURE 5
Clouds

The three main types of clouds are cirrus, cumulus, and stratus. A cloud's name contains clues about its height and structure.
Interpreting Diagrams *What type of cloud is found at the highest altitudes?*

Cirrus

Cirrocumulus

Altocumulus

Cumulonimbus

Altostratus

Cumulus

Nimbostratus

Stratus

Fog

(km)
13
12
11
10
9
8
7
6
5
4
3
2
1

FIGURE 6
Fog Around the Golden Gate Bridge
The cold ocean water of San Francisco Bay is often covered by fog in the early morning.
Predicting What will happen as the sun rises and warms the air?

Altocumulus and Altostratus Part of a cloud's name may be based on its height. The names of clouds that form between 2 and 6 kilometers above Earth's surface have the prefix *alto-*, which means "high." The two main types of these clouds are altocumulus and altostratus. These are "middle-level" clouds that are higher than regular cumulus and stratus clouds, but lower than cirrus and other "high" clouds.

Fog Clouds that form at or near the ground are called fog. Fog often forms when the ground cools at night after a warm, humid day. The ground cools the air just above the ground to the air's dew point. The next day the heat of the morning sun "burns" the fog off as its water droplets evaporate. Fog is more common in areas near bodies of water or low-lying marshy areas. In mountainous areas, fog can form as warm, moist air moves up the mountain slopes and cools.

 **Reading Checkpoint**) **What is fog?**

Section 1 Assessment

S 6.4.a, 6.4.e,
E-LA: Reading 6.1.2

Vocabulary Skill Identify Multiple Meanings
Review the two meanings of the word *relative*.
Then use the scientific meaning in a sentence.

Reviewing Key Concepts

1. **a. Reviewing** What is humidity?
   b. Comparing and Contrasting How are humidity and relative humidity different?
   c. Calculating Suppose a sample of air can at most hold 10 grams of water vapor. If the sample actually has 2 grams of water vapor, what is its relative humidity?

2. **a. Identifying** What process is involved in cloud formation?
   b. Summarizing What two conditions are needed for clouds to form?
   c. Inferring When are clouds formed by ice crystals instead of drops of liquid water?

3. **a. Listing** What are the three main types of clouds?
   b. Describing Briefly describe each of the three main types of clouds.
   c. Classifying Classify each of the following cloud types as low-level, medium-level, or high-level: altocumulus, altostratus, cirrostratus, cirrus, cumulus, fog, nimbostratus, and stratus.

Lab zone **At-Home Activity**

Water in the Air Fill a large glass half full with cold water. Show your family members what happens as you add ice cubes to the water. Explain to your family that the water that appears on the outside of the glass comes from water vapor in the atmosphere. Also explain why the water on the outside of the glass only appears after you add ice to the water in the glass.

Section 2

Precipitation

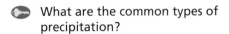

CALIFORNIA
Standards Focus

S 6.4.e Students know differences in pressure, heat, air movement, and humidity result in changes in weather.

🔑 What are the common types of precipitation?

Key Term
• precipitation

Lab zone Standards **Warm-Up**

How Can You Make Hail?

1. Put on your goggles.
2. 🧪 Put 15 g of salt into a beaker. Add 50 mL of water. Stir the solution until most of the salt is dissolved
3. Put 15 ml of cold water in a clean test tube.
4. Place the test tube in the beaker.
5. Fill the beaker almost to the top with crushed ice. Stir the ice mixture every minute for six minutes.
6. Remove the test tube from the beaker and drop an ice chip into the test tube. What happens?

Think It Over

Inferring Based on your observation, what conditions are necessary for hail to form?

In Arica, Chile, the average rainfall is less than 1 millimeter per year. But in Hawaii, the average rainfall on Mount Waialeale is about 12 meters per year. As you can see, rainfall varies greatly around the world.

Water evaporates from every water surface on Earth and from living things. This water eventually returns to the surface as precipitation. **Precipitation** (pree sip uh TAY shun) is any form of water that falls from clouds and reaches Earth's surface.

Not all clouds produce precipitation. For precipitation to occur, cloud droplets or ice crystals must grow heavy enough to fall through the air. One way that cloud droplets grow is by colliding and combining with other droplets. As the droplets grow larger, they move faster and collect more small droplets. Finally, the droplets become heavy enough to fall out of the cloud as raindrops.

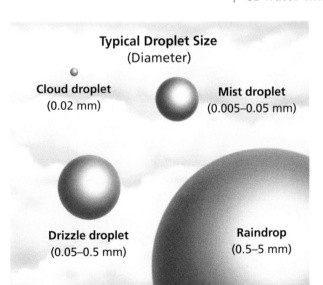

Typical Droplet Size
(Diameter)

Cloud droplet
(0.02 mm)

Mist droplet
(0.005–0.05 mm)

Drizzle droplet
(0.05–0.5 mm)

Raindrop
(0.5–5 mm)

FIGURE 7
Water Droplets
Droplets come in many sizes. Believe it or not, a raindrop has about one million times as much water in it as a cloud droplet.

For: Links on precipitation
Visit: www.SciLinks.org
Web Code: scn-0925

Types of Precipitation

In warm parts of the world, precipitation is almost always in the form of rain. In colder regions, precipitation may fall as snow or ice. 🔵 **Common types of precipitation include rain, hail, snow, sleet, and freezing rain.**

Rain The most common kind of precipitation is rain. Drops of water are called rain if they are at least 0.5 millimeter in diameter. Precipitation made up of smaller drops of water is called drizzle. Precipitation of even smaller drops is called mist. Drizzle and mist usually fall from stratus clouds.

Hail Round pellets of ice larger than 5 millimeters in diameter are called hailstones. Hail forms only inside cumulonimbus clouds during thunderstorms. A hailstone starts as an ice pellet inside a cold region of a cloud. Strong updrafts carry the hailstone up through the cold region many times. Each time the hailstone goes through the cold region, a new layer of ice forms around it. Eventually the hailstone becomes heavy enough to fall to the ground. If you cut a hailstone in half, you often see shells of ice, like the layers of an onion, as shown in Figure 8. Because hailstones can grow quite large before finally falling to the ground, hail can cause tremendous damage to crops, buildings, and vehicles.

FIGURE 8
How Hail Forms
Hailstones start as small pellets of ice in cumulonimbus clouds. They grow larger as they are repeatedly tossed up and down, until they become so heavy that they fall to the ground.
Interpreting Diagrams *Why do hailstones grow larger as they are tossed up and down in a cloud?*

Tiny ice pellets are tossed up and down in cumulonimbus clouds, growing larger as they gain layers of ice.

Eventually the ice pellets grow heavy enough to fall to the ground as hail.

Snow Often water vapor in a cloud is converted directly into ice crystals called snowflakes. Snowflakes have an endless number of different shapes and patterns, all with six sides or branches. Powdery snow is produced when snow falls through cold, dry air. When snow falls through humid air that is close to freezing, the snowflakes tend to join together into larger clumps in which the individual crystals are hard to see.

Sleet Sometimes raindrops fall through a layer of air that is below 0°C, the freezing point of water. As they fall, the raindrops freeze into solid particles of ice. Ice particles smaller than 5 millimeters in diameter are called sleet.

Freezing Rain Sometimes raindrops falling through cold air near the ground do not freeze in the air. Instead, they freeze when they touch a cold surface. This kind of precipitation is called freezing rain.

In an ice storm, a smooth, thick layer of ice builds up on every surface. This can produce beautiful effects as it coats trees and bushes. However, the weight of the ice may break tree branches and cause them to fall onto power lines, causing power failures. Freezing rain and sleet can make sidewalks and roads slippery and dangerous.

FIGURE 9
Snowflake
Snowflakes are tiny ice crystals. They all have six sides or branches.

 **Reading Checkpoint** What is sleet?

Section 2 Assessment

S 6.4.e, E-LA: Reading 6.2.2, Writing 6.2.1

Target Reading Skill Compare and Contrast Make a compare/contrast table for types of precipitation. How do rain, sleet, and hail form?

Reviewing Key Concepts

1. **a.** Listing Name the five common types of precipitation.
   b. Comparing and Contrasting Compare and contrast freezing rain and sleet.
   c. Classifying A thunderstorm produces precipitation in the form of ice particles that are about 6 millimeters in diameter. What type of precipitation would this be?

   d. Relating Cause and Effect How do hailstones become so large in cumulonimbus clouds?

Writing in Science

Firsthand Account Think about the most exciting experience you have had with precipitation. Write a paragraph about that event. Make sure you describe the precipitation itself as well as the effect it had on you.

Section 3
Air Masses and Fronts

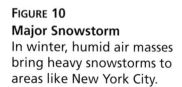
CALIFORNIA
Standards Focus

S 6.4.e Students know differences in pressure, heat, air movement, and humidity result in changes in weather.

- What are the major types of air masses in North America, and how do they move?
- What are the main types of fronts?
- What type of weather is associated with cyclones and anticyclones?

Key Terms
- air mass
- tropical
- polar
- maritime
- continental
- front
- occluded
- cyclone
- anticyclone

Lab zone Standards **Warm-Up**

How Do Fluids of Different Densities Behave?

1. Put on your apron. Place a cardboard divider across the middle of a plastic shoe box.
2. Add a few drops of red food coloring to a liter of warm water. Pour the red liquid, which represents low-density warm air, into the shoe box on one side of the divider.

3. Add about 100 mL of table salt and a few drops of blue food coloring to a liter of cold water. Pour the blue liquid, which represents high-density cold air, into the shoe box on the other side of the divider.
4. What do you think will happen if you remove the divider?
5. Now quickly remove the divider. Watch carefully from the side. What happens?

Think It Over
Developing Hypotheses Based on this activity, write a hypothesis stating what would happen if a mass of cold air ran into a mass of warm air.

Listen to the evening news in the winter and you may hear a weather forecast like this: "A huge mass of Arctic air is moving our way, bringing freezing temperatures." Today's weather can be influenced by air from thousands of kilometers away—perhaps from Canada or the Pacific Ocean. A huge body of air that has similar temperature, humidity, and air pressure at any given height is called an **air mass.** A single air mass may spread over millions of square kilometers and be up to 10 kilometers deep.

FIGURE 10
Major Snowstorm
In winter, humid air masses bring heavy snowstorms to areas like New York City.

Types of Air Masses

Scientists classify air masses according to two characteristics: temperature and humidity. ⬤ **Four major types of air masses influence the weather in North America: maritime tropical, continental tropical, maritime polar, and continental polar.**

The characteristics of an air mass depend on the temperatures and moisture content of the region over which the air mass forms. Remember that temperature affects air pressure. Cold, dense air has a higher pressure, while warm, less dense air has a lower pressure. **Tropical,** or warm, air masses form in the tropics and have low air pressure. **Polar,** or cold, air masses form north of 50° north latitude and south of 50° south latitude. Polar air masses have high air pressure.

Whether an air mass is humid or dry depends on whether it forms over water or land. **Maritime** air masses form over oceans. Water evaporates from the oceans, so the air can become very humid. **Continental** air masses form over land. Continental air masses have less exposure to large amounts of moisture from bodies of water. Therefore, continental air masses are drier than maritime air masses.

Maritime Tropical Warm, humid air masses form over tropical oceans. Maritime tropical air masses that form over the Gulf of Mexico and the Atlantic Ocean move first into the southeastern United States. These air masses then move north and northeast, where they influence weather in the central and eastern United States. In the west, maritime tropical air masses form over the Pacific Ocean. They mainly affect the weather on the West Coast. As they cross the coastal mountain ranges, the Pacific air masses lose moisture.

In summer, maritime tropical air masses usually bring hot, humid weather. Many summer showers and thunderstorms in the eastern United States develop in air masses that have formed over the Gulf of Mexico. In winter, a humid air mass can bring heavy rain or snow.

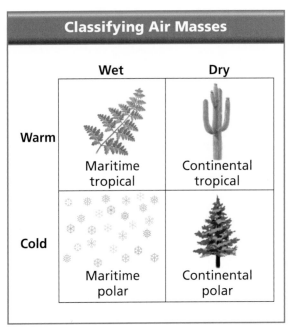

Classifying Air Masses

	Wet	Dry
Warm	Maritime tropical	Continental tropical
Cold	Maritime polar	Continental polar

FIGURE 11
Air masses can be classified according to their temperature and humidity. **Identifying** *What type of air mass consists of warm, moist air?*

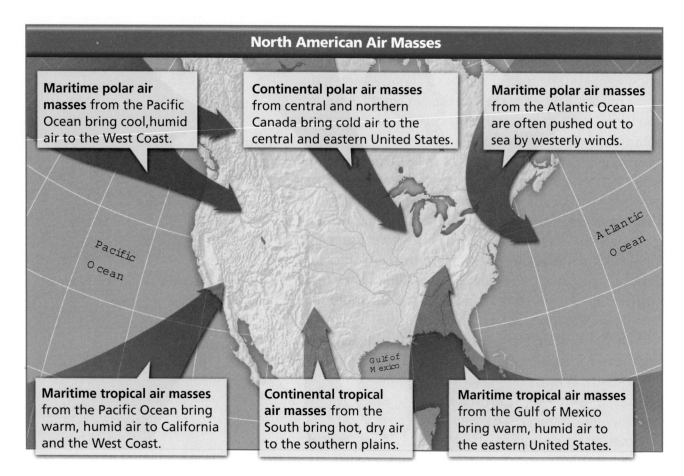

North American Air Masses

Maritime polar air masses from the Pacific Ocean bring cool, humid air to the West Coast.

Continental polar air masses from central and northern Canada bring cold air to the central and eastern United States.

Maritime polar air masses from the Atlantic Ocean are often pushed out to sea by westerly winds.

Pacific Ocean

Atlantic Ocean

Gulf of Mexico

Maritime tropical air masses from the Pacific Ocean bring warm, humid air to California and the West Coast.

Continental tropical air masses from the South bring hot, dry air to the southern plains.

Maritime tropical air masses from the Gulf of Mexico bring warm, humid air to the eastern United States.

FIGURE 12
Air masses can be warm or cold, and humid or dry. As an air mass moves into an area, the weather changes.

Maritime Polar Cool, humid air masses form over the icy cold North Pacific and North Atlantic oceans. Maritime polar air masses affect the West Coast more than the East Coast. Even in summer, these masses of cool, humid air often bring fog, rain, and cool temperatures to the West Coast.

Continental Tropical Hot, dry air masses form mostly in summer over dry areas of the Southwest and northern Mexico. Continental tropical air masses cover a smaller area than other air masses. They occasionally move northeast, bringing hot, dry weather to the southern Great Plains.

Continental Polar Large continental polar air masses form over central and northern Canada and Alaska, as shown in Figure 12. Air masses that form near the Arctic Circle can bring bitterly cold weather with very low humidity. In winter, continental polar air masses bring clear, cold, dry air to much of North America. In summer, the air mass is milder. Storms may occur when continental polar air masses move south and collide with maritime tropical air masses moving north.

 **Reading Checkpoint** Where do continental polar air masses come from?

How Air Masses Move

When an air mass moves into an area and interacts with other air masses, it causes the weather to change. 🔄 **In the continental United States, air masses are commonly moved by the prevailing westerlies and jet streams.**

Prevailing Westerlies The prevailing westerlies, the major wind belts over the continental United States, generally push air masses from west to east. For example, maritime polar air masses from the Pacific Ocean are blown onto the West Coast, bringing low clouds and showers.

Jet Streams Embedded within the prevailing westerlies are jet streams. Recall that jet streams are bands of high-speed winds about 10 kilometers above Earth's surface. As jet streams blow from west to east, air masses are carried along their tracks.

Fronts As huge masses of air move across the land and the oceans, they collide with each other. But the air masses do not easily mix. Think about a bottle of oil and water. The less dense oil floats on top of the denser water. Something similar happens when two air masses with different temperatures and humidities collide. The air masses do not easily mix. The boundary where the air masses meet becomes a **front.** Storms and changeable weather often develop along fronts, as shown in Figure 13.

Lab zone | Skills **Activity**

Calculating

When planes fly from west to east, they fly with the jet stream, and therefore can fly faster. When traveling from east to west, planes fly against the jet stream, and travel slower. To calculate the rate at which the planes fly, divide the distance traveled by the time it takes.

$$Rate = \frac{Distance}{Time}$$

If a plane flies from Denver, Colorado, to New York City, a distance of about 2,618 kilometers, it takes about 3 hours and 30 minutes. The return flight takes about 4 hours. Calculate the rates of air travel, in km/h, in each direction. How much extra speed does the jet stream add to the west-to-east flight?

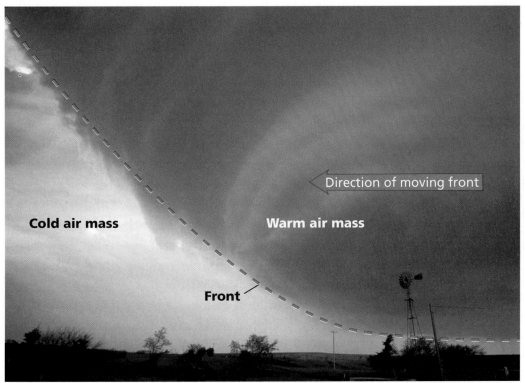

Cold air mass

Warm air mass

Direction of moving front

Front

FIGURE 13
How a Front Forms
The boundary where unlike air masses meet is called a front. A front may be 15 to 600 kilometers wide and extend high into the troposphere.

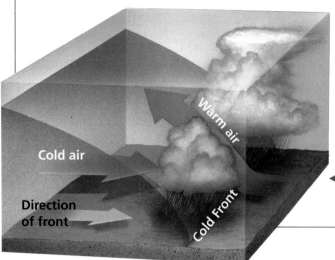

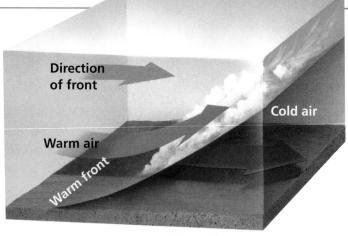

FIGURE 14
Types of Fronts
There are four types of fronts: cold fronts, warm fronts, stationary fronts, and occluded fronts.
Interpreting Diagrams *What kind of weather occurs at a warm front?*

Direction of front

Cold air

Warm air

Warm front

▲ **Warm Front**
A warm air mass overtakes a slow-moving cold air mass.

Cold air

Warm air

Direction of front

Warm Front

Cold Front

◄ **Cold Front**
A fast-moving cold air mass overtakes a warm air mass.

Lab zone Skills **Activity**

Classifying
At home, watch the weather forecast on television. Make a note of each time the weather reporter mentions a front. Classify the fronts mentioned or shown as cold, warm, stationary, or occluded. What type of weather is predicted to occur when the front arrives? Note the specific weather conditions, such as temperature and air pressure, associated with the front. Is each type of front always associated with the same type of weather?

Types of Fronts

🖰 Colliding air masses can form four types of fronts: cold fronts, warm fronts, stationary fronts, and occluded fronts. The kind of front that develops depends on the characteristics of the air masses and how they are moving.

Cold Fronts As you have learned, cold air is dense and tends to sink. Warm air is less dense and tends to rise. When a rapidly moving cold air mass runs into a slowly moving warm air mass, the denser cold air slides under the lighter warm air. The warm air is pushed upward along the leading edge of the colder air, as shown in Figure 14. A cold front forms.

As the warm air rises, it expands and cools. Remember that warm air can hold more water vapor than cool air. The rising air soon reaches the dew point, the temperature at which the water vapor in the air condenses into droplets of liquid water or forms tiny ice crystals. Clouds form. If there is a lot of water vapor in the warm air, heavy rain or snow may fall. If the warm air mass contains only a little water vapor, then the cold front may be accompanied by only cloudy skies.

Since cold fronts tend to move quickly, they can cause abrupt weather changes, including thunderstorms. After a cold front passes through an area, colder, drier air moves in, often bringing clear skies, a shift in wind, and lower temperatures.

✓ **Reading Checkpoint** **What type of weather do cold fronts bring?**

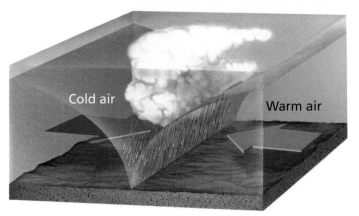

Stationary Front
Cold and warm air masses meet, but neither can move the other.

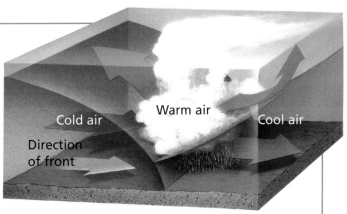

Occluded Front
A warm air mass is caught between two cooler air masses.

Go Online
active art

For: Weather Fronts activity
Visit: PHSchool.com
Web Code: cfp-4031

Warm Fronts Clouds and precipitation also accompany warm fronts. At a warm front, a fast-moving warm air mass overtakes a slowly moving cold air mass. Because cold air is denser than warm air, the warm air moves over the cold air. If the warm air is humid, light rain or snow falls along the front. If the warm air is dry, scattered clouds form. Because warm fronts move slowly, the weather may be rainy or cloudy for several days. After a warm front passes through an area, the weather is likely to be warm and humid.

Stationary Fronts Sometimes cold and warm air masses meet, but neither one can move the other. The two air masses face each other in a "standoff." In this case, the front is called a stationary front. Where the warm and cool air meet, water vapor in the warm air condenses into rain, snow, fog, or clouds. If a stationary front remains stalled over an area, it may bring many days of clouds and precipitation.

Occluded Fronts The most complex weather situation occurs at an occluded front, where a warm air mass is caught between two cooler air masses. The denser cool air masses move underneath the less dense warm air mass and push the warm air upward. The two cooler air masses meet in the middle and may mix. The temperature near the ground becomes cooler. The warm air mass is cut off, or **occluded,** from the ground. As the warm air cools and its water vapor condenses, the weather may turn cloudy and rain or snow may fall.

FIGURE 15

Structure of Cyclones and Anticyclones
Winds spiral inward toward the low-pressure center of a cyclone. Winds spiral outward from the high-pressure center of an anticyclone.
Interpreting Diagrams *Do cyclone winds spin clockwise or counterclockwise in the Northern Hemisphere?*

Cyclone (Low)

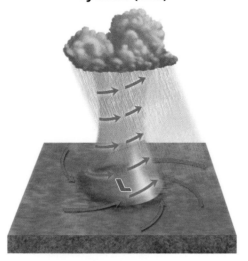

Anticyclone (High)

Cyclones and Anticyclones

As air masses collide to form fronts, the boundary between the fronts sometimes becomes distorted. This distortion can be caused by surface features, such as mountains, or strong winds, such as the jet stream. When this happens, bends can develop along the front. The air begins to swirl. The swirling air can cause a low-pressure center to form.

Cyclones If you look at a weather map, you will see areas marked with an *L*. The L stands for "low," and indicates an area of relatively low air pressure. A swirling center of low air pressure is called a **cyclone,** from a Greek word meaning "wheel."

As warm air at the center of a cyclone rises, the air pressure decreases. Cooler air blows toward this low-pressure area from nearby areas where the air pressure is higher. As shown in Figure 15, winds spiral inward toward the center of the system. Winds in a cyclone spin counterclockwise in the Northern Hemisphere when viewed from above. In the Southern Hemisphere, cyclone winds spin in a clockwise direction.

Cyclones play a large part in the weather of the United States. As air rises in a cyclone, the air cools, forming clouds and precipitation. ☁ **Cyclones and decreasing air pressure are associated with clouds, wind, and precipitation.**

Anticyclones As its name suggests, an anticyclone is the opposite of a cyclone. **Anticyclones** are high-pressure centers of dry air. Anticyclones are usually called "highs"—*H* on a weather map. Winds spiral outward from the center of an anticyclone, moving toward areas of lower pressure. Because of the Coriolis effect, winds in an anticyclone spin clockwise in the Northern Hemisphere. Because air moves out from the center of the anticyclone, cool air moves downward from higher in the troposphere. As the cool air falls, it warms up, so its relative humidity drops. ☁ **The descending air in an anticyclone generally causes dry, clear weather.**

Reading Checkpoint What is an anticyclone?

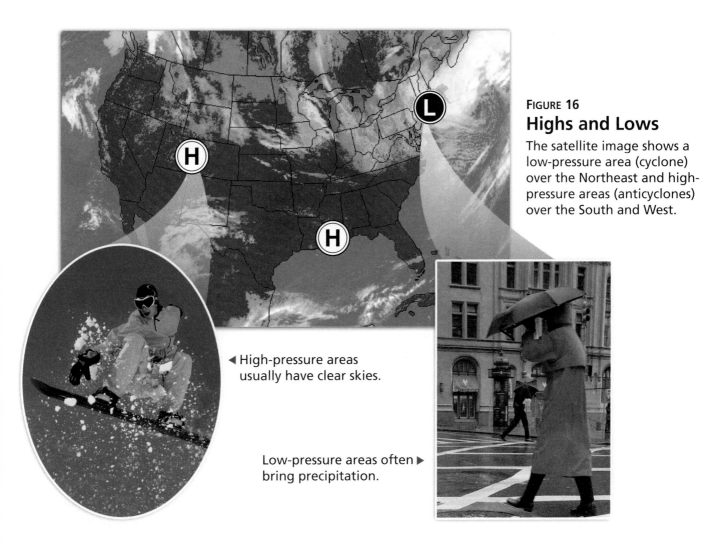

FIGURE 16
Highs and Lows
The satellite image shows a low-pressure area (cyclone) over the Northeast and high-pressure areas (anticyclones) over the South and West.

◄ High-pressure areas usually have clear skies.

Low-pressure areas often ► bring precipitation.

Section 3 Assessment

S 6.4.e, E-LA: Reading 6.1.2, Writing 6.2.0

Vocabulary Skill Identify Multiple Meanings
Use the scientific meaning of *front* in a sentence. Then use the everyday meaning in a sentence.

Reviewing Key Concepts

1. a. **Reviewing** What two characteristics are used to classify air masses?
   b. **Classifying** Classify the four major types of air masses according to whether they are dry or humid.
   c. **Applying Concepts** What type of air mass would form over the northern Atlantic Ocean?
2. a. **Defining** What is a front?
   b. **Describing** Name the four types of fronts and describe the type of weather each brings.
   c. **Classifying** What type of front would most likely be responsible for several days of rain and clouds?

3. a. **Identifying** What is a cyclone?
   b. **Relating Cause and Effect** How does air move in an anticyclone? How does this movement affect the weather?
   c. **Comparing and Contrasting** Compare cyclones and anticyclones. What type of weather is associated with each?

Writing in Science

News Report Suppose you are a television weather reporter covering a severe thunderstorm. Write a brief report to explain to viewers the conditions that caused the thunderstorm.

Section 4
Storms

CALIFORNIA Standards Focus

S 6.2.d Students know earthquakes, volcanic eruptions, landslides, and floods change human and wildlife habitats.

S 6.4.e Students know differences in pressure, heat, air movement, and humidity result in changes in weather.

- What are the main kinds of storms, and how do they form?
- What measures can you take to ensure safety in a storm?

Key Terms
- storm
- thunderstorm
- lightning
- tornado
- hurricane
- storm surge

Lab zone Standards Warm-Up

Can You Make a Tornado?

1. Fill a large jar three-quarters full with water. Add a drop of liquid dish detergent and a penny or a marble.
2. Put the lid on the jar tightly. Now move the jar in a circle until the water inside begins to spin.

Think It Over

Observing What happens to the water in the jar? Describe the pattern that forms. How is it like a tornado? Unlike a tornado?

As a storm rages, lightning flashes and thunder rumbles. After the sky clears, dripping trees and numerous puddles are the only evidence of the passing storm. Right? Not always. Scientists search for other evidence—"fossil lightning"! When lightning strikes sand or sandy soil, the sand grains are fused together to form a fulgurite. The shape of the fulgurite reflects the path of the lightning bolt that formed it, as shown in Figure 17. These structures clearly show the tremendous power of storms.

A **storm** is a violent disturbance in the atmosphere. Storms involve sudden changes in air pressure, which in turn cause rapid air movements. Conditions that bring one kind of storm often cause other kinds of storms in the same area. For example, the conditions that cause thunderstorms can also cause tornadoes. There are several types of severe storms.

FIGURE 17
Fulgurites
A fulgurite forms when lightning strikes sand or sandy soil. The temperature of the lightning is so high that it melts the sand and forms a tube.

FIGURE 18
Thunderstorm Formation
A thunderstorm forms when warm, humid air rises rapidly within a cumulonimbus cloud.
Applying Concepts Why do cumulonimbus clouds often form along cold fronts?

Labels in figure: Storm movement; Cold air moves downward; Warm, humid air rises; Heavy rain

Thunderstorms

Do you find thunderstorms frightening? Exciting? As you watch the brilliant flashes of lightning and listen to long rolls of thunder, you may wonder what caused them.

How Thunderstorms Form A **thunderstorm** is a small storm often accompanied by heavy precipitation and frequent thunder and lightning. **Thunderstorms form in large cumulonimbus clouds, also known as thunderheads.** Most cumulonimbus clouds form on hot, humid afternoons. They also form when warm air is forced upward along a cold front. In both cases, the warm, humid air rises rapidly. The air cools, forming dense thunderheads. Heavy rain falls, sometimes along with hail. Within the thunderhead are strong upward and downward winds—updrafts and downdrafts—as shown in Figure 18. Many thunderstorms form in the spring and summer in southern states or on the Western Plains.

Lightning and Thunder During a thunderstorm, areas of positive and negative electric charges build up in the storm clouds. **Lightning** is a sudden spark, or electric discharge, as these charges jump between parts of a cloud, between nearby clouds, or between a cloud and the ground. Lightning is similar to the shocks you sometimes feel when you touch a metal object on a very dry day, but on a much larger scale.

What causes thunder? A lightning bolt can heat the air near it to as much as 30,000°C, much hotter than the sun's surface. The rapidly heated air expands suddenly and explosively. Thunder is the sound of the explosion. Because light travels much faster than sound, you see lightning before you hear thunder.

FIGURE 19
Lightning Striking Earth
Lightning occurs when electric charges jump within clouds, between clouds, or between clouds and the ground. Lightning can cause fires or serious injuries.

For: More on thunder and lightning
Visit: PHSchool.com
Web Code: cfd-4032

Thunderstorm Damage Thunderstorms can cause severe damage. The heavy rains associated with thunderstorms can flood low-lying areas. Lightning can also cause damage. When lightning strikes the ground, the hot, expanding air can shatter tree trunks or start forest fires. When lightning strikes people or animals, it acts like a powerful electric shock. Lightning can cause unconsciousness, serious burns, or even heart failure.

Floods A major danger during severe thunderstorms is flooding. Floods occur when so much water pours into a stream or river that its banks overflow, covering the surrounding land. In urban areas, floods can occur when the ground is already saturated by heavy rains. The water can't soak into the water-logged ground or the many areas covered with buildings, roads, and parking lots.

Floods can bury or wash away human and wildlife habitats. However, floods may also have benefits. For example, river floods can provide rich new soil for agriculture.

Thunderstorm Safety The safest place to be during a thunderstorm is indoors. If you are inside a house, avoid touching telephones, electrical appliances, or plumbing fixtures, all of which can conduct electricity. It is usually safe to stay in a car with a hard top during a thunderstorm. The electricity will move along the metal skin of the car and jump to the ground.  **During thunderstorms, avoid places where lightning may strike. Also avoid objects that can conduct electricity, such as metal objects and bodies of water.**

How can you stay safe if you are caught outside during a thunderstorm? Don't seek shelter under a tree, because lightning may strike the tree and you. Instead, find a low area away from trees, fences, and poles. If you are swimming or in a boat, get to shore and find shelter away from the water.

Reading Checkpoint How can lightning be dangerous?

Tornadoes

A tornado is one of the most frightening and destructive types of storms. A **tornado** is a rapidly whirling, funnel-shaped cloud that reaches down from a storm cloud to touch Earth's surface. If a tornado occurs over a lake or ocean, the storm is known as a waterspout. Tornadoes are usually brief, but can be deadly. They may touch the ground for 15 minutes or less and be only a few hundred meters across. But wind speeds in the most intense tornadoes may approach 500 kilometers per hour.

FIGURE 20
Tornado Formation

Tornadoes can form when warm, humid air rises rapidly in a cumulonimbus cloud. Varying winds at different heights can spin the rising air like a top.

2 The warm air begins to rotate as it meets winds blowing in different directions at different altitudes.

Cumulonimbus cloud

1 Warm, moist air flows in at the bottom of a cumulonimbus cloud and moves upward. A low pressure area forms inside the cloud.

3 A tornado forms as part of the cloud descends to earth in a funnel.

Rain

How Tornadoes Form Tornadoes can form in any situation that produces severe weather. ⊙ **Tornadoes most commonly develop in thick cumulonimbus clouds—the same clouds that bring thunderstorms.** Tornadoes are most likely to occur when thunderstorms are likely—in spring and early summer, often late in the afternoon when the ground is warm. The Great Plains often have the kind of weather pattern that is likely to create tornadoes: A warm, humid air mass moves north from the Gulf of Mexico into the lower Great Plains. A cold, dry air mass moves south from Canada. When the air masses meet, the cold air moves under the warm air, forcing it to rise. A squall line, or narrow band of thunderstorms, is likely to form, with storms traveling from southwest to northeast. A single squall line can produce ten or more tornadoes.

Tornado Alley About 800 tornadoes occur in the United States every year. Weather patterns on the Great Plains result in a "tornado alley," as shown in Figure 21. However, tornadoes can and do occur in nearly every part of the United States, including California.

Tornado Safety ⊙ **The safest place to be during a tornado is in a storm shelter or the basement of a well-built building.** Stay away from windows and doors to avoid flying debris. Lie on the floor under a sturdy piece of furniture, such as a large table. If you are outdoors, lie flat in a ditch.

FIGURE 21
Tornado Alley

Tornadoes in the U.S. are most likely to occur in a region known as Tornado Alley. **Interpreting Maps** *Name five states that Tornado Alley crosses.*

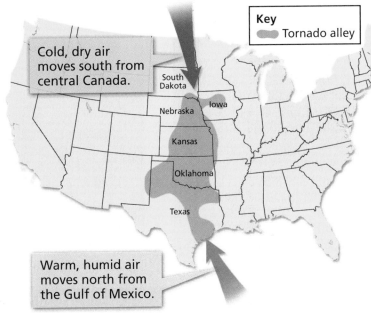

Cold, dry air moves south from central Canada.

South Dakota
Nebraska
Iowa
Kansas
Oklahoma
Texas

Key
Tornado alley

Warm, humid air moves north from the Gulf of Mexico.

Snowstorms

In the winter in the northern United States and at high elevations, a large amount of precipitation falls as snow. All year round, most precipitation begins in clouds as snow. If the air is colder than 0°C all the way to the ground, the precipitation falls as snow.

In California, snowstorms generally occur only at high elevations, such as on Mount Shasta or the Sierra Nevada mountain range. However, Californians depend on snow to provide part of their fresh water needs. Much of the snow that accumulates in the mountains during the winter months melts in the spring and summer. This snowmelt provides fresh water for a variety of needs, including irrigation and electricity production.

Science and **History**

Weather That Changed History

Unanticipated storms have caused incredible damage, killed large numbers of people, and even changed the course of history.

1588 England
King Philip II of Spain sent the Spanish Armada, a fleet of 130 ships, to invade England. Strong winds in the English Channel trapped the Armada near shore. Some Spanish ships escaped, but storms wrecked most of them.

1281 Japan
In an attempt to conquer Japan, Kublai Khan, the Mongol emperor of China, sent a fleet of ships carrying a huge army. A hurricane from the Pacific brought high winds and towering waves that sank the ships. The Japanese named the storm *kamikaze*, meaning "divine wind."

1620 Massachusetts
English Pilgrims set sail for the Americas in the *Mayflower*. They had planned to land near the mouth of the Hudson River, but turned back north because of rough seas and storms. When the Pilgrims landed farther north, they decided to stay and so established Plymouth Colony.

1200	1600	1700

Reading a Weather Map

Problem How does a weather map communicate data?

Skills Focus interpreting maps, observing, drawing conclusions

Procedure

1. Examine the symbols on the weather map below. For more information about the symbols used on the map, refer to Figure 26 and Figure 27 earlier in this section.

2. Observe the different colors on the weather map below.

3. Find the symbols for snow and rain.

4. Locate the warm fronts and cold fronts.

5. Locate the symbols for high and low pressure.

Analyze and Conclude

1. **Interpreting Maps** What color represents the highest temperatures? What color represents the lowest temperatures?

2. **Interpreting Maps** Which city has the highest temperature? Which city has the lowest temperature?

3. **Interpreting Maps** Where on the map is it raining? Where on the map is it snowing?

4. **Interpreting Maps** How many different kinds of fronts are shown on the map?

5. **Observing** How many areas of low pressure are shown on the map? How many areas of high pressure are shown on the map?

6. **Drawing Conclusions** What season does this map represent? How do you know?

7. **Communicating** The triangles and semicircles on the front lines show which way the front is moving. What type of front is moving toward Minneapolis? What kind of weather do you think it will bring?

More to Explore

Compare this weather map to one shown on a television news report. Which symbols on these maps are similar? Which symbols are different?

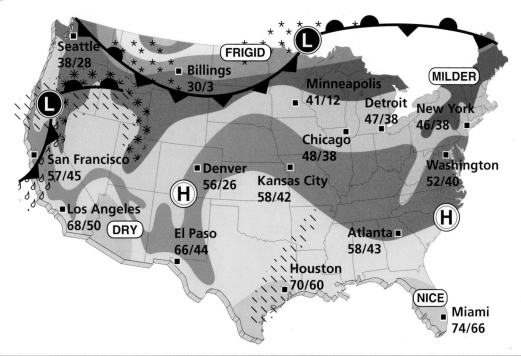

Doppler Radar

"Let's look at our Doppler radar screen," says a TV meteorologist pointing to a weather map with moving blotches of color. The colors represent different locations and intensities of precipitation. "The purple area here shows a severe storm moving rapidly into our area." Doppler radar helps meteorologists make more accurate weather forecasts by tracking the speed and direction of precipitation.

What Is Doppler Radar?

Doppler radar gets its name from the "Doppler effect," which describes the changes that occur in radio waves as they bounce off a moving object. Nearly 150 Doppler radar stations throughout the United States continuously send out radio waves. These waves bounce off particles in the air, such as raindrops, snowflakes, hail, and even dust. Some of these radio waves are reflected back to the Doppler radar station where computers process the data.

Transmitter sends out radio waves that bounce off particles, such as raindrops, in the air. Some waves are reflected back to the stations.

Antenna picks up the returning radio waves. Data from incoming waves are sent to a computer.

Computer is used to process data and generate a Doppler radar image for meteorologist.

Doppler Radar Station
Rotating continuously inside the protective housing, the station is supported by a tower that may be as tall as 30 meters.

How Effective Is Doppler Radar?

Before Doppler radar, it was hard to track fast-moving storms such as tornadoes. Tornado warnings were issued an average of just five minutes in advance. Today, Doppler radar can give people several extra minutes to prepare. People also use Doppler images to make decisions about everyday activities.

But the technology does have limitations. Doppler radar doesn't "see" everything. Sometimes mountains or buildings block the radio waves. In addition, Doppler radar doesn't always pick up light precipitation such as drizzle. Meteorologists must review the completeness of the data and decide how it might affect the forecast.

Tornado
Doppler radar can detect the air movements in thunderstorms that may lead to tornadoes. A tornado is a rapidly spinning, funnel-shaped cloud formed of condensed water particles.

Weigh the Impact

1. **Identify the Need** How is Doppler radar an important technology in weather forecasting?
2. **Research** Using the Internet, research Doppler radar reports for your city. Examine a Doppler image and explain each element on the map, including the different colors and the direction of motion.
3. **Write** As a TV meteorologist, write the script for a local weather forecast. Describe areas with precipitation, the amount of precipitation, and the direction of weather systems.

Go Online
PHSchool.com

For: More on Doppler radar
Visit: PHSchool.com
Web Code: cfh-4030

Doppler Radar Screens

The amount of precipitation is shown above by using different colors.

The different colors above show the speed and direction of precipitation.

🔑 The **BIG Idea** — Differences in air pressure, air temperature, winds, and humidity produce changes in weather.

1 Water in the Atmosphere

🔑 Key Concepts   🏴 S 6.4.a, 6.4.e

● Relative humidity can be measured with an instrument called a psychrometer.

● Clouds form when water vapor in the air condenses to form liquid water or ice crystals.

● Scientists classify clouds into three main types based on their shape: cirrus, cumulus, and stratus. Clouds are also classified by altitude.

Key Terms
• water cycle • evaporation • humidity
• relative humidity • psychrometer
• condensation • dew point • cirrus
• cumulus • stratus

2 Precipitation

🔑 Key Concept   🏴 S 6.4.e

● Common types of precipitation include rain, hail, snow, sleet, and freezing rain.

Key Term
• precipitation

3 Air Masses and Fronts

🔑 Key Concepts   🏴 S 6.4.e

● Maritime tropical, continental tropical, maritime polar, and continental polar air masses influence the weather in North America.

● In the continental United States, air masses are commonly moved by the prevailing westerlies and jet streams.

● Colliding air masses can form four types of fronts: cold fronts, warm fronts, stationary fronts, and occluded fronts.

● Cyclones and decreasing air pressure are associated with clouds, wind, and precipitation.

● The descending air in an anticyclone generally causes dry, clear weather.

Key Terms
• air mass • tropical • polar • maritime
• continental • front • occluded • cyclone
• anticyclone

4 Storms

🔑 Key Concepts   🏴 S 6.2.d, 6.4.e

● Thunderstorms form in large cumulonimbus clouds, also known as thunderheads.

● During thunderstorms, avoid places where lightning may strike.

● Tornadoes most commonly develop in thick cumulonimbus clouds.

● The safest place during a tornado is a storm shelter or the basement of a well-built building.

● All year round, most precipitation begins in clouds as snow.

● If you are caught in a snowstorm, try to find shelter from the wind.

● A hurricane begins over warm ocean water as a low-pressure area, or tropical disturbance.

● If you hear a hurricane warning and are told to evacuate, leave the area immediately.

Key Terms
• storm • thunderstorm • lightning
• tornado • hurricane • storm surge

5 Predicting the Weather

🔑 Key Concepts   🏴 S 6.4.e

● Meteorologists use maps, charts, and computers to prepare weather forecasts.

● Symbols on weather maps show fronts, pressure, precipitation, and temperatures.

Key Terms
• meteorologist • isobar • isotherm

Review and Assessment

Target Reading Skill

Compare and Contrast The table compares and contrasts thunderstorms, tornadoes, and hurricanes. Copy the table on a separate sheet of paper. Then complete it and add a title.

Type of Storm	Where Forms	Typical Time of Year	Safety Rules
Thunderstorm	Within large cumulonimbus clouds	a.____?____	b.____?____
Tornado	c.____?____	Spring, early summer	d.____?____
Hurricane	e.____?____	f.____?____	Evacuate or move inside a well-built building

Reviewing Key Terms

Choose the letter of the best answer.

1. A type of cloud that forms in flat layers and often covers much of the sky is
   a. cirrus.　　　　**b.** cumulus.
   c. fog.　　　　　**d.** stratus.

2. Rain, sleet, and hail are all forms of
   a. evaporation.
   b. condensation.
   c. precipitation.
   d. convection.

3. Cool, clear weather usually follows a(n)
   a. warm front.
   b. cold front.
   c. stationary front.
   d. occluded front.

4. Very large tropical cyclones with high winds are called
   a. hurricanes.
   b. tornadoes.
   c. air masses.
   d. anticyclones.

5. Lines joining places that have the same temperature are
   a. isobars.
   b. isotherms.
   c. fronts.
   d. occluded.

Complete the following sentences so that your answers clearly explain the key terms.

6. The process of **condensation** occurs when _____.

7. **Cyclones,** which are _____, often bring clouds, winds, and precipitation.

8. **Lightning,** which is _____, often occurs during thunderstorms.

9. **Tornadoes,** which are _____, commonly develop in thick cumulonimbus clouds.

10. Weather maps may include **isobars,** which are _____.

Writing in Science

Descriptive Paragraph Imagine that you are a hurricane hunter—a scientist who flies into a hurricane to collect data. Describe what it would feel like as you flew through the hurricane's eyewall into its eye.

Video Assessment
Discovery Channel School
Weather Patterns

Review and Assessment

Checking Concepts

11. Why do clouds usually form high in the air instead of near Earth's surface?

12. Describe sleet, hail, and snow in terms of how each one forms.

13. Describe how wind patterns affect the movement of air masses in North America.

14. How does a cold front form?

15. Describe two situations in which floods can occur.

16. What happens to a hurricane when it moves onto land? Why?

Thinking Critically

17. **Problem Solving** A psychrometer gives the same reading on both thermometers. What is the relative humidity?

18. **Relating Cause and Effect** How do differences in air density influence the movement of air along cold and warm fronts?

19. **Interpreting Diagrams** Describe the journey of a small particle of water through the water cycle, using the terms in the diagram below.

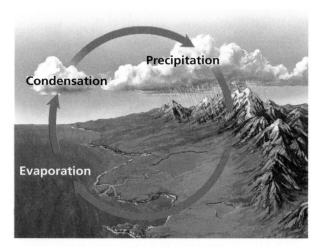
Precipitation
Condensation
Evaporation

20. **Comparing and Contrasting** Compare thunderstorms and tornadoes. How are they similar? How are they different?

21. **Predicting** If air pressure is decreasing, what kind of weather is likely to occur?

22. **Applying Concepts** Would you expect hurricanes to form over the oceans off the northeast or northwest coasts of the United States? Explain.

23. **Applying Concepts** Why can't meteorologists accurately forecast the weather a month in advance?

Applying Skills

Use the map to answer Questions 24–27.

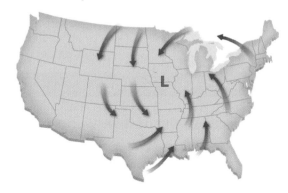

24. **Interpreting Maps** Does the map show a cyclone or an anticyclone? How can you tell?

25. **Interpreting Data** What do the arrows show about the movement of the winds in this pressure center? What else indicates wind direction?

26. **Making Models** Using this diagram as an example, draw a similar diagram to illustrate a high-pressure area. Remember to indicate wind direction in your diagram.

27. **Posing Questions** If you saw a pressure center like the one shown above on a weather map, what could you predict about the weather? What questions would you need to ask in order to make a better prediction?

Lab zone Standards Investigation

Performance Assessment Present your weather maps and weather forecasts to the class. Discuss how accurate your weather predictions were. Explain any inaccuracies in your forecasts.

Choose the letter of the best answer.

1. The major source of energy for the water cycle is
   A the ocean.   B the sun.
   C the wind.   D surface runoff.   *S 6.4.a*

2. How are air masses classified?
   A by temperature and pressure
   B by pressure and humidity
   C by temperature and density
   D by temperature and humidity   *S 6.4.e*

3. A rapidly moving cold air mass meets a slowly moving warm air mass and forms a front. What will most likely occur at this front?
   A The two air masses will mix together.
   B The warm air will slide under the cold air. The cold air will rise and get warmer.
   C Cold air will slide under the warm air. Warm air will rise and cool. Clouds will form.
   D The less dense warm air will sink and cool. Clouds will form.   *S 6.4.e*

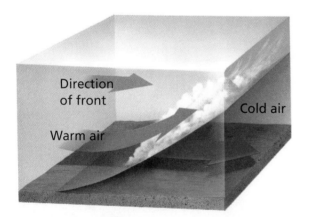

4. The diagram above shows a(n)
   A cold front.
   B warm front.
   C occluded front.
   D stationary front.   *S 6.4.e*

5. Thunderstorms can cause severe damage through
   A lightning and thunder.
   B hurricanes and flooding.
   C flooding and lightning.
   D thunder and hurricanes.   *S 6.2.d*

Use the graph below and your knowledge of science to answer Questions 6 and 7.

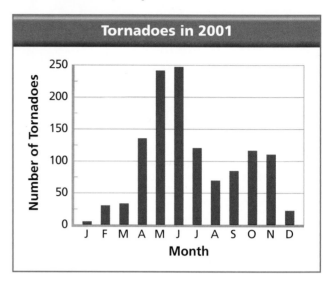

6. According to the graph, which two months in 2001 had the most tornadoes?
   A April and May
   B May and July
   C May and June
   D June and July   *S 6.4.e*

7. Which statement best summarizes the trend shown in the graph?
   A Tornadoes always occur most frequently in May and June.
   B Tornadoes occur when the weather is warmest.
   C In 2001, tornadoes were most frequent in April, May, and June.
   D Tornadoes are generally most frequent in the winter.   *S 6.4.e*

Apply the **BIG Idea**

8. Compare and contrast cyclones and anticyclones in terms of air pressure, temperature, wind direction, and humidity. What type of weather does each bring? *S 6.4.e*

Chapter 9

Climate and Climate Change

Emperor penguins live in Antarctica. Their dense network of feathers helps to protect them from extreme cold and strong winds. ▶

S 6.4.e

Focus on the BIG Idea

What are the major factors that influence a region's climate?

Check What You Know

Think about how the weather changes with the seasons where you live. Is there a dry season and a rainy season? Are certain months usually hotter than others? Write a paragraph describing how the weather changes over the course of a year where you live and in one other location with very different seasonal changes. Explain why you think these seasonal changes occur.

Build Science Vocabulary

The images shown here represent some of the key terms in this chapter. You can use this vocabulary skill to help you understand the meaning of some key terms in this chapter.

Vocabulary Skill

High-Use Academic Words

High-use academic words are words that are used frequently in academic reading, writing, and discussions.

Word	Definition	Example Sentence
major (MAY jur) p. 376	*adj.* Great in size, amount, number, or importance	Hurricanes often cause <u>major</u> damage in Florida.
positive (PAHZ uh tiv) p. 377	*adj.* Having a good or useful effect; hopeful	She received <u>positive</u> comments on her science project.
range (raynj) p. 347	*v.* To extend or reach in a given direction	The temperature in our nation's capital can <u>range</u> from about –3˚C to 32˚C.
region (REE jun) p. 346	*n.* Part of the surface of Earth; an area	The southern <u>region</u> of the United States has the warmest weather.

Apply It!

Choose the word from the table that best completes the sentence.

1. The age of the students at the science conference _____ from 12 to 17.
2. What states are included in the Pacific _____ of the United States?
3. The rain is a _____ sign that the dry period is over.

microclimate

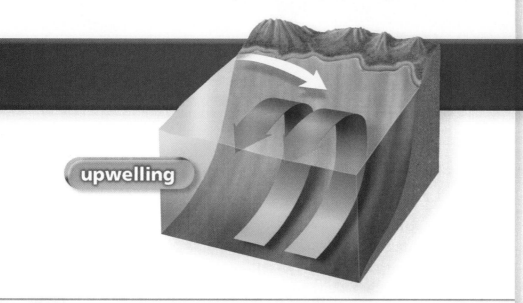
upwelling

rain forest

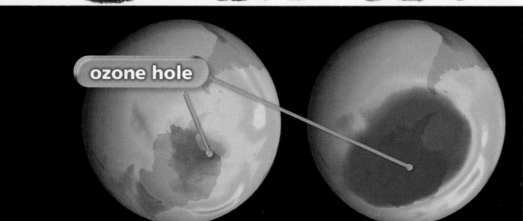
chaparral

ozone hole

Chapter 9 Vocabulary

Interactive Textbook

Build Science Vocabulary
Online
Visit: PHSchool.com
Web Code: cwj-3090

How to Read Science

 ## Create Outlines

You have learned to use headings and to identify main ideas and details to guide you as you read. An outline uses these skills to show the relationship between main ideas and supporting details.

An outline usually is set up like the one below. Roman numerals show the main topics or headings. Capital letters show the subheadings. Numbers show supporting details and key terms.

Look at the sample outline of the first part of Section 1.

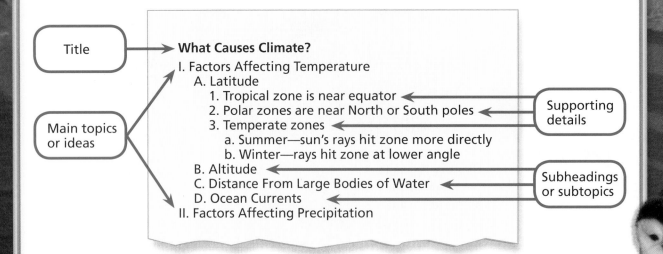

What Causes Climate?

Title

Main topics or ideas

I. Factors Affecting Temperature
  A. Latitude
      1. Tropical zone is near equator
      2. Polar zones are near North or South poles
      3. Temperate zones
          a. Summer—sun's rays hit zone more directly
          b. Winter—rays hit zone at lower angle
  B. Altitude
  C. Distance From Large Bodies of Water
  D. Ocean Currents
II. Factors Affecting Precipitation

Supporting details

Subheadings or subtopics

Apply It!

Use the outline above to answer the following questions.
  1. What are the main topics in this outline?
  2. What details describe how latitude affects temperature?

Copy the outline above into your notebook. Use the headings, subheadings, and key terms to help you select information to complete the outline for Section 1. Then create outlines for Section 2 and Section 3.

Investigating Microclimates

A microclimate is a small area with its own climate. As you work through this chapter, you will investigate microclimates in your community.

Your Goal

To compare weather conditions from at least three microclimates

To complete your investigation, you must

- hypothesize how the microclimates in three areas differ from each other
- collect data from your locations at the same time each day
- relate each microclimate to the plants and animals found there

Plan It!

Begin by brainstorming a list of nearby places that may have different microclimates. How are the places different? Keep in mind weather factors such as temperature, precipitation, humidity, wind direction, and wind speed. Consider areas that are grassy, sandy, sunny, or shaded.

You will need to measure daily weather conditions and record them in a logbook. Collect the instruments you need before you begin your investigation. Once you have collected all the data, construct your graphs and look for patterns. Then plan your presentation.

What Causes Climate?

CALIFORNIA
Standards Focus

S 6.4.a Students know the sun is the major source of energy for phenomena on Earth's surface; it powers winds, ocean currents, and the water cycle.

S 6.4.e Students know differences in pressure, heat, air movement, and humidity result in changes in weather.

- What factors influence temperature?
- What factors influence precipitation?
- What causes the seasons?

Key Terms
- climate • microclimate
- tropical zone • polar zone
- temperate zone
- marine climate
- continental climate
- ocean current • windward
- leeward • monsoon

An oasis in the Mojave Desert ▼

Lab zone Standards **Warm-Up**

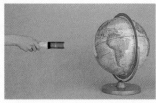

How Does Latitude Affect Climate?

1. On a globe, tape a strip of paper from the equator to the North Pole. Divide the tape into three equal parts. Label the top section *poles,* the bottom section *equator,* and the middle section *mid-latitudes.*

2. Tape the end of an empty toilet paper roll to the end of a flashlight. Hold the flashlight about 30 cm from the equator. Turn on the flashlight to represent the sun. On the paper strip, have a partner draw the area the light shines on.

3. Move the flashlight up slightly to aim at the "mid-latitudes." Keep the flashlight horizontal and at the same distance from the globe. Again, draw the lighted area.

4. Repeat Step 3, but this time aim the light at the "poles."

Think It Over

Observing How does the size of the illuminated area change? Do you think the sun's rays heat Earth's surface evenly?

The weather in an area changes every day. At a given location, the weather may be cloudy and rainy one day and clear and sunny the next. **Climate,** on the other hand, refers to the long-term, average conditions of temperature, precipitation, winds, and clouds in an area. For example, California's Mojave Desert, shown below, has a hot, dry climate.

Scientists use two main factors—precipitation and temperature—to describe the climate of a region. A climate region is a large area that has similar climate conditions throughout. For example, the climate in the southwestern United States is dry, with hot summers.

The factors that affect large climate regions also affect smaller areas. Have you ever noticed that it is cooler and more humid in a grove of trees than in an open field? A small area with climate conditions that differ from those around it may have its own **microclimate.**

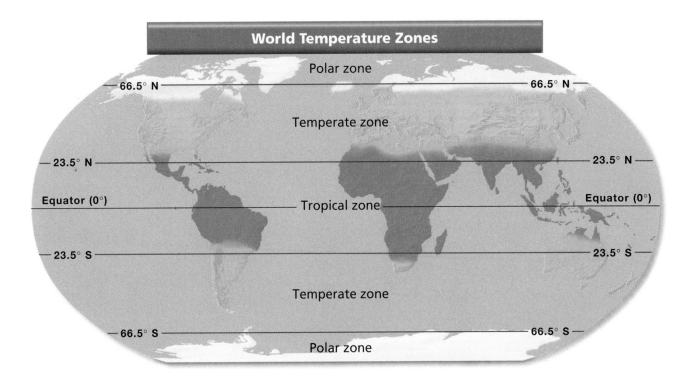

World Temperature Zones

Polar zone

66.5° N   66.5° N

Temperate zone

23.5° N   23.5° N

Equator (0°)   Equator (0°)

Tropical zone

23.5° S   23.5° S

Temperate zone

66.5° S   66.5° S

Polar zone

Factors Affecting Temperature

Why are some places warm and others cold? ⬡ **The main factors that influence temperature are latitude, altitude, distance from large bodies of water, and ocean currents.**

Latitude In general, climates of locations near the equator are warmer than climates far from the equator. The main reason is that the sun's rays hit Earth's surface most directly at the equator. At the poles, the same amount of solar radiation is spread over a larger area, and therefore brings less warmth.

Recall that latitude is the distance from the equator, measured in degrees. Based on latitude, Earth's surface can be divided into the three temperature zones shown in Figure 1. The **tropical zone** is the area near the equator, between about 23.5° north latitude and 23.5° south latitude. The tropical zone receives direct or nearly direct sunlight all year round, making climates there warm.

In contrast, the sun's rays always strike at a lower angle near the North and South poles. As a result, the areas near both poles have cold climates. These **polar zones** extend from about 66.5° to 90° north and 66.5° to 90° south latitudes.

Between the tropical zones and the polar zones are the **temperate zones.** In summer, the sun's rays strike the temperate zones more directly. In winter, the sun's rays strike at a lower angle. As a result, the weather in the temperate zones ranges from warm or hot in summer to cool or cold in winter.

FIGURE 1
The tropical zone has the warmest climates. Cold climates occur in the polar zone. In between lies the temperate zone, where climates vary from warm to cool.
Interpreting Maps *In which temperature zone is most of the United States located?*

FIGURE 2
Effect of Altitude
Mount Kilimanjaro, in Tanzania, is near the equator.
Relating Cause and Effect
What factor is responsible for the difference between the climate at the mountaintop and the climate at the base?

Altitude The peak of Mount Kilimanjaro towers high above the plains of East Africa. Kilimanjaro is covered in snow all year round, as shown in Figure 2. Yet it is located near the equator, at 3° south latitude. Why is Mount Kilimanjaro so cold?

In the case of high mountains, altitude is a more important climate factor than latitude. In the troposphere, temperature decreases about 6.5 Celsius degrees for every 1-kilometer increase in altitude. As a result, highland areas everywhere have cool climates, no matter what their latitude. At nearly 6 kilometers, the air at the top of Kilimanjaro is about 39 Celsius degrees colder than the air at sea level at the same latitude.

Distance From Large Bodies of Water Oceans or large lakes can also affect temperatures. Oceans greatly moderate, or make less extreme, the temperatures of nearby land. Water heats up more slowly than land. It also cools down more slowly. Therefore, winds off the ocean often prevent extremes of hot and cold in coastal regions. Much of the west coasts of North America, South America, and Europe have mild **marine climates,** with relatively mild winters and cool summers. The Pacific Ocean moderates the temperatures of coastal California.

The centers of North America and Asia are too far inland to be warmed or cooled by the ocean. Most of Canada and of Russia, as well as the central United States, have continental climates. **Continental climates** have more extreme temperatures than marine climates. Winters are cold, while summers are warm or hot.

Ocean Currents Marine climates are influenced by **ocean currents,** streams of water within the oceans that move in regular patterns. As you will learn in the next section, ocean currents may flow either near the surface or deep below it.

Some warm surface currents move heat from the tropics toward the poles. This affects climate as the warm ocean water warms the air above it. The warmed air then moves over nearby land. In the same way, cold currents bring cold water from the polar zones toward the equator. A cold surface current brings cool air.

The best-known warm-water current is the Gulf Stream. As shown in Figure 3, the Gulf Stream begins in the Gulf of Mexico and then flows north along the east coast of the United States. When it crosses the North Atlantic, it becomes the North Atlantic Drift. This warm surface current brings mild, humid air to Iceland, Ireland, and southern England. As a result, these areas have a mild, wet climate despite their relatively high latitude.

The cool California Current and warm Davidson Current affect the climates of coastal California. You will learn more about these currents in the next section.

 **Reading Checkpoint** What effect do oceans have on the temperatures of nearby land areas?

Go Online
SciLINKS NSTA

For: Links on ocean currents
Visit: www.SciLinks.org
Web Code: scn-0834

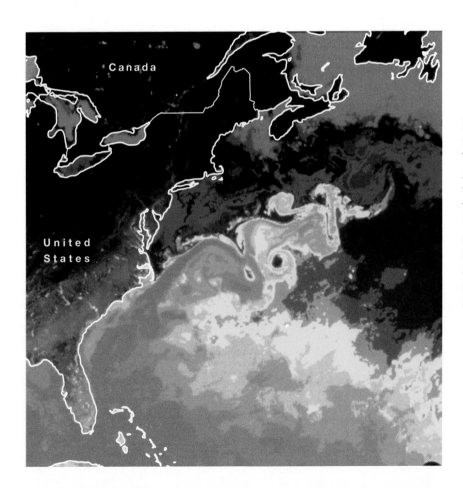

FIGURE 3
Surface Currents and Climate
This satellite image of the Atlantic Ocean has been enhanced with colors that show water temperature. Red and orange indicate warmer water, while green and blue indicate colder water.
Interpreting Maps The Gulf Stream flows around Florida in the lower left of the map. Is the Gulf Stream a warm or a cold current?

Factors Affecting Precipitation

The air masses that pass over an area may bring rain or snow. The amount of precipitation varies from year to year. But over time, total precipitation tends toward a yearly average. What determines the amount of precipitation an area receives? ⬤ **The main factors that affect precipitation are prevailing winds, the presence of mountains, and seasonal winds.**

Prevailing Winds As you know, weather patterns depend on the movement of huge air masses. Air masses are moved from place to place by prevailing winds, the directional winds that usually blow in a region. Air masses can be warm or cool, dry or humid. The amount of water vapor in the air mass influences how much rain or snow will fall. The amount of water vapor in prevailing winds also depends on where the winds come from. Winds that blow inland from oceans or large lakes carry more water vapor than winds that blow from over land.

Mountain Ranges A mountain range in the path of prevailing winds can also influence where precipitation falls. When humid winds blow from the ocean toward coastal mountains, they are forced to rise, as shown in Figure 4. The rising air cools and its water vapor condenses, forming clouds. Rain or snow falls on the **windward** side of the mountains, the side the wind hits first.

By the time the air has moved over the mountains, it has lost much of its water vapor, so it is cool and dry. The land on the **leeward** side of the mountains—downwind—is in a rain shadow. Little precipitation falls there.

The Sierra Nevada mountains have a major effect on California's climate. As shown in Figure 4, a great deal of precipitation falls on the western, windward side of the mountain range. Extremely dry areas such as Death Valley are located on the leeward side of the mountains.

FIGURE 4
Rain Shadow
A mountain range can form a barrier to the movement of humid air. Humid air cools as it is blown up the side of a mountain range.
Applying Concepts *Where does the heaviest rainfall occur?*

Warm, moist air blows in from the ocean and is pushed up by the mountains.

Warm, moist air

As the air rises, it cools and water vapor condenses. Moisture in the air is released as precipitation.

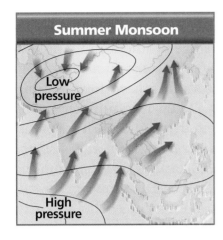

Summer Monsoon

Low pressure

High pressure

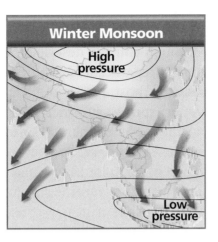

Winter Monsoon

High pressure

Low pressure

FIGURE 5
Monsoons
In a summer monsoon, wind blows from the ocean to the land. In the winter, the monsoon reverses and blows from the land to the ocean. Summer monsoons in Nepal cause heavy rain (above).

Seasonal Winds A seasonal change in wind patterns can affect precipitation. These seasonal winds are similar to land and sea breezes, but occur over a wider area. Sea and land breezes over a large region that change direction with the seasons are called **monsoons.** What produces a monsoon? In the summer in South and Southeast Asia, the land gradually gets warmer than the ocean. A "sea breeze" blows steadily inland from the ocean all summer, even at night. The air blowing from the ocean during this season is very warm and humid. As the humid air rises over the land, the air cools. This causes water vapor to condense into clouds, producing heavy rains.

Thailand and parts of India receive much of their rain from the summer monsoons. Monsoon winds also bring rain to coastal areas in West Africa and northeastern South America.

Regions affected by monsoon winds receive very little rain in winter. In the winter, the land cools and becomes colder than the ocean. A "land breeze" blows steadily from the land to the ocean. These winds carry little moisture.

The Santa Ana winds are hot, dry winds that often blow in Southern California during fall and early winter. Cool air from the desert blows toward the coast. As air flows down the mountains, it is compressed and warms up. The humidity of the air drops and vegetation dries out, creating a potential fire hazard.

 Reading Checkpoint   **Why does precipitation fall mainly on the windward sides of mountains?**

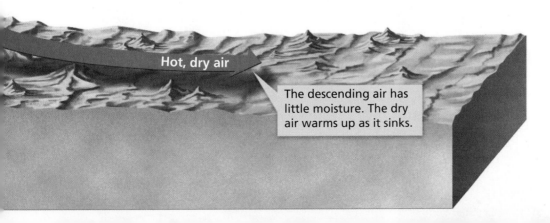

Hot, dry air

The descending air has little moisture. The dry air warms up as it sinks.

Math Skills

Percentage Light from the sun strikes Earth's surface at different angles. An angle is made up of two lines that meet at a point. Angles are measured in degrees. A full circle has 360 degrees.

When the sun is directly overhead near the equator, it is at an angle of 90° to Earth's surface. A 90° angle is called a right angle. What percentage of a circle is it?

$$\frac{90 \text{ degrees}}{360 \text{ degrees}} = \frac{d\%}{100\%}$$

$$90 \times 100 = 360 \times d$$

$$\frac{90 \times 100}{360} = d = 25$$

A 90° angle is 25 percent of a full circle.

Practice Problem Earth's axis is tilted at an angle of 23.5°. About what percentage of a right angle is this?

FIGURE 6
Summer and Winter
There can be a striking difference between summer and winter in the same location. **Inferring**
During which season does the area shown receive more solar energy?

The Seasons

Although you can describe the average weather conditions of a climate region, these conditions are not constant all year long. Instead, most places outside the tropics have four seasons: winter, spring, summer, and fall. When it is summer in the Northern Hemisphere it is winter in the Southern Hemisphere. So the seasons are not a result of changes in the distance between Earth and the sun. In fact, Earth is farthest from the sun during the summer in the Northern Hemisphere. The sun itself transfers a nearly constant amount of energy to Earth throughout the year.

Tilted Axis ◯ **The seasons are caused by the tilt of Earth's axis as Earth travels around the sun.** The axis is an imaginary line through Earth's center that passes through both poles. Earth rotates, or turns, around this axis once each day. Earth's axis is not straight up and down, but is tilted at an angle of 23.5°. As Earth travels around the sun, its axis always points in the same direction. So the north end of the axis is pointed away from the sun for one part of the year and toward the sun for another part of the year.

Effect of the Tilted Axis Look at Figure 7. Which way is the north end of Earth's axis tilted in June? Notice that the Northern Hemisphere receives radiation from the sun at a more direct angle. Also, in June the days in the Northern Hemisphere are longer than the nights. The combination of more direct solar radiation and longer days makes Earth's surface warmer in the Northern Hemisphere than at any other time of the year. It is summer in the Northern Hemisphere. At the same time, the Southern Hemisphere is experiencing winter.

In December, on the other hand, the north end of Earth's axis is tilted away from the sun. It is winter in the Northern Hemisphere and summer in the Southern Hemisphere.

Reading Checkpoint In June, what season is it in the Southern Hemisphere?

FIGURE 7
The Seasons

The seasons are a result of Earth's tilted axis. The seasons change as the amount of energy each hemisphere receives from the sun changes.

March

June

December

23.5°

June
The north end of Earth's axis is tilted toward the sun. It is summer in the Northern Hemisphere and winter in the Southern Hemisphere.

September

March and September
Neither end of Earth's axis is tilted toward the sun. Both hemispheres receive the same amount of energy.

December
The south end of Earth's axis is tilted toward the sun. It is summer in the Southern Hemisphere and winter in the Northern Hemisphere.

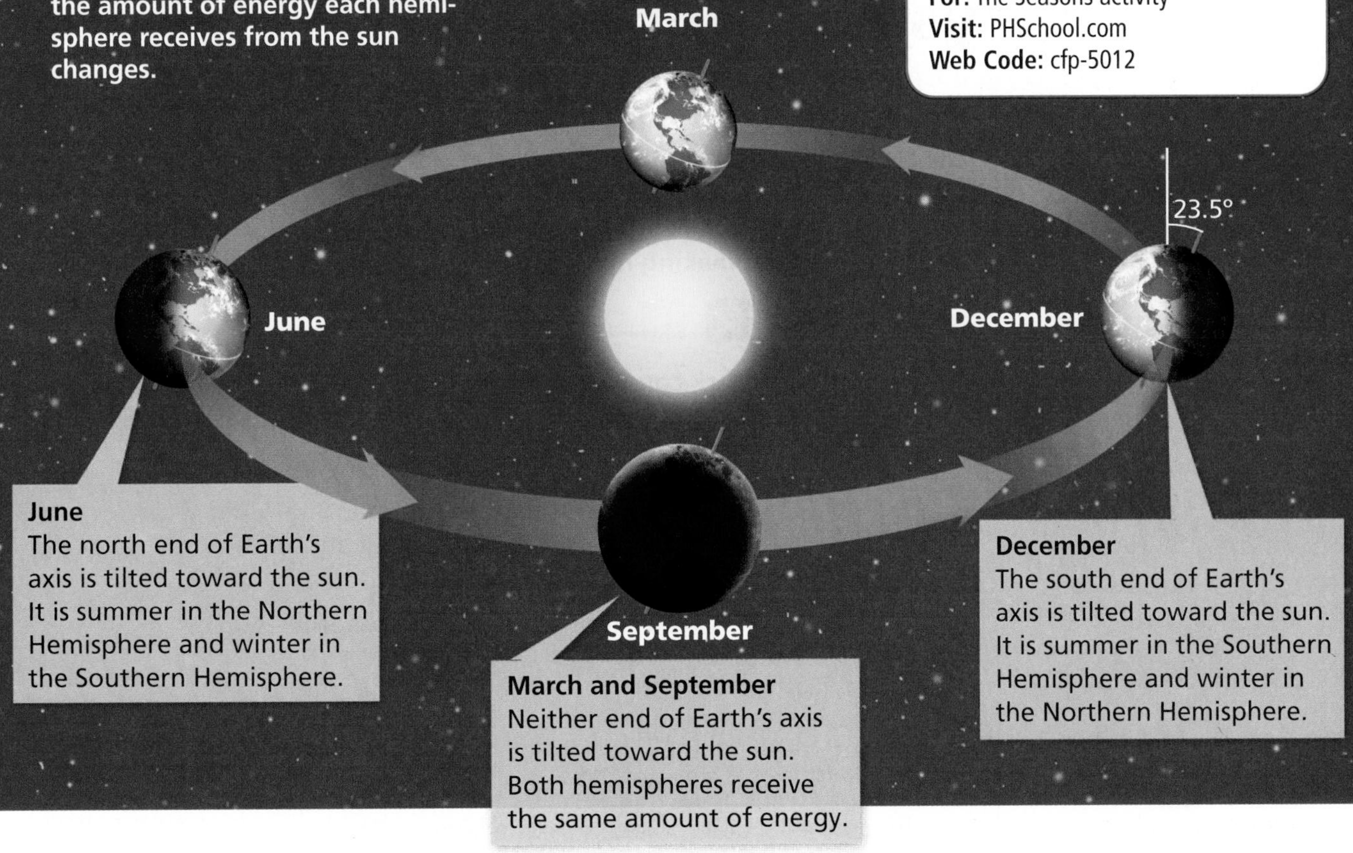

Section ① Assessment

S 6.4.a, 6.4.e,
E-LA: Reading 6.1.0

Vocabulary Skill High-Use Academic Words
Complete the sentence to show you understand the meaning of the word *range*. The weather in the temperate zones can range _____.

🔑 Reviewing Key Concepts

1. a. **Identifying** Name four factors that affect temperature.
   b. **Describing** How does temperature vary in Earth's temperature zones?
   c. **Comparing and Contrasting** Two locations are at the same latitude in the temperate zone. One is in the middle of a continent. The other is on a coast affected by a warm ocean current. How will their climates differ?

2. a. **Listing** List three factors that affect precipitation.
   b. **Summarizing** How do prevailing winds affect the amount of precipitation an area receives?

c. **Relating Cause and Effect** How does a mountain range in the path of prevailing winds affect precipitation on either side of the mountains?

3. a. **Reviewing** What causes the seasons?
   b. **Describing** Describe how the seasons are related to Earth's orbit around the sun.
   c. **Developing Hypotheses** How might Earth's climates be different if Earth were not tilted on its axis?

Math Practice

4. **Percentage** At noon at a particular location, the sun makes an angle of 66.5° with Earth's surface. What percentage of a full circle is this?

Sunny Rays and Angles

Materials

black construction paper

pencil and ruler

clear tape and scissors

3 thermometers or temperature probes

books and protractor

100-W incandescent lamp

graph paper

clock or watch

Problem
How does the angle of a light source affect the rate at which the temperature of a surface changes?

Skills Focus
controlling variables, graphing, interpreting data, making models

Procedure

1. Cut a strip of black construction paper 5 cm by 10 cm. Fold the paper in half and tape two sides to form a pocket.

2. Repeat Step 1 to make two more pockets.

3. Place the bulb of a thermometer inside each pocket. If youre usin g a temperature probe, see your teacher for instructions.

4. Place the pockets with thermometers close together, as shown in the photo. Place one thermometer in a vertical position (90° angle), one at a 45° angle, and the third one in a horizontal position (0° angle). Use a protractor to measure the angles. Support the thermometers with books.

5. Position the lamp so that it is 30 cm from each of the thermometer bulbs. Make sure the lamp will not move during the activity.

Data Table

Time (min.)	Temperature (°C)		
	0° Angle	45° Angle	90° Angle
Start			
1			
2			
3			
4			
5			

Sample Graph

Key

0° angle – – – –

45° angle ——

90° angle • • • • • •

6. Copy a data table like the one above into your notebook.

7. In your data table, record the temperature on all three thermometers. (All three temperatures should be the same.)

8. Switch on the lamp. In your data table, record the temperature on each thermometer every minute for 15 minutes. **CAUTION:** *Be careful not to touch the hot lampshade.*

9. After 15 minutes, switch off the lamp.

Analyze and Conclude

1. **Controlling Variables** In this experiment, what was the manipulated variable? What was the responding variable?

2. **Graphing** Graph your data. Label the horizontal axis and vertical axis of your graph as shown on the sample graph. Use solid, dashed, and dotted lines to show the results from each thermometer, as shown in the key.

3. **Interpreting Data** Based on your data, at which angle did the temperature increase the most?

4. **Interpreting Data** At which angle did the temperature increase the least?

5. **Making Models** What part of Earth's surface does each thermometer represent?

6. **Drawing Conclusions** Why is air at the North Pole still very cold in the summer even though the Northern Hemisphere is tilted toward the sun?

7. **Communicating** Write a paragraph explaining what variables were held constant in this experiment.

Design an Experiment

Design an experiment to find out how the results of the investigation would change if the lamp were placed farther from the thermometers. Then, design another experiment to find out what would happen if the lamp were placed closer to the thermometers.

Currents and Climate

S 6.4.d Students know that convection currents distribute heat in the atmosphere and oceans.

S 6.4.e Students know differences in pressure, heat, air movement, and humidity result in changes in weather.

- What causes surface currents and deep currents, and what effects do they have?
- What are El Niño and La Niña?
- How does upwelling affect the distribution of nutrients in the ocean?

Key Terms
- El Niño
- La Niña
- salinity
- upwelling

Lab zone Standards **Warm-Up**

Which Is More Dense?

1. Fill a plastic container three-quarters full with warm water. Wait for the water to stop moving.
2. Add several drops of food coloring to a cup of ice water and stir.
3. Gently dribble colored water down the inside of the container. Observe.

Think It Over

Inferring Describe what happened to the cold water. Which is more dense, warm water or cold water? Explain.

One spring day, people strolling along a beach in Washington State saw an amazing sight. Hundreds of sneakers of all colors and sizes were washing ashore from the Pacific Ocean! This "sneaker spill" was eventually traced to a cargo ship accident. Containers of sneakers had fallen overboard and now the sneakers were washing ashore.

But the most amazing part of the story is this—scientists could predict where the sneakers would wash up next. And just as the scientists had predicted, sneakers washed up in Oregon, and then thousands of kilometers away in Hawaii!

How did the scientists know that the sneakers would float all the way to Hawaii? The answer is that the sneakers were transported by a well-known ocean current. Recall from Section 1 that a current is a large stream of moving water that flows through the oceans. Unlike waves, currents carry water from one place to another. Some currents move water at the surface of the ocean, while other currents move water deep in the ocean.

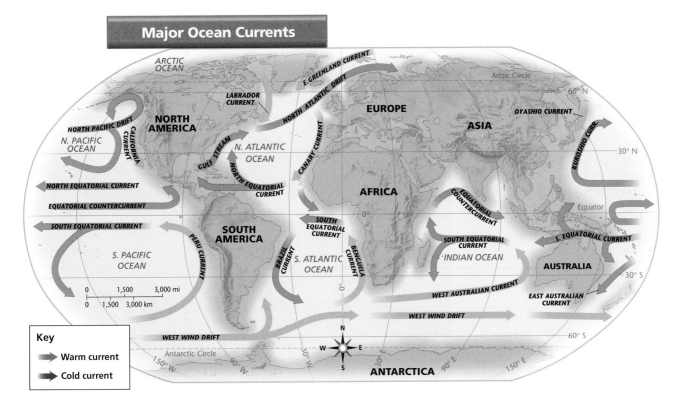

Major Ocean Currents

ARCTIC OCEAN

Arctic Circle

60° N

LABRADOR CURRENT

E. GREENLAND CURRENT

NORTH ATLANTIC DRIFT

EUROPE

ASIA

OYASHIO CURRENT

NORTH PACIFIC DRIFT

NORTH AMERICA

N. PACIFIC OCEAN

CALIFORNIA CURRENT

GULF STREAM

N. ATLANTIC OCEAN

CANARY CURRENT

KUROSHIO CURR.

30° N

NORTH EQUATORIAL CURRENT

NORTH EQUATORIAL CURRENT

AFRICA

EQUATORIAL COUNTERCURRENT

Equator

EQUATORIAL COUNTERCURRENT

SOUTH EQUATORIAL CURRENT

SOUTH AMERICA

SOUTH EQUATORIAL CURRENT

S. EQUATORIAL CURRENT

S. PACIFIC OCEAN

PERU CURRENT

BRAZIL CURRENT

S. ATLANTIC OCEAN

BENGUELA CURRENT

SOUTH EQUATORIAL CURRENT

INDIAN OCEAN

AUSTRALIA

30° S

0   1,500   3,000 mi
0   1,500   3,000 km

WEST AUSTRALIAN CURRENT

EAST AUSTRALIAN CURRENT

WEST WIND DRIFT

Key
→ Warm current
→ Cold current

WEST WIND DRIFT

Antarctic Circle

60° S

ANTARCTICA

N W E S

150° W   90° W   30° W   30° E   90° E   150° E

Surface Currents

Figure 8 shows the major surface currents in Earth's oceans. Notice that surface currents move in circular patterns in the major oceans. Most of the currents flow east or west, and then double back to complete the circle.

🔑 **Surface currents, which affect water to a depth of several hundred meters, are driven mainly by winds.** For example, in the mid-latitudes of the Northern Hemisphere, the prevailing westerlies blow from the southwest and push water at the ocean's surface eastward.

Recall from Chapter 7 that winds are caused by differences in air pressure, which are in turn the result of the unequal heating of the atmosphere by the sun. Thus, the sun's radiation is the ultimate source of energy that powers global winds and surface currents in the ocean.

Coriolis Effect Global winds are not the only factors that influence surface currents. Continents block and redirect the flow of currents. In addition, the Coriolis effect, which you learned about in Chapter 7, also influences surface currents. Recall that the Coriolis effect causes global winds to curve as a result of Earth's rotation. In the same way as the Coriolis effect changes global winds, it causes surface currents to curve to the right in the Northern Hemisphere and to the left in the Southern Hemisphere. For example, the Gulf Stream curves eastward across the Atlantic as a result of the Coriolis effect.

FIGURE 8
Large surface currents generally move in circular patterns in Earth's oceans. **Interpreting Maps** *Name four currents that flow along the coasts of North America. State whether each current is warm or cold.*

Lab zone Skills **Activity**

Inferring

Look at the currents in Figure 8 in the South Pacific, South Atlantic, and Indian oceans. What pattern can you observe? Now compare currents in the South Atlantic to those in the North Atlantic. What might be responsible for differences in the current patterns?

FIGURE 9
California Surfer
Mild temperatures due to the surface currents off the coast of California allow surfers to surf year round.

Effects on Climate Currents affect climate by moving cold and warm water around the globe. In general, surface currents carry warm water from the tropics toward the poles and bring cold water back toward the equator. **A surface current warms or cools the air above it, influencing the climate of the land near the coast.**

Winds pick up moisture as they blow across warm-water currents. In contrast, cold-water currents cool the air above them. Since cold air holds less moisture than warm air, these currents tend to bring cool, dry weather to the land areas in their path.

The California Current and, in winter, the Davidson Current are very important to people who live near coastal California. These currents help to moderate the temperatures of coastal California throughout the year.

The cool California Current flows southward approximately 3,000 kilometers from southern Canada to near Baja California. The California Current carries cool water toward the equator, making summer climates along the West Coast cooler than you would expect at those latitudes.

Although the California Current flows all year long, the direction of the prevailing winds changes in winter. The weak Davidson Current carries warmer water northward during the winter months, closer to the coast than the California Current. This helps to keep coastal climates in California mild in winter.

FIGURE 10
Viewing El Niño and La Niña From Space

In these false-color satellite images, warmer water is red and white. Cooler water is blue and purple.

El Niño and La Niña

Changes in ocean currents and winds can greatly affect climate. El Niño and La Niña are short-term changes in the tropical Pacific Ocean caused by changes in ocean surface currents and prevailing winds. El Niño and La Niña both influence weather patterns all over the world.

El Niño The warm-water event known as **El Niño** begins when an unusual pattern of winds forms over the western Pacific. This causes a vast sheet of warm water to move eastward toward the South American coast, as shown in Figure 10. El Niño causes the surface of the ocean in the eastern Pacific to be unusually warm. El Niño typically occurs every two to seven years.

The arrival of El Niño's warm surface water disrupts the cold ocean currents along the western coast of South America and changes weather patterns there. El Niño also affects weather patterns around the world, often bringing severe conditions such as heavy rains or droughts. For example, in 1997–1998, a major El Niño caused an especially warm winter in the northeastern United States. However, it was also responsible for heavy rains, flooding, and mudslides in California. El Niño conditions can last for one to two years before normal winds and currents return.

La Niña When surface waters in the eastern Pacific are colder than normal, a climate event known as **La Niña** occurs. A La Niña event is the opposite of an El Niño event. La Niña typically brings colder than normal winters and greater precipitation to the Pacific Northwest and the north central states. La Niña also causes greater hurricane activity in the western Atlantic.

 **Reading Checkpoint** How often does El Niño typically occur?

▲ In **normal years**, water in the eastern Pacific is kept relatively cool by currents along the coast of North and South America.

▲ When **El Niño** occurs, warm surface water from the western Pacific moves east toward the coast of South America.

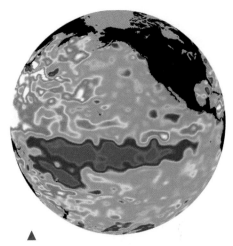

▲ **La Niña** occurs when surface waters in the eastern Pacific Ocean are colder than normal.

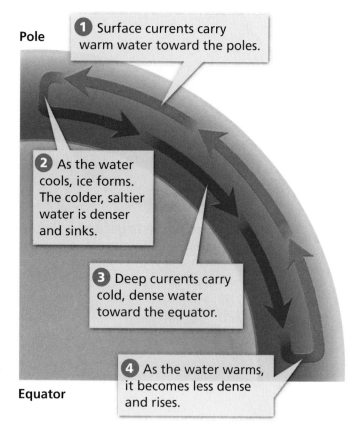

Pole

1 Surface currents carry warm water toward the poles.

2 As the water cools, ice forms. The colder, saltier water is denser and sinks.

3 Deep currents carry cold, dense water toward the equator.

4 As the water warms, it becomes less dense and rises.

Equator

FIGURE 11
Deep Currents
Deep currents are caused by differences in the density of ocean water.
Relating Cause and Effect Why does ocean water sink near the poles and rise near the equator?

Deep Currents

Deep below the ocean's surface, another type of current causes chilly waters to creep slowly across the ocean floor. ⬤ **Deep currents are caused by differences in the density of ocean water.**

Ocean Water Density The density of ocean water depends on its temperature and its salinity. **Salinity** is the total amount of dissolved salts in a water sample.

When a warm surface current moves from the equator toward one of the poles, it gradually cools. As ice forms near the poles, the salinity of the water increases from the salt left behind during freezing. As its temperature decreases and its salinity increases, the water becomes denser and sinks. Then, the cold water flows back along the ocean floor toward the equator as a deep current. Like surface currents, deep currents are affected by the Coriolis effect, which causes them to curve.

A Global Conveyer Belt ⬤ **Deep currents move and mix water around the world. They carry cold water from the poles toward the equator.** Deep currents flow slowly. They may take as long as 1,000 years to flow from the pole to the equator and back again!

The conveyer belt at a supermarket checkout counter moves objects from one place to another as it turns in a continuous path. Similarly, surface currents and deep currents together form a global "conveyer belt" in which water circulates through the oceans.

As Figure 11 shows, this "conveyer belt" is actually a series of convection currents that move warm water from the tropics toward the poles and cold water toward the equator. As these currents flow, heat is transferred through the ocean. This process influences global climates by altering ocean water temperatures and by releasing heat into the atmosphere.

As dense water sinks near the poles, it slowly spreads out and mixes with surrounding waters in the deep ocean. This process brings dissolved oxygen down into the ocean depths, where it helps to sustain life.

 **Reading Checkpoint** What is salinity?

Upwelling

In most parts of the ocean, surface waters do not usually mix with deep ocean waters. However, mixing sometimes occurs when winds cause upwelling. **Upwelling** is the movement of cold water upward from the deep ocean. As winds blow away the warm surface water, cold water rises to replace it.

🔑 **Upwelling brings up tiny ocean organisms, minerals, and other nutrients from the deeper layers of the water.** Without this motion, the surface waters of the open ocean would be very scarce in nutrients. Because nutrients are plentiful, zones of upwelling are usually home to huge schools of fish.

Upwelling occurs in the Pacific Ocean off the west coasts of North America and South America. Many people depend on this rich fishing area for food and jobs. Along the California coast, upwelling generally takes place from March through September as prevailing winds push surface waters offshore. The arrival of El Niño prevents upwelling from occurring. Without the nutrients brought by upwelling, fish die or go elsewhere to find food, reducing the fishing catch that season and hurting people's livelihoods.

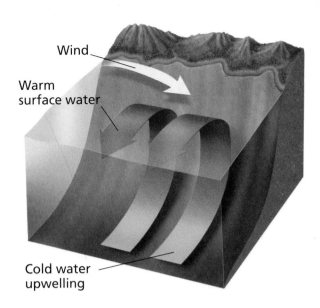

Wind

Warm surface water

Cold water upwelling

FIGURE 12
Upwelling
As cold water rises from the deep ocean, it brings a new supply of nutrients to the surface.

Section 2 Assessment

S 6.4.d, 6.4.e, E-LA: Reading 6.2.4

🔄 **Target Reading Skill** Create Outlines
Complete your outline for this section. What details did you include about El Niño and La Niña?

🔑 **Reviewing Key Concepts**

1. a. **Describing** How do surface currents affect the climate of coastal areas?
   b. **Predicting** What type of climate might a coastal area have if nearby currents are cold?
   c. **Explaining** Explain how deep currents form and move in the ocean.
   d. **Comparing and Contrasting** Compare the causes and effects of deep currents and surface currents.
2. a. **Describing** Describe the changes that occur in the Pacific Ocean and the atmosphere above it during El Niño.
   b. **Relating Cause and Effect** What effects does El Niño have on weather and climate?

3. a. **Reviewing** What causes upwelling?
   b. **Explaining** Why are huge schools of fish usually found in zones of upwelling?
   c. **Applying Concepts** Why would the ability to predict the occurrence of El Niño be important for the fishing industry on the western coast of South America?

Lab zone At-Home **Activity**

Modeling the Coriolis Effect With the help of a family member, use chalk and a globe to model the Coriolis effect. Have your family member slowly rotate the globe in an easterly direction. As the globe rotates, draw a line from the North Pole to the equator. Use your knowledge of the Coriolis effect to explain why the line is curved.

Climate Regions

CALIFORNIA
Standards Focus

S 6.4.e Students know differences in pressure, heat, air movement, and humidity result in changes in weather.

- What factors are used to classify climates?
- What are the six main climate regions?

Key Terms
- rain forest
- savanna
- desert
- steppe
- chaparral
- humid subtropical
- subarctic
- tundra
- permafrost

Lab zone **Standards Warm-Up**

How Do Climates Differ?

1. Collect pictures from magazines and newspapers of a variety of land areas around the world.
2. Sort the pictures into categories according to common weather characteristics.

Think It Over

Forming Operational Definitions Choose several words that describe the typical weather for each category. What words would you use to describe the typical weather where you live?

Suppose you lived for an entire year near the equator. It would be very different from where you live now. The daily weather, the amount of sunlight, and the pattern of seasons would all be new to you. You would be in another climate region.

Scientists classify climates according to two major factors: temperature and precipitation. They also consider the distinct vegetation in different areas. This system, developed around 1900 by Wladimir Köppen, identifies broad climate regions, each of which has smaller subdivisions.

There are six main climate regions: tropical rainy, dry, temperate marine, temperate continental, polar, and highlands. California has a wide variety of climate regions, including dry, temperate marine, and highlands.

Maps show boundaries between the climate regions. In the real world, of course, no clear boundaries mark where one climate region ends and another begins. Each region blends gradually into the next.

Tropical Rainy Climates

🔑 **The tropics have two types of rainy climates: tropical wet and tropical wet-and-dry.** Tropical wet climates are found in low-lying lands near the equator.

Tropical Wet In areas that have a tropical wet climate, many days are rainy, often with afternoon thunderstorms. These thunderstorms are triggered by midday heating. Another source of precipitation is prevailing winds. In many areas with a tropical wet climate, the trade winds bring moisture from the oceans. With year-round heat and heavy rainfall, vegetation grows lush and green. Dense rain forests grow in these rainy tropical climates. **Rain forests** are forests in which large amounts of rain fall year-round. Tropical rain forests are important because it is thought that at least half of the world's species of land plants and animals are found there.

In the United States, only the windward sides of the Hawaiian islands have a tropical wet climate. Rainfall is very heavy—over 10 meters per year on the windward side of the Hawaiian island of Kauai. The rain forests of Hawaii have a large variety of plants, including ferns, orchids, and many types of vines and trees.

Tropical Wet-and-Dry Areas that have tropical wet-and-dry climates receive slightly less rain than tropical climates and have distinct dry and rainy seasons. Instead of rain forests, there are tropical grasslands called **savannas.** Scattered clumps of trees that can survive the dry season dot the coarse grasses. Only a small part of the United States—the southern tip of Florida—has a tropical wet-and-dry climate. The graphs in Figure 14 show how temperature and precipitation vary in Makindu, Kenya, in East Africa.

✓ **Reading Checkpoint** What parts of the United States have tropical rainy climates?

FIGURE 13
Tropical Rain Forests
Lush tropical rain forests grow in the tropical wet climate.

FIGURE 14
Climate Graphs
A graph of average temperature (left) can be combined with a graph of average precipitation (middle) to form a climate graph. These graphs show data for a tropical wet-and-dry region.

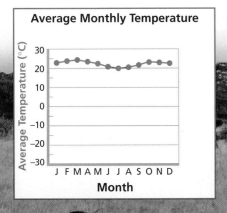

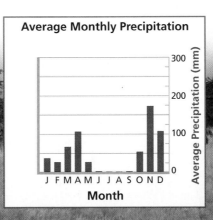

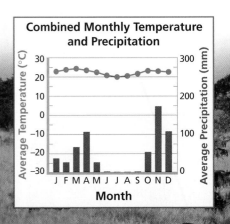

FIGURE 15
Climate Regions

Climate regions are classified according to a combination of temperature and precipitation. Climates in highland regions change rapidly as altitude changes.

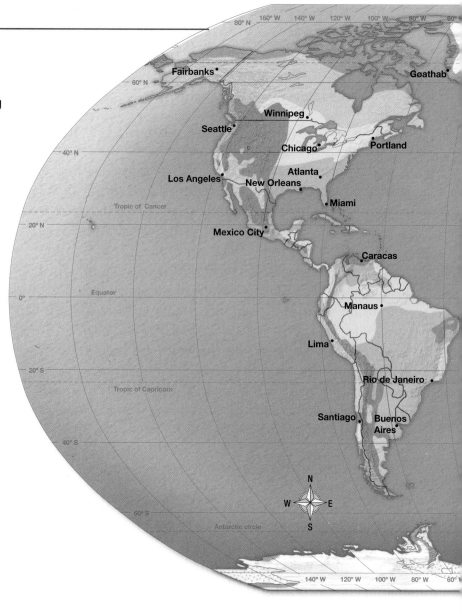

Key

Tropical Rainy
- Tropical wet
- Tropical wet-and-dry

Dry
- Semiarid
- Arid

Temperate Marine
- Mediterranean
- Humid subtropical
- Marine west coast

Temperate Continental
- Humid continental
- Subarctic

Polar
- Tundra
- Ice cap

Highlands

Tropical Rainy
Temperature always 18°C or above

■ **Tropical wet** Always hot and humid, with heavy rainfall (at least 6 centimeters per month) all year round

■ **Tropical wet-and-dry** Always hot; alternating wet and dry seasons; heavy rainfall in the wet season

Dry
Occurs wherever potential evaporation is greater than precipitation; may be hot or cold

■ **Semiarid** Dry but receives about 25 to 50 centimeters of precipitation per year

■ **Arid** Desert, with little precipitation, usually less than 25 centimeters per year

Temperate Marine
Averages 10°C or above in warmest month, between –3°C and 18°C in the coldest month

■ **Mediterranean** Warm, dry summers and rainy winters

■ **Humid subtropical** Hot summers and cool winters

■ **Marine west coast** Mild winters and cool summers, with moderate precipitation all year

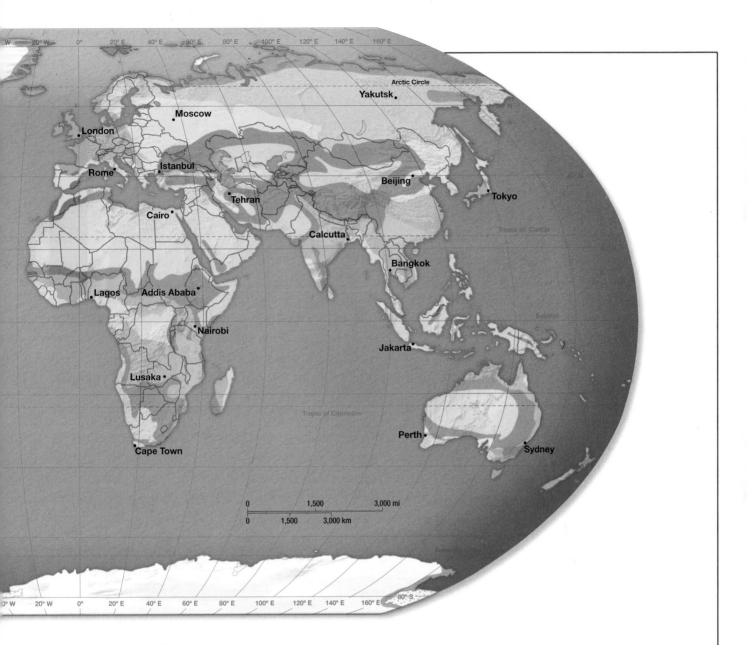

Temperate Continental
Average temperature 10°C or above in the warmest month, −3°C or below in the coldest month

Humid continental Hot, humid summers and cold winters, with moderate precipitation year round

Subarctic Short, cool summers and long, cold winters; light precipitation, mainly in summer

Polar
Average temperature below 10°C in the warmest month

Tundra Always cold with a short, cool summer—warmest temperature about 10°C

Ice cap Always cold, average temperature at or below 0°C

Highlands
Generally cooler and wetter than nearby lowlands; temperature decreasing with altitude

FIGURE 16
Arid Climate
California's deserts are home to a variety of animals, including the kit fox.
Interpreting Graphs Which month has the highest average temperature?

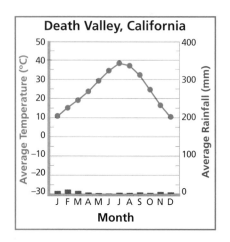

Death Valley, California

Dry Climates

A climate is "dry" if the amount of precipitation that falls is less than the amount of water that could potentially evaporate. Because water evaporates more slowly in cool weather, a cool place with low rainfall may not be as dry as a warmer place that receives the same amount of rain. ☞ **Dry climates include arid and semiarid climates.**

Look at the map of world climate regions in Figure 15. What part of the United States is dry? Why is precipitation in this region so low? As you can see, dry regions often lie inland, far from oceans that are the source of humid air masses. In addition, much of the region lies in the rain shadow east of the Sierra Nevada and Rocky Mountains. Humid air masses from the Pacific Ocean lose much of their water as they cross the mountains. Little rain or snow is carried to dry regions.

Arid When you think about **deserts,** or arid regions, you may picture blazing heat and drifting sand dunes. Some deserts are hot and sandy, but others are cold or rocky. On average, arid regions, or deserts, get less than 25 centimeters of rain a year. Some years may bring no rain at all. Only specialized plants such as cactus and yucca can survive the desert's dryness and extremes of hot and cold. Much of California's southeast, including Death Valley and the rest of the Mojave Desert, has an arid climate.

Semiarid Locate the semiarid regions in Figure 15. As you can see, large semiarid areas are usually located on the edges of deserts. These semiarid areas are called steppes. A **steppe** is dry but gets enough rainfall for short grasses and low bushes to grow. For this reason, a steppe may also be called a prairie or grassland. The Great Plains are the major steppe region of the United States. Portions of southeastern California are considered semiarid.

 **Reading Checkpoint** What is a desert?

Temperate Marine Climates

Look once again at Figure 15. Along the coasts of continents in the temperate zones, you will find the third main climate region, temperate marine. ⬤ **There are three kinds of temperate marine climates: marine west coast, Mediterranean, and humid subtropical.** Because of the moderating influence of oceans, all three are humid and have mild winters.

Marine West Coast The coolest temperate marine climates are found on the west coasts of continents north of 40° north latitude and south of 40° south latitude. Humid ocean air brings mild, rainy winters. Summer precipitation can vary considerably.

In North America, the marine west coast climate extends from northern California to southern Alaska. In the northwestern United States, humid air from the Pacific Ocean hits the western slopes of the Coastal Ranges. The air rises up the slopes of the mountains, and it cools. As the air cools, large amounts of rain or snow fall on the western slopes. The eastern slopes lie in the rain shadow of the mountains and receive little precipitation.

Because of the heavy precipitation, thick forests of tall trees grow in this region, including coniferous, or cone-bearing, trees such as Sitka spruce, Douglas fir, redwoods, and Western red cedar, as shown in Figure 17. One of the main industries of this region is harvesting and processing wood for lumber, paper, and furniture.

Eugene, Oregon

FIGURE 17
Marine West Coast Climate
Redwoods, Douglas firs, and Sitka spruce dominate the lush forests found in marine west coast climates.

Santa Barbara, California

FIGURE 18
Mediterranean Climate
Santa Barbara, on the coast of southern California, has a Mediterranean climate. Mild temperatures throughout the year make the area ideal for growing olives and citrus fruits.
Interpreting Graphs How much precipitation does Santa Barbara receive in July? In January?

Mediterranean A coastal climate that is drier and warmer than west coast marine is known as Mediterranean. Most areas with this climate are found around the Mediterranean Sea. In the United States, much of coastal California has a Mediterranean climate. This climate is mild, with two seasons. In winter, marine air masses bring cool, rainy weather. Summers are somewhat warmer, with little rain.

Mediterranean climates have two main vegetation types. One is made up of dense shrubs and small trees, called **chaparral** (shap uh RAL). The other vegetation type includes grasses with a few large trees.

Agriculture is important to the economy of California's Mediterranean climate region. Using irrigation, farmers grow many different crops, including rice, many vegetables, fruits, and nuts.

Humid Subtropical The warmest temperate marine climates are along the edges of the tropics. **Humid subtropical** climates are wet and warm, but not as constantly hot as the tropics. Locate the humid subtropical climates in Figure 15.

The southeastern United States has a humid subtropical climate. Summers are hot, with much more rainfall than in winter. Maritime tropical air masses move inland, bringing tropical weather conditions, including thunderstorms and occasional hurricanes, to southern cities such as Houston, New Orleans, and Atlanta. Winters are cool to mild, with more rain than snow. However, polar air masses moving in from the north can bring freezing temperatures and frosts.

Mixed forests of oak, ash, hickory, and pines grow in the humid subtropical region of the United States. Important crops in this region include oranges, peaches, peanuts, sugar cane, and rice.

 **Reading Checkpoint** What region of the United States has a humid subtropical climate?

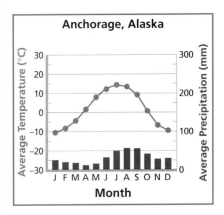

Temperate Continental Climates

Temperate continental climates are not influenced very much by oceans, so they commonly have extremes of temperature. 🔑 **Temperate continental climates are only found on continents in the Northern Hemisphere, and include humid continental and subarctic.** The parts of continents in the Southern Hemisphere south of 40° south latitude are not far enough from oceans for dry continental air masses to form.

Humid Continental Shifting tropical and polar air masses bring constantly changing weather to humid continental climates. In winter, continental polar air masses move south, bringing bitterly cold weather. In summer, tropical air masses move north, bringing heat and high humidity. Humid continental climates receive moderate amounts of rain in the summer. Smaller amounts of rain or snow fall in winter.

What parts of the United States have a humid continental climate? The eastern part of the region—the Northeast—has a range of forest types, from mixed forests in the south to coniferous forests in the north. Much of the western part of this region—the Midwest—was once tall grasslands, but is now farmland.

Subarctic The subarctic climates lie north of the humid continental climates. Summers in the subarctic are short and cool. Winters are long and bitterly cold.

In North America, coniferous trees such as spruce and fir make up a huge northern forest that stretches from Alaska to eastern Canada. Wood products from this forest are an important part of the economy. Many large mammals, including bears and moose, live in the forest. Birds of many species breed in the subarctic.

 **Reading Checkpoint** Which area of the United States has a subarctic climate?

FIGURE 19
Subarctic Climate
Subarctic climates have cool summers and cold winters. The world's largest subarctic regions are in Russia, Canada, and Alaska. This emperor goose is breeding in the subarctic climate region in Alaska.

Polar Climates

The polar climate is the coldest climate region, and includes the ice cap and tundra climates. Ice cap and tundra climates are found only in the far north and south, near the North and South poles. Most polar climates are relatively dry, because the cold air holds little moisture.

Ice Cap As Figure 15 shows, ice cap climates are found mainly on Greenland and in Antarctica. With average temperatures always at or below freezing, the land in ice cap climate regions is covered with ice and snow. Intense cold makes the air dry. Lichens and a few low plants may grow on the rocks.

Tundra The **tundra** climate region stretches across northern Alaska, Canada, and Russia. Short, cool summers follow bitterly cold winters. Because of the cold, some layers of the tundra soil are always frozen. This permanently frozen tundra soil is called **permafrost.** Because of the permafrost, water cannot drain away, so the soil is wet and boggy in summer.

It is too cold on the tundra for trees to grow. Despite the harsh climate, during the short summers the tundra is filled with life. Mosquitoes and other insects hatch in the ponds and marshes above the frozen permafrost. Mosses, grasses, lichens, wildflowers, and shrubs grow quickly during the short summers. In North America, herds of caribou eat the vegetation and are in turn preyed upon by wolves. Some birds, such as the white-tailed ptarmigan, live on the tundra year-round. Others, such as the arctic tern and many waterfowl, spend only their summer breeding seasons there.

Reading Checkpoint   **What type of vegetation is found on the tundra?**

FIGURE 20
Tundra Climate
The Nenet people are reindeer herders on the tundra of northern Russia. These reindeer are grazing on some short shrubs typical of tundra plants.

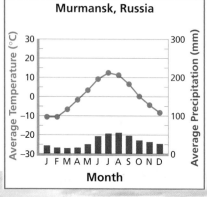

Murmansk, Russia

Highlands

Why are highlands a distinct climate region? **Temperature falls as altitude increases, so highland regions are colder than the regions that surround them.** Increasing altitude produces climate changes similar to the climate changes you would expect with increasing latitude. Precipitation also increases as air masses carrying moisture pass over highland areas.

The climate on the lower slopes of a mountain range is like that of the surrounding countryside. The Rocky Mountain foothills, for instance, share the semiarid climate of the Great Plains. But as you go higher up into the mountains, temperatures become lower and precipitation increases. Climbing 1,000 meters up in elevation is like traveling 1,200 kilometers toward the poles. The climate higher in the mountains is like that of the subarctic: cool with coniferous trees. The high mountains of California, including the Sierra Nevada, have a highland climate.

Above a certain elevation—the tree line—temperatures are too low for trees to grow. The climate above the tree line is like that of the tundra. Only low plants, mosses, and lichens can grow there.

FIGURE 21
Highland Climate
Highland climates are generally cooler than surrounding regions. The Mount Ranier area in Washington State has short summers and long, severe winters.
Classifying *What climate zone does the mountaintop resemble?*

Section 3 Assessment

S 6.4.e, E-LA: Reading 6.2.4

Target Reading Skill Create Outlines Complete your outline for this section. What important ideas did you include about temperate marine climates?

Reviewing Key Concepts

1. a. **Listing** What two major factors are used to classify climates?
   b. **Reviewing** What other factor did Köppen use in classifying climates?
2. a. **Identifying** What are the six main climate regions?
   b. **Comparing and Contrasting** How is a tropical wet climate similar to a tropical wet-and-dry climate? How are they different?
   c. **Inferring** In what climate region would you find plains covered with short grasses and small bushes? Explain.
   d. **Relating Cause and Effect** Why do marine west coast climates have much precipitation?

   e. **Predicting** Which place would have more severe winters—central Russia or the west coast of France? Why?
   f. **Sequencing** Place the following climates in order from coldest to warmest: tundra, subarctic, humid continental, ice cap.
   g. **Relating Cause and Effect** How could a forest grow on a mountain that is surrounded by a desert?

Lab zone At-Home **Activity**

What's Your Climate? Describe to your family the characteristics of the climate region in which you live. What plants and animals live in your climate region? What characteristics do these plants and animals have that make them well adapted to the region?

Cool Climate Graphs

Materials

3 pieces of graph paper

black, blue, red, and green pencils

ruler

calculator

Problem Based on climate data, what is the best time of year to visit various cities to enjoy particular recreational activities?

Skills Focus graphing, interpreting data

Procedure

1. Work in groups of three. Each person should graph the data for a different city, A, B, or C.

2. On graph paper, use a black pencil to label the axes as on the climate graph below. Title your climate graph City A, City B, or City C.

3. Use your green pencil to make a bar graph of the monthly average amount of precipitation. Place a star below the name of each month that has more than a trace of snow.

4. Use a red pencil to plot the average monthly maximum temperature. Make a dot for the temperature in the middle of each space for the month. When you have plotted data for all 12 months, connect the points into a smooth curved line.

5. Use a blue pencil to plot the average monthly minimum temperature for your city. Use the same procedure as in Step 4.

6. Calculate the total average annual precipitation for this city and include it in your observations. Do this by adding the average precipitation for each month.

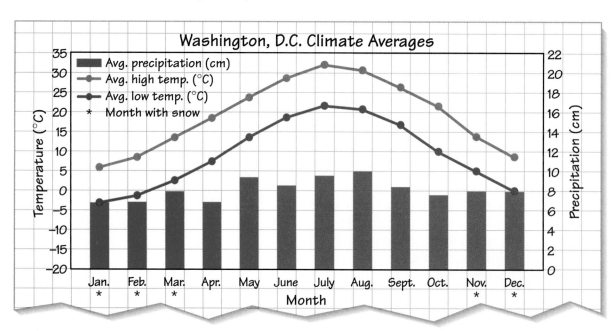

Climate Data												
Washington, D.C.	Jan.	Feb.	Mar.	April	May	June	July	Aug.	Sept.	Oct.	Nov.	Dec.
Average High Temp. (°C)	6	8	14	19	24	29	32	31	27	21	14	8
Average Low Temp. (°C)	–3	–2	3	8	14	19	22	21	17	10	5	0
Average Precipitation (cm)	6.9	6.9	8.1	6.9	9.4	8.6	9.7	9.9	8.4	7.6	7.9	7.9
Months With Snow	*	*	*	trace	—	—	—	—	trace	*	*	*
City A	Jan.	Feb.	Mar.	April	May	June	July	Aug.	Sept.	Oct.	Nov.	Dec.
Average High Temp. (°C)	13	16	16	17	17	18	18	19	21	21	17	13
Average Low Temp. (°C)	8	9	9	10	11	12	12	13	13	13	11	8
Average Precipitation (cm)	10.4	7.6	7.9	3.3	0.8	0.5	0.3	0.3	0.8	3.3	8.1	7.9
Months With Snow	trace	trace	trace	—	—	—	—	—	—	—	—	trace
City B	Jan.	Feb.	Mar.	April	May	June	July	Aug.	Sept.	Oct.	Nov.	Dec.
Average High Temp. (°C)	5	7	10	16	21	26	29	27	23	18	11	6
Average Low Temp. (°C)	–9	–7	–4	1	6	11	14	13	8	2	–4	–8
Average Precipitation (cm)	0.8	1.0	2.3	3.0	5.6	5.8	7.4	7.6	3.3	2.0	1.3	1.3
Months With Snow	*	*	*	*	*	—	—	—	trace	*	*	*
City C	Jan.	Feb.	Mar.	April	May	June	July	Aug.	Sept.	Oct.	Nov.	Dec.
Average High Temp. (°C)	7	11	13	18	23	28	33	32	27	21	12	8
Average Low Temp. (°C)	–6	–4	–2	1	4	8	11	10	5	1	–3	–7
Average Precipitation (cm)	2.5	2.3	1.8	1.3	1.8	1	0.8	0.5	0.8	1	2	2.5
Months With Snow	*	*	*	*	*	trace	—	—	trace	trace	*	*

Analyze and Conclude

Use all three climate graphs, plus the graph for Washington, D.C., to answer these questions.

1. **Interpreting Data** Which of the four cities has the least change in average temperatures during the year?

2. **Interpreting Maps** Use the climate map on pages 364–365 to help find the climate region in which each city is located.

3. **Applying Concepts** Which of the cities below matches each climate graph?
   Colorado Springs, Colorado; latitude 39° N
   San Francisco, California; latitude 38° N
   Reno, Nevada; latitude 40° N

4. **Inferring** The four cities are at approximately the same latitude. Why are their climate graphs so different?

5. **Graphing** What factors do you need to consider when setting up and numbering the left and right y-axes of a climate graph so that your data will fit on the graph?

6. **Communicating** Imagine that you are writing a travel brochure for one of the four cities. Write a description of the climate of the city and discuss the best time to visit to do a selected outdoor activity.

More to Explore

What type of climate does the area where you live have? Find out what outdoor recreational opportunities your community has. How is each activity particularly suited to the climate of your area?

Section 4
Climate Change

CALIFORNIA
Standards Focus

S 6.4.e Students know differences in pressure, heat, air movement, and humidity result in changes in weather.

🔑 How might human activities be affecting the temperature of Earth's atmosphere?

🔑 How have human activities affected the ozone layer?

Key Terms
- ice age
- global warming
- greenhouse gas
- ozone hole
- chlorofluorocarbon

Lab zone Standards **Warm-Up**

What Is the Greenhouse Effect?

1. ✂ Cut two pieces of black construction paper to fit the bottoms of two shoe boxes.
2. 🧪 Place a thermometer in each box. Record the temperatures on the thermometers. Cover one box with plastic wrap.
3. Place the boxes together where sunlight or a light bulb can shine on them equally. Make sure the thermometers are shaded by the sides of the boxes.
4. Wait 15 minutes and read the thermometers again. Record the temperatures.

Think It Over

Inferring How can you explain any temperature difference between the two boxes?

Video Field Trip
Discovery Channel School
Climate and Climate Change

The amount of energy transferred from the sun to Earth remains nearly constant over time. As a result, Earth's climates tend to be fairly stable for thousands of years. However, climates have gradually changed throughout Earth's history. Over millions of years, warm periods have alternated with cold periods known as **ice ages.** During an ice age, huge sheets of ice called glaciers cover large parts of Earth's surface.

In the past two million years there have been many major ice ages. Each one lasted 100,000 years or longer. Long, warmer periods occurred between the ice ages. Some scientists think that we are now in a warm period between ice ages.

The last ice age ended only about 10,500 years ago. Ice sheets covered much of northern Europe and North America, reaching as far south as present-day Iowa and Nebraska. In some places, the ice was more than 3 kilometers thick. So much water was frozen in the ice sheets that the average sea level was much lower than it is today. When the ice sheets melted, the rising oceans flooded coastal areas. Inland, the Great Lakes and many smaller bodies of water formed.

Global Warming

Most past changes in world climates were caused by natural factors, such as volcanic activity and the motion of the continents. But recently scientists have observed climate changes that may be the result of human activities. For example, over the last 120 years, the average temperature of the troposphere has risen by about 0.7 Celsius degree. This gradual increase in the temperature of Earth's atmosphere is called **global warming.**

The Greenhouse Hypothesis Recall that gases in Earth's atmosphere hold in heat from the sun, keeping the atmosphere at a comfortable temperature for living things. Recall that the process by which gases in Earth's atmosphere trap this energy is called the greenhouse effect. Look at the greenhouse in Figure 22. Notice that sunlight does not heat the air in the greenhouse directly. Instead, sunlight first heats the soil, benches, and pots. Then infrared radiation from these surfaces heats the air in the greenhouse. The greenhouse effect in Earth's atmosphere is similar in some ways.

Gases in the atmosphere that trap energy are called **greenhouse gases.** Carbon dioxide, water vapor, and methane are some of the greenhouse gases. 🔑 **Many scientists have hypothesized that human activities that add greenhouse gases to the atmosphere are warming Earth's atmosphere.**

FIGURE 22
Greenhouse Effect
Sunlight enters a greenhouse and is absorbed. The interior of the greenhouse radiates back energy in the form of infrared radiation, or heat. Much of the heat is trapped and held inside the greenhouse, warming it.
Applying Concepts *What gases in Earth's atmosphere can trap heat like a greenhouse?*

Infrared radiation cannot pass through the greenhouse roof.

Sunlight

Key

Sunlight

Infrared radiation

FIGURE 23
Ice Core Samples
These scientists are taking an ice core from the glacier that covers Antarctica. Data from ice cores enable scientists to measure changing levels of carbon dioxide in the atmosphere.

Changing Levels of Carbon Dioxide Scientists think that an increase in carbon dioxide is a major factor in global warming. Until the late 1800s, the level of carbon dioxide in the atmosphere remained about the same. How did scientists determine this? They measured the amount of carbon dioxide in air bubbles trapped in Antarctic ice. They obtained these samples of ancient air from ice cores, as shown in Figure 23. The glacier that covers Antarctica formed over millions of years. Gas bubbles in the ice cores provide samples of air from the time the ice formed.

Is global warming caused by human activities, or does it have a natural cause? Scientists have done a great deal of research to try to answer this question.

Since the late 1800s, the level of carbon dioxide in the atmosphere has increased steadily. Most scientists think that this change is a result of increased human activities. For example, the burning of wood, coal, oil, and natural gas adds carbon dioxide to the air. During the last 100 years, these activities have increased greatly in many different countries. Some scientists predict that the level of carbon dioxide could double by the year 2100. If that happens, then global temperature could rise by 1.5 to 4.5 Celsius degrees.

Math: Algebra and Functions 6.2.0

Math ▶ Analyzing Data

Carbon Dioxide Levels

The graph shows estimated carbon dioxide levels in the atmosphere over the last 1,000 years.

1. **Reading Graphs** What variable is shown on the x-axis of the graph? On the y-axis?

2. **Interpreting Data** What pattern do you see in these data? How would you explain this pattern?

3. **Interpreting Data** How much did carbon dioxide levels increase between 1800 and 1900? Between 1900 and 2000?

4. **Predicting** Given the trend in carbon dioxide levels between 1900 and 2000, predict the level of carbon dioxide in the atmosphere in 2100. If your prediction is correct, what might be the result?

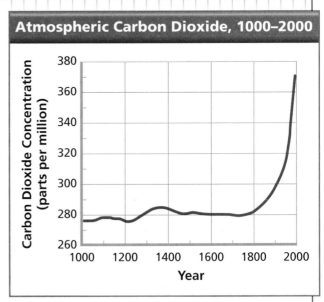

Atmospheric Carbon Dioxide, 1000–2000

1960

1990

Climate Variation Hypothesis Not all scientists agree about the causes of global warming. Some scientists think that the 0.7 Celsius degree rise in global temperatures over the past 120 years may be due in part to natural variations in climate.

Satellite measurements have shown that the amount of energy the sun produces increases and decreases slightly from year to year. Even such minor changes in solar energy could be causing periods of warmer and cooler climates. Climate change could be a result of changes in both carbon dioxide levels and the amount of solar energy.

Possible Effects Global warming could have some positive effects. Farmers in some areas that are now cool could plant two crops a year instead of one. Places that are too cold for farming today could become farmland. However, many effects of global warming are likely to be less positive. Higher temperatures would cause water to evaporate from exposed soil, such as plowed farmland. Dry soil blows away easily. Thus, some fertile fields might become "dust bowls."

A rise in temperatures of even a few degrees will warm up water in the oceans. Some scientists think warmer ocean water would increase the strength of hurricanes.

As the water warms, it would expand, raising sea level around the world. The melting of glaciers and polar ice caps could also increase sea level. Sea level has already risen by 10 to 20 centimeters over the last 100 years, and could rise another 25 to 80 centimeters by the year 2100. Even such a small rise in sea level would flood low-lying coastal areas.

 **Reading Checkpoint** What are three possible effects of global warming?

FIGURE 24
Melting Glaciers
The photos show the Burroughs glacier in Alaska. The photo on the left was taken in 1960. The photo on the right, taken in1990, shows the large amount of melting that has taken place. **Developing Hypotheses** *What do you think was responsible for the melting shown in the photos?*

Go Online
PLANET DIARY

For: More on the greenhouse effect
Visit: PHSchool.com
Web Code: cfd-4044

Ozone Depletion

Another global change in the atmosphere involves the ozone layer. Ozone in the stratosphere filters out much of the harmful ultraviolet radiation from the sun, as shown in Figure 25.

In the 1970s, scientists noticed that the ozone layer over Antarctica was growing thinner each spring. A large area of reduced ozone, or **ozone hole,** was being created. In 2000, the ozone hole reached a record size of more than 28.5 million km^2—almost the size of Africa. By 2004, the maximum size of the ozone hole decreased to about 20 million km^2. What created the ozone hole? **Chemicals produced by humans have been damaging the ozone layer.**

Chlorofluorocarbons A major cause of ozone depletion is a group of compounds called **chlorofluorocarbons,** or CFCs. CFCs were used in air conditioners and refrigerators, as cleaners for electronic parts, and in aerosol sprays, such as deodorants.

Most chemical compounds released into the air eventually break down. CFCs, however, can last for decades and rise all the way to the stratosphere. In the stratosphere, ultraviolet radiation breaks down the CFC molecules into atoms, including chlorine. The chlorine atoms then break ozone down into oxygen atoms.

Results of Ozone Depletion Because ozone blocks ultraviolet radiation, a decrease in ozone means an increase in the amount of ultraviolet radiation that reaches Earth's surface. Ultraviolet radiation can cause eye damage and several kinds of skin cancer.

In the late 1970s, the United States and many other countries banned most uses of CFCs in aerosol sprays. In 1990, many nations agreed to phase out the production and use of CFCs. Because ozone depletion affects the whole world, such agreements must be international to be effective. Worldwide production of the chemicals has greatly decreased. In the United States, at the current rate it will take until 2010 to completely eliminate the use of CFCs. The size of the ozone hole is expected to gradually shrink over time as these agreements take effect.

 **Reading Checkpoint** What are CFCs?

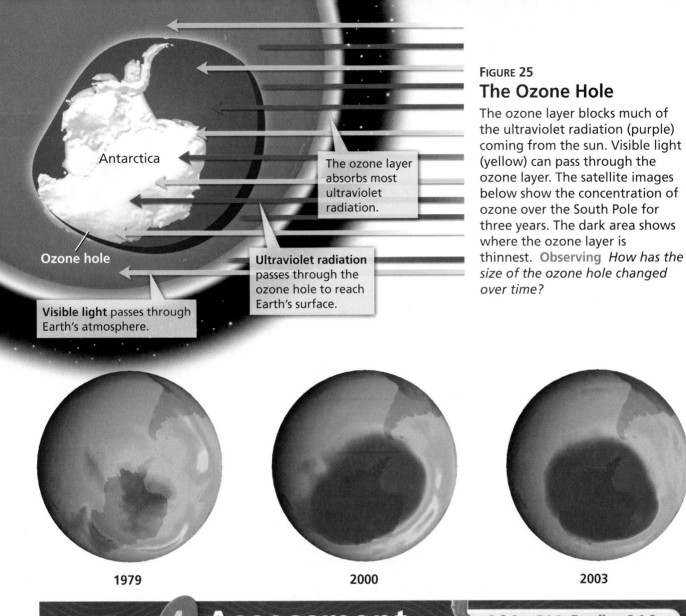

FIGURE 25

The Ozone Hole

The ozone layer blocks much of the ultraviolet radiation (purple) coming from the sun. Visible light (yellow) can pass through the ozone layer. The satellite images below show the concentration of ozone over the South Pole for three years. The dark area shows where the ozone layer is thinnest. **Observing** *How has the size of the ozone hole changed over time?*

Antarctica

The ozone layer absorbs most ultraviolet radiation.

Ozone hole

Ultraviolet radiation passes through the ozone hole to reach Earth's surface.

Visible light passes through Earth's atmosphere.

| 1979 | 2000 | 2003 |

Section 4 Assessment　　S 6.4.e, E-LA: Reading 6.1.0

Vocabulary Skill High-Use Academic Words
Complete the following sentence to show you understand the word *major*. Some major factors that scientists believe are affecting global warming are _____.

Reviewing Key Concepts

1. a. Defining What is global warming?
   b. Identifying What human actions increase the amount of carbon dioxide in the atmosphere?
   c. Relating Cause and Effect How do scientists think that increased carbon dioxide levels are contributing to global warming?
   d. Inferring Much of the atmosphere of the planet Venus is made up of carbon dioxide. How do you think this influences the surface temperatures on Venus?

2. a. Reviewing What effect have human activities had on the ozone layer?
   b. Summarizing Summarize the cause of ozone depletion and the steps taken to reverse it.
   c. Relating Cause and Effect Explain the effect of ozone depletion on human health.

Lab zone At-Home Activity

Sun Protection Visit a drugstore with your family. Compare the SPF (sun protection factor) of the various sunscreens for sale. Explain why it is important to protect your skin from ultraviolet radiation. Determine the best value for the money in terms of SPF rating and price.

Study Guide

🔑 The **BIG Idea**

The main factors that influence a region's climate include latitude, altitude, distance from large bodies of water, ocean currents, prevailing winds, the presence of mountains, and seasonal winds.

1 What Causes Climate?

🔑 **Key Concepts**　　　🔧 S 6.4.a, 6.4.e

- The main factors that influence temperature are latitude, altitude, distance from large bodies of water, and ocean currents.
- The main factors that influence precipitation are prevailing winds, the presence of mountains, and seasonal winds.
- The seasons are caused by the tilt of Earth's axis as Earth travels around the sun.

Key Terms

climate	continental climate
microclimate	ocean current
tropical zone	windward
polar zone	leeward
temperate zone	monsoon
marine climate	

2 Currents and Climate

🔑 **Key Concepts**　　　🔧 S 6.4.a, 6.4.d

- Surface currents are driven mainly by winds. A surface current warms or cools the air above it, influencing the climate of the land near the coast.
- El Niño and La Niña are short-term changes in the tropical Pacific Ocean caused by changes in ocean surface currents and prevailing winds.
- Deep currents are caused by differences in the density of ocean water. Deep currents move and mix water around the world. They carry cold water from the poles toward the equator.
- Upwelling brings up tiny ocean organisms, minerals, and other nutrients from the deeper layers of the water.

Key Terms

El Niño	salinity
La Niña	upwelling

3 Climate Regions

🔑 **Key Concepts**　　　🔧 S 6.4.e

- Scientists classify climates according to two major factors: temperature and precipitation.
- There are six main climate regions: tropical rainy, dry, temperate marine, temperate continental, polar, and highlands.
- The tropics have two types of rainy climates: tropical wet and tropical wet-and-dry.
- Dry climates can be arid and semiarid climates.
- There are three kinds of temperate marine climates: marine west coast, Mediterranean, and humid subtropical.
- Temperate continental climates are only found on continents in the Northern Hemisphere, and include humid continental and subarctic.
- The polar climate is the coldest climate region, and includes the ice cap and tundra climates.
- Temperature falls as altitude increases, so highland regions are colder than regions that surround them.

Key Terms

rain forest	chaparral	tundra
savanna	humid	permafrost
desert	subtropical	
steppe	subarctic	

4 Climate Change

🔑 **Key Concepts**　　　🔧 S 6.4.e

- Many scientists have hypothesized that human activities that add greenhouse gases to the atmosphere are warming Earth's atmosphere.
- Chemicals produced by humans have been damaging the ozone layer.

Key Terms

ice age	ozone hole
global warming	chlorofluorocarbon
greenhouse gas	

Review and Assessment

⊙ **Target Reading Skill**
Create Outlines Complete your outline for Section 1.

What Causes Climate?

I. Factors Affecting Temperature
    A. Latitude
    B. Altitude
    C. Distance From Large Bodies of Water
    D. Ocean Currents
II. Factors Affecting Precipitation
    A.
    B.

Reviewing Key Terms

Choose the letter of the best answer.

1. The average conditions of temperature, precipitation, wind, and clouds in an area over a period of years make up its
   a. weather.
   b. latitude.
   c. climate.
   d. season.

2. Winds and currents move in curved paths because of
   a. the Coriolis effect.
   b. El Niño.
   c. upwelling.
   d. tides.

3. A wet, warm climate zone on the edge of the tropics is
   a. humid subtropical.
   b. tundra.
   c. subarctic.
   d. continental climate.

4. A tropical grassland with scattered clumps of trees is a
   a. steppe.
   b. desert.
   c. savanna.
   d. rain forest.

5. The main cause of ozone depletion is
   a. global warming.
   b. chlorofluorocarbons.
   c. greenhouse gases.
   d. sunspots.

Complete the following sentences so that your answers clearly explain the key terms.

6. **Climate** is different than weather because _____.

7. **El Niño,** which is _____, can disrupt weather patterns around the world.

8. **Upwelling,** which is _____, provides nutrients that attract huge schools of fish.

9. Rain or snow often falls on the **windward** side of a mountain range, meaning _____ .

10. Higher levels of carbon dioxide in the atmosphere may produce **global warming,** which is _____.

Writing in Science

Expedition Plan Suppose that you are preparing to take a trip back in time to the last ice age. Write a list of the equipment you will need to bring with you and describe what the climate will be like.

Video Assessment
Discovery Channel School
Climate and Climate Change

Review and Assessment

Checking Concepts

11. Explain how distance from large bodies of water can affect the temperature of nearby land areas.

12. What are monsoons, and how do they affect climate in the regions where they occur?

13. What causes Earth's seasons?

14. What is the Coriolis effect? How does it influence ocean currents?

15. How do warm-water currents influence climate?

16. How are "dry" climates defined? How do the two types of dry climate differ?

17. To be effective, why must agreements aimed at preventing or reducing ozone depletion be international?

Thinking Critically

18. **Relating Cause and Effect** Describe three ways in which water influences climate.

19. **Comparing and Contrasting** How are El Niño and La Niña similar? How are they different?

20. **Relating Cause and Effect** Why do parts of the United States have a semiarid climate while neighboring areas have a humid continental climate?

21. **Reading Graphs** Which month shown on the graph has the warmest average temperature? Which month is the wettest? What type of climate is indicated by the graph?

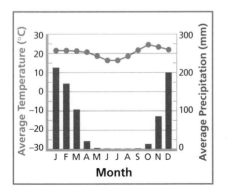

Math Practice

22. **Percentage** Suppose a city receives an average of 35 cm of precipitation each November. If an average of 140 cm of precipitation falls there in a year, what percentage falls in November?

Applying Skills

Use the map of world temperature zones to answer Questions 23–26.

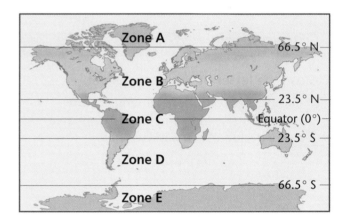

23. **Interpreting Maps** Name each of the five zones shown on the map.

24. **Measuring** What is the name of the temperature zone that includes the equator? How many degrees of latitude does this zone cover?

25. **Interpreting Data** Which of the five zones shown on the map has the greatest amount of land area suitable for people to live?

26. **Drawing Conclusions** Which zone has the highest average temperatures all year round? Explain why.

Standards Investigation

Performance Assessment Now share your investigation with your class. In your presentation, describe the patterns you found in your graphs. Then explain what you think causes different microclimates. After your presentation, think about how you could have improved your investigation.

Choose the letter of the best answer.

The graphs below show average monthly precipitation for two locations in Arizona. Use the information and your knowledge of science to answer Questions 1–2.

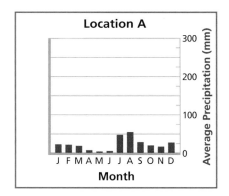

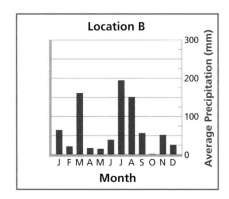

1. During which months do these locations receive the most precipitation?
   A January through March
   B April through June
   C July through September
   D October through December   **S 6.4.e**

2. Although they are only a few kilometers apart, Location B receives nearly three times as much precipitation as Location A. What is the best explanation for this fact?
   A Location B is in a rain shadow.
   B Location B is near a mountain top.
   C Location A is dried by prevailing winds.
   D Location A is much colder than Location B.

   S 6.4.e

3. Predict what type of climate would be the most likely in an area located in the interior of a large continent, on the east side of a major mountain range. Winds in the area commonly blow from west to east.
   A dry
   B polar
   C temperate marine
   D tropical rainy   **S 6.4.e**

4. What two major factors are usually used to classify climates?
   A precipitation and altitude
   B temperature and air pressure
   C temperature and precipitation
   D air pressure and humidity   **S 6.4.e**

5. The major method by which heat flows between the ocean's surface and the deep ocean is
   A conduction.
   B convection.
   C radiation.
   D global warming.   **S 6.3.c, 6.4.d**

6. Heat is carried through the ocean from the tropics to the polar regions mainly by
   A waves.
   B upwelling.
   C surface currents.
   D deep currents.   **S 6.3.a, 6.4.d**

7. What is the major result at Earth's surface of ozone depletion in the stratosphere?
   A an increase in the amount of ultraviolet radiation reaching the surface
   B a decrease in the amount of ultraviolet radiation reaching the surface
   C an increase in global temperatures
   D a decrease in global temperatures   **S 6.4.e**

Apply the **BIG Idea**

8. Identify three factors that can have a significant effect on a region's climate. Explain how each of these factors can influence climate.

   S 6.4.d, 6.4.e

Weather and Climate
Unit 3 Review

Chapter 7
The Atmosphere
The BIG Idea

Air pressure and temperature vary with altitude and location, resulting in distinct atmospheric layers and predictable wind patterns.

🔑 What is the composition of Earth's atmosphere?

🔑 What are the four main layers of the atmosphere?

🔑 How is heat transferred in the troposphere?

🔑 What causes winds?

Chapter 8
Weather
The BIG Idea

Differences in air pressure, air temperature, winds, and humidity produce changes in weather.

🔑 How do clouds form?

🔑 What are the common types of precipitation?

🔑 What are the main types of fronts?

🔑 What are the main kinds of storms, and how do they form?

🔑 What type of weather is associated with cyclones and anticyclones?

Chapter 9
Climate and Climate Change
The BIG Idea

The main factors that influence a region's climate include latitude, altitude, distance from large bodies of water, ocean currents, prevailing winds, the presence of mountains, and seasonal winds.

🔑 What causes surface currents and deep currents, and what effects do they have?

🔑 What factors are used to classify climates?

Connecting the BIG Ideas

The graphs below show the average maximum temperature and the average precipitation each month in four California locations. The table also shows the altitude and latitude for each location. Eureka and Santa Barbara are coastal locations, and Death Valley and Tahoe are inland locations.

Altitude and Latitude		
Location	Altitude	Latitude
Death Valley	82 m below sea level	36° N
Eureka	14 m above sea level	41° N
Santa Barbara	13 m above sea level	34° N
Tahoe	1,902 m above sea level	39° N

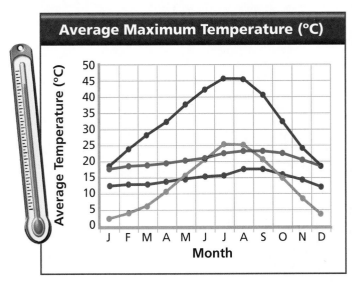

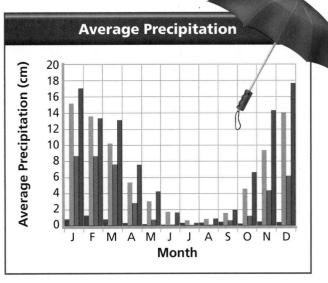

■ Death Valley ■ Santa Barbara
■ Tahoe ■ Eureka

1. On average, at which location would you expect to find the lowest air pressure ? *(Chapter 7)*
   a. Death Valley   b. Eureka
   c. Santa Barbara   d. Tahoe

2. What type of precipitation would most likely occur in Eureka in March? *(Chapter 8)*
   a. freezing rain   b. rain
   c. sleet   d. snow

3. What type of climate is found in Death Valley? *(Chapter 9)*
   a. arid   b. highlands
   c. Mediterranean   d. tundra

4. **Summary** Write a paragraph comparing and contrasting the climate of the four locations. What factors affect the climate in each location?

Chapter 10

Ecosystems

CALIFORNIA
Standards Preview

S 6.2 Topography is reshaped by the weathering of rock and soil and by the transportation and deposition of sediment. As a basis for understanding this concept:

d. Students know earthquakes, volcanic eruptions, landslides, and floods change human and wildlife habitats.

S 6.5 Organisms in ecosystems exchange energy and nutrients among themselves and with the environment. As a basis for understanding this concept:

a. Students know energy entering ecosystems as sunlight is transferred by producers into chemical energy through photosynthesis and then from organism to organism through food webs.

b. Students know matter is transferred over time from one organism to others in the food web and between organisms and the physical environment.

c. Students know populations of organisms can be categorized by the functions they serve in an ecosystem.

e. Students know the number and types of organisms an ecosystem can support depends on the resources available and on abiotic factors, such as quantities of light and water, a range of temperatures, and soil composition.

This population of monarch butterflies is made up of thousands of individual butterflies. ▶

Focus on the BIG Idea

S 6.5.c.

What relationships exist between living things and the environment?

Check What You Know

A tidepool at the seashore is home to a small community of organisms. In the shallow, salty water of the tidepool is seaweed called kelp. The kelp requires sunlight to grow. The tidepool also contains small crabs that eat kelp, and an octopus that eats crabs. What is the source of energy for this community? What would happen to the octopus if the kelp were removed from the tidepool? Explain.

The images shown here represent some of the key terms in this chapter. You can use this vocabulary skill to help you understand the meaning of some key terms in this chapter.

Vocabulary Skill

Identify Related Word Forms

You can increase your vocabulary by learning related forms of a word. If you know that the verb *collect* means "to gather together," then you can figure out the meaning of the noun *collection* and the adjective *collective*.

Example Students will *collect* (verb) cans and take the *collection* (noun) to a recycling center.

Verb	Noun	Adjective
inhabit To live in	**habitat** The place where an organism lives	**habitable** Fit to be lived in
limit To keep within or below a certain amount	**limit** An amount that is within or below a certain level or number	**limited** Kept within a certain amount
prey To hunt or kill for food	**predator** An organism that hunts or kills	**predatory** Living by hunting or killing
produce To make one's own food	**producer** An organism that can make its own food	**productive** Capable of making its own food

Apply It!

Review the words related to *prey*. Complete the following sentences with the correct form of the word.

1. Owls _____ on mice, moles, and rabbits.
2. How could a rabbit avoid being killed by a _____?
3. Eagles, hawks, and owls are _____ animals.

ecosystem

Chapter 10
Vocabulary

population

mutualism

nitrogen cycle

carnivore

primary succession

Interactive Textbook

Build Science Vocabulary
Online
Visit: PHSchool.com
Web Code: cwj-4100

How to Read Science

Sequence

Sequence is the order in which a series of events occurs. In Chapter 3, you used a flowchart to show events in a process that has a beginning and an end. Sequence can also be a continuous process, or cycle, that does not have an end. The paragraph below shows a continuous sequence. As you read, look for signal words, such as *first*, *next*, and *then*, that indicate sequence.

The Water Cycle

The water cycle is a continuous process by which water moves from Earth's surface to the atmosphere and back. <u>First</u>, water evaporates from oceans, rivers and lakes. <u>Next</u>, water vapor in the atmosphere condenses, forming clouds. <u>Then</u>, water returns to Earth's surface as precipitation—rain or snow. <u>Finally</u>, streams flow back to the ocean.

Use a cycle diagram like this one to help you understand the text. In your notebook, write the first event in the circle at the top of the page. Then write each event in sequence, moving clockwise.

The Water Cycle

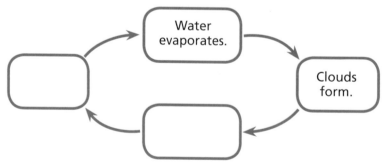

Apply It!

Review the water cycle diagram above.
1. Why is a cycle diagram a good way to explain what happens to water on Earth?
2. Fill in the sequence of the next two events in the water cycle.

After you read Section 5, prepare a cycle diagram showing the carbon cycle.

Standards **Investigation**

S 6.5.c, 6.7.c

What's a Crowd?

In this chapter, you will explore how living things obtain the things they need from their surroundings. You will also learn how living things interact with the living and nonliving things around them. As you work on this investigation, you will observe interactions among growing plants.

Your Goal

To design and conduct an experiment to determine the effect of crowding on plant growth

To complete this investigation, you must

- develop a planting plan
- develop a hypothesis relating the growth of plants in a container to the number of plants
- observe and collect data on the growing plants
- present your results in a written report and a graph
- follow the safety guidelines in Appendix A

Plan It!

With your group, brainstorm ideas for your plan. What conditions do plants need to grow? How will you arrange your seeds in their containers? What types of measurements will you make when the plants begin to grow? Submit your draft plan to your teacher. When your teacher has approved your plan, plant your seeds. Then collect and analyze the growth data and present your results.

Living Things and the Environment

S 6.5.e Students know the number and types of organisms an ecosystem can support depends on the resources available and on abiotic factors, such as quantities of light and water, a range of temperatures, and soil composition.

- What needs are met by an organism's environment?

- What are the two parts of an organism's habitat with which it interacts?

- What are the levels of organization within an ecosystem?

Key Terms

- organism
- habitat
- biotic factor
- abiotic factor
- photosynthesis
- species
- population
- community
- ecosystem
- ecology

Black-Tailed Prairie Dog

Lab zone Standards Warm-Up

What Does It Depend On?

1. Choose a magazine picture of a nature scene. Paste the picture onto a sheet of paper, leaving space all around the picture.

2. Locate everything in the picture that is alive. Use a colored pencil to draw a line from each living thing. If you know its name, write it on the line.

3. Using a different colored pencil, label each nonliving thing.

Think It Over

Inferring How do the living things in the picture depend on the nonliving things? Using a third color, draw lines connecting the living things to the nonliving things they need.

As the sun rises on a warm summer morning, the Nebraska town is already bustling with activity. Some residents are hard at work building homes for their families. They are working underground, where it is dark and cool. Other inhabitants are collecting seeds for breakfast. Some of the town's younger residents are at play, chasing each other through the grass.

Suddenly, an adult spots a threatening shadow—an enemy has appeared in the sky! The adult cries out several times, warning the others. Within moments, the town's residents disappear into their underground homes. The town is silent and still, except for a single hawk circling overhead.

Have you guessed what kind of town this is? It is a prairie dog town on the Nebraska plains. As these prairie dogs dug their burrows, searched for food, and hid from the hawk, they interacted with their environment, or surroundings.

FIGURE 1
Red-Tailed Hawk
This red-tailed hawk obtains food, water, and shelter from its habitat. Prairie dogs are a source of food for red-tailed hawks.

Habitats

A prairie dog is one type of **organism**, or living thing. Different types of organisms must live in different types of environments. 🗝 **An organism obtains food, water, shelter, and other things it needs to live, grow, and reproduce from its environment.** An environment that provides the things the organism needs to live, grow, and reproduce is called its **habitat.**

One area may contain many habitats. For example, in a forest, mushrooms grow in the damp soil, salamanders live on the forest floor, and woodpeckers build nests in tree trunks.

Organisms live in different habitats because they have different requirements for survival. A prairie dog obtains the food and shelter it needs from its habitat. It could not survive in a tropical rain forest or on the rocky ocean shore. Likewise, the prairie would not meet the needs of a spider monkey or hermit crab.

 **Reading Checkpoint** Why do different organisms live in different habitats?

Biotic Factors

To meet its needs, a prairie dog must interact with more than just the other prairie dogs around it. 🗝 **An organism interacts with both the living and nonliving parts of its habitat.** The living parts of a habitat are called **biotic factors** (by AHT ik). Biotic factors in the prairie dogs' habitat include the grass and plants that provide seeds and berries. The hawks, ferrets, badgers, and eagles that hunt the prairie dogs are also biotic factors. In addition, worms, fungi, and bacteria are biotic factors that live in the soil underneath the prairie grass.

 **Reading Checkpoint** Name a biotic factor in your environment.

Lab zone Try This **Activity**

Observing a Habitat

1. With your teacher's permission, visit an area such as a schoolyard or park that contains habitats for a variety of organisms. **CAUTION:** *Avoid insect bites or contact with harmful plants that may cause allergic reactions.*

2. Select appropriate tools, such as binoculars or a hand lens. Use them to observe a particular organism and the biotic factors in its habitat.

3. Record your observations. To display your data, make a poster showing your organism and the biotic factors you identified.

Predicting How do you think the organism interacts with the habitat's biotic factors?

FIGURE 2

Abiotic Factors

The nonliving things in an organism's habitat are abiotic factors. **Applying Concepts** *Name three abiotic factors you interact with each day.*

▲ This orangutan is enjoying a drink of water.

▲ Sunlight enables this plant to make its own food.

▲ This banjo frog burrows in the soil to stay cool.

Abiotic Factors

Abiotic factors (ay by AHT ik) are the nonliving parts of an organism's habitat. They include water, sunlight, oxygen, temperature, and soil.

Water All living things require water to carry out their life processes. Water also makes up a large part of the bodies of most organisms. Your body, for example, is about 65 percent water. Plants and algae need water, along with sunlight and carbon dioxide, to make their own food in a process called **photosynthesis** (foh toh SIN thuh sis). Other living things depend on plants and algae for food.

Sunlight Because sunlight is needed for photosynthesis, it is an important abiotic factor for most living things. In places that do not receive sunlight, such as dark caves, plants and algae cannot grow. Because there are no plants or algae to provide food, few other organisms can live in such places.

Oxygen Most living things require oxygen to carry out their life processes. Oxygen is so important to the functioning of the human body that you can live only a few minutes without it. Organisms that live on land obtain oxygen from air, which is about 20 percent oxygen. Fish and other water organisms obtain oxygen that is dissolved in the water around them.

Temperature The typical range of temperatures in an area determines the types of organisms that can live there. For example, if you took a trip to a warm tropical island, you might see colorful orchid flowers and tiny lizards. These organisms could not survive on the frozen plains of Siberia.

Some animals alter their environments so they can survive very hot or very cold temperatures. Prairie dogs, for example, dig underground dens to find shelter from the hot summer sun and cold winter winds.

Soil Soil is a mixture of rock fragments, nutrients, air, water, and the decaying remains of living things. Soil in different areas consists of varying amounts of these materials. The composition of soil in an area influences the kinds of plants that can grow there. Many animals, such as the prairie dogs, use the soil itself as a home. Billions of microscopic organisms such as bacteria also live in the soil.

 **Reading Checkpoint** How do abiotic factors differ from biotic factors?

Levels of Organization

Of course, organisms do not live all alone in their habitat. Instead, organisms live together in populations and communities, and with abiotic factors in their ecosystems.

Populations In 1900, travelers saw a prairie dog town in Texas that covered an area twice the size of the city of Dallas. The town contained more than 400 million prairie dogs! These prairie dogs were all members of one species, or single kind, of organism. A **species** (SPEE sheez) is a group of organisms that are physically similar and can mate with each other and produce offspring that can also mate and reproduce.

All the members of one species in a particular area are referred to as a **population.** The 400 million prairie dogs in the Texas town are one example of a population. All the pigeons in New York City make up a population, as do all the bees that live in a hive. In contrast, all the trees in a forest do not make up a population, because they do not all belong to the same species. There may be pines, maples, birches, and many other tree species in the forest.

Communities A particular area usually contains more than one species of organism. The prairie, for instance, includes prairie dogs, hawks, grasses, badgers, and snakes, along with many other organisms. All the different populations that live together in an area make up a **community.**

To be considered a community, the different populations must live close enough together to interact. One way the populations in a community may interact is by using the same resources, such as food and shelter. For example, the tunnels dug by prairie dogs also serve as homes for burrowing owls and black-footed ferrets. The prairie dogs share the grass with other animals. Meanwhile, prairie dogs themselves serve as food for many species.

FIGURE 3
A Population
All these zebras make up a population.

Ecosystems The community of organisms that live in a particular area, along with their nonliving surroundings, make up an **ecosystem.** A prairie is just one of the many different ecosystems found on Earth. Other ecosystems in which living things make their homes include mountain streams, deep oceans, and evergreen forests.

Figure 4 shows the levels of organization in an ecosystem. **The smallest level of organization is a single organism, which belongs to a population that includes other members of its species. The population belongs to a community of different species. The community and abiotic factors together form an ecosystem.**

Because the populations in an ecosystem interact with one another, any change affects all the different populations that live there. The study of how living things interact with each other and with their environment is called **ecology.** Ecologists are scientists who study ecology. As part of their work, ecologists study how organisms react to changes in their environment. An ecologist, for example, may look at how a fire affects a prairie ecosystem.

Reading Checkpoint What is ecology?

Section 1 Assessment

S 6.5.e; E-LA: Reading 6.1.0; Writing 6.2.0

Vocabulary Skill Use Related Words
Complete the sentence by using the correct form of *habitat* or *inhabit.* An organism must live in a _____ that meets its needs for survival.

Reviewing Key Concepts

1. **a. Listing** What basic needs are provided by an organism's habitat?
   b. Predicting What might happen to an organism if its habitat could not meet one of its needs?
2. **a. Defining** Define the terms *biotic factors* and *abiotic factors.*
   b. Interpreting Illustrations List all the biotic and abiotic factors in Figure 4.
   c. Making Generalizations Explain why water and sunlight are two abiotic factors that are important to most organisms.

3. **a. Sequencing** List these terms in order from the smallest level to the largest: *population, organism, ecosystem, community.*
   b. Classifying Would all the different kinds of organisms in a forest be considered a population or a community? Explain.
   c. Relating Cause and Effect How might a change in one population affect other populations in a community?

Writing in Science

Descriptive Paragraph What habitat do you live in? Write a one-paragraph description of your habitat. Describe how you obtain the food, water, and shelter you need from your habitat. How does this habitat meet your needs in ways that another would not?

FIGURE 4

Ecological Organization

The smallest level of organization is the organism. The largest is the entire ecosystem.

Organism: Prairie dog

Population: Prairie dog town

Community: All the living things that interact on the prairie

Ecosystem: All the living and nonliving things that interact on the prairie

A World in a Bottle

Materials

pre-cut, clear
plastic bottle

gravel and soil

plastic spoon and
large rubber band

charcoal

2 vascular plants

spray bottle

moss plants

clear plastic wrap

Problem How do organisms survive in a closed ecosystem?

Skills Focus Making models, observing

Procedure

1. In this lab, you will place plants in moist soil in a bottle that then will be sealed. This setup is called a terrarium. Predict whether the plants can survive in this habitat.

2. Spread about 2.5 cm of gravel on the bottom of a pre-cut bottle. Then sprinkle a spoonful or two of charcoal over the gravel.

3. Use the spoon to layer about 8 cm of soil over the gravel and charcoal. After you add the soil, tap it down to pack it.

4. Scoop out two holes in the soil. Remove the vascular plants from their pots. Gently place their roots in the holes. Then pack the loose soil firmly around the plants' stems.

5. Fill the spray bottle with water. Spray the soil until you see water collecting in the gravel.

6. Cover the soil with the moss plants, including the areas around the stems of the vascular plants. Lightly spray the mosses with water.

7. Tightly cover your terrarium with plastic wrap. Secure the cover with a rubber band. Place the terrarium in bright, indirect light.

8. Observe your terrarium daily for two weeks. Record your observations in your notebook. If its sides fog, move the terrarium to an area with a different amount of light. You may need to move it a few times. Note any changes you make in your terrarium's location.

Analyze and Conclude

1. **Making Models** List all of the biotic factors and abiotic factors that are part of your ecosystem model.

2. **Observing** Are any biotic or abiotic factors able to enter the terrarium? If so, which ones?

3. **Predicting** Suppose a plant-eating insect were added to the terrarium. Predict whether it would be able to survive. Explain your prediction.

4. **Communicating** Write a paragraph that explains how the plant depends on each of the abiotic factors you listed in Question 1. Are there any factors the plant could survive without? Explain.

Design an Experiment

Plan an experiment that would model a freshwater ecosystem. How would this model be different from the land ecosystem? *Obtain your teacher's approval before carrying out your plan.*

Section 2

Populations

CALIFORNIA
Standards Focus

S 6.5.e Students know the number and types of organisms an ecosystem can support depends on the resources available and on abiotic factors, such as quantities of light and water, a range of temperatures, and soil composition.

- What causes populations to change in size?
- What factors limit population growth?

Key Terms
- birth rate
- death rate
- immigration
- emigration
- limiting factor
- carrying capacity

Lab zone Standards **Warm-Up**

How Can Population Size Change?

A population of 30 deer lives in a forest. In your notebook, calculate how the population size changes during the five years listed below.

1. In the first year, 10 deer are born and 5 die.
2. In the second year, 8 deer are born and none die.
3. In the third year, 7 deer are born and 2 die.
4. In the fourth year, 12 deer are born, 8 die, and 10 leave the forest.
5. In the fifth year, 6 deer are born, 10 die, and 12 leave the forest.
6. Make a graph of the changes in population size.

Think It Over

Interpreting Graphs Describe how the population size of the deer herd changed over time. Did the overall population size increase, stay the same, or decrease?

How would you like to be an ecologist today? Your assignment is to study the albatross population on an island. One question you might ask is how the size of the albatross population is changing. Is the number of albatrosses on the island increasing, decreasing, or remaining about the same? To answer this question, an ecologist must observe how the size of the albatross population changes over several years.

FIGURE 5
Studying Populations
These young albatrosses are part of a larger albatross population in the Falkland Islands.

Changes in Population Size

The size of any population does not remain the same for very long. **Populations can change in size when new members join the population or when members leave the population.**

Births and Deaths The main way in which new individuals join a population is by being born into it. The **birth rate** of a population is the number of births in a population in a certain amount of time. For example, suppose that a population of 100 rabbits produces 600 young in a year. The birth rate in this population would be 600 young per year.

The main way that individuals leave a population is by dying. The **death rate** is the number of deaths in a population in a certain amount of time. If 400 rabbits die in a year in the population, the death rate would be 400 rabbits per year.

The Population Statement When the birth rate in a population is greater than the death rate, the population will generally increase. This can be written as a mathematical statement using the "is greater than" sign:

If birth rate > death rate, population size increases.

However, if the death rate in a population is greater than the birth rate, the population size will generally decrease. This can also be written as a mathematical statement:

If death rate > birth rate, population size decreases.

Immigration and Emigration The size of a population also can change when individuals move into or out of the population. **Immigration** (im ih GRAY shun) means moving into a population. **Emigration** (em ih GRAY shun) means leaving a population. For instance, if food is scarce, some members of an antelope herd may wander off in search of better grassland. If they become permanently separated from the original herd, they will no longer be part of that population.

Graphing Changes in Population Changes in a population's size can be displayed on a line graph. Figure 6 shows a graph of the changes in a rabbit population. The vertical axis shows the numbers of rabbits in the population, while the horizontal axis shows time. The graph shows the size of the population over a ten-year period.

 **Reading Checkpoint** How does emigration affect population size?

FIGURE 6
This line graph shows how the size of a rabbit population changed over a ten-year period.
Interpreting Graphs *In what year did the rabbit population reach its highest point? What was the size of the population in that year?*

▼ Young rabbits in a nest

From Year 0 to Year 4, more rabbits joined the population than left it, so the population increased.

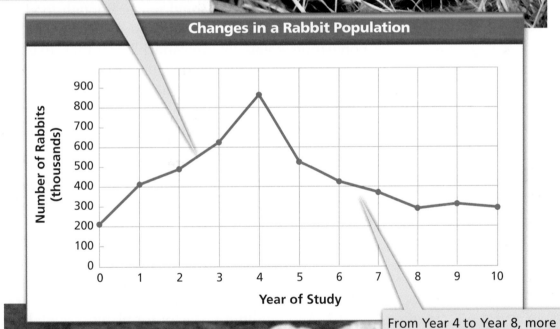

Changes in a Rabbit Population

From Year 4 to Year 8, more rabbits left the population than joined it, so the population decreased.

◀ Rabbit caught by a fox

Limiting Factors

When the living conditions in an area are good, a population will generally grow. But eventually some environmental factor will cause the population to stop growing. The number of organisms an ecosystem can support depends on the amount of resources available and on abiotic factors. A **limiting factor** is an environmental factor that causes a population to stop growing. 🔎 **Some limiting factors for populations are food and water, space, light, soil composition, and weather conditions.**

Food and Water Organisms require food and water to survive. Since food and water are often in limited supply, they are often limiting factors. Suppose a giraffe must eat 10 kilograms of leaves each day to survive. The trees in an area can provide 100 kilograms of leaves a day while remaining healthy. Five giraffes could live easily in this area, since they would only require a total of 50 kilograms of food. But 15 giraffes could not all survive—there would not be enough food. No matter how much shelter, water, and other resources there were, the population would not grow much larger than 10 giraffes.

The largest population that an area can support is called its **carrying capacity.** The carrying capacity of this giraffe habitat would be 10 giraffes. A population usually stays near its carrying capacity because of the limiting factors in its habitat.

Space Space is also a limiting factor. For example, nesting space is a limiting factor for seabirds such as gannets. The rocky shores where gannets nest get very crowded. If a pair does not find space to nest, they will not be able to add to the population.

Space is also a limiting factor for plant populations. The amount of space in which a plant grows determines whether the plant can obtain the water and nutrients it needs.

Light Another limiting factor for plants is light. For example, tree seedlings may not get enough light if branches from other trees block the sunlight.

FIGURE 7
Space as a Limiting Factor
The amount of space available in this tidepool limits the number of sea stars and anemones that can live there.

Soil Composition The composition of the soil is also a limiting factor that affects plant growth. To support vigorous plant growth, soils must contain sufficient nitrogen and minerals, including phosphorus and potassium. The soil must also contain enough humus without excess acidity or alkalinity.

Weather Weather conditions can limit population growth. Many types of organisms require a particular range of temperatures and amount of rainfall to live and reproduce. For example, the saguaro cactus can withstand the heat and dryness of the Arizona desert. But the saguaro will not grow where winter temperatures fall much below freezing.

The number of organisms that an ecosystem can support varies from season to season. For example, more organisms thrive during temperate summers than can survive icy winters.

Unusual weather events can also affect population size. A cold snap in late spring can kill the young of many species of birds and mammals. A hurricane or flood can wash away nests and burrows.

FIGURE 8
Weather as a Limiting Factor
A snowstorm can limit the size of an orange crop.
Applying Concepts *What other weather conditions can limit population growth?*

 **Reading Checkpoint** How can unusual weather affect population size?

Section 2 Assessment

S 6.5.e, E-LA: Reading 6.1.0, Math: 6 NS 2.3

Vocabulary Skill Use Related Words Complete the sentence by using the correct form of *limit* and *limiting*. A _____ factor will stop the growth of an animal population because it may _____ food, water, or space for that population.

Reviewing Key Concepts

1. a. **Identifying** Name two ways organisms join a population and two ways organisms leave a population.
   b. **Calculating** Suppose a population of 100 mice has produced 600 young. If 200 mice have died, how many mice are in the population now? (Assume for this question that no mice have moved into or out of the population for other reasons.)
   c. **Drawing Conclusions** Suppose that you discovered that there were actually 750 mice in the population. How could you account for the difference?

2. a. **Reviewing** Name five limiting factors for populations.
   b. **Describing** Choose one of the limiting factors and describe how it limits population growth.
   c. **Inferring** How might the limiting factor you chose affect the pigeon population in your town?

Math Practice

3. **Inequalities** Complete the following inequality showing the relationship between carrying capacity and population size. Then explain why the inequality is true.

   If population size ■ carrying capacity, then population size will decrease.

Energy Flow in Ecosystems

CALIFORNIA
Standards Focus

S 6.5.a Students know energy entering ecosystems as sunlight is transferred by producers into chemical energy through photosynthesis and then from organism to organism through food webs.

S 6.5.c Students know populations of organisms can be categorized by the functions they serve in an ecosystem.

🔑 What energy roles do organisms play in an ecosystem?

🔑 How does energy move through an ecosystem?

🔑 How much energy is available at each level of an energy pyramid?

Key Terms

- producer
- consumer
- herbivore
- carnivore
- omnivore
- scavenger
- decomposer
- food chain
- food web
- energy pyramid

Lab zone Standards **Warm-Up**

Where Did Your Dinner Come From?

1. Across the top of a sheet of paper, list the different types of foods you ate for dinner last night.
2. Under each item, write the name of the plant, animal, or other organism that was the source of that food. Some foods have more than one source. For example, macaroni and cheese contains flour (which is made from a plant such as wheat) and cheese (which comes from an animal).

Think It Over
Classifying How many of your food sources were plants? How many were animals?

Do you play an instrument in your school band? If so, you know that each instrument has a role in a piece of music. For instance, the flute may provide the melody while the drum provides the beat.

Just like the instruments in a band, each organism has a role in the movement of energy through its ecosystem. A bluebird's role, for example, is different from that of the giant oak tree where it is perched. But all parts of the ecosystem, like all parts of a band, are necessary for the ecosystem to work.

Energy Roles

An organism's energy role, or ecological function, is determined by how it obtains energy and how it interacts with other organisms. 🔑 **Each of the organisms in an ecosystem fills the energy role of producer, consumer, or decomposer.**

Producers Energy enters most ecosystems as sunlight. Some organisms, such as plants, algae, and some bacteria, capture the energy of sunlight and store it as food energy. These organisms use the sun's energy to turn water and carbon dioxide into chemical energy in a process called photosynthesis. This chemical energy is stored as food within the organism.

An organism that can make its own food is a **producer.** Producers, such as plants, algae, and some bacteria, are the source of all the food in an ecosystem. In a few ecosystems, producers obtain energy from a source other than sunlight. One such ecosystem is found in rocks deep beneath the ground. How is energy brought into this ecosystem? Certain bacteria in this ecosystem produce their own food using the energy in a gas, hydrogen sulfide, that is found in their environment.

Consumers Some members of an ecosystem cannot make their own food. An organism that obtains energy by feeding on other organisms is a **consumer.**

Consumers are classified by what they eat. Consumers that eat only plants are **herbivores.** Familiar herbivores are caterpillars and deer. Consumers that eat only animals are **carnivores.** Lions and spiders are some examples of carnivores. Consumers that eat both plants and animals are **omnivores.** Crows, bears, and most humans are omnivores.

Some carnivores are scavengers. A **scavenger** is a carnivore that feeds on the bodies of dead organisms. Scavengers include catfish and vultures.

Decomposers If an ecosystem had only producers and consumers, the raw materials of life would stay locked up in wastes and the bodies of dead organisms. Luckily, there are organisms in ecosystems that prevent this problem. **Decomposers** break down wastes and dead organisms and return the raw materials to the ecosystem.

You can think of decomposers as nature's recyclers. While obtaining energy for their own needs, decomposers return simple molecules to the environment. These molecules can be used again by other organisms. Mushrooms and bacteria are common decomposers.

Reading Checkpoint What do herbivores and carnivores have in common?

Consumer—Herbivore

Producer

Consumer—Omnivore

Decomposer

FIGURE 9
Energy Roles
Producers, such as oak trees, obtain energy by making their own food. Consumers, such as luna moth larvae and eastern bluebirds, obtain energy by feeding on other organisms. **Classifying** *What role do decomposers play in ecosystems?*

Lab zone **Try This Activity**

Weaving a Food Web

This activity shows how the organisms in a food web are interconnected.

1. Your teacher will assign you a role in the food web.
2. Hold one end of each of several pieces of yarn in your hand. Give the other ends of your yarn to the other organisms to which your organism is linked.
3. Your teacher will now eliminate an organism. All the organisms connected to the missing organism should drop the yarn that connects them.

Making Models How many organisms were affected by the removal of just one organism? What does this activity show about the importance of each organism in a food web?

Food Chains and Food Webs

As you have read, energy enters most ecosystems as sunlight and is converted into chemical energy by producers. This energy is transferred to each organism that eats a producer, and then to other organisms that feed on these consumers. ⬤ **The transfer of energy from organism to organism in an ecosystem can be shown in diagrams called food chains and food webs.**

Food Chains A **food chain** is a series of events in which one organism eats another and obtains energy. You can follow one food chain in Figure 10. The first organism in a food chain is always a producer, such as the tree. The second organism feeds on the producer and is called the first-level consumer. The carpenter ant is a first-level consumer. Next, a second-level consumer eats the first-level consumer. The second-level consumer in this example is the woodpecker.

Food Webs A food chain shows only one possible path along which energy can move through an ecosystem food web. But just as you do not eat the same thing every day, neither do most other organisms. Most producers and consumers are part of many food chains. A more realistic way to show the flow of energy through an ecosystem is a food web. As shown in Figure 10, a **food web** consists of the many overlapping food chains in an ecosystem.

In Figure 10, you can trace the many food chains in a woodland ecosystem food web. Note that an organism may play more than one role in an ecosystem. For example, an omnivore such as the mouse is a first-level consumer when it eats grass. But when the mouse eats a grasshopper, it is a second-level consumer.

Just as food chains overlap and connect, food webs interconnect as well. While a gull might eat a fish at the ocean, it might also eat a mouse at a landfill. The gull, then, is part of two food webs—an ocean food web and a land food web. All the world's food webs interconnect in what can be thought of as a global food web.

 **Reading Checkpoint** What energy role is filled by the first organism in a food chain?

Food Chain

Woodpecker

Carpenter ant

Tree

FIGURE 10

A Food Web

A food web consists of many interconnected food chains. Trace the path of energy through the producers, consumers, and decomposers.
Interpreting Diagrams *Which organisms in the food web are acting as herbivores? Which are carnivores?*

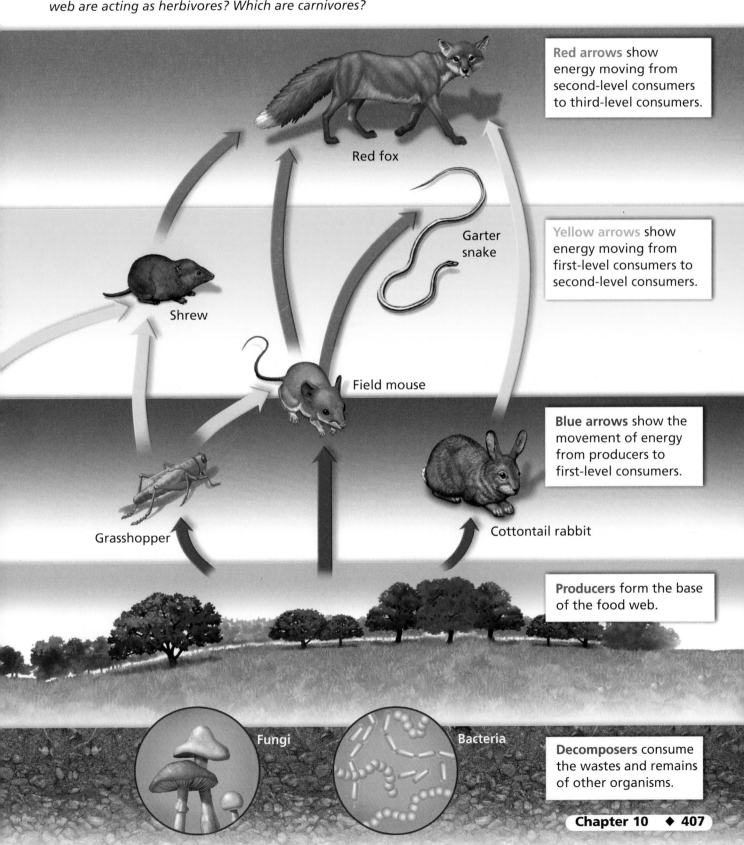

Red arrows show energy moving from second-level consumers to third-level consumers.

Red fox

Garter snake

Yellow arrows show energy moving from first-level consumers to second-level consumers.

Shrew

Field mouse

Blue arrows show the movement of energy from producers to first-level consumers.

Grasshopper

Cottontail rabbit

Producers form the base of the food web.

Fungi

Bacteria

Decomposers consume the wastes and remains of other organisms.

FIGURE 11
Energy Pyramid
This energy pyramid shows the amount of energy available at each level of a food web. Energy is measured in kilocalories, or kcal.
Calculating *How many times more energy is available at the producer level than at the second-level consumer level?*

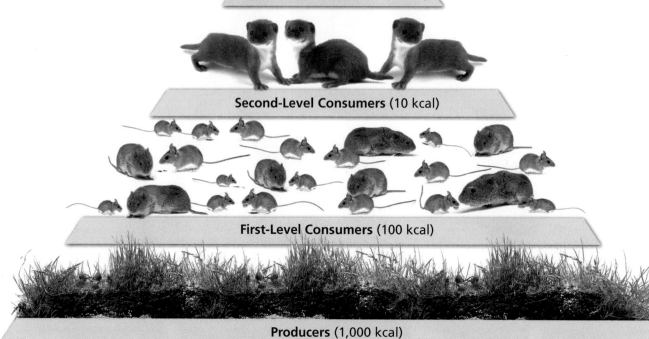

Third-Level Consumers (1 kcal)

Second-Level Consumers (10 kcal)

First-Level Consumers (100 kcal)

Producers (1,000 kcal)

Energy Pyramids

When an organism in an ecosystem eats, it obtains energy. The organism uses some of this energy to move, feed, grow, and reproduce. This means that only some of the energy it obtains will be available to the next organism in the food web.

A diagram called an **energy pyramid** shows the amount of energy that moves from one feeding level to another in a food web. You can see an energy pyramid in Figure 11. **The most energy is available at the producer level of the pyramid. As you move up the pyramid, each level has less energy available than the level below.** An energy pyramid is wider at the base and narrower at the top.

Energy Flow in Ecosystems The wide base of the pyramid represents the ecosystem's producers—in this case, plants. The richness of plant growth controls the number of organisms that can be supported at higher feeding levels in the ecosystem. In turn, abiotic factors control the richness of plant growth.

In general, only about 10 percent of the chemical energy at one level of a food web is transferred to the next higher level. The other 90 percent of the energy is used for the organism's life processes or is lost to the environment as heat. Since about 90 percent of the energy is lost at each step, there is not enough energy to support many feeding levels in an ecosystem.

The organisms at higher feeding levels of an energy pyramid do not necessarily require less energy to live than do the organisms at lower levels. Since so much energy is lost at each level, the amount of energy available at the producer level limits the number of consumers that the ecosystem is able to support. As a result, there are usually few organisms at the highest level in a food web.

Scavengers and Decomposers Scavengers and decomposers are also part of an energy pyramid. They feed on the remains or wastes of organisms at each level of the pyramid.

FIGURE 12
Energy Flow
This barn owl will soon use the energy contained in the rat to carry out its own life processes.

Section 3 Assessment

S 6.5.a, 6.5.c; E-LA: Reading 6.1.0

Vocabulary Skill Use Related Words Complete the sentence by using the correct form of *produce* or *producers*. Organism called _____, which include plants, algae, and some bacteria, _____ all the food in an ecosystem.

Reviewing Key Concepts

1. a. **Identifying** Name the three energy roles that organisms fill in an ecosystem.
   b. **Explaining** How do organisms in each of the three energy roles obtain chemical energy?
   c. **Classifying** Identify the energy roles of the following organisms in a pond ecosystem: tadpole, algae, heron.
2. a. **Defining** What is a food chain? What is a food web?
   b. **Comparing and Contrasting** Why is a food web a more realistic model of an ecosystem than is a food chain?
3. a. **Reviewing** What does an energy pyramid show?
   b. **Describing** How does the amount of chemical energy available at one level of an energy pyramid compare to the amount of energy available at the next level up?
   c. **Relating Cause and Effect** Why are there usually few organisms at the top of an energy pyramid?

Lab zone **At-Home Activity**

Energy-Role Walk Take a short walk outdoors with a family member to look for producers, consumers, and decomposers. Create a list of the organisms and their energy roles. For each consumer, try to classify it further according to what it eats and its level. Then explain to your family member how energy flows in ecosystems.

Interactions Among Living Things

CALIFORNIA
Standards Focus

S 6.5.c Students know populations of organisms can be categorized by the functions they serve in an ecosystem.

🔑 How do an organism's adaptations help it to survive?

🔑 What are the major ways in which organisms in an ecosystem interact?

🔑 What are the three types of symbiotic relationships?

Key Terms
- natural selection
- adaptations
- niche
- competition
- predation
- predator
- prey
- symbiosis
- mutualism
- commensalism
- parasitism
- parasite
- host

Lab zone Standards **Warm-Up**

Can You Hide a Butterfly?

1. Trace a butterfly on a piece of paper, using the outline shown here.
2. Look around the classroom and pick a spot where you will place your butterfly. You must place your butterfly out in the open. Color your butterfly so it will blend in with the spot you choose.
3. Tape your butterfly down. Someone will now have one minute to find the butterflies. Will your butterfly be found?

Think It Over

Predicting Over time, do you think the population size of butterflies that blend in with their surroundings would increase or decrease?

Can you imagine living in a cactus like the one in Figure 13? Ouch! You probably wouldn't want to live in a house covered with sharp spines. But many species live in, on, and around saguaro cactuses.

As day breaks, a twittering sound comes from a nest tucked in one of the saguaro's arms. Two young red-tailed hawks are preparing to fly for the first time. Farther down the stem, a tiny elf owl peeks out of its nest in a small hole. This owl is so small it could fit in your palm! A rattlesnake slithers around the base of the saguaro, looking for lunch. Spying a shrew, the snake strikes it with its needle-like fangs. The shrew dies instantly.

Activity around the saguaro continues after sunset. Long-nosed bats come out to feed on the nectar from the saguaro's blossoms. The bats stick their faces into the flowers to feed, dusting their long snouts with white pollen. As they move from plant to plant, they carry the pollen to other saguaros. This enables the cactuses to reproduce.

Adapting to the Environment

Each organism in the saguaro community has unique characteristics. These characteristics affect the individual's ability to survive in its environment.

Natural Selection A characteristic that makes an individual better suited to its environment may eventually become common in that species through a process called **natural selection.** Natural selection works like this: Individuals whose unique characteristics are best suited for their environment tend to survive and produce offspring. Offspring that inherit these characteristics also live to reproduce. In this way, natural selection results in **adaptations,** the behaviors and physical characteristics that allow organisms to live successfully in their environments.

Individuals with characteristics that are poorly suited to the environment are less likely to survive and reproduce. Over time, poorly suited characteristics may disappear from the species.

Niche 🔵 **Every organism has a variety of adaptations that are suited to its specific living conditions.** The organisms in the saguaro community have adaptations that result in specific ecological roles. For example, the organism may be a producer, consumer, or decomposer. The role of an organism in its habitat, or how it makes its living, is called its **niche.** A niche includes the type of food the organism eats, how it obtains this food, and which other organisms use the organism as food. A niche also includes when and how the organism reproduces and the physical conditions it requires to survive.

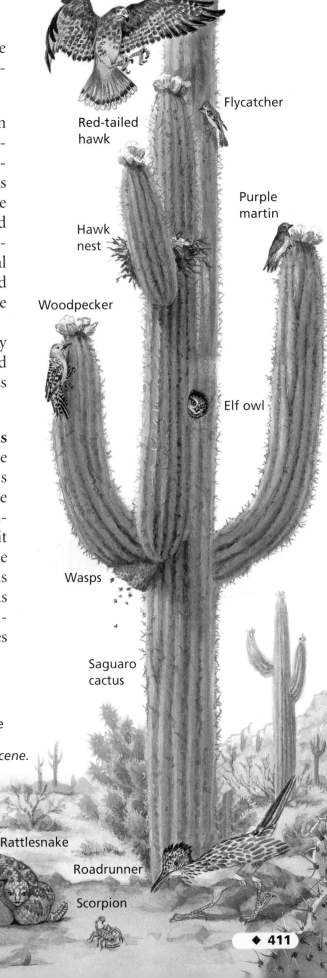

Red-tailed hawk

Flycatcher

Purple martin

Hawk nest

Woodpecker

Elf owl

Wasps

Saguaro cactus

Rattlesnake

Roadrunner

Scorpion

Gila monster

FIGURE 13
Saguaro Community
The organisms in the saguaro community are well adapted to their desert environment.
Observing *Identify two interactions in this scene.*

Cape May Warbler
This species feeds at the tips of branches near the top of the tree.

Bay-Breasted Warbler
This species feeds in the middle part of the tree.

Yellow-Rumped Warbler
This species feeds in the lower part of the tree and at the bases of the middle branches.

FIGURE 14
Niche and Competition
Each of these warblers occupies a different niche in its spruce tree habitat. By feeding in different areas of the tree, the birds avoid competing for food. *Comparing and Contrasting How do the niches of these three warblers differ?*

For: More on population interactions
Visit: PHSchool.com
Web Code: ced-5013

Competition

During a typical day in the saguaro community, a range of interactions takes place among organisms.  **There are three major types of interactions among organisms: competition, predation, and symbiosis.**

Different species can share the same habitat and food requirements. For example, the roadrunner and the elf owl both live on the saguaro and eat insects. However, these two species do not occupy exactly the same niche. The roadrunner is active during the day, while the owl is active mostly at night. If two species occupy the same niche, one of the species will eventually die off. The reason for this is **competition,** the struggle between organisms to survive as they attempt to use the same limited resource.

In any ecosystem, there is a limited amount of food, water, and shelter. Organisms that survive have adaptations that enable them to reduce competition. For example, the three species of warblers in Figure 14 live in the same spruce forest habitat. They all eat insects that live in the spruce trees. How do these birds avoid competing for the limited insect supply? Each warbler "specializes" in feeding in a certain part of a spruce tree. This is how the three species coexist.

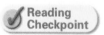 **Reading Checkpoint** Why can't two species occupy the same niche?

Predation

A tiger shark lurks below the surface of the clear blue water, looking for shadows of albatross chicks floating above. The shark spots a chick and silently swims closer. Suddenly, the shark bursts through the water and seizes the albatross with one snap of its powerful jaw. This interaction between two organisms has an unfortunate ending for the albatross.

An interaction in which one organism kills another for food is called **predation.** The organism that does the killing, in this case the tiger shark, is the **predator.** The organism that is killed, in this case the albatross, is the **prey.**

The Effect of Predation on Population Size Predation can have a major effect on the size of a population. Recall from Section 2 that when the death rate exceeds the birth rate in a population, the size of that population usually decreases. So if there are many predators, the result is often a decrease in the size of the population of their prey. But a decrease in the number of prey results in less food for their predators. Without adequate food, the predator population starts to decline. So, generally, populations of predators and their prey rise and fall in related cycles.

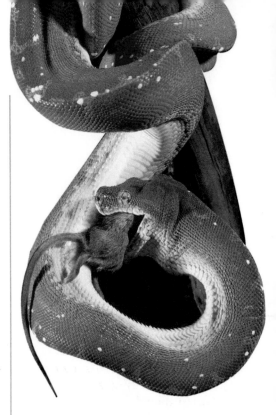

FIGURE 15
Predation
This green tree python and mouse are involved in a predator-prey interaction.

Math: Statistics, Data Analysis, and Probability 6.3.2

Math / Analyzing Data

Predator-Prey Interactions

On Isle Royale, an island in Lake Superior, the populations of wolves (the predator) and moose (the prey) rise and fall in cycles. Use the graph to answer the questions.

1. **Reading Graphs** What variable is plotted on the x-axis? What two variables are plotted on the y-axis?

2. **Interpreting Data** How did the moose population change between 1965 and 1972? What happened to the wolf population from 1973 through 1976?

3. **Inferring** How might the change in the moose population have led to the change in the wolf population?

4. **Drawing Conclusions** What is one likely cause of the dip in the moose population between 1974 and 1981?

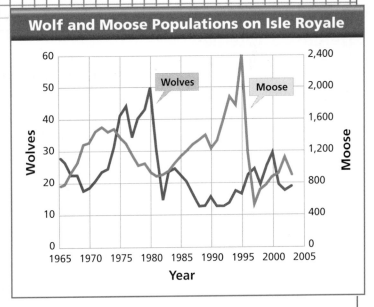

5. **Predicting** How might a disease in the wolf population one year affect the moose population the next year?

◀ Mimicry
If you're afraid of snakes, you'd probably be terrified to see this organism staring at you. Because this caterpillar looks like a snake, it can trick would-be predators into staying away.

False Coloring ▲
The large false eyespots on the moth's wings scare potential predators away.

▼ Camouflage
This insect might fool a predator into looking elsewhere for a meal.

◀ Warning Coloring
Like many brightly colored animals, this grasshopper is poisonous. Its bright blue and yellow colors warn predators not to eat it.

FIGURE 16
Defense Strategies

Organisms display a wide array of adaptations that help them avoid becoming prey. **Inferring** *What other adaptations might contribute to the grasshopper's ability to escape a predator?*

Video Field Trip
Discovery Channel School
Populations and Communities

Predator Adaptations Predators have adaptations that help them catch and kill their prey. For example, a cheetah can run very fast for a short time, enabling it to catch its prey. A jellyfish's tentacles contain a poisonous substance that paralyzes tiny water animals. Some plants, too, have adaptations for catching prey. The sundew is covered with sticky bulbs on stalks—when a fly lands on the plant, it remains snared in the sticky goo while the plant digests it.

Some predators have adaptations that enable them to hunt at night. For example, the big eyes of an owl let in as much light as possible to help it see in the dark. Insect-eating bats can hunt without seeing at all. Instead, they locate their prey by producing pulses of sound and listening for the echoes. This precise method enables a bat to catch a flying moth in complete darkness.

Prey Adaptations How do organisms avoid being killed by such effective predators? Organisms have many kinds of adaptations that help them avoid becoming prey. The alertness and speed of an antelope help protect it from its predators. And you're probably not surprised that the smelly spray of a skunk helps keep its predators at a distance. As you can see in Figure 16, other organisms also have some very effective ways to avoid becoming a predator's next meal.

Reading Checkpoint What are two predator adaptations?

Symbiosis

Many of the interactions in the saguaro community you read about are examples of symbiosis. **Symbiosis** (sim bee OH sis) is a close relationship between two species that benefits at least one of the species. ⬤ **The three types of symbiotic relationships are mutualism, commensalism, and parasitism.**

Mutualism A relationship in which both species benefit is called **mutualism** (MYOO choo uh liz um). The relationship between the saguaro and the long-eared bats is an example of mutualism. The bats benefit because the cactus flowers provide them with food. The saguaro benefits as its pollen is carried to another plant on the bat's nose.

In some cases of mutualism, two species are so dependent on each other that neither could live without the other. This is true for some species of acacia trees and stinging ants in Central and South America. The stinging ants nest only in the acacia tree, whose thorns discourage the ants' predators. The tree also provides the ants' only food. The ants, in turn, attack other animals that approach the tree and clear competing plants away from the base of the tree. To survive, each species needs the other.

Commensalism A relationship in which one species benefits and the other species is neither helped nor harmed is called **commensalism** (kuh MEN suh liz um). The red-tailed hawks' interaction with the saguaro is an example of commensalism. The hawks benefit by having a place to build their nest, while the cactus is not affected by the hawks.

Commensalism is not very common in nature because two species are usually either helped or harmed a little by any interaction. For example, by creating a small hole for its nest in the cactus stem, the elf owl slightly damages the cactus.

FIGURE 17
Mutualism
Three yellow-billed oxpeckers get a cruise and a snack aboard an obliging hippopotamus. The oxpeckers eat ticks living on the hippo's skin. Since both the birds and the hippo benefit from this interaction, it is an example of mutualism.

Parasitism **Parasitism** (PA ruh sit iz um) involves one organism living on or inside another organism and harming it. The organism that benefits is called a **parasite,** and the organism it lives on or in is called a **host.** The parasite is usually smaller than the host. In a parasitic relationship, the parasite benefits from the interaction while the host is harmed.

Some common parasites are fleas, ticks, and leeches. These parasites have adaptations that enable them to attach to their host and feed on its blood. Other parasites live inside the host's body, such as tapeworms that live inside the digestive systems of dogs, wolves, and some other mammals.

Unlike a predator, a parasite does not usually kill the organism it feeds on. If the host dies, the parasite loses its source of food. An interesting example of this rule is shown by a species of mite that lives in the ears of moths. The mites almost always live in just one of the moth's ears. If they live in both ears, the moth's hearing is so badly affected that it is likely to be quickly caught and eaten by its predator, a bat.

FIGURE 18
Parasitism
Ticks feed on the blood of certain animals. *Predicting How will the tick affect its host?*

 Reading Checkpoint **Why doesn't a parasite usually kill its host?**

Section 4 Assessment

S 6.5.c; E-LA: Reading 6.1.0

Vocabulary Skill Use Related Words Complete the sentence by using the correct form of *prey* or *predation.* _____ affects the population size of owls, mice, rabbits, and other animals.

Reviewing Key Concepts

1. a. **Defining** What are adaptations?
   b. **Explaining** How are a snake's sharp fangs an adaptation that helps it survive in the saguaro community?
   c. **Developing Hypotheses** Explain how natural selection in snakes might have led to adaptations such as sharp fangs.

2. a. **Reviewing** What are three main ways in which organisms interact?
   b. **Classifying** Give one example of each type of interaction.

3. a. **Listing** List the three types of symbiotic relationships.
   b. **Comparing and Contrasting** For each type of symbiotic relationship, explain how the two organisms are affected.

c. **Applying Concepts** Some of your classroom plants are dying. Others that you planted at the same time and cared for in the same way are growing well. When you look closely at the dying plants, you see tiny mites on them. Which symbiotic relationship is likely occurring between the plants and mites? Explain.

Lab zone At-Home **Activity**

Feeding Frenzy You and your family can observe interactions among organisms at a bird feeder. Fill a clean, dry, 2-liter bottle with birdseed. With paper clips, attach a plastic plate to the neck of the bottle. Then hang your feeder outside where you can see it easily. Observe the feeder at different times of the day, using binoculars if available. Keep a log of all the organisms you see near it and of how they interact.

Section 5

Cycles of Matter

CALIFORNIA Standards Focus

S 6.5.b Students know matter is transferred over time from one organism to others in the food web and between organisms and the physical environment.

- What processes are involved in the water cycle?
- How are carbon and oxygen recycled in ecosystems?
- What is the nitrogen cycle?

Key Term
- nitrogen fixation

FIGURE 19
Water Cycle
This cheetah is drinking from a pool of fresh water that formed as part of the water cycle.

Lab zone Standards Warm-Up

What's the Matter?

1. Hold a small mirror a few centimeters from your mouth.
2. Exhale onto the mirror.
3. Observe the surface of the mirror.

Think It Over
Inferring What is the substance that forms on the mirror? Where did this substance come from?

A pile of crumpled cars is ready for loading into a giant compactor. The aluminum and copper pieces have already been removed so that they can be recycled, or used again. Now the steel will be reclaimed at a recycling plant. Earth has a limited supply of aluminum, copper, and the iron used in steel. Recycling old cars is one way to ensure a steady supply of these materials.

Like the supply of metal for building cars, the supply of matter in an ecosystem is limited. Matter in an ecosystem includes water, carbon, oxygen, nitrogen, and many other substances. Matter is transferred from one organism to another in the food web and between organisms and the environment. If matter could not be recycled in this way, ecosystems would quickly run out of the raw materials necessary for life. In this section, you will learn about some cycles of matter: the water cycle, the carbon and oxygen cycles, and the nitrogen cycle.

The Water Cycle

Water is essential for life. To ensure a steady supply, Earth's water must be recycled. Recall that the water cycle is the continuous process by which water moves from Earth's surface to the atmosphere and back. **The processes of evaporation, condensation, and precipitation make up the water cycle.** The heat of the sun provides the energy for the water cycle.

Living things are also involved in the water cycle. For example, plants absorb water from the soil through their roots and then release water vapor into the air through pores in their leaves. You release liquid water in your wastes and water vapor when you exhale.

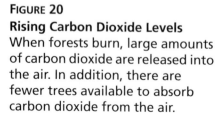

Lab zone Try This **Activity**

Carbon and Oxygen Blues

This activity explores the role of producers in the carbon and oxygen cycles.

1. Your teacher will provide you with two plastic cups containing bromthymol blue solution. Bromthymol blue solution appears blue in the absence of carbon dioxide and appears yellow in the presence of carbon dioxide. Note the color of the solution.

2. Place two sprigs of an *Elodea* plant into one of the cups. Do not put any *Elodea* into the second cup. Cover both cups with plastic wrap. Wash your hands.

3. Place the cups where they will not be disturbed. Observe the two cups over the next few days. Note any color changes.

Inferring What do your observations indicate about the role of producers in the carbon and oxygen cycles?

The Carbon and Oxygen Cycles

Two other substances necessary for life are carbon and oxygen. Carbon is a major building block in the bodies of living things. Most organisms use oxygen for their life processes. **In ecosystems, the processes by which carbon and oxygen are recycled are linked. Producers, consumers, and decomposers play roles in recycling carbon and oxygen.**

The Carbon Cycle Producers take in carbon dioxide gas from the air during photosynthesis. They use carbon from the carbon dioxide to make food molecules—carbon-containing molecules such as sugars and starches. When consumers eat producers, they take in the carbon-containing food molecules. When consumers break down these food molecules to obtain energy, they release carbon dioxide and water as waste products. When producers and consumers die, decomposers break down their remains and return carbon compounds to the soil. Some decomposers also release carbon dioxide as a waste product.

The Oxygen Cycle Like carbon, oxygen cycles through ecosystems. Producers release oxygen as a result of photosynthesis. Most organisms take in oxygen from the air or water and use it to carry out their life processes.

Human Impact Human activities also affect the levels of carbon and oxygen in the atmosphere. When humans burn oil and other fuels, carbon dioxide is released into the atmosphere. When humans clear forests for lumber, fuel, and farmland, carbon dioxide levels also rise. As you know, producers take in carbon dioxide during photosynthesis. When trees are removed from the ecosystem, there are fewer producers to absorb carbon dioxide. There is a greater effect if trees are burned down to clear a forest. If trees are burned down to clear a forest, additional carbon dioxide is released in the burning process.

Reading Checkpoint What role do producers play in the carbon and oxygen cycles?

FIGURE 20
Rising Carbon Dioxide Levels
When forests burn, large amounts of carbon dioxide are released into the air. In addition, there are fewer trees available to absorb carbon dioxide from the air.

FIGURE 21
Carbon and Oxygen Cycles

This scene shows how the carbon and oxygen cycles are linked. Producers, consumers, and decomposers all play a role in recycling these two substances.
Interpreting Diagrams *How do human activities affect the carbon and oxygen cycles?*

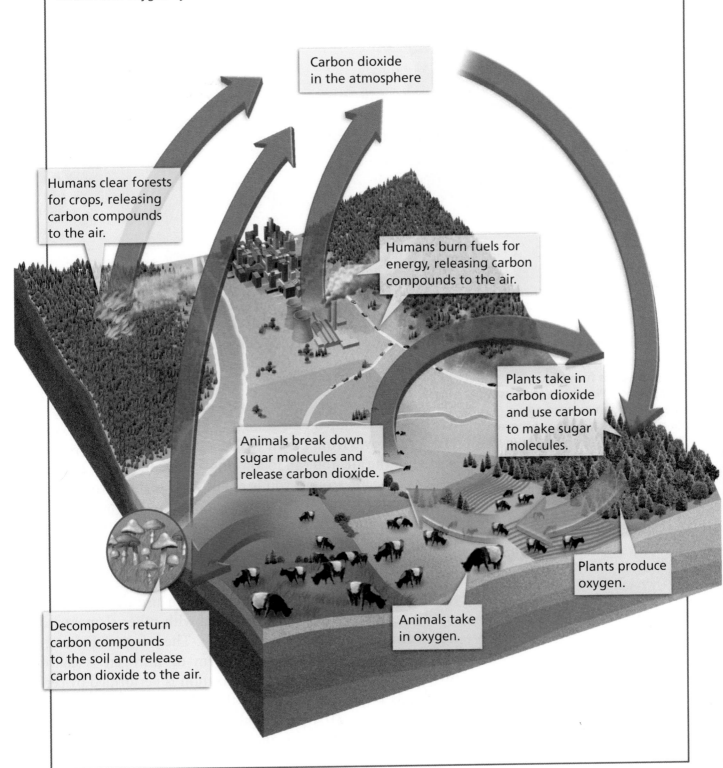

Carbon dioxide in the atmosphere

Humans clear forests for crops, releasing carbon compounds to the air.

Humans burn fuels for energy, releasing carbon compounds to the air.

Plants take in carbon dioxide and use carbon to make sugar molecules.

Animals break down sugar molecules and release carbon dioxide.

Plants produce oxygen.

Decomposers return carbon compounds to the soil and release carbon dioxide to the air.

Animals take in oxygen.

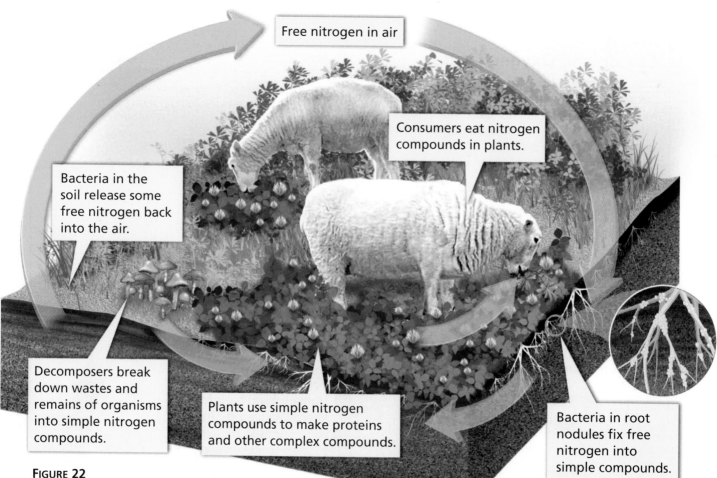

Free nitrogen in air

Consumers eat nitrogen compounds in plants.

Bacteria in the soil release some free nitrogen back into the air.

Decomposers break down wastes and remains of organisms into simple nitrogen compounds.

Plants use simple nitrogen compounds to make proteins and other complex compounds.

Bacteria in root nodules fix free nitrogen into simple compounds.

FIGURE 22
Nitrogen Cycle

In the nitrogen cycle, free nitrogen from the air is fixed into compounds. Plants can then use these nitrogen compounds in carrying out their life processes.
Relating Cause and Effect *How does nitrogen get returned to the environment?*

The Nitrogen Cycle

Like carbon, nitrogen is a necessary building block in the matter that makes up living things. 🔵 **In the nitrogen cycle, nitrogen moves from the air to the soil, into living things, and back into the air.** You can follow this process in Figure 22.

Since the air around you is about 78 percent nitrogen gas, you might think that it would be easy for living things to obtain nitrogen. However, most organisms cannot use nitrogen gas. Nitrogen gas is called "free" nitrogen because it is not combined with other kinds of atoms.

Nitrogen Fixation Most organisms can use nitrogen only once it has been "fixed," or combined with other elements to form nitrogen-containing compounds. The process of changing free nitrogen into a usable form of nitrogen is called **nitrogen fixation.** Most nitrogen fixation is performed by certain kinds of bacteria. Some of these bacteria live in bumps called nodules (NAHJ oolz) on the roots of certain plants. These plants, known as legumes, include clover, beans, peas, alfalfa, and peanuts.

The relationship between the bacteria and the legumes is an example of mutualism. Both the bacteria and the plant benefit from this relationship: The bacteria feed on the plant's sugars, and the plant is supplied with nitrogen in a usable form.

Return of Nitrogen to the Environment

Once nitrogen has been fixed, producers can use it to build proteins and other complex compounds. Decomposers, in turn, break down these complex compounds in animal wastes and the bodies of dead organisms. Decomposition returns simple nitrogen compounds to the soil. Nitrogen can cycle from the soil to producers and then to consumers many times. At some point, however, bacteria break down the nitrogen compounds completely. These bacteria then release free nitrogen back into the air. The cycle continues from there.

 **Reading Checkpoint** Where do some nitrogen-fixing bacteria live?

FIGURE 23
Growth in Nitrogen-Poor Soil
Pitcher plants can grow in nitrogen-poor soil because they have another way of obtaining nitrogen. Insects become trapped in the plant's tube-shaped leaves. The plant then digests the insects and uses their nitrogen compounds for its functions.

Section 5 Assessment

S 6.5.b; E-LA: Reading 6.2.0, Writing 6.2.1

Target Reading Skill Sequence Review the text that follows the blue heading The Carbon Cycle on page 418. Create a diagram of the cycle.

Reviewing Key Concepts

1. **a. Defining** Define the three major processes that occur during the water cycle.
   b. Making Generalizations Defend this statement: The sun is the driving force behind the water cycle.
2. **a. Reviewing** Which two substances are linked in one recycling process?
   b. Comparing and Contrasting What role do producers play in the carbon and oxygen cycles? What role do consumers play in these cycles?
   c. Developing Hypotheses How might the death of all the producers in a community affect the carbon and oxygen cycles?

3. **a. Reviewing** Why do organisms need nitrogen?
   b. Sequencing Outline the major steps in the nitrogen cycle.
   c. Predicting What might happen in a community if all the nitrogen-fixing bacteria died?

Writing in Science

Comic Strip Choose one of the cycles discussed in this section. Then draw a comic strip with five panels that depicts the important events in the cycle. Remember that the last panel must end with the same event that begins the first panel.

Section 6
Changes in Communities

How do primary and secondary succession differ?

Key Terms
- succession
- primary succession
- pioneer species
- secondary succession

In 1988, huge fires raged through the forests of Yellowstone National Park. The fires were so hot that they jumped from tree to tree without burning along the ground. It took months for the fires to burn out. All that remained were thousands of blackened tree trunks sticking out of the ground like charred toothpicks.

Could a forest community recover from such disastrous fires? It might seem unlikely. But within just a few months, signs of life had returned. First, tiny green shoots of new grass poked through the sooty ground. Then, small tree seedlings began to grow. The forest was coming back! After 15 years, young forests were flourishing in many areas.

Fires, earthquakes, volcanic eruptions, landslides, floods, and other natural disasters can change human and wildlife habitats very quickly. But even without such disasters, communities change. The series of predictable changes that occur in a community over time is called **succession.**

Changes in a
Yellowstone community ▼

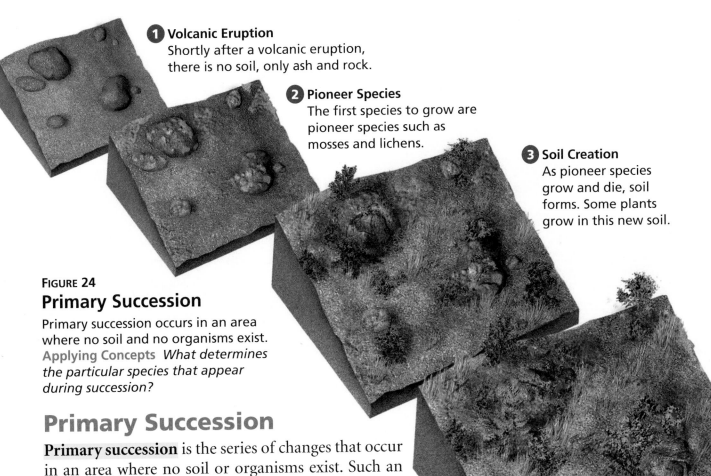

1 **Volcanic Eruption**
Shortly after a volcanic eruption, there is no soil, only ash and rock.

2 **Pioneer Species**
The first species to grow are pioneer species such as mosses and lichens.

3 **Soil Creation**
As pioneer species grow and die, soil forms. Some plants grow in this new soil.

4 **Fertile Soil and Maturing Plants**
As more plants die, they decompose and make the soil more fertile. New plants grow, and existing plants mature in the fertile soil.

FIGURE 24
Primary Succession
Primary succession occurs in an area where no soil and no organisms exist. Applying Concepts *What determines the particular species that appear during succession?*

Primary Succession

Primary succession is the series of changes that occur in an area where no soil or organisms exist. Such an area might be a new island formed by the eruption of an undersea volcano or an area of rock uncovered by a melting sheet of ice.

Figure 24 shows the series of changes in an area after a violent volcanic eruption. The first species to populate the area are called **pioneer species.** They are often carried to the area by wind or water. Typical pioneer species are mosses or lichens, which are fungi and algae growing in a symbiotic relationship. As pioneer species grow, they help break up the rocks and form soil. When the organisms die, they provide nutrients that enrich the thin layer of soil that is forming on the rocks.

Over time, plant seeds land in the new soil and begin to grow. The specific plants that grow depend on the climate of the area. For example, in a cool, northern area, early seedlings might include alder and cottonwood trees. Eventually, succession may lead to a community of organisms that does not change unless the ecosystem is disturbed. Reaching this mature community can take centuries.

Reading Checkpoint **What are some pioneer species?**

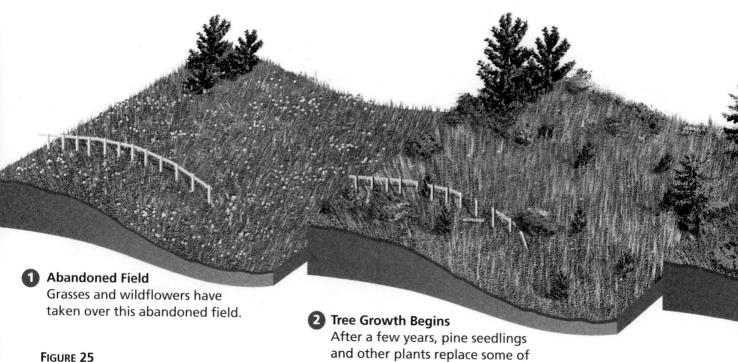

1 Abandoned Field
Grasses and wildflowers have taken over this abandoned field.

2 Tree Growth Begins
After a few years, pine seedlings and other plants replace some of the grasses and wildflowers.

FIGURE 25
Secondary Succession

Secondary succession occurs following a disturbance to an ecosystem, such as clearing a forest for farmland.

Go Online
SciLINKS NSTA

For: Links on succession
Visit: www.SciLinks.org
Web Code: scn-0514

Secondary Succession

The changes following the Yellowstone fire were an example of secondary succession. **Secondary succession** is the series of changes that occur in an area where the ecosystem has been disturbed, but where soil and organisms still exist. Natural disturbances that have this effect include fires, hurricanes, and tornadoes. Human activities, such as farming, logging, or mining, may also disturb an ecosystem. 🔑 **Unlike primary succession, secondary succession occurs in a place where an ecosystem currently exists.**

Secondary succession usually occurs more rapidly than primary succession. Consider, for example, an abandoned field in the southeastern United States. You can follow the process of succession in such a field in Figure 25. After a century, a hardwood forest is developing. This forest community may remain for a long time.

 **Reading Checkpoint** What are two natural events that can disturb an ecosystem?

3 **A Forest Develops**
As tree growth continues, the trees begin to crowd out the grasses and wildflowers.

4 **Mature Community**
Eventually, a mixed forest of pine, oak, and hickory dominates the landscape.

Section 6 Assessment

S 6.2.d, 6.5.e; E-LA: Reading 6.2.0

Target Reading Skill Sequence Review the steps in Figure 25 Secondary Succession. Would you use a cycle diagram or a flowchart to show this proccess. Why?

Reviewing Key Concepts

1. a. Defining What is primary succession? What is secondary succession?
   b. Comparing and Contrasting How do primary succession and secondary succession differ?
   c. Classifying Grass poking through a crack in a sidewalk is an example of succession. Is it primary succession or secondary succession? Explain.

Lab zone **At-Home Activity**

Community Changes Interview a family member or neighbor who has lived in your neighborhood for a long time. Ask the person to describe how the neighborhood has changed over time. Have areas that were formerly grassy been paved or developed? Have any farms, parks, or lots returned to a wild state? Write a summary of your interview. Can you classify any of the changes as examples of succession?

Lab zone Skills Lab
Guided Inquiry

Change in a Tiny Community

Materials

small baby-food jar

wax pencil

hay solution

pond water

plastic dropper

microscope slide

coverslip

microscope

Problem How can you observe energy roles in a pond community?

Skills Focus observing, classifying

Procedure

1. Use a wax pencil to label a small jar with your name.

2. Fill the jar about three-fourths full with hay solution. Add pond water until the jar is nearly full. Examine the mixture and record your observations in your notebook.

3. Place the jar in a safe location out of direct sunlight where it will remain undisturbed. Always wash your hands thoroughly with soap after handling the jar or its contents.

4. After two days, examine the contents of the jar and record your observations.

5. Use a plastic dropper to collect a few drops from the surface of the solution in the jar. Make a slide following the procedures in the yellow box at the right. **CAUTION:** *Slides and coverslips are fragile, and their edges are sharp. Handle them carefully.*

6. Examine the slide under a microscope, using both low and high power and following the procedures in the box at the right. Draw each type of organism you observe. Estimate the number of each type in your sample. The illustration below shows some of the organisms you might see.

7. Repeat Steps 5 and 6 with a drop of solution taken from the side of the jar beneath the surface.

8. Repeat Steps 5 and 6 with a drop of solution taken from the bottom of the jar. When you are finished, follow your teacher's directions about cleaning up.

9. After 3 days, repeat Steps 5 through 8.

10. After 3 more days, repeat Steps 5 through 8 again. Then follow your teacher's directions for returning the solution.

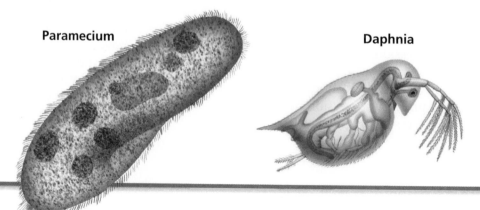

Paramecium

Daphnia

Analyze and Conclude

1. **Classifying** Identify as many of the organisms you observed as possible. Use the diagrams on the facing page and any other resources your teacher provides.

2. **Observing** Producers usually contain chlorophyll, a substance that helps them capture sunlight for photosynthesis. Chlorophyll makes an organism look green. Which organisms appear to be producers?

3. **Inferring** Which organisms appear to be consumers? Explain your answer.

4. **Observing** How did the community change over the period of time that you made your observations?

5. **Inferring** What biotic factors may have influenced the changes in this community? Explain.

6. **Communicating** Based on what you have observed in this lab, draw a simple food chain from this community.

More to Explore

Use library materials to research the organisms you observed in your sample of pond water. Based on your research, draw a food web showing how food energy is transferred from organism to organism in the pond community. Classify the organisms in your food web as producers and consumers (herbivores, omnivores, or carnivores).

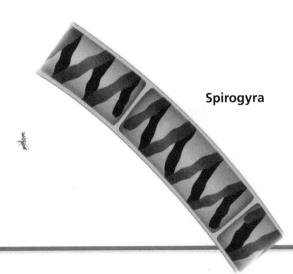

Spirogyra

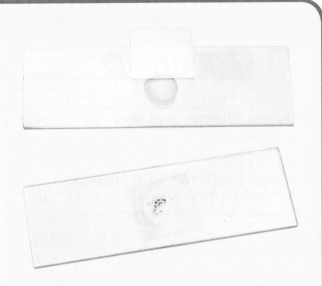

Making and Viewing a Slide

A. Place one drop of the solution to be examined in the middle of a microscope slide. Place one edge of a coverslip at the edge of the drop, as shown in the photo. Gently lower the coverslip over the drop. Try not to trap any air bubbles

B. Place the slide on the stage of a microscope so the drop is over the opening in the stage. Adjust the stage clips to hold the slide.

C. Look from the side of the microscope, and use the coarse adjustment knob to move the low-power objective close to, but not touching, the coverslip.

D. Look through the eyepiece and use the coarse adjustment knob to raise the body tube and bring the slide into view. Use the fine adjustment knob to bring the slide into focus.

E. To view the slide under high power, look from the side of the microscope and revolve the nosepiece until the high-power objective clicks into place just over, but not touching, the slide.

F. While you are looking through the eyepiece, use the fine adjustment knob to bring the slide into focus.

Chapter 10

Study Guide

The BIG Idea Organisms in ecosystems exchange energy and nutrients among themselves and with the environment.

1 Living Things and the Environment

Key Concepts   S 6.5.e

- An organism obtains food, water, shelter, and other things it needs to live, grow, and reproduce from its environment.

- An organism interacts with both the living and nonliving parts of its habitat.

- The smallest unit of organization is a single organism, which belongs to a population of its species. The population belongs to a community of different species. The community and abiotic factors together form an ecosystem.

Key Terms
- organism   • habitat   • biotic factor
- abiotic factor   • photosynthesis   • species
- population   • community   • ecosystem
- ecology

2 Populations

Key Concepts   S 6.5.e

- Populations can change in size when new members join the population or when members leave the population.

- Some limiting factors for populations are food and water, space, light, soil, and weather.

Key Terms
- birth rate   • death rate   • immigration
- emigration   • limiting factor
- carrying capacity

3 Energy Flow in Ecosystems

Key Concepts   S 6.5.a, c

- Each organism in an ecosystem fills the energy role of producer, consumer, or decomposer.

- The transfer of energy from organism to organism in an ecosystem can be shown in diagrams called food chains and food webs.

- The most energy is available at the producer level of an energy pyramid.

Key Terms
- producer   • consumer   • herbivore
- carnivore   • omnivore   • scavenger
- decomposer   • food chain   • food web
- energy pyramid

4 Interactions Among Living Things

Key Concepts   S 6.5.c

- Every organism has a variety of adaptations that are suited to its specific living conditions.

- The major types of interactions among organisms are competition, predation, and symbiosis.

- The three types of symbiotic relationships are mutualism, commensalism, and parasitism.

Key Terms
- natural selection   • adaptations   • niche
- competition   • predation   • predator   • prey
- symbiosis   • mutualism   • commensalism
- parasitism   • parasite   • host

5 Cycles of Matter

Key Concepts   S 6.5.b

- The processes of evaporation, condensation, and precipitation make up the water cycle.

- In ecosystems, the processes by which carbon and oxygen are recycled are linked. Living things recycle carbon and oxygen.

- In the nitrogen cycle, nitrogen moves from the air to soil, to living things, and back to the air.

Key Term
- nitrogen fixation

6 Changes in Communities

Key Concept   S 6.2.d; 6.5.e

- Unlike primary succession, secondary succession occurs in an existing ecosystem.

Key Terms
- succession   • primary succession
- pioneer species   • secondary succession

Review and Assessment

🎯 Target Reading Skill

Sequence In your notebook, copy the graphic organizer for the Nitrogen Cycle. Then complete it.

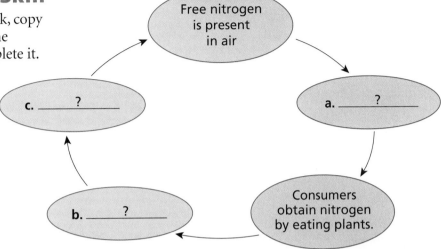

The Nitrogen Cycle

Free nitrogen is present in air

a. ___?___

Consumers obtain nitrogen by eating plants.

b. ___?___

c. ___?___

Reviewing Key Terms

Choose the letter of the best answer.

1. A prairie dog, a hawk, and a badger all are members of the same
   - **a.** niche.
   - **b.** community.
   - **c.** species.
   - **d.** population.

2. All of the following are examples of limiting factors for populations *except*
   - **a.** space.
   - **b.** food.
   - **c.** time.
   - **d.** weather.

3. In which type of interaction do both species benefit?
   - **a.** predation
   - **b.** mutualism
   - **c.** commensalism
   - **d.** parasitism

4. A diagram that shows how much energy is available at each feeding level in an ecosystem is a(n)
   - **a.** food chain.
   - **b.** food web.
   - **c.** energy cycle.
   - **d.** energy pyramid.

5. Which of these relationships is an example of parasitism?
   - **a.** a bird building a nest on a tree branch
   - **b.** a bat pollinating a saguaro cactus
   - **c.** a flea living on a cat's blood
   - **d.** ants protecting a tree that produces the ants' only food

Complete the following sentences so that your answers clearly explain the key terms.

6. You would expect to find an organism in its **habitat,** which is _____.

7. Any plants and animals in an organism's habitat are **biotic factors,** which are _____.

8. The flow of energy through an ecosystem can be shown in a **food web,** which is _____.

9. An organism's **niche,** or ecological role, can also be described as its _____.

10. One major type of interaction between organisms is **competition,** which is _____.

Writing in Science

Descriptive Paragraph Use what you have learned about predators and prey to write about an interaction between two organisms. For each organism, describe at least one adaptation that helps it either catch prey or fend off predators.

Video Assessment

Discovery Channel School
Populations and Communities

Review and Assessment

Checking Concepts

11. Name two biotic and two abiotic factors you might find in a forest ecosystem.

12. Explain how plants and algae use sunlight. How is this process important to other living things in an ecosystem?

13. Give an example showing how space can be a limiting factor for a population.

14. Describe two adaptations that prey organisms have developed to protect themselves. Tell how each adaptation protects the organism.

15. Name and describe each of the three energy roles organisms can play in an ecosystem.

16. How are food chains and food webs different?

Thinking Critically

17. Classifying Which organisms in the illustration at the right are producers? Consumers?

18. Relating Cause and Effect In the nitrogen cycle, how does free nitrogen become available for organisms to use?

19. Inferring What is the source of energy for most ecosystems? Explain.

20. Classifying Lichens and mosses have just begun to grow on the rocky area below. Which type of succession is occurring? Explain.

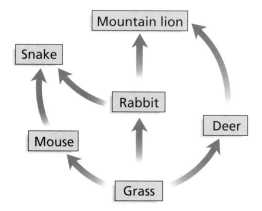

Math Practice

21. Inequalities Review the two inequalities about population size. Then revise each inequality to include immigration and emigration in addition to birth rate and death rate.

Applying Skills

Use the data in the food web below to answer Questions 22-25.

```
            Mountain lion
  Snake
              Rabbit
                          Deer
  Mouse
              Grass
```

22. Interpreting Diagrams Which organism in this food web fills the role of producer?

23. Classifying Specify whether each consumer in this food web is a first-level, second-level, or third-level consumer.

24. Inferring Which level of the food web has the greatest amount of available energy?

25. Predicting If a disease were to kill most of the rabbits in this area, predict how the snakes, deer, and mountain lions would be affected?

Lab zone **Standards Investigation**

Performance Assessment Review your report and graph to be sure that they clearly state your conclusion about the effects of crowding on plant growth. With your group, decide how you will present your results. After your presentation, list some improvements to your experimental plan.

Choose the letter of the best answer.

1. In the food chain shown in the diagram below, which of the following organisms obtains its energy directly from the frog?

   A grass
   B grasshopper
   C snake
   D owl

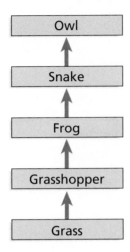

   S 6.5.a

2. A freshwater lake has a muddy bottom, which is home to different types of algae and other organisms. Many species of fish feed on the algae. Which of the following is an abiotic factor in this ecosystem?

   A the temperature of the water
   B the color of the algae
   C the number of species of fish
   D the amount of food available to the fish

   S 6.5.e

3. Although three different bird species all live in the same tree in an area, competition between the birds rarely occurs. The most likely explanation for this lack of competition is that these birds

   A occupy different niches.
   B eat the same food.
   C have a limited supply of food.
   D live in the same part of the trees.   *S 6.5.c*

4. Which pair of terms could apply to the same organism?

   A carnivore and producer
   B omnivore and producer
   C scavenger and herbivore
   D carnivore and consumer   *S 6.5.c*

Use the energy pyramid below and your knowledge of science to answer Questions 5 and 6.

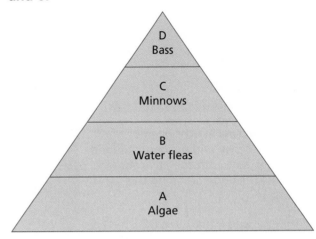

5. Which organisms are the producers in this ecosystem?

   A algae
   B minnows
   C water fleas
   D bass   *S 6.5.c*

6. At which level of this energy pyramid is the LEAST energy available?

   A level A
   B level B
   C level C
   D level D   *S 6.5.b*

7. Which of the following events would most likely lead to primary succession?

   A a hurricane
   B a volcanic eruption
   C a fire
   D abandonment of a farm field   *S 6.2.d*

8. Describe the path of carbon as it travels through the carbon cycle. Begin with the atmosphere. Include the role of producers, consumers, and decomposers.

   S 6.5.b

Chapter 11

Living Resources

The migrating salmon in this Alaska river provide food for grizzly bears. ▶

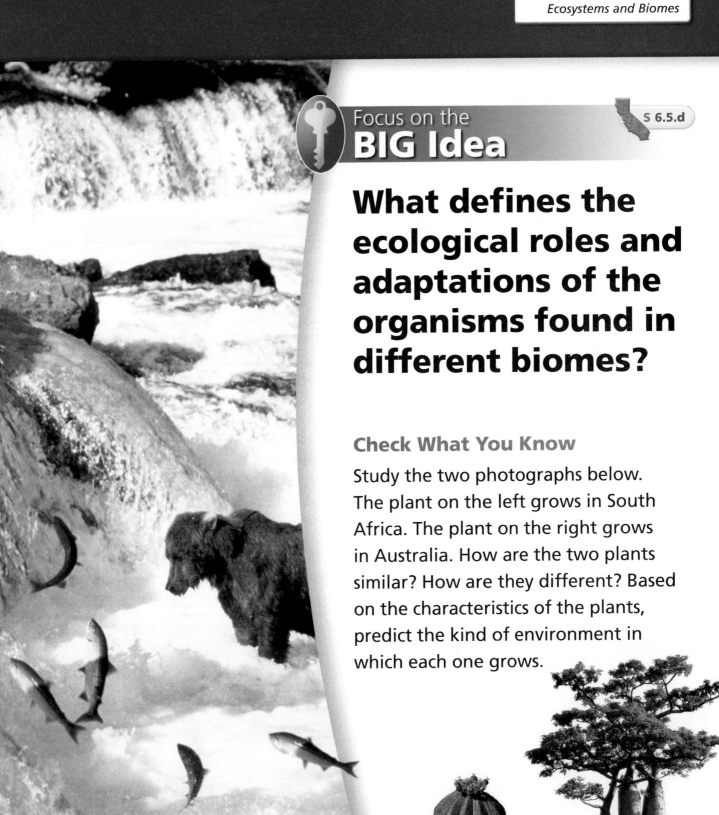

Focus on the
BIG Idea

S 6.5.d

What defines the ecological roles and adaptations of the organisms found in different biomes?

Check What You Know

Study the two photographs below. The plant on the left grows in South Africa. The plant on the right grows in Australia. How are the two plants similar? How are they different? Based on the characteristics of the plants, predict the kind of environment in which each one grows.

Build Science Vocabulary

The images shown here represent some of the key terms in this chapter. You can use this vocabulary skill to help you understand the meaning of some key terms in this chapter.

Vocabulary Skill

High-Use Academic Words

Knowing these high-use academic words will help you understand, discuss, and write about the science content in this chapter.

Word	Definition	Example Sentence
source (sawrs) p. 453	*n.* The beginning; the origin	The sun is our main <u>source</u> of energy.
resource (REE sawrs) p. 453	*n.* A material or living thing that people can use	Coal and oil are <u>resources</u> that we depend on.
sustain (suh STAYN) p. 455	*v.* To keep up; to maintain	Food and water are necessary to <u>sustain</u> humans.
distinct (dih STINKT) p. 436	*adj.* Different; not the same	Each type of bird is <u>distinct</u>.

Apply It!

Choose the word from the table that best completes the sentence.
1. Forests are a natural _____.
2. Trees in the rain forest form several _____ layers.
3. We can _____ our forests by planting new trees to replace those that we cut down.
4. Insects are a _____ of food for reptiles, birds, and mammals.

grassland

estuary

selective cutting

endangered species

Chapter 11
Vocabulary

Build Science Vocabulary
Online
Visit: PHSchool.com
Web Code: cwj-4110

How to Read Science

Identify Main Ideas

The main idea in a paragraph is the most important, or biggest, idea. Sometimes the main idea is stated directly. At other times you must identify the main idea yourself. Here are some tips.

- Read carefully the first and last few sentences in the paragraph.
- Identify the main idea of the paragraph.
- Identify a few important details about the topic.

Read the paragraph below. In your notebook, write the main idea in the first box. Under it, write a few supporting details.

Freshwater ecosystems provide habitats for an amazing variety of organisms. Streams and rivers are home to animals like trout that are adapted to fast-moving water. Ponds are bodies of still, fresh water where dragonflies, turtles, and frogs live. In the open water of lakes and ponds, sunfish feed on insects.

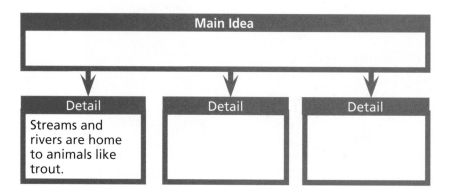

Main Idea

Detail	Detail	Detail
Streams and rivers are home to animals like trout.		

Apply It!

Complete your graphic organizer by answering the following questions.

1. What is the main idea of the paragraph?
2. What details support the main idea?

Complete a graphic organizer like the one above for paragraphs in Sections 2 and 4.

Breaking It Down

Nothing in an ecosystem is wasted. Even when living things die, organisms such as mushrooms recycle them. This natural process of breakdown is called decomposition. When fallen leaves and other waste products decompose, a fluffy brown mixture called compost is formed. You can observe decomposition firsthand in this chapter project by building a compost chamber.

Your Goal

To design and conduct an experiment to learn more about the process of decomposition

To complete this investigation, you must

- build two compost chambers
- investigate the effect of one of the following variables on decomposition: moisture, oxygen, temperature, or activity of soil organisms
- analyze your data and present your results
- follow the safety guidelines in Appendix A

Plan It!

Your teacher will provide you with a sample of compost material. Observe the wastes in the mixture with a hand lens. Write a hypothesis about which kinds of waste will decay and which will not. Next, decide which variable you will test and plan how you will test it. Once your teacher approves your plan, build your compost chambers and begin the experiment.

Biomes

CALIFORNIA
Standards Focus

S 6.5.d Students know different kinds of organisms may play similar ecological roles in similar biomes.

S 6.5.e Students know the number and types of organisms an ecosystem can support depends on the resources available and on abiotic factors, such as quantities of light and water, a range of temperatures, and soil composition.

- What factors determine the type of biome found in an area?
- What are the six major biomes?

Key Terms

- biome
- desert
- canopy
- understory
- grassland
- savanna
- deciduous tree
- coniferous tree
- tundra
- permafrost

Video Field Trip
Discovery Channel School
Ecosystems and Biomes

Lab zone Standards Warm-Up

How Much Rain Is That?

The table shows the typical amount of precipitation that falls each year in four locations. With your classmates, you will create a full-sized bar graph on a wall to represent these amounts.

Location	Precipitation (cm)
Mojave Desert	15
Illinois Prairie	70
Great Smoky Mountains	180
Costa Rican Rain Forest	350

1. Using a meter stick, measure a strip of adding-machine paper 15 centimeters long. Label this strip "Mojave Desert."
2. Repeat Step 1 for the other locations. Label each strip.
3. Follow your teacher's instructions on hanging your strips.

Think It Over
Developing Hypotheses What effect might the amount of precipitation have on the types of plants that live in a location?

Congratulations! You've been selected to go on a world expedition to explore Earth's biomes. A **biome** is a region with a certain climate and certain forms of vegetation. You'll be visiting places ranging from steamy tropical forests to frozen Arctic plains. **It is mostly the climate—temperature and precipitation—in an area that determines its biome.** Climate limits the species of plants that can grow in an area, which in turn determine what other organisms can live there.

Different organisms living in similar biomes may play similar ecological roles. For example, most continents have a large area of flat, grassy plains. So these continents have organisms that fill the role, or niche, of "large, grazing herbivore." In North America, these herbivores are the bison. In Africa, they are wildebeests and antelopes. And in Australia, they are kangaroos.

Ecologists classify biomes in different ways. **The six major biomes are the desert, rain forest, grassland, deciduous forest, boreal forest, and tundra.**

Desert Biomes

The first stop on your expedition is a desert. You step off the bus into searing summer heat. At midday, it is too hot to walk outside in the desert.

A **desert** is an area that receives less than 25 centimeters of rain per year. The amount of evaporation in a desert is greater than the amount of precipitation. Some of the driest deserts may not receive any precipitation in a year!

Deserts often undergo large shifts in temperature during the course of a day. A scorching hot desert like the Namib Desert in Africa cools rapidly each night when the sun goes down. Other deserts, such as the Mojave in the southwestern United States, are very hot in the summer but often experience freezing temperatures in the winter.

Organisms that live in the desert must be adapted to the lack of rain and extreme temperatures. For example, the stem of a saguaro cactus has folds that work like the pleats in an accordion. The stem expands to store water when it is raining. Gila monsters can spend weeks at a time in their cool underground burrows. Many other desert animals are most active at night when the temperatures are cooler.

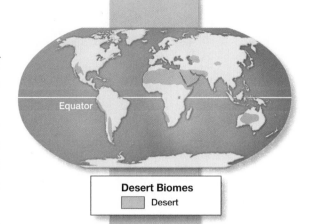

Desert Biomes
☐ Desert

FIGURE 1
Desert
The Mojave Desert in California is a typical hot desert.
Making Generalizations *Describe the climate conditions of a typical desert.*

Gambel's quail

Australian Rain Forest

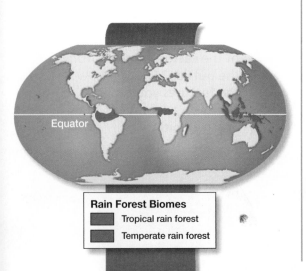

▲ Lumholtz's tree kangaroo

FIGURE 2

Rain Forest Roles
Tree kangaroos and spider monkeys live in different rain forests on opposite sides of the world. But both are consumers living in the forest canopy.

Equator

Rain Forest Biomes
■ Tropical rain forest
■ Temperate rain forest

Rain Forest Biomes

The next stop on your trip is a rain forest. This biome is living up to its name—it's pouring! After just a short shower, however, the sun reappears. Surprisingly, though, very little sunlight reaches you through the thick leaves above. Plants are everywhere in the rain forest. And animals are flying, creeping, and slithering all around you. Although tropical rain forests cover only a small part of the planet, they probably contain more species of plants and animals than all the other biomes combined.

Tropical Rain Forests As you can see on the map, tropical rain forests are found in regions close to the equator. The climate is warm and humid all year long, and there is a lot of rain—over 200 centimeters per year. Because of these climate conditions, an astounding variety of plants grow in tropical rain forests.

Trees in the rain forest form several distinct layers. The tall trees form a leafy roof called the **canopy.** A few giant trees poke out above the canopy. Below the canopy, a second layer of shorter trees and vines forms an **understory.** Understory plants grow well in the shade formed by the canopy. The forest floor is nearly dark, so only a few plants live there.

The rich plant life in tropical rain forests provides food and habitat for many species of animals. Ecologists estimate that millions of species of insects live in tropical rain forests. In fact, the most abundant animals are ants and termites. These and other insects serve as a source of food for many reptiles, birds, and mammals. These animals are, in turn, food for other animals.

South American Rain Forest

▲ Spider monkey

Ecological Roles in Rain Forests Very different animals may play similar ecological roles in rain forests around the world. For example, mammalian consumers in South American rain forests include sloths, deer, monkeys, rodents, and cats. Consumers in Australian rain forests include kangaroos, wallabies, and bandicoots, all of which belong to a different group of mammals altogether.

The animals that live in the rain forest canopy have similar adaptations. For example, spider monkeys have hands with thumbs and tails that can grasp onto branches as they move about in the canopy. Tree kangaroos do not have grasping tails. But they use their long tails to keep their balance as they move about in the trees. Their feet have sharp claws and spongy pads that help them in climbing.

Temperate Rain Forests When you hear the term *rain forest*, you probably think of the warm, humid, tropical rain forests. But there is another type of rain forest. The northwestern coast of the United States receives more than 300 centimeters of rain per year. Huge trees grow there, including cedars, redwoods, and Douglas firs. But it is difficult to classify this region. Many ecologists refer to this ecosystem as a temperate rain forest. The term *temperate* means having moderate temperatures. The redwood forests of the northern California coast are temperate rain forests.

 **What is an understory?**

Cheetah

FIGURE 3
Savanna
Migrating wildebeests make their way across a vast Kenyan savanna. A savanna is a type of grassland that has scattered shrubs and small trees.

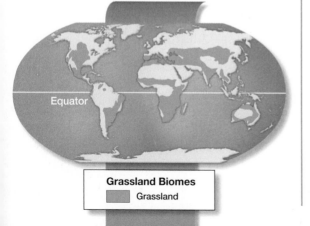

Equator

Grassland Biomes
Grassland

Grassland Biomes

The next stop on the trip is quite a change from the rain forest. You are now in a grassy plain called a prairie. The breeze carries the scent of soil warmed by the sun. The rich soil can support grasses as tall as you. Startled by your approach, sparrows dart into hiding places among the waving grass stems.

Ecologists classify prairies, which are generally found in the middle latitudes, as grasslands. A **grassland** is an area that is populated mostly by grasses and other nonwoody plants. Most grasslands receive 25 to 75 centimeters of rain each year. This amount of rain is not enough for trees to grow. Fires and droughts are common in this biome. Grasslands that are located closer to the equator than prairies are known as savannas. A **savanna** receives as much as 120 centimeters of rain per year. Scattered shrubs and small trees grow on savannas, along with grass.

Grasslands are home to many of the largest animals on Earth. Herbivores include elephants, antelopes, zebras, rhinoceroses, and giraffes in Africa, bison in North America, and kangaroos in Australia. Grazing by these large herbivores helps to maintain the grasslands. The animals keep young trees and bushes from sprouting and competing with the grass for water and sunlight.

 **Reading Checkpoint** **Which type of grassland usually receives more rainfall, a prairie or a savanna?**

Deciduous Forest Biomes

Your trip to the next biome takes you to another forest. It is now late summer. Cool mornings here give way to warm days. Several members of your group are busy recording the many plant species. Others are looking through their binoculars, trying to identify the songbirds. You step carefully to avoid a small frog.

You are now in a deciduous forest biome. Many of the trees here are **deciduous trees** (dee SIJ oo us), trees that shed their leaves and grow new ones each year. Oaks and maples are deciduous trees. Deciduous forests receive enough rain—at least 50 centimeters per year—to support the growth of trees and other plants. Temperatures in the deciduous forest vary greatly during the year. The growing season usually lasts five to six months.

The variety of plants in a deciduous forest creates many different habitats. Different species of birds live in different parts of the forest, eating the insects and fruits in their own areas. Mammals such as chipmunks and skunks live in deciduous forests. In a North American deciduous forest you might also see large herbivores that browse on leaves, such as white-tailed deer. Black bears are omnivores that eat plants and animals.

If you were to return to this biome in the winter, you would not see much wildlife. Many of the bird species migrate to warmer areas. Some of the mammals hibernate, or enter a state of greatly reduced body activity similar to sleep. Animals that hibernate rely on fat stored in their bodies during the winter months. For example, the American black bear and the Asiatic black bear store fat in late summer for use in the winter.

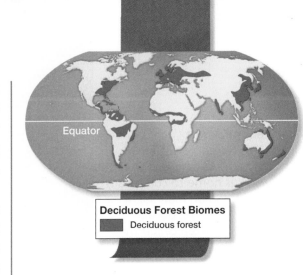

Deciduous Forest Biomes
Deciduous forest

FIGURE 4
Deciduous Forest
This forest is a beautiful example of a deciduous forest in autumn. Most of the trees in a deciduous forest have leaves that change color and drop each autumn. **Comparing and Contrasting** *How do deciduous forests differ from rain forests?*

▼ Southern flying squirrel

▼ Red fox

Lynx

FIGURE 5
Boreal Forest
This boreal forest in Alaska's Denali National Park is home to coniferous trees and animals such as moose. The boreal forest is often called the "sprucemoose" forest.

Lab zone Skills Activity

Inferring

Both the great horned owl and the golden eagle live in boreal forest biomes. The great horned owl is found in the boreal forests of North America, while the golden eagle lives in North America, Europe, and Asia. What ecological roles do you think these two birds play in their boreal habitats?

Boreal Forest Biomes

You now head north into a colder climate. The expedition leaders claim they can identify the next biome, a boreal forest, by its smell. When you arrive, you catch a whiff of the spruce and fir trees that blanket the hillsides. Feeling the chilly early fall air, you pull a jacket out of your bag.

Boreal Forest Plants Most of the trees in the boreal forest are **coniferous trees** (koh NIF ur us), trees that produce their seeds in cones and have leaves shaped like needles. The boreal forest is sometimes referred to by its Russian name, the *taiga* (TY guh). Winters in these forests are very cold. The snow can reach heights well over your head! Even so, the summers are rainy and warm enough to melt all the snow.

Trees in the boreal forest are well adapted to the cold climate. Since the water is frozen for much of the year, trees in the boreal forest have adaptations that prevent water loss. Fir, spruce, hemlock, and other coniferous trees all have thick, waxy needles that prevent water from evaporating.

Boreal Forest Animals Many of the animals of the boreal forest eat the seeds produced by the coniferous trees. These animals include red squirrels, insects, and birds such as finches and chickadees. Some herbivores, such as snowshoe hares, moose, and beavers, eat tree bark and new shoots. The variety of herbivores in the boreal forest supports many large predators, including wolves, bears, falcons, owls, and lynxes. The boreal forests of Asia even have Siberian tigers!

Equator

Boreal Forest Biomes
■ Boreal forest

Reading Checkpoint How are needles an advantage to trees in the boreal forest?

Tundra Biomes

As you arrive at your next stop, you feel the driving, chilly wind right away. The **tundra** is an extremely cold and dry biome. But don't expect deep snow. Many people are surprised to learn that the tundra receives about as much precipitation as a desert.

Most of the soil in the tundra is frozen all year. This frozen soil is called **permafrost.** During the short summer, the top layer of soil thaws, but the underlying soil remains frozen. Because rainwater cannot soak into the permafrost, there are many shallow ponds and marshy areas on the tundra in the summer.

Tundra Plants Plants of the tundra include mosses, grasses, shrubs, and dwarf forms of a few trees, such as willows. Most of the plant growth takes place during the long days of the short summer season. North of the Arctic Circle, the sun does not set during midsummer.

Tundra Animals In summer, the animals you might remember most are insects. Insect-eating birds take advantage of the plentiful food. Large numbers of waterfowl nest in the marshes. When winter approaches, these birds migrate south. Mammals of the tundra include caribou, musk oxen, foxes, wolves, and Arctic hares. The mammals that remain on the tundra during the winter grow thick fur coats. What can these animals find to eat on the tundra in winter? The caribou scrape snow away to find lichens. Wolves follow the caribou and look for weak members of the herd to prey upon.

Reading Checkpoint What is permafrost?

Tundra Biomes

Tundra

FIGURE 6
Tundra
Although it is frozen and seemingly barren in winter, the tundra in Alaska explodes with color in autumn.
Relating Cause and Effect *Why are there no tall trees on the tundra?*

Musk ox ▲

FIGURE 7
Ice
Polar bears live for much of the year on sea ice that covers the Arctic Ocean.

Go Online
active art

For: Earth's Biomes activity
Visit: PHSchool.com
Web Code: cep-5024

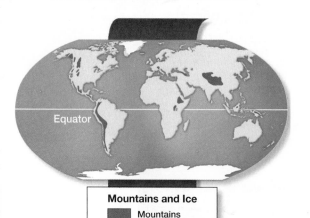

Equator

Mountains and Ice
◼ Mountains
☐ Ice

Mountains and Ice

Some areas of land are not part of any major biome. These areas include land that is covered with thick sheets of ice and mountain ranges.

Ice Near Earth's poles, the climate is very cold and the land is covered year-round with thick ice sheets. These places include most of the island of Greenland in the Arctic (the region around the North Pole) and the continent of Antarctica around the South Pole. Organisms that are adapted to life on the Arctic ice include polar bears and harp seals. Leopard seals and emperor penguins are adapted to the Antarctic. Fish living in the icy waters produce chemicals that keep their blood from freezing.

Mountains As you read in Chapter 9, altitude, or elevation, has a great effect on climate. The greater the elevation, the colder the climate is. As a result, high mountains are cool. And because air cools as it rises, the top of a mountain usually receives more rainfall than its base. Thus the climate of a mountain changes from its base to its top. An area's climate determines what plants will grow there. As a result, the types of plants on a mountain can vary greatly from its base to its peak. It is as if different elevations on a mountain have different biomes.

 **Reading Checkpoint** **Why do different plants grow at different elevations on a mountain?**

California Mountains If you were to hike from the Central Valley of California to the top of the Sierra Nevada, you would pass through a series of areas, or zones. Each zone has a different climate and a different community of plants, as shown in Figure 8.

The Central Valley is a dry grassland. As you enter the foothills, you see an open woodland of live oak and pine trees. At this elevation, you might also see dense thickets of shrubs. Higher up, you pass through a region of taller trees, including yellow pines, Douglas fir, and black oak. Next you reach a zone that is similar to the boreal forest, with lodgepole pine and fir trees. When you finally reach the peaks of the mountains, it is so cold and windy that only short plants can grow. The tiny flowering plants and dwarf willow trees at the top are similar to those in the tundra.

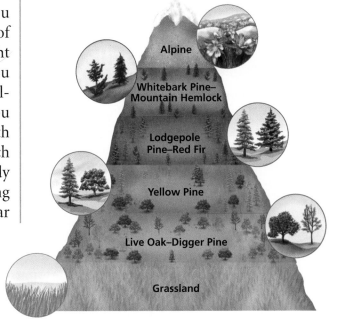

Alpine

Whitebark Pine–Mountain Hemlock

Lodgepole Pine–Red Fir

Yellow Pine

Live Oak–Digger Pine

Grassland

FIGURE 8
Climate Differences on Mountains
The climate changes dramatically as you move up a tall mountain. Climate determines the distribution of species on the mountain. *Inferring Which zone on the mountain is warmest? Coldest? Explain.*

Section (**1**) **Assessment**

S 6.5.d, 6.5.e; E-LA: Reading 6.1.0, Writing 6.2.3

Vocabulary Skill High-Use Academic Words In a complete sentence, explain what the *source* of food is for animals in the tundra.

 Reviewing Key Concepts

1. a. **Reviewing** What two factors are most important in determining an area's biome?
   b. **Relating Cause and Effect** If deserts and tundras receive similar amounts of rainfall, why are these two biomes so different?
   c. **Applying Concepts** Why would hiking up a tall mountain be a good way to observe how climate determines an area's biome?
2. a. **Listing** What are the six major biomes found on Earth?
   b. **Comparing and Contrasting** How are the three forest biomes (rain forests, deciduous forests, and boreal forests) alike? How are they different?
   c. **Inferring** What biome might you be in if you were standing on a bitterly cold, dry plain with only a few, short plants scattered around?

Writing in Science

Research Report Choose two different biomes, such as a desert and a rain forest. Then, select a niche you would like to learn more about. Compare organisms that fill the niche in the biomes you selected. Use a variety of research materials, such as the Internet, CD-ROM reference materials, videos, or periodicals. Summarize your findings in a report.

Biomes in Miniature

Materials

empty, clean cardboard milk carton

scissors and tape

sandy soil or potting soil

10 impatiens seed and 5 lima bean seeds

about 30 rye grass seeds

index card and water

clear plastic wrap

lamp and stapler

Problem How do organisms in a biome depend on abiotic factors?

Skills Focus observing, making models

Procedure 🎋

1. Your teacher will assign your group a biome. You will also observe the other groups model biomes. Based on the chart below, predict how well you think each of the three kinds of seeds will grow in each set of conditions. Record these predictions in your notebook. Then copy the data table on the facing page four times, once for each biome.

2. Staple the spout of the milk carton closed. Completely cut away one of the four sides of the carton. Poke a few holes in the opposite side for drainage, and then place that side down.

3. Fill the carton to 3 centimeters from the top with the type of soil given in the table. Divide the surface of the soil into three sections by making two lines in it with a pencil.

4. In the section near the spout, plant the impatiens seeds. In the middle section, plant the lima bean seeds. In the third section, scatter the rye grass seeds on the surface.

5. Water all the seeds well. Then cover the open part of the carton with plastic wrap.

6. On an index card, write the name of your biome, the names of the three types of seeds in the order you planted them, and the names of your group members. Tape the card to the carton. Put the carton in a warm place where it will not be disturbed.

7. Once the seeds sprout, provide your biome with light and water as specified in the chart. Keep the carton covered with plastic wrap except when you add water.

8. Observe all the model biomes daily for at least one week. Record your observations.

Growing Conditions			
Biome	Soil Type	Hours of Light per Day	Watering Instructions
Forest	Potting soil	1–2 hours of direct light	Let the surface dry; then add water.
Desert	Sandy soil	5–6 hours of direct light	Let the soil dry to a depth of 2.5 cm below the surface.
Grassland	Potting soil	5–6 hours of direct light	Let the surface dry; then add water.
Rain forest	Potting soil	No direct light; indirect light for 5–6 hours	Keep the surface of the soil moist.

Analyze and Conclude

1. **Observing** In which model biome did each type of seed grow best? In which model biome did each type of seed grow least well?

2. **Making Models** In this experiment, how did you model the following abiotic factors: sunlight, water, and temperature?

3. **Inferring** How was each type of seed affected by the soil type, amount of light, and availability of water?

4. **Classifying** Why do you think that ecologists who study biomes often focus on identifying the key abiotic factors and typical plants in an area?

5. **Communicating** Write a paragraph explaining how your miniature biomes modeled real-life biomes. Which features of real-life biomes were you able to model well? Which features of real-life biomes were more difficult to model? Explain what your models showed about the dependence of organisms on specific abiotic factors.

Data Table			
Name of Biome: _____			
Day	Impatiens	Lima Beans	Rye Grass
1			
2			
3			
4			
5			
6			
7			

Grassland

rye grass / lima beans / impatiens

Design an Experiment

Write a plan for setting up a model rain forest or desert terrarium. Include typical plants found in that biome. Obtain your teacher's approval before carrying out your investigation.

Section 2
Aquatic Ecosystems

CALIFORNIA Standards Focus

S 6.5.b. Students know matter is transferred over time from one organism to others in the food web and between organisms and their physical environment.

- What abiotic factors influence aquatic ecosystems?
- What are the major types of aquatic ecosystems?
- What are the ecological roles of organisms in aquatic food webs?

Key Terms
- estuary
- intertidal zone
- neritic zone
- kelp forests
- coral reefs
- plankton

Lab zone **Standards Warm-Up**

What's in Pond Water?

1. Using a hand lens, observe a sample of pond water.
2. Make a list of everything you see in the water. If you don't know the name of something, write a short description or draw a picture.
3. Your teacher has set up a microscope with a slide of pond water. Observe the slide under the microscope and add any new items to your list. Wash your hands with soap when you are done.

Think It Over
Classifying Use one of these systems to divide the items on your list into two groups: moving/still, biotic/abiotic, or microscopic/visible without a microscope. What does your classification system tell you about pond water?

FIGURE 9
Humpback Whale
Whales like this humpback whale are the largest consumers in marine ecosystems.

No trip around the world would be complete without exploring Earth's waters. Since almost three quarters of Earth's surface is covered with water, don't be surprised at how much there is to see. Many organisms make their homes in aquatic, or water-based, ecosystems. Your travels will take you to both freshwater ecosystems and marine (or saltwater) ecosystems.

All aquatic ecosystems are affected by the same abiotic factors: sunlight, temperature, oxygen, and salt content. Sunlight is a key factor in aquatic ecosystems. Sunlight is needed for photosynthesis in the water just as it is on land. Because water absorbs sunlight, there is only enough light for photosynthesis near the surface or in shallow water.

Freshwater Ecosystems

On this part of the expedition, you will explore Earth's waters. Most of Earth's surface is covered with water, but only a tiny fraction is fresh water. **Freshwater ecosystems include streams, rivers, ponds, and lakes.** These ecosystems provide habitats for an amazing variety of organisms, from tiny algae to huge bears.

Streams and Rivers Your first stop is a mountain stream. Where the stream begins, the cold, clear water flows rapidly. Animals that live here are adapted to the strong current. For example, insects and other small animals have hooks or suckers that help them cling to rocks. Trout have streamlined bodies that allow them to swim despite the rushing water. Few plants or algae can grow in this fast-moving water. Instead, first-level consumers rely on leaves and seeds that fall into the stream.

As the stream flows along, other streams join it. The current slows, and the water becomes cloudy with soil. The slower-moving water is warmer and contains less oxygen. This larger stream might now be called a river. Different organisms are adapted to life in a river. Plants take root among the pebbles on the river bottom. These producers provide food for young insects and homes for frogs and their tadpoles. These consumers, in turn, provide food for many larger consumers.

Ponds and Lakes Your next stop is a pond. Ponds and lakes are bodies of standing, or still, fresh water. Most lakes are larger and deeper than ponds. Ponds are often shallow enough that sunlight can reach the bottom even in the center of the pond, allowing plants to grow there. In large ponds and most lakes, however, algae floating at the surface are the major producers.

Many animals are adapted for life in the still water. Along the shore of the pond, you observe dragonflies, turtles, snails, and frogs. Sunfish live in the open water, feeding on insects and algae from the surface. Scavengers such as catfish live near the pond bottom. Bacteria and other decomposers also feed on the remains of other organisms.

 **Reading Checkpoint** What is a lake?

FIGURE 10
A Pond Ecosystem
Ponds and lakes are freshwater ecosystems characterized by still water. Pickerelweed and herons are typical pond organisms.
Interpreting Photographs *How is the heron well suited to its aquatic environment?*

◄ Tricolored heron

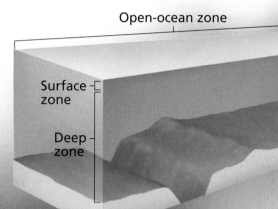

FIGURE 11
Marine Ecosystems

The ocean is home to a number of different ecosystems. Factors such as water temperature and the amount of sunlight determine what types of organisms can live in each zone.

Open-ocean zone

Neritic zone

Open-ocean zone

Intertidal zone

Surface zone

Deep zone

Deep zone

Marine Ecosystems

Now you head to the coast to explore some marine ecosystems. On your way, you'll pass through an estuary. An **estuary** (ES choo ehr ee) is found where the fresh water of a river meets the salt water of the ocean. Algae and plants such as marsh grasses provide food and shelter for many animals, including crabs, worms, clams, and fish. Many of these animals use the calm waters of estuaries for breeding grounds. ☞ **Marine ecosystems include estuaries, intertidal zones, neritic zones, and the open ocean. These zones are classified largely by the depth of water.** Figure 11 shows the major ocean zones.

Intertidal Zone Next, you walk along a rocky shore. Here, between the highest high-tide line and the lowest low-tide line, is the **intertidal zone.** Organisms here must be able to survive pounding waves and the sudden changes in water level and temperature that occur with high and low tides. Animals such as barnacles and sea stars cling to the rocks. Clams and crabs burrow in the sand.

Neritic Zone Below the low-tide line is the **neritic zone** (nuh RIT ik), the shallow region that extends over the continental shelf. Here sunlight can pass through the shallow water, allowing photosynthesis to occur. Mineral nutrients, such as nitrogen and phosphorus, often well up from the continental shelf. Plenty of sunlight and nutrients make this zone rich in living things.

452 ◆

Intertidal zone

Kelp forest

Neritic zone

Kelp forests grow in cold neritic waters where the bottom is rocky. They can be found off California's coast. The major producers are giant kelp—algae that grow up to 30 meters long. Kelp forests are home to many animals, including large schools of fish and gray whales. Sea otters feed on sea urchins.

In tropical regions, coral reefs may form. **Coral reefs** are created by colonies of tiny coral animals. Algae live in the bodies of the coral animals and provide food for the corals. Because the algae need warm temperatures and sunlight, coral reefs form only in warm shallow water. Large numbers of fish and other animals live around a coral reef. Coral reefs are one of the most diverse ecosystems on Earth.

The Open Ocean Out in the open ocean, light reaches only to a depth of a few hundred meters. Near the surface, floating algae carry out photosynthesis. Marine animals, such as tuna, swordfish, and some whales, depend on the algae for food. However, this region does not have the nutrient resources of the neritic zone, so it supports fewer living things.

The deep zone is located below the surface zone. The deep zone is almost totally dark. Most animals in this zone feed on the remains of organisms that sink down from the surface. The deepest parts of the deep zone are home to bizarre-looking animals, such as giant squid with eyes that glow in the dark.

Go Online
SciLINKS

For: Links on aquatic ecosystems
Visit: www.SciLinks.org
Web Code: scn-0525

 Reading Checkpoint **What two zones make up the open ocean?**

FIGURE 12

An Ocean Food Web

This ocean food web includes typical organisms found in the Arctic Ocean. The arrows indicate what each organism eats.
Interpreting Diagrams Which organisms feed directly on the Arctic cod? Which organisms depend indirectly on the cod?

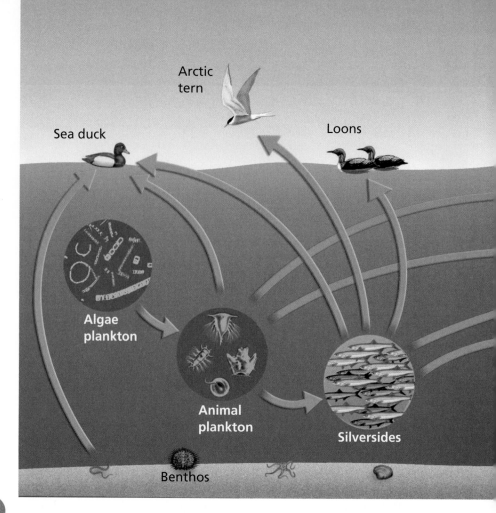

Arctic tern

Sea duck

Loons

Algae plankton

Animal plankton

Silversides

Benthos

Lab zone Try This Activity

Model a Food Web

1. Form a circle of five students. Each student will represent a marine organism: algae, animal plankton, fish, seal, or whale. Write the name of your organism on a card.

2. Discuss the feeding relationships among the five organisms.

3. Use pieces of string to connect your card to the cards of organisms that may have feeding relationships with your organism.

Inferring Based on your results in Step 3, are the feeding relationships among ocean organisms simple or complex? Explain.

Ocean Food Webs

🔑 **As on land, organisms in the ocean are connected by food chains and food webs. But in the ocean, the producers are algae rather than plants.** Most algae are **plankton**—tiny organisms that float in the water.

Throughout the ocean, plankton are a source of food for organisms of all sizes. For example, much of the algae is eaten by tiny single-celled consumers called protozoans. These primary consumers are then eaten by secondary consumers— larger protozoans or animal plankton, such as jellyfish, crustaceans, and worms. Animal plankton, in turn, is eaten by fish. Finally, fish are eaten by top-level predators such as birds and seals.

Figure 12 shows a food web of organisms living in the Arctic Ocean. Notice how each organism depends either directly or indirectly on food produced by algae plankton. Wastes from the food chain drift to the ocean floor, where many decomposers live. Some of these decomposers are scavengers, such as crabs. Other decomposers include bacteria and worms.

✓ **Reading Checkpoint** In an ocean food web, which organisms are decomposers?

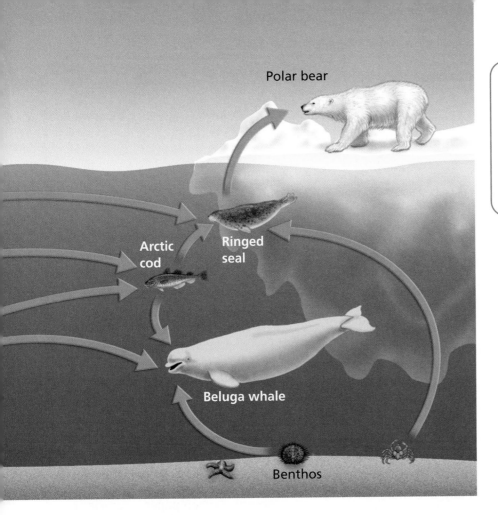

Polar bear

Arctic cod

Ringed seal

Beluga whale

Benthos

Go Online *active art*

For: Ocean Food Web activity
Visit: PHSchool.com
Web Code: cfp-3042

Section 2 Assessment

S 6.5.b; E-LA: Reading 6.2.0, Writing 6.2.0

Target Reading Skill **Identify Main Ideas** Reread the paragraphs under the heading Ocean Food Webs. Identify the main idea and two important details.

Reviewing Key Concepts

1. a. **Reviewing** What four abiotic factors are important in all aquatic ecosystems?
   b. **Explaining** Why is sunlight important in aquatic ecosystems?
   c. **Predicting** Would you expect to find many organisms living at the bottom of a deep lake? Explain.

2. a. **Identifying** Identify the three ocean zones.
   b. **Sequencing** List the ocean zones in order. Begin with the most shallow zone and end with the zone in the deepest water.
   c. **Inferring** Which zone probably has the greatest variety of living things? How is variety related to water depth?

3. a. **Defining** What is plankton?
   b. **Describing** What is the role of algae plankton in an ocean food web?
   c. **Classifying** A great blue whale is a filter feeder that eats mostly plankton. Is a blue whale a primary consumer, a secondary consumer, or a top-level consumer? Explain.

Writing in Science

Cause-and-Effect Paragraph Write a brief paragraph describing how the ocean food web in Figure 12 might be affected by a decrease in the Arctic cod population. Which populations might increase as a result? Which populations might decrease? Explain your answers. To help plan your writing, you might use a cause-and-effect graphic organizer.

Recycling Paper

Materials

newspaper

microscope and microscope slide

plastic wrap and mixing bowl

water

eggbeater

screen

square pan

heavy book

Problem Is paper a renewable resource?

Skills Focus observing, predicting

Procedure

1. Tear off a small piece of newspaper. Place it on a microscope slide and examine it under a microscope. Record your observations.

2. Tear a sheet of newspaper into pieces about the size of postage stamps. Place the pieces in the mixing bowl. Add enough water to cover the newspaper. Cover the bowl and let the mixture stand overnight.

3. The next day, add more water to cover the paper if necessary. Use the eggbeater to mix the wet paper until it is smooth. This thick liquid is called paper pulp.

4. Place the screen in the bottom of the pan. Pour the pulp onto the screen, spreading it out evenly. Then lift the screen above the pan, allowing most of the water to drip into the pan.

5. Place the screen and pulp on several layers of newspaper to absorb the rest of the water. Lay a sheet of plastic wrap over the pulp. Place a heavy book on top of the plastic wrap to press more water out of the pulp.

6. After 30 minutes, remove the book. Carefully turn over the screen, plastic wrap, and pulp. Remove the screen and plastic wrap. Let the pulp sit on the newspaper for one or two more days to dry. Replace the newspaper layers if necessary.

7. When the pulp is dry, observe it closely. Record your observations.

Analyze and Conclude

1. **Observing** What kind of structures did you observe when you examined torn newspaper under a microscope?

2. **Inferring** What are these structures made of? Where do they come from?

3. **Predicting** What do you think happens to the structures you observed when paper is recycled? How do you think this affects the number of times paper can be recycled?

4. **Communicating** Based on what you learned in this lab, do you think paper should be classified as a renewable or nonrenewable resource? Defend your answer with evidence and sound reasoning.

Design an Experiment

Using procedures like those in this lab, design an experiment to recycle three different types of paper, such as shiny magazine paper, paper towels, and cardboard. *Obtain your teachers permission before carrying out your investigation.* How do the resulting papers differ?

Forests and Fisheries

CALIFORNIA
Standards Focus

S 6.6.b Students know different natural energy and material resources, including air, soil, rocks, petroleum, fresh water, wildlife, and forests, and know how to classify them as renewable or nonrenewable.

S 6.6.c Students know the natural origin of the materials used to make common objects.

- How can forests be managed as renewable resources?
- How can fisheries be managed for a sustainable yield?

Key Terms
- renewable resource
- clear-cutting
- selective cutting
- sustainable yield
- fishery
- aquaculture

Lab zone Standards **Warm-Up**

What Happened to the Tuna?

1. Use the data in the table to make a line graph. Label the axes of the graph and add a title.
2. Mark the high and low points on the graph.

Think It Over

Inferring Describe the changes in the tuna population during this period. Can you suggest a reason for these changes?

Year	Bluefin Tuna Population
1970	218,000
1975	370,000
1980	67,000
1985	58,000
1990	46,000
1995	63,000
2000	67,000

At first glance, an oak tree and a bluefin tuna may not seem to have much in common. But oak trees and tuna are both examples of living resources that people can use. People use oak trees to make furniture, lumber, and cork. Tuna are a source of food for people.

Oak trees and tuna reproduce and grow relatively quickly, replacing those that people use. For this reason, they are considered renewable resources. A **renewable resource** is one that is either always available or is naturally replaced in a relatively short time. In this section, you will read about two major types of renewable resources: forests and fisheries.

Forest Resources

Forests contain many valuable resources. Many products are made from the fruits, seeds, and other parts of forest plants. Some of these products, such as maple syrup, rubber, and nuts, come from living trees. Other products, such as lumber and wood pulp for making paper, require cutting down trees. Coniferous trees, including pine and spruce, are used for construction and for making paper. Hardwoods, such as oak, cherry, and maple, are used for furniture because of their strength and beauty.

Trees and other plants produce oxygen that organisms need to survive. They also absorb carbon dioxide and many pollutants from the air. Trees help prevent flooding and control soil erosion. Their roots absorb rainwater and hold soil in place.

Go Online
active art

For: Logging Methods activity
Visit: PHSchool.com
Web Code: cep-5032

FIGURE 13
Logging Methods

Clear-cutting involves cutting down all the trees in an area at once. **Interpreting Diagrams** *What is selective cutting?*

Managing Forests

There are about 300 million hectares of forests in the United States. That's nearly a third of the nation's area! Many forests are located on public land. Others are owned by individuals or by private timber and paper companies. Forest industries in the United States provide jobs for more than 1 million people.

🔑 **Because new trees can be planted to replace trees that are cut down, forests can be renewable resources.** The United States Forest Service and environmental organizations work with forestry companies to conserve forest resources. They try to develop logging methods that maintain forests as renewable resources.

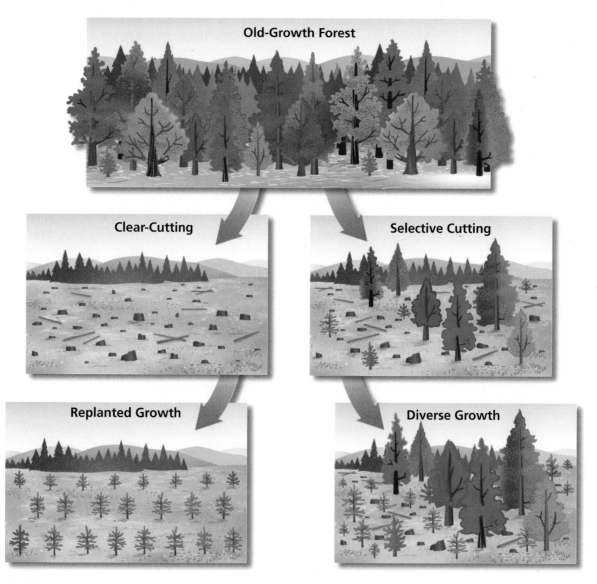

Logging Methods There are two major methods of logging: clear-cutting and selective cutting. **Clear-cutting** is the process of cutting down all the trees in an area at once. Cutting down only some trees in a forest and leaving a mix of tree sizes and species behind is called **selective cutting.**

Each logging method has advantages and disadvantages. Clear-cutting is usually quicker and cheaper than selective cutting. It may also be safer for the loggers. In selective cutting, the loggers must move the heavy equipment and logs around the remaining trees in the forest. But selective cutting is usually less damaging to the forest environment than clear-cutting. When an area of forest is clear-cut, the ecosystem changes. After clear-cutting, the soil is exposed to wind and rain. Without the protection of the tree roots, the soil is more easily blown or washed away. Soil washed into streams may harm the fish and other organisms that live there.

Sustainable Forestry Forests can be managed to provide a sustainable yield. A **sustainable yield** is an amount of a renewable resource such as trees that can be harvested regularly without reducing the future supply. Sustainable forestry works sort of like a book swap: as long as you donate a book each time you borrow one, the total supply of books will not be affected. Planting a tree to replace one that was cut down is like donating a book to replace a borrowed one.

In sustainable forestry, after trees are harvested, young trees are planted. Trees must be planted frequently enough to keep a constant supply. Different species grow at different rates. Forests containing faster-growing trees, such as pines, can be harvested and replanted every 20 to 30 years. On the other hand, some forests containing hardwood trees, such as hickory, oak, and cherry, may be harvested only every 40 to 100 years. One sustainable approach is to log small patches of forest. This way, different sections of forest can be harvested every year.

 **What is sustainable yield?**

FIGURE 14
Sustainable Forestry
Sustainable forestry practices include the planting of young trees after mature trees have been harvested.

Lab zone Skills Activity

Calculating

In a recent year, the total catch of fish in the world was 112.9 million metric tons. Based on the data below, calculate the percent of this total each country caught.

Country	Catch (millions of metric tons)
China	24.4
Japan	6.8
United States	5.6
Peru	8.9

What do you think might happen to the world's fish supply if each country increased its annual catch?

FIGURE 15
Fisheries
Even though fisheries are renewable resources, they must be managed for sustainable yields, or the supply of fish may run out.

Fisheries

An area of ocean with many valuable ocean organisms is called a **fishery.** Some major fisheries include the Grand Banks off Newfoundland, Georges Bank off New England, and Monterey Canyon off California. Fisheries like these are valuable renewable resources.

Until recently, fisheries seemed like an unlimited resource. The waters held such huge schools of fish. And fish reproduce in great numbers. A single codfish can lay as many as 9 million eggs in a single year! But people have found that this resource has limits. After many years of big catches, huge populations of cod off the New England coast declined greatly. What caused these changes?

The fish were caught faster than they could breed, so the population decreased. This situation is known as overfishing. Scientists estimate that 70 percent of the world's major fisheries have been overfished. But if fish populations recover, a sustainable yield can again be harvested. **Managing fisheries for a sustainable yield includes setting fishing limits, changing fishing methods, developing aquaculture techniques, and finding new resources.**

Fishing Limits Laws can ban the fishing of certain species. Laws may also limit the number or size of fish that can be caught or require that fish be within a certain range of sizes. These laws ensure that young fish survive long enough to reproduce and that all of the largest adult fish aren't caught. If a fishery has been severely overfished, however, the government may ban fishing completely until the populations recover.

Fishing Methods Today many fishing crews use nets with a larger mesh size that allow small, young fish to escape. In addition, many other fishing practices are regulated by laws. Some fishing methods have been outlawed. Outlawed methods include poisoning fish with cyanide and stunning them by exploding dynamite underwater. These techniques harm all the fish in an area rather than targeting certain fish.

Aquaculture The practice of raising fish and other water-dwelling organisms for food is called **aquaculture.** The fish may be raised in artificial ponds or bays. Salmon, catfish, and shrimp are farmed in this way in the United States.

But aquaculture has drawbacks. The artificial ponds and bays often replace natural habitats such as salt marshes. Maintaining the farms can cause pollution and spread diseases into wild fish populations.

New Resources Today about 9,000 different fish species are harvested for food. More than half the animal protein eaten by people throughout the world comes from fish. One way to help feed a growing human population is to fish for new species. Scientists and chefs are working together to introduce people to deep-water species such as monkfish and tile fish, as well as easy-to-farm freshwater fish such as tilapia.

FIGURE 16
Aquaculture
Aquaculture is helping to meet the demand for fish. This fish farm in Hawaii raises tilapia.
Applying Concepts *What costs and benefits does aquaculture involve?*

 **Reading Checkpoint** What is aquaculture?

Section 3 Assessment

S 6.6.b, 6.6.c
E-LA: Reading 6.1.0

Vocabulary Skill High-Use Academic Words
Use the meaning of the word *sustain* to explain the meaning of *sustainable forestry*.

Reviewing Key Concepts

1. **a. Reviewing** Why are forests considered renewable resources?
   b. Comparing and Contrasting How does the clear-cutting logging method differ from selective cutting?
   c. Developing Hypotheses You are walking in a clear-cut section of forest a few days after a heavy rainstorm. A nearby stream is very muddy and has many dead fish. What may have happened?

2. **a. Listing** What are four ways fisheries can be managed for a sustainable yield?

   b. Explaining What are two kinds of laws that regulate fishing? How can they help ensure the health of a fishery?
   c. Predicting What might happen to a fish population over time if all the largest fish in the population were caught? Explain.

Lab zone **At-Home Activity**

Renewable Resource Survey With a family member, conduct a "Forest and Fishery" survey of your home. Make a list of all the things that are made from either forest or fishery products. Then ask other family members to predict how many items are on the list. Are they surprised by the answer?

Biodiversity

S 6.6.b Students know different natural energy and material resources, including air, soil, rocks, petroleum, fresh water, wildlife, and forests, and know how to classify them as renewable or nonrenewable.

- In what ways is biodiversity valuable?
- What factors affect an area's biodiversity?
- Which human activities threaten biodiversity?
- How can biodiversity be protected?

Key Terms

- biodiversity
- keystone species
- extinction
- endangered species
- threatened species
- habitat destruction
- poaching
- captive breeding

FIGURE 17

Organisms of many kinds are part of Earth's biodiversity.

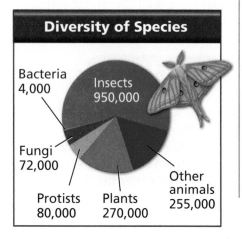

Diversity of Species

Bacteria 4,000

Insects 950,000

Fungi 72,000

Protists 80,000

Plants 270,000

Other animals 255,000

Lab zone Standards **Warm-Up**

How Much Variety Is There?

1. You will be given two cups of seeds. The seeds in cup A represent the trees in a section of tropical rain forest. The seeds in cup B represent the trees in a section of deciduous forest.
2. Pour the seeds from cup A onto a plate. Sort the seeds by type. Count the different types of seeds. This number represents the number of different kinds of trees in that forest.
3. Repeat Step 2 with the seeds in cup B.
4. Share your results with your class. Use the class results to calculate the average number of different kinds of trees in each type of forest.

Think It Over

Inferring How does the variety of trees in the two forests differ? Can you suggest any advantages of having a wide variety of species?

No one knows exactly how many species live on Earth. As you can see in Figure 17, more than 1.5 million species have been identified so far. The number of different species in an area is called its **biodiversity.** It is difficult to estimate the total biodiversity on Earth because many areas of the planet have not been thoroughly studied. Some experts think that the deep oceans alone could contain 10 million new species!

Preserving biodiversity is important. **People value wildlife and ecosystems for their beauty and as a source of recreation. In addition, biodiversity has both economic value and ecological value within an ecosystem.**

Many plants, animals, and other organisms can be valuable resources. They provide food and raw materials for medicines, clothing, and other products. For example, forests provide wood for fuel and building material, and fisheries provide fish for food. But these resources can only be renewable if they are used in a sustainable way. If habitats and species are lost when a resource is harvested, then the resource can become nonrenewable. Ecosystems themselves can also be valuable. People enjoy wildlife tours in rain forests and other locations.

Factors Affecting Biodiversity

Biodiversity varies from place to place. ⊙ **Factors that affect biodiversity in an ecosystem include area, climate, diversity of niches, and keystone species.**

Area Within a given biome, a large area will contain more species than a small area. For example, a large island such as New Guinea is home to more bird species than a smaller island such as Bali.

Climate Many scientists hypothesize that the great biodiversity in the tropics may be related to climate. The number of species generally increases from the poles toward the equator. Tropical rain forests are the most diverse ecosystems in the world. Why is this? Tropical rain forests have fairly constant temperatures and large amounts of rainfall throughout the year. Many plants in these regions grow year-round, providing a continuous food supply for other organisms.

Niche Diversity Coral reefs are the second most diverse ecosystems in the world. Found only in shallow, warm waters, coral reefs are often called the rain forests of the sea. A reef supports many different niches for organisms that live under, on, and among the coral. More species are able to live in the reef than in a more uniform habitat, such as a flat sandbar.

Keystone Species All the species in an ecosystem are interconnected. Some species play a particularly crucial role. A **keystone species** is a species that influences the survival of many other species in an ecosystem. For example, the sea otter, which eats sea urchins, is a keystone species in kelp forests. In the 1800s, hunters on the Pacific coast killed most of the sea otters for fur. The sea urchins were able to reproduce without control and ate up all the kelp. When sea otters were reintroduced, the kelp population recovered. The ecosystem's balance was restored.

 **Reading Checkpoint** What is a keystone species?

FIGURE 18

Land and Ocean Ecosystems

Three factors that affect the biodiversity of an ecosystem are area, climate, and niche diversity. *Inferring* *Which factor is most likely responsible for the biodiversity of coral reefs? Of tropical rain forests?*

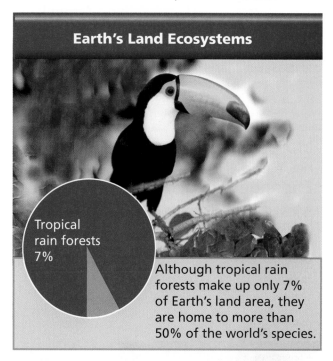

Earth's Land Ecosystems

Tropical rain forests 7%

Although tropical rain forests make up only 7% of Earth's land area, they are home to more than 50% of the world's species.

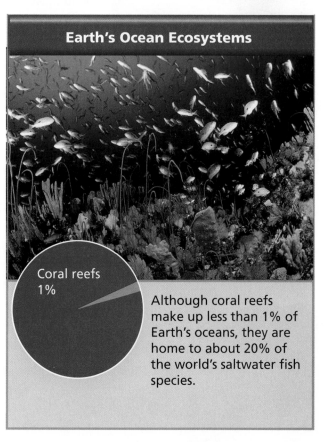

Earth's Ocean Ecosystems

Coral reefs 1%

Although coral reefs make up less than 1% of Earth's oceans, they are home to about 20% of the world's saltwater fish species.

Biodiversity in Danger

In the 1800s, there were millions of passenger pigeons in the United States. Then, in less than a century, people hunted the birds until there were no passenger pigeons left.

Extinction The disappearance of all members of a species from Earth is called **extinction**. Extinction is a natural process. But in the last few centuries, the number of species becoming extinct has increased dramatically. Species in danger of becoming extinct in the near future are called **endangered species**. Species that could become endangered in the near future are called **threatened species**. Threatened and endangered species are found on every continent and in every ocean.

A natural event, such as an earthquake or a volcanic eruption, can damage an ecosystem, wiping out populations or even species. **Human activities can also threaten biodiversity. These activities include habitat destruction, poaching, pollution, and the introduction of nonnative species.**

Reading Checkpoint What is an endangered species?

Figure 19
Endangered Species

A broad range of species and habitats are represented on the endangered list in the United States.

◀ **Tennessee Purple Coneflower**
These daisy-like plants grow only in cedar forests in central Tennessee. Conservation organizations and landowners are working together to protect these plants.

▲ **Schaus Swallowtail Butterfly**
This butterfly is threatened by habitat loss and pollution in the Florida Keys.

◀ **Peninsular Bighorn Sheep**
This herbivore of southern California's deserts grazes on grasses and shrubs. Predation, diseases, and habitat loss threaten the bighorn.

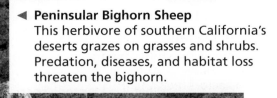

Habitat Destruction The major cause of extinction is **habitat destruction,** the loss of a natural habitat. This can occur when forests are cleared to create grazing land or when wetlands are filled in to build towns. Some species are not able to survive such changes to their habitat.

Poaching Poaching is the illegal killing or removal of wildlife from their habitats. Many endangered animals are killed and sold for their skin or fur. Others are taken and sold as pets.

Pollution Some species are endangered because of pollution. Substances that cause pollution, called pollutants, may reach animals through the water or air. Pollutants may harm or kill organisms.

Nonnative Species Introducing a nonnative species, or exotic, into an ecosystem threatens biodiversity. Without its natural predators and consumers, the introduced species often outcompetes or harms the native organisms.

Go Online
PLANET DIARY

For: More on biodiversity
Visit: PHSchool.com
Web Code: ced-5033

Whooping Crane ▶
Threatened by habitat destruction and disease, about half of the remaining whooping cranes are in zoos. The species is recovering well since its lowest point in the 1940s.

California Tiger Salamander ▲
This salamander is threatened by habitat loss.

Steller's Sea Lion ▶
Overfishing has led to a decline in this mammal's sources of food. Other factors may also be threatening this species.

Math
Analyzing Data

California Peregrine Falcon Recovery

The peregrine falcon, the world's fastest bird of prey, was nearly extinct in the United States in 1970. The pesticide DDT weakened peregrine eggshells, so the eggs rarely hatched. In 1972, the United States banned DDT. Use the graph to answer the questions.

1. **Reading Graphs** What variable is plotted on the *x*-axis? What variable is plotted on the *y*-axis?

2. **Interpreting Data** How did California's peregrine population change from 1976 to 1998?

3. **Inferring** Why do you think the peregrine population grew fairly slowly at first?

4. **Predicting** What might this graph have looked like if DDT had not been banned?

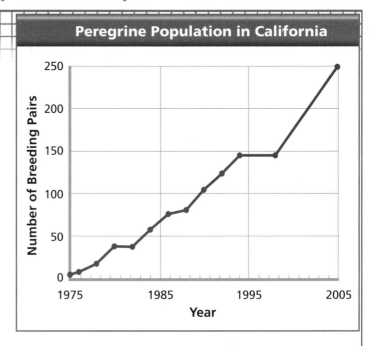

Peregrine Population in California

(Graph: x-axis "Year" from 1975 to 2005; y-axis "Number of Breeding Pairs" from 0 to 250)

Protecting Biodiversity

Some people who work to preserve biodiversity focus on protecting just one endangered species. Others try to protect entire ecosystems, such as the Great Barrier Reef in Australia. **Three successful approaches to protecting biodiversity are captive breeding, laws and treaties, and habitat preservation.**

Captive Breeding **Captive breeding** is the mating of animals in zoos or wildlife preserves. Scientists care for the young and then release them into the wild when they are grown.

Captive breeding was the only hope for the California condor, the largest bird in North America. Condors became endangered due to habitat destruction, poaching, and pollution. By 1984, there were only 27 California condors. Scientists captured all the wild condors and brought them to zoos to breed. Today, there are more than 200 California condors.

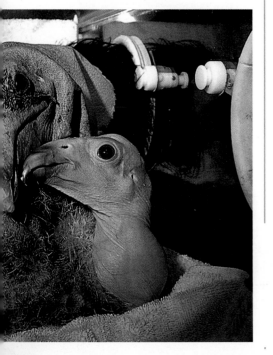

FIGURE 20
Captive Breeding
California condor chicks raised in captivity need to learn what adult condors look like. Here, a scientist uses a puppet to feed and groom a chick.

Laws and Treaties Laws can help protect species. In the United States, the Endangered Species Act prohibits trade in products made from threatened or endangered species. Internationally, wildlife is protected by the Convention on International Trade in Endangered Species. This treaty lists more than 800 species that cannot be traded for profit.

Habitat Preservation The best way to preserve biodiversity is to protect whole ecosystems. Protecting whole ecosystems saves endangered species and the other species in their community. Many countries have set aside wildlife habitats as parks, reserves, and refuges.

To succeed, reserves must have the characteristics of diverse ecosystems. For example, they must be large enough to support the populations that live there. The reserves must contain a variety of niches. And of course, it is still necessary to keep the air, land, and water clean, control poaching, and remove nonnative species.

FIGURE 21
Habitat Preservation
Habitat preservation is the aim of national parks such as Channel Islands National Park in California.

Section 4 Assessment

S 6.6.b; E-LA: Reading 6.2.0

Target Reading Skill Identify Main Ideas Reread the paragraphs under the heading The Value of Biodiversity. Identify two or three details that support the main idea that preserving biodiversity is important.

Reviewing Key Concepts

1. a. **Identifying** What are three factors that affect the biodiversity in an ecosystem?
   b. **Explaining** How does each of these factors affect biodiversity?
   c. **Developing Hypotheses** Would you expect to find great biodiversity in the tundra biome? Why or why not?
2. a. **Listing** Name four human activities that can threaten biodiversity.
   b. **Applying Concepts** Black bears are roaming through a new housing development in search of food, even though the housing development is still surrounded by forest. How can you account for the bears' behavior?

3. a. **Reviewing** What are three approaches to protecting biodiversity?
   b. **Relating Cause and Effect** For each approach to protecting biodiversity, list at least one factor that might limit its success.
   c. **Making Judgments** List some ways in which those limitations might be dealt with.

Lab zone At-Home **Activity**

Species Refuges Obtain a map of your community or state. With a family member, identify any city, state, or national parks or refuges in your area. Choose one location and find out whether there are endangered or threatened species living there. Research the ecological role of these organisms. Then prepare a five-minute presentation for your class on what you learned.

The BIG Idea The environment defines the characteristics and ecological roles of the organisms found in different biomes. Therefore, similar biomes may contain organisms that play similar ecological roles.

1 Biomes

Key Concepts
S 6.5.d, 6.5.e

- It is mostly the climate—temperature and precipitation—in an area that determines its biome.

- The six major biomes are the desert, rain forest, grassland, deciduous forest, boreal forest, and tundra.

Key Terms

biome	savanna
desert	deciduous tree
canopy	coniferous tree
understory	tundra
grassland	permafrost

2 Aquatic Ecosystems

Key Concepts
S 6.5.b

- All aquatic ecosystems are affected by the same abiotic factors: sunlight, temperature, oxygen, and salt content.

- Freshwater ecosystems include streams, rivers, ponds, and lakes.

- As on land, organisms in the ocean are connected by food chains and food webs. But in the ocean, the producers are algae rather than plants.

Key Terms

estuary	kelp forests
intertidal zone	coral reefs
neritic zone	plankton

3 Forests and Fisheries

Key Concepts
S 6.6.b, 6.6.c

- Because new trees can be planted to replace trees that are cut down, forests can be renewable resources.

- Managing fisheries for a sustainable yield includes setting fishing limits, changing fishing methods, developing aquaculture techniques, and finding new resources.

Key Terms

renewable resource	sustainable yield
clear-cutting	fishery
selective cutting	aquaculture

4 Biodiversity

Key Concepts
S 6.6.b

- Biodiversity has both economic value and ecological value within an ecosystem.

- Factors that affect biodiveristy in an ecosystem include area, climate, and diversity of niches.

- Human activities can threaten biodiversity. These activities include habitat destruction, poaching, pollution, and the introduction of exotic species.

- Three successful approaches to protecting biodiversity are captive breeding, laws and treaties, and habitat preservation.

Key Terms

biodiversity	threatened species
keystone species	habitat destruction
extinction	poaching
endangered species	captive breeding

Review and Assessment

Target Reading Skill

Identify Main Ideas Reread the paragraphs under the heading Protecting Biodiversity in Section 4. Complete the graphic organizer.

Protecting Biodiversity

Three approaches to protecting biodiversity are captive breeding, laws and treaties, and habitat preservation.

Detail	Detail	Detail

Reviewing Key Terms

Choose the letter of the best answer.

1. Much of Canada is covered in fir and spruce forests. The winter is cold and long. What is this biome?
   a. tundra
   b. boreal forest
   c. deciduous forest
   d. grassland

2. The leafy roof formed by tall trees in a rain forest is called the
   a. understory.
   b. canopy.
   c. temperate rain forest.
   d. savanna.

3. The area between the highest high-tide line and lowest low-tide line is called the
   a. estuary.
   b. fishery.
   c. intertidal zone.
   d. neritic zone.

4. The practice of raising fish for food is called
   a. aquaculture.   b. overfishing.
   c. poaching.   d. captive breeding.

5. If all members of a species disappear from Earth, that species is
   a. extinct.   b. endangered.
   c. renewable.   d. threatened.

Complete the following sentences so that your answers clearly explain the key terms.

6. The Mojave is considered to be a **desert** because _____.

7. In the tundra, rainwater cannot soak through the **permafrost,** which is _____.

8. Sunlight can pass through the **neritic zone,** which is _____.

9. Many fishes are primary consumers that feed on **plankton,** which are _____.

10. A species of frog that is rapidly disappearing is an **endangered species** because _____.

Writing in Science

Encyclopedia Entry Write a half-page encyclopedia entry about life in the desert. Describe at least two plants and animals that live in the desert. Focus on the adaptations that allow these organisms to thrive in the harsh environment.

Video Assessment
Discovery Channel School
Ecosystems and Biomes

Review and Assessment

Checking Concepts

11. Why is the tropical rain forest able to support so many species?

12. In which biome would you find large herbivores such as elephants and zebras? Explain.

13. Which abiotic factors are important to aquatic ecosystems?

14. How does the idea of a sustainable yield pertain to forestry? How does it apply to fisheries?

15. Explain how habitat destruction affects species.

Thinking Critically

16. **Inferring** Polar bears are well adapted to life around the Arctic Ocean. Their white fur camouflages them in the snow. They can withstand freezing temperatures for a long time. They can swim and hunt in very cold water. Is the distribution of polar bears limited by physical barriers, competition, or climate? Explain your answer.

17. **Comparing and Contrasting** How are boreal forests and deciduous forests similar? How are they different?

18. **Predicting** A chemical spill has just killed off all the algae in a part of the surface zone in the open ocean. How will this accident affect the food webs in that part of the surface zone?

19. **Comparing and Contrasting** Which logging method is shown below? Compare the effects of this method with those of selective cutting.

Applying Skills

Use the table to answer Questions 20–24.

A study was done to identify the reasons why mammal and bird species become endangered or threatened. The data are shown in the table below.

Reason	Mammals	Birds
Poaching	31%	20%
Habitat loss	32%	60%
Exotic species	17%	12%
Other causes	20%	8%

20. **Graphing** Make a bar graph comparing the reasons why mammals and birds become endangered or threatened. Show reasons on the horizontal axis and percentages of animal groups on the vertical axis.

21. **Interpreting Data** What is the major reason that mammals become endangered or threatened? What is the main threat to birds?

22. **Predicting** Would stricter laws against poaching be likely to benefit mammal species or bird species more? Explain.

23. **Applying Concepts** An exotic species of mammal escapes from a cargo ship and invades a new habitat. How might this affect the percentage of endangered mammals in this habitat? Explain.

24. **Developing Hypotheses** Suggest two explanations for the differences between the data for mammals and birds.

Lab zone | Standards Investigation

Performance Assessment In your presentation, clearly describe the biodiversity you observed in your plot. You can use drawings, video, photos, or a computer for your presentation. Be sure to include the data you collected on abiotic factors as well.

CALIFORNIA Standards Practice

Choose the letter of the best answer.

1. Wildebeests, which live in the African savanna, graze on grasses. Which of the following animals most likely plays a similar ecological role to that of the wildebeest?

   A sheep in the plains of the Midwestern United States

   B monkeys in the Amazon rain forest

   C lions in the grasslands of Africa

   D owls in a boreal forest   **S 6.5.d**

2. In some areas, foresters plant one tree for every tree they cut for paper production. This activity is an example of

   A a nonsustainable approach to a nonrenewable natural resource.

   B a sustainable approach to a nonrenewable natural resource.

   C a nonsustainable approach to a renewable natural resource.

   D a sustainable approach to a renewable natural resource.   **S 6.6.c**

Use the table below and your knowledge of science to answer Question 3.

Biome	Average Annual Rainfall (cm)
1	30
2	10
3	350
4	75

3. Which biome is most likely a tropical rain forest?

   A Biome 1   **B** Biome 2

   C Biome 3   **D** Biome 4   **S 6.5.e**

4. In an ocean ecosystem, a jellyfish, which feeds on plankton, is an example of a

   A producer.

   B primary consumer.

   C secondary consumer.

   D top-level predator.   **S 6.5.b**

Use the graph below to answer Questions 5 and 6.

The graph below shows how the population of one kind of fish, haddock, changed in Georges Bank between 1980 and 2000.

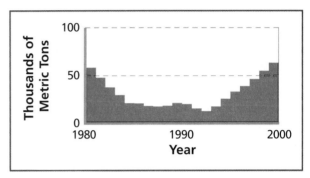

5. Which of the following statements best explains the graphed data?

   A The population of haddock increased from 1980 to 1990.

   B By 2000, the haddock population reached the same level as in 1980.

   C The haddock population changed little from 1980 to 1990.

   D The haddock population is decreasing steadily.   **S 6.6.b**

6. Which of the following probably accounts for the trend shown between 1992 and 2000?

   A laws regulating haddock fishing

   B overfishing

   C niche diversity

   D habitat fragmentation   **S 6.6.b**

7. You are in an area in California where the fresh water of a river delta meets the Pacific Ocean. What type of habitat are you in?

   A a neritic zone   **B** the coral reef zone

   C an estuary   **D** the tundra

                                     S 6.5.e

Apply the BIG Idea

8. A desert in Africa and a tropical rain forest in Asia lie along the same latitude. Compare the resources and abiotic factors available in these two biomes. Explain why biodiversity is greater in the rain forest than in the desert.   **S 6.5.e**

Energy and Material Resources

These California wind turbines use the energy of the wind to generate electricity. ▶

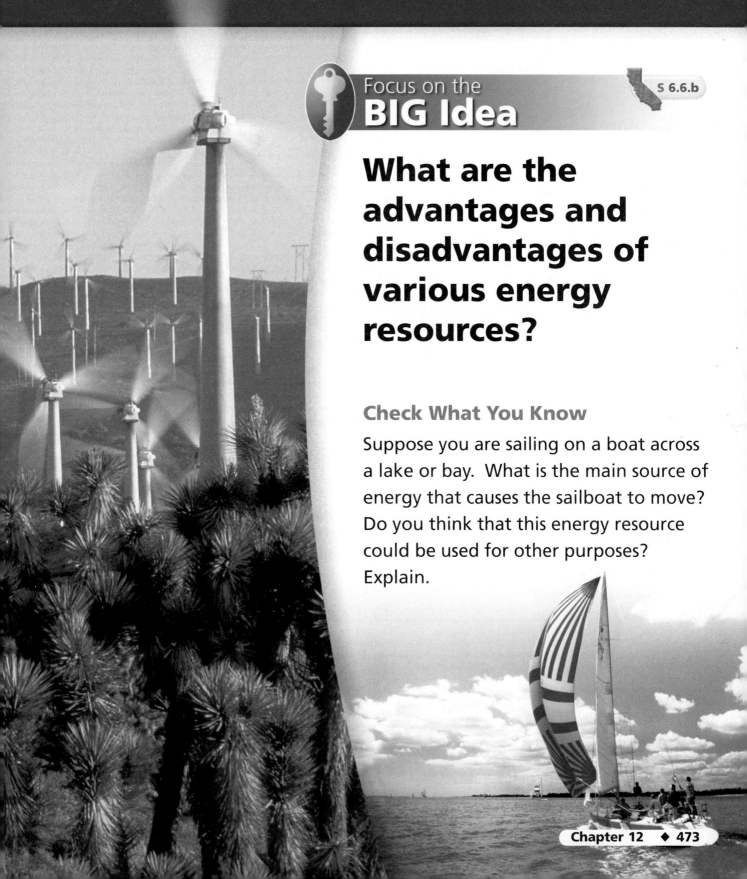

Focus on the
BIG Idea

S 6.6.b

What are the advantages and disadvantages of various energy resources?

Check What You Know

Suppose you are sailing on a boat across a lake or bay. What is the main source of energy that causes the sailboat to move? Do you think that this energy resource could be used for other purposes? Explain.

Build Science Vocabulary

The images shown here represent some of the key terms in this chapter. You can use this vocabulary skill to help you understand the meaning of some key terms in this chapter.

Vocabulary Skill

Prefixes

A prefix is a word part that is added at the beginning of a word to change its meaning. For example, *re-* meaning "again" is a prefix that is frequently used in science. In the word *rewrite*, the prefix *re-* is added to the word *write* to form *rewrite*, meaning "to write again."

re-	+	**write**	=	**rewrite**
again		write		write again

Use the prefixes below to help you learn the key terms.

Prefix	Meaning	Key Terms
bio-	Life	Biomass, biodegradable
com-	With, together	Combustion
con-	With, together	Conservation
hydro-	Water	Hydrocarbon, hydroelectric
re-	Again, back	Recycling

Apply It!

Review the prefixes above. Then predict what the word *recycling* means using what you know about the prefix *re-*. After reading the chapter, revise your definition as needed.

Look for these prefixes as you read the chapter.

hydrocarbon

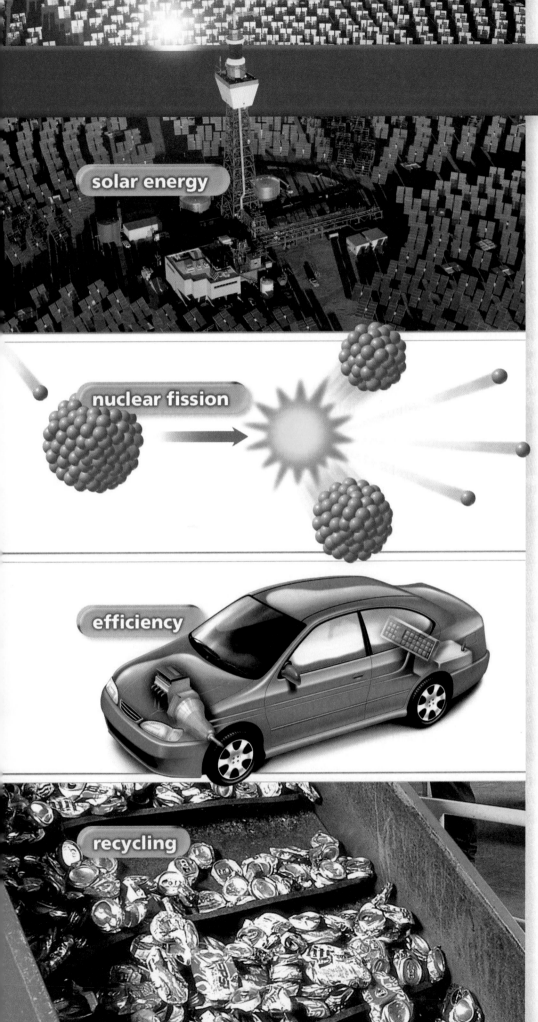

solar energy

nuclear fission

efficiency

recycling

Chapter 12
Vocabulary

Interactive Textbook

Build Science Vocabulary
Online
Visit: PHSchool.com
Web Code: cwj-4120

How to Read Science

Compare and Contrast

Science texts often make comparisons. When you compare and contrast, you examine the similarities and differences between things. You can compare and contrast by using a table.

Follow these steps to set up a compare/contrast table.
- List the characteristics or features to be compared across the top of the table.
- List the items to be compared in the left column.
- Complete the table by filling in information about each characteristic or feature.

In this chapter, you will learn about coal, oil, and natural gas—three major sources of energy. Look at the compare/contrast table. Complete the table after reading Section 1.

Energy Type	Advantages	Disadvantages
Coal	Low cost, plentiful	
Oil		Nonrenewable, mostly imported
Natural gas		

Apply It!

Review the compare/contrast table and answer the questions.
1. What energy resources are being compared in the table?
2. What characteristics are being compared?
3. In what column would you place additional energy types to be compared?

After reading Section 2, create a table comparing solar energy, hydroelectric power, and wind power. After reading Section 3, create a table comparing nuclear fission and nuclear fusion.

Standards **Investigation**

Energy Audit

How much energy does it take to keep your school running? In this chapter's investigation, you will work in a group to study energy use in your school.

Your Goal

To report on one type of energy use in your school and make suggestions for saving energy

To complete this investigation, you must

- survey the types of energy used in one area of your school
- classify each type of energy used as renewable or nonrenewable
- identify ways to conserve energy in that area
- prepare a written report summarizing your observations and proposing your suggestions
- follow the safety guidelines in Appendix A

Plan It!

With your group, brainstorm a list of the ways in which you think energy is used in and around your school. Select an area of the school to study, such as a classroom, the cafeteria, or the school grounds. You could also consider the school's heating or cooling system or transportation to and from school.

Then decide what type of data you will collect. When you begin your study, look for ways to reduce energy use. At the end of the chapter, you will present your group's proposal to make your school more energy-efficient.

Fossil Fuels

CALIFORNIA
Standards Focus

S 6.3.b Students know that when fuel is consumed, most of the energy released becomes heat energy.

S 6.6.a Students know the utility of energy sources is determined by factors that are involved in converting these sources to useful forms and the consequences of the conversion process.

- How do fuels provide energy?
- What are the three major fossil fuels?
- Why are fossil fuels considered nonrenewable resources?

Key Terms
- fuel
- energy transformation
- combustion
- fossil fuel
- hydrocarbon
- petroleum
- refinery
- petrochemical

Lab zone Standards **Warm-Up**

What's in a Piece of Coal?

1. Observe a chunk of coal. Record your observations in as much detail as possible, including its color, texture, and shape.
2. Now use a hand lens to observe the coal more closely.
3. Examine your coal for fossils—imprints of plant or animal remains.

Think It Over

Observing What did you notice when you used the hand lens compared to your first observations? What do you think coal is made of?

How did you travel to school today? Whether you traveled in a car or a bus, walked, or rode your bike, you used some form of energy. The source of that energy was a fuel. A **fuel** is a substance that provides energy—such as heat, light, motion, or electricity—as the result of a chemical change.

Energy Transformation and Fuels

Rub your hands together quickly for several seconds. Did they become warmer? When you moved your hands, they had kinetic energy, the energy of motion. The friction of your hands rubbing together converted the kinetic energy to thermal energy, which you felt as heat. A change from one form of energy to another is called an **energy transformation,** or an energy conversion.

Gasoline is a fossil fuel. ▶

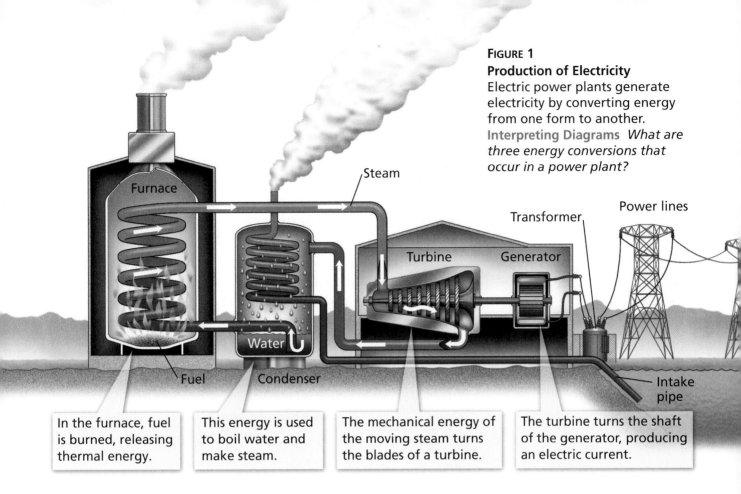

FIGURE 1
Production of Electricity
Electric power plants generate electricity by converting energy from one form to another.
Interpreting Diagrams *What are three energy conversions that occur in a power plant?*

In the furnace, fuel is burned, releasing thermal energy.

This energy is used to boil water and make steam.

The mechanical energy of the moving steam turns the blades of a turbine.

The turbine turns the shaft of the generator, producing an electric current.

Combustion Fuels contain stored chemical energy, which can be released by **combustion,** or burning. ● **When fuels are burned, chemical energy is released as heat and light. These forms of energy can be used to generate other forms of energy, such as motion or electricity.** Ultimately, however, most of the released energy is converted into heat.

For example, when the gasoline in a car's engine is burned, some of the chemical energy stored in the gasoline is converted into thermal energy. This thermal energy is then converted to kinetic energy that moves the car. Then when the brakes are applied, the car's kinetic energy is converted into heat as the brake pads rub against part of the wheels.

Production of Electricity The chemical energy stored in fuels can be used to generate electricity. In a typical electric power plant, the thermal energy produced by burning fuel is used to boil water, making steam, as shown in Figure 1. The mechanical energy of the steam then turns a turbine. The turbine is connected to a generator, which consists of powerful magnets surrounded by coils of copper wire. As the magnets turn inside the wire coil, an electric current is produced. This current flows through power lines to homes and industries.

 **Reading Checkpoint** What energy transformations occur in a car's engine?

For: Links on fossil fuels
Visit: www.SciLinks.org
Web Code: scn-0551

Lab zone Skills Activity

Graphing

Use the data in the table below to make a circle graph showing the uses of energy in the United States. (To review circle graphs, see the Skills Handbook.)

End Use of Energy	Percent of Total Energy
Transportation	26.5
Industry	38.1
Homes and businesses	35.4

What Are Fossil Fuels?

Most of the energy used today comes from organisms that lived hundreds of millions of years ago. As these plants, animals, and other organisms died, their remains piled up. Layers of sand, rock, and mud buried the dead organisms. Over time, heat and the pressure of sediments changed the material into other substances. **Fossil fuels** are the energy-rich substances formed from the remains of organisms.  **The three major fossil fuels are coal, oil, and natural gas.**

Fossil fuels are made of hydrocarbons. **Hydrocarbons** are chemical compounds that contain carbon and hydrogen. During combustion, carbon and hydrogen combine with oxygen from the air to form carbon dioxide and water. Combustion releases energy in the forms of heat and light. The combustion of fossil fuels provides more energy per kilogram than the combustion of other fuels such as wood.

✓ **Reading Checkpoint** What are hydrocarbons?

Coal

Coal is a solid fossil fuel formed from plant remains. Figure 2 shows the process by which coal forms. People have burned coal to produce heat for thousands of years. Today, coal makes up about 23 percent of the fuel used in the United States. Most of that coal fuels electrical power plants.

Before coal can be used to produce energy, it has to be mined, or removed from the ground. Miners use machines to chop the coal into chunks and lift it to the surface. Coal mining can be a dangerous job. Thousands of miners have been killed or injured in accidents in the mines. Many more suffer from lung diseases. Fortunately, modern safety procedures and better equipment have made coal mining safer.

Coal is the most plentiful and inexpensive fossil fuel in the United States. It is fairly easy to transport and provides a lot of energy when burned. But coal also has some disadvantages. Coal mining can increase erosion. One type of coal mining leaves large open pits in the ground, and runoff from these coal mines can cause water pollution.

Burning most types of coal results in more air pollution than other fossil fuels. This pollution can be reduced to some extent by treating the coal before burning. Many pollutants can also be filtered out after combustion before they can reach the atmosphere. Nevertheless, concerns about pollution continue to limit the widespread use of coal.

FIGURE 2

Coal Formation

Coal is formed from the remains of trees and other plants that grew in swamps hundreds of millions of years ago. **Relating Diagrams and Photos** *What are two ways that peat and coal differ?*

Decomposing Plant Matter
When swamp plants die, their decomposing remains build up.

Peat
Over time, plant remains pile up and form peat. Peat can be burned as fuel.

Coal
Under increasing pressure from sediments, peat is compacted. Eventually, peat becomes coal. Coal is a more efficient fuel than peat.

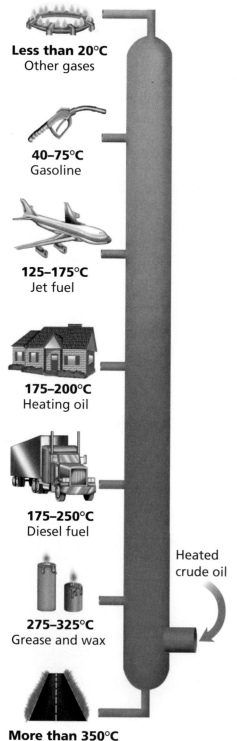

FIGURE 3
Oil Production
Crude oil is first pumped out of the ground and then refined. In the refining process, crude oil is heated and separated to make different products.

Less than 20°C
Other gases

40–75°C
Gasoline

125–175°C
Jet fuel

175–200°C
Heating oil

175–250°C
Diesel fuel

Heated crude oil

275–325°C
Grease and wax

More than 350°C
Asphalt

Oil

Oil is a thick, black, liquid fossil fuel. It formed from the remains of small organisms that lived in oceans and shallow inland seas hundreds of millions of years ago. **Petroleum** is another name for oil, from the Latin words *petra* (rock) and *oleum* (oil). Petroleum accounts for more than one third of the world's energy production. Fuel for most cars, airplanes, trains, and ships comes from petroleum. In addition, many homes are heated by oil.

Most oil deposits are located underground in tiny holes in sandstone or limestone. Because oil deposits are usually located deep below the surface, finding oil is difficult.

Oil Products When oil is first pumped out of the ground, it is called crude oil. To be made into useful products, such as gasoline, crude oil must undergo a process called refining. A factory in which crude oil is heated and separated into fuels and other products is called a **refinery.**

In Figure 3, you can see some of the products made by refining crude oil. Many other products you use every day are also made from crude oil. **Petrochemicals** are compounds that are made from oil. Petrochemicals are used to make plastics and the synthetic materials used in many common objects. Petrochemicals are also used in paints, medicines, and cosmetics.

Oil Resources Oil's low cost in the past and its ease-of-use have made it an important resource in our modern economy. However, as with the combustion of all fossil fuels, the combustion of oil in cars and power plants produces air pollution. Accidental oil spills sometimes pollute the oceans and harm sea life. Also, existing oil supplies are being used up faster than new supplies are being discovered.

Natural Gas

Natural gas is a mixture of methane and other gases. Natural gas forms from some of the same organisms as oil. Because it is less dense than oil, natural gas often rises above an oil deposit, forming a pocket of gas.

Pipelines are often used to transport natural gas from its source to the places where it is used. If all the gas pipelines in the United States were connected, they would reach to the moon and back—twice! Natural gas can also be compressed into a liquid and transported in huge ships. Compressed natural gas is also used in trucks and buses.

Natural gas has several advantages. It produces large amounts of energy but lower levels of many air pollutants than coal or oil. It is also easy to transport once a network of pipelines is built. One disadvantage of natural gas is that it is highly flammable. A gas leak can cause a violent explosion and fire.

Gas companies help to prevent dangerous explosions from leaks. If you use natural gas in your home, you probably are familiar with the "gas" smell that alerts you whenever there is unburned gas in the air. Natural gas actually has no odor at all. Gas companies add a chemical with a distinct smell to the gas so that people can detect a gas leak.

FIGURE 4
Natural Gas Pipelines
More than 2,500,000 kilometers of natural gas pipelines run underground in the United States. Here, a technician prepares a new section of pipe.

 **Reading Checkpoint** **What is one advantage of using natural gas?**

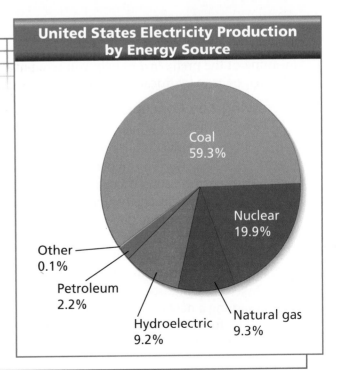

Math: Statistics, Data Analysis, and Probability 6.3.2

Math Analyzing Data

Fuels and Electricity

The circle graph shows which energy sources are used to produce electricity in the United States.

1. **Reading Graphs** What does each wedge of the circle represent?

2. **Interpreting Data** Which energy source is used to generate most of the electricity in the United States?

3. **Drawing Conclusions** What percentage of the electricity production in the United States relies on fossil fuels?

4. **Predicting** How might the circle graph differ 50 years from now? Give reasons to support your prediction.

United States Electricity Production by Energy Source

Coal 59.3%
Nuclear 19.9%
Other 0.1%
Petroleum 2.2%
Hydroelectric 9.2%
Natural gas 9.3%

Fuel Supply and Demand

As natural resources, fuels can be classified as either renewable or nonrenewable. Renewable resources are either always available or are naturally replaced in a short time. Nonrenewable resources cannot be replaced in a useful time frame.

The many advantages of using fossil fuels as an energy source have made them essential to modern life. ⬤ **But since fossil fuels take hundreds of millions of years to form, they are considered nonrenewable resources.** For example, Earth's known oil supplies took some 500 million years to form.

Many nations that consume large amounts of fossil fuels have relatively small supplies. They have to buy oil, natural gas, or coal from other nations. The United States, for example, uses about one third of all the oil produced in the world. But only 3 percent of the world's oil supply is located in this country. The difference must be purchased from other countries. The uneven distribution of oil supplies has often been a cause of political problems in the world.

Known coal supplies are high compared to current demand. However, the world's demand for oil and natural gas has been growing faster than new supplies are being found. This could lead to higher prices in the future as these resources become scarcer. Eventually, other types of energy resources will be needed to help meet the world's energy needs.

FIGURE 5
Supply and Demand
In the 1970s, a group of oil-exporting nations reduced their oil exports to the United States. Gasoline shortages resulted.

Section 1 Assessment

S 6.3.b, 6.6.a
E-LA: Reading 6.1.0

Vocabulary Skill Prefixes How does knowing the meaning of the prefix *hydro-* help you remember what happens to hydrocarbons during combustion?

⬤ **Reviewing Key Concepts**

1. **a. Defining** What is a fuel?
   b. Explaining How do fuels provide energy?
   c. Sequencing Describe in order the energy transformations that occur in the production of electricity at a power plant.
2. **a. Listing** What are the three main fossil fuels?
   b. Comparing and Contrasting List an advantage and a disadvantage of each fossil fuel discussed in this section.
   c. Making Judgments Suppose you were designing a new fossil fuel power plant. Which fossil fuel would you recommend? Give two reasons for your answer.

3. **a. Reviewing** Why are fossil fuels considered nonrenewable resources?
   b. Problem Solving List three things you can do to reduce your dependence on fossil fuels.

Lab zone **At-Home Activity**

Heating Fuel Pros and Cons Talk to an adult family member to find out what type of energy source is used to heat or cool your home. Then, with the family member, list some advantages and disadvantages of that type of fuel. Share what you learned with your classmates. What fuel source is used by the majority of students in your class?

Renewable Sources of Energy

CALIFORNIA
Standards Focus

S 6.6.a Students know the utility of energy sources is determined by factors that are involved in converting these sources to useful forms and the consequences of the conversion process.

S 6.6.b Students know different natural energy and material resources, including air, soil, rocks, minerals, petroleum, fresh water, wildlife, and forests, and know how to classify them as renewable or nonrenewable.

- What forms of energy does the sun provide?
- What are some renewable sources of energy?

Key Terms
- solar energy
- hydroelectric power
- biomass fuel
- gasohol
- geothermal energy
- tide

Lab zone **Standards Warm-Up**

Can You Capture Solar Energy?

1. Pour 250 milliliters of water into each of two resealable, clear plastic bags.
2. Record the water temperature in each bag. Seal the bags.
3. Put one bag in a dark or shady place. Put the other bag in a place where it will receive direct sunlight.
4. Predict what the temperature of the water in each bag will be after 30 minutes.
5. Record the temperatures after 30 minutes.

Think It Over

Developing Hypotheses How did the water temperature in each bag change? What could account for these results?

You've just arrived at the campsite for your family vacation. The sun streaming through the trees warms your face. A breeze stirs, carrying with it the smell of a campfire. Maybe you'll start your day with a dip in the warm water of a nearby hot spring.

You might be surprised to learn that even in these woods, you are surrounded by energy resources. The sun warms the air, the wind blows, and heat from inside Earth warms the waters of the spring. These sources of energy are all renewable—they are constantly being supplied. Scientists are trying to find ways to put these renewable energy resources to work to meet people's energy needs.

Campers surrounded by ▶
renewable resources

FIGURE 6
Solar Collector
This mirror collects energy from the sun and powers an electric plant in New South Wales, Australia. *Inferring Why is the Australian desert a practical location for a solar power plant?*

Video Field Trip
Discovery Channel School
Energy Resources

Harnessing the Sun's Energy

The warmth you feel on a sunny day is **solar energy,** or energy from the sun. 🔷 **The sun constantly gives off energy in the forms of light and heat.** Solar energy is the source, directly or indirectly, of most other renewable energy resources. In one day, Earth receives enough solar energy to meet the energy needs of the entire world for 40 years. Solar energy does not cause pollution, and it will not run out for billions of years.

One problem with solar energy is that it is only available when the sun is shining. Efficient, low-cost solar energy storage systems are not readily available. Another problem is that sunlight is very spread out. To obtain a large amount of power, it is necessary to collect solar energy from a large area. For this reason, it remains expensive to produce electricity using solar energy.

Solar Power Plants One way to capture the sun's energy involves using giant mirrors. In a solar power plant, rows of mirrors focus the sun's rays to heat a tank of water. The water boils, creating steam, which can then be used to generate electricity.

Solar Cells Solar energy can be converted directly into electricity in a solar cell. A solar cell has a negative and a positive terminal, like a battery. When light hits the cell, an electric current is produced. Solar cells power some calculators, lights, and other small devices. However, it would take more than 5,000 solar cells the size of your palm to produce enough electricity for a typical American home.

Passive Solar Heating Solar energy can be used to heat buildings with passive solar systems. A passive solar system converts sunlight into thermal energy, which is then distributed without using pumps or fans. Passive solar heating is what occurs in a parked car on a sunny day. Solar energy passes through the car's windows and heats the seats and other car parts. These parts transfer heat to the air, and the inside of the car warms. The same principle can be used to heat a home.

Active Solar Heating An active solar system captures the sun's energy, and then uses pumps and fans to distribute the heat. First, light strikes the dark metal surface of a solar collector. There, it is converted to thermal energy. Water is pumped through pipes in the solar collector to absorb the thermal energy. The heated water then flows to a storage tank. Finally, pumps and fans distribute the heat throughout the building.

 **Reading Checkpoint** How do solar cells work?

FIGURE 7

Solar House

A solar house uses passive and active heating systems to convert solar energy into heat and electricity.

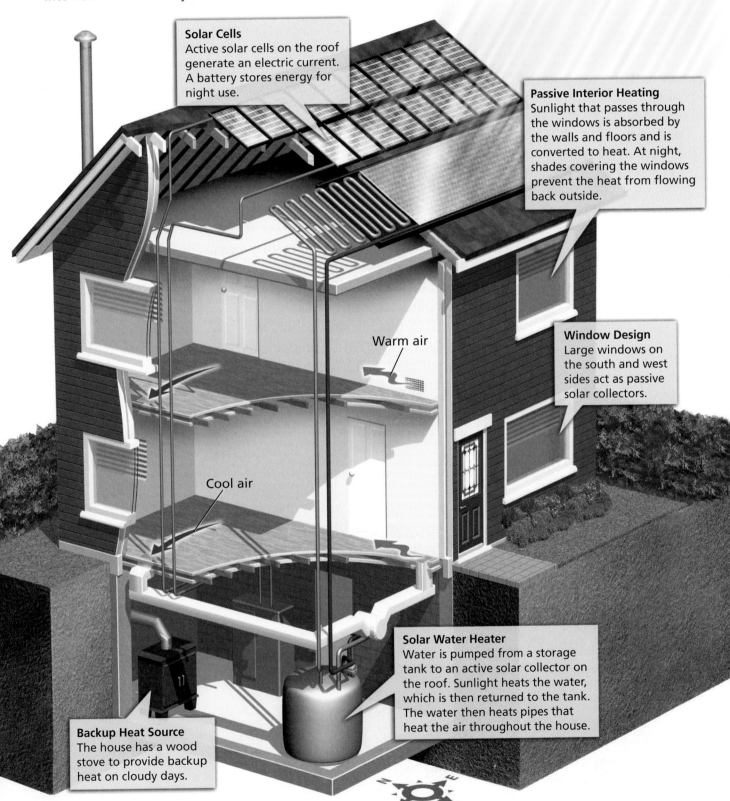

Solar Cells
Active solar cells on the roof generate an electric current. A battery stores energy for night use.

Passive Interior Heating
Sunlight that passes through the windows is absorbed by the walls and floors and is converted to heat. At night, shades covering the windows prevent the heat from flowing back outside.

Warm air

Window Design
Large windows on the south and west sides act as passive solar collectors.

Cool air

Solar Water Heater
Water is pumped from a storage tank to an active solar collector on the roof. Sunlight heats the water, which is then returned to the tank. The water then heats pipes that heat the air throughout the house.

Backup Heat Source
The house has a wood stove to provide backup heat on cloudy days.

Hydroelectric Power

The sun is one source of renewable energy.  **Other renewable sources of energy include water, the wind, biomass fuels, geothermal energy, and the tides.**

Solar energy is the indirect source of water power. Recall that in the water cycle, energy from the sun heats water on Earth's surface, forming water vapor. The water vapor condenses and falls back to Earth as rain and snow. As the water flows over the land, it provides another source of energy.

Hydroelectric power is electricity produced by flowing water. A dam across a river blocks the flow of water, creating a body of water called a reservoir. When a dam's control gates are opened, water flows through tunnels at the bottom of the dam. As the water moves through the tunnels, it turns turbines, which are connected to a generator.

Today, hydroelectric power is the most widely used source of renewable energy. Unlike solar energy, flowing water provides a steady supply of energy. Once a dam and power plant are built, producing electricity is inexpensive and does not create air pollution. But hydroelectric power has limitations. In the United States, most suitable rivers have already been dammed. And dams can have negative effects on the environment, such as sediment build-up and the potential for disaster caused by dam failure.

Reading Checkpoint What is hydroelectric power?

Wind Power

Like water power, wind power is also an indirect form of solar energy. The sun heats Earth's surface unevenly. As a result of this uneven heating, different areas of the atmosphere have different temperatures and air pressures. The differences in pressure cause winds as air moves from one area to another.

FIGURE 8
Renewable Energy Sources

This dam and wind farm use renewable sources of energy to generate power. The car runs on vegetable oil, a type of biomass fuel that is also renewable.

Comparing and Contrasting *How are biomass fuels similar to energy sources such as wind and water? How are they different?*

Wind can be used to turn a turbine and generate electricity. Large wind farms consist of many wind turbines, which are modern versions of windmills. These wind farms are located in regions such as Central California where the wind blows strongly and steadily, so the most power can be produced.

Wind is perhaps the fastest growing energy resource. Wind power is renewable and does not cause pollution. The cost of energy produced by wind turbines has been falling steadily thanks to improvements in technology. In areas with strong winds, wind turbines can produce electricity at a cost that is competitive with those of fossil-fuel plants.

But wind power does have some drawbacks. Many areas do not have sufficiently strong and steady winds to support wind farms. Wind farms require a lot of land, although the land can often be used for other purposes. Also, the wind often blows the strongest in scenic areas, such as along the shore or on mountaintops, where people may object to building wind turbines.

Biomass Fuels

Wood was probably the first fuel ever used for heat and light. Wood belongs to a group of fuels called **biomass fuels,** which are made from material that was once part of a living thing. Other biomass fuels include leaves, food wastes, and manure.

Aside from being burned as fuel, biomass materials can also be converted into other fuels. For example, some crops can be used to make alcohol. Adding the alcohol to gasoline forms a mixture called **gasohol.** Gasohol can be used as fuel for cars. Bacteria can produce methane gas when they decompose biomass materials in landfills. That methane can be used to heat buildings.

Biomass fuels are renewable resources. But it takes time for new trees to replace those that have been cut down. And producing alcohol and methane in large quantities is expensive. As a result, biomass fuels are not widely used today in the United States. But as fossil fuels become scarcer, biomass fuels may play a larger role in meeting energy needs.

Tapping Earth's Energy

Below Earth's surface are pockets of very hot liquid rock called magma. In some places, magma is very close to the surface. The intense heat from Earth's interior that warms the magma is called **geothermal energy.**

In certain regions, such as Iceland and New Zealand, magma heats underground water to the boiling point. In these places, the hot water and steam can be valuable sources of energy. For example, in Reykjavík, Iceland, 90 percent of homes are heated by water warmed underground in this way. Geothermal energy can also be used to generate electricity, as shown in Figure 9.

Geothermal energy is an unlimited source of cheap energy. But it does have disadvantages. There are only a few places where magma comes close to Earth's surface. Elsewhere, very deep wells would be needed to tap this energy. Drilling deep wells is very expensive. Even so, geothermal energy is likely to play a growing part in meeting energy needs in some regions.

Reading Checkpoint How can geothermal energy be used to generate electricity?

FIGURE 9
Geothermal Energy
A geothermal power plant uses heat from Earth's interior as an energy source. Cold water is piped deep into the ground, where it is heated by magma. The resulting steam and hot water can be used for heat or to generate electricity.
Making Generalizations *What are one advantage and one disadvantage of geothermal energy?*

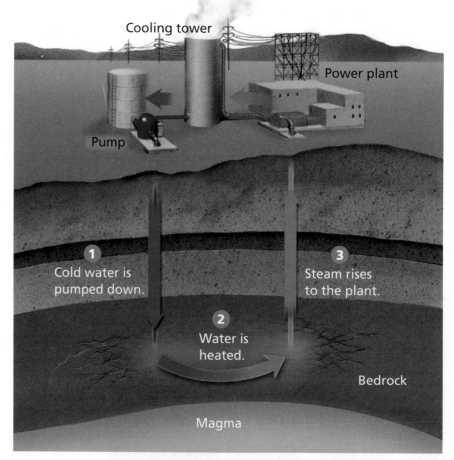

Cooling tower
Power plant
Pump

1 Cold water is pumped down.
2 Water is heated.
3 Steam rises to the plant.

Bedrock
Magma

Tidal Energy

You have already learned that flowing water in a river can be used to produce electricity. Another source of moving water is the tides. The **tides** are the regular rise and fall of Earth's waters along its shores. The tides are caused by the gravitational pull of the moon and sun. Along some coastlines, enormous amounts of water move into bays and river mouths at high tide. This water flows back out to sea when the tide falls.

A few tidal power plants have been built to take advantage of this regular motion. Such power plants typically consist of a low, gated dam across the entrance to a shallow bay or river. As the tide rises, the dam's gates open so that water flows in. As the tide retreats, the gates shut to trap the water behind. Gravity pulls the trapped water back to the sea through tunnels. The energy of the water flowing through these tunnels generates electricity, as in a hydroelectric power plant.

Although tidal power is a clean, renewable source of energy, it has several limitations. Harnessing tidal power is practical only where there is a large difference between high and low tides—at least 4 or 5 meters. There are only a few places in the world where such a large difference occurs. Also, a dam across a bay would block boats and fish from passing through. Therefore, tidal power is likely to remain a limited source of energy.

FIGURE 10
Tidal Power Plant
This large tidal power plant in France is used to generate electricity.

Section 2 Assessment

S 6.6.a, 6.6.b, E-LA: Reading 6.2.2, Writing 6.2.3

Target Reading Skill Comparing and Contrasting Complete a table comparing the pros and cons of solar, water, wind, and geothermal energy resources.

Reviewing Key Concepts

1. a. **Identifying** What two forms of energy does the sun supply?
   b. **Explaining** What are two reasons that solar energy has not replaced energy from fossil fuels?
   c. **Applying Concepts** A friend of yours argues that shopping malls should use solar energy to conserve fossil fuels. How would you respond?

2. a. **Listing** List five renewable energy sources other than solar energy.
   b. **Classifying** Which of the renewable energy sources that you listed are actually indirect forms of solar energy? Explain.
   c. **Predicting** Which source of renewable energy do you think is most likely to be used in your community within the next 20 years? Explain your answer.

Writing in Science

Research Report Use published materials and Internet resources to write a one-page research report about one of the energy resources discussed in this chapter. Discuss the energy resource's advantages and disadvantages. Be sure to also discuss its current status and environmental impacts. Include a brief bibliography.

Technology Lab
Full Inquiry

Design and Build a Solar Cooker

Materials

glue and tape

3 sheets of aluminum foil

3 sheets of oaktag paper

3 thermometers and wooden or plastic stirrers

clock or watch

scissors

frozen vegetables

Problem What is the best shape for a solar cooker?

Skills Focus designing a solution, evaluating the design

Procedure

PART 1 Research and Investigate

1. Glue a sheet of aluminum foil, shiny side up, to each sheet of oaktag paper. Before the glue dries, gently smooth out any wrinkles in the foil.

2. Bend one sheet into a U shape. Leave another sheet flat. Bend another sheet into a shape of your own choosing.

3. Predict which shape will produce the largest temperature increase when placed in the sun. Write down your prediction and explain your reasons.

4. Place the aluminum sheets in direct sunlight. Use wood blocks or books to hold the sheets in position, if necessary.

5. Record the starting temperature on each thermometer.

6. Place the thermometer bulbs in the center of the aluminum shapes. After 15 minutes, record the final temperature on each thermometer.

PART 2 Design and Build

7. Using what you learned in Part 1, design a solar cooker that can cook frozen vegetables. Your solar cooker should
   • be no larger than 50 cm on any side
   • cook the vegetables in less than 10 minutes
   • be made of materials approved by your teacher

8. Prepare a written description of your plan that includes a sketch of your cooker. Include a list of materials and an operational definition of a "well-cooked" vegetable. Obtain your teacher's approval for your design. Then build your solar cooker.

PART 3

Evaluate and Redesign

9. Test your solar cooker by spearing some frozen vegetables on the stirrers. Time how long it takes to cook the vegetables. Make note of any problems with your solar cooker design.

10. Based on your test, decide how you could improve the design of your cooker. Then make any desired changes to your cooker and test how the improved cooker functions.

Analyze and Conclude

1. **Identifying a Need** In what situations might it be important to have an efficient cooker that does not use fuel?

2. **Designing a Solution** How did you incorporate what you learned in Part 1 into your design in Part 2? For example, which shape did you use in your cooker design?

3. **Evaluating the Design** When you tested your solar cooker, what problems did you encounter?

4. **Redesigning** In what ways did you change your design for your second test? How did the redesign improve the performance of your cooker?

5. **Working With Design Constraints** Why might it be important for solar cookers to use inexpensive, readily available materials?

6. **Evaluating the Impact on Society** How can solar-powered devices help meet the world's future energy needs? What limitation do solar-powered devices have?

Communicate

Design an advertisement for your solar cooker that will appear in a camping magazine. Make sure your ad describes the benefits of solar cookers in general, and of your design in particular.

Nuclear Energy

CALIFORNIA
Standards Focus

S 6.6.a Students know the utility of energy sources is determined by factors that are involved in converting these sources to useful forms and the consequences of the conversion process.

S 6.6.b Students know different natural energy and material resources, including air, soil, rocks, minerals, petroleum, fresh water, wildlife, and forests, and know how to classify them as renewable or nonrenewable.

- What happens during a nuclear fission reaction?
- How does a nuclear power plant produce electricity?
- How does a nuclear fusion reaction occur?

Key Terms

- nucleus
- nuclear fission
- reactor vessel
- fuel rod
- control rod
- meltdown
- nuclear fusion

Lab zone Standards **Warm-Up**

Why Do They Fall?

1. Line up 15 dominoes to form a triangle.
2. Knock over the first domino so that it falls against the second row of dominoes. Observe the results.
3. Set up the dominoes again, but then remove the dominoes in the third row from the lineup.
4. Knock over the first domino again. Observe what happens.

Think It Over

Inferring Suppose each domino produced a large amount of energy when it fell over. Why might it be helpful to remove the dominoes as you did in Step 3?

Wouldn't it be great if people could use the same method as the sun to produce energy? The kind of reactions that power the sun involve the central cores of atoms. The central core of an atom that contains the protons and neutrons is called the **nucleus** (plural *nuclei*). Reactions that involve nuclei, called nuclear reactions, result in tremendous amounts of energy. Two types of nuclear reactions are fission and fusion.

Nuclear Fission

Nuclear reactions convert matter into energy. As part of his theory of relativity, Albert Einstein developed a formula that described the relationship between energy and matter. You have probably seen this famous equation: $E = mc^2$. In the equation, the E represents energy and the m represents mass. The c, which represents the speed of light, is a very large number. This equation states that when matter is changed into energy, an enormous amount of energy is released.

▲ **Albert Einstein**
1879–1955

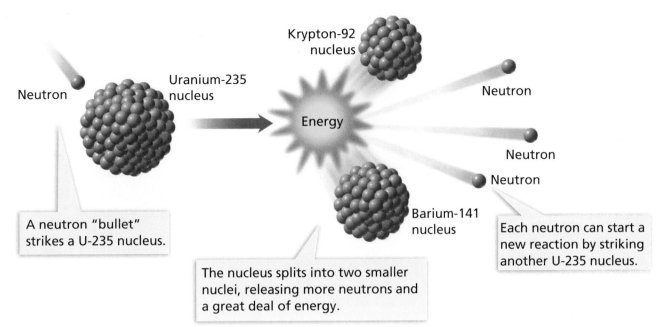

Neutron

Uranium-235 nucleus

Krypton-92 nucleus

Energy

Neutron

Neutron

Neutron

Barium-141 nucleus

A neutron "bullet" strikes a U-235 nucleus.

The nucleus splits into two smaller nuclei, releasing more neutrons and a great deal of energy.

Each neutron can start a new reaction by striking another U-235 nucleus.

FIGURE 11
Nuclear Fission
A great deal of energy is released in a nuclear fission reaction.
Interpreting Diagrams *How does a nuclear fission reaction begin?*

Fission Reactions Nuclear fission is the splitting of an atom's nucleus into two smaller nuclei. The fuel for the reaction is a large atom that has an unstable nucleus, such as uranium-235 (U-235). A neutron is shot at the U-235 atom at high speed. **When the neutron hits the U-235 nucleus, the nucleus splits apart into two smaller nuclei and two or more neutrons.** The total mass of all these particles is a bit less than the mass of the original nucleus. The small amount of mass that makes up the difference has been converted into energy—a lot of energy, as described by Einstein's equation.

Meanwhile, the fission reaction has produced more neutrons. If any of these neutrons strikes another nucleus, the fission reaction is repeated. More neutrons and more energy are released. If there are enough nuclei nearby, the process repeats in a chain reaction, just like a row of dominoes falling. In a nuclear chain reaction, the amount of energy released increases rapidly with each step in the chain.

Energy From Fission What happens to all the energy released by these fission reactions? If a nuclear chain reaction is not controlled, the released energy causes a huge explosion. The explosion of an atomic bomb is an uncontrolled nuclear fission reaction. A few kilograms of matter explode with more force than several thousand tons of dynamite. However, if the chain reaction is controlled in a power plant, the energy is released as heat, which can then be used to generate electricity.

Reading Checkpoint   **What happens in a nuclear chain reaction?**

Lab zone Skills **Activity**

Calculating
A pellet of U-235 produces as much energy as 615 liters of fuel oil. An average home uses 5,000 liters of oil a year. How many U-235 pellets would be needed to supply the same amount of energy?

Nuclear Power
Nuclear power plants generate much of the world's electricity. The inset photo shows autunite, a uranium ore.

Nuclear Power Plants

Controlled nuclear fission reactions take place inside nuclear power plants. Nuclear power plants generate much of the world's electricity—about 20 percent in the United States and more than 70 percent in France.

Nuclear Fuel The uranium fuel for nuclear power plants is refined from uranium ores. Uranium ore is fairly abundant. However, since new uranium ore is not being created, uranium is considered a nonrenewable resource.

Energy Production Look at the nuclear power plant diagram in Figure 13. 🗝 **In a nuclear power plant, the heat released from fission is used to change water into steam. The steam then turns the blades of a turbine to generate electricity.**

The **reactor vessel** is the part of the nuclear reactor where nuclear fission occurs. The reactor contains **fuel rods** that hold pellets of uranium. When several fuel rods are placed close together, a series of fission reactions occurs.

If the reactor vessel gets too hot, control rods are used to slow down the chain reactions. **Control rods,** made of the metal cadmium, are inserted between the fuel rods to slow the speed of the chain reactions.

Heat is removed from the reactor vessel by water or another fluid that is pumped through the reactor. This fluid passes through a heat exchanger. There, the fluid boils water to produce steam, which runs the electrical generator. The steam is condensed again and pumped back to the heat exchanger.

 **Reading Checkpoint** What is the purpose of a control rod?

Pros and Cons Accidents at nuclear power plants have led to safety concerns. In 1986, the reactor vessel in a nuclear power plant in Chernobyl, Ukraine, overheated. The fuel rods generated so much heat that they started to melt, a condition called a **meltdown.** The excess heat caused a series of explosions, which injured or killed dozens of people. In addition, radioactive materials escaped into the environment.

Another problem is the disposal of highly radioactive wastes. Some radioactive wastes remain dangerous for many thousands of years. Scientists must find a way to store these wastes safely for a long period of time.

Nuclear plants also emit large amounts of heat to the air and nearby bodies of water. However, because nuclear plants don't burn fossil fuels, they don't produce air pollution. Since these plants don't emit carbon dioxide, some suggest that they could help to solve the problem of global warming.

Go Online
active art

For: Nuclear Power Plant activity
Visit: PHSchool.com
Web Code: cep-5053

FIGURE 13
Nuclear Power Plant
Nuclear fission provides the energy to generate electricity in a nuclear power plant. **Interpreting Diagrams** *In what part of the power plant does nuclear fission occur?*

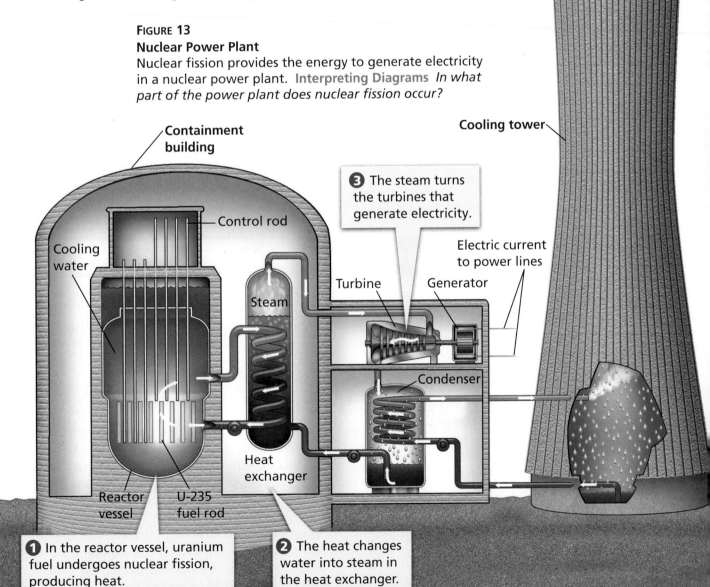

Containment building

Cooling tower

❸ The steam turns the turbines that generate electricity.

Control rod

Cooling water

Electric current to power lines

Turbine   Generator

Steam

Condenser

Heat exchanger

Reactor vessel   U-235 fuel rod

❶ In the reactor vessel, uranium fuel undergoes nuclear fission, producing heat.

❷ The heat changes water into steam in the heat exchanger.

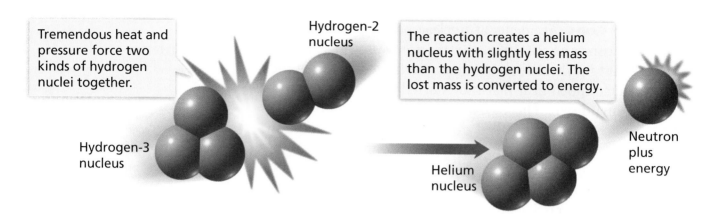

Tremendous heat and pressure force two kinds of hydrogen nuclei together.

Hydrogen-2 nucleus

The reaction creates a helium nucleus with slightly less mass than the hydrogen nuclei. The lost mass is converted to energy.

Hydrogen-3 nucleus

Helium nucleus

Neutron plus energy

FIGURE 14
Nuclear Fusion
In nuclear fusion, two hydrogen nuclei are forced together, forming a helium nucleus, a neutron, and energy.
Interpreting Diagrams *What is released during a fusion reaction?*

The Quest to Control Fusion

Nuclear fusion is the combining of two atomic nuclei to produce a single larger nucleus. 🔑 **In nuclear fusion, two hydrogen nuclei combine to create a helium nucleus, which has slightly less mass than the two hydrogen nuclei. The lost mass is converted to large amounts of energy.**

Nuclear fusion is the process by which the sun produces energy. On Earth, fusion is a promising future energy source. Fusion fuels are readily available—water contains a form of hydrogen that could be used. Since its fuel can be found in water, fusion is considered a renewable energy source. Fusion would not produce air pollution. And unlike fission, fusion would not produce long-lived radioactive wastes. However, fusion can take place only at extremely high pressures and temperatures. The construction of a practical fusion reactor is a major engineering challenge that may take many years to complete.

Section 3 Assessment

S 6.6.a, 6.6.b,
E-LA: Reading 6.2.2

🎯 **Target Reading Skill** Comparing and Contrasting Create a compare/contrast table showing the similarities and differences in nuclear fission and nuclear fusion.

🔑 **Reviewing Key Concepts**

1. **a. Defining** What is nuclear fission?
   b. Sequencing Describe the steps that occur in a nuclear fission reaction.
   c. Classifying Is uranium a renewable or nonrenewable resource? Explain.
2. **a. Identifying** What type of nuclear reaction produces electricity in a nuclear power plant?
   b. Explaining Explain how electricity is produced in a nuclear power plant.
   c. Predicting What might happen in a nuclear plant if too many control rods were removed?

3. **a. Reviewing** Define nuclear fusion.
   b. Relating Cause and Effect How is energy produced during a nuclear fusion reaction?

Lab zone **At-Home Activity**

Shoot the Nucleus With a family member, make a model of a nuclear fission reaction. Place a handful of marbles on the floor in a tight cluster, so that they touch one another. Step back about a half meter from the marbles. Shoot a marble at the cluster. Note what effect the moving marble has on the cluster. Then using a diagram, explain how this event models a nuclear fission reaction.

Energy Conservation

CALIFORNIA
Standards Focus

S 6.3.a Students know energy can be carried from one place to another by heat flow or by waves, including water, light and sound waves, or by moving objects.

S 6.3.b Students know that when fuel is consumed, most of the energy released becomes heat energy.

What are two ways to preserve our current energy sources?

Key Terms
- efficiency
- insulation
- energy conservation

Lab zone Standards **Warm-Up**

Which Bulb Is More Efficient?

1. Record the light output (listed in lumens) from the packages of a 60-watt incandescent light bulb and a 15-watt compact fluorescent bulb.

2. Place the fluorescent bulb in a lamp socket. **CAUTION:** *Make sure the lamp is unplugged.*

3. Plug in the lamp and turn it on. Hold the end of a thermometer about 8 centimeters from the bulb.

4. Record the temperature after five minutes.

5. Turn off and unplug the lamp. When the bulb is cool, remove it. Repeat Steps 2, 3, and 4 with the incandescent light bulb.

Think It Over

Inferring The 60-watt bulb uses four times as much energy as the 15-watt bulb. Does it also provide four times as much light output? If not, how can you account for the difference?

What would happen if the world ran out of fossil fuels today? The heating and cooling systems in most buildings would cease to function. Forests would disappear as people began to burn wood for heating and cooking. Cars, buses, and trains would be stranded wherever they ran out of fuel. About 70 percent of the world's electric power capacity would be idled. Since televisions, computers, and telephones depend on electricity, communication would be greatly reduced.

Although fossil fuels won't run out soon, they also won't last forever. Most people think that it makes sense to use fuels more wisely now to avoid possible fuel shortages in the future. **One way to preserve energy resources is to increase the efficiency of energy use. Another way is to conserve energy whenever possible.**

Energy Efficiency

One way to make energy resources last longer is to use fuels more efficiently. **Efficiency** is the percentage of energy that is actually used to perform work. The rest of the energy is "lost" to the surroundings, usually as heat. This heat can pollute the water and air. People have developed many ways to increase energy efficiency.

Heating and Cooling One method of increasing the efficiency of heating and cooling systems is insulation. **Insulation** is a layer of material that traps air to help block heat flow between the air inside and outside a building. You have probably seen insulation made of fiberglass, which looks like pink cotton candy.

Trapped air can act as insulation in windows, too. Many windows consist of two panes of glass with space between them. The air between the panes of glass acts as insulation.

• Tech & Design in History •

Energy-Efficient Products

Scientists and engineers have developed many technologies that improve energy efficiency and reduce energy use.

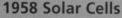

1958 Solar Cells
More than 150 years ago, scientists discovered that silicon can convert light into electricity. The first useful application of solar cells was to power the radio on a satellite. Now solar cells are even used on experimental cars like the one above.

1936 Fluorescent Lighting
Fluorescent bulbs were introduced to the public at the hundredth anniversary celebration of the United States Patent Office. Because these bulbs use less energy than incandescent bulbs, most offices and schools use fluorescent lights today.

1932 Fiberglass Insulation
Long strands of glass fibers trap air and keep buildings from losing heat. Less fuel is used for heating.

| 1930 | 1940 | 1950 | 1960 |

Lighting Much of the electricity used for home lighting is wasted. For example, less than 10 percent of the electricity that an incandescent light bulb uses is converted into light. The rest is given off as heat. In contrast, compact fluorescent bulbs use about one fourth as much energy to provide the same amount of light.

Transportation Engineers have improved the energy efficiency of cars by designing better engines and tires. Another way to save energy is to reduce the number of cars on the road. In many communities, public transit systems provide an alternative to driving. Other cities encourage carpooling. Many cities now set aside lanes for cars containing two or more people.

 **Reading Checkpoint** **What are two examples of insulation?**

1967 Microwave Ovens
The first countertop microwave oven for the home was introduced. Microwaves cook food by heating the water the food contains. Unlike a conventional oven, a microwave oven heats only the food. And preheating is unnecessary, saving even more energy.

1981 High-Efficiency Window Coatings
Materials that reflect sunlight were first used to coat windows in the early 1980s. This coating reduces the air conditioning needed to keep the inside of the building cool.

1997 Hydrogen-Powered Vehicles
Hydrogen fuel cells produce no polluting emissions. In 1997, two major automakers unveiled experimental hydrogen-powered cars. The first mass-produced hydrogen-powered cars are expected around 2010.

| 1970 | 1980 | 1990 | 2000 |

FIGURE 15
Energy Conservation
There are many ways you can conserve energy.

Ways I can conserve energy:

✓ *Walk or ride a bike for short trips*

✓ *Recycle*

✓ *Use fans instead of air conditioners when it's hot*

✓ *Turn off the lights and television when leaving a room*

Energy Conservation

Another approach to making energy resources last longer is conservation. **Energy conservation** means reducing energy use.

You can reduce your personal energy use by changing your behavior in some simple ways. For example, if you walk to the store instead of getting a ride, you are conserving the gasoline it would take to drive to the store. You can also follow some of the suggestions in Figure 15.

While these suggestions seem like small things, multiplied by millions of people they add up to a lot of energy saved for the future.

 **Reading Checkpoint** What are two ways you can reduce your personal energy use?

Section 4 Assessment

S 6.3.a, 6.3.b, E-LA: Reading 6.1.0, Writing 6.2.0

Vocabulary Skill Prefixes The prefix *con-* and the Latin root *servare* form *conserve*, meaning "keep together" or "preserve." What is the meaning of *energy conservation*?

Reviewing Key Concepts

1. **a. Identifying** What are the two keys to preserving our current energy resources?
   b. Applying Concepts How does insulating buildings help to preserve energy resources? How does carpooling preserve resources?
   c. Predicting One office building contains only incandescent lights. The building next door contains only fluorescent lights. Predict which building has higher energy bills. Explain your answer.

Writing in Science

Energy Savings Brochure
Conduct an energy audit of your home. Look for places where energy is being lost, such as cracks around doors. Also look for ways to reduce energy use, such as running the dishwasher only when it is full. Then create a short, illustrated brochure of energy-saving suggestions. Keep the brochure where everyone can see it.

Consumer Lab
Guided Inquiry

S 6.3.a, 6.7.c

Keeping Comfortable

Materials

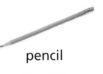

containers and lids made of paper, glass, plastic, plastic foam, and metal

pencil

ice water

thermometers or temperature probes

beakers

hot water

clock or watch

Problem How well do different materials prevent heat flow?

Skills Focus measuring, controlling variables

Procedure

1. Use a pencil to poke a hole in the lid of a paper cup. Fill the cup halfway with cold water.

2.  Put the lid on the cup. Insert a thermometer into the water through the hole. (If you are using a temperature probe, see your teacher for instructions.) When the temperature stops dropping, place the cup in a beaker. Add hot water to the beaker until the water level is about 1 cm below the lid.

3. Record the water temperature once every minute until it has increased by 5°C. Use the time it takes for the temperature to increase 5°C as a measure of the effectiveness of the paper cup in preventing heat transfer.

4. Choose three other containers and their matching lids to test. Design an experiment to compare how well those materials prevent heat transfer. You can use a similar procedure to the one you used in Steps 1–3.

Analyze and Conclude

1. **Measuring** In Step 2, what was the starting temperature of the cold water? How long did it take for the temperature to increase by 5°C? In which direction did the heat flow? Explain.

2. **Making Models** If the materials in Steps 1–3 represented your home in very hot weather, which material would represent the rooms in your home? The outdoor weather? The building walls?

3. **Controlling Variables** In the experiment you conducted in Step 4, what were the manipulated and responding variables? What variables were kept constant?

4. **Drawing Conclusions** Which material was most effective at preventing the transfer of heat? Which was the least effective? Explain how your data support your conclusion.

5. **Communicating** Write a paragraph explaining why the results of your experiment could be useful to people building energy-efficient structures.

Design an Experiment

Design an experiment to compare how well the materials you tested would work if the hot water were inside the cup and the cold water were outside. *Obtain your teacher's permission before carrying out your investigation.*

Go Online
PHSchool.com

For : Data sharing
Visit: PHSchool.com
Web Code: ced-5054

The Hybrid Car

How do you get from here to there? Like most people, you probably rely on cars or buses. Engines that burn fossil fuels power most of these vehicles. To conserve fossil fuels, as well as to reduce air pollution, some car companies have begun to produce hybrid vehicles.

How Are Hybrid Cars Different?

The power source for most cars is a gasoline engine that powers the transmission. Unlike conventional cars, hybrid cars use both a gasoline engine and an electric motor to turn the transmission. The generated power can be used by the transmission to turn the wheels. Or power can be converted into electricity for later use by the electric motor. Any extra electricity is stored in the car's battery. The gasoline engine in a hybrid car is smaller, more efficient, and less polluting than the engine in a conventional car.

Gasoline Engine The engine burns fuel to provide energy to the car.

Electric Motor and Generator In this model, the electric motor draws energy from the car's battery to help the car speed up. As the car slows down, the generator produces electricity to recharge the car's battery.

Transmission This device transmits power from the engine to the axle that turns the wheels.

Start The car uses power from its battery to start the gasoline engine.

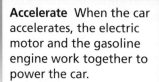

Accelerate When the car accelerates, the electric motor and the gasoline engine work together to power the car.

Brake When the car brakes, the motor acts like a generator and stores electrical energy in the battery.

Are Hybrid Cars the Way to Go?

Hybrid cars consume less gas per mile and emit fewer pollutants than cars that run on gasoline alone. In spite of the benefits, there are some drawbacks to hybrid cars. In general, hybrid cars have less power for climbing steep hills and less acceleration than cars with larger engines. In addition, the large batteries could be an environmental hazard if they end up in a landfill. Drivers must make trade-offs in buying any car.

Mileage per Tank of Gas

Gasoline stored in the fuel tank flows to the engine, where it is burned.

Battery The car's electric motor uses energy stored in the battery.

Stop When the car stops or idles, the gasoline engine stops. It restarts when the driver steps on the gas pedal.

You Decide

1. **Identify the Need** Why are some car companies developing hybrid cars?
2. **Research** Research hybrid cars currently on the market. Use your findings to list the advantages and disadvantages of hybrid-car technology.
3. **Write** Should your family's next car be a conventional or hybrid model? Use the information here and your research findings to write several paragraphs supporting your opinion.

Go Online PHSchool.com **For:** More on hybrid cars
Visit: PHSchool.com
Web Code: ceh-5050

Recycling Material Resources

CALIFORNIA
Standards Focus

S 6.6.c Students know the natural origin of the materials used to make common objects.

🔑 What are three methods of handling solid waste?

🔑 What can people do to help control the solid waste problem?

Key Terms
- municipal solid waste
- incineration
- leachate
- sanitary landfill
- recycling
- biodegradable
- composting

Lab zone | Standards Warm-Up

What's in the Trash?
Your teacher will give you a trash bag. The items in the bag represent the most common categories of household waste in the United States.

1. Before you open the bag, predict what the two most common categories are.

2. Put on some plastic gloves. Open the bag and sort the trash items into categories based on what they are made of.

3. 🖐️ Count the number of trash items in each category. Construct a bar graph showing the number of pieces of trash in each category.

Think It Over

Interpreting Data Based on your graph, what are the two most common types of household waste? Was your prediction correct?

How much trash does your family throw away in a year? If it's your job to take the trash out, you might say that it's a large amount. Now imagine that amount multiplied by every family in the United States! Consider these facts:

- Every hour, people throw away about 2.5 million plastic bottles.

- Every day, the average person produces about 2 kilograms of trash.

- Every year, people throw away 2.8 million metric tons of plastic bags and 230 million automobile tires.

You can see why some people call the United States a "throw-away society"! Disposable products can be cheap and convenient. But they have created a big problem—what to do with all the trash.

The Problem of Waste Disposal

In their daily activities, people generate many types of waste, including used paper, empty packages, and food scraps. The waste materials produced in homes, businesses, schools, and other places in a community are called **municipal solid waste.** Other sources of solid waste include construction debris and certain agricultural and industrial wastes. ◯ **Three methods of handling solid waste are burning, burying, and recycling. Each method has advantages and disadvantages.**

Incineration The burning of solid waste is called **incineration** (in sin ur AY shun). Incineration has some advantages. The burning facilities, or incinerators, do not take up much space. They do not pose a risk of polluting ground-water. The heat produced by burning solid waste can be used to generate electricity. These "waste-to-energy" plants supply electricity to many homes in the United States.

Unfortunately, incinerators do have drawbacks. Even the best incinerators release some pollution into the air. And although incinerators reduce the volume of waste by as much as 90 percent, some waste still remains. This waste needs to be disposed of somewhere. Finally, incinerators are expensive to build.

FIGURE 16
Waste Disposal
Billions of tons of municipal solid waste are created in the United States each year. More than one third of that waste is paper.
Reading Graphs *What percentage of solid waste does food waste represent?*

Landfill Wastes

Paper and cardboard 38%

Yard wastes 13%

Food wastes 10%

Plastics 9%

Metals 8%

Glass 6%

Other wastes 16%

FIGURE 17
Sanitary Landfill

A well-designed sanitary landfill contains the waste and prevents it from polluting the surrounding land and water.

Landfills Until fairly recently, people usually disposed of waste in open holes in the ground. But these open dumps were dangerous and unsightly. Rainwater falling on a dump dissolved chemicals from the wastes, forming a polluted liquid called **leachate.** Leachate could run off into streams and lakes, or trickle down into the groundwater below the dump.

In 1976, the government banned open dumps. Now much solid waste is buried in landfills that are constructed to hold the wastes more safely. A **sanitary landfill** holds municipal solid waste, construction debris, and some types of agricultural and industrial waste. Figure 17 shows the parts of a well-designed sanitary landfill. Once a landfill is full, it is covered with a clay cap to keep rainwater from entering the waste.

However, even well-designed landfills still pose a risk of polluting groundwater. And while capped landfills can be reused in certain ways, including as parks and sites for sports arenas, they cannot be used for housing or agriculture.

Reading Checkpoint **What are two possible uses of a capped sanitary landfill?**

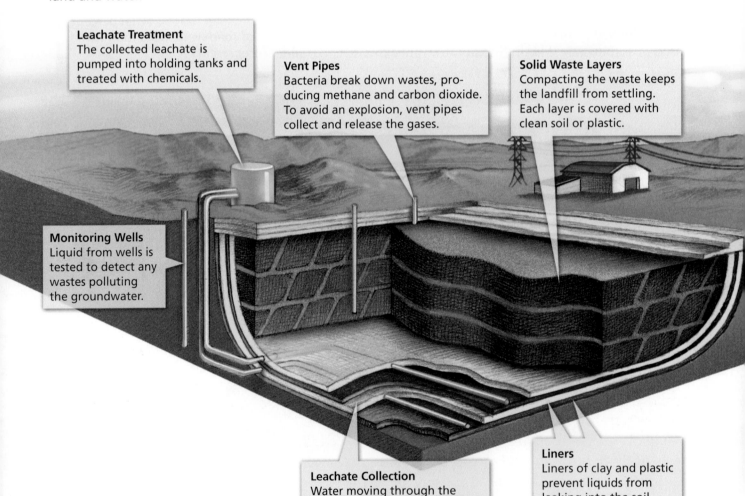

Leachate Treatment
The collected leachate is pumped into holding tanks and treated with chemicals.

Vent Pipes
Bacteria break down wastes, producing methane and carbon dioxide. To avoid an explosion, vent pipes collect and release the gases.

Solid Waste Layers
Compacting the waste keeps the landfill from settling. Each layer is covered with clean soil or plastic.

Monitoring Wells
Liquid from wells is tested to detect any wastes polluting the groundwater.

Leachate Collection
Water moving through the landfill dissolves some wastes, forming leachate at the bottom.

Liners
Liners of clay and plastic prevent liquids from leaking into the soil.

FIGURE 18
Metal Recycling
Metal is a commonly recycled material. Here, crumpled aluminum cans ride up a conveyor belt in a recycling center.
Predicting Without recycling, what might eventually happen to the supply of aluminum?

Recycling

The process of reclaiming raw materials and reusing them to create new products is called **recycling.** Recycling reduces the volume of solid waste by enabling people to use the materials in wastes again. While recycling uses some energy, it also saves the energy that would be needed to obtain and process raw materials.

As you know, matter in ecosystems is naturally recycled through the water cycle, carbon cycle, and other processes. Any material that can be broken down and recycled by bacteria and other decomposers is **biodegradable** (by oh dih GRAY duh bul). Unfortunately, many of the products people use today are not biodegradable. Plastic containers, metal cans, rubber tires, and glass jars are examples of products that do not naturally decompose. Instead, people have developed techniques to recycle the raw materials in these products.

A wide range of materials, including motor oil, tires, and batteries, can be recycled. Most recycling focuses on four major categories of products: metal, plastic, glass, and paper.

Metal In your classroom, you are surrounded by metal objects that can be recycled. Your desk, scissors, staples, and paper clips are probably made of steel. Another very common metal, aluminum, is used to make soda cans, house siding, window screens, and many other products.

Metals such as iron and aluminum can be recycled. Recycling metal saves money and causes less pollution than making new metal. With recycling, no ore needs to be mined, transported to factories, or processed. In addition, recycling metals helps conserve these nonrenewable resources.

Lab zone Skills Activity

Graphing

What happens to trash? Use the data in the table below to construct a circle graph of methods of municipal solid waste disposal in the United States. Give your circle graph a title. (For help making a circle graph, see the Skills Handbook.)

Method of Disposal	Percentage of Waste
Landfills	56%
Recycling	27%
Incineration	17%

FIGURE 19
Plastic Recycling
Plastic bottles can be recycled and made into many products, including polyester fleece for jackets.

Lab zone Try This **Activity**

It's in the Numbers

Plastic bottles and other plastic products usually have a number inside a triangle indicating the type of plastic they are made of. Plastics must be sorted by type before they can be recycled.

Sort the plastic products your teacher gives you into groups according to their recycling numbers.

Classifying Compare and contrast the pieces in each group with one another and with the pieces in other groups. Describe the characteristics of each group.

Plastic When oil is refined to make gasoline and other petroleum products, solid materials called resins are left over. Resins can be heated, stretched, and molded into plastic products. Common plastic products that can easily be recycled include milk jugs, detergent containers, and soda bottles. When these products are recycled, they take on very different forms: as fleece jackets, carpeting, floor tiles, trash cans, or even dock pilings!

Glass Glass is made from sand, soda ash, and limestone mixed together and heated. Glass is one of the easiest products to recycle because glass pieces can be melted down over and over to make new glass containers.

Recycling glass is less expensive than making glass from raw materials. Because the recycled pieces melt at a lower temperature than the raw materials, less energy is required. Recycling glass also reduces the environmental damage caused by mining for soda and limestone.

Paper It takes about 17 trees to make one metric ton of paper. Paper mills turn wood into a thick liquid called pulp. Pulp is spread out and dried to produce paper. Pulp can also be made from old newspapers and old used paper. Most paper products can only be recycled a few times. Each time paper is recycled, the new paper is rougher, weaker, and darker.

Is Recycling Worthwhile? Besides conserving resources, recycling also saves energy. For example, making aluminum products from recycled aluminum rather than from raw materials uses about 90 percent less energy overall. For certain materials, recycling is usually worthwhile.

But recycling is not a complete answer to the solid waste problem. For some cities, recycling is not cost-effective. Scientists have not found good ways to recycle some materials. The value of recycling must be judged on a case-by-case basis.

What People Can Do

The good news is that there are ways individuals can help control the solid waste problem. 🔑 **These are sometimes called the "three R's"—reduce, reuse, and recycle.** *Reduce* refers to creating less waste in the first place. For example, you can use a cloth shopping bag rather than a disposable paper or plastic bag. *Reuse* refers to finding another use for an object rather than discarding it. For example, you could refill plastic drink bottles with drinking water instead of buying new bottles of water.

As you have read, *recycle* refers to reclaiming raw materials to create new products. You can take the first step in the recycling process by recycling at home and by encouraging others to recycle. You can also make an effort to buy products made from recycled materials. This encourages companies to use recycled materials in their products.

Another way to reduce the amount of solid waste your family produces is to start a compost pile. **Composting** is the process of helping biodegradable wastes to decompose naturally. The moist, dark conditions in a compost pile allow natural decomposers to break down waste more quickly. Compost piles can be used to recycle grass clippings, raked leaves, and some food wastes. Compost is an excellent natural fertilizer for plants.

FIGURE 20
Composting
Many kinds of food and yard waste can be composted.
Interpreting Photographs How does composting help reduce household waste?

 **Reading Checkpoint** What is composting?

Section 5 Assessment

S 6.6.c, E-LA: Reading 6.1.0

Vocabulary Skill Prefixes Use what you know about the prefix *bio-* to help you define the word *biodegradable.*

🔑 **Reviewing Key Concepts**

1. **a. Reviewing** Name three ways of dealing with solid waste.
   b. Comparing and Contrasting Describe an advantage and a disadvantage of each method.
   c. Developing Hypotheses Near a former open dump, there is a stream in which your older relatives used to fish. No one fishes there anymore, however, because there are no fish. What might have happened?

2. **a. Identifying** What is meant by the "three R's"?
   b. Problem Solving Give one example of how you could practice each of the "three R's."

Lab zone At-Home **Activity**

Trash Weigh-In For one week, have your family collect its household trash in large bags. Do not include food waste. At the end of the week, hold a trash weigh-in. Multiply the total amount by 52 to show how much trash your family produces in a year. Can you come up with any ways to reduce your family trash load?

The BIG Idea

Energy and material resources differ in a variety of ways, including their costs, availability of supplies, and environmental impacts to produce and use.

① Fossil Fuels

🔑 **Key Concepts**   🏴 S 6.3.b, 6.6.a

- When fuels are burned, the chemical energy that is released can be used to generate another form of energy, such as heat, light, motion, or electricity.

- The three major fossil fuels are coal, oil, and natural gas.

- Since fossil fuels take hundreds of millions of years to form, they are considered nonrenewable resources.

Key Terms

fuel
energy transformation
combustion
fossil fuel
hydrocarbon
petroleum
refinery
petrochemical

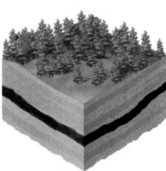

② Renewable Sources of Energy

🔑 **Key Concepts**   🏴 S 6.6.a, 6.6.b

- The sun constantly gives off energy in the forms of light and heat.

- In addition to solar energy, renewable sources of energy include water, the wind, biomass fuels, geothermal energy, and the tides.

Key Terms

solar energy
hydroelectric power
biomass fuel
gasohol
geothermal energy
tide

③ Nuclear Energy

🔑 **Key Concepts**   🏴 S 6.6.a, 6.6.b

- During nuclear fission, the nucleus splits apart into smaller nuclei and two or more neutrons.

- In a nuclear power plant, the heat released from fission reactions is used to change water into steam. The steam then turns the blades of a turbine to generate electricity.

- In nuclear fusion, two hydrogen nuclei combine to create a helium nucleus, which has slightly less mass than the two hydrogen nuclei. The lost mass is converted to energy.

Key Terms

nucleus
nuclear fission
reactor vessel
fuel rod
control rod
meltdown
nuclear fusion

④ Energy Conservation

🔑 **Key Concepts**   🏴 S 6.3.a, 6.3.b

- One way to preserve energy resources is to increase the efficiency of energy use. Another way is to conserve energy whenever possible.

Key Terms

• efficiency • insulation • energy conservation

⑤ Waste Disposal and Recycling

🔑 **Key Concepts**   🏴 S 6.6.c

- Three methods of handling solid waste are burning, burying, and recycling. Each method has advantages and disadvantages.

- One way to help solve the solid waste problem is to practice the "three R's"—reduce, reuse, and recycle.

Key Terms

• municipal solid waste • incineration
• leachate • sanitary landfill • recycling
• biodegradable • composting

Review and Assessment

For: Self-Assessment
Visit: PHSchool.com
Web Code: cwa-4120

↻ Target Reading Skill

Compare and Contrast The table compares and contrasts various sources of energy. Copy the table onto a separate sheet of paper and then complete it.

Sources of Energy		
Energy Type	**Advantages**	**Disadvantages**
Coal	Low cost, plentiful	
Oil		Nonrenewable, mostly imported
Solar		
Wind		
Hydroelectric		
Geothermal		
Nuclear fission		
Nuclear fusion		

Reviewing Key Terms

Choose the letter of the best answer.

1. Which of the following is *not* a fossil fuel?
   a. coal
   b. wood
   c. oil
   d. natural gas

2. Wind and biomass energy are both indirect forms of
   a. nuclear energy.
   b. electrical energy.
   c. solar energy.
   d. geothermal energy.

3. The particle used to start a nuclear fission reaction is a(n)
   a. neutron.   **b.** electron.
   c. proton.   **d.** atom.

4. The part of a nuclear power plant where fission takes place is the
   a. turbine.   **b.** control rod.
   c. heat exchanger. **d.** reactor vessel.

5. The process of reclaiming raw materials and reusing them to create new products is called
   a. incineration.   **b.** recycling.
   c. composting.   **d.** combustion.

Complete the following sentences so that your answers clearly explain the key terms.

6. In the process of **combustion,** a fuel such as coal undergoes _____.

7. Gasoline is a **petrochemical,** which means it is a(n) _____.

8. **Geothermal energy** is a renewable energy source that is produced from _____.

9. **Energy conservation** means that _____ .

10. **Composting** is a process in which _____.

Writing in Science

Letter In a letter to a friend, predict how solar energy will change your life over the next 20 years. Include specific details in your description.

Video Assessment
Discovery Channel School
Energy Resources

Review and Assessment

Checking Concepts

11. Describe how coal forms.

12. What is natural gas? How is natural gas transported to where it is needed?

13. Describe three features of a solar home. (Your answer may include passive and active solar systems.)

14. Explain how wind can be used to generate electricity.

15. How is a nuclear fission reaction controlled in a nuclear reactor?

16. Define energy efficiency. Give three examples of inventions that increase energy efficiency.

17. Name and define the "three R's" of solid waste management.

Thinking Critically

18. **Comparing and Contrasting** Compare the recycling of metal and paper. How are they similar? How are they different?

19. **Predicting** Do you think you will ever live in a solar house? Support your prediction with details about the climate in your area.

20. **Classifying** State whether each of the following energy sources is renewable or nonrenewable: coal, solar power, natural gas, hydroelectric power. Give a reason for each answer.

21. **Making Judgments** Write a short paragraph explaining why you agree or disagree with the following statement: "The United States should build more nuclear power plants to prepare for the future shortage of fossil fuels."

22. **Relating Cause and Effect** In the nuclear reaction shown below, a neutron is about to strike a U-235 nucleus. What will happen next?

Neutron

Uranium-235 nucleus

Applying Skills

Use the information in the table to answer Questions 23–27.

The table below shows the world's energy production in 1973 and today.

Energy Source	Units Produced 1973	Units Produced Today
Oil	2,861	3,574
Natural gas	1,226	2,586
Coal	2,238	3,833
Nuclear	203	2,592
Hydroelectric	1,300	2,705
Total	7,828	15,290

23. **Interpreting Data** How did the total energy production change from 1973 to today?

24. **Calculating** What percentage of the total world energy production did nuclear power provide in 1973? What percentage does it provide today?

25. **Classifying** Classify the different energy sources according to whether they are renewable or nonrenewable.

26. **Inferring** How has the importance of hydroelectric power changed from 1973 to the present?

27. **Predicting** How do you think the world's energy production will change over the next 40 years? Explain.

Lab zone Standards Investigation

Performance Assessment Share your energy-audit report with another group. The group should review the report for clarity, organization, and detail. Make revisions based on feedback from the other group. As a class, discuss each group's findings. Then prepare a class proposal with the best suggestions for conserving energy in your school.

Choose the letter of the best answer.

1. When a fuel is consumed, most of the energy released eventually ends up as
   A light.
   B sound.
   C heat.
   D electricity.   **S 6.3.b**

2. Many plastics and paints are made from
   A gasohol.
   B biomass.
   C uranium.
   D petrochemicals.   **S 6.6.c**

3. The interior of your car heats up on a sunny day because of
   A passive solar heating.
   B solar cells.
   C active solar heating.
   D indirect solar heating.   **S 6.6.a**

4. The main function of a dam in producing electricity is to
   A form a reservoir for recreation.
   B prevent flooding after a heavy rain.
   C provide a source of fast-moving water.
   D provide a source of wind.   **S 6.6.a**

5. Which of the following steps in producing electricity in a nuclear reactor comes first?
   A Steam turns the blades of a turbine.
   B Water boils to produce steam.
   C Uranium atoms are split.
   D Heat is released.   **S 6.6.a**

6. Heat flow from a warm house to the cold outdoors can be reduced by
   A insulation.
   B combustion.
   C recycling.
   D incineration.   **S 6.3.a**

7. Which of the following is a renewable energy source?
   A oil
   B coal
   C wind
   D natural gas   **S 6.6.b**

Use the graph to answer Questions 8 and 9.

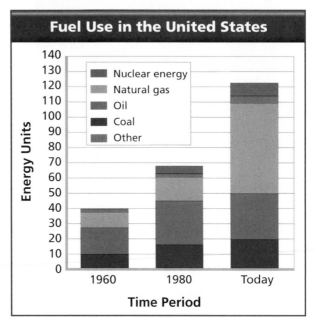

8. According to the graph, most of the fuel sources used in the United States today are
   A renewable fuels.
   B nuclear fuels.
   C fossil fuels.
   D solar energy.   **S 6.6.a, 6.6.b**

9. Which statement about fuel use in the United States is best supported by the graph?
   A Natural gas has become the most widely used fuel source.
   B The use of nuclear energy is decreasing.
   C Coal is becoming the main source of fuel.
   D The amount of oil being used today has greatly decreased since 1980.   **S 6.6.a**

Apply the BIG Idea

10. State two advantages and two disadvantages of using coal to generate electricity. Do the same for using solar energy to produce electricity. Classify each as either a renewable or nonrenewable energy resource. Explain your reasoning in each case.   **S 6.6.a, 6.6.b**

Ecology and Resources
Unit 4 Review

Unit 4 Assessment

Connecting the BIG Ideas

A small city at the edge of California's Central Valley is growing quickly. The council must choose either a coal, wind, or nuclear power plant to meet the increasing energy demands. An expert on energy resources and an ecologist give the council advice.

Power Plant Choices			
Type of Power Plant	Advantage/ Disadvantage	Renewable/ Nonrenewable	Effects on Ecosystem
Coal			
Wind			
Nuclear			

The energy expert says that although a coal power plant will be expensive, coal is a relatively cheap fuel. She also says that the plant will cause some air pollution.

Next, she explains that wind energy will not pollute the air. In addition, the cost of power produced by wind turbines is about the same as that of the coal plant. However, dozens of wind turbines would have to be built.

Finally, the energy expert says that a nuclear power plant is expensive, but will not pollute the air. However, radioactive waste must be disposed of safely. Also, the water used to cool the plant will be warm when released back into the environment.

The ecologist explains that a nearby river flows through a marsh that floods in winter. The marsh is home to many fish, insects, amphibians, migrating birds, and mammals. Grasses, tall rushes, and shrubs cover the marsh. Large trees line the riverbanks.

The ecologist suggests that pollution from a coal power plant could make the water more acidic and injure marsh organisms. The wind turbines might kill migrating birds. Warm water from a nuclear plant may harm some animals, but could benefit others.

1. Which organisms are the primary producers in the marsh? *(Chapter 10)*
   a. birds
   b. amphibians and mammals
   c. insects
   d. grasses, rushes, and shrubs

2. To which biome do the freshwater marshes of the Central Valley belong? *(Chapter 11)*
   a. deciduous   b. tundra
   c. grassland   d. temperate rain forest

3. Which type of power plant considered by the city council uses renewable energy? *(Chapter 12)*
   a. coal   b. wind
   c. natural gas   d. oil

4. **Summary** Summarize the three power plant choices. Include the advantages and disadvantages of each type of power plant, whether the energy source is renewable or nonrenewable, and how it may affect the marsh ecosystem.

Think Like a Scientist

Scientists have a particular way of looking at the world, or scientific habits of mind. Whenever you ask a question and explore possible answers, you use many of the same skills that scientists do. Some of these skills are described on this page.

Observing

When you use one or more of your five senses to gather information about the world, you are **observing.** Hearing a dog bark, counting twelve green seeds, and smelling smoke are all observations. To increase the power of their senses, scientists sometimes use microscopes, telescopes, or other instruments that help them make more detailed observations.

An observation must be an accurate report of what your senses detect. It is important to keep careful records of your observations in science class by writing or drawing in a notebook. The information collected through observations is called evidence, or data.

Inferring

When you interpret an observation, you are **inferring,** or making an inference. For example, if you hear your dog barking, you may infer that someone is at your front door. To make this inference, you combine the evidence—the barking dog—and your experience or knowledge—you know that your dog barks when strangers approach—to reach a logical conclusion.

Notice that an inference is not a fact; it is only one of many possible interpretations for an observation. For example, your dog may be barking because it wants to go for a walk. An inference may turn out to be incorrect even if it is based on accurate observations and logical reasoning. The only way to find out if an inference is correct is to investigate further.

Predicting

When you listen to the weather forecast, you hear many predictions about the next day's weather—what the temperature will be, whether it will rain, and how windy it will be. Weather forecasters use observations and knowledge of weather patterns to predict the weather. The skill of **predicting** involves making an inference about a future event based on current evidence or past experience.

Because a prediction is an inference, it may prove to be false. In science class, you can test some of your predictions by doing experiments. For example, suppose you predict that larger paper airplanes can fly farther than smaller airplanes. How could you test your prediction?

Activity

Use the photograph to answer the questions below.

Observing Look closely at the photograph. List at least three observations.

Inferring Use your observations to make an inference about what has happened. What experience or knowledge did you use to make the inference?

Predicting Predict what will happen next. On what evidence or experience do you base your prediction?

Classifying

Could you imagine searching for a book in the library if the books were shelved in no particular order? Your trip to the library would be an all-day event! Luckily, librarians group together books on similar topics or by the same author. Grouping together items that are alike in some way is called **classifying.** You can classify items in many ways: by size, by shape, by use, and by other important characteristics.

Like librarians, scientists use the skill of classifying to organize information and objects. When things are sorted into groups, the relationships among them become easier to understand.

Activity

Classify the objects in the photograph into two groups based on any characteristic you choose. Then use another characteristic to classify the objects into three groups.

Making Models

Have you ever drawn a picture to help someone understand what you were saying? Such a drawing is one type of model. A model is a picture, diagram, computer image, or other representation of a complex object or process. **Making models** helps people understand things that they cannot observe directly.

Scientists often use models to represent things that are either very large or very small, such as the planets in the solar system, or the parts of a cell. Such models are physical models—drawings or three-dimensional structures that look like the real thing. Other models are mental models—mathematical equations or words that describe how something works.

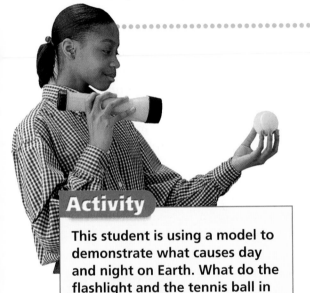

Activity

This student is using a model to demonstrate what causes day and night on Earth. What do the flashlight and the tennis ball in the model represent?

Communicating

Whenever you talk on the phone, write a report, or listen to your teacher at school, you are communicating. **Communicating** is the process of sharing ideas and information with other people. Communicating effectively requires many skills, including writing, reading, speaking, listening, and making models.

Scientists communicate to share results, information, and opinions. Scientists often communicate about their work in journals, over the telephone, in letters, and on the Internet.

They also attend scientific meetings where they share their ideas with one another in person.

Activity

On a sheet of paper, write out clear, detailed directions for tying your shoe. Then exchange directions with a partner. Follow your partner's directions exactly. How successful were you at tying your shoe? How could your partner have communicated more clearly?

Making Measurements

By measuring, scientists can express their observations more precisely and communicate more information about what they observe.

Measuring in SI

The standard system of measurement used by scientists around the world is known as the International System of Units, which is abbreviated as SI (**Système International d'Unités,** in French). SI units are easy to use because they are based on multiples of 10. Each unit is ten times larger than the next smallest unit and one tenth the size of the next largest unit. The table lists the prefixes used to name the most common SI units.

Common SI Prefixes		
Prefix	**Symbol**	**Meaning**
kilo-	k	1,000
hecto-	h	100
deka-	da	10
deci-	d	0.1 (one tenth)
centi-	c	0.01 (one hundredth)
milli-	m	0.001 (one thousandth)

Length To measure length, or the distance between two points, the unit of measure is the **meter (m).** The distance from the floor to a doorknob is approximately one meter. Long distances, such as the distance between two cities, are measured in kilometers (km). Small lengths are measured in centimeters (cm) or millimeters (mm). Scientists use metric rulers and meter sticks to measure length.

Common Conversions	
1 km	= 1,000 m
1 m	= 100 cm
1 m	= 1,000 mm
1 cm	= 10 mm

Liquid Volume To measure the volume of a liquid, or the amount of space it takes up, you will use a unit of measure known as the **liter (L).** One liter is the approximate volume of a medium-size carton of milk. Smaller volumes are measured in milliliters (mL). Scientists use graduated cylinders to measure liquid volume.

Activity

The larger lines on the metric ruler in the picture show centimeter divisions, while the smaller, unnumbered lines show millimeter divisions. How many centimeters long is the shell? How many millimeters long is it?

Activity

The graduated cylinder in the picture is marked in milliliter divisions. Notice that the water in the cylinder has a curved surface. This curved surface is called the *meniscus*. To measure the volume, you must read the level at the lowest point of the meniscus. What is the volume of water in this graduated cylinder?

Common Conversion
1 L = 1,000 mL

Mass To measure mass, or the amount of matter in an object, you will use a unit of measure known as the **gram (g).** One gram is approximately the mass of a paper clip. Larger masses are measured in kilograms (kg). Scientists use a balance to find the mass of an object.

> **Common Conversion**
>
> 1 kg = 1,000 g

Activity

The mass of the potato in the picture is measured in kilograms. What is the mass of the potato? Suppose a recipe for potato salad called for one kilogram of potatoes. About how many potatoes would you need?

Temperature To measure the temperature of a substance, you will use the **Celsius scale.** Temperature is measured in degrees Celsius (°C) using a Celsius thermometer. Water freezes at 0°C and boils at 100°C.

Time The unit scientists use to measure time is the **second (s).**

Activity

What is the temperature of the liquid in degrees Celsius?

Converting SI Units

To use the SI system, you must know how to convert between units. Converting from one unit to another involves the skill of **calculating,** or using mathematical operations. Converting between SI units is similar to converting between dollars and dimes because both systems are based on multiples of ten.

Suppose you want to convert a length of 80 centimeters to meters. Follow these steps to convert between units.

1. Begin by writing down the measurement you want to convert—in this example, 80 centimeters.

2. Write a conversion factor that represents the relationship between the two units you are converting. In this example, the relationship is 1 meter = 100 centimeters. Write this conversion factor as a fraction, making sure to place the units you are converting from (centimeters, in this example) in the denominator.

3. Multiply the measurement you want to convert by the fraction. When you do this, the units in the first measurement will cancel out with the units in the denominator. Your answer will be in the units you are converting to (meters, in this example).

Example

80 centimeters = ■ meters

$$80 \text{ centimeters} \times \frac{1 \text{ meter}}{100 \text{ centimeters}} = \frac{80 \text{ meters}}{100}$$

$$= 0.8 \text{ meters}$$

Activity

Convert between the following units.

1. 600 millimeters = ■ meters
2. 0.35 liters = ■ milliliters
3. 1,050 grams = ■ kilograms

Conducting a Scientific Investigation

In some ways, scientists are like detectives, piecing together clues to learn about a process or event. One way that scientists gather clues is by carrying out experiments. An experiment tests an idea in a careful, orderly manner. Although experiments do not all follow the same steps in the same order, many follow a pattern similar to the one described here.

Posing Questions

Experiments begin by asking a scientific question. A scientific question is one that can be answered by gathering evidence. For example, the question "Which freezes faster—fresh water or salt water?" is a scientific question because you can carry out an investigation and gather information to answer the question.

Developing a Hypothesis

The next step is to form a hypothesis. A **hypothesis** is a possible explanation for a set of observations or answer to a scientific question. A hypothesis may incorporate observations, concepts, principles, and theories about the natural world. Hypotheses lead to predictions that can be tested. A prediction can be worded as an *If . . . then . . .* statement. For example, a prediction might be *"If I add salt to fresh water, then the water will take longer to freeze."* A prediction worded this way serves as a rough outline of the experiment you should perform.

Designing an Experiment

Next you need to plan a way to test your hypothesis. Your plan should be written out as a step-by-step procedure and should describe the observations or measurements you will make.

Two important steps involved in designing an experiment are controlling variables and forming operational definitions.

Controlling Variables In a well-designed experiment, you need to keep all variables the same except for one. A **variable** is any factor that can change in an experiment. The factor that you change is called the **manipulated variable**. In this experiment, the manipulated variable is the amount of salt added to the water. Other factors, such as the amount of water or the starting temperature, are kept constant.

The factor that changes as a result of the manipulated variable is called the **responding variable.** The responding variable is what you measure or observe to obtain your results. In this experiment, the responding variable is how long the water takes to freeze.

An experiment in which all factors except one are kept constant is called a **controlled experiment.** Most controlled experiments include a test called the control. In this experiment, Container 3 is the control. Because no salt is added to Container 3, you can compare the results from the other containers to it. Any difference in results must be due to the addition of salt alone.

Forming Operational Definitions Another important aspect of a well-designed experiment is having clear operational definitions. An **operational definition** is a statement that describes how a particular variable is to be measured or how a term is to be defined. For example, in this experiment, how will you determine if the water has frozen? You might decide to insert a stick in each container at the start of the experiment. Your operational definition of "frozen" would be the time at which the stick can no longer move.

Experimental Procedure
1. Fill 3 containers with 300 milliliters of cold tap water.
2. Add 10 grams of salt to Container 1; stir. Add 20 grams of salt to Container 2; stir. Add no salt to Container 3.
3. Place the 3 containers in a freezer.
4. Check the containers every 15 minutes. Record your observations.

Interpreting Data

The observations and measurements you make in an experiment are called **data.** At the end of an experiment, you need to analyze the data to look for any patterns or trends. Patterns often become clear if you organize your data in a data table or graph. Then think through what the data reveal. Do they support your hypothesis? Do they point out a flaw in your experiment? Do you need to collect more data?

Drawing Conclusions

A **conclusion** is a statement that sums up what you have learned from an experiment. When you draw a conclusion, you need to decide whether the data you collected support your hypothesis or not. You may need to repeat an experiment several times before you can draw any conclusions from it. Conclusions often lead you to pose new questions and plan new experiments to answer them.

Activity

Is a ball's bounce affected by the height from which it is dropped? Using the steps just described, plan a controlled experiment to investigate this problem.

Technology Design Skills

Engineers are people who use scientific and technological knowledge to solve practical problems. To design new products, engineers usually follow the process described here, even though they may not follow these steps in the exact order. As you read the steps, think about how you might apply them in technology labs.

Identify a Need

Before engineers begin designing a new product, they must first identify the need they are trying to meet. For example, suppose you are a member of a design team in a company that makes toys. Your team has identified a need: a toy boat that is inexpensive and easy to assemble.

Research the Problem

Engineers often begin by gathering information that will help them with their new design. This research may include finding articles in books, magazines, or on the Internet. It may also include talking to other engineers who have solved similar problems. Engineers often perform experiments related to the product they want to design.

For your toy boat, you could look at toys that are similar to the one you want to design. You might do research on the Internet. You could also test some materials to see whether they will work well in a toy boat.

Drawing for a boat design ▼

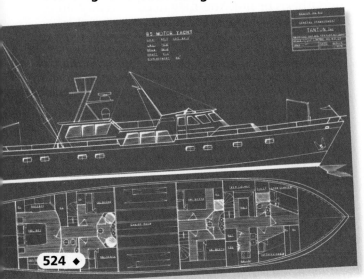

Design a Solution

Research gives engineers information that helps them design a product. When engineers design new products, they usually work in teams.

Generating Ideas Often design teams hold brainstorming meetings in which any team member can contribute ideas. **Brainstorming** is a creative process in which one team member's suggestions often spark ideas in other group members. Brainstorming can lead to new approaches to solving a design problem.

Evaluating Constraints During brainstorming, a design team will often come up with several possible designs. The team must then evaluate each one.

As part of their evaluation, engineers consider constraints. **Constraints** are factors that limit or restrict a product design. Physical characteristics, such as the properties of materials used to make your toy boat, are constraints. Money and time are also constraints. If the materials in a product cost a lot, or if the product takes a long time to make, the design may be impractical.

Making Trade-offs Design teams usually need to make trade-offs. In a **trade-off,** engineers give up one benefit of a proposed design in order to obtain another. In designing your toy boat, you will have to make trade-offs. For example, suppose one material is sturdy but not fully waterproof. Another material is more waterproof, but breakable. You may decide to give up the benefit of sturdiness in order to obtain the benefit of waterproofing.

Build and Evaluate a Prototype

Once the team has chosen a design plan, the engineers build a prototype of the product. A **prototype** is a working model used to test a design. Engineers evaluate the prototype to see whether it works well, is easy to operate, is safe to use, and holds up to repeated use.

Think of your toy boat. What would the prototype be like? Of what materials would it be made? How would you test it?

Troubleshoot and Redesign

Few prototypes work perfectly, which is why they need to be tested. Once a design team has tested a prototype, the members analyze the results and identify any problems. The team then tries to **troubleshoot,** or fix the design problems. For example, if your toy boat leaks or wobbles, the boat should be redesigned to eliminate those problems.

Communicate the Solution

A team needs to communicate the final design to the people who will manufacture and use the product. To do this, teams may use sketches, detailed drawings, computer simulations, and word descriptions.

Activity

You can use the technology design process to design and build a toy boat.

Research and Investigate

1. Visit the library or go online to research toy boats.
2. Investigate how a toy boat can be powered, including wind, rubber bands, or baking soda and vinegar.
3. Brainstorm materials, shapes, and steering for your boat.

Design and Build

4. Based on your research, design a toy boat that
   - is made of readily available materials
   - is no larger than 15 cm long and 10 cm wide
   - includes a power system, a rudder, and an area for cargo
   - travels 2 meters in a straight line carrying a load of 20 pennies
5. Sketch your design and write a step-by-step plan for building your boat. After your teacher approves your plan, build your boat.

Evaluate and Redesign

6. Test your boat, evaluate the results, and troubleshoot any problems.
7. Based on your evaluation, redesign your toy boat so it performs better.

Creating Data Tables and Graphs

How can you make sense of the data in a science experiment?
The first step is to organize the data to help you understand them.
Data tables and graphs are helpful tools for organizing data.

Data Tables

You have gathered your materials and set up your experiment. But before you start, you need to plan a way to record what happens during the experiment. By creating a data table, you can record your observations and measurements in an orderly way.

Suppose, for example, that a scientist conducted an experiment to find out how many Calories people of different body masses burn while doing various activities. The data table shows the results.

Notice in this data table that the manipulated variable (body mass) is the heading of one column. The responding variable (for

Calories Burned in 30 Minutes			
Body Mass	Experiment 1: Bicycling	Experiment 2: Playing Basketball	Experiment 3: Watching Television
30 kg	60 Calories	120 Calories	21 Calories
40 kg	77 Calories	164 Calories	27 Calories
50 kg	95 Calories	206 Calories	33 Calories
60 kg	114 Calories	248 Calories	38 Calories

Experiment 1, the number of Calories burned while bicycling) is the heading of the next column. Additional columns were added for related experiments.

Bar Graphs

To compare how many Calories a person burns doing various activities, you could create a bar graph. A bar graph is used to display data in a number of separate, or distinct, categories. In this example, bicycling, playing basketball, and watching television are the three categories.

To create a bar graph, follow these steps.

1. On graph paper, draw a horizontal, or *x*-, axis and a vertical, or *y*-, axis.

2. Write the names of the categories to be graphed along the horizontal axis. Include an overall label for the axis as well.

3. Label the vertical axis with the name of the responding variable. Include units of measurement. Then create a scale along the axis by marking off equally spaced numbers that cover the range of the data collected.

4. For each category, draw a solid bar using the scale on the vertical axis to determine the height. Make all the bars the same width.

5. Add a title that describes the graph.

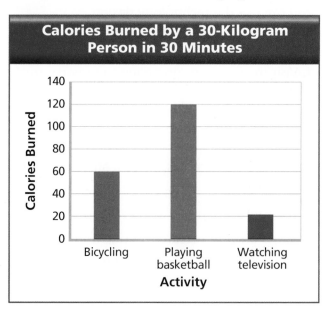

Calories Burned by a 30-Kilogram Person in 30 Minutes

Line Graphs

To see whether a relationship exists between body mass and the number of Calories burned while bicycling, you could create a line graph. A line graph is used to display data that show how one variable (the responding variable) changes in response to another variable (the manipulated variable). You can use a line graph when your manipulated variable is **continuous,** that is, when there are other points between the ones that you tested. In this example, body mass is a continuous variable because there are other body masses between 30 and 40 kilograms (for example, 31 kilograms). Time is another example of a continuous variable.

Line graphs are powerful tools because they allow you to estimate values for conditions that you did not test in the experiment. For example, you can use the line graph to estimate that a 35-kilogram person would burn 68 Calories while bicycling.

To create a line graph, follow these steps.

1. On graph paper, draw a horizontal, or *x*-, axis and a vertical, or *y*-, axis.

2. Label the horizontal axis with the name of the manipulated variable. Label the vertical axis with the name of the responding variable. Include units of measurement.

3. Create a scale on each axis by marking off equally spaced numbers that cover the range of the data collected.

4. Plot a point on the graph for each piece of data. In the line graph above, the dotted lines show how to plot the first data point (30 kilograms and 60 Calories). Follow an imaginary vertical line extending up from the horizontal axis at the 30-kilogram mark. Then follow an imaginary horizontal line extending across from the vertical axis at the 60-Calorie mark. Plot the point where the two lines intersect.

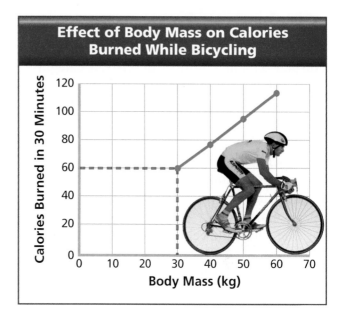

Effect of Body Mass on Calories Burned While Bicycling

5. Connect the plotted points with a solid line. (In some cases, it may be more appropriate to draw a line that shows the general trend of the plotted points. In those cases, some of the points may fall above or below the line. Also, not all graphs are linear. It may be more appropriate to draw a curve to connect the points.)

6. Add a title that identifies the variables or relationship in the graph.

Activity

Create line graphs to display the data from Experiment 2 and Experiment 3 in the data table.

Activity

You read in the newspaper that a total of 4 centimeters of rain fell in your area in June, 2.5 centimeters fell in July, and 1.5 centimeters fell in August. What type of graph would you use to display these data? Use graph paper to create the graph.

Circle Graphs

Like bar graphs, circle graphs can be used to display data in a number of separate categories. Unlike bar graphs, however, circle graphs can only be used when you have data for *all* the categories that make up a given topic. A circle graph is sometimes called a pie chart. The pie represents the entire topic, while the slices represent the individual categories. The size of a slice indicates what percentage of the whole a particular category makes up.

The data table below shows the results of a survey in which 24 teenagers were asked to identify their favorite sport. The data were then used to create the circle graph at the right.

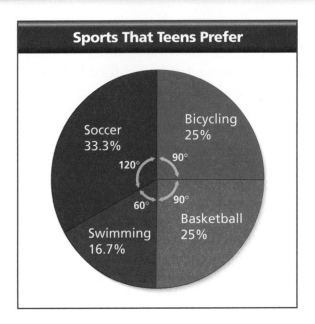

Sports That Teens Prefer

Favorite Sports	
Sport	Students
Soccer	8
Basketball	6
Bicycling	6
Swimming	4

To create a circle graph, follow these steps.

1. Use a compass to draw a circle. Mark the center with a point. Then draw a line from the center point to the top of the circle.

2. Determine the size of each "slice" by setting up a proportion where *x* equals the number of degrees in a slice. (*Note:* A circle contains 360 degrees.) For example, to find the number of degrees in the "soccer" slice, set up the following proportion:

$$\frac{\text{Students who prefer soccer}}{\text{Total number of students}} = \frac{x}{\text{Total number of degrees in a circle}}$$

$$\frac{8}{24} = \frac{x}{360}$$

Cross-multiply and solve for x.

$$24x = 8 \times 360$$
$$x = 120$$

The "soccer" slice should contain 120 degrees.

3. Use a protractor to measure the angle of the first slice, using the line you drew to the top of the circle as the 0° line. Draw a line from the center of the circle to the edge for the angle you measured.

4. Continue around the circle by measuring the size of each slice with the protractor. Start measuring from the edge of the previous slice so the wedges do not overlap. When you are done, the entire circle should be filled in.

5. Determine the percentage of the whole circle that each slice represents. To do this, divide the number of degrees in a slice by the total number of degrees in a circle (360), and multiply by 100%. For the "soccer" slice, you can find the percentage as follows:

$$\frac{120}{360} \times 100\% = 33.3\%$$

6. Use a different color for each slice. Label each slice with the category and with the percentage of the whole it represents.

7. Add a title to the circle graph.

Activity

In a class of 28 students, 12 students take the bus to school, 10 students walk, and 6 students ride their bicycles. Create a circle graph to display these data.

Math Review

Scientists use math to organize, analyze, and present data.
This appendix will help you review some basic math skills.

Mean, Median, and Mode

The **mean** is the average, or the sum of the data divided by the number of data items. The middle number in a set of ordered data is called the **median**. The **mode** is the number that appears most often in a set of data.

> **Example**
>
> A scientist counted the number of distinct songs sung by seven different male birds and collected the data shown below.
>
> | Male Bird Songs | | | | | | | |
> |---|---|---|---|---|---|---|---|
> | Bird | A | B | C | D | E | F | G |
> | Number of Songs | 36 | 29 | 40 | 35 | 28 | 36 | 27 |
>
> To determine the mean number of songs, add the total number of songs and divide by the number of data items—in this case, the number of male birds.
>
> $$\text{Mean} = \frac{231}{7} = 33 \text{ songs}$$
>
> To find the median number of songs, arrange the data in numerical order and find the number in the middle of the series.
>
> **27 28 29 35 36 36 40**
>
> The number in the middle is 35, so the median number of songs is 35.
>
> The mode is the value that appears most frequently. In the data, 36 appears twice, while each other item appears only once. Therefore, 36 songs is the mode.

> **Practice**
>
> Find out how many minutes it takes each student in your class to get to school. Then find the mean, median, and mode for the data.

Probability

Probability is the chance that an event will occur. Probability can be expressed as a ratio, a fraction, or a percentage. For example, when you flip a coin, the probability that the coin will land heads up is 1 in 2, or $\frac{1}{2}$, or 50 percent.

The probability that an event will happen can be expressed in the following formula.

$$P(\text{event}) = \frac{\text{Number of times the event can occur}}{\text{Total number of possible events}}$$

> **Example**
>
> A paper bag contains 25 blue marbles, 5 green marbles, 5 orange marbles, and 15 yellow marbles. If you close your eyes and pick a marble from the bag, what is the probability that it will be yellow?
>
> $$P(\text{yellow marbles}) = \frac{15 \text{ yellow marbles}}{50 \text{ marbles total}}$$
>
> $$P = \frac{15}{50}, \text{ or } \frac{3}{10}, \text{ or } 30\%$$

> **Practice**
>
> Each side of a cube has a letter on it. Two sides have *A*, three sides have *B*, and one side has *C*. If you roll the cube, what is the probability that *A* will land on top?

Area

The **area** of a surface is the number of square units that cover it. The front cover of your textbook has an area of about 600 cm².

Area of a Rectangle and a Square To find the area of a rectangle, multiply its length times its width. The formula for the area of a rectangle is

$$A = \ell \times w, \text{ or } A = \ell w$$

Since all four sides of a square have the same length, the area of a square is the length of one side multiplied by itself, or squared.

$$A = s \times s, \text{ or } A = s^2$$

Example

A scientist is studying the plants in a field that measures 75 m × 45 m. What is the area of the field?

$$A = \ell \times w$$
$$A = 75 \text{ m} \times 45 \text{ m}$$
$$A = 3{,}375 \text{ m}^2$$

Area of a Circle The formula for the area of a circle is

$$A = \pi \times r \times r, \text{ or } A = \pi r^2$$

The length of the radius is represented by r, and the value of π is approximately $\frac{22}{7}$.

Example

Find the area of a circle with a radius of 14 cm.

$$A = \pi r^2$$
$$A = 14 \times 14 \times \frac{22}{7}$$
$$A = 616 \text{ cm}^2$$

Practice

Find the area of a circle that has a radius of 21 m.

Circumference

The distance around a circle is called the circumference. The formula for finding the circumference of a circle is

$$C = 2 \times \pi \times r, \text{ or } C = 2\pi r$$

Example

The radius of a circle is 35 cm. What is its circumference?

$$C = 2\pi r$$
$$C = 2 \times 35 \times \frac{22}{7}$$
$$C = 220 \text{ cm}$$

Practice

What is the circumference of a circle with a radius of 28 m?

Volume

The volume of an object is the number of cubic units it contains. The volume of a wastebasket, for example, might be about 26,000 cm³.

Volume of a Rectangular Object To find the volume of a rectangular object, multiply the object's length times its width times its height.

$$V = \ell \times w \times h, \text{ or } V = \ell w h$$

Example

Find the volume of a box with length 24 cm, width 12 cm, and height 9 cm.

$$V = \ell w h$$
$$V = 24 \text{ cm} \times 12 \text{ cm} \times 9 \text{ cm}$$
$$V = 2{,}592 \text{ cm}^3$$

Practice

What is the volume of a rectangular object with length 17 cm, width 11 cm, and height 6 cm?

Fractions

A **fraction** is a way to express a part of a whole. In the fraction $\frac{4}{7}$, 4 is the numerator and 7 is the denominator.

Adding and Subtracting Fractions To add or subtract two or more fractions that have a common denominator, first add or subtract the numerators. Then write the sum or difference over the common denominator.

To find the sum or difference of fractions with different denominators, first find the least common multiple of the denominators. This is known as the least common denominator. Then convert each fraction to equivalent fractions with the least common denominator. Add or subtract the numerators. Then write the sum or difference over the common denominator.

Example

$$\frac{5}{6} - \frac{3}{4} = \frac{10}{12} - \frac{9}{12} = \frac{10 - 9}{12} = \frac{1}{12}$$

Multiplying Fractions To multiply two fractions, first multiply the two numerators, then multiply the two denominators.

Example

$$\frac{5}{6} \times \frac{2}{3} = \frac{5 \times 2}{6 \times 3} = \frac{10}{18} = \frac{5}{9}$$

Dividing Fractions Dividing by a fraction is the same as multiplying by its reciprocal. Reciprocals are numbers whose numerators and denominators have been switched. To divide one fraction by another, first invert the fraction you are dividing by—in other words, turn it upside down. Then multiply the two fractions.

Example

$$\frac{2}{5} \div \frac{7}{8} = \frac{2}{5} \times \frac{8}{7} = \frac{2 \times 8}{5 \times 7} = \frac{16}{35}$$

Practice

Solve the following: $\frac{3}{7} \div \frac{4}{5}$.

Decimals

Fractions whose denominators are 10, 100, or some other power of 10 are often expressed as decimals. For example, the fraction $\frac{9}{10}$ can be expressed as the decimal 0.9, and the fraction $\frac{7}{100}$ can be written as 0.07.

Adding and Subtracting With Decimals To add or subtract decimals, line up the decimal points before you carry out the operation.

Example

$$\begin{array}{r} 27.4 \\ +\ 6.19 \\ \hline 33.59 \end{array} \qquad \begin{array}{r} 278.635 \\ -\ 191.4 \\ \hline 87.235 \end{array}$$

Multiplying With Decimals When you multiply two numbers with decimals, the number of decimal places in the product is equal to the total number of decimal places in each number being multiplied.

Example

$$\begin{array}{r} 46.2 \text{ (one decimal place)} \\ \times\ 2.37 \text{ (two decimal places)} \\ \hline 109.494 \text{ (three decimal places)} \end{array}$$

Dividing With Decimals To divide a decimal by a whole number, put the decimal point in the quotient above the decimal point in the dividend.

Example

$$15.5 \div 5$$
$$\begin{array}{r} 3.1 \\ 5\overline{)15.5} \end{array}$$

To divide a decimal by a decimal, you need to rewrite the divisor as a whole number. Do this by multiplying both the divisor and dividend by the same multiple of 10.

Example

$$1.68 \div 4.2 = 1.68 \div 4.2$$
$$\begin{array}{r} 0.4 \\ 42\overline{)16.8} \end{array}$$

Practice

Multiply 6.21 by 8.5.

Ratio and Proportion

A **ratio** compares two numbers by division. For example, suppose a scientist counts 800 wolves and 1,200 moose on an island. The ratio of wolves to moose can be written as a fraction, $\frac{800}{1,200}$, which can be reduced to $\frac{2}{3}$. The same ratio can also be expressed as 2 to 3 or 2 : 3.

A **proportion** is a mathematical sentence saying that two ratios are equivalent. For example, a proportion could state that $\frac{800 \text{ wolves}}{1,200 \text{ moose}} = \frac{2 \text{ wolves}}{3 \text{ moose}}$. You can sometimes set up a proportion to determine or estimate an unknown quantity. For example, suppose a scientist counts 25 beetles in an area of 10 square meters. The scientist wants to estimate the number of beetles in 100 square meters.

Example

1. Express the relationship between beetles and area as a ratio: $\frac{25}{10}$, simplified to $\frac{5}{2}$.

2. Set up a proportion, with x representing the number of beetles. The proportion can be stated as $\frac{5}{2} = \frac{x}{100}$.

3. Begin by cross-multiplying. In other words, multiply each fraction's numerator by the other fraction's denominator.

$$5 \times 100 = 2 \times x, \text{ or } 500 = 2x$$

4. To find the value of x, divide both sides by 2. The result is 250, or 250 beetles in 100 square meters.

Practice

Find the value of x in the following proportion: $\frac{6}{7} = \frac{x}{49}$.

Percentage

A **percentage** is a ratio that compares a number to 100. For example, there are 37 granite rocks in a collection that consists of 100 rocks. The ratio $\frac{37}{100}$ can be written as 37%. Granite rocks make up 37% of the rock collection.

You can calculate percentages of numbers other than 100 by setting up a proportion.

Example

Rain falls on 9 days out of 30 in June. What percentage of the days in June were rainy?

$$\frac{9 \text{ days}}{30 \text{ days}} = \frac{d\%}{100\%}$$

To find the value of d, begin by cross-multiplying, as for any proportion:

$$9 \times 100 = 30 \times d \qquad d = \frac{900}{30} \qquad d = 30$$

Practice

There are 300 marbles in a jar, and 42 of those marbles are blue. What percentage of the marbles are blue?

Significant Figures

The **precision** of a measurement depends on the instrument you use to take the measurement. For example, if the smallest unit on the ruler is millimeters, then the most precise measurement you can make will be in millimeters.

The sum or difference of measurements can only be as precise as the least precise measurement being added or subtracted. Round your answer so that it has the same number of digits after the decimal as the least precise measurement. Round up if the last digit is 5 or more, and round down if the last digit is 4 or less.

> **Example**
>
> Subtract a temperature of 5.2°C from the temperature 75.46°C.
>
> **75.46 − 5.2 = 70.26**
>
> 5.2 has the fewest digits after the decimal, so it is the least precise measurement. Since the last digit of the answer is 6, round up to 3. The most precise difference between the measurements is 70.3°C.

> **Practice**
>
> Add 26.4 m to 8.37 m. Round your answer according to the precision of the measurements.

Significant figures are the number of nonzero digits in a measurement. Zeroes between nonzero digits are also significant. For example, the measurements 12,500 L, 0.125 cm, and 2.05 kg all have three significant figures. When you multiply and divide measurements, the one with the fewest significant figures determines the number of significant figures in your answer.

> **Example**
>
> Multiply 110 g by 5.75 g.
>
> **110 × 5.75 = 632.5**
>
> Because 110 has only two significant figures, round the answer to 630 g.

Scientific Notation

A **factor** is a number that divides into another number with no remainder. In the example, the number 3 is used as a factor four times.

An **exponent** tells how many times a number is used as a factor. For example, $3 \times 3 \times 3 \times 3$ can be written as 3^4. The exponent ^{4} indicates that the number 3 is used as a factor four times. Another way of expressing this is to say that 81 is equal to 3 to the fourth power.

> **Example**
>
> $3^4 = 3 \times 3 \times 3 \times 3 = 81$

Scientific notation uses exponents and powers of ten to write very large or very small numbers in shorter form. When you write a number in scientific notation, you write the number as two factors. The first factor is any number between 1 and 10. The second factor is a power of 10, such as 10^3 or 10^6.

> **Example**
>
> The average distance between the planet Mercury and the sun is 58,000,000 km. To write the first factor in scientific notation, insert a decimal point in the original number so that you have a number between 1 and 10. In the case of 58,000,000, the number is 5.8.
>
> To determine the power of 10, count the number of places that the decimal point moved. In this case, it moved 7 places.
>
> **58,000,000 km = 5.8 × 10^7 km**

> **Practice**
>
> Express 6,590,000 in scientific notation.

Safety Symbols

These symbols warn of possible dangers in the laboratory and remind you to work carefully.

 Safety Goggles Wear safety goggles to protect your eyes in any activity involving chemicals, flames or heating, or glassware.

 Lab Apron Wear a laboratory apron to protect your skin and clothing from damage.

 Breakage Handle breakable materials, such as glassware, with care. Do not touch broken glassware.

 Heat-Resistant Gloves Use an oven mitt or other hand protection when handling hot materials such as hot plates or hot glassware.

 Plastic Gloves Wear disposable plastic gloves when working with organisms and harmful chemicals. Keep your hands away from your face, and dispose of the gloves according to your teacher's instructions.

 Heating Use a clamp or tongs to pick up hot glassware. Do not touch hot objects with your bare hands.

 Flames Before you work with flames, tie back loose hair and clothing. Follow instructions from your teacher about lighting and extinguishing flames.

 No Flames When using flammable materials, make sure there are no flames, sparks, or other exposed heat sources present.

 Corrosive Chemical Avoid getting acid or other corrosive chemicals on your skin or clothing or in your eyes. Do not inhale the vapors. Wash your hands after the activity.

 Poison Do not let any poisonous chemical come into contact with your skin, and do not inhale its vapors. Wash your hands when you are finished with the activity.

 Fumes Work in a ventilated area when harmful vapors may be involved. Avoid inhaling vapors directly. Only test an odor when directed to do so by your teacher, and use a wafting motion to direct the vapor toward your nose.

 Sharp Object Scissors, scalpels, knives, needles, pins, and tacks can cut your skin. Always direct a sharp edge or point away from yourself and others.

 Animal Safety Treat live or preserved animals or animal parts with care to avoid harming the animals or yourself. Wash your hands when you are finished with the activity.

 Plant Safety Handle plants only as directed by your teacher. If you are allergic to certain plants, tell your teacher; do not do an activity involving those plants. Avoid touching harmful plants such as poison ivy. Wash your hands when you are finished with the activity.

 Electric Shock To avoid electric shock, never use electrical equipment around water, or when the equipment is wet or your hands are wet. Be sure cords are untangled and cannot trip anyone. Unplug equipment not in use.

 Physical Safety When an experiment involves physical activity, avoid injuring yourself or others. Alert your teacher if there is any reason you should not participate.

 Disposal Dispose of chemicals and other laboratory materials safely. Follow the instructions from your teacher.

 Hand Washing Wash your hands thoroughly when finished with the activity. Use soap and warm water. Rinse well.

 General Safety Awareness When this symbol appears, follow the instructions provided. When you are asked to develop your own procedure in a lab, have your teacher approve your plan before you go further.

Science Safety Rules

General Precautions

Follow all instructions. Never perform activities without the approval and supervision of your teacher. Do not engage in horseplay. Never eat or drink in the laboratory. Keep work areas clean and uncluttered.

Dress Code

Wear safety goggles whenever you work with chemicals, glassware, heat sources such as burners, or any substance that might get into your eyes. If you wear contact lenses, notify your teacher.

Wear a lab apron or coat whenever you work with corrosive chemicals or substances that can stain. Tie back long hair. Remove or tie back any article of clothing or jewelry that can hang down and touch chemicals, flames, or equipment. Roll up long sleeves. Never wear open shoes or sandals.

First Aid

Report all accidents, injuries, or fires to your teacher, no matter how minor. Be aware of the location of the first-aid kit, emergency equipment such as the fire extinguisher and fire blanket, and the nearest telephone. Know whom to contact in an emergency.

Heating and Fire Safety

Keep all combustible materials away from flames. When heating a substance in a test tube, make sure that the mouth of the tube is not pointed at you or anyone else. Never heat a liquid in a closed container. Use an oven mitt to pick up a container that has been heated.

Using Chemicals Safely

Never put your face near the mouth of a container that holds chemicals. Never touch, taste, or smell a chemical unless your teacher tells you to.

Use only those chemicals needed in the activity. Keep all containers closed when chemicals are not being used. Pour all chemicals over the sink or a container, not over your work surface. Dispose of excess chemicals as instructed by your teacher.

Be extra careful when working with acids or bases. When mixing an acid and water, always pour the water into the container first and then add the acid to the water. Never pour water into an acid. Wash chemical spills and splashes immediately with plenty of water.

Using Glassware Safely

If glassware is broken or chipped, notify your teacher immediately. Never handle broken or chipped glass with your bare hands.

Never force glass tubing or thermometers into a rubber stopper or rubber tubing. Have your teacher insert the glass tubing or thermometer if required for an activity.

Using Sharp Instruments

Handle sharp instruments with extreme care. Never cut material toward you; cut away from you.

Animal and Plant Safety

Never perform experiments that cause pain, discomfort, or harm to animals. Only handle animals if absolutely necessary. If you know that you are allergic to certain plants, molds, or animals, tell your teacher before doing an activity in which these are used. Wash your hands thoroughly after any activity involving animals, animal parts, plants, plant parts, or soil.

During field work, wear long pants, long sleeves, socks, and closed shoes. Avoid poisonous plants and fungi as well as plants with thorns.

End-of-Experiment Rules

Unplug all electrical equipment. Clean up your work area. Dispose of waste materials as instructed by your teacher. Wash your hands after every experiment.

English and Spanish Glossary

A

abiotic factor A nonliving part of an organism's habitat. (p. 394)
factor abiótico La parte no viva del hábitat de un organismo.

abrasion The grinding away of rock by other rock particles carried in water, ice, or wind. (p. 59)
abrasión Desgaste de la roca por otras partículas de roca llevadas por el agua, el viento o el hielo.

acid rain Rain that contains more acid than normal. (p. 260)
lluvia ácida Lluvia que contiene más acidez de la normal.

acidic Describes a substance that reacts strongly with metals and changes blue litmus paper red. (p. 69)
ácido Describe a una sustasncia que reacciona fuertemente con metales y hace que el papel de tornasol azul cambie a rojo.

adaptation A behavior or physical characteristic that helps an organism survive in its environment.
adaptación Comportamiento o característica física que permite a un organismo vivir en su medio ambiente. (p. 411)

aftershock An earthquake that occurs after a larger earthquake in the same area. (p. 199)
réplica Sismo que ocurre después de un terremoto mayor en la misma área.

air mass A huge body of air that has similar temperature, humidity, and air pressure throughout.
masa de aire Gran volumen de aire que tiene temperatura, humedad y presión similares en todos sus puntos. (p. 310)

air pressure The pressure caused by the weight of a column of air pushing down on an area. (p. 263)
presión de aire Presión causada por el peso de una columna de aire que empuja hacia abajo en un área.

alluvial fan A wide, sloping deposit of sediment formed where a stream leaves a mountain range. (p. 99)
abanico aluvial Depósito ancho de sedimento en declive, que se forma donde un arroyo sale de una cordillera.

altitude Elevation above sea level. (p. 265)
altitud Elevación sobre el nivel del mar.

anemometer An instrument used to measure wind speed. (p. 283)
anemómetro Instrumento que se usa para medir la velocidad del viento.

aneroid barometer An instrument that measures changes in air pressure without using a liquid. (p. 264)
barómetro aneroide Instrumento que mide los cambios en la presión del aire sin usar líquido.

anticyclone A high-pressure center of dry air. (p. 316)
anticiclón Centro de aire seco de alta presión.

aquaculture The farming of water organisms. (p. 461)
acuicultura Crianza de organismos de agua salada y dulce.

asthenosphere The soft layer of the mantle on which the lithosphere floats. (p. 137)
astenosfera Capa suave del manto en la que flota la litosfera.

atmosphere Earth's envelope of gases. (pp. 15, 256)
atmósfera Capa de gases que rodea la Tierra.

B

barometer An instrument used to measure changes in air pressure. (p. 264)
barómetro Instrumento que se usa para medir cambios en la presión del aire.

base-isolated building A building mounted on bearings that absorb an earthquake's energy. (p. 202)
edificio de base aislada Edificio montado sobre soportes diseñados para absorber la energía liberada por los terremotos.

basic A word used to describe a substance that feels slippery and changes red litmus paper blue. (p. 69)
base Describe a una sustasncia resbalosa al tacto y hace que el papel de tornasol rojo cambie a azul.

basin A broad, bowl-shaped valley formed where the crust is bent downward. (p. 236)
cuenca Valle amplio, en forma de tazón, formado donde la corteza está hundida.

batholith A mass of rock formed when a large body of magma cools inside the crust. (p. 234)
batolito Masa de roca formada cuando una gran masa de magma se enfría dentro de la corteza.

beach Wave-washed sediment along a coast. (p. 111)
playa Sedimento depositado por las olas a lo largo de una costa.

bedrock The solid rock beneath the soil. (p. 66)
lecho rocoso Capa sólida de roca debajo del suelo.

biodegradable Capable of being broken down by bacteria and other decomposers. (p. 509)
biodegradable Sustancia que las bacterias y otros descomponedores pueden descomponer.

biodiversity The number of species in an area.
biodiversidad Número de diferentes especies en un área. (p. 462)

biomass fuel Fuel made from living things. (p. 489)
combustible de biomasa Combustible formado a partir de seres vivos.

biome A group of land ecosystems with similar climates and organisms. (p. 438)
bioma Grupo de ecosistemas terrestres con climas y organismos similares.

biosphere All living things. One of the four spheres into which scientists divide Earth. (p. 15)
biosfera Todos los seres vivos; una de las cuatro esferas en las cuales los científicos dividen la Tierra.

biotic factor A living part of an organism's habitat.
factor biótico La parte viva del hábitat de un organismo. (p. 393)

birth rate The number of births in a population in a certain amount of time. (p. 400)
tasa de natalidad Número de nacimientos en una población en un período determinado.

C

caldera The large hole at the top of a volcano formed when the roof of a magma chamber collapses.
caldera Gran agujero en la parte superior de un volcán que se forma cuando la tapa de la cámara magmática del volcán se desploma. (p. 232)

canopy A leafy roof formed by tall trees in a forest. (p. 440)
bóveda arbórea Cubierta densa formada por las cimas hojeadas de los árboles altos de un bosque.

captive breeding The mating of animals in zoos or wildlife preserves. (p. 466)
reproducción en cautiverio Apareamiento de animales en zoológicos y reservas naturales.

carnivore A consumer that eats only animals. (p. 405)
carnívoro Consumidor que come sólo animales.

carrying capacity The largest population that an area can support. (p. 402)
capacidad de carga La mayor población que puede sustentar un área.

Central Valley The large basin in California between the Coast Ranges and the Sierra Nevada. (p. 236)
Valle Central La gran cuenca en California, que queda entre las cordilleras costera y Sierra Nevada.

chaparral An area of dense shrubs and small trees found in Mediterranean climates. (p. 368)
chaparral Área de densos arbustos y pequeños árboles que se halla en los climas mediterráneos.

chemical weathering The process that breaks down rock through chemical changes. (p. 60)
desgaste químico Proceso que erosiona la roca mediante cambios químicos.

chlorofluorocarbons Chlorine compounds that are the main cause of ozone depletion. (p. 378)
clorofluorocarbonos Compuestos de cloro que son la causa principal de la destrucción del ozono.

cinder cone A steep, cone-shaped hill or small mountain made of volcanic ash, cinders, and bombs.
cono de escoria Colina o pequeña montaña escarpada en forma de cono que se forma cuando ceniza volcánica, escoria y bombas se acumulan alrededor de la boca de un volcán. (p. 230)

cirrus Wispy, feathery clouds made mostly of ice crystals that form at high levels. (p. 304)
cirros Nubes parecidas a plumas o pinceladas blancas formadas principalmente por cristales de hielo que se crean a grandes altitudes.

clear-cutting The process of cutting down all the trees in an area at once. (p.459)
tala total Proceso de cortar simultáneamente todos los árboles de un área.

climate The average, long-term conditions of temperature, precipitation, winds, and clouds in an area.
clima Promedio, año a año, de las condiciones de temperatura, precipitación, viento y nubes en un área. (p. 346)

colliding boundary A plate boundary where two plates move toward each other. (p. 161)
borde convergente Borde de placa donde dos placas se deslizan una hacia la otra.

combustion The process of burning a fuel. (p. 479)
combustión Proceso en el que se quema un combustible.

commensalism A relationship in which one species benefits and the other is neither helped nor harmed.
comensalismo Relación entre dos especies donde una se beneficia y la otra no obtiene ni beneficio ni perjuicio. (p. 415)

community All the different populations that live together in an area. (p. 395)
comunidad Todas las diferentes poblaciones que viven juntas en un área.

competition The struggle between organisms to survive using the same limited resource. (p. 412)
competencia Lucha entre organismos por sobrevivir a medida que usan los recursos limitados en un mismo hábitat.

composite volcano A tall, cone-shaped mountain in which layers of lava and ash alternate. (p. 231)
volcán compuesto Montaña alta con forma de cono en la que las capas de lava se alternan con capas de ceniza y otros materiales volcánicos.

composting The process of helping biodegradable wastes to decompose naturally. (p. 511)
compostaje Proceso de ayudar a que los desechos biodegradables se descompongan de manera natural.

compression Stress that squeezes rock, causing folding.
compresión Esfuerzo que oprime una roca hasta que ésta se pliega o rompe. (p. 175)

condensation The process by which molecules of water vapor in the air become liquid water. (p. 303)
condensación Proceso por el cual las moléculas de vapor de agua se convierten en agua líquida.

conduction The direct transfer of heat between two substances that are touching. (pp. 141, 280)
conducción Transferencia directa de energía térmica de una sustancia a otra que la toca.

coniferous tree A tree that produces its seeds in cones and that has needle-shaped leaves. (p. 444)
árbol conífero Árbol que produce sus semillas en conos y sus hojas tienen forma de aguja.

conservation plowing Soil conservation method in which the dead stalks from the previous year's crop are left in the ground to hold the soil in place. (p. 77)
arada de conservación Método de conservación del suelo en el cual los tallos muertos de la cosecha del año anterior se dejan en la tierra para que sujeten el suelo en su lugar.

consumer An organism that obtains energy by feeding on other organisms. (p. 405)
consumidor Organismo que obtiene energía alimentándose de otros organismos.

continental (air mass) A dry air mass that forms over land. (p. 311)
masa de aire continental Masa de aire seco que se forma sobre la tierra.

continental climate The climate of the centers of continents, with cold winters and warm or hot summers. (p. 348)
clima continental Clima del centro de los continentes, con inviernos fríos y veranos templados o calurosos.

continental drift The hypothesis that the continents slowly move across Earth's surface.
deriva continental Hipótesis según la cual los continentes se desplazan lentamente en la superficie de la Tierra. (p. 145)

continental glacier A glacier that covers much of a continent or large island. (p. 116)
glaciar continental Glaciar que cubre gran parte de un continente o una isla grande.

contour interval The difference in elevation from one contour line to the next. (p. 29)
intervalo entre curvas de nivel Diferencia de elevación de una curva de nivel a otra.

contour line A line on a topographic map that connects points of equal elevation. (p. 29)
curva de nivel Línea en un mapa topográfico que conecta puntos de igual elevación.

contour plowing Plowing fields along the curves of a slope to prevent soil loss. (p. 77)
arada en contorno Arar los campos siguiendo las curvas de una pendiente para evitar que el suelo se suelte.

control rod A cadmium rod used in a nuclear reactor to absorb neutrons from fission reactions. (p. 496)
varilla de control Varilla de cadmio que se usa en un reactor nuclear para absorber los neutrones emitidos por las reacciones de la fisión.

controlled experiment An experiment in which only one variable is manipulated at a time. (p. 9)
experimento controlado Experimento en el cual sólo una variable es manipulada a la vez.

convection The transfer of heat by the movement of a fluid. (pp. 142, 280)
convección Transferencia de energía térmica por el movimiento de un líquido.

convection current The movement of a fluid that transfers heat from one part of the fluid to another.
corriente de convección Movimiento de un líquido que transfiere calor de un punto del líquido a otro. (pp. 142, 280)

coral reef A structure of calcite skeletons built up by coral animals in warm, shallow ocean water. (p. 453)
arrecife de coral Estructura de esqueletos calcáreos formada por corales en aguas oceánicas templadas y poco profundas.

Coriolis effect The effect of Earth's rotation on the direction of winds and currents. (p. 285)
efecto de Coriolis Efecto de la rotación terrestre sobre la dirección de los vientos y las corrientes.

crater A bowl-shaped area that forms around a volcano's central opening. (p. 222)
cráter Área en forma de tazón que se forma alrededor de la entrada central de un volcán.

crop rotation The planting of different crops in a field each year to maintain the soil's fertility. (p. 77)
rotación de cultivos Plantación de cultivos diferentes en un campo cada año para mantener la fertilidad del suelo.

crust The layer of rock that forms Earth's outer surface. (p. 135)
corteza Capa de rocas que forma la superficie externa de la Tierra.

crystal A solid in which the atoms are arranged in a pattern that repeats again and again. (p. 49)
cristal Sólido en el que los átomos están dispuestos en un patrón que se repite una y otra vez.

cumulus Fluffy, white clouds, usually with flat bottoms, that look like rounded piles of cotton. (p. 304)
cúmulos Nubes blancas, que normalmente tienen la parte inferior plana, que parecen grandes masas de algodón esponjosas y redondas.

cyclone A swirling center of low air pressure.
ciclón Centro de un remolino de aire de baja presión. (p. 316)

data Facts, figures, and other evidence gathered through observations. (p. 10)
dato Hecho, cifra u otra evidencia reunida por medio de las observaciones.

death rate The number of deaths in a population in a certain amount of time. (p. 400)
tasa de mortalidad Número de muertes en una población en un período determinado.

deciduous tree A tree that sheds its leaves and grows new ones each year. (p. 443)
árbol caducifolio Árbol cuyas hojas caen y vuelven a crecer anualmente.

decomposer An organism that breaks down wastes and dead organisms. (pp. 71, 405)
descomponedor Organismo que descompone desechos y organismos muertos.

deep-ocean trench A deep valley along the ocean floor beneath which oceanic crust slowly sinks toward the mantle. (p. 154)
fosa oceánica profunda Valle profundo a lo largo del suelo oceánico debajo del cual la corteza oceánica se hunde lentamente hacia el manto.

deflation Wind erosion that removes surface soil.
deflación Erosión por viento que se lleva materiales superficiales. (p. 113)

degree A unit used to measure distances around a circle. One degree equals 1/360 of a full circle. (p. 25)
grado Unidad usada para medir distancias alrededor de un círculo. Un grado es igual a 1/360 de un círculo completo.

delta A landform made of sediment that is deposited where a river flows into an ocean or lake. (p. 99)
delta Accidente geográfico formado por sedimentos que se depositan en la desembocadura de un río a un océano o lago.

density The amount of mass of a substance in a given volume; mass per unit volume. (pp. 142, 263)
densidad Cantidad de masa en un espacio dado; masa por unidad de volumen.

deposition Process in which sediment is laid down in new locations. (p. 89)
sedimentación Proceso por el cual se asientan sedimentos en sitios nuevos.

desert An arid region that on average receives less than 25 cm of rain a year. (pp. 366, 439)
desierto Región árida que, como promedio, recibe menos de 25 centímetros de lluvia al año.

dew point The temperature at which condensation begins. (p. 303)
punto de rocío Temperatura a la que comienza la condensación

dike A slab of volcanic rock formed when magma forces itself across rock layers. (p. 233)
dique discordante Placa de roca volcánica formada cuando el magma se abre paso a través de las capas de roca.

dormant A volcano that is not currently active, but that may become active in the future. (p. 227)
inactivo Volcán que en la actualidad no está activo, pero que puede volver a ser activo en el futuro.

Dust Bowl The area of the Great Plains where wind erosion caused soil loss during the 1930s. (p. 76)
Cuenca del polvo Área de las Grandes Llanuras donde la erosión por el viento causó la pérdida de suelo durante la década de 1930.

Earth science The science that focuses on planet Earth and its place in the universe. (p. 18)
ciencia de la Tierra Ciencia que se centra en el planeta Tierra y en su lugar en el universo.

earthquake The shaking that results from the movement of rock beneath Earth's surface. (p. 181)
terremoto Temblor que resulta del movimiento de la roca debajo de la superficie de la Tierra.

ecology The study of how living things interact with each other and their environment. (p. 396)
ecología Estudio de cómo interactúan los seres vivos entre sí y con su medio ambiente.

ecosystem The community of organisms in an area, along with their nonliving surroundings. (p. 396)
ecosistema Comunidad de organismos que viven en un área determinada, junto con su medio ambiente no vivo.

efficiency The percentage of energy that is used to perform work. (p. 500)
eficiencia Porcentaje de energía usada para realizar trabajo.

El Niño A climate event that occurs every two to seven years in the Pacific Ocean, during which winds shift and push warm water toward South America.
El Niño Fenómeno climático que ocurre cada dos a siete años en el Océano Pacífico, durante el cual los vientos se desvían y empujan el agua templado hacia la costa de América del Sur. (p. 359)

electromagnetic wave Wave that can transfer energy through the vacuum of space. (p. 272)
ondas electromagnéticas Ondas que transfieren energía a través del vacío.

elevation Height above sea level. (p. 21)
elevación Altura sobre el nivel del mar.

emigration Leaving a population. (p. 400)
emigración Abandono de una población.

endangered species A species in danger of becoming extinct in the near future. (p. 464)
especie en peligro de extinción Especie que corre el riesgo de desaparecer en el futuro próximo.

energy The ability to do work or cause change. (pp. 14, 96)
energía Capacidad para realizar trabajo o producir cambios.

energy conservation The practice of reducing energy use. (p. 502)
conservación de la energía Práctica de reducción del uso de energía.

energy pyramid A diagram that shows the amount of energy that moves from one feeding level to another in a food web. (p. 408)
pirámide de la energía Diagrama que muestra la cantidad de energía que pasa de un nivel de alimentación a otro en una red alimentaria.

energy transformation A change from one form of energy to another; also called an energy conversion. (p. 478)
transformación de la energía Cambio de una forma de energía a otra; también se le llama conversión de energía.

epicenter The point on Earth's surface directly above an earthquake's focus. (p. 181)
epicentro Punto en la superficie de la Tierra directamente sobre el foco de un terremoto.

erosion The process by which water, ice, wind, or gravity moves weathered rock or soil. (p. 57, 88)
erosión Proceso por el cual el agua, el hielo, el viento, o la gravedad desplazan rocas degastadas y suelo.

estuary A habitat in which the fresh water of a river meets the salt water of the ocean. (p. 452)
estuario Hábitat en el cual el agua dulce de un río se encuentra con el agua salada del mar.

evaporation The process by which water molecules in liquid water escape into the air as water vapor. (p. 300)
evaporación Proceso por el cual las moléculas de agua líquida son liberadas al aire como vapor de agua.

exosphere The outer layer of the thermosphere.
exosfera Capa externa de la termosfera. (p. 271)

extinct A volcano that is no longer active and is unlikely to erupt again. (p. 227)
extinto Volcán que ya no es activo y es poco probable que haga erupción otra vez; describe un tipo de organismo que ya no existe en la Tierra.

extinction The disappearance of all members of a species from Earth. (p. 464)
extinción Desaparición de la Tierra de todos los miembros de una especie.

fault A break or crack in Earth's lithosphere along which the rocks move. (p. 160)
falla Fisura o grieta en la litosfera de la Tierra a lo largo de la cual se mueven las rocas.

fertility A measure of how well soil supports plant growth. (p. 67)
fertilidad Medida de lo apropiado de un suelo para mantener el crecimiento de las plantas.

fishery An area with a large population of valuable ocean organisms. (p. 460)
pesquería Área con una gran población de organismos marinos aprovechables.

flood plain Wide valley through which a river flows.
llanura de aluvión Valle ancho por el cual fluye un río. (p. 97)

focus The point beneath Earth's surface where rock breaks under stress and causes an earthquake. (p. 181)
foco Punto debajo de la superficie de la Tierra en el que la roca se rompe a raíz del esfuerzo, y causa un terremoto.

food chain A series of events in which one organism eats another and obtains energy. (p. 406)
cadena alimentaria Serie de sucesos en los que un organismo se come a otro y obtiene energía.

food web The pattern of overlapping food chains in an ecosystem. (p. 406)
red alimentaria Patrón de cadenas alimentarias sobrepuestas en un ecosistema.

footwall The block of rock that forms the lower half of a fault. (p. 176)
labio inferior Bloque de roca que constituye la mitad inferior de una falla.

fossil A trace of an ancient organism that has been preserved in rock. (p. 146)
fósil Vestigio de un organismo de la antigüedad que se ha preservado en la roca u otra sustancia.

fossil fuel An energy-rich substance formed from the remains of organisms. (p. 480)
combustible fósil Sustancia rica en energía que se forma a partir de los restos de organismos.

friction The force that opposes the motion of one surface as it moves across another surface. (p. 194)
fricción Fuerza que se opone al movimiento de una superficie a medida que se mueve a través de otra superficie.

front The boundary where unlike air masses meet but do not mix. (p. 313)
frente Límite en donde se encuentran masas de aire diferentes, pero no se mezclan.

fuel A substance that provides energy as the result of a chemical change. (p. 478)
combustible Sustancia que libera energía como resultado de un cambio químico.

fuel rod A uranium rod that undergoes fission in a nuclear reactor. (p. 496)
varilla de combustible Varilla de uranio que se somete a la fisión en un reactor nuclear.

gasohol A mixture of gasoline and alcohol. (p. 489)
gasohol Mezcla de gasolina y alcohol.

geothermal energy Heat from Earth's interior.
energía geotérmica Calor del interior de la Tierra. (p. 490)

geyser A fountain of water and steam that builds up pressure underground and erupts at regular intervals. (p. 228)
géiser Fuente de agua y vapor que acumula presión subterránea y hace erupción a intervalos regulares.

glacier A large mass of moving ice and snow on land.
glaciar Gran masa de hielo y nieve que se mantiene en movimiento sobre la tierra. (p. 116)

global warming A gradual increase in the temperature of Earth's atmosphere. (p. 375)
calentamiento global Aumento gradual en la temperatura promedio de la atmósfera terrestre.

global winds Winds that blow steadily from specific directions over long distances. (p. 285)
vientos globales Vientos que soplan constantemente desde direcciones específicas por largas distancias.

grassland An area populated by grasses and other nonwoody plants. Most grasslands get 25 to 75 centimeters of rain each year. (p. 442)
pradera Área poblada de pastos y de otras plantas no leñosas. La mayoría de las praderas recibe de 25 a 75 centímetros de lluvia al año.

gravity A force that moves rocks and other materials downhill; the force that pulls objects toward each other. (p. 89)
gravedad Fuerza que mueve rocas y otros materiales cuesta abajo; fuerza que atrae objectos entre sí.

greenhouse effect The process by which heat is trapped in the atmosphere by water vapor, carbon dioxide, methane, and other gases that form a "blanket" around Earth. (p. 275)
efecto invernadero Proceso por el cual el calor queda atrapado en la atmósfera por gases que forman una "manta" alrededor de la Tierra.

greenhouse gases Gases in the atmosphere, such as carbon dioxide, that trap solar energy. (p. 375)
gases de invernadero Gases de la atmósfera, como el dióxido de carbono, que atrapan la energía solar.

gully A large channel in soil formed by erosion.
barranco Canal grande en el suelo, formado por la erosión. (p. 96)

habitat The place where an organism lives and where it obtains all the things it needs to survive. (p. 393)
hábitat Lugar donde vive un organismo y donde obtiene todo lo que necesita para sobrevivir.

habitat destruction Loss of a natural habitat. (p. 465)
destrucción del hábitat Pérdida de un hábitat natural.

hanging wall The block of rock that forms the upper half of a fault. (p. 176)
labio superior Bloque de roca que constituye la mitad superior de una falla.

headland A part of the shore that sticks out into the ocean. (p. 109)
promontorio Parte de la costa que se interna en el mar.

heat The transfer of thermal energy between objects because of a difference in temperature. (pp. 17, 280)
calor Transferencia de energía térmica de un objeto a otro debido a una diferencia de temperatura.

herbivore A consumer that eats only plants. (p. 405)
herbívoro Consumidor que come sólo plantas.

host Organism that a parasite lives in or on. (p. 416)
huésped Organismo dentro o fuera del cual vive un parásito en una interacción de parasitismo.

hot spot An area where magma from deep within the mantle melts through the crust above it. (p. 219)
punto caliente Área por donde el magma de las profundidades del manto atraviesa la corteza.

humid subtropical A wet and warm climate found on the edges of the tropics. (p. 368)
subtropical húmedo Clima húmedo y templado que se encuentra en los límites de los trópicos.

humidity The amount of water vapor in a given volume of air. (p. 301)
humedad Cantidad de vapor de agua en un volumen de aire definido.

humus Dark-colored organic material in soil. (p. 67)
humus Material orgánico de color oscuro en el suelo.

hurricane A tropical storm that has winds of about 119 kilometers per hour or higher. (p. 324)
huracán Tormenta tropical que tiene vientos de cerca de 119 kilómetros por hora o mayores.

hydrocarbon An energy-rich chemical compound that contains carbon and hydrogen atoms. (p. 480)
hidrocarburo Compuesto químico rico en energía que contiene átomos de carbono e hidrógeno.

hydroelectric power Electricity produced using the energy of flowing water. (p. 488)
energía hidroeléctrica Electricidad que se produce usando la energía de una corriente de agua.

hydrosphere Earth's water and ice. One of the four spheres into which scientists divide Earth. (p. 15)
hidrosfera El agua y el hielo de Tierra; una de las cuatro esferas en las cuales los científicos dividen la Tierra.

hypothesis A possible explanation for an observation or answer to a scientific question; must be testable. **hipótesis** Explicación posible para un conjunto de observaciones o respuesta a una pregunta científica; debe ser verificable. (p. 8)

ice age Time in the past when continental glaciers covered large parts of Earth's surface. **glaciación** Época del pasado en la que glaciares continentales cubrieron grandes extensiones de la superficie terrestre. (pp. 116, 374)

ice wedging Process that splits rock when water seeps into cracks, then freezes and expands. (p. 59) **efecto cuña de hielo** Proceso que parte la roca cuando el agua penetra en las grietas, y luego se congela y expande.

igneous rock A type of rock that forms from the cooling of molten rock at or below the surface. (p. 50) **roca ígnea** Tipo de roca que se forma cuando se enfrían las rocas fundidas en la superficie o debajo de la superficie.

immigration Moving into a population. (p. 400) **inmigración** Ingreso a una población.

incineration The burning of solid waste. (p. 507) **incineración** Quema de desechos sólidos.

index contour On a topographic map, a heavier contour line that is labeled with elevation of that contour line in round units. (p. 29) **curva de nivel índice** En un mapa topográfico, una curva de nivel más gruesa que lleva rotulada la elevación de esa curva de nivel en unidades redondeadas.

inferring Making an inference; an interpretation based on observations and prior knowledge. **inferir** Proceso de realizar una inferencia; interpretación basada en observaciones y en el conocimiento previo. (p. 7)

infrared radiation Electromagnetic waves with wavelengths that are longer than red light. (p. 273) **radiación infrarroja** Ondas electromagnéticas con longitudes de onda más largas que la luz visible.

inner core A dense sphere of solid iron and nickel at the center of Earth. (p. 138) **núcleo interno** Densa esfera de hierro y níquel situada en el centro de la Tierra.

insulation Material that blocks heat transfer between the air inside and outside a building. (p. 500) **aislante** Material que impide la transferencia de calor entre el interior y el exterior de un edificio.

intertidal zone An area that stretches from the highest high-tide line on land out to the point exposed by the lowest low tide. (p. 452) **zona intermareal** Área que se extiende desde la línea más alta de pleamar en tierra hasta el punto de la plataforma continental expuesto por la bajamar más baja.

intrusion An igneous rock layer formed when magma hardens beneath Earth's surface. (p. 233) **intrusión** Capa de roca ígnea formada cuando el magma se endurece bajo la superficie de la Tierra.

ionosphere The lower part of the thermosphere. **ionosfera** Parte inferior de la termosfera. (p. 271)

island arc A string of islands formed by the volcanoes along a deep-ocean trench. (p. 218) **arco de islas** Cadena de islas formadas por los volcanes que se encuentran a lo largo de una fosa oceánica profunda.

isobar A line on a weather map that joins places that have the same air pressure. (p. 330) **isobara** Línea en un mapa del tiempo que une lugares que tienen la misma presión de aire.

isotherm A line on a weather map that joins places that have the same temperature. (p. 330) **isoterma** Línea en un mapa del tiempo que une lugares que tienen la misma temperatura.

jet streams Bands of high-speed winds about 10 kilometers above Earth's surface. (p. 288) **corriente de chorro** Banda de vientos de alta velocidad a unos 10 kilómetros sobre la superficie de la Tierra.

kelp forest Marine ecosystem where large, brown algae called giant kelp grow. (p. 453) **bosque de kelp** Ecosistema marino donde crece un alga grande y café llamada kelp gigante.

kettle A small depression that forms when a chunk of ice is left in glacial till. (p. 118) **marmita** Pequeña depresión que se forma cuando queda un trozo de hielo en la tillita.

keystone species A species that influences the survival of many other species in an ecosystem. (p. 463)
especie clave Especie que influye en la supervivenia de muchas otras en un ecosistema.

La Niña A climate event in the eastern Pacific Ocean in which surface waters are colder than normal. (p. 359)
La Niña Fenómeno climático que ocurre en la parte este del océano Pacífico, en el cual las aguas superficiales están más frías que lo normal.

land breeze The flow of air from land to a body of water. (p. 284)
brisa terrestre Flujo de aire desde la tierra a una masa de agua.

latitude The distance in degrees from the equator. (pp. 26, 286)
latitud Distancia en grados del ecuador.

lava Liquid magma that reaches the surface; also, the rock formed when liquid lava hardens. (p. 216)
lava Magma líquida que sale a la superficie; también, la roca que se forma cuando la lava líquida se solidifica.

lava flow Area covered by lava from a volcano's vent. (p. 222)
colada de lava Área cubierta de lava a medida que ésta sale por la boca del volcán. (p. 222)

leachate Polluted liquid produced by water passing through buried wastes in a landfill. (p. 508)
lixiviado Líquido contaminado que se produce por el paso del agua a través de los desechos enterrados en un relleno sanitario.

leeward The side of a mountain range that faces away from the oncoming wind. (p. 350)
sotavento Lado de una cadena montañosa que está resguardado del viento.

lightning A sudden spark, or energy discharge, caused when electrical charges jump between parts of a cloud, between nearby clouds, or between a cloud and the ground. (p. 319)
rayo Chispa repentina o descarga de energía causada por cargas eléctricas que saltan entre partes de una nube, entre nubes cercanas o entre una nube y la tierra.

limiting factor An environmental factor that causes a population to decrease. (p. 402)
factor limitante Factor ambiental que impide el crecimiento de una población.

liquefaction The process by which an earthquake's violent movement suddenly turns loose soil into liquid mud. (p. 199)
licuefacción Proceso mediante el que las violentas sacudidas de un terremoto de pronto convierten la tierra suelta en lodo líquido.

lithosphere A rigid layer made up of the uppermost part of the mantle and the crust. (pp. 15, 136)
litosfera Capa rígida constituida por la parte superior del manto y la corteza.

litter The loose layer of dead plant leaves and stems on the surface of the soil. (p. 70)
mantillo Capa suelta de hojas y tallos de plantas muertas en la superficie del suelo.

load The amount of sediment that a river carries.
carga La cantidad de sedimento que lleva un río o arroyo. (p. 102)

loam Rich, fertile soil that is made up of about equal parts of clay, sand, and silt. (p. 67)
limo arcilloso arenoso Suelo rico y fértil que está formado por partes casi iguales de arcilla, arena y limo.

local winds Winds that blow over short distances.
vientos locales Vientos que soplan por distancias cortas. (p. 284)

loess A wind-formed deposit made of fine particles of clay and silt. (p. 114)
loes Depósito de partículas finas de arcilla y limo arrastradas por el viento.

longitude The distance in degrees east or west of the prime meridian. (p. 26)
longitud Distancia en grados al este o al oeste del primer meridiano.

longshore drift The movement of water and sediment down a beach caused by waves coming in to shore at an angle. (p. 111)
deriva litoral Movimiento de agua y sedimentos paralelo a una playa debido a la llegada de olas inclinadas respecto a la costa.

magma The molten mixture of rock-forming substances, gases, and water from the mantle. (p. 216)
magma Mezcla fundida de las sustancias que forman las rocas, gases y agua, proveniente del manto.

magma chamber The pocket beneath a volcano where magma collects. (p. 222)
cámara magmática Bolsa debajo de un volcán en la que se acumula el magma.

magnitude The measurement of an earthquake's strength based on seismic waves and movement along faults. (p. 184)
magnitud Medida de la fuerza de un sismo basada en las ondas sísmicas y en el movimiento que ocurre a lo largo de las fallas.

manipulated variable The one factor that a scientist changes during an experiment; also called independent variable. (p. 9)
variable manipulada Único factor que un científico cambia durante un experimento; también llamada variable independiente.

mantle The layer of hot, solid material between Earth's crust and core. (p. 136)
manto Capa de material caliente y sólido entre la corteza terrestre y el núcleo.

map A flat model of all or part of Earth's surface as seen from above. (p. 24)
mapa Modelo plano de toda la superficie de la Tierra o parte de ella tal y como se ve desde arriba.

marine climate The climate of some coastal regions, with relatively warm winters and cool summers.
clima marino Clima de algunas regiones costeras, con inviernos relativamente templados y veranos fríos. (p. 348)

maritime (air mass) A humid air mass that forms over oceans. (p. 311)
masa de aire marítima Masa de aire húmedo que se forma sobre los océanos.

mass movement Any one of several processes by which gravity moves sediment downhill. (p. 89)
movimiento de masas Cualquiera de varios procesos por los cuales la gravedad desplaza sedimentos cuesta abajo.

matter Anything that has mass and takes up space.
materia Cualquier cosa que tiene masa y ocupa un espacio. (p. 16)

meander A looplike bend in the course of a river.
meandro Curva muy pronunciada en el curso de un río. (p. 98)

mechanical weathering The type of weathering in which rock is physically broken into smaller pieces.
desgaste mecánico Tipo de desgaste en el cual una roca se rompe físicamente en trozos más pequeños. (p. 58)

meltdown A dangerous condition in which fuel rods inside a nuclear reactor melt. (p. 497)
fusión (del núcleo de un reactor) Condición peligrosa en la cual las varillas de combustible dentro del reactor nuclear se derriten.

Mercalli scale A scale that rates earthquakes according to their intensity and how much damage they cause at a particular place. (p. 184)
escala de Mercalli Escala con la que se miden los sismos basándose en la intensidad y el daño que ocasionan.

mercury barometer An instrument that measures changes in air pressure, consisting of a glass tube partially filled with mercury, with its open end resting in a dish of mercury. (p. 264)
barómetro de mercurio Instrumento que mide los cambios en la presión del aire; consiste de un tubo de vidrio parcialmente lleno de mercurio con su extremo abierto posado en un recipiente con mercurio.

mesosphere The layer of Earth's atmosphere immediately above the stratosphere. (p. 270)
mesosfera Capa de la atmósfera de la Tierra inmediatamente sobre la estratosfera.

metamorphic rock Rock that forms when a rock is changed by heat, pressure, or chemical reactions.
roca metamórfica Tipo de roca que se forma cuando una roca es transformada por el calor, presión o reacciones químicas. (p. 51)

meteorologist A scientist who studies the causes of weather and tries to predict it. (pp. 19, 329)
meteorólogo Científico que estudia las causas del tiempo e intentan predecirlo.

microclimate Climate conditions within a small area that differ from those in the surrounding area.
microclima Condiciones climáticas en una área pequeña que son diferentes del clima de las áreas de alrededor. (p. 346)

mid-ocean ridge An undersea mountain chain where new ocean floor is produced. (p. 150)
dorsal oceánica Cordillera montañosa submarina donde se produce nuevo suelo oceánico.

mineral A natural inorganic solid with a crystal structure and definite chemical composition.
mineral Sólido inorgánico que ocurre en la naturaleza, de estructura cristalina y composición química definida. (p. 49)

moment magnitude scale A scale that rates an earthquake by estimating the total energy released. (p. 185)
escala de magnitud del momento Escala con la que se miden los sismos estimando la cantidad total de energía liberada por un terremoto. (p. 185)

monsoon Sea or land breeze over a large region that changes direction with the seasons. (p. 351)
monzón Vientos marinos o terrestres que cambian de dirección según las estaciones.

moraine A ridge formed by the till deposited at the edge of a glacier. (p. 118)
morrena Montículo formado por la tillita depositada en el borde de un glaciar.

mountain A landform with high elevation and high relief. (p. 23)
montaña Accidente geográfico con una elevación alta y un relieve alto.

municipal solid waste Waste produced in homes, businesses, and schools. (p. 507)
desechos sólidos urbanos Desechos producidos en hogares, oficinas y escuelas.

mutualism A relationship between two species in which both species benefit. (p. 415)
mutualismo Relación entre dos especies de la cual ambas se benefician.

natural resource Anything in the environment that humans use. (p. 75)
recurso natural Cualquier cosa de la naturaleza que usan los humanos.

natural selection A process by which characteristics that make an individual better suited to its environment become more common in a species.
selección natural Proceso por el cual las características que permiten a un individuo adaptarse mejor a su medio ambiente se hacen más comunes en una especie. (p. 411)

neritic zone The region of shallow ocean water over the continental shelf. (p. 452)
zona nerítica Región sobre la placa continental donde el agua del océano es poco profunda.

niche The role of an organism in its habitat, or how it makes its living. (p. 411)
nicho Función de un organismo en su hábitat, o cómo sobrevive.

nitrogen fixation The process of changing free nitrogen gas into a usable form. (p. 420)
fijación del nitrógeno Proceso de conversión del gas nitrógeno libre en una forma aprovechable.

nonrenewable resource A natural resource that is not replaced in a useful time frame. (p. 53)
recurso no renovable Recurso natural que no se restaura una vez usado, en un período relativamente corto.

normal fault A type of fault where the hanging wall slides downward; caused by tension in the crust.
falla normal Tipo de falla en la cual el labio superior se desliza hacia abajo como resultado de la tensión en la corteza. (p. 176)

nuclear fission The splitting of an atom's nucleus into two smaller nuclei and neutrons. (p. 495)
fisión nuclear División del núcleo de un átomo en dos núcleos más pequeños y neutrones.

nuclear fusion The combining of two nuclei to produce a single larger nucleus and much energy.
fusión nuclear Unión de dos núcleos para producir un núcleo único más grande y liberar energía. (p. 498)

nucleus The central core of an atom that contains the protons and neutrons (p. 494)
núcleo Parte central de un átomo, que contiene protones y neutrones.

observing The process of using one or more of your senses to gather information. (p. 7)
observar Proceso de usar uno o más de tus sentidos para reunir información.

occluded Cut off, as in a front where warm air mass is caught between two cooler air masses. (p. 315)
ocluido Aislado o cerrado, como cuando la masa de aire cálido queda atrapada entre dos masas de aire más frío.

ocean current A large stream of moving water that flows through the ocean in a regular pattern. (p. 349)
corriente oceánica Gran corriente de agua que fluye a través del océano en un patrón regular.

omnivore A consumer that eats both plants and animals. (p. 405)
omnívoro Consumidor que come tanto plantas como animales.

ore Rock that contains a metal or useful mineral.
mena Rocaque contiene un metal o un mineral de importancia económica. (p. 54)

organism A living thing. (p. 393)
organismo Un ser viviente.

outer core A layer of molten iron and nickel that surrounds the inner core of Earth. (p. 138)
núcleo externo Capa de hierro y níquel fundidos que rodea el núcleo interno de la Tierra.

oxbow lake A meander cut off from a river. (p. 98)
meandro abandonado Meandro que ha quedado aislado de un río.

oxidation A chemical change in which a substance combines with oxygen, as when iron forms rust.
oxidación Cambio químico en el cual una sustancia se combina con el oxígeno, como cuando el hierro se oxida y se forma herrumbre. (p. 61)

ozone A form of oxygen that has three oxygen atoms in each molecule instead of the usual two. (p. 257)
ozono Forma de oxígeno que tiene tres átomos de oxígeno en cada molécula.

ozone hole A large area of reduced ozone concentration in the stratosphere, found over Antarctica. (p. 378)
agujero en la capa de ozono Una gran área de reducida concentración de ozono en la estratosfera, que se halla sobre la Antártica.

P wave A type of seismic wave that compresses and expands the ground. (p. 183)
onda P Tipo de onda sísmica que comprime y expande el suelo.

Pangaea Landmass that broke apart 200 million years ago and gave rise to today's continents. (p. 145)
Pangea Nombre de la masa terrestre única que se dividió hace 200 millones de años, dando origen a los continentes actuales.

parasite Organism that benefits by living on or in a host.
parásito Organismo que se beneficia de vivir en la superficie o en el interior de un huésped en una interacción de parasitismo. (p. 416)

parasitism A relationship in which one organism lives on or in a host and harms it. (p. 416)
parasitismo Relación en la cual un organismo vive en la superficie o en el interior de un huésped y lo perjudica.

permafrost Permanently frozen soil found in the tundra climate region. (pp. 370, 445)
permagélido Suelo permanentemente helado que se encuentra en la región climática de la tundra.

permeable Characteristic of a material full of tiny, connected air spaces that water can seep through.
permeable Característica de un material que está lleno de diminutos espacios de aire conectados entre sí, por los que puede penetrar el agua. (p. 62)

petrochemical A compound made from oil. (p. 482)
petroquímico Compuesto que se obtiene del petróleo.

petroleum Liquid fossil fuel; oil. (p. 482)
petróleo Combustible fósil líquido.

photochemical smog A brownish haze formed when pollutants react with each other in the presence of sunlight. (p. 260)
neblina tóxica fotoquímica Densa bruma pardusca que se forma cuando los contaminantes reaccionan entre ellos en presencia de luz solar.

photosynthesis The process in which organisms use water along with sunlight and carbon dioxide to make their own food. (p. 394)
fotosíntesis Proceso por el cual los organismos usan el agua junto con la luz solar y el dióxido de carbono para producir su alimento.

pioneer species The first species to populate an area.
especies pioneras Primeras especies en poblar una región. (p. 423)

pipe A long tube through which magma moves from the magma chamber to Earth's surface. (p. 222)
chimenea Largo tubo por el que el magma sube desde la cámara magmática hasta la superficie.

English and Spanish Glossary

plain Landform of flat land with low relief.
llanura Accidente geográfico que consiste en un terreno plano o ligeramente ondulado con un relieve bajo. (p. 22)

plankton Tiny algae and animals that float in water and are carried by waves and currents. (p. 454)
plancton Algas y animales diminutos que flotan en el agua a merced de las olas y las corrientes.

plate A section of the lithosphere that slowly moves over the asthenosphere, carrying pieces of continental and oceanic crust. (p. 158)
placa Sección de la litosfera que se desplaza lentamente sobre la astenosfera, llevando consigo trozos de la corteza continental y de la oceánica.

plate tectonics The theory that pieces of Earth's lithosphere are in constant motion, driven by convection currents in the mantle. (p. 159)
tectónica de placas Teoría según la cual las partes de la litosfera de la Tierra están en continuo movimiento, impulsadas por las corrientes de convección del manto.

plateau A landform that has high elevation and a more or less level surface. (pp. 23, 180)
meseta Accidente geográfico que tiene una elevación alta y cuya superficie está más o menos nivelada.

plucking The process by which a glacier picks up rocks as it flows over the land. (p. 117)
arranque glaciar Proceso por el cual un glaciar arranca rocas al fluir sobre la tierra.

poaching Illegal killing or removal of wildlife.
caza ilegal Matanza o eliminación de la fauna silvestre de su hábitat. (p. 465)

polar (air mass) A cold air mass that forms north of 50° north latitude or south of 50° south latitude and has high air pressure. (p. 311)
masa de aire polar Masa de aire frío que se forma al norte de los 50° de latitud norte o al sur de los 50° de latitud sur y que tiene presión alta.

polar zone The areas near both poles, from about 66.5° to 90° north and 66.5° to 90° south latitudes. (p. 347)
zona polar Áreas cercana a los polos, desde unos 66.5° a 90° de latitud norte y 66.5° a 90° de latitud sur.

pollutant A harmful substance in the air, water, or soil.
contaminante Sustancia dañina en el aire, agua o suelo. (p. 259)

population All the members of one species in a particular area. (p. 395)
población Todos los miembros de una especie en un área particular.

precipitation Any form of water that falls from clouds and reaches Earth's surface. (p. 307)
precipitación Cualquier forma de agua que cae desde las nubes y llega a la superficie de la Tierra.

predation An interaction in which one organism kills another for food. (p. 413)
depredación Interacción en la cual un organismo mata y se come a otro.

predator The organism that does the killing in a predation interaction. (p. 413)
depredador Organismo que mata en la depredación.

predicting Forecasting what will happen in the future based on past experience or evidence. (p. 7)
predecir Proceso de pronosticar lo que va a suceder en el futuro, basado en la experiencia pasada o en evidencia.

pressure The force exerted on a surface divided by the total area over which the force is exerted.
presión Fuerza ejercida sobre una superficie dividida por el área total sobre la cual se ejerce la fuerza. (pp. 134, 263)

prey An organism that is killed and eaten by another organism. (p. 413)
presa Organismo que otro organismo mata y come.

primary succession The series of changes that occur in an area where no soil or organisms exist. (p. 423)
sucesión primaria Serie de cambios que ocurren en un área en donde no existe suelo ni organismos.

producer An organism that can make its own food.
productor Organismo que puede elaborar su propio alimento. (p. 405)

psychrometer An instrument used to measure relative humidity, consisting of a wet-bulb thermometer and a dry-bulb thermometer. (p. 302)
psicrómetro Instrumento que se usa para medir la humedad relativa y que consiste de un termómetro de bulbo húmedo y de un termómetro de bulbo seco.

pyroclastic flow An explosive volcanic eruption of ash, cinders, bombs, and gases. (p. 225)
flujo piroclástico Emisión de ceniza, escoria, bombas y gases durante una erupción volcánica explosiva.

radiation The direct transfer of energy through space by electromagnetic waves. (pp. 141, 272)
radiación Transferencia directa de energía a través del espacio por ondas electromagnéticas.

rain forest A forest in the tropical wet climate zone in which large amounts of rain fall year-round.
bosque tropical Selva ubicada dentro de la zona de clima tropical húmedo en la cual caen grandes cantidades de lluvia todo el año. (p. 363)

reactor vessel The part of a nuclear reactor where nuclear fission occurs. (p. 496)
cuba de reactor Parte de un reactor nuclear donde ocurre la fisión nuclear.

recycling The process of reclaiming and reusing raw materials. (p. 509)
reciclaje Proceso de recuperar y volver a usar materias primas.

refinery A factory in which crude oil is heated and separated into fuels and other products. (p. 482)
refinería Planta en la que el petróleo crudo se calienta y fracciona en combustibles y otros productos.

relative humidity The percentage of water vapor in the air compared to the maximum amount of water vapor that air can contain at a given temperature.
humedad relativa Porcentaje de vapor de agua en el aire comparado con la cantidad máxima de vapor de agua que puede contener el aire a una temperatura particular. (p. 301)

relief The difference in elevation between the highest and lowest parts of an area. (p. 21)
relieve Diferencia en la elevación entre las partes más altas y más bajas en un área.

renewable resource A resource that is either always available or is naturally replaced relatively quickly.
recurso renovable Recurso que está siempre disponible o que es restituido de manera natural en un período relativamente corto. (p. 457)

responding variable The factor that changes as a result of changes to the manipulated, or independent, variable in an experiment; also called dependent variable. (p. 9)
variable respuesta Factor que cambia como resultado de cambios a la variable manipulada, o independiente, en un experimento; también llamada variable dependiente.

reverse fault A type of fault where the hanging wall slides upward; caused by compression in the crust.
falla inversa Tipo de falla en la cual el labio superior se desliza hacia arriba como resultado de compresión en la corteza. (p. 177)

Richter scale A scale that rates an earthquake's magnitude based on the size of its seismic waves.
escala de Richter Escala con la que se mide la magnitud de un terremoto basándose en el tamaño de sus ondas sísmicas. (p. 184)

rift valley Valley form where plates move apart.
valle de fisura Valle profundo que se forma cuando dos placas se separan. (p. 160)

rill A tiny groove in soil made by flowing water.
arroyuelo Pequeño surco en el suelo que deja el agua al fluir. (p. 96)

Ring of Fire Volcano belt that rims the Pacific Ocean.
Cinturón de Fuego Gran cadena de volcanes que rodea el océano Pacífico. (p. 217)

rock cycle A series of processes on the surface and inside Earth that slowly changes rocks from one kind to another. (p. 50)
ciclo de las rocas Serie de processos en la superficie y dentro de la Tierra que lentamente transforman las rocas de un tipo de roca a otro.

runoff Water that flows over the ground surface rather than soaking into the ground. (p. 95)
escorrentía Agua que fluye sobre la superficie del suelo en lugar de ser absorbida por éste.

S wave A type of seismic wave that moves the ground up and down or side to side. (p. 183)
onda S Tipo de onda sísmica que hace que el suelo se mueva de arriba abajo, o de lado a lado.

salinity The total amount of dissolved salts in a water sample. (p. 360)
salinidad Cantidad total de sales disueltas en una muestra de agua.

sand dune A deposit of wind-blown sand. (p. 112)
duna de arena Depósito de arena arrastrada por el viento.

sanitary landfill A landfill that holds nonhazardous waste such as municipal solid waste and construction debris. (p. 508)
relleno sanitario Relleno que contiene desechos no peligrosos, como desechos sólidos urbanos y escombros de la construcción.

English and Spanish Glossary

savanna A tropical grassland with scattered clumps of trees. (pp. 363, 442)
sabana Pradera tropical con grupos de árboles.

scale Used to compare distance on a map or globe to distance on Earth's surface. (p. 24)
escala Se usa para comparar la distancia en un mapa o globo terráqueo con la distancia en la superficie de la Tierra.

scattering Reflection of light in all directions. (p. 274)
dispersión Reflexión de luz en todas las direcciones.

scavenger A carnivore that feeds on the bodies of dead organisms. (p. 405)
carroñero Carnívoro que se alimenta del cuerpo de animales muertos.

science A way of learning about the natural world through observations and logical reasoning; leads to a body of knowledge. (p. 7)
ciencia Método para aprender acerca del mundo natural a través de observaciones y del razonamiento lógico; conduce a un conjunto de conocimientos.

scientific inquiry The process of discovery in science; the ways in which scientists study the natural world and propose explanations based on evidence. (p. 8)
investigación científica Proceso continuo de descubrimiento en la ciencia; diversidad de métodos con los que los científicos estudian el mundo natural y proponen explicaciones del mismo basadas en la evidencia que reúnen.

scientific notation A mathematical method of writing numbers using powers of ten. (p. 533)
notación científica Método matemático de escritura de números que usa la potencia de diez.

scientific theory A well-tested concept that explains a wide range of observations. (p. 12)
teoría científica Concepto bien comprobado que explica un amplia gama de observaciones.

sea breeze The flow of cooler air from over an ocean or lake toward land. (p. 284)
brisa marina Flujo de aire más frío desde un océano o lago hacia la costa.

sea-floor spreading The process by which molten material adds new oceanic crust to the ocean floor.
expansión del suelo oceánico Proceso mediante el cual la materia fundida añade nueva corteza oceánica al suelo oceánico. (p. 151)

secondary succession The series of changes that occur in an area where the ecosystem has been disturbed, but where soil and organisms still exist. (p. 424)
sucesión secundaria Serie de cambios que ocurren en un área después de la perturbación de un ecosistema, pero donde todavía hay suelo y organismos.

sediment Small, solid pieces of material from rocks or organisms; earth materials deposited by erosion.
sedimento Partículas sólidas de materiales que provienen de rocas u organismos; materiales terrestres depositados por la erosión. (pp. 50, 89)

sedimentary rock A type of rock that forms when particles from other rocks or the remains of plants and animals are pressed and cemented together. (p. 50)
roca sedimentaria Tipo de roca que se forma cuando las partículas de otras rocas o los restos de plantas y animales son presionados y cementados.

seismic waves Vibrations that travel through Earth carrying the energy released during an earthquake.
ondas sísmicas Vibraciones que se desplazan por la Tierra, llevando la energía liberada durante un terremoto. (p. 133)

seismogram The record of an earthquake's seismic waves produced by a seismograph. (p. 191)
sismograma Registro producido por un sismógrafo de las ondas sísimicas de un terremoto.

seismograph A device that records ground movements caused by seismic waves. (p. 184)
sismógrafo Aparato con el que se registran los movimientos del suelo ocasionados por las ondas sísmicas a medida que éstas se desplazan por la Tierra.

selective cutting The process of cutting down only some trees in an area. (p. 459)
tala selectiva Proceso de cortar sólo algunos árboles de un área.

shearing Stress that pushes masses of rock in opposite directions, in a sideways movement. (p. 175)
cizallamiento Esfuerzo que presiona masas de roca en sentidos opuestos.

shield volcano A wide, gently sloping mountain made of layers of lava; formed by quiet eruptions.
volcán en escudo Montaña ancha de pendientes suaves, compuesta por capas de lava y formada durante erupciones no violentas. (p. 230)

silica A material found in magma that is formed from the elements oxygen and silicon. (p. 224)
sílice Material presente en el magma, compuesto por los elementos oxígeno y silicio.

sill A slab of volcanic rock formed when magma squeezes between layers of rock. (p. 233)
dique concordante Placa de roca volcánica formada cuando el magma se mete entre las capas de roca.

sliding boundary A plate boundary where two plates move past each other in opposite directions. (p. 161)
borde de transformación Borde de placa donde dos placas se deslizan una respecto a la otra, pero en sentidos opuestos.

smelting The process by which ore is melted to separate the useful metal from other elements. (p. 54)
fundición Proceso mediante el que una mena se funde para separar el mineral útil de otros elementos.

sod A thick mass of grass roots and soil. (p. 74)
tepe Masa gruesa de raíces de hierbas y suelo.

soil The loose, weathered material on Earth's surface in which plants can grow. (p. 66)
suelo Material suelto y desgastado sobre la superficie de la Tierra en donde crecen las plantas.

soil conservation The management of soil to prevent its destruction. (p. 77)
conservación del suelo Cuidado del suelo para prevenir su destrucción.

soil horizon The layer of soil that differs in color and texture from the layers above or below it. (p. 68)
horizonte de suelo Capa de suelo que se diferencia en color y textura de las capas que tiene encima o debajo.

solar energy Energy from the sun. (p. 486)
energía solar Energía del Sol.

sonar Device to determine the distance of an object under water by recording echoes of sound waves.
sonar Aparato con el cual se determina la distancia de un objeto sumergido en el agua mediante el registro del eco de las ondas sonoras. (p. 150)

species A group of organisms that are physically similar and can mate with each other and produce offspring that can also mate and reproduce. (p. 395)
especie Grupo de organismos que son físicamente semejantes, se pueden cruzar y producen crías que también se pueden cruzar y reproducir.

spit A beach formed by longshore drift that projects like a finger out into the water. (p. 112)
banco de arena Playa formada por la deriva litoral; que se interna como un dedo dentro del agua.

spreading boundary A plate boundary where two plates move away from each other. (p. 160)
borde divergente Borde de placa donde dos placas se separan.

steppe A prairie or grassland found in the semiarid climate region. (p. 366)
estepa Pradera o pastizal que se encuentra en las regiones semiáridas.

storm A violent disturbance in the atmosphere. (p. 318)
tormenta Alteración violenta en la atmósfera.

storm surge A "dome" of water that sweeps across the coast where a hurricane lands. (p. 325)
marejadas "Cúpula" de agua que se desplaza a lo largo de la costa donde aterriza un huracán.

stratosphere The second-lowest layer of Earth's atmosphere. (p. 268)
estratosfera Segunda capa inferior de la atmósfera de la Tierra.

stratus Clouds that form in flat layers and often cover much of the sky. (p. 304)
estratos Nubes que forman capas planas y que a menudo cubren gran parte del cielo.

stream A channel through which water is continually flowing downhill. (p. 96)
arroyo Canal por el cual fluye continuamente agua cuesta abajo.

stress A force that acts on an area of rock to change its shape or volume. (p. 174)
esfuerzo Fuerza que al actuar sobre una roca cambia su forma o volumen.

strike-slip fault A type of fault where rocks on either side move past each other sideways with little up-or-down motion. (p. 177)
falla transcurrente Tipo de falla en la cual las rocas a ambos lados se deslizan horizontalmente en sentidos opuestos, con poco desplazamiento hacia arriba o abajo.

subarctic A climate zone that lies north of the humid continental climates, with short, cool summers and long, cold winters. (p. 369)
subártico Zona climática que se encuentra al norte de los climas continentales húmedos.

subduction The process by which oceanic crust sinks beneath a deep-ocean trench and back into the mantle at a colliding plate boundary. (p. 154)
subducción Proceso mediante el cual la corteza oceánica se hunde debajo de una fosa oceánica profunda y vuelve al manto por el borde de una placa convergente.

subsoil The layer of soil beneath the topsoil. (p. 68)
subsuelo Capa del suelo bajo el suelo superior que contiene principalmente arcilla y otros minerales.

succession The series of predictable changes that occur in a community over time. (p. 422)
sucesión Serie de cambios predecibles que ocurren en una comunidad a través del tiempo.

surface wave A type of seismic wave that forms when P waves and S waves reach Earth's surface. (p. 183)
onda superficial Tipo de onda sísmica que se forma cuando las ondas P y las ondas S llegan a la superficie de la Tierra.

sustainable yield Amount of a renewable resource harvested regularly without reducing future supply.
rendimiento sostenible Cantidad de un recurso renovable que puede ser recolectado constantemente sin reducir el abastecimiento futuro. (p. 459)

symbiosis A close relationship between two species that benefits at least one of the species. (p. 415)
simbiosis Relación estrecha entre dos especies de la que se beneficia al menos una de ellas.

temperate zones The areas between the tropical and the polar zones, from about 23.5° to 66.5° north and 23.5° to 66.5° south latitude. (p. 347)
zonas templadas Áreas entre las zonas tropicales y polares, que se encuentran entre 23.5° a 66.5° latitud norte y 23.5° a 66.5° latitud sur.

temperature A measure of how hot or cold an object is compared to a reference point. (p. 271)
temperatura Medida de lo caliente o frío que está un objeto comparado con un punto de referencia.

tension Stress that stretches rock so that it becomes thinner in the middle. (p. 175)
tensión Esfuerzo que estira una roca, haciéndola más delgada en el centro.

thermal energy The total energy of motion in the particles of a substance. (pp. 17, 279)
energía térmica Energía de movimiento total en las partículas de una sustancia.

thermometer An instrument used to measure temperature, consisting of a thin glass tube with a bulb on one end that contains a liquid. (p. 279)
termómetro Instrumento que se usa para medir la temperatura; consiste en un tubo de fino vidrio con un bulbo en un extremo que contiene un líquido.

thermosphere The outermost layer of Earth's atmosphere. (p. 270)
termosfera Capa exterior de la atmósfera.

threatened species A species that could become endangered in the near future. (p. 464)
especie amenazada Especie que puede llegar a estar en peligro de extinción en el futuro próximo.

thunderstorm A small storm with heavy precipitation and frequent thunder and lightning. (p. 319)
tronada Pequeña tormenta acompañada de fuerte precipitación y frecuentes rayos y truenos.

tides The daily rise and fall of Earth's waters on its coastlines. (p. 491)
mareas Ascenso y descenso diario de las aguas de la Tierra en las costas.

till The sediments deposited directly by a glacier. (p. 118)
tillita Sedimentos depositados directamente por un glaciar.

topographic map A map that shows the surface features of an area. (p. 28)
mapa topográfico Mapa que muestra los accidentes geográficos de la superficie terrestre de un área.

topography The shape of the land determined by elevation, relief, and landforms. (p. 21)
topografía Forma del terreno determinada por la elevación, el relieve y los accidentes geográficos.

topsoil Mixture of humus, clay, and other minerals that forms the crumbly, topmost layer of soil. (p. 68)
suelo superior Mezcla de humus, arcilla y otros minerales que forman la capa superior y suelta del suelo.

tornado A rapidly whirling, funnel-shaped cloud that reaches down to touch Earth's surface. (p. 320)
tornado Nube con forma de embudo que gira rápidamente y que desciende hasta la superficie.

tropical (air mass) A warm air mass that forms in the tropics and has low air pressure. (p. 311)
masa de aire tropical Masa de aire templado que se forma en los trópicos y tiene presión baja.

tropical zone The area near the equator, between about 23.5° north latitude and 23.5° south latitude.
zona tropical Área cercana al ecuador, entre aproximadamente los 23.5° de latitud norte y los 23.5° de latitud sur. (p. 347)

troposphere The lowest layer of Earth's atmosphere.
troposfera Capa más inferior de la atmósfera de la Tierra. (p. 268)

tsunami A giant wave usually caused by an earthquake beneath the ocean floor. (p. 200)
tsunami Ola gigantesca, casi siempre causada por un sismo bajo el suelo oceánico.

tundra A polar climate region, found across northern Alaska, Canada, and Russia, with short, cool summers and bitterly cold winters (p. 370); an extremely cold, dry biome. (p. 445)
tundra Región climática polar que se encuentra en el norte de Alaska, Canadá y Rusia, que tiene veranos cortos y fríos, e inviernos extremadamente fríos; bioma extremadamente frío y seco.

ultraviolet radiation Electromagnetic waves with wavelengths that are shorter than visible light. (p. 273)
radiación ultravioleta Ondas electromagnéticas con longitudes de onda más cortas que la luz visible.

understory A layer of shorter plants that grow in the shade of a forest canopy. (p. 440)
sotobosque Estrato de plantas de baja estatura que crecen a la sombra de la bóveda arbórea.

uniformitarianism The geologic principle that the same geologic processes that operate today operated in the past to change Earth's surface. (p. 57)
uniformismo Principio geológico que enuncia que los mismos procesos geológicos que cambian la superficie de la Tierra en la actualidad, ocurrían en el pasado.

upwelling The movement of cold water upward from the deep ocean that is caused by wind. (p. 361)
afloramiento Movimiento ascendente de aguas frías desde las profundidades del mar.

valley glacier A long, narrow glacier that forms when snow and ice build up in a mountain valley. (p. 116)
glaciar de valle Glaciar largo y angosto que se forma por acumulación de hielo y nieve en un valle de montaña.

variable A factor that can change in an experiment.
variable Factor que puede cambiar en un experimento. (p. 9)

vent Opening through which magma leaves a volcano.
boca Abertura a través de la que la roca en fusión y los gases salen de un volcán. (p. 222)

volcanic neck Hardened magma in a volcano's pipe.
cuello volcánico Depósito de magma solidificada en la chimenea de un volcán. (p. 233)

volcano A weak spot in the crust where magma has come to the surface. (p. 216)
volcán Punto débil en la corteza por donde el magma escapa hacia la superficie.

water cycle The continual movement of water among Earth's atmosphere, oceans, and land through evaporation, condensation, and precipitation.
ciclo del agua Movimiento continuo de agua entre la atmósfera, los océanos y la superficie de la Tierra mediante la evaporación, condensación y precipitación. (p. 300)

water vapor Water in the form of a gas. (p. 258)
vapor de agua Agua en forma de gas.

wave A disturbance that transfers energy from place to place; the movement of energy through a body of water. (p.16)
onda Perturbación que transfiere energía de un lugar a otro; **ola** Movimiento de energía a través de un cuerpo de agua.

weather The condition of Earth's atmosphere at a particular time and place. (p. 256)
tiempo meteorológico Condición de la atmósfera de la Tierra en un tiempo y lugar determinados.

weathering The chemical and physical processes that break down rock at Earth's surface. (p. 57)
desgaste Procesos químicos y físicos que rompen las rocas de la superficie de la Tierra.

wind The horizontal movement of air from an area of high pressure to an area of lower pressure. (p. 283)
viento Movimiento horizontal de aire de un área de alta presión a un área de menor presión.

wind-chill factor A measure of cooling combining the effects of temperature and wind speed. (p. 283)
factor de sensación térmica Medida de enfriamiento que combina la temperatura y la velocidad del viento.

windward The side of a mountain range that faces the oncoming wind. (p. 350)
barlovento Lado de una cadena montañosa donde pega el viento de frente.

Index

Index

Page numbers for key terms are printed in **boldface** type.
Page numbers for illustrations, maps, and charts are printed in *italics*.

Index

Index

Page numbers for key terms are printed in **boldface** type.
Page numbers for illustrations, maps, and charts are printed in *italics*.

Index

Index

Page numbers for key terms are printed in **boldface** type.
Page numbers for illustrations, maps, and charts are printed in *italics*.

Acknowledgments

Science Content Standards for California Public Schools reproduced by permission, California Department of Education, CDE Press, 1430 N Street, Suite 3207, Sacramento, CA 95814.

Acknowledgment for pages 238–239: "Gelatin Volcanoes" by R. Fisk and D. Jackson from *Exploring Planets in the Classroom*. Copyright by Hawaii Space Grant Consortium, based on experiments done by R. Fisk and D. Jackson, U.S. Geological Survey.

Staff Credits

Ernest Albanese, Scott Andrews, Becky Barra, Peggy Bliss, Anne M. Bray, Katherine Bryant, Michael A. Burstein, Sara Castrignano, Kenneth Chang, Jonathan Cheney, Bob Craton, Patricia M. Dambry, Glen Dixon, Jonathan Fisher, Kathryn Fobert, Paul Gagnon, Elizabeth Good, Robert M. Graham, Christian Henry, Anne Jones, Kelly Kelliher, Toby Klang, Russ Lappa, Greg Lam, Dotti Marshall, Tim McDonald, Brent McKenzie, Ranida McKneally, Julia Osborne, Caroline Power, Gerry Schrenk, Siri Schwartzman, Malti Sharma, Laurel Smith, Emily Soltanoff, Paul Ramos, Linda Zust Reddy, Rashid Ross, Marcy Rose, Diane Walsh

Additional Credits

Michelle Chaison, Lisa Clark, Angela Clarke, Paula Gogan-Porter, Tom Greene, Kama Holder, Robyn Salbo, Chris Willson, Heather Wright

Illustration

Articulate Graphics, Morgan Cain & Associates, David Corrente, Warren Cutler, Dorling Kindersley, John Edwards & Associates, Forge FX, Chris Forsey, Geosystems Global Corporation, Dale Gustafson, Robert Hynes, Kevin Jones Associates, Jared D. Lee, Martucci Design, Steve McEntee, Rich McMahon, Rich McMahon with J/B Woolsey Associates, Karen Minot, Paul Mirocha, Ortelius Design, Inc., Matthew Pippin, Brucie Rosch, Ted Smykal, Walter Stuart, J/B Woolsey Associates, XNR Productions, Rose Zgodzinski

Tables and Graphs

Matt Mayerchak, Ernest Albanese

Photography

Photo Research Sue McDermott, John Judge, Paula Wehde, Kerri Hoar
Cover Images: Prentice Hall ISBN 0-13-201274-X **Poppy**, Foreground r, Corbis; **Poppy**, Foreground l, Charles O'Rear/Corbis; **Poppy Field**, Ralph A. Clevenger/Corbis; **Mountain**, Galen Rowell/Corbis.
Scott Foresman ISBN 0-328-24653-0 **Front cover and spine**, bluestripe snapper, Dave Fleetham/Pacific Stock; **background**, coral reef, coral detail, Stuart Westmorland/Corbis. **Back Cover, top**, DK images; **middle**, Bruce Davidson/Nature Picture Library; **bottom**, Cameron/Corbis; **background coral detail**, Stuart Westmorland/Corbis.

CHAPTER 1

Pages 0–1, STS-108 Crew, NASA; **1r**, Prentice Hall; **2b**, Richard Haynes; **3t**, Gary Braasch/Corbis; **4–5**, STS-108 Crew, NASA; **6 inset**, Ben Hankins/USGS; **6-7b**, G. Brad Lewis/Getty Images, Inc.; **8l**, Phil Schermeister/National Geographic; **8–9c**, Raymond K. Gehman/National Geographic; **10tl**, Robert W. Christopherson; **10ml**, Dorling Kindersley Media Library; **11tl**, Richard Haynes; **11tm**, Richard Haynes; **11tr**, Richard Haynes; **11br**, Richard Haynes; **11bm**, Richard Haynes; **11bl**, Richard Haynes; **12tl**, ML Sinibaldi/Corbis; **13b**, Panoramic Images/Getty; **14–15b**, Corbis; **16tl**, AP/Wide World Photos; **16tr**, Natalie Fobes/Corbis; **17tl** PunchStock; **17tr**, Michael Zagaris/Major League Baseball/Getty; **18l**, M.W. Franke/Peter Arnold, Inc.; **18r**, L. Gould/OSF/Animals Animals/Earth Scenes; **19t**, Bob Crandall/Stock Boston; **19b**, Frank Pederick/The Image Works; **22l**, Tom Bean; **23l**, David Muench; **23r**, Tom Bean; **28t**, Richard Haynes; **28b**, Mitch Wojnarowicz/The Image Works; **29tl**, Galen Rowell/Corbis; **33t**, Russ Lappa; **33b**, Tom Stewart/Corbis; **34–35b**, Richard Haynes; **36tl**, Getty Images, Inc.; **36tm**, Getty Images, Inc.; **36bm**, Richard Haynes; **36m**, Getty Images, Inc.; **36bl**, Getty Images, Inc.; **36ml**, Royalty-Free/Corbis.

CHAPTER 2

Pages 42–43, David Keaton/Corbis; **43br**, Prentice Hall; **44b**, Tasa Graphic Arts, Inc.; **45t**, Breck P. Kent/Animals Animals/Earth Scenes; **45b**, Larry Lefever/Grant Heilman Photography, Inc.; **46–47**, David Keaton/Corbis; **48b**, Dick Durrance II/Corbis; **49br**, Tasa Graphic Arts, Inc.; **50l**, Breck P. Kent; **50r**, E. R. Degginger; **51mr**, Barry Runk/Grant Heilman Photography, Inc.; **51br**, Andrew J. Martinez/Photo Researchers, Inc.; **53t**, DK/ Judith Miller Archive; **53b**, Donald C. Johnson/Corbis; **54bl**, Paul A. Souders/Corbis; **56t**, Richard Haynes; **57t**, Jerry D. Greer;

57b, Ron Watts/Corbis; **58tr**, Susan Rayfield/Photo Researchers, Inc.; **58br**, E.R. Degginger/Photo Researchers, Inc.; **58l**, Breck P. Kent/Animals Animals/Earth Scenes; **59l**, John Sohlden /Visuals Unlimited; **59r**, Jim Steinberg/Animals Animals/Earth Scenes; **61t**, Mike Mazzaschi/Stock Boston; **63tl**, Thomas C. Meierding; **63tr**, Thomas C. Meierding; **66t**, Richard Haynes; **66–67b**, Tom Bean; **69tl**, Photodisc/Getty; **69tr**, Photodisc/Getty; **72t**, J.M. Labat/Jacana/Photo Researchers, Inc.; **74t**, Richard Haynes; **74b**, Tom Bean; **75t**, Corbis; **75b**, Grant Heilman; **76t**, AP/Wide World Photos; **77r**, Larry Lefever/Grant Heilman Photography, Inc.; **78br**, Mike Mazzaschi/Stock Boston.

CHAPTER 3

Pages 82–83, David Keaton/Corbis; **83br**, Prentice Hall; **84b**, Scott T. Smith; **85t**, Tom Bean; **85m**, Jack Dykinga/Stone Allstock/Getty; **85b**, Marc Muench/Muench Photography, Inc.; **86–87**, David Keaton/Corbis; **87br**, Prentice Hall; **87bl**, Oswald Eckstein/Zefa/Corbis; **88b**, AP/Wide World Photos; **90r**, Thomas G. Rampton/Grant Heilman Photography, Inc.; **90l**, AP Photo/Kevork Djansezian; **91t**, Steven Holt/Stockpix.com; **97b**, Dorling Kindersley; **98tr**, Tom Bean; **99t**, Martin Miller; **99b**, NASA/SADO/Tom Stack & Associates, Inc.; **106t**, Smiley N. Pool/Dallas Morning News/Corbis; **107tl**, Vincent Laforet/Pool/ Reuters/Corbis; **107b**, Vincent Laforet/Pool/Reuters/Corbis; **108t**, Richard Haynes; **108bl**, Royalty-Free/Corbis; **109tr**, Buddy Mays/Corbis; **112tl**, Martin Miller; **113b**, Tom Bean; **115t**, Richard Haynes; **115b**, Marc Muench/Muench Photography, Inc.; **124t**, STS-108 Crew, NASA; **124m**, David Keaton/Corbis; **124b**, David Keaton/Corbis; **125tr**, F. Gilson/ Peter Arnold.

CHAPTER 4

Pages 126–127, Craig Aurness/Corbis; **127br**, Prentice Hall; **129m**, Lester V. Bergman/Corbis; **130–131**, Craig Aurness/Corbis; **134b**, Tracy Frankel/Getty Images, Inc.; **135t**, Dean Conger/Corbis; **136br**, Dorling Kindersley; **136–137**, Getty Images, Inc.; **139tl**, Runk/Schoenberger/Grant Heilman Photography, Inc.; **140t**, Richard Haynes; **141br**, Richard Haynes; **142b**, Richard Haynes; **144mr**, Dorling Kindersley/Stephen Oliver; **147tr**, Ken Lucas/Visuals Unlimited; **148tl**, Bettmann/Corbis; **149bl**, Jeffrey L. Rotman/Corbis; **152-153**, SIO Archives/UCSD; **157t**, Richard Haynes; **158bl**, Russ Lappa.

CHAPTER 5

Pages 168–169, AP/Wide World Photos; **169br**, Prentice Hall **170**, Tom & Susan Bean/ DRK Photo; **173-174**, AP/Wide World Photos; **173 inset**, Richard Haynes; **174b**, Wang Yuan-Mao/AP/Wide World Photos; **174t**, Russ Lappa; **176bl**, Tom and Susan Bean, Inc./DRK Photo; **177r**, W. Kenneth Hamblin; **177l**, Martin Miller/Visuals Unlimited; **179b**, Jim Wark/Airphoto; **180t**, Tom Bean; **181t**, Richard Haynes; **182r**, Kevin Fleming/Corbis; **184tl**, Lauren McFalls/AP/Wide World Photos; **184ml**, Tim Crosby/Getty Images, Inc.; **184br**, AP/Wide World Photos; **185t**, Peter Griffiths/Dorling Kindersley Images; **186tl**, Roger Ressmeyer/Corbis; **190b**, Michael Holford; **190t**, Russ Lappa; **195tr**, Reuters NewMedia Inc./Corbis; **196t**, Richard Haynes; **196b**, Tom Szlukovenyi/Reuters/Corbis; **199bl**, Roger Ressmeyer/ Corbis; **205mr**, IFA/eStock Photography/PictureQuest; **206br**, AP/Wide World Photos.

CHAPTER 6

Pages 210–211, Douglas Peebles/Corbis; **211br**, Prentice Hall; **213t**, Paul Souders/ Getty; **213 second from top**, Greg Vaughn/Tom Stack & Associates, Inc.; **213 third from top**, Danny Lehman/Corbis; **213b**, NASA; **214–215 background**, Douglas Peebles/Corbis; **215t**, Prentice Hall; **215b**, Prentice Hall; **216b**, Bettmann/Corbis; **221tr**, Breck P. Kent; **221mr**, E.R. Degginger/Color Pic, Inc.; **221bl**, DK Picture Library; **222b**, G. Brad Lewis/Getty Images, Inc.; **223t**, Dorling Kindersley Media Library; **224t**, Dave B. Fleetham/Tom Stack & Associates, Inc.; **224b**, Tui De Roy/ Minden Pictures; **225t**, Richard Thom/Visuals Unlimited; **225t inset**, Pat and Tom Leeson/Photo Researchers, Inc.; **225b inset**, P. Lipman/U.S. Geological Survey/Geologic Inquiries Group; **226l**, North Wind Picture Archives; **226m**, Robert Fried Photography; **226r**, Kim Heacox/Peter Arnold, Inc.; **227m**, Alberto Garcia/ Saba Press; **227br**, Fabrizio Villa/AP/Wide World Photos; **227tl**, Alberto Garcia/Saba Press; **227ml**, Alberto Garcia/Saba Press; **227bl**, Alberto Garcia/Saba Press; **228tl**, Linda Bailey/Animals Animals/Earth Scenes; **229t**, Richard Haynes; **229b**, Helga Lade/Peter Arnold, Inc.; **230–231**, AFP/Corbis; **231t inset**, Earth Observatory/NASA; **231b inset**, Manfred Gottschalk/Tom Stack & Associates, Inc.; **232tr**, Greg Vaughn/Tom Stack & Associates, Inc.; **233b**, Danny Lehman/Corbis; **233 inset**, David Hosking/Photo Researchers, Inc.; **234tr**, Carr Clifton/Minden Pictures; **235b**, Ron Niebrugge/Alamy; **237tr**, Philip Wallick/ Corbis; **237mr**, Corbis; **239br**, David Muench/ Corbis; **240bl**, Alberto Garcia/Saba Press; **244–245**, Roger Ressmeyer/Corbis; **245br**, Erich Lessing/Art Resource, NY; **245mr**, Scala/Art Resource, NY; **245tl**, Museo Archeologico Nazionale, Naples, Italy/Scala/Art Resource, NY.; **246t**, Private Collection/Bridgeman Art Library; **247t**, Dorling Kindersley; **247b**, Sean Sexton Collection/Corbis; **248t**, Craig Aurness/ Corbis; **248m**, AP/Wide World Photos; **248b**, Douglas Peebles/Corbis.

CHAPTER 7
Pages 250–251, Wayne R. Bilenduke/Getty Images, Inc.; **251br,** Tobias Bernhard/ Getty; **252b,** NASA/Photo Researchers, Inc.; **253t,** Prentice Hall; **253** second from top, Matton Images; **253** third from top, David Lawrence/Panoramic Images; **253b,** James Schwabel/Panoramic Images; **254–255,** Wayne R. Bilenduke/Getty Images, Inc.; **255br,** Richard Haynes; **256tr,** Russ Lappa; **256b,** NASA/Photo Researchers, Inc.; **257br,** Steve Mason/Getty Images, Inc.; **258t,** Tom Bean/DRK Photo; **258b,** Karl H. Switak/Photo Researcher, Inc.; **259l,** Michael Fogden/DRK Photo; **259r,** Gail Shumway/Getty Images, Inc.; **260b,** Will McIntyre/Photo Researchers, Inc.; **261t,** AP/Wide World Photos; **262t,** Russ Lappa; **262b,** Royalty-Free/Corbis; **265tr,** Prentice Hall; **267t,** Russ Lappa; **267b,** Steve Vidler/Superstock, Inc.; **268t,** Marc C. Burnett/Photo Researchers, Inc.; **271t,** Photographer's Choice/Getty Images, Inc.; **273t,** David Lawrence/Panoramic Images; **278b,** Yang Liu/Corbis; **279r,** Russ Lappa; **282t,** Richard Haynes; **282b,** Anna Zieminski/AFP/Getty Images, Inc.; **284t,** James Schwabel/Panoramic Images; **284b,** James Schwabel/Panoramic Images; **286b,** Austin Brown/Getty Images, Inc.

CHAPTER 8
Pages 294–295, NASA; **295br,** Prentice Hall; **296b,** Barry Runk/Grant Heilman/ Photography; **297t,** William Johnson/Stock Boston; **297m,** Gene Rhoden/Peter Arnold, Inc.; **297** third from top, Oxford Scientific Films; **298–299,** NASA; **299** inset, Richard Haynes; **300–301,** Jeremy Horner/Corbis; **302tl,** Barry Runk/Grant Heilman/Photography; **303br,** Bruce Coleman, Inc.; **304t,** Scott Nielsen/Bruce Coleman, Inc.; **304m,** John Shaw/Bruce Coleman, Inc.; **304b,** Claudia Parks/Corbis; **306t,** Ed Pritchard/Getty Images, Inc.; **307t,** Richard Haynes; **308** inset, Nuridsany et Perennou/Photo Researchers, Inc.; **308b,** Phil Degginger/ Bruce Coleman, Inc.; **309t,** Gerben Oppermans/Getty Images, Inc.; **310t,** Russ Lappa; **310–311,** Benjamin Lowy/Corbis; **313b,** Gene Rhoden/Peter Arnold, Inc.; **317tm,** Accuweather; **317** inset left, Mike Chew/Corbis; **317** inset right, Getty Images Inc.; **318t,** Richard Haynes; **318b,** Peter Menzel; **320l,** Warren Faidley/DRK Photo; **321t,** Oxford Scientific Films; **322l,** The Granger Collection, NY; **322m,** The Granger Collection, NY; **322r,** The Granger Collection; **323l,** Roger de la Harpe/ Dorling Kindersley; **323m,** North Wind Picture Archives; **323r,** Corbis; **325t,** NASA; **328–329,** Photo Researchers, Inc; **329t,** Bob Daemmrich/Stock Boston; **335b,** David Frazier; **336** Scott Nielsen/Bruce Coleman, Inc.

CHAPTER 9
Pages 340–341, Tim Davis/Corbis; **341br,** Andreas Pollok/Getty; **342b,** Michael S. Bisceglie/Animals Animals-Earth Scenes; **343** third from top, Royalty-Free/Corbis; **343** second from top, Craig Tuttle/Corbis; **343b,** TOMS; **344–345,** Tim Davis/ Corbis; **345br,** Richard Haynes; **346b,** David Muench Photography; **346b,** Richard Haynes; **348t,** David Madison/Bruce Coleman, Inc.; **349b,** Raven/Explorer/Photo Researchers, Inc.; **351tr,** Steve McCurry/Magnum Photos; **352l,** Bruce Coleman, Inc.; **352r,** Bruce Coleman, Inc.; **354b,** Richard Haynes; **356b,** Russ Lappa; **358t,** Larry Beard/Acclaim Images; **359t,** NOAA; **359m,** NOAA; **359b,** NOAA; **362t,** Russ Lappa; **362–364b,** Royalty Free/Corbis; **363tr,** Getty Images, Inc.; **364bl,** Bruce Forster/ Getty Images Inc.; **364br,** David Muench; **364bm,** Jess Stock/Getty Images, Inc.; **365bl,** Tom Till/DRK Photo; **365br,** David Muench; **365bm,** Ragnar Th. Sigurdsson/ Artic-Images; **366** inset, Gibson, Mickey/Animals Animals-Earth Scenes; **366t,** Tony Craddock/Getty; **367bl,** Tom Bean/DRK Photo; **368t,** Charlie Waite/Getty Images, Inc.; **369tl,** Liz Hymans/Corbis; **369** inset, DRK Photo; **370b,** Bryan & Cherry Alexander/Artic Images; **371tr,** Adam Jones/Photo Researchers, Inc.; **374tr,** Richard Haynes; **376tl,** Anne Howard/Artic Images.; **377l,** Larry Taylor; **377r,** Kent Syverson; **379l,** TOMS; **379m,** TOMS; **379r,** TOMS; **384t,** Wayne R. Bilenduke/Getty; **384m,** NASA; **384b,** Tim Davis/Corbis.

CHAPTER 10
Pages 386–387, Frans Lanting/Minden Pictures; **387br,** Brandon D. Cole/Corbis; **389t,** Tony Craddock/Getty Images, Inc.; **390–391,** Frans Lanting/Minden Pictures; **391** inset, Richard Haynes; **392t,** Richard Haynes; **392b,** C.K. Lorenz/Photo Researchers; **393t,** C.W. Schwartz/Animals Animals/Earth Scenes; **394t,** Konrad Wothe/Minden Pictures; **394m,** Christoph Burki/Getty Images, Inc.; **394b,** John Cancalosi/Tom Stack & Associates; **395b,** Getty Images, Inc.; **399br,** Frans Lanting/ Minden Pictures; **401t,** Alan D. Carey/Photo Researchers, Inc.; **401b,** Leonard Lee Rue III/Photo Researchers, Inc.; **402b,** Darrell Gulin/Dembinsky Photo Associates; **403t,** Tom & Pat Leeson/Photo Researchers, Inc.; **404–405,** Kent Foster/Photo Researchers, Inc.; **405t** inset, David Northcott/DRK Photo; **405m** inset, Adam Jones/Photo Researchers, Inc.; **405b** inset, S. Nielsen/DRK Photo; **409t,** Andy Rouse/DRK Photo; **412r,** Wally Eberhart/Visuals Unlimited; **412tl,** Ron Willocks/ Animals Animals/Earth Scenes; **412ml,** Patti Murray/Animals Animals/Earth Scenes; **412bl,** Rob Simpson/Vsuals Unlimited; **413t,** F. Stuart Westmorland/Photo Researchers, Inc.; **414tl,** Leroy Simon/Visuals Unlimited; **414bl,** Brian Rogers/ Visuals Unlimited; **414br,** Art Wolfe; **415b,** Daryl Balfour/Getty Images, Inc.; **416t,** Volker Steiger/SPL/Photo Researchers, Inc.; **416b,** Richard Haynes; **417tr,** Richard Haynes; **417bl,** Joe McDonald/Corbis; **418b,** Asa C. Thoresen/Photo Researchers, Inc.; **421t,** E. R. Degginger/Photo Researchers, Inc.; **422bl,** Tom & Pat Leeson/ Photo Researchers, Inc.; **422br,** Tom & Pat Leeson/Photo Researchers.

CHAPTER 11
Pages 432–433, Kennan Ward/Corbis; **433bl,** M P LAND/Science Photo Library/ Photo Researchers; **433br,** Thomas Scmitt/Image Bank/Getty; **434b,** Panoramic Images/Getty; **435t,** J. Pfaff/zefa/Corbis; **435m,** Steffen Thalemann/ Getty; **435b,** Photodisc/ Getty; **436–437,** Kennan Ward/Corbis; **437** inset, Richard Haynes; **439b,** Barbara Gerlach/DRK Photo; **439** inset, Maslowski/Photo Researchers; **440t,** T. Allofs/ zefa/Corbis; **440** inset, Dave Watts/Nature Picture Library; **441t,** Macduff Everton/Getty; **441** inset, Art Wolfe, Inc.; **442t,** Art Wolfe/Getty Images, Inc.; **442** inset, Gerry Ellis/Minden Pictures; **443b,** Carr Clifton/ Minden Pictures; **443t** inset, Nick Bergkessel/Photo Researchers, Inc.; **443b** inset, Stephen J. Krasemann/DRK Photo; **444l,** Stephen J. Krasemann/DRK Photo; **444r,** Jeff Lepore/ Photo Researchers, Inc.; **445b,** Michio Hoshino/Minden Pictures; **445** inset, Yva Momatiuk/John Eastcott/Minden Pictures; **446t,** D. Robert & Lorri Franz/Corbis; **450b,** Stuart Westmorland/Corbis; **451r,** David Weintraub/Photo Researchers, Inc.; **451** inset, Steven David Miller/Animals Animals/Earth Scenes; **459br,** Inga Spence/ Visuals Unlimited; **460b,** G.R. Robinson/Visuals Unlimited; **461tl,** Greg Vaughn/ Tom Stack & Associates; **462tr,** Richard Haynes; **463t,** Wayne Lynch/DRK Photo; **463b,** Fred Bavendam/Minden Pictures; **464l,** David Sieren/ Visuals Unlimited; **464r,** David Liebman; **464b,** Joseph Van Os/Getty Images, Inc.; **465l,** Stephen J. Krasemann/DRK Photo; **465b** inset, Marilyn Kazmers/Peter Arnold, Inc.; **465r,** Ken Lucas/Visuals Unlimited; **466bl,** Roy Toft/Tom Stack & Associates; **467tr,** Nik Wheeler/Corbis; **468br,** David Dennis/Animals Animals/Earth Scenes.

CHAPTER 12
Pages 472–473, Richard Hamilton Smith/Corbis; **473br,** Simon Bruty/Getty images; **474bl,** Andreas Einsiedel/Dorling Kindersley Media Library; **475b,** David Joel/Getty Images, Inc.; **475t,** George Steinmetz/Corbis; **476–477** background, Richard Hamilton Smith/Corbis; **477** inset, Visuals Unlimited; **478t,** E.R. Degginger; **478b,** Toby Talbot/AP/Wide World Photos; **481tl,** Colin Keates/Dorling Kindersley Media Library; **481ml,** Andreas Einsiedel/Dorling Kindersley Media Library; **481bl,** Andreas Einsiedel /Dorling Kindersley Media Library; **482t,** Bill Ross/Corbis; **483t,** Roger Ball/Corbis; **484t,** Owen Franken/Corbis; **485b,** Lawrence Migdale/ Photo Researchers, Inc.; **486tl,** Nadia MacKenzie/Getty Images, Inc.; **488bl,** Royalty-Free/Corbis; **489br,** Brian Branch-Price/ AP/Wide World Photos; **491t,** Yann Arthus-Bertrand/Corbis; **493b,** Richard Haynes; **494t,** Russ Lappa; **494b,** Bettman/Corbis; **496t,** Joseph Sohm/ ChromoSohm Inc./ Corbis; **496** inset, E.R. Degginger/Color Pic. Inc.; **499t,** Richard Haynes; **500bl,** Mitch Kezar/Getty Images, Inc.; **500bm,** Tony Freeman/PhotoEdit; **500br,** Scott Olson/Getty Images, Inc.; **501bl,** Anthony Meshkinyar/Getty Images, Inc.; **501bm,** Yves Marcoux/Getty Images, Inc.; **501br,** Mike Fiala/Getty Images; **502t,** Michael Newman/Photo Edit; **506–507,** Nick Vedros, Vedros & Assoc./Getty Images, Inc.; **509tl,** David Joel/Getty Images, Inc.; **510tr,** Randy Faris/Corbis; **510tl,** Richard Haynes; **511t,** Larry Lefever/Grant Heilman Photography, Inc.; **512bl,** Nadia MacKenzie/Getty Images, Inc.; **516t,** Frans Lanting/Minden Pictures; **516m,** Kennan Ward/Corbis; **516b,** Richard Hamilton Smith/Corbis.